ISABELLA OF CASTILE

Ghosts of Spain
Catherine of Aragon

ISABELLA OF CASTILE

Europe's First Great Queen

Giles Tremlett

BLOOMSBURY

NEW YORK · LONDON · OXFORD · NEW DELHI · SYDNEY

Bloomsbury USA
An imprint of Bloomsbury Publishing Plc

1385 Broadway
New York
NY 10018
USA

50 Bedford Square
London
WC1B 3DP
UK

www.bloomsbury.com

BLOOMSBURY and the Diana logo are trademarks of Bloomsbury Publishing Plc

First published in Great Britain 2017
First U.S. edition 2017

© Giles Tremlett, 2017
Map by ML Design
Family tree by Phillip Beresford

ISBN: HB: 978-1-63286-520-5
            EPUB: 978-1-63286-522-9

Library of Congress Cataloging-in-Publication Data is available.

2 4 6 8 10 9 7 5 3 1

Typeset by Newgen Knowledge Works (P) Ltd., Chennai, India
Printed and bound in the U.S.A. by Berryville Graphics Inc., Berryville, Virginia

To find out more about our authors and books visit www.bloomsbury.com. Here you will find
extracts, author interviews, details of forthcoming events, and the option to sign up for our
newsletters.Bloomsbury books may be purchased for business or promotional use.
For information on bulk purchases please contact Macmillan Corporate and
Premium Sales Department at specialmarkets@macmillan.com.

'No woman in history has exceeded her achievement.'
Hugh Thomas, *Rivers of Gold: The Rise of the Spanish Empire*

'Probably the most important person in our history.'
Manuel Fernández Álvarez, *Isabel la Católica*

To Katharine Blanca Scott, for all we have done and made.

CONTENTS

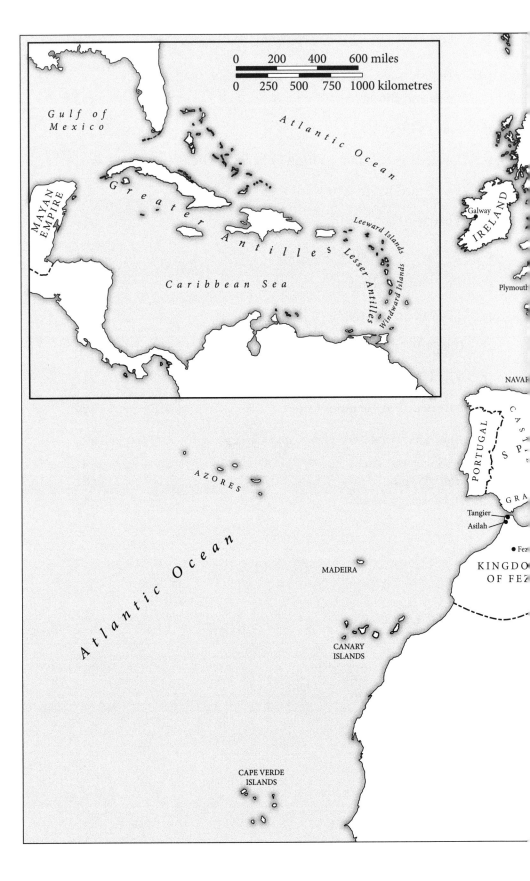

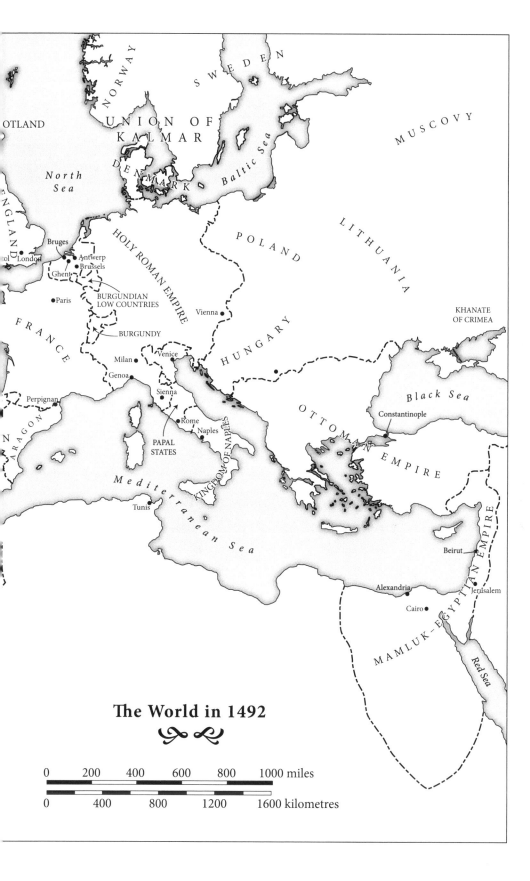

The World in 1492

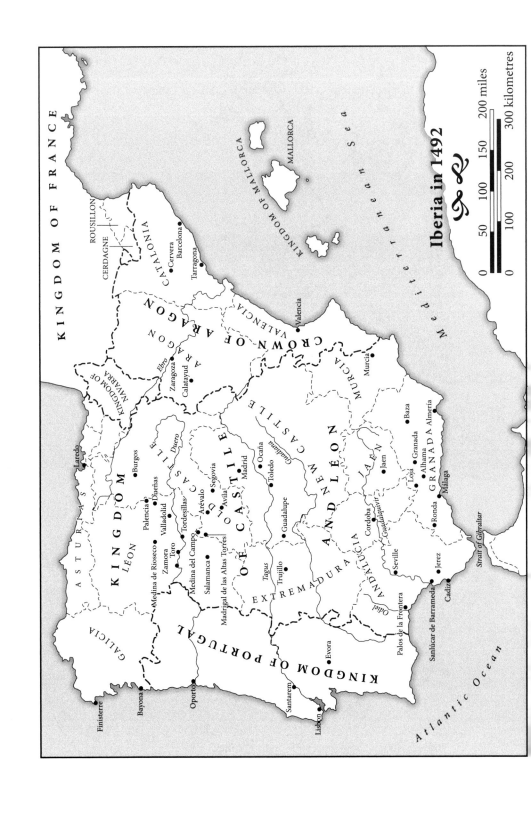

KINGDOM OF FRANCE

ROUSILLON
CERDAGNE

CATALONIA
Cervera
Barcelona
Tarragona

Mediterranean Sea

KINGDOM OF MALLORCA
MALLORCA

Iberia in 1492

0 50 100 150 200 miles

0 100 200 300 kilometres

KINGDOM OF NAVARRA

Zaragoza
Calatayud
ARAGON
Ebro

CROWN OF ARAGON

VALENCIA
Valencia

MURCIA
Murcia

Baza
GRANADA Almeria
Granada
Alhama
Loja
Ronda Malaga

Strait of Gibraltar

ASTURIAS
Laredo

KINGDOM OF LEÓN

Burgos
Dueñas
Palencia
Valladolid
Medina de Rioseco
Zamora
Toro
Medina del Campo
Salamanca
Madrigal de las Altas Torres

Duero

CASTILE

OLD CASTILE

Segovia
Arévalo
Avila
Madrid
Ocaña
Toledo
Guadalupe

NEW CASTILE

Guadiana

ANDLÉON

JAEN
Jaen
Cordoba
Guadalquivir
ANDALUCIA
Seville

EXTREMADURA
Trujillo
Tagus

GALICIA
Finisterre
Bayona
Oporto

KINGDOM OF PORTUGAL

Santarem
Lisbon
Evora

Palos de la Frontera
Odiel
Sanlúcar de Barrameda
Cadiz
Jerez

Atlantic Ocean

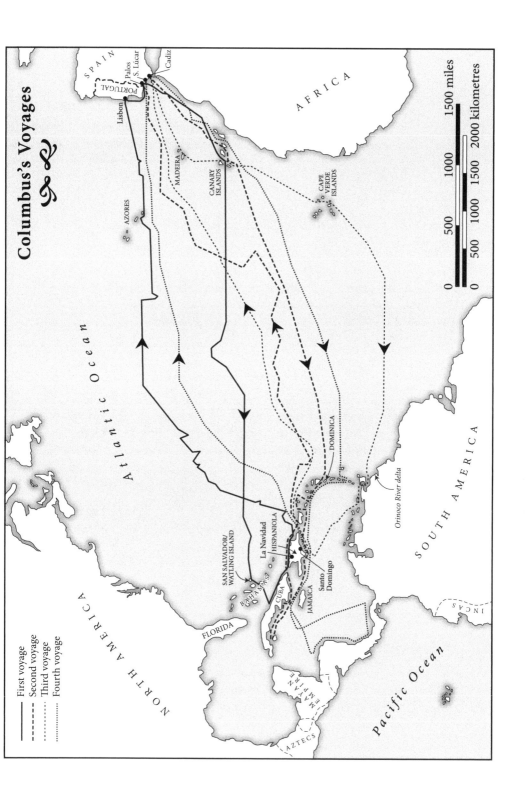

Columbus's Voyages

First voyage
Second voyage
Third voyage
Fourth voyage

NORTH AMERICA

Atlantic Ocean

Pacific Ocean

SOUTH AMERICA

AFRICA

SPAIN
PORTUGAL
Lisbon
Palos
S. Lucar
Cadiz

AZORES

MADEIRA

CANARY ISLANDS

CAPE VERDE ISLANDS

FLORIDA

SAN SALVADOR/ WATLING ISLAND

BAHAMAS

CUBA

La Navidad
HISPANIOLA

JAMAICA

Santo Domingo

DOMINICA

Orinoco River delta

MAYA

AZTECS

INCAS

0   500   1000   1500 miles

0   500   1000   1500   2000 kilometres

FAMILY TREE OF ISABELLA OF CASTILE

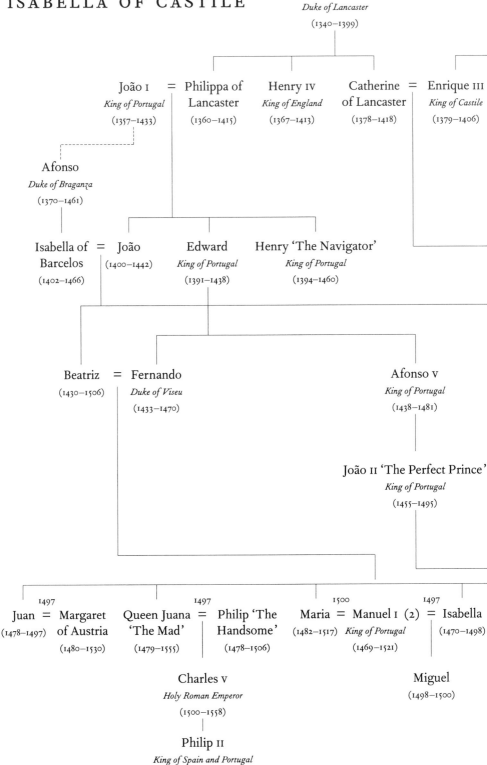

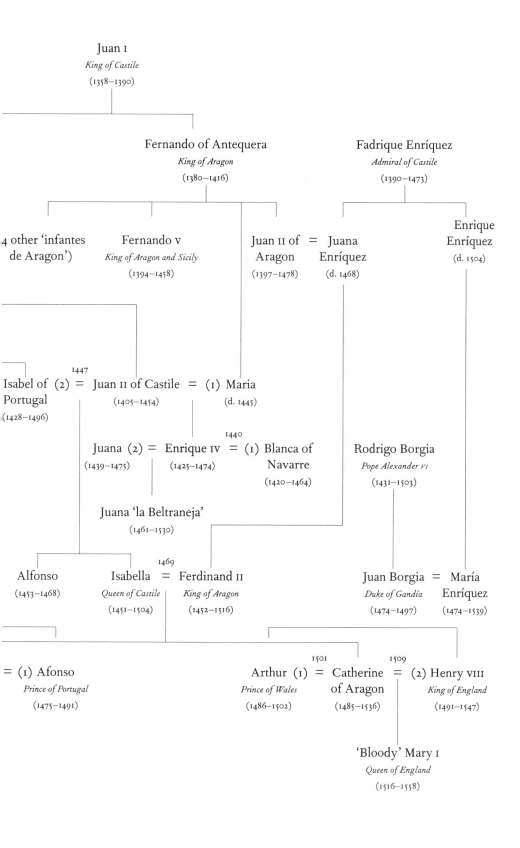

Juan I
King of Castile
(1358–1390)

Fernando of Antequera
King of Aragon
(1380–1416)

Fadrique Enríquez
Admiral of Castile
(1390–1473)

4 other 'infantes
de Aragon')

Fernando V
King of Aragon and Sicily
(1394–1458)

Juan II of = Juana
Aragon   Enríquez
(1397–1478) (d. 1468)

Enrique
Enríquez
(d. 1504)

Isabel of (2) = Juan II of Castile = (1) Maria
Portugal   (1405–1454)   (d. 1445)
(1428–1496)
              1447

Juana (2) = Enrique IV = (1) Blanca of
(1439–1475) (1425–1474)   Navarre
                        (1420–1464)
                    1440

Rodrigo Borgia
Pope Alexander VI
(1431–1503)

Juana 'la Beltraneja'
(1461–1530)

Alfonso
(1453–1468)

Isabella = Ferdinand II
Queen of Castile | *King of Aragon*
(1451–1504) (1452–1516)
        1469

Juan Borgia = María
Duke of Gandía Enríquez
(1474–1497) (1474–1539)

= (1) Afonso
Prince of Portugal
(1475–1491)

Arthur (1) = Catherine = (2) Henry VIII
Prince of Wales of Aragon *King of England*
(1486–1502) (1485–1536) (1491–1547)
        1501   1509

'Bloody' Mary I
Queen of England
(1516–1558)

Europe's First Great Queen

Segovia, 13 December 1474

The sight was shocking. Gutierre de Cárdenas walked solemnly down the chilly, windswept streets of Segovia, the royal sword held firmly in front of him with its point towards the ground. Behind him came a new monarch, a twenty-three-year-old woman of short-to-middling height with light auburn hair and green-blue eyes whose air of authority was accentuated by the menace of Cárdenas's weapon. This was a symbol of royal power as potent as any crown or sceptre. Those who braved the thin, wintry air of Segovia to watch the procession knew that it signified the young woman's determination to impart justice, and impose her will, through force. Isabella of Castile's glittering jewels spoke of regal magnificence, while Cárdenas's sword threatened violence. Both indicated power and a willingness to exercise it.[1]

Onlookers were amazed. Isabella's father and half-brother, the two kings who had ruled fractious Castile for the previous seventy years, were not famed for their use of power. They had let others rule for them. Yet here was a woman, of all things, declaring her determination to govern them herself. 'Some of those in the crowd muttered that they had never seen such a thing,' reported one contemporary. The grumblers felt no compunction about challenging the right of a woman to rule over them, and little need to keep their mouths shut. Castile's weak monarchy had become the subject of derision, disobedience and outright rebellion. For decades the country's kings had been playthings for a section of those mighty, arrogant, land-owning aristocrats who already referred to themselves as the 'Grandees'. This woman who claimed to be their new queen on a December day in 1474 may have appeared in her most magnificent, bejewelled finery, but only a modest number of Grandees, churchmen and other senior officials accompanied her. It was a sign that her problems went beyond her gender and the fragile state of Castile's monarchy. For Isabella was not the only claimant to the throne, nor was she the person who had been designated as such by the previous monarch. This was, in short, a usurper's pre-emptive coup. Nobody could be sure that it would work.[2]

Castile was the largest, strongest and most populous kingdom in what the Romans (and their Visigoth heirs) had called Hispania and which today is divided between the two countries of the Iberian peninsula, Spain and Portugal. With upwards of 4 million inhabitants it was significantly more populous than England and one of the larger countries in western Europe. The kingdom that Isabella claimed was the result of a slow, six-centuries-long conquest of land occupied by the Muslims – known to Christians as *moros*, or Moors – who had crossed the nine miles of water that separate Spain from north Africa at the Strait of Gibraltar and swept through Iberia early in the eighth century. Castile's recent history was less than glorious and its experience of queens regnant was both distant and, by reputation, dismal.[3] No one alive could recall what it was like to have a strong monarch, while infighting and troublesome neighbours – Aragon to the east, the Muslim kingdom of Granada to the south and Portugal to the west – continued to absorb much of its energy. Dealing with these three countries and the small but often irritating northern kingdom of Navarre was about all it was able to manage in terms of foreign adventures – though the royal family had often looked abroad for marriage partners and Isabella herself boasted both a Portuguese mother and, in Catherine of Lancaster, an English grandmother. To the north, France remained a far more potent power – one that Castile was careful not to upset.

Those watching Isabella process through the cold streets of Segovia could not know that they were witnessing the first steps of a queen destined to become the most powerful woman Europe had seen since Roman times. 'This queen of Spain, called Isabella, has had no equal on this earth for 500 years,' one awestruck visitor from northern Europe would eventually proclaim, admiring the fear and loyalty she provoked among the lowliest of Castilians and the mightiest of Grandees.[4] This was not hyperbole. Europe had limited experience of queens regnant, and even less of successful ones. Few of those who followed Isabella have had such a lasting impact. Only Elizabeth I of England, Archduchess María Theresa of Austria, Russia's Catherine the Great (outshining a formidable predecessor, the Empress Elizabeth) and Britain's Queen Victoria can rival her, each in their own era. All faced the challenges of being a female ruler in an otherwise overwhelmingly male-dominated world and all had long, transformative reigns, leaving legacies that would be felt for centuries. Only Isabella did this by leading a country as it emerged from the troubled late middle ages, harnessing the ideas and tools of the early Renaissance to start transforming a fractious, ill-disciplined nation into a European powerhouse with a clear-minded and ambitious monarchy at its centre.[5] She was, in other words, the first in that still-small club of great European queens. To some she remains the greatest. 'No woman in history has exceeded her achievement,' says the historian of Spain, Hugh Thomas.[6] This author agrees, at least as far as female European monarchs and their impact on the world is concerned.

Isabella's achievements are not just remarkable because of her sex, merely more so. Isabella appeared after more than a century of crisis in Europe. In 1346, a force of besieging Tartars had catapulted the blotchy, plague-ridden bodies of Black Death victims into a Genoese garrison in the Crimea. This forced them into galleys which carried the disease into Europe, or so the Genoese writer Gabriele de' Mussi claimed after watching the plague devastate his home town of Piacenza. In fact, the Black Death took many other routes into

Europe, where it killed a third of the population. This accelerated the demise of the feudal system in much of western Europe, starving it of manpower and provoking everything from peasants' revolts to the abandonment of productive land.[7] Then in 1453, the handsome, dashing, twenty-year-old Ottoman sultan Mehmet II ordered that his galleys be pulled overland into the Golden Horn, cutting off the capital of eastern Christendom, Constantinople. This soon fell into his hands. Muslim armies then completed their occupation of Greece and much of the Balkans, marking a new low point in the history of western, Christian Europe. The explanation for all this, in a world dominated by religion and superstition, was simple and widely shared. God was angry. His wrath had fallen on a sinful world and, in some parts, it was believed that he had slammed shut the door to heaven. Christians had long dreamed of a mythical, redeeming leader, the Last World Emperor or Lion King, who would recover Jerusalem and convert the world to the true faith.[8] Now, with Islam on the rise and themselves faced with apparently irreversible decline, they needed such a leader even more urgently.

Castilians hoped that the great saviour of Christianity would be one of their own monarchs, but weak kings brought constant disappointment. Foreigners saw squabbling Spain as shrouded in 'natural darkness',[9] and Castile remained a volatile, unsettled society. A whole new social category, the 'new Christians' or *conversos*, was still being assimilated amid frequent outbursts of violence. The *conversos* were the children and grandchildren of what had once been the world's largest community of Jews, most of whom appear to have been forcibly converted eighty years earlier. In the cities a growing bourgeoisie of wool traders, bankers, merchants and local oligarchs struggled to assert itself. Elsewhere many strived to attain or maintain the privileges of class – often personified by the broad, if sometimes impoverished, category of *hidalgos*, whose name derived from the term *hijos de algo*, or 'sons-of-something'.[10] But real power still lay in the vast, untaxed estates of Grandees, military orders and the church – which were also the biggest threat to royal authority.[11]

Yet in a continent split into dozens of quarrelsome kingdoms, city states, principalities and duchies, Castile was one of the few countries with the potential to produce a leader who could reverse the flagging fortunes of western Christendom. Vast flocks of hardy, fine-haired merino sheep – some 5 million animals – had turned it into what one historian called 'the Australia of the Middle Ages', with wool travelling north to the sophisticated textile centres of Europe.[12] In Rome, the spiritual capital of Europe, the pope was only too aware of the importance of this wealth since Iberia provided a third of the papacy's income.

No one had ever imagined that the Last World Emperor would be a woman, but Isabella, in alliance with her husband King Ferdinand of Aragon, did more than any other monarch of her time to reverse Christendom's decline. Despite this, appreciation of Isabella has remained a largely Spanish thing. There are many reasons why. One is her use of violence. This is a legitimate and necessary tool for exercising power, but is often deemed disturbing when used by queens – as if those who usurp the male role of leadership are driven by dark and vicious forces that annul a supposedly natural, gentle femininity. Isabella had no qualms about employing violence, feeling the hand of God behind every blow delivered in her name. Nowhere was this more so than in her attempt to finish off the so-called *Reconquista* by defeating the ancient Muslim kingdom of Granada. Isabella admired Joan of Arc, but made no attempt to imitate her by leading troops into battle. That was man's work, and she believed firmly in the division of the sexes (and classes, faiths and ethnic groups). In that, and many other things, she was not just a woman of her time, but a ferociously conservative one. Nor did she feel it necessary to feign any form of masculinity, though men often found they could explain her extraordinary success only by attributing to her some of their own, male qualities. Where Elizabeth I would later proclaim herself to have 'the heart and stomach of a king', Isabella preferred to express angry astonishment that 'as a weak woman' she was so much more audacious and belligerent than the men who served her.

The Castile she claimed the right to rule owed its name to the castles, or *castillos*, that dotted a kingdom carved out over centuries of warfare and conquest of Muslim lands. Her country's self-identity was shaped around its role as a crusading nation and defender of Christianity's southern frontier. The distinct regions of Castile owed their existence, too, to the different stages of a *Reconquista* which had started in the mountains that loomed over the Cantabrian coast in the north, and spread slowly into the wider area known as Old Castile. This lay north of a central chain of snow-capped mountains and sierras that included both the Guadarrama and Gredos ranges. Old Castile (together with the lands where the *Reconquista* was launched and had its first successes, in Asturias, the Basque country and Galicia) was fringed to the north and west by a wild, dangerous coastline. It included Spain's own Land's End, or Finisterre, where wonderstruck Romans had come to marvel at the sun sinking below the western edge of the known world. This most ancient section of her realms was structured around a network of handsome, walled cities like Segovia, Avila, Burgos and Valladolid that had grown wealthy on the back of the wool trade. Every autumn the flocks of sheep traipsed south across the mountains – or 'over the passes' as Isabella herself put it – to their winter pastures in the area that had become known as New Castile. This was presided over by ancient Toledo, with its magnificent churches, converted mosques and synagogues that jointly symbolised centuries of religious coexistence in Spain. Further to the south and west lay booming Andalusia, with its fertile plains, Atlantic ports and the country's biggest city Seville as its thriving capital. Far off to the east lay the thinly populated frontier land of Murcia, which provided Castile with ports on the Mediterranean. Extremadura, on Castile's western border with Portugal, also owed much of its character to its own frontier status.

Across the varied and often rugged landscapes of Castile – from the green, damp north-west to the arid, desert-like south-east – Isabella's violence was directed against those who opposed her usurper's coup, challenged royal authority or threatened the purity of her kingdom.

Religious and ethnic cleansing saw thousands burned, tens of thousands expelled[13] and many more forcibly converted to Christianity. Jews and Muslims were erased from the official population of Spain, forcing many to hide their real faith. Her novel, royal-directed state Inquisition used flimsy evidence or confessions extracted under torture to burn *conversos* whose racial impurity was often the only real basis for suspicion about their beliefs. And it was during her reign that Christian Spaniards with a Jewish bloodline began to find themselves formally categorised as second-rate subjects. These are terrible acts by the morals of today, but were widely applauded in a Europe which looked scornfully upon Spain's mix of religions. Many wondered why it had waited so long to do what they themselves had done centuries before.

Religious or ethnic cleansing, enslavement and intolerance were not frowned upon. They could, in fact, be virtuous. Yet even by the measures of her own era Isabella was deemed severe. Machiavelli himself commented on the 'pious cruelty'[14] practised in her kingdoms. In public she perfected a distant form of impassive regality, but behind this lay a woman of intense and stubborn convictions. Only Ferdinand and the handful of stern, austere Christian friars to whom she turned for moral guidance seemed capable of changing her mind. And yet many people were grateful, for that same single-minded severity brought stability and security to their daily lives – shielding them from the violence of mobs, the greed of the Grandees and the casual cruelty of those who rode roughshod over Castile's laws.

Isabella's calm exterior hid not just a strong will but also an elevated idea of her place in history and a desire for lasting fame that drove her ambition far beyond the traditional frontiers of Castile. Ships from neighbouring Portugal were already nosing their way deep into the Atlantic and south down the coast of Africa. Under her leadership, with the help of the talented and eccentric Genoese sailor Christopher Columbus, Castile would push further and deeper west, discovering an entire 'New World' that won it glory, power and gold.

This also wrought a fourfold increase in the geographical size of what would eventually be termed 'Western civilisation' and helped provoke a tectonic shift in global power. It was, in many ways, the miracle for which embattled Christendom had been waiting.

All this was achieved, in part, because Isabella began the process of imposing what other princes and monarchs across Europe were also battling to install – a new kind of royal dominance that reduced the political power of feudal lords and handed more to a new class of loyal and dependent royal bureaucrats. It was a bold, clever transition, not revolutionary but still profoundly transformative, and all done by appealing, ironically, to tradition. In her desire to draw as much power as possible to the crown – a precursor to the absolutist monarchies of later centuries – she saw eye to eye with her husband Ferdinand, whose lesser kingdoms of Aragon eventually gave them joint control of most of contemporary Spain, though this kind of rule was much easier to implant in Castile. Indeed, her greatest political act was to forge an alliance with Ferdinand that was at once unique and clearly understood by both, though it provoked – and continues to provoke – confusion. 'Some people may be astonished, and say, "How! Are there two monarchs in Castile?"' asked one befuddled visitor from England, writing in French.[15] 'I write "monarchs" because the king is king on account of the queen, by right of marriage, and because they jointly term themselves "monarchs".' Even contemporary observers, then, struggled to understand this unique phenomenon, with wilder explanations painting the queen either as a silent and subservient companion to Ferdinand or, alternatively, as a man-dominating harridan. Yet the royal 'we' employed in their letters reflected reality, for Isabella's signature was also her husband's, and vice versa – at least in Castile, for Aragon's laws made her queen consort and, in practice, the junior partner there.

One of the greatest problems for a biographer writing about Isabella is separating out the role of husband and wife, though this is often a pointless task. If one of Isabella's most important early decisions was to marry Ferdinand and another was to share power as near equals, then she also deserves credit for her husband's actions. His triumphs were hers (just as hers were his) and must add to, rather than subtract from, her individual achievements. Their failures and excesses must also be shared, but the couple's early discovery that two people whose partnership is grounded in absolute trust and confidence in each other's abilities can do much more than one person on their own is key to understanding Isabella's reign. This was fifteenth-century love – mostly a question of respect – at its best. In Isabella's case it was accompanied by a possessive, jealous passion for her husband that was a further mark of her intense, single-minded character.

Another difficulty in divining the truth about Isabella's life is her embrace of propaganda. She intuitively understood, as Machiavelli would put it, that 'to govern is to make believe'. She also wanted to ensure that her version of history – in which she appears as a sainted figure, delivering tough, redeeming love to a lost nation – would triumph. For this, Isabella counted on a group of tame chroniclers who not only depended on her for their livelihoods but often had to present their work for approval. This biographer has tried to use these chronicles judiciously, taking into account their authors' prejudices without ignoring the fact that they were often witnesses to the most important moments in Isabella's career. Where possible these have been contrasted against more impartial observers, be they letter writers, foreign visitors or the dry but revealing church, state and municipal records which Spanish scholars continue to mine.

For many Roman Catholics, Isabella's ability to cleanse her own country – including weeding out much of the church corruption that would drive people elsewhere into the arms of Protestantism – was crucial in turning Spain into a bulwark against Lutheranism and heresy. Witch-hunts carried out by both Protestants and Catholics across the rest of Europe, they point out, proved just as cruel as and more murderous than her most terrifying invention, the Spanish Inquisition. Even today her more fervent supporters campaign for her beatification. Among the reasons they give is that Columbus's voyage to the Americas, a venture that saw entire populations wiped out, delivered so many converts to Christianity.

A black legend, built around the Inquisition and bolstered by both Protestant disdain and Italian envy, shaped the vision of a queen who laid the foundations of the world's first global empire and prepared Spain to become Europe's dominant power for much of the sixteenth century. In Spain, an opposite process of glorification happened. Isabella became a model of every possible virtue and a ready symbol for religious conservatives and authoritarians ('The inspiration for our Africa policy' says a plaque put up by dictator General Francisco Franco's regime in 1951, in the small convent room in Madrigal de Las Altas Torres where she was born 500 years previously). That black legend, together with Spain's later dramatic decline, has helped to marginalise her in the dominant narratives of European history. Sexual prurience, meanwhile, has kept her out of literature and the popular imagination. Isabella could be a coquette, but she had no known or suspected lovers – carnal or otherwise. She stayed belligerently faithful to her wandering husband Ferdinand, struggling with her own jealousy while scorning women of lesser morality (and there were plenty). The heat of hidden love or lust did nothing to fire her reign. Passion was for God, her husband and her country. Her story is not about sex. It is about power.

No Man Ever Held Such Power

The Stúñiga family's house, Valladolid, 3 June 1453

Castile's greatest man rose at dawn, heard mass and took holy communion. Then Álvaro de Luna picked at a plate of bitter cherries and washed down with wine the few that his tightened, fearful throat allowed him to swallow. Outside, the streets of Valladolid were beginning to absorb the first rays of the harsh Castilian summer sun. The sixty-three-year-old noble who had governed the kingdom for as long as many could remember knew this was his last meal. Soon they brought a mule to the house where he was being kept prisoner in this wealthy city of silversmiths and merchants. With a black cape over his shoulders and his hat in place, they led him up the busy commercial street known as La Costanilla, over a small, smelly tributary of the River Esgueva and into the main plaza. 'This is the justice that our Lord King orders for this cruel tyrant and usurper of the royal crown, as punishment for his wickedness and service, ordering that his head be chopped off!' shouted the crier – nervously forgetting to say *dis*service. Luna's sharp mind produced a quick, sardonic riposte. 'Well said,' he quipped. 'This is how I am being paid for my service.'[1]

Even at this early hour a large crowd jostled to view the morbid procession through one of the kingdom's biggest cities – which lay amid grain fields and rough pastures in the broad, thin-aired flatlands of Spain's high, central *meseta*. Windows were packed with onlookers. For years Luna had ruled in the name of the true monarch,

Juan II, accruing not just power but also vast wealth. His lands, and those of the mighty Santiago military order that he led, stretched across the length and breadth of Castile. Juan had hero-worshipped and loved him when he was a child king. 'No man . . . ever reached so high, or held such power, or was so loved by his king,' wrote a contemporary chronicler called 'the Hawksman'.[2] Few, he might have added, were so hated by their enemies. These had spread a scurrilous rumour that the relationship between the young man who was appointed a page to the three-year-old monarch when he himself was eighteen had developed into something sexual and improper. As soon as Juan was old enough to rule on his own Luna became his *privado*, or favourite, exercising royal power in the monarch's name. Now that he was heading to his death, the city's people were both thrilled and appalled to witness the eternally enticing drama of a great man's downfall. Torches burned on two large crucifixes each side of a stage covered in black cloth where the executioner awaited. There was no axe or heavy sword for a swift death. The executioner had brought, instead, a *puñal* – a sharp-tipped, sometimes blunt-edged, dagger. 'I beg you to check that it is sharp,' said Luna, as he paced nervously around the stage. He had brought his own cord to bind his hands, but wanted to know what the iron hoop attached to a wooden stand was for. The executioner informed him that it was to display his head, just as soon as it had been detached from his body. 'Do what you will!' he retorted. The collar of his blue, pressed-woollen doublet, lined with the luxurious, steel-grey fur of Arctic foxes, was loosened and he was forced to lie on the stage. The executioner begged his forgiveness, then plunged the *puñal* into his neck and hacked off his head.

Two royal Isabellas were not far from Valladolid on that dramatic summer's day in 1453, probably in their recently built palace home forty miles away in the walled town of Madrigal de Las Altas Torres – an unpretentious square of narrow, two-storey buildings around a large courtyard. One of them was King Juan's daughter Isabella, the future queen of Castile, aged just two. The little girl with light auburn hair, greenish-blue eyes and unusually pale skin was too young to know what was happening. But her mother, Isabella of Portugal, was immensely pleased by the bloody spectacle being enacted in Valladolid. The queen consort, who was Juan's second wife, had helped orchestrate the downfall of the man who kept them apart for much of their six-year marriage. Other Grandees were also pleased. They had come to hate not just Luna's power, but also the way he justified it as a mere continuation of the king's own rightful and absolute supremacy over all his people. They did not like him preaching that the king was so far above the Grandees themselves. They believed that they should also have a major say in the running of the kingdom, and a bigger slice of its wealth. Luna's crime had been not his control of the king but his failure to share. The common folk of Valladolid were in two minds about his death. A silver tray placed in front of the stage for contributions to his funeral costs soon filled up with coins, bearing the king's figure or his lion and castle symbols. King Juan himself could not bear to be in the city for the death of the man whom he had adored as a child and trusted as a monarch. He stayed away, while others carried out his orders.[3]

Juan's forty-seven-year reign had started with his strapping English mother, Catherine of Lancaster, acting as co-regent for the toddler monarch. The six-foot-tall, increasingly obese daughter of John of Gaunt was a compulsive eater and drinker. Her imposing stature, ruddy cheeks, manly walk and continually expanding frame had a startling impact on those who saw her.[4] Men were not used to being towered over in such a fashion. But Catherine died, her muscles withering away, when Juan was just thirteen. Her death only increased the orphaned boy's emotional dependence on Luna. Catherine's main contributions to her husband's Trastámara dynasty were the very English complexion and light-coloured eyes passed on to her granddaughter.

Isabella's father was tall, sturdy, clever and deeply cultured. 'He spoke and understood Latin; he read very well; he liked books and stories a great deal. He took great pleasure in listening to poems and was a fine critic of them,' said Fernan Pérez de Guzmán, one of Castile's many talented poets. He was, however, a feeble king who preferred hunting or listening to music to the business of government, submitting to Luna's orders 'more obediently and humbly than any son ever did to his father'. There were huge obstacles to overcome, especially with the troublesome neighbouring kingdom of Aragon, which was now ruled by an uppity branch of the Trastámara family. Aragon occupied a large, triangular wedge of Iberia, including most of its east coast and the two great maritime trading cities of Barcelona and Valencia, as well as owning Sicily and Sardinia. Its ruling family, especially a group of young sibling princes known as the *infantes* of Aragon, claimed numerous lands in Castile. But Castile was wealthier, more populous and mightier. Luna eventually defeated the *infantes*, though the most successful of them – the wily, ruthless and long-lived future king of Aragon, Juan the Great – remained a thorn in Castile's side for decades to come.

After Juan II's first wife had died, leaving him with a lone son and heir called Enrique, a new marriage had been arranged to Isabella of Portugal. The court's many warrior poets were impressed by the nineteen-year-old granddaughter of Portugal's King João I. She was beautiful, sweet-natured and demure. Iñigo López de Mendoza, Marquess of Santillana and the greatest poet of the time, deemed her 'genteel person and face' worthy of a Giotto fresco. This apparent coyness hid a strength of character and willingness to enter the political fray that Luna would come to rue. Juan was forty-two when he remarried, and the young woman who stepped into his bed excited him enormously. 'The result was very different to that expected, as the monarch became passionate about the sweet young lady and began to enjoy with great freedom the honest [sexual] treatment of his beautiful wife,' said the acerbic royal official Alfonso de Palencia, one of the great chroniclers of Isabella's later reign.[5] Some worried that this infatuation was bad for his health. He was already considered 'close to old age', but reportedly partook of 'uninterrupted pleasures' with his young wife. His counsellors fretted that she would wear him out. That may have been one of the excuses used for keeping Juan away from her. For much of the time Isabella remained in the drab little palace in Madrigal de Las Altas Torres with her court of Portuguese ladies, while affairs of state kept her husband constantly on the move. The vast, open skies of the Castilian *meseta* – the highest region in Europe, after Switzerland – and the busy traffic of storks and other birdlife migrating to and from Africa must have provided little consolation to a woman used to the greenery and seascapes of Portugal. At one stage the queen saw her husband just twice in two years. It was in Madrigal de Las Altas Torres – famous for the uniquely Iberian *mudéjar* style of architecture that blended Arabic decorative and structural work with Romanesque and Gothic shapes – that her daughter Isabella had been born on 22 April 1451.[6] The appearance of a second heir to the throne, after her twenty-six-year-old half-brother Enrique, was celebrated, but there must have been disappointment about the child's sex. A second son would have been much better for the safe continuity of the Trastámara family dynasty. One duly appeared nineteen months later, when Isabella's brother Alfonso was born.

Isabella of Portugal was of haughty, noble stock and was about the only person apart from Luna with private access to the king. 'The young lady found opportunities to counsel him in secret, which was good for both the king's own honour and the security of the throne,' observed a royal chronicler. When he began to have second thoughts about acting against his favourite, she both pushed him to keep going and enlisted Grandee support. It was a sign of the forceful, proud and tenacious side of the royal Portuguese women who would serve as little Isabella's role models. The downfall of Luna brought only temporary relief. Juan soon fell ill, but not badly enough to give up his infatuation with his young wife. 'Nobody dared to warn him of the threat to his life posed by his uncontrolled passions . . . weakened, but a slave to sensuality and daily given over to the caresses of a young and beautiful wife,' recorded Palencia.[7]

Unpractised as he was, Isabella's father found ruling his lands without Luna more difficult than he had expected. He may have enjoyed more time with his wife, but his stamina was waning. A year later he also died and her half-brother Enrique was on the throne. Little Isabella's reaction is not recorded, though in his will her father had carefully named her third in succession to his crown, after Enrique and her young full sibling Alfonso. Nobody expected that she would ever become queen. She would, in any case, hold her position in the line of succession only until the new king Enrique could produce his own offspring.

2

The Impotent

The Royal Court of Castile 1454–1461

The king's sperm was disappointing. Physicians had brought Enrique IV to orgasm by masturbating him themselves. The result was considered 'watery and sterile', if good enough to make an attempt at artificial insemination. Enrique's second wife Juana of Portugal was given a thin gold tube with which to introduce the semen that her husband had produced into her vagina. 'It was to see if [via the tube] she could receive the semen, but she could not,' a German doctor who travelled to Castile's court, Hieronymus Münzer, reported later. A respected and wealthy Jewish doctor called Samaya, who had been a royal physician for decades, oversaw the extraordinary procedure. History's first recorded experiment in attempted human artificial insemination was a sign of just how desperate Isabella of Castile's half-brother was to produce an heir to his crown.[1] The problems he was experiencing were enough to generate a cruel nickname that served, also, as a metaphor for his reign – he was Enrique 'the Impotent'.

At Isabella's birth her half-brother Enrique had been married to Blanca, a princess from the independent kingdom of Navarre. Long-suffering Blanca had emerged from their wedding bed 'in the same state she had arrived in, which worried everyone', the son of a royal physician later wrote.[2] Tradition demanded that the sheets be displayed afterwards, so the humiliation of the fifteen-year-old prince and his sixteen-year-old bride must have been public. Later attempts at sex had been equally disastrous and the thirteen-year marriage was discreetly annulled on the basis of non-consummation after a hearing at a church in the small Segovian town of Alcazarén in May 1453. 'They can freely remarry . . . so that the prince can become a father and the princess a mother,' declared the Vatican-appointed official Luis de Acuña. Enrique blamed bewitchment for their problems, with his lawyers claiming that the couple suffered 'reciprocal impotence due to malign influences'. They also wanted the king's subjects to know that the problem was temporary and specific, presenting the evidence gathered by an 'honest priest' who had interviewed a number of the king's alleged lovers in Segovia. 'With each of them he had carnal relations just like any other potent male and his virile member was firm and duly produced manly seed,' the hearing was told. Enrique's enemies muttered that he must be homosexual. Others said his problem was physiological, caused by an unfortunately shaped penis with a bulbous head and narrow base that made it hard to maintain an erection. He had been a sickly, strange-looking youth, perhaps because his parents were first cousins.[3]

Isabella was moved even further away from the royal court when Enrique came to the throne in July 1454,[4] travelling with her mother Isabella of Portugal and little brother Alfonso to the walled town of Arévalo, not far from Madrigal de Las Altas Torres. There, in a sleepy Castilian backwater, the younger Isabella spent seven happy years. The two-storey Arévalo house was smaller than the palace in Madrigal de Las Altas Torres, but it was generous by the standards of such a modest town. The skyline of Arévalo, as in Madrigal, was dominated by its walls, defensive turrets and square church towers. These were often wrought in *mudéjar* style, the brickwork laid out in pretty patterns or with uncut stones, pebbles and mud filling regular, oblong spaces between columns and rows of red bricks. An Arab-built bridge ran across pointed arches at the bottom of the steep slope down to the River Adaja. Although well watered, the town was far from the moderating force of the sea and, sitting above the steep valleys of two rivers, it was fully exposed to the harsh weather of the *meseta* plateau.

Long, cold winters and short, baking-hot summers came almost back to back, separated only by brief autumns and springs. It was a tranquil and famously healthy place, surrounded by fields of cereal crops, vines and carefully tended pine woods, with vegetable gardens along the river banks.[5] 'The plague has rarely been known here, because of its clean and pure air,' wrote a later chronicler of the town. The most exotic aspect of Arévalo was its unusually large population of *mudéjar* Muslims (as those living in Christian Castile were known) and of Jews, perhaps a quarter of the total. These had enthusiastically taken part in the town's celebrations when Isabella's half-brother Enrique came to the throne, with their play-acting preceding the general cry of 'Castile! Castile for King Enrique!' Young princesses were not supposed to mix with such people. Visitors from northern Europe who frowned on Castile's unusual mix of religions complained that in some places Muslims were difficult to tell apart from Christians. Castilian visitors here, and to other towns with *mudéjar* Muslims, obviously suffered the same problems. Attempts to make them cut their hair differently and wear blue crescent symbols so that they would be recognisable to outsiders appear to have failed. But the Alis, Yussufs, Fatimas and Isaacs of Arévalo were easily identifiable to the townsfolk themselves, with clear differences in customs, dances, days of worship and the way they cooked their food using oil rather than pig fat or lard.[6]

Isabella of Portugal went into severe decline after Juan's death, reportedly shutting herself 'in a dark room, condemning herself to silence'. Palencia talks of her 'growing madness'. Her daughter was protective but seems to have responded to her mother's derangement by growing a hard, protective skin and attaching herself to the simple, tidy certainties provided by religion, tradition and social hierarchy. The appearance in Arévalo of yet another Portuguese Isabella – the young *infanta*'s widowed grandmother Isabella de Barcelos – mitigated the pain and confusion of growing up with such a deep depressive. Barcelos was part of a self-confident Portuguese royal family that was enjoying the fruits of international conquest thanks to its intrepid explorers and navigators. Her Castilian son-in-law had esteemed her so highly that she became one of his counsellors. Her Portuguese family were all that little Isabella would eventually seek to be – noble, conquering and devout. Barcelos appears to have been the most influential of the women who oversaw Isabella's early childhood, giving her an unshakeable sense of status and confidence in her own abilities. It was here, too, in the protected environment of the modest U-shaped palace with its closed patio and garden in Arévalo, that she developed a strong sisterly attachment to her childhood playmate Alfonso. The measure of Isabella's overall happiness in Arévalo was the bitterness with which she later recalled their departure.[7]

Young Isabella was surrounded by Portuguese retainers, but one of Luna's men – Gonzalo Chacón, another propagandist[8] for royal supremacy – was put in charge of her education. He may have reminded the young girl of her father's reasons for executing Luna, which had included 'usurping my royal pre-eminence' and ignoring 'royal superiority'.[9] She must also have heard the local legends of how Arévalo had been the home of Hercules, who would star-gaze from here into the clear *meseta* night, or how a nearby palace had housed Spain's Christian Gothic kings before the Muslim armies swept across the country in the eighth century.[10] Castile's poets and historians wrote wistfully about those virile, valiant and vice-free kings, claiming they were descendants of Hercules himself and awaiting the moment when God would allow their country to reclaim its natural glory. Castile's fall from grace had been divine punishment for sins that, with the Moors still occupying the large southern kingdom of Granada, had not been fully purged. Where Juan II had failed, they hoped, Enrique might now succeed. Isabella may have enjoyed the romantic tales of Castile's past, but she would not have seen them as an educational lesson for a future monarch. She was, after all, just a girl. Not only did she have two brothers, but in the unlikely event that she were to inherit Castile's crown, a husband could be expected to govern for her.[11]

Like his father Juan II, Enrique also relied on a *privado* to do the work of governing – in this case the greedy and ambitious Juan Pacheco, Marquess of Villena, who had ruled over him since he was a boy. Pacheco had 'encouraged the prince's lust, allowing him to fall into all kinds of lascivious behaviour and blindly following degenerates into depravity',[12] wrote one of his many detractors. Pacheco had been placed at Enrique's side by Álvaro de Luna and came to imitate him in many respects, while also learning from his errors.[13] Where Luna preached an early form of royal absolutism, with himself as the wielder of the monarch's power, Pacheco claimed to be the leader of a faction of nobles who would help the king rule in a more collegiate and allegedly time-honoured fashion. His real interest was personal enrichment, using conspiracy, chaos and a constant reshuffling of alliances with the grasping Grandees as his main tools.

Pacheco soon fixed a second marriage for Enrique. His new wife was another Iberian princess, Juana of Portugal. She was just sixteen, a noted beauty and, like so many other European princesses, a simple bargaining chip used to seal an alliance with her brother, King Afonso V. Some saw a marriage between beauty and beast. Enrique proclaimed that he wanted her to bear children who would 'add greater authority to my royal status', but he also took the precaution of abolishing the law that made royal wedding nights a public spectacle.[14] A court wit joked that the king would never father a child and 'laughed at that farcical marriage night, saying there were three things he wouldn't bend over to pick up in the street: the king's virility, the Marquess's pronunciation [the stuttering Pacheco][15] and the Archbishop of Seville's gravity'.[16]

Enrique was twenty-six years older than his half-sister, Isabella. He was a kindly, shy and cultured man with a penchant for tragic ballads.[17] A gifted singer and musician, collector of exotic animals and a superb horseman, he was temperamentally unsuited to the public role of a king. There was nothing he liked more than to hide himself away with his animals or lose himself deep inside a thick forest, accompanied by his loyal personal guard of *mudéjar*

Muslims. A childhood accident had left him with a deformed nose, squashed flat on to his face, but he was tall, athletic and blue-eyed with a bushy beard and fair hair. To his admirers this made him look like a fierce lion. To his enemies he looked 'like a monkey'.[18] Enrique suffered a form of acromegaly or gigantism, which left him with outsized hands and feet along with an abnormally large head and thick facial features. His massive forehead stood above strangely staring eyes and wide, strong cheeks that flattened out as they descended into a long, unwieldy jaw.[19] He was a king with no airs and limited self-esteem, who rejected the daily trappings of royalty. 'He never allowed people to kiss his hand, and made little of himself . . . He dressed simply, in woollen cloth, with long tunics and hooded cloaks: royal insignias and ceremony were not to his taste,' said Diego Enríquez del Castillo, his admiring official chronicler. A portrait by a German traveller showed him in a simple, hooded cloak and riding boots, two lynx-like felines at his feet and his head covered with a red cap. He was, in short, a gentle giant – intimidating but cripplingly overwhelmed by his own physical defects and only properly happy when out of public view. Nor was he terribly interested in his half-siblings, with Isabella seeing little of the king in the early years of her life.[20]

Pacheco was an able, if self-serving, *privado* and together he and Enrique made a promising start. The end of the Hundred Years War in France brought increased trade and a small economic boom as they renewed Castile's traditional French alliance.[21] Enrique also poured money into a new war against the Moorish kingdom of Granada, which was as much a point of honour as it was an opportunity for territorial growth and personal enrichment for the crown, the lesser aristocracy and the families of the Grandees. It also offered wider prestige in a Europe traumatised by the loss of Constantinople to the Muslim Turks the year before Enrique came to the throne.

His greatest problem was a powerful and wealthy faction of the Grandees. As Álvaro de Luna had stood on that stage waiting for his head to be hacked off in Valladolid a few years earlier, he had spotted one of Enrique's gentleman grooms in the crowd. 'Tell the prince to give better rewards to his servants than the king has ordered for me,' he said. Enrique did exactly that, giving away to the Grandees and others much of his royal wealth – especially the income from the so-called *realengo* lands and towns that belonged directly to the crown. As their wealth and power grew, so his declined. Greedy Pacheco pulled the strings, took his cut and made sure his family rose above the rest. Enrique's war on Granada, for which he raised a large army, was less adventurous than many liked. He preferred attrition to open warfare and set-piece battles. 'He was pious rather than cruel and loved his people's lives more than the spilling of blood, saying that a man's life was priceless,' according to del Castillo. 'He preferred to inflict damage on his enemies little by little, rather than see his people killed or wounded.'[22] This was a sensible strategy, but some thought it cowardly, especially as the Moors were refusing to pay the tributes that Castile normally demanded from Granada.

All the time Pacheco and the other nobles schemed behind his back, encouraging chaos. In the wilder, northern fringes of his kingdom, in rainy Galicia and along the storm-swept Cantabrian seaboard, arch-priests, bishops, nobles and lesser gentlemen fought each other for land or took control of royal territory with virtual impunity.[23] Similar chaos ruled in the south-eastern frontier lands of Murcia, while Grandees and other local strongmen tussled with one another for power over southern Seville and much of Andalusia. And where royal power was weak and nobles were busy fighting one another, crime flourished, justice was absent and people were unhappy.

Those looking for reasons to criticise Enrique found many, especially his lack of regal grandeur. 'He covered that lovely hair with common hats, hoods or tasteless caps,' said one of his chief detractors, Isabella's future chronicler Alfonso de Palencia. 'His great height was vulgarised . . . by clothes that were beneath his dignity and shoes that were even shabbier.' We do not know what Isabella was told about her half-brother, but his slovenly, unregal appearance is unlikely to have impressed her proud Portuguese grandmother. There were even rumours that his commitment to Christianity was suspect and he was accused of allowing his Muslim personal guards to 'snatch young men and women from their parents' arms and corrupt them'.[24] Muslim families liked to bring him delicacies as he travelled, pandering to the king's sweet tooth. 'They came out to meet him with figs, raisins, butter, milk and honey, which the king ate with delight, seated on the ground in the Moorish fashion. In this, as in all things, he adapted himself to their habits, and that made them feel stronger while, at the same time, the concerns of our own people grew and grew,'[25] Palencia wrote with evident disdain. The Muslims in Enrique's kingdoms, like Castile's Jews, fell under his personal protection, which he maintained despite growing popular pressure against them both. A populist preacher called Friar Alonso de Espina whipped up hatred with invented tales about kidnapped Christian children having their hearts torn out by Jews, who burned them to ashes, mixed them with wine and drank them.[26] The age-old 'blood libel' against the Jews – that they used the blood of murdered Christian children in secret rituals – which had been circulating around Europe for centuries despite attempts by various popes to quash it, thus made its way into Castile.[27] 'Just as the devil has a thousand ways of causing harm, so has the Jew, his son,' Espina proclaimed.[28]

Nobles seeking to stir up trouble also encouraged attacks[29] on the large community of *conversos* or 'new' Christians, who were mostly descended from Jewish families that had converted en masse during outbreaks of anti-Jewish violence sixty years earlier. Here again, Friar Espina[30] fanned the flames of hatred towards what, for blood reasons, some still saw as a group that formed part of the 'Jewish race'.[31] A fellow friar, Fernando de la Plaza, even claimed to have collected 100 foreskins from secret *converso* circumcision ceremonies.[32] 'Friar Fernando told the King that he did not have the foreskins in his possession, but that the matter was related to him by people of authority . . . but refused to mention their names, so that it was all found to be a lie,' del Castillo said.[33] As popular worry about 'secret Jews' grew, the *converso* head of the Jeronymite order, Friar Alfonso de Oropesa, was asked to investigate their existence in the archbishopric of Toledo. He concluded that the few cases of so-called 'judaising' (following Jewish rites and beliefs) were mostly due to ignorance, while complaints were largely the result of envy or the economic self-interest of so-called 'old' Christians.[34]

As the years dragged on, Enrique's power disintegrated and chaos spread. The lack of a direct heir did not help. Then, seven years after he had married Juana of Portugal, his wife finally became pregnant. No one expressed surprise, at least in public, at the king's sudden ability to sire children. Perhaps the experiments in artificial insemination had worked. Castile celebrated, but for his half-sister Isabella this was one of the most traumatic moments of her life. If Juana was to give birth to a new heir, Enrique wanted any challengers kept close. Isabella and her little brother Alfonso, now aged ten and seven, were ordered to leave Arévalo and join his court. 'Alfonso and I, who were just children at the time, were inhumanely and forcibly torn from our mother's arms and taken into Queen Juana's power,' she complained later.[35]

3

The Queen's Daughter

Segovia, 1461–1464

Queen Juana swore loudly and grabbed doña Guiomar de Castro, the rising star of Castile's court and her husband's formal lover, by the hair. With her other hand the queen picked up a *chapín*, the clog-like, wooden-soled platform shoes that she wore to paddle through muddy courtyards and that usefully added several inches to her normal height. Then she brought the heavy shoe crashing down on Guiomar's head. 'She hit her many times on the head and shoulders,' one chronicler reported.[1] Life at court, the ten-year-old Isabella would soon find, was considerably more eventful than it had been in sleepy, safe Arévalo.

Isabella and Alfonso had waved goodbye to their mother and grandmother late in 1461, travelling the forty miles from Arévalo to Segovia through the bitter winter cold.[2] It is impossible to know how her mother coped with the separation. In years to come Isabella would visit whenever she could, but in the short term the ten-year-old girl was in Queen Juana's hands. Later in her life, Isabella would hold the queen up as a sort of evil stepmother figure, abusing the young girl who came to her court, though Enrique's official chronicler del Castillo – whose role was to glorify his king as far as possible – claimed otherwise. 'She was always treated with love and sisterliness,' he wrote.[3]

Segovia was a far bigger city than Arévalo, perched on a windswept hill with an impressive Roman aqueduct bearing water from hillside to hillside on rows of double arches ninety-five feet high.

The change in atmosphere, from protected, childish naivety to a world of sophisticated political and sexual intrigue, was absolute. Isabella's sister-in-law Juana had brought with her to the city's San Martín palace a group of young, aristocratic Portuguese ladies-in-waiting famed for flirtatious behaviour and outlandish clothes.[4] 'Never before has such a group of girls so totally lacking in discipline been seen,' the curmudgeonly chronicler Palencia reported.

> Their provocative dress titillated, an effect that was magnified even more by their provocative words. Giggling was a frequent part of their conversation . . . They gorged themselves day and night with greater abandon than if they had been in a tavern. Sleep took up the rest of their time, apart from that which they set aside for cosmetics and perfumes; and they made no secret of doing that, but went uncovered in public from their nipples down to their belly button, painting themselves with white make-up from their toes, ankles and shins to their upper thighs and groin so that, when they fell from their horses – as happened all too frequently – their limbs would shine with uniform whiteness.[5]

Palencia's unfettered misogyny and desire to destroy Enrique IV's reputation undoubtedly made him exaggerate the plunging necklines and flirtatious behaviour of these teenage Portuguese *damas*, but neutral observers were also shocked. 'The queen of Castile is here. And with her are many ladies in varying headgear: one wore a bonnet, the other a *carmagnole* jacket, another's hair was loose, or in a hat, or done up with a piece of silk or a Moorish turban,' one stunned Navarran noble reported. 'Some carry daggers, others have swords or even lances, darts and Castilian capes. I, sir, have never seen so many outfits before.'

Isabella soon discovered that life at Juana of Portugal's court in the solid, if higgledy-piggledy San Martín palace, was boisterously competitive, but it was also fun. The queen loved partying and believed, like many, that a royal court should do so intensely.

That made her an attractive social counterweight to her withdrawn, misanthropic husband – who kept one half of the palace for his own household. Courtly love, the theatrical and ritualistic game of conquest and rapture played out in royal courts across Europe, was an essential part of the entertainment and intrigue. It was, at least in theory, a safe form of recreation. Courtly love relied not on physical seduction, but on elaborate rituals and exaggerated declarations of infatuation. These were as much about posturing as about passion. Isabella saw plenty of it and, despite the routine condemnations of Juana's infamous court by later chroniclers who were in her pay, never expressed dislike or disapproval. One of her envoys famously had to be carried out of an English banquet after fainting at the sight of the lady he was wooing. It was, too, a perfectly honourable pastime for married men and women. Isabella's own heart raced fastest to tales of the mortal dangers faced by knights in battle, but poets and troubadours had long told tales of lovesickness and hopeless adoration, and she certainly did not complain of being the love focus for an outpouring of Spanish chivalric poetry later in her life.[6]

Isabella learned that kings were allowed, even expected, to play the courtly love game. So were queens. At jousts the young knights were meant to flatter Queen Juana by wearing her colours, sending her gifts and proclaiming their devotion and utmost willingness to die in combat for her – or for one of her ladies-in-waiting. Courtly love was safe terrain, too, for the sexually inhibited Enrique. Kings could take their lovers to bed, but this was by no means necessary. Doña Guiomar was the best-known – but not the only – of Enrique's formal lovers. She certainly kept Enrique interested, and their dalliance allowed him to project himself as a man of sexual vigour, though no offspring were engendered. The spiteful Palencia thought that Enrique deliberately tormented the queen with his lovers, hoping to push her into the arms of someone else who might leave her pregnant with a child he could claim was his own. 'He judged that the jealousy [provoked by] these false [sexual] relations was the most powerful tool for breaking down the queen's resistance,' Palencia claimed. It is more likely that the insecure king was putting on a show, in much the same way as he insisted on having three 'formal' wedding nights, in separate years, with Juana. Either way, there was nothing shocking about it. The relationship was deemed by gentler commentators to be of 'good honour and profit'.[7]

Yet the lines around courtly love were blurred and could cause problems. Such was the case with the upstart and cavalier doña Guiomar. Her crime, in Juana's eyes, was the lack of respect she showed to her, the queen. The young bucks who had previously worn the queen's colours at jousts and other tournaments had begun to wear Guiomar's colours instead. Presents and other tokens of courtly love went to Guiomar, not Juana. 'Those seeking royal favour made doña Guiomar their target, rather than her [the queen],' said Palencia. Supporters of one woman or another squabbled continually, and the whole thing threatened to get out of hand. Enrique's right-hand man Pacheco favoured Juana while his other close adviser, the archbishop of Seville, sided with Guiomar. It was all part of the irrevocable breakdown of morality, Palencia tutted as he later wrote – for Isabella's judgemental eyes – the blackest possible version of her half-brother's life. 'It was insufferable for her to see his favourite receiving all the good fortune and the praise of the courtesan, thereby wounding her dignity,' he said. Enrique was furious with his wife for her attack on Guiomar. His response was to deposit his haughty mistress in luxurious accommodation two leagues away while showering her with gifts and income. 'The king went often to see her,' reported del Castillo.[8]

Becoming the king's formal mistress was a good career move for an ambitious court lady like Guiomar, who went on to marry the powerful Duke of Treviño and have ten children with him (while he also acquired a further half-dozen illegitimate offspring from his own mistresses).[9] Enrique's other known 'lover', Catalina de Sandoval, would become an abbess – a position of power and wealth – despite her wild reputation for 'freely seeking out men'. In this case, Palencia claimed, Enrique placed her in charge of a notorious convent just outside Toledo's city walls, where the nuns were famed for their 'dissolute and frenetic life'. Palencia's malicious imagination added scabrous detail to his black propaganda. Not only did Enrique send armed men to evict the reformist abbess then in residence, he claimed, but the king also ordered the beheading of one of Catalina's other lovers – a handsome young man called Alfonso de Córdoba – out of impotent spite.[10]

While kings could bed their lovers, queens were permitted to play the love game only if they reserved their bodies for their husbands. Even Palencia admitted that, for the time being, Juana remained a good, modest and faithful queen consort. 'No one was ever such a good friend of gentility and virtue as you are,' wrote the poet Gómez Manrique.[11]

The queen's wing in the palace in Segovia was independent and separated from the king's side by the animal house that was home to Enrique's roaring lions.[12] Isabella saw little of Enrique, as the queen's side had its own doorway through a large granite arch on to a small square. A row of shops selling fish, meat and bread sat opposite one side of the palace and nearby streets would have bustled with commerce. Thick walls kept out the summer heat and fires must have roared in the winter as bitter, freezing winds whipped into the city. In architectural terms, Isabella had swapped the *mudéjar* towers of Arévalo's churches for the solid, Romanesque forms of Segovia. Enrique's court was nomadic, but Juana's pregnancies also meant there were periods when the king was afraid to move her, and Isabella's first two years with the queen saw them spend long periods in Segovia or Madrid.[13]

As the due date drew nearer in February 1462, the king sent a litter to carry Juana as gently as possible to his Alcazar palace in the then small and relatively unimportant city of Madrid. Isabella probably travelled the sixty-odd miles of bumpy road too, for she followed the queen's court almost wherever it went.[14]

The birth was difficult. Unlike in other European courts where royal women retired to their rooms accompanied by an entirely female entourage, in Castile men attended. In fact, Juana went through labour with a crowd of men around her, including the king, his favourite Pacheco and various other senior members of the royal household.[15] Enrique, Count of Alva de Liste, wrapped his arms around her for support as she squatted to give birth.[16] After a long struggle, the baby was finally born. It was a cause of both joy and disappointment. Instead of a boy who would be an uncontested heir, Juana produced a girl. In Castile this was less of a problem than elsewhere, where women were banned from ruling. The girl could inherit the throne if necessary, though her husband could be expected to rule in her name. Nevertheless, after seven years of barren marriage, the birth was also a triumph. Enrique had proved that he could sire children. If one had been engendered, more could surely come. The court celebrated with jousts, bull-runs and the tourney-style game of *cañas*, inherited from the Moors, where groups of riders on swift ponies would hurl long cane poles at one another.[17] Eight days later the baby girl was christened Juana, like her mother. It was a suitably grand affair. The mighty archbishop of Toledo, a feudal churchman and political heavyweight from the powerful Carrillo family, baptised the girl. Isabella was there too, the ten-year-old girl becoming godmother to her baby niece.[18] 'The whole kingdom rejoiced,' reported del Castillo.[19]

Three months later Enrique ordered that the parliament, the Cortes, made up of representatives, or *procuradores*, from seventeen important cities, assemble in Madrid together with most of the great lords, bishops and gentlemen to swear acceptance of Juana as heiress. 'I order that you swear here to my daughter Princess doña Juana, my first-born child, that you are faithful and loyal to her as is the custom with the first-born children of kings, so that when God is done with me there is someone to inherit and reign over these kingdoms,' Enrique told them.[20] Isabella and Alfonso were the first to swear. Isabella walked up to their baby cousin as she lay in the arms of the archbishop of Toledo, said the oath and kissed the tiny hands of her future rival. Some nobles, including Pacheco, claimed they had sworn against their free will. Secret documents were signed, declaring as much, but without explaining why. Isabella later claimed that she knew exactly why they had objected to swearing the oath, blaming Queen Juana. 'It was something she [the queen] had demanded because she knew the truth about her pregnancy and was taking precautions,' she said, referring to the baby's allegedly dubious paternity.[21]

It is impossible to either prove or disprove the theory that saw the baby Juana later given the nickname of 'La Beltraneja', after her putative father Beltrán de la Cueva, Enrique's *mayordomo*, or royal steward.[22] Isabella would later amplify and broadcast the theory, but two telling pieces of evidence suggest that the baby girl really was Enrique's daughter. The most persuasive is that Juana was pregnant again within a year. In this case it was a boy, but the queen miscarried at six months. A curious letter sent to Enrique by an official in Juana's household, keeping him up to date on goings-on there while he was away, sees the doctors themselves swearing that another pregnancy could be engendered soon. The Jewish doctor Samaya had been sent to look after Juana as she was nursed back to health after the miscarriage in Aranda de Duero, accompanied by Isabella and the rest of her court. This was a densely packed, walled town 100 miles north of Madrid, where the houses stood atop a labyrinth of cool cellars that stored what was already, and still is, one of the most precious products from the *ribera,* or banks, of the west-flowing River Duero – the rich red wine made from local vines grown on limestone soils. Samaya had done his work well. 'He has cured her so well that her ladyship is now very healthy,' the letter writer, called Guinguelle, said. '*Maestre* Samaya says that he would bet his own neck that, if your highness came today, the queen would get pregnant again.'[23] Perhaps, with his thin golden tube for artificial insemination, Samaya had found a way to help them past the king's physical problems or the psychological traumas that might have come with them. Either way, the fact that little Juana was born in matrimony and never repudiated as his biological daughter was enough to ensure her legal position as his heiress.[24]

Concern about the paternity issue made its way to Rome, where a report from Pope Pius II to his secretary Gobellino within eighteen months of the birth laid out all the possibilities then being discussed in hushed tones at the court and which Isabella, now aged twelve, must also have heard. 'It was said that the queen . . . was impregnated without losing her virginity. Some said that the semen poured into the entrance [of her vagina] had penetrated into the most hidden places inside her. Others believed a man other than Enrique was responsible and that he so ardently desired an heir that he treated the girl as his own because it was that woman who had given birth.'[25] The rumours that had reached Rome now gave the troublesome Grandees an excuse for rebellion.[26] A bogus heiress was being foisted on Castile, they could argue. It was their duty to act.

4

Two Kings, Two Brothers

Avila, 5 June 1465

The rebellion was staged on a summer's day outside the cren-
ellated and turreted walls of Avila – an imposing mass of
grey granite, studded with eighty-seven bulging towers that ran
for two miles around the hilltop city. A wooden stage had been
erected and a crowd gathered to see the show. An effigy of the
king, dressed in mourning, was placed on a mock throne. Around
it stood a gang of Grandees, with Pacheco, the belligerent archbishop of Toledo, Alfonso Carrillo, and the Manriques, another
powerful noble clan, leading them.[1] 'He had a crown on his head,
the sword of justice in front of him, and a rod in his hands,' the
chronicler Enríquez del Castillo, who remained loyal to Enrique,
reported. The archbishop stepped up to the dummy and tore
off the crown, loudly insisting that it no longer deserved royal
treatment. Then Pacheco[2] snatched away its sceptre while others
grabbed the sword. Enrique had forfeited his right to reign or
administer justice, they told the crowd. Then they kicked over
the king's chair and booted him off the stage. Some onlookers
burst into tears. But nobleman Diego López de Zúñiga and others
continued to hurl insults at the broken toy, shouting '¡A tierra,
puto!'[3] ('Down on the ground, faggot!').

With Enrique's dummy lying in the dust, they brought their new
king on to the stage. He was Isabella's brother Alfonso, a boy who was
just eleven years old.[4] Too young to rule himself, he would obviously
need them, the Grandees, to do the job for him. They hoisted the boy

on to their shoulders amid shouts of 'Castile for King Alfonso!' The country now had two kings. Civil war had been proclaimed.

Isabella was not on the walls of Avila to see her beloved little brother declared king in June, 1465. She was still with Enrique and Juana's court, but her status now changed. The battle between Enrique IV and Alfonso had two major secondary actors – their respective heirs, the infant Juana and Isabella – and control of them was part of the new game.

In the run-up to this piece of theatre, the nobles had discussed various ways to excuse their lust for power. Among the more absurd suggestions was that Enrique be charged with heresy for secretly trying to convert them to Islam. Wiser heads said the pope, who would have to decide, was unlikely to fall for that. Others claimed that Enrique should be accused of breaking with the supposed tradition that Castile's kings were historically elected by the nobility and public acclaim.[5]

Isabella was now an important piece on the complex chessboard of Castilian politics. She had turned twelve in 1463 and so was already of marrying age.[6] Whoever married her would become one of the most powerful men in the kingdom. As Castile separated into two factions, Enrique sought the support of Portugal, while the seditious nobles looked to Aragon and its king, Juan the Great. The best way to seal an alliance was with a marriage, especially if the bride-to-be was of Castilian royal blood. In April 1464 Isabella had found herself being transported to a town on the Portuguese border to meet Queen Juana's thirty-one-year-old brother, King Afonso V of Portugal. Isabella appears to have spoken to him in Portuguese, learned both at her mother's house and among Queen Juana's ladies. 'Her beauty so captivated him that he immediately wanted to make her his wife,' reported a fawning Palencia.[7]

Those plotting rebellion accused Enrique of holding Isabella and her brother against their will. They even made a clumsy attempt at kidnapping them from Madrid's Alcázar fortress, which was easily foiled, as was a second attempt a few months later. 'We are sure that certain people, with wicked intent, have taken control of the illustrious prince Alfonso and, at the same time, of the illustrious princess Isabella. And not only that, we are also sure that these people have agreed to and planned to kill the said prince and marry off the princess,' the disgruntled group of Grandees wrote in the May 1464 manifesto which fired the first shot of rebellion. 'And this will be done without the agreement of the Grandees of this kingdom as is the custom when such matches are made, all with the aim of allowing succession [of the crown] in this kingdom to pass to someone who has no right to it.' They demanded that the young prince and princess, whom they now termed 'the rightful heirs' to the crown, should be taken away from Queen Juana and handed over to them.[8]

As royal authority disintegrated, superstitious Castilians began to see bad omens. A tornado swept through southern Seville, a city divided between violent political factions, knocking down buildings and killing people. Frightened *sevillanos* stared up into the sky to see what looked like rows of soldiers lined up to fight one another. Many saw their own future painted there, in the tumultuous skies above Castile's most populous city. Ordinary people knew that while the spirit of rebellion was confined to the noble class, it was they who would suffer if the latter unleashed the chaos of war. Rampant inflation, epidemics and bad harvests made things worse. They were right to worry. Civil war sputtered into life on September 1464, with Enrique retreating behind Segovia's thick walls.[9]

Pacheco's gang extended its list of complaints, which already included the restoration of the custom that royal wedding nights be public events, with notaries and witnesses. Now they took aim at the *conversos*, accusing Enrique of surrounding himself with heretics. They added colour to their gripes by claiming that his Moorish guard was given both to raping women and to indulging in homosexual acts. He raised unwarranted taxes, failed to consult with his nobles, allowed coinage to be debased and failed to administer proper justice, they added. Above all, they complained that he was now the captive of his *mayordomo*, Beltrán de la Cueva. For the first time, they dared to claim openly that the king was a cuckold and his daughter the result of adultery. 'Both your royal highness and he [Beltrán] know that she is not your daughter and cannot be your lawful successor,' they said. This first public allegation of Juana's illegitimacy was to be key to the future of Castile, and to that of Isabella.[10]

Enrique dilly-dallied. The aged bishop of Cuenca, Lope de Barrientos, had raised a large army and urged him to fight. 'Otherwise you will go down in history as the most useless king there has ever been in Spain,' he said. Instead, at least initially, he chose to give way, reneging on Juana's right to inherit the throne and declaring Alfonso his heir. The boy was handed to Pacheco. Isabella, who was told she would be given her own household, must have briefly clung to a promise that she could also return to her mother in Arévalo. But Enrique then went back on his word, demanding that Alfonso be returned to him and preparing for war. Isabella had to remain in Segovia, her hopes of joining her mother dashed. Instead she was watched over by Queen Juana while her brother was raised on the Grandees' shoulders in Avila and proclaimed king.[11]

Pacheco soon sought to make personal gain out of the chaos. His messengers now told Enrique that the best way to buy his family's loyalty back and quash the rebellion was to marry Isabella to his brother and fellow rebel, Pedro Girón – a powerful magnate in Andalusia and head of the Calatrava military order. He was prepared to pay a handsome price, offering to bring 3,000 lancers and lend Enrique 70,000 *doblas* (as Castile's higher-value gold coins were called), and promising that he and his brother would switch their allegiance and 'bring the prince, his brother, and place him [back] in his power'. Enrique agreed, urging Girón to 'come as fast as possible'. The move was at once brilliant and fraught with danger. It put Pacheco's scheming, ruthless family within arm's reach of the crown. Girón set out for Segovia armed with money and a large escort of men designed to impress those who saw it with his power and magnificence.[12] Isabella, now realising that she had become a simple item for barter, was to be his prize.

Isabella had raised no complaint against the proposed Portugal match, probably because marrying a monarch did not seem beneath her dignity. Now she reacted with horror, sinking to her knees and begging God to free her from the Girón match. Her prayers worked. As Girón rode towards her, he fell ill and ten days later he died. Enrique was crestfallen, but Isabella, who had just turned fifteen, was delighted. Her Portuguese match was now also forgotten as chaos ruled on both sides of a conflict that neither side was strong enough to win. The experience seems to have marked her, and she began to draw her own conclusions about allowing others to decide her fate.[13]

Civil war, meanwhile, dragged on. Battles were few and far between and, by the standards of other confrontations in Europe, remarkably low in casualties. With royal authority now either completely absent or contested, the kingdom descended into a series of mostly local feuds. Some were old rivalries come back to life, others reflected the new conflict between the king and the Grandees or the growing intolerance towards *conversos*, while rogue elements and ambitious nobles stole or claimed whatever they could. Anti-*converso* rioting broke out in Toledo, which had long been a focus of rivalry between 'old' and 'new' Christians, with both sides taking up arms and fire consuming part of the city. Two *converso* leaders were hanged by the mob. 'They opposed the church and so it was ordered that they be hung by their feet, head down,' a crier called out as their naked bodies were paraded around the city. Nobles switched this way and that, some trying to stay on both sides at once. Pacheco was the master of this. 'With one foot planted on the shoulder of one king and the other foot planted on the shoulder of the other king he pisses over us all,' a fellow noble complained.[14]

A battle at Olmedo in August 1467 produced a narrow but inconclusive victory for Enrique. It was, by the standards of this messy, still inchoate war, a big battle – but only forty-five soldiers died. The archbishop of Toledo, leading Alfonso's army, was wounded. A month later Alfonso turned the tide, riding into Segovia almost without a fight after traitors opened the gates to his troops. The shock-waves soon reached the San Martín palace. A frightened Queen Juana dashed for the cathedral and then for the fortified safety of the mighty Alcázar, a fairytale fortress with pointed towers which crowned an unassailable spur jutting out over the confluence of the Eresma and Clamores rivers. But the sixteen-year-old Isabella found, for almost the first time, that she had to make her own decision. Would she go with Juana, or back her brother against her half-brother? This does not seem to have been too difficult to resolve. Isabella's loyalty lay firmly with her childhood companion from Arévalo rather than with the weak, if kindly, half-brother who was twenty-six years her senior. 'I stayed in my palace, against the queen's will, in order to leave her dishonest custody that was bad for my honour and dangerous for my life,' Isabella explained later in life, adding more than a touch of righteous drama. Her meeting with Alfonso, who appeared later at the San Martín palace, was a happy one, according to the chroniclers – 'both were contented, with joyous faces'.[15]

Backing Alfonso was a life-changing decision, though she could not know it. It was also brave. No one knew how the civil war would end, or who would suffer most. But, for the first time, Isabella now also showed her mettle. She would go with her brother, but only on certain conditions. These she spelled out quite clearly. Alfonso's most important counsellors, including Pacheco and the archbishop of Toledo, were to sign a document agreeing that she would not be forced into a marriage she did not want. She also demanded that she be allowed to return to her mother's house in Arévalo.[16] She had lived with Juana in Enrique's court for six years, but the modest dowager's palace and the *mudéjar* towers of Arévalo were her real home.

Enrique had lost Segovia, his favourite city. It was too much. He began negotiating once more with Pacheco and his allies, who demanded that Queen Juana be handed over to them. This was the end of Juana's political career and she responded by living up to the reputation already attributed to her. She began an enduring relationship with Pedro de Castilla, nephew of the man whose charge she was put into – the notoriously untrustworthy archbishop of Seville, Alfonso de Fonseca. Now Juana really did fall pregnant by her lover Pedro de Castilla. She tried to hide the pregnancy under a special wire contraption, but there was no point. A son, Andrés, was born. She did not stop there, for a second son would be called Apóstol. Such brazenly scandalous behaviour would fuel Isabella's later furious assault on her half-sister-in-law's reputation, but Enrique did not seem too upset and continued to send his wife gifts, including a silver service and even a bed.[17]

Isabella, meanwhile, was enjoying her return to Arévalo. When Alfonso turned fourteen on 17 December 1467, they celebrated the birthday in their mother's house, with Isabella organising the mummery and dressing up as one of the muses. She asked Gómez Manrique, the great court poet, to write the verses that she and her ladies acted out for her brother. They remained there for several months, but an outbreak of plague saw Alfonso, accompanied by Isabella and a body of troops, flee Arévalo at the end of June 1468.[18]

They stopped for the night at the village of Cardeñosa, where Alfonso was served breaded trout. That night he slept badly and the following morning was unable to talk. Isabella stayed by his bedside for part of the next four days. As the hours went by, and doctors tried to bleed him, it became clear that her brother was dying. Isabella had time to discuss with Pacheco and the archbishop of Toledo what should happen next. She herself wrote letters on 4 July. 'According to what the doctors say, and as a result of the sins of this kingdom, his life is in such great danger that he is unlikely to survive,' she said. 'And you all know that in the moment that the Lord decides to take his life, succession of the kingdoms and royal lands of Castile and León will, as his legitimate heiress and successor, pass to me.'[19]

5

Bulls

Toros de Guisando, 19 September 1468

I t was a cool, clear day in the open land at the foot of the Cerro de Guisando, a first, gentle rampart rising towards the southern side of central Spain's soaring Gredos mountains. Four giant, granite bulls stood among what, given the time of year, must have been a parched landscape of yellowed grass and bush, the trees still full leaved and a snaking line of greenery marking the course of a narrow, gently gurgling stream. This was a special place. A handful of contemplative Jeronymite monks had chosen to take refuge from the world in a small, rustic monastery on a wooded hillside near by. No one knew what the mysterious, long-backed bulls were doing here, or who had so carefully and laboriously carved them out of massive blocks of raw granite. Their presence spoke of physical power and centuries of unwritten history. It was an appropriate place for Isabella to seal an historic agreement.

The princess rode a handsomely garnished mule. It was led by the archbishop of Toledo, Alfonso Carrillo, who walked unwillingly and suspiciously ahead of her as they approached the king. The bellicose archbishop had come with 200 of his own lancers. But this meeting was not about war. It was about bringing peace to a kingdom that had lived in a state of anguished uncertainty for three years. It was a peace that Isabella had chosen and which, despite her youth and dependence on others, bore the stamp of self-confidence and assertiveness that some already found unsettling in a person of her sex and age.

Enrique arrived with far greater pomp, accompanied by more than a thousand horsemen. The fanfares blasted out by his trumpeters must have sent the terrified local wildlife scurrying into holes, lairs and thickets, or flocks of startled birds flying into the distance. The show of might was real, since Enrique had the power to destroy Isabella and her supporters. Some wished he would. But he, too, preferred peace, even if that meant bending to the will of the young woman approaching him on her splendid mule. He was tired of trouble and, anyway, had long shaped his behaviour around the avoidance of conflict, armed or otherwise. Isabella dismounted. She approached Enrique, bent down and made to kiss his hand. It was a public sign of obedience, designed to be seen by all. Enrique, following both custom and a pre-agreed script, signalled that it was not necessary. The message was clear. Isabella was not going to challenge Enrique for his crown, but she was not to be humiliated.[1]

There were three other acts to this public performance in September, 1468, that would change the history of Spain. First of all a letter written by Enrique was read out. In it, he recognised that Isabella was now the rightful heir to his throne. Enrique then asked all those present to swear recognition of Isabella's position as heiress, while the papal nuncio Antonio Giacomo Venier freed them from their previous oath of allegiance to La Beltranaja. His words bore the authority of the pope himself. All those present then pledged loyalty to Enrique. Carrillo, at his own insistence, was the last to do so.[2]

The obstinate archbishop had tried hard to dissuade Isabella from making this agreement with Enrique, arguing against it right up until the night before. Carrillo was primate of Spain and a formidable warrior priest who wore a bright scarlet cloak with a white cross over his armour when leading his men into battle. His archbishopric brought with it huge temporal power, with 19,000 vassals in its extensive lands, as well as twenty-one castles and an army of 2,000 men. He was also an inveterate plotter and occasional ally of Aragon's King Juan the Great. Yet Isabella had held firm against one of the most powerful men in Castile, effectively rejecting the military might he and the extended Carrillo clan offered. In order to soften the archbishop's sense of humiliation and calm his notoriously bad temper she had, after morning mass, signed a written pledge that she would make sure Enrique and his men did not punish Carrillo or his men for their loyalty to her. This decision, and the others she had taken during negotiations over the agreement, provided those involved with a first glimpse of the strong personality of the young woman whom fate had suddenly thrust into the front line of Castilian affairs.[3]

Isabella may have uttered a private prayer that morning during mass. In later years she would, through her propagandists, claim that it was this: 'If I do have this right, give me the sense and energy, with the help of Your arm, to pursue and achieve it and bring peace to this kingdom.'[4] The 'sense and energy' provide a useful guide to how Isabella saw herself, at least in retrospect. Modesty about her abilities did not rank as a major concern. The 'arm' she referred to belonged to the entity she thought had led her to this position, God. Divine help or, rather, divine approval of her actions was to become a common stance in Isabella's life. That underpinned her self-confidence and made false – or even real – humility unnecessary. A usefully circular argument was shaping in her head. If she had been appointed the future queen of Castile, that was God's choice. And if God had chosen her to do his work, then she only had to abide by his tenets in order for him to approve of her actions, which were divinely sanctioned. In the wrong hands, that could be a recipe for tyranny. The only problem, indeed, was knowing exactly what those tenets were. The judgement day that came after death was, she knew, both real and frightening. For guidance on that, she turned away from worldly churchmen like the archbishop to a series of stern friars, several of them also her confessors, who shunned mundane pleasures and embraced the strictest versions of Christian morality. During her sojourns in Segovia she had already encountered one of them, the sulphurous prior of Spain's oldest Dominican monastery, the Convento of Santa Cruz – Tomás de Torquemada. He had clear ideas about the ills that afflicted the kingdom. They included the Jews, those *conversos* who he believed were still secret Jews, soothsayers, simony in the church and corrupt or inept city officials.[5] The kingdom was sick, he told her, and needed purifying. Only strong medicine would achieve that.

There were a few notable absences at the Guisando bulls. Neither six-year-old Juana la Beltraneja, who had been stripped of her rightful place as heiress, nor her mother Queen Juana were there. Their protectors from the powerful Mendoza family, who often acted more like jailers, protested vehemently against the agreement. A few weeks earlier, Queen Juana had been the protagonist of a fairytale flight from the town of Alaejos. She was now unable to hide the fact that she was seven months pregnant by her lover Pedro de Castilla, yet her presence had been needed at court as negotiations over her daughter's future progressed. Enrique sent for her in mid-August, but she claimed to need a bigger, better escort befitting her queenly status. Reports about what happened next are as colourful and unreliable as the undoubtedly accurate reason (that she now really had cuckolded the king) for her decision to flee. According to one account, a few nights later she was lowered down the town's walls in a basket, which toppled over as it neared the ground. The heavily pregnant Juana, who survived the fall relatively unscathed, was scooped up by Pedro de Castilla and a young friend who had been waiting with horses. They rode off through the dark and eventually installed themselves in Buitrago, a town held by the Mendozas.[6]

Juana had placed herself in mortal danger with this liaison. Women who strayed could be killed by their husbands, fathers, brothers or cousins to save the family honour. A court in the southern city of Murcia, for example, had pardoned a man called Diego del Poyo for murdering his wife after she slept with another man. 'Given the reputation of that bad woman, he had very good reasons for doing so,' it said. But Enrique displayed neither the interest nor the malice needed to pursue his wife. Perhaps he really had encouraged her to take lovers in the past and was afraid she would now speak out. Or perhaps he felt guilty about breaking the most important political and sentimental bond of their marriage – little Juana, whose paternity he had publicly claimed as his, whatever the biological truth. The queen's behaviour may, in fact, have been convenient for him as it was an impediment to her defending herself and her daughter. Juana's baby boy, Andrés, would not be born until November. The situation was so extraordinary that Castile's law code simply did not contemplate the possibility of a pregnant, adulterous queen.[7]

The agreement struck at Guisando came after a rapid volte-face by Isabella. Some of her supporters had assumed, on Alfonso's death, that she would proclaim herself queen. Isabella herself had, after all, sent out letters while waiting for her brother to die, stating that this was her intention. Immediately after his death, however, her letters had become less assertive about a direct claim on the throne. 'I am the legitimate heiress,' she wrote to the authorities in Murcia, a pro-Alfonso city. 'Hold this city for me as you held it for my brother the king.' They were also to send counsellors, however, to help decide what should happen next. Murcia responded with an elaborate funeral ceremony, banning townspeople from singing, playing music or wearing gaudy clothes. The city's dignitaries sat by an empty, ceremonial death-bed before dressing themselves in coarse woollen cloth and carrying a coffin through the streets to the main church. The torchlit procession – accompanied by the sound of wailing – included five ceremonial shields, one of which was carried by representatives of the city's Jews and another by its Moors. Castile's cities and the local oligarchies who ran them formed a political stratum of their own, much like the nobles or the church. Those that had backed Alfonso remained largely expectant, waiting to see what would happen. Murcia set up a provisional council while Jerez chose 'not to raise the flag of a king or a queen until all are in agreement'.[8]

Realism had quickly forced Isabella into avoiding a head-on confrontation with her half-brother. Now aged seventeen, she was in the hands of the same puppeteer nobles who had manipulated her brother to their own ends. With no money of her own and no guarantee that the rebels would automatically transfer their support to a woman, she chose caution, good sense and – within the limitations of her difficult situation – the most independent route possible. From now on she would limit her claim to that of 'princess and legitimate heir in these kingdoms of Castile and León'. She would be heiress to King Enrique – though, with typical and inconsistent obstinacy, she would always insist that her brother Alfonso had been the rightful king.[9]

Instead of proudly, if foolishly, challenging her half-brother for the crown, Isabella elected to fight a different sort of battle. She wanted to be able to choose her own husband. It was a sign of her precocious political awareness that she so quickly identified this as the crucial issue for all involved. Her most powerful backer, the archbishop of Toledo, was in cahoots with Juan the Great of Aragon, who had already identified Isabella as the ideal bride for his son and heir, Ferdinand. But Pacheco, who did much of the negotiating for Enrique, secretly hoped to marry his own daughter Beatriz to Ferdinand, thereby advancing his family's status even further. Once more, he now sought to divide, confuse and come out top. The best way to end the rebellion, he told Enrique, was to recognise Isabella as his heiress, then marry her off to a foreign prince and send her away to a distant court.[10] All Enrique needed to do was ensure that he maintained the right to decide on her husband.

Isabella soon became aware of the rivalries between the nobles for control over her and, above all, the choice of her future husband. Pacheco warned her against the archbishop, who also happened to be his uncle, whom he deemed 'obstinate by nature and stiff-necked'. The latter, meanwhile, warned her that his nephew was secretly planning to marry her off to Afonso of Portugal. While all around her plotted ways to wed her to their favourite contender,

Isabella told her half-brother that she was happy for him to search for a husband for her, but the last word would have to be hers. And the agreement must be in writing. 'She must marry whoever the king decides on, with the volition of the lady princess and by agreement with the council [made up] of the archbishop [of Seville], the Master [of the Santiago order, Pacheco] and the Count [of Plasencia, Álvaro de Stúñiga],' one version of the agreement states.[11] That allowed Isabella, Enrique and Pacheco's gang of Grandees to walk away each convinced that they, and they alone, would eventually decide on Isabella's husband.

The change of heiress from Juana to Isabella was much more than a question of oaths and pledges. Isabella insisted that she be given the full rights and properties due to an heir to Castile's throne. That meant she became princess of Asturias, the traditional title held by the heir. With the title came lands and income. She was also given rights over the cities of Avila, Ubeda, Alcaraz and Huete, and the towns of Molina, Medina del Campo and Escalona and the income from them. Isabella's new position made her, at least in theory, financially independent and gave her a personal power base. All this had formed part of the negotiations done by messengers and proxies, with last-minute alterations made after Isabella and Enrique had installed themselves in two nearby towns, Cebreros and Cadalso, that were near to the Guisando bulls.[12]

In the brief period between Alfonso's death and the meeting beside the Guisando bulls, Isabella had shown herself worthy of her new status as heir apparent. She had known when to bend, especially in the face of superior might, but she had also shown that she knew when to dig her heels in. Her patron, the archbishop of Toledo, may not have liked it, but she had asserted her authority. She was already displaying some of the qualities that Enrique and her father Juan had famously lacked. Shrewd observers might have realised that something was changing. But there were few such observers. The decades of submissive monarchs and centuries of mostly submissive women weighed too heavily. While her chances of becoming queen had increased dramatically, most would have expected her to reign as little more than a figurehead. Government would be a task for her husband and his advisers. Neither Enrique nor Pacheco, the apparent winners at Guisando, nor her own supporters like the archbishop, showed any sign of understanding the woman they were dealing with. In fact the young Isabella was emerging as a powerfully intense, decisive and sometimes unbending character. She knew how to set her own objectives and, more importantly, how to stand up for herself. Hers was a self-confidence built on simple, straightforward beliefs, unfettered by self-examination or the need to add shades of grey to those things she viewed in black and white.

An awkward but vital question remained unanswered. Who would Isabella marry? The treaty gave Enrique the right to choose, while the senior nobles still believed they had a right to approve that choice and Isabella herself had, crucially, obtained her own right of veto. The Guisando agreement also stated that Isabella must stay with Enrique and his counsellors until a husband was found.[13] As the two siblings and those used to forcing their opinions on Enrique turned their backs on the stone bulls and rode off together, the unity of Castile and of the Trastámara family apparently restored, each already had different thoughts on what all that might mean.

6

Choosing Ferdinand

Colmenar de Oreja, 24 October 1468

T he five horsemen who galloped into the town of Colmenar de Oreja must have looked like just another group of courtiers joining Isabella and Enrique as the apparently happy royal court of Castile settled here and in the neighbouring town of Ocaña to administer a newly peaceful country. The group headed towards the town's largest church, Santa María, and pinned a document to the door. Having achieved their aim, they fled at full gallop, for they knew that the explosive words laboriously written out would shatter the illusion of calm that had descended on both court and country. News of its contents must have spread like wildfire, with Isabella among the first to know.[1]

The riders were led by the Count of Tendilla, a senior member of the Mendoza clan and legal guardian to the six-year-old Princess Juana – now a rival to her cousin and godmother, Isabella. He had brought with him to this town thirty miles from Madrid a formal protest against the agreement that had been silently notarised a month earlier by the stone bulls at Guisando. Pinning it to the church door was a safe way to make it public and, in effect, to serve a writ on both Isabella and Enrique. 'It is public knowledge that the said lady princess, my ward, as legitimate daughter of the king was long ago proclaimed and accepted, at the time of her birth, as princess and first in line to inherit these kingdoms,'[2] the letter stated. It was a reminder to Isabella that her rival had never been declared illegitimate by either her father or her mother.

Princess Juana was, the count reminded those who gathered at the church door, born into a proper marriage. 'She is the legitimate daughter of the king and was born into a legitimate marriage approved by our very holy Pope Pius, of great fame, and by Pope Paul II,' the writ stated.[3] And that meant she could not be disinherited without the pope's direct approval, 'because he was the source of approval of the marriage into which she was born and within which she was confirmed as the legitimate heiress'.[4] Tendilla and his fellow riders[5] had chosen to nail the letter to the church door out of fear of reprisals, according to del Castillo, because 'such was the might of those to whom it was directed that, given the contents of the appeal, they did not dare give it directly to them in person'.[6] It was a warning that the coexistence in Castile of a king, a queen consort, the queen's lover, her future illegitimate child and two potential heiresses to the crown – both seen as needing husbands – was unlikely to be simple.

The appearance of stability generated at Guisando was only skin deep, and the senior nobles were already manoeuvring to undermine it. Pacheco continued his self-interested scheming, an angry archbishop of Toledo was preparing a bold strategy to win Isabella back and the offended, ambitious Mendozas were looking to turn their possession of her rival Juana to their advantage. Aragon, Portugal and France watched closely, awaiting the opportunities that can be plucked from chaos. The court had moved to Colmenar de Oreja and to the neighbouring town of Ocaña because this was Pacheco territory, controlled by the military order of Santiago of which he was now Master. Pacheco had never been so mighty, or Enrique so dependent. It was here, according to Palencia, that they began plotting to marry Isabella off to a foreign prince, with Portugal's Afonso V still the favourite. Neither man counted on Isabella being anything other than acquiescent.[7]

Isabella spent the Christmas of 1468 in Ocaña with her small court of loyal officials and ladies, a virtual prisoner in Pacheco's fiefdom. Less than a year had gone by since her brother's death, but already she found herself having to make one of the most important decisions of her life. She must either bow to Enrique, accept the Grandees' power over the monarchy and marry the Portuguese king – a widower whose children were older than Isabella herself and who would expect to rule in her place[8] – or she could rebel, marry a man of her own choice and risk sparking yet another civil war.

The obvious alternative candidate was Juan the Great of Aragon's precocious son Ferdinand, who would soon turn seventeen. The scheming Aragonese monarch ruled over a collection of semi-independent kingdoms that often had a fractious relationship with their bellicose king, who fought frequent border wars with France and had complex interests in Italy. His Italian lands included Sardinia and Sicily, which Juan the Great had gifted to Ferdinand six months earlier, in June 1468 – allowing him to use the title of king of Sicily, though he remained in Aragon and the task of governing the island kingdom was carried out by a viceroy. Among the reasons that Juan the Great, who was two weeks away from celebrating his seventieth birthday, gave for making the appointment was the support Ferdinand had already given him in 'the sweat of war during his old age'. That same month he had formally appointed Ferdinand as his lieutenant in all his kingdoms, allowing him to exercise royal power during his father's absence. The Aragonese king now imagined his son, already experienced in battle and accustomed to making important decisions, as future king of a vast part of Iberia. Only Portugal, little Navarre and the Muslim kingdom of Granada would be outside his realms. A single marriage treaty could achieve immeasurably more than the old wars between his branch of the Trastámara family and Isabella's father. Ferdinand's future wife, it was assumed, would remain in the background – allowing him to govern alone. He sent Pierres de Peralta, the *condestable* of Navarre, into Castile as his envoy, his bags full of written offers of gold to Isabella's closest advisers.[9]

While secret negotiations were carried out at night-time meetings with the Aragonese envoys in Isabella's rooms, the Portuguese king sent the archbishop of Lisbon to finalise a wedding treaty that he had been led to believe was a mere formality. His envoys were entertained lavishly by Pacheco, but Isabella politely refused to commit herself to them, while also avoiding an outright 'no'. As the *procuradores*, representing the cities, and the Grandees gathered for a Cortes meeting called by Enrique at Ocaña, the town seethed with plots and counter-plots. Everybody seemed to sense this was an historic moment. The king's grip on power continued to weaken, with the rebels who had raised Alfonso as a rival monarch now governing in Enrique's name. Some of Spain's powerful cities pinned their hopes for the future on Isabella. Those *procuradores* who were worried about growing Grandee power over the cities, and over the kingdom, found Isabella ready to listen to their complaints, if powerless to do anything about them. They were not even offered the opportunity of fulfilling the terms of the Guisando agreement by publicly swearing loyalty to Isabella as heiress. A campaign of bullying was then ordered with a thuggish noble called Pedro de Velasco sent to threaten Isabella with imprisonment if she did not agree to the Portuguese match. 'Velasco expressed himself in such excessive terms that he forced tears from the lady and she, full of embarrassment, begged God's protection from such shamefulness and cruel infamy,' wrote Palencia, who also claimed that an angry Enrique ordered his soldiers to arrest anyone singing pro-Aragonese songs on the streets of Ocaña.[10]

Enrique must have been aware of the presence of Pierres de Peralta, who based himself at the archbishop of Toledo's residence in nearby Yepes. He had been sent with blank pieces of paper signed by Juan the Great, so desperate was the Aragonese king to make this marriage happen. The archbishop's illegitimate son Troilo, now Peralta's son-in-law, acted as go-between. One legend talks of a secret meeting between Isabella and the intrepid ambassador, who had waded across the strong-running River Tagus in the dark, at which the future queen finally swore to marry Ferdinand. In fact, the exact moment when Isabella decided to marry Ferdinand is impossible to pinpoint, but she had clearly made her mind up by the end of January 1469, only four months after signing the Guisando bulls' accord, when one of Juan the Great's envoys wrote informing him of her choice. 'It must be him [Ferdinand] and no other,' the envoy said. A few days later Isabella sent a trusted adviser, Gómez Manrique, with Peralta to Ferdinand in the Catalan town of Cervera. She was not prepared, however, to put her pledge in writing, in case it was intercepted. Instead, she wrote him a cryptic note.

> To my cousin, the king of Sicily. *Señor* cousin: as the *condestable* is on his way to you it is not necessary for me to put this in writing, but only to ask forgiveness for the late reply. He will explain the delay to your majesty. I beg you to trust him and you must now order me to do your will, and I will have to do it. And the reason for that you will find out from him this very day, because it is not something that should be written down. From the hand that will now do whatever you command. The princess.[11]

Enrique and his *privado* Pacheco remained convinced that they had the eighteen-year-old princess under control. After all, the Guisando treaty stated that the king must choose, that his counsellors must approve and that, only then, Isabella herself could agree, or not, on her husband. The king and his entourage now set out southwards for Andalusia, making Isabella swear not to move from Ocaña or make marriage plans without them. Some of Isabella's officials were bribed to spy on her and Pacheco's men were ordered to ensure that she stayed put. As Isabella plotted for herself, she had a distinct advantage over the men she was dealing with. They simply could not imagine that a young woman, however royal her blood, might operate independently of them. That also went for those, like Palencia, who were now in favour of the Ferdinand match. The defect was not in her individually, but in women as a whole. 'Women have been the downfall of Spain,' is how Palencia, attributing the idea to the people of Burgos, would put it.[12]

In later years a romantic narrative of Isabella's choice evolved which saw her excitedly and girlishly fall in love with the dashing young Ferdinand from a distance. In fact, Isabella was a far harder-nosed political player than that. Her choice was pragmatic, not emotional. A Portuguese marriage would place Isabella firmly, perhaps permanently, in the hands of Pacheco's power-hungry band of Grandees. These were already secretly offering to proclaim Afonso of Portugal heir, and Isabella a mere consort, just as soon as she was wedded to the Portuguese king. But marriage to Ferdinand brought similar problems. She would place herself in the self-interested hands of Juan the Great and the archbishop of Toledo – two bullying old men who also expected her to cede all protagonism to her husband. The kingdom of Aragon did not allow women to occupy the throne and Ferdinand, as one of the few male Trastámaras available to rule Castile, was a direct rival to Isabella as well as a potential ally, even within marriage. Several of her senior advisers, like Chacón and Gutierre de Cárdenas, had been handsomely bribed by the Aragonese king, but he needed the match far more than Portugal. That put Isabella in a stronger bargaining position. The desire of the archbishop of Toledo and her other allies to keep as much power as possible in Castile rather than giving it away to Aragon also played in her favour. Like the Grandees who dominated Enrique, they imagined themselves exercising power for her. So when it came to bargaining with Juan the Great they could be trusted to press hard for Castile's rights, which were also hers.[13]

Once again, Isabella was aided by the basic belief among the men involved that – whatever was pledged or written down on paper – it was inconceivable that, once married, she would not simply hand power over to her husband, a council of Grandees or both. Nor was there anything in her calm and apparently demure outward demeanour – a cloak under which Isabella was learning to hide her steely character – to make them think otherwise. On 7 March, exactly two months before Enrique set out for Andalusia, a secret marriage agreement was finalised in Cervera.[14] It permitted Ferdinand, who would turn seventeen two days later, to administer justice in Castile, but everything else would have to be agreed, signed or done with the permission of his wife. He could not even leave Castile without her permission. He would also provide 100,000 florins once the marriage was consummated and an army of 4,000 lancers to defend Isabella against the enemies she was now creating. A further 20,000 florins must be paid up front along with a valuable pearl and ruby necklace which the cash-strapped Aragonese royals had pawned in Valencia.[15]

Attempts were made to limit the damage to Enrique's royal pride. In an early draft, signed only by Ferdinand and his father, the young prince had pledged 'to observe and uphold the peace signed between King Enrique and her [Isabella], and allow and ensure that his highness reigns peacefully for the rest for his days'. Both he and his father would forget any previous insults from their past enemies in Castile, including Enrique, and 'forgive all, in the service of God and out of consideration for her serene princess'. Enrique was also to be given 'full filial obedience' by his future brother-in-law. 'We will go personally to live in those kingdoms to be there with the princess, and we will not leave without her approval, nor will we take her from those kingdoms without her consent,' Ferdinand had pledged, with their offspring also to remain in Castile.[16] 'We will never take them away from her, nor take them out of those kingdoms against her will.'

By Aragonese standards, it was a humiliating document. It left Ferdinand a virtual prisoner in the hands of Isabella and her counsellors. The idea that a prince of Aragon and king of Sicily should need a wife's permission to be in his own kingdoms, or those of his father, was shocking. But it was just the start, and a man could still be expected to prevail over his wife. Juan and Ferdinand were, in any case, not in a position to demand any more. They could not, at first, even provide the necklace that was meant to be given to Ferdinand's fiancée. Isabella now had to keep her part of the bargain. Promises had been given, but in the liquid, turbulent world of Castilian politics, alliances were made and unmade with exasperating ease. Aragonese messengers were ready with money to buy support among the nobility, but she had to prove that she was committed by openly rebelling against Enrique and fleeing Ocaña. Her eventual excuse for leaving the town was that she wanted to oversee preparations for the ceremonies in Arévalo, her mother's town, to mark the anniversary of her brother Alfonso's death. Arévalo had been occupied by Enrique's allies, however, so she and her mother travelled on to her birthplace of Madrigal de Las Altas Torres.[17] Once more, her choice was to return to the landscapes, people and simple certainties of her childhood.

The decision, however, was anything but childlike. Isabella had left the historic Guisando agreement in tatters and civil war now threatened. Worse still, she had allied herself with Juan the Great, a long-time foe of both Enrique and her father. Castile could remember still the awful, uncertain days of the wars against the *infantes* of Aragon. Juan the Great, now aged seventy, was one of those *infantes*. The engagement to Ferdinand, however, remained a secret and Enrique's reaction to Isabella's disobedient departure from Ocaña was not nearly as aggressive as it might have been. His appetite for bloody confrontation was limited and he preferred to leave things in the hands of Pacheco, who had a natural liking for ill-defined, chaotic situations. These were the moments when the king needed him most, and which could best be played out to his personal benefit.

Rather than make war on a princess whose only crime so far was to disobey his instructions and leave Ocaña, Enrique now sent her a different marriage proposal. This time it came from France's King Louis XI, who wanted her to marry his brother, and heir apparent, the Duke of Berry. A French ambassador, the bishop of Arras, arrived in Madrigal, hoping that a marriage would help him settle an alliance with Castile against England's King Edward IV. The self-important bishop so maddened Isabella with his pomposity, arrogance and sly verbal attacks on Ferdinand that she could barely contain herself. She kept calm, however, making non-committal replies that left the bishop thinking he had received a half-promise. Palencia later claimed that Isabella had sent her chaplain, Alfonso de Coca, to cast an eye over both the French duke and Ferdinand. 'He described the immense advantages that don Ferdinand had over the other, given that – even discounting the larger size of his dominions and the union of the kingdoms – he was far better looking. The Duke [of Berry] scarcely warranted comparison, as he was made ugly by the extreme thinness of his legs and a certain accumulation of liquids that made him half-blind.' Palencia claimed a 'bloated and arrogant' France would force Castile to submit to its will while warning that its 'repugnant customs' clashed with Castile's supposed seriousness. Isabella appears to have carried away from the meeting a life-long dislike of France. 'You showed that you desired any other, less useful, marriage to be arranged in order to prevent a wedding with the honest and dutiful prince [Ferdinand],' Isabella scolded Enrique later.[18]

In the meantime, Palencia himself was chosen to travel to Aragon to collect the pearl and ruby necklace that had been pledged to her as an advance on the wedding dowry payment. Ferdinand travelled south to Valencia in person to recover the bulky necklace in mid-July and hand it to Palencia. He also made a chivalrous offer that must have warmed Isabella's heart and which certainly fitted her idea of proper knightly behaviour. 'He called me to see him on his own,' said Palencia, 'and asked whether I thought he should head as soon as possible for Madrigal, taking two companions and myself as a guide, in order to console the anxious lady with his presence, and to run the same risks that she was running.' The chronicler must have been conscious of the necklace's weight, both physical and emblematic, as he rode back into Castile. The thick knot of gold strings weighed more than three *marcos* (twenty-five ounces) and was hung with seven fat rubies and eight oval-shaped, greyish pearls. An enormous ruby dangled from its centre, decorated with a beautiful pear-shaped pearl.[19] The jewels were proof, if she needed it, of Ferdinand's commitment.

Isabella must have lived in a state of acute anxiety. Her husband-to-be was more than 300 miles away in his father's kingdoms. If they were to marry, he would somehow have to infiltrate himself into a Castile that was mostly hostile. She was also in personal danger, asking her handful of Grandee allies to send troops to Madrigal, and the atmosphere in her small court began to sour. Not everyone wanted to join her rebellion and some of her *damas*, or ladies-in-waiting, fearing the worst, slipped away. They included some of her most intimate friends. 'They knew how you had already ordered that I be captured and deprived of my freedom, as was also clear in certain letters that came into my hands, including one to the town council of Madrigal ordering that they arrest me,' Isabella wrote to Enrique later. Eventually she decided it was safer to leave the town, setting off on a journey that would see her settle in Valladolid.[20] She wanted a safe place where Ferdinand could reach her.

7

Marrying Ferdinand

Zaragoza, 5 October 1469

T he dark-haired, full-lipped young man who finally set out from
Zaragoza dressed as a lowly groom was a convincing actor. Riding
with five others, Ferdinand stayed in role for two days and two nights,
serving meals and looking after the horses. The seventeen-year-old
prince had waited impatiently for a sign from Isabella that he should
set out. This had finally arrived in the form of Palencia and Gutierre de
Cárdenas, who had ridden via back routes and through the dark of the
night so as to avoid Enrique's spies. Along the way they had realised
that the first sixty-five miles of Ferdinand's journey into Castile would
be through extremely hostile territory. Once in Zaragoza, Isabella's
envoys acted as if they had no business with Ferdinand, with Cárdenas
hiding in their lodgings while Palencia set out for a secret meeting with
the young prince in a monk's cell at the magnificent San Francisco
monastery, whose chapel boasted a 245-foot nave. Ferdinand, they
decided, should loudly proclaim that he was setting out to see his father
in Catalonia and then, disguised as a servant, would join a supposed
Aragonese embassy heading into Castile. Palencia and Cárdenas,
meanwhile, left Zaragoza in a pretend huff, loudly complaining that
Ferdinand had told them he had urgent business in Catalonia.[1]

After two days the riders made it to Burgo de Osma, where the
Duke of Treviño – now married to Enrique's former mistress doña
Guiomar – awaited them with an escort of lancers. Ferdinand insisted
they push straight on, setting out again at 3 a.m. By 9 October 1469
the energetic young prince was at Dueñas where, among others, his

aunt Teresa Enríquez greeted him. It was a reminder that Ferdinand was, via his mother, half-Castilian. Cárdenas and Palencia pressed on to Valladolid, just eighteen miles away, knowing that Isabella would be anxiously awaiting news. They seem to have bickered along the way, about which of them deserved the glory for their successful mission.[2]

Ferdinand and his seventy-one-year-old father, still battling rebellions in the north of Catalonia, were now taking risks far bigger than those taken by Isabella. 'The king [Juan] has no other son or support in his old age in this world other than the king of Sicily [Ferdinand] and on him hangs the health, wellbeing and succession of all these kingdoms,' Juan's secretary Felip Climent wrote.[3] 'The mere fact that the king says with his own mouth that he [his son] should risk travelling with just three or four men to Valladolid, especially considering the vague promises of safety that he has . . . should make the king of Sicily [Ferdinand] believe that his toughness and strength defy description.'

Enrique had no reason to be surprised by Ferdinand's arrival. A month earlier, on 8 September 1469, Isabella had written to him from Valladolid announcing that she was set to marry. She now claimed that she, Enrique and the nobles had agreed to study four potential candidates for husband to determine which would be best for the kingdom. Isabella named the four, in order, as Ferdinand, Afonso V of Portugal, the French Duke of Berry and the future Richard III of England. She chided her half-brother for trying to bully her into a Portuguese marriage, claiming that an agreement had been negotiated behind her back. Isabella blamed 'certain people', meaning Pacheco, for duping King Afonso into thinking that she was willing to marry him and claimed that the will of other nobles and *procuradores* had been ignored, while others had been cowed into approval of the match by threats. Her right to decide on her own future, with 'just and due freedom', agreed at Guisando, had also been ignored.[4]

She, meanwhile, claimed to have conducted her own consultations with the nobles. 'They praised and approved of a marriage with the Prince of Aragon, King of Sicily, giving very obvious reasons as to why,' she told Enrique. Ferdinand's obvious virtues, including his age and Trastámara blood, were being deliberately besmirched by those with 'sinister intent' who surrounded the king. Even more shocking had been the attempt to foist the French Duke of Berry on her. The French, she said, would treat Castile like a mere province and use it in its wars with Aragon.[5]

Isabella's defiant anger shines through her letter to Enrique. She is, nevertheless, acutely aware of the trouble she is about to cause and of the dangers to herself and the young man who was coming into a foreign land to marry her against the monarch's wishes. Ferdinand, she said, would come in peace and as a faithful servant to Enrique. She reminded him that they all shared great-grandparents and that their own grandfather, Castile's King Enrique III, had expressly asked in his will that the Castilian and Aragonese lines should inter-marry to keep the family close. Those who claimed that Ferdinand would cause trouble were misleading him. 'You can be sure that, from now on, I will comply with my promises,' she added. 'And you can be secure in the obedience that the said prince of Aragon should owe, and understands that he owes, to your highness, if you are prepared to receive him as an obedient son.'[6] She wanted, in other words, both to rebel and to be forgiven. Pacheco and Enrique may not have planned to stick to the Guisando agreement, but they had not blatantly torn it up like this.

Isabella wrote to Enrique again on 12 October, telling him that Ferdinand was already in Castile and assuring him that her husband-to-be came in peace. This time she pleaded for his blessing. 'I beg that you may approve of his coming and approve of the [good] intentions underpinning my plans,' she said. Enrique did not bother to reply. It was, in any case, too late for him to object. Two days later Isabella met her future husband for the first time. The only image she had ever seen of Ferdinand was a roughly engraved medallion showing a young, bearded face and little more. Gutierre de Cárdenas had to point out which of the group of riders that entered Valladolid was Isabella's future husband. An apocryphal story has Isabella excitedly shouting, 'That is he! That is he!',[7] and she must have been overjoyed that Ferdinand had made it to her successfully, especially as he had been ready to run such risks to get to her. The only surviving portrait from around this time, or copied from an original, shows him sporting a wispy, young man's beard of fine dark hairs that only sparsely cover his chin and cheeks, while thick black straight hair hangs lankly over his ears – as it does in other portraits – and down to the base of his neck. Brown eyes below a straight fringe of black hair add to the overall swarthiness.

The tension provoked by the appearance of a son of the infamous *infantes* of Aragon was immediately patent, even among Isabella's followers. Some of the Castilian nobles insisted that Ferdinand kiss his wife's hand to prove his obeisance and show that, in this match, he was the lucky one. Isabella herself was inclined to agree, but the archbishop of Toledo was scandalised. Ferdinand already held the title of king (of Sicily) and so would elevate her to the rank of queen. More importantly, he was a man. 'He put a stop to this shameful and insulting adulation by pointing out the insolence that some people were trying to instil in the wife, who had to obey her husband and hand over to the male the symbols of power,' wrote Palencia, who agreed with his friend the archbishop on this. But the extraordinary agreement signed at Cervera was read out, leaving little doubt about Ferdinand's subordinate role. Palencia claimed that the young couple, aged eighteen and seventeen, were so smitten with each other that only the presence of the archbishop during their two-hour meeting prevented them from misbehaving. More importantly, they also signed a joint document with the archbishop, recognising their dependence on his support by stating that he was now their chief counsellor. 'Without you, archbishop, we will not do or order anything, but instead will govern and do things by mutual agreement between the three of us as if we were one body and soul,' they said.[8] The archbishop took them literally. He was, at least in his own mind, their *privado* – the true power behind the throne.

The religious part of the wedding was celebrated three days later in the presence of the archbishop of Toledo, who somehow managed to represent the interests of God, Castile, Aragon and himself all at the same time. It was a modest affair, made more so by the urgency with which it was conducted. The Cervera agreement was read out once more, hammering home the superior status of Isabella, and of Castile, in the marriage. The bride and bridegroom were second cousins. As such, they needed a papal dispensation to marry. But Pope Paul II was on Enrique's side. Only four months earlier he had provided written permission for Isabella to marry another distant cousin, Afonso V of Portugal. The problem was solved with the public reading of an entirely false dispensation, allegedly given by an earlier pope, Pius II. The papal nuncio Venier let it all happen, his pockets weighed down with Aragonese gold and his mouth firmly shut. He was the only man with the authority to override Toledo – or to expose the enormous lie that had just been uttered. Perhaps he, like Juan the Great, believed that the pope would come up with a dispensation once the marriage had already been celebrated. More likely, however, he was thinking of the 1,000 ounces of gold he was to receive yearly from Ferdinand's kingdom of Sicily and the additional promise of an even richer bishopric than his current one in León.[9]

Isabella was complicit in the cheating. 'As for what you say in your letter about me marrying without a dispensation, there is no need for a long reply as you are not the judge in this matter,' she wrote in a circular letter addressed to Enrique eighteen months later. 'My conscience is fully clean, as can be shown by the authentic bulls and documents, whenever and wherever necessary.'[10] She was bluffing. She had never seen any 'authentic' documents. They did not exist. Her later reputation for both piety and scrupulous legality, busily promoted by her propagandists, does not hold up at this stage of her life. Neither does that of Ferdinand. Politics and power clearly came first. In that, she was displaying considerable prowess.

8

Rebel Princess

Juan de Vivero's Palace, Valladolid, 19 October 1469

The sheets from the wedding bed were displayed, in all their bloodied glory, to the crowd waiting outside Isabella's bedroom in Juan de Vivero's palace near the gate of San Pedro in Valladolid. The stained bedlinen had been handed to the select group of officials who had inspected the chamber before the couple went in and then stood at its door. 'Trumpets, drums and minstrels played as they showed them [the sheets] to all those people who were waiting in the [adjoining] room, which was packed full,' reported the royal chronicler Diego de Valera. Isabella was determined not to repeat the errors of Enrique, who had changed Castilian royal tradition by banning people from his wedding-night chamber. She wanted people to know both that the marriage had been consummated and that she had come to it as a virgin. The blood on the sheets proved both. There was evident satisfaction that the tradition had been reinstated. 'Evidence of her virginity and nobility was properly presented before the judges, city councillors and gentlemen as is apt for monarchs,' Dr Toledo, their physician, noted in his diary. Isabella's husband was equally keen to let it be known that the marriage would not suffer from the kind of bedroom problems that had blighted Enrique's reign and reputation. 'Last night, in the service of God, we consummated the marriage,' he wrote to the city council of Valencia the following day. When Enrique later spread false rumours claiming that consummation had never happened, Isabella held her head high. 'This subject is embarrassing and hateful to noble women,' she sniffed.[1] 'All I can say is that our actions are the evidence that we must present to both God and the world.'

The marriage celebrations lasted for seven days, with dances, fires and merrymaking in the streets of Valladolid as Enrique's spies watched closely. There were street processions and public fiestas across Aragon and even in far-off Sicily. In the rest of Castile, however, the celebrations were either muted or non-existent.[2] A country that had lived through three years of civil war found itself, after a single year of peace, back on the precipice. One person was ultimately responsible for that. It was the eighteen-year-old heiress to the crown, Isabella, who had torn up the peace agreement. That may have been a wise pre-emptive move, from her point of view, but it left the rest of her country in a state of nervous, fearful expectation.

Awaking in Juan de Vivero's palace on 20 October 1469, the morning after consummating her marriage, Isabella may have reflected with satisfaction on just how completely she had imposed her will. The rebel princess was not generally given to regret over her actions. She and no one else had chosen her husband. An agreement had been broken, but men like the archbishop of Toledo were telling her this did not matter. The king had broken it first, she said to herself, by trying to marry her off to princes she did not like and who were bad for the future of Castile. That was stretching the truth to breaking point, but it was the story she would now promote.

She must also, however, have been aware of some major weaknesses in their position. Cities, with their thick stone walls, fortresses, towers and taxes were crucial for anyone wanting to exercise control over Castile and its countryside. She and her husband had the support of just a handful of significant cities, and holding on to them would be difficult. Valladolid, where they had married, was already subject to an increasingly tense, and potentially violent, confrontation between the local nobles who wanted to control it – with the well-connected Vivero just one of those tussling for power. Important towns like Tordesillas and Olmedo remained in their orbit, but they were under pressure to switch allegiance, and the lands Isabella and her husband controlled directly covered only a small piece of Castile.[3] The other sources of power were the nobles and the church, but support from those quarters was sparse. Isabella's real might came from the archbishop's vast lands, income and private army and from those of Ferdinand's Castilian grandfather, the admiral of Castile, Fadrique Enríquez. The dormant power of Aragon, with its long frontier, was available to her in case of emergency, but only if the often overstretched Juan the Great had the resources and the will to do so. The young couple were, in other words, completely dependent on other people.

Three old men looked on with satisfaction. Juan the Great, Fadrique Enríquez and the archbishop of Toledo were men of weight, experience and tradition. Their unusual longevity was matched by equally remarkable vigour. The archbishop was about to turn sixty. The others were a decade or more older. They had been born at the end of the previous century, before Isabella's father had come to the throne. They were also wealthy and could raise their own armies. In that sense they were classic medieval magnates, entirely comfortable with and confident of their power. The contrast between them and the young princes when it came to experience, power and military might was blatantly in their favour. Without them, the marriage simply would not have happened. As if to drive the point home, Ferdinand wrote to his father explaining that they were worried King Enrique would attack. Archbishop Carrillo had advised them to gather a cavalry force of 1,000 men as protection, but they had no money and needed 40,000 florins urgently. 'They asked the king for this money . . . because his son had gone to Castile with no money and the princess also had none,' reported the great Aragonese historian and chronicler Jerónimo Zurita. 'But they needed to maintain their court and so needed the 100,000 florins that had been promised.'[4]

The bellicose archbishop, above all, thought that he was in command of the situation. Carrillo was stubborn, opinionated, fanciful and ambitious. He did not like to be argued with and accrued great wealth and power, but spent beyond his means in a constant quest for fame and glory. He liked, in short, to be in control – distributing orders and largesse, being obeyed, admired and, if necessary, feared. The fantasies about his own grandiosity were accompanied by others – including a belief in alchemy, that infinite riches could be found by discovering the secret of turning base metals into gold or silver. This made him easy prey for the hustlers and charlatans who turned up at the doors of his great episcopal palace in Alcalá de Henares asking him to fund their attempts to discover such secrets. 'He was a big-hearted man, whose main desire was to do great things and have a grand status, to be acclaimed and of great reputation,' said the future royal chronicler Fernando del Pulgar, who was close to the rival Mendoza family. 'His gifts were distributed out of a desire for fame, not from the use of reason . . . and he always needed more [money].' As primate of Spain, ruling over the country's wealthiest archbishopric,[5] he had long been one of the most powerful men in the land – but that was not enough. He saw the document he had signed with Isabella and Ferdinand shortly before their marriage, in which they vowed to act as one, as proof that the teenage princes were in his hands. 'In handing out positions, grants and gifts we will follow your counsel and await your approval,'[6] they had pledged. Nothing could be decided without him. Or so he imagined.

Isabella and Ferdinand were of a different school. They might still be very young, but they were bold, self-confident, intelligent and mature for their ages. More importantly, they quickly recognised that together they were something far greater than they were as separate individuals. Both were acutely aware of their own royal status and of the dangers of allowing others to exercise power, however slight, in their name. They had already defied the king of Castile. Now they seemed to encourage one another in an increasingly rebellious attitude towards the bullying and imperious archbishop. Ferdinand's father had told him to be strictly obedient, but soon he was angrily telling the archbishop that 'he was not going to be ordered about by anyone'.[7] Zurita explained that the young prince was already clear that he and his wife should not be dominated by the nobility. 'And [he said] neither the archbishop nor anyone else should think otherwise, as many Castilian kings had lost their way by doing that.' Isabella travelled the same path, and Archbishop Carrillo blamed her officials for the young couple's attitude. This was not yet royal absolutism, as they had no kingdom to rule and the concept was not as well developed as it would be in later centuries, but it was certainly a statement of intent. The young couple, indeed, encouraged each other in their single-mindedness. Juan the Great could barely believe they would behave so recklessly, but the counsellors he had sent with Ferdinand wrote back saying they too were losing influence. 'He is so set in his ways that it seems nothing other than the things he believes are right or which he desires are any good or of use,' they complained.[8]

The young couple also became increasingly desperate for money. Isabella had already pawned the ruby necklace to pay her own retainers and she and her husband were now as good as bankrupt. Ferdinand wrote to his father warning him that some of Isabella's followers 'are ready to leave and join the other side'.[9] If their situation worsened further, he warned, all might soon be lost.

Isabella wrote letters begging other nobles for their support, urging them to help calm Enrique's ire and reminding them of Ferdinand's own Castilian blood. 'As you know, Ferdinand is a *natural* of these kingdoms, and direct descendant of the kings of Castile. And, as is well known in these kingdoms and outside them, one serves the king best by choosing the most useful and profitable [options] for these kingdoms,' she wrote.[10]

The first signs of tension between the Castilian and Aragonese factions of their small court also appeared. Isabella fought with her new husband over their officials. *Mayordomos*, chaplains and confessors were jostling for power and status in their new joint venture, where some senior posts were now covered twice over. Isabella's no-nonsense attitude extended even to her new father-in-law, who soon discovered that she did not like to be pushed about. Without money of her own, she could have no independence. So she immediately insisted that Juan the Great pay out the rest of her dowry, giving her both a share of the income generated by Sicily and the taxes paid by the towns of Borja and Magallón in Aragon, and Elche and Crevillent in Valencia. She eventually sent her own officials to oversee her affairs in Aragonese lands and when her overstretched father-in-law tried to wriggle out of their agreement she insisted there was nothing to negotiate. 'Do not change a single letter' of the agreement, she retorted, warning him not to act in her affairs without her permission. 'Let me do what I think is best in the [lands] that you gave me . . . I will only do what is right.'[11]

Their situation soon deteriorated further. Valladolid was increasingly unstable and they left for nearby Dueñas on 8 March 1470. It was a wise decision. At the end of the summer rioting broke out, as the mob turned on the city's *conversos*. Their host Juan de Vivero encouraged the rioters, hoping to settle his own scores with other nobles who wanted control of the city – including Isabella and Ferdinand's protector Fadrique Enríquez. The latter 'was ready to lose one of his eyes if that meant Juan de Vivero lost both', wrote one observer, in what could have been a summary of the many rivalries that simmered among Castile's Grandees. Some of the king's supporters threatened to storm Vivero's house, seeing the rebel princes as the potential spark for even greater chaos across the kingdom. 'They had good reasons,' del Castillo claimed, 'as all towns had suffered badly during earlier wars and they feared that more suffering would now come.' Enrique and Pacheco had also encouraged the mayhem, seeing it as an opportunity to regain control of the biggest city that supported Isabella. By mid-September, they had done just that.[12]

The archbishop, meanwhile, became increasingly angry with Isabella and her husband. They were under his protection in well-fortified Dueñas and, he thought, owed him both gratitude and obedience. He knew that the truculent young princes were nothing without him, but also that the rights he was fighting over were Isabella's, not his. He resorted to threats, reminding them that he had once been loyal to Enrique and could easily return to the king's side. Then he blamed Isabella directly, showing himself angrier with her than with Ferdinand. In meetings with Juan the Great's envoys the archbishop gave full rein to his wrath. 'If they [dared] hurt him, he would turn the queen over just as he had turned over her brother, King Enrique,' they reported after one bitter encounter. Isabella, in turn, began to see Dueñas as a prison.[13]

They had few other places to go. Ferdinand's grandfather, the admiral, offered them refuge in Medina de Rioseco, which belonged to one of his sons, but that would displease the archbishop even more. Most other nobles backed Enrique or sat on the fence waiting to see what would happen next. Isabella continued to write to her royal half-brother, begging him to accept the marriage. As rumours spread that he was preparing to act against them, she and Ferdinand wrote again. They admitted marrying without his consent, but reminded him that they had previously sent envoys pledging obedience and begging him 'to accept us as true children'. They proposed a grand meeting at some neutral place, to thrash out their differences. Any that remained unresolved could be put before a council of wise men, made up of the four heads of Spain's largest religious orders – the Jeronymites, the Franciscans, the Dominicans and the Carthusians. Otherwise, they knew, war threatened. 'And before such troubles start, given that they would be difficult to stop once they had begun, that they could bring terrible offence to God and irreparable damage to these kingdoms of yours and that we believe these would even extend across a large part of Christendom, we beg you to hear us out,' they added.[14] Enrique replied to their multiple pleas with either silence or vague promises to discuss the matter with his council.

The young couple, meanwhile, enjoyed each other's company in the privacy of the bedroom. Around the time of their move to Dueñas, they made a dramatic announcement that forced everyone to reassess their strategies. Isabella was pregnant. If she gave birth to a boy, the Trastámara line in Castile would finally have a male descendant. Her son would not only be in line to succeed to the throne, but would also be a valuable future husband.[15] An uneasy stand-off developed as all sides waited for the child to be born. 'It was awaited with extraordinary impatience . . . as importance was attached to the birth of a male child,' Palencia reported. 'Even the Master of Santiago [Pacheco] and most of his allies kept their hostility more under control than usual.'

The lull ended just as soon as Isabella gave birth on 2 October 1470. The child, when it came, was a girl, also named Isabella. Almost everyone was disappointed, except for Enrique. Little is known of Isabella's reaction, though she must have found pleasure in adding her daughter's grandiose title – '*infanta* of Castile *and* Aragon' – to the letters announcing her birth. The fact that her daughter was a princess in both principal kingdoms of Spain was a sign of just how powerful her family could become if Isabella herself ever ascended to the throne. If a woman was to be measured by the way in which she gave birth, Isabella was already displaying an ability to overcome even the most painful of physical tests. 'She neither showed nor expressed the pain that, at such a time, women feel and show,' said the chronicler Pulgar. This fortitude became legendary. 'I have been informed by the ladies who serve her in her chamber that, neither when in pain through illness nor during the pains of childbirth . . . did they ever see her complain, and that, rather, she suffered them with marvellous fortitude,' one visitor to her court reported later. Isabella herself was far less dramatic about it all. 'Thanks to the immense generosity of God, my health was fine after the birth,' she wrote in one letter. She handed the child over to a governess and a wet nurse. The latter was meant to be 'good looking and of good stock, with plentiful milk', according to one court commentator.[16]

In political terms, the birth of a girl was a disaster. 'Enrique's followers . . . who, while waiting to see whether doña Isabella would give birth to a boy or a girl had ceased their violent attacks on the princes, [now] openly threw themselves into fighting them,' said Palencia. There were also doubts over the legitimacy of a daughter born into a marriage between close relatives which, in the eyes of the church, remained unsanctioned. Isabella and Ferdinand knew they were on thin ground with the papal dispensation they had claimed to possess. Juan the Great's ambassadors in Rome were now busily trying to obtain one. Ferdinand was horrified. That spoiled the narrative they had promoted in Castile – that the dispensation had already been given. 'I understand they have been seeking an audience with the Pope and, among other things, planned to ask for a dispensation for the marriage,' he said. 'It is important that those in charge of our affairs at the court in Rome . . . do not seek or petition for anything that I myself have not written to them about.'[17]

If the birth was a disappointment, a fall from his horse by Ferdinand must have been deeply disturbing. The young prince was a keen, skilled rider who loved the sometimes dangerous pastime of jousting. The game of *cañas*, with the teams of riders on nimble, lightweight horses, was another favourite. His doctor reported in November that Ferdinand had taken one too many falls and these had somehow 'corrupted his blood'. They had feared for his life, but he recovered a few days later. Isabella's fortunes, meanwhile, continued to spiral downwards. She soon lost the important trading town of Medina del Campo – a valuable part of her personal wealth – and her officials there were sent packing by Enrique's followers.[18] All this paled, however, in comparison to the king's next move.

Enrique had raised Isabella to the status of heiress. Now he was determined to cast her back down. In the broad, well-watered Lozoya Valley, fifty miles north of Madrid, a ceremony similar to that carried out before the Guisando bulls took place late in October 1470.[19] This time those arriving to do homage to the king were the mighty Mendozas, together with Queen Juana and her daughter, the younger Juana, now aged eight. Crucially, foreigners were also present. Raising Juana to the status of heiress again was not just about punishing Isabella for her insolence and disobedience. It was also about securing an alliance with France that would help Enrique counter the return of the historically troublesome Aragonese Trastámaras to his kingdom. Juana was to be given the husband whom Isabella had turned down – the same Duke of Berry, now known as the Duke of Guyenne, who was heir to the French crown. Some 100 Frenchmen accompanied Enrique's court, and the same French bishop of Arras, the envoy who had so irritated Isabella before, now bearing the title of Cardinal Albi, oversaw the ceremony in which Enrique and Juana declared that the little girl was their true daughter and legitimate heir. The nobles and bishops queued to kiss the girl's hand. The Count of Boulogne then stepped forward and, as the Duke of Guyenne's stand-in, held the eight-year-old's hand while Albi officially declared them to be engaged. The pendulum had swung all the way back. Isabella was no longer princess of Asturias[20] and a Frenchman was well placed to rule, one day, both France and, through his wife, much of Spain.

The wording of the document signed by Enrique and Queen Juana (who, presumably, had left her illegitimate son behind) leaves no doubt about Isabella's future status. The king starts by recalling how he named little Juana as heiress shortly after her birth. The reason for doing this had been straightforward. 'According to divine and human right and to the laws of this kingdom, the inheritance and succession is due to and belongs to our very dear and beloved legitimate and *natural* [meaning biological] daughter Princess Juana,' he states. The document repeatedly emphasises that Juana is his heir not just because she is the queen's daughter but also because she is his biological offspring. Queen Juana, reaching out her right hand to touch the cross held by Cardinal Albi, swore the same thing: 'I am certain that the said Princess doña Juana is the legitimate and *natural* daughter of my lord the king and mine, and as such I treat her and have always considered her.'[21]

Princess Juana had lost her title, Enrique admitted, at the Guisando bulls. But his decision to declare Isabella as heiress had been taken solely to avoid civil war and had come with strict conditions. 'In order to stop certain warring and divisions that existed in these kingdoms at the time and more of which was expected, and because the said *infanta* [Isabella] promised and publicly swore to obey and serve me as her king . . . and to marry whomsoever I chose . . . I ordered that my sister the *infanta* should be entitled and sworn in as princess and heiress,' he explained. 'She did the opposite, doing me a great and damaging disservice, disrespecting me, breaking both her own sworn oath and the laws of these kingdoms while creating great upheaval and scandal.' She must now pay the price. 'As a result, and given that her swearing in [as heiress] prejudiced my daughter Princess Juana and her rights, that second oath to my sister is declared invalid.' Those present were ordered to transfer their allegiance, with Cardinal Albi reading out a bull from Pope Paul II freeing them from their earlier oath to Isabella. 'From now on you must not in any way call, entitle, consider or hold the *infanta* doña Isabella to be my heir and successor,'[22] Enrique commanded.

One royal command could be undone by another and those who had gathered in the Lozoya Valley were clear about what had happened. 'She [Isabella] had married the king of Sicily, prince of Aragon, even though she had been warned not to,' one Mendoza official wrote. 'As a result, given the lack of loyalty and disobedience she showed by marrying on her own authority and without any agreement or permission, and for many other reasons, [the king] disinherited her.' A keen observer might have noticed, however, that the only thing binding the Grandees who lined up behind the manipulative and untrustworthy Pacheco in the green valley beside the River Lozoya was their dislike of strong monarchs.[23]

Isabella had received what, by any considered measurement, was a just reward for her rebellion. Enrique had been preparing to undermine the Guisando agreement, but she had reneged on it first. Isabella now had a husband, but had lost her future kingdom and her chosen path was leading towards disaster. She continued to squabble with Archbishop Carrillo, the one man with the power to keep her ambitions afloat. The relationship became so tense that she and Ferdinand finally moved out of Dueñas to fortified Medina de Rioseco[24] and the protection of Ferdinand's Castilian relatives. The archbishop saw that as an insult and went off angrily to deal with his own feudal lands.

All this was a coup for France's devious King Louis XI, whose reputation for intrigue saw him dubbed 'the Cunning'. The new arrangement with France, indeed, obliged Enrique to declare war on England – a measure that was bound to anger Castile's traders and sailors operating out of its northern ports. Enrique himself eagerly awaited the arrival of French troops led by Juana's new fiancé.[25]

Isabella now wrote angrily to her brother. 'You complain about the breaking of promises, but forget the promises made to me that were then broken,' she wrote. 'For which reason I was no longer obliged to abide by anything that had been pledged.' Her list of complaints was long and, in places, imaginary. Although she and Ferdinand had shown peaceful intent, Isabella claimed, she had been disinherited without her case being heard and with the aid of none other than the 'odious and suspect' Cardinal Albi of France. She reminded Enrique that certain nobles (without mentioning Pacheco) had secretly protested against their first oath to Juana. The idea that the little girl was his real daughter was a ridiculous lie. 'She is not, as the people of these kingdoms know,' Isabella said. 'From many other pieces of evidence and from trustworthy witnesses and authentic documents it would seem that things are quite the opposite, and I am amazed that in such a short space of time you have displayed so many contradictions,' she added. 'You are trying to sell copper as gold, iron as silver and an illegitimate heiress as legitimate.'[26] Yet those supposedly trustworthy witnesses and authentic documents were never made public.

Isabella claimed to have inherited her rights from her brother Alfonso. Enrique's broken promises included the fact that he had failed to ask the Cortes to swear an oath to her, that the lands she was due were not handed over and that he had promised to divorce Queen Juana and exile her. She pretended to be too refined to go into the full extent of Juana's shameful behaviour while also claiming, falsely, that she herself could show a dispensation for her marriage to Ferdinand. More importantly, Enrique had tried to ignore the pledge not to force her into marriage. Among her other reasons for turning the elderly Portuguese monarch down, she said, was that she would have become stepmother to his adult children. 'Because if all stepmothers are loathsome to their stepchildren and daughters-in-law, how much greater I would be with such a vast inheritance awaiting me,' she wrote. The French match had been especially bad. 'The French nation is, and always has been, so odious to our own Castilian nation,' she said, ignoring a long history of alliances.[27]

With so many broken promises, she had felt free to choose her own husband, following the advice of those nobles who recommended Ferdinand. This was selfless on her part, Isabella claimed, and her only interest had been the wellbeing of Castile. She also suggested that Ferdinand was, thanks to his Trastámara blood, next in line to the throne after herself. Her choice had been made 'because he was a son of these kingdoms [of Castile] and that if God disposed of me, the right to succeed in them would belong to him [anyway] and because he was close in age to me and because of the kingdoms he would inherit, which were so neighbourly and matched these kingdoms.'[28]

She finished her letter with what could be read as either a warning or a threat. 'If you carry on like this and robbery, arson and death are the result, our Lord God will put those responsible and all of you who consent to such wickedness on trial,' she wrote. 'And the prince, my Lord [Ferdinand], and I and our followers will be without blame, as we have behaved according to reason and justice, as everyone can clearly see.' The letter was circulated freely across the kingdom. A copy was pinned to the doors of the handsome Gothic cathedral in Burgos, with its two octagonal spires, decorated with airy stonework tracery, soaring heavenwards. Burgos was the great wool centre of Spain (and one of the cities that had sent representatives to the Lozoya Valley ceremony) whose mighty cathedral spires outreached even those of Paris and Reims. The letter pinned to the cathedral doors was a demonstration of bravura, mixing fact, conjecture, fantasy and outright lies.[29] But it also laid out the arguments on which Isabella based her future insistence that she, not Juana, was the rightful heiress. She would never let go of them. God could be her judge.

9

The Borgias

Rome, 8 August 1471

Isabella and her husband Ferdinand were not the only Spaniards trying to manoeuvre themselves into Europe's seats of power. In Rome, a smooth and adaptable Spanish cardinal called Rodrigo Borgia emerged, once more, as a winner in the summer of 1471. A new pope, Sixtus IV, was elected in August, with the young cardinal from Valencia a crucial supporter in the conclave that had voted for him. Pope Paul II, famously secretive and immensely wealthy, had died two weeks earlier. Some said he had stuffed himself with melon and died of indigestion. Others claimed he had had a massive heart attack while being sodomised by one of his pageboys. Either way, his death had been one of the few pieces of good news received by Isabella as she sat in Medina de Rioseco[1] with her husband and infant daughter while Enrique IV set about disinheriting her. The previous pope had been a staunch Enrique ally, issuing a dispensation that would enable Isabella to marry Afonso V of Portugal if necessary but failing to produce one that would make her marriage to Ferdinand legal.

Borgia had been raised to cardinal at the age of twenty-five by his uncle, the Spanish pope Calixtus III, and the high-living young Valencian had proved to be a shrewd operator. He had enjoyed the lively, dissolute days of Pope Paul II, but could see the wind was blowing in the direction of a more austere and obviously religious figure, the apparently pious Franciscan monk Francesco della Rovere. Borgia had secretly pledged to back his bid for the papacy, pretending to support a different candidate until his vote became crucial – when he dramatically switched sides. Temperamentally the new pope and the powerful Spanish cardinal may have seemed very different, but they had more in common than was outwardly visible. What mattered most, they knew, was to be on the winning side. Rome was a place of power, ambition and opportunity. The pope was 'Supreme Lord of Rome and of the Papal States', effectively making him the monarch of a large coast-to-coast block of land that covered a quarter of mainland Italy. He also held the key to the vast wealth of the church across western Europe. The fifty-four silver cups filled with pearls, alongside the gold, diamonds and silver that Borgia and his fellow cardinals were shown in the treasure room of the pope's castle of Sant'Angelo a few days later, were proof of that.[2] The pope's spiritual might came with extraordinary legal powers. It was he who presided over the Rota, the final court of appeal on the church laws that extended across all of Christendom, directly touching the lives of great and small. This was only too obvious to Isabella, who had married illegally and badly needed a papal dispensation to make right the lies that so weakened her position in Castile.

Borgia was as charismatic as he was ambitious. 'Beautiful women are attracted to him in a most remarkable way, more powerfully than iron is drawn to the magnet,' recorded one observer. His officials claimed he was also a man of 'endless virility'. A previous pope, Pius II, had felt obliged to scold him over rumours that he and another cardinal had attended a particularly lewd garden party in Siena. 'We are told that the dances were immodest and the seduction of love beyond bounds and that you yourself behaved as though you were one of the most vulgar men of the age . . . you forbade entry to the husbands, fathers, brothers and other male relations who came with these young women.'

When Sixtus IV was formally crowned, it was Borgia who placed the glittering, wedding-cake tiara of Gregorio Magno on the pope's head, reminding him that he was the 'father of princes and kings, the ruler of the world, the vicar of our Saviour Jesus Christ on earth' (though in rowdy Rome the solemnity was spoiled by riotous behaviour among the crowd in Piazza di San Giovanni in Laterano). Cardinals who were in the pope's favour could expect to accrue vast power and wealth. For some, indeed, that was the whole purpose of being in Rome. Borgia, whose loyalty was rewarded with the lucrative cardinal-bishopric of Albano and the abbey of Subiaco, was the epitome of the worldly, venal power-merchants produced by this system. As vice-chancellor of the Holy Roman Church since 1457, he was already one of the wealthiest and most powerful men in Rome. 'His plate, his pearls, his clothes embroidered with silk and gold, and his books in every department of learning are very numerous, and all are magnificent,' commented the Roman diarist Jacopo Gherardi da Volterra.[3] The word nepotism (from the Latin word *nepos*, or grandson) was coined to describe the way he and other members of popes' families were created cardinals. He was a so-called 'cardinal-nephew', a category that had first appeared in the eleventh century. For the previous two centuries almost all popes had appointed at least one nephew, or other close relative (and some so-called 'nephews' were thought to be illegitimate sons), as cardinal. Several popes, indeed, had once been cardinal-nephews themselves. Borgia, now aged forty, knew that the papacy itself might eventually be his, but there was no rush. Cardinal-nephews did not need to be priests and Borgia himself had not been ordained as such until twelve years after being made both cardinal and deacon of Rome's San Nicola in Carcere church. He was, however, a brilliant lawyer and diplomat. He was also, crucially for Isabella and her husband, Spanish.

The rumours about the causes of Paul II's death were almost certainly wrong, but they fitted the atmosphere of the time. Alfonso de Palencia had travelled to Rome in the early days of Paul II's papacy and came back disgusted, painting a picture of corruption and venality in his usual uninhibited and exaggerated style. He may well have shared his stories, later, with Isabella, who was often outraged by the goings-on in Rome. Paul II, he claimed, had spent his days gazing on the vast hoard of gold coins and statues that he had collected and cared little for the moral purity of a corrupt church. 'He paid more attention to the celebration of public entertainments than to correcting customs,' said Palencia. 'He organised depraved games in which prostitutes, Jews and donkeys received prizes.' Youths had charged semi-naked along the running course, slipping in the wet and reaching the finishing line caked in mud while the well-fed cardinals, whose party had despatched thirty oxen, laughed uproariously.[4]

The cardinals had increased their daily displays of luxury under Paul II, with the pope ordering that they dress in new silk robes with their caps trimmed in gold. 'And when was this change made?' asked Palencia. 'Precisely at a time when vain ornamentation was the last thing they should boast about.' Under recent popes, Christendom had seen its eastern frontiers retreat as the Ottoman Turks extended their power. Constantinople had fallen only eighteen years previously and the Turks now threatened to head north and west into the kingdom of Hungary. For a Castilian like Isabella, brought up with the crusader mentality of a front-line state, the decadence of Rome helped explain the shrinking borders of Christendom. Palencia, too, painted a picture of the cardinals behaving like the Emperor Nero and playing while Rome burned.

> In the days when almost the whole world followed the Catholic religion, the church's prelates dressed decorously; but now, when all of Asia, Africa and a third of Europe follow the crescent moon [of Islam], when the Great Turk is attacking Catholics and daily putting us in greater difficulty so that the fear now extends to inside the very walls of Rome, our exemplary men give themselves over to luxury and, as if they had no cares in the world, are busy with their scandalous outfits and given over to a dissoluteness worthy of total condemnation.[5]

It was a reminder of the corrupt, parlous state of Christendom and, for some, of the need for strong new leaders who could reverse the long-lasting period of decline.

With Borgia's support, the new pope now set about uniting Christian Europe so that it could defend itself, sending legates out to deal with the most powerful princes of the time.[6] Crucially, he chose Borgia as his legate to Spain. The latter's natural sympathy must have lain towards Aragon, his country of birth, even though Castile was more powerful. Borgia knew that Aragon had major interests in Italy – both via Sardinia and Sicily and through the large kingdom of Naples. The latter covered the half of Italy directly south of the papal states and was ruled by a bastard branch of the Aragonese royal family. With that in mind, Sixtus decided to back Isabella rather than Enrique. By December 1471 he had signed the dispensation for Isabella's marriage. This was a momentous decision for the young princess, which meant that her half-brother could no longer accuse her of throwing away her virginity, and honour, uselessly.[7] It was a first glimmer of light at the end of what had become a long, dark tunnel.

With the help of her father-in-law, Isabella fought to hold on to supporters. Juan the Great had worked hard to keep Archbishop Carrillo onside. The two old men shared a similar vision of the world and one can only imagine them, via their envoys, tutting together about the cheeky, impetuous behaviour of a generation whom they tripled in age. Isabella had publicly snubbed Toledo by moving into lands belonging to Ferdinand's maternal family, but arduous negotiations eventually saw them agree to return to Dueñas late in 1471.[8] The new *entente* almost unravelled instantly after the superstitious archbishop fell under the spell of a fraudster and alchemist called Alarcón who claimed to know the secret of the philosopher's stone. This was alchemy's greatest prize, allowing the person who eventually discovered it to turn base metals into gold and silver and even to heal all illnesses and prolong life.

The bilious Palencia, normally one of the archbishop's greatest allies, claimed that Alarcón had seduced nuns, indulged in incest and left wives behind in Sicily, Cyprus and Rhodes while also promising everyone who loaned him money that they could share the gold that he would soon produce. In fact, said Palencia, Alarcón had laid a subtle trap, knowing the archbishop's weakness for alchemy. The trickster put out word that he was scared some greedy prince would kidnap him in order to get his hands on the gold and so thought the only place he could be safe would be in the archbishop's luxurious palaces. The free-spending archbishop fell for him completely. 'He became the prelate's most beloved, trusted and befriended person,' said Palencia, who was damning about the archbishop's stupidity. 'There is no proof capable of convincing the minds of those suffering from this sickness of the truth, given that all over there are unfortunates who, in the midst of their own poverty, imagine themselves powerful by dreaming of future treasures,' he wrote. 'He wasted much of his bountiful income on this futile business, with the hope [of a discovery] allowing him to make his naturally free-spending nature even more prodigious.' Palencia was correct in identifying Toledo's spending as a problem. Money poured into his exchequer from the archbishopric's lands, but it gushed out at an even faster rate. That was what happened, explained Juan de Lucena, a Castilian contemporary, if you spent like a king on an archbishop's income. 'However great the incomings are, the outgoings will always be higher,' he said. The archbishop just borrowed more, relying on Alarcón's promises of limitless wealth and in the knowledge that his enormous debts were as much a problem for his creditors as they were for him. 'Such is our ambition that, dissatisfied with our income, we try to turn iron into gold and end up turning gold into iron,' said Lucena.[9]

'His [the archbishop's] empty exchequer, however, did not allow him to pay out the money [Alarcón] needed and so he turned to Doña Isabella, begging her to give the alchemist 500 Aragonese florins of the income received from Sicily,' Palencia reported. Isabella gave way and, to keep Toledo happy, even allowed Alarcón a daily audience. This provoked fierce encounters with Friar Alonso de Burgos,

Isabella's brash, irascible confessor. Neither man knew how to back down and their rows became legendary, even turning to violence.[10]

It was not surprising that Isabella, who harboured a strong dislike of sorcery, should have been irritated by the archbishop's dysfunctional household, though it was Friar Alonso's ability to make enemies that brought things to a head, with a meeting to try resolve their differences almost ending in disaster. 'In Dueñas Princess Isabella looked poorly upon the archbishops' followers and those who opposed Friar Alfonso,' said Palencia. 'The archbishop did not like that, which only annoyed the princess more and meant that instead of producing a solution the meeting nearly made things much worse.'[11]

While Enrique tried, and failed, to woo the archbishop, Juan the Great sent envoys to attract other nobles to Isabella and Ferdinand's cause. The main target was the mighty Mendoza clan. If they could be won over, the balance of power would shift dramatically. Little progress was made, but a small victory elsewhere provided a sign of how things might change. When Enrique ceded the royal rights over the town of Sepulveda to Pacheco, further augmenting the latter's wealth, his decision provoked a rebellion among the townsfolk. Ferdinand and Isabella sent a detachment of lancers, who were happily received and saw Sepulveda transfer its allegiance to Isabella. The townsfolk had, in effect, rebelled against the grasping nobles, seeing a threat to their traditions. It was a reflection of a wider rivalry, between citizens of towns (or, often, the local oligarchs who controlled them) and the nobles. A similar sense of outrage was developing among the Basques, where the Count of Haro was trampling over local rights. The Basques also looked angrily on Enrique's new deal with France.[12] They were frontier people, harbouring age-old hatreds and memories of numerous border and other disputes.

Isabella may be expected to have prayed for divine intervention to ease her worries. If so, she soon had further reasons for thanking her God. As Borgia set out by boat for Spain, death once more came to her rescue. It had once freed her of an undesirable future husband in the form of Pacheco's brother, Pedro Girón, and had recently given her a friendly pope. Now it struck on her behalf in France. The Duke of Guyenne died in May 1472, just eighteen months after the deal at the Lozoya Valley and before he had managed to muster an army to bring to Spain. Juana la Beltraneja had lost her future husband. That did not change the girl's status as legitimate heiress, but it robbed Enrique of a valuable ally as France's interest in sending an army to expel Isabella disappeared.[13]

A few weeks later, Borgia arrived in Valencia. The port city had grown wealthy from Mediterranean trade, its city walls enclosing impressive Gothic palaces and an imposing, domed cathedral. But it had rarely, if ever, seen the sort of opulence brought by the cardinal to impress his kinsmen, with the city chronicler later declining to write down how much had been spent on throwing parties, 'so as not to embarrass St Peter'.[14]

Borgia brought with him immense powers. After a month of celebrations he set off north towards Catalonia where Ferdinand was staying with his exultant father – who was on the point of quashing a long-running rebellion. That allowed Juan to increase Ferdinand's allowance from Sicily, helping alleviate the young couple's penury. His father's optimism extended to Castile, where he believed Isabella's position was growing stronger and 'we expect good news shortly'. Ferdinand met Borgia halfway, at Tarragona, where the Spanish cardinal placed in his hands that most precious of documents – the papal bull that not only permitted the marriage but, in an aside that proved the illegality of what Isabella and Ferdinand had done, freed them from the threat of excommunication for breaking church laws. In meetings with Ferdinand and his father, Borgia appears to have pledged to back Isabella's claim to the crown and, crucially, to help win over the Mendozas.[15]

Borgia began working on the man who was both a senior figure in the family and the weak link in its support for Enrique, the bishop of Sigüenza, Pedro González de Mendoza. Slippery, arrogant and ambitious, the bishop had his eyes set on personal grandeur. He wanted what Borgia already had – a cardinal's red, wide-brimmed and tasselled *galero* hat. He had assiduously attended Enrique's court, waiting for Pacheco to deliver on a promise to lobby for him with the previous pope.[16] But the new pope favoured Juan the Great more, so now he was ready to switch sides.

Ferdinand and Borgia eventually met Mendoza in Valencia, a city that had been in a state of almost permanent fiestas – first for Borgia and then for Ferdinand, though the collapse of a stand of seats during a bullfight had spoiled the latter. The city, presumably, had greeted both with the raucous displays of fireworks for which it was already known.[17] Mendoza tried to outdo them both on his arrival with a spectacular procession preceded by two black Africans banging huge drums and a noisy band of trumpeters and other drummers. In exchange for his cardinal's hat and a promise from Ferdinand that his family would be allowed to hold on to Castilian lands that had once belonged to the Aragonese Trastámara clan, the bishop appears to have secretly pledged the Mendozas' allegiance to Isabella – at least when Enrique died. Borgia, who had been given powers to appoint two Spanish cardinals, also seems to have promised not to give the other one to the Mendozas' traditional rival, the archbishop of Toledo. Mendoza now began publicly to express doubts 'about whether Princess Juana was the king's daughter, given the dissolute lifestyle of her mother, the queen'. The Mendozas, who had looked after the queen through her first illegitimate pregnancy, probably knew that she was pregnant with Pedro de Castilla's child once more.[18]

These were dizzying days in Valencia. Soon the city found itself celebrating again, the cathedral bells ringing out because of news that had arrived from Barcelona. After a decade of rebellion, the *barceloneses* had accepted Juan the Great as their king once more. Isabella was overjoyed, though her jarring letter of congratulations to her father-in-law showed a personal idea of victory as a form of vengeance and humiliation. 'This provides you with revenge over all those who do not wish you to prosper,' she said.[19]

Borgia's magnificent cavalcade, now boosted by the splendour of the Mendozas, travelled towards Madrid late in 1472. The proud, spendthrift archbishop of Toledo was not about to be outdone and the impact of Borgia's stay at his palace in Alcalá de Henares was felt for miles around. Flocks of sheep and herds of cattle were driven into the town to be slaughtered and consumed. Turkeys, geese and other poultry arrived in such quantities that Palencia joked that, 'in the villages and towns around, there wasn't a single cock who did not look out desolately the next morning at the empty steps of the hen-house'. He worried that the Catalans and Valencians who accompanied Borgia would take away a poor impression. 'They are the most sober of Spaniards, and this will give Castilians a reputation for gluttony,' he wrote.[20]

Borgia encouraged his hosts to spend wantonly. 'I will not go into all the things that the Cardinal did, or failed to do, in spite of the dignity required of such high rank,' wrote Palencia, before listing them anyway. Top of the list were: 'His love of luxury and other uncontrolled passions . . . [and] the puffed-up pomposity'. It was remarkably easy for Borgia to raise vast sums. He simply sold titles, honours and remission from sins. 'They knew that Spaniards are more attached to the titles of things than to their real substance, and so willingly spend to obtain ambitious honours . . . the clergy [who had come] from Rome were prodigious granting things in exchange for money, thereby debasing ancient integrity,' grumbled Palencia. Money, not reform, was top of Borgia's agenda as he pursued his main aim of funding a war against the Turks. 'Nothing was refused for money; by sacrificing a large sum one could obtain whatever one wanted and the remission of sins or the gifting of unwarranted honours was proportional to the amount given. Those who had never been learned, were awarded doctorates, jettisoning all the rigour of examinations.' A typical bull issued by Borgia promised to restore the recipient 'to the state of purity and innocence in which you were when you were baptised'. Isabella was among the buyers.[21]

More importantly, Borgia arrived with instructions to sort out the Castilian inheritance crisis, which threatened to keep an important part of Christendom engaged in civil war rather than fighting Muslim encroachment. He was able to persuade Enrique to appoint him as mediator. But Borgia hit two immovable rocks. One was the archbishop, who hated the Mendozas and looked on with envy at the new cardinal from their ranks. The other was the combination of Isabella and Ferdinand, who did not trust Pacheco or those who continually plotted to take power away from the monarchy. So Borgia headed slowly home. He had failed to resolve the problem, but crucially had helped push the Mendozas towards Isabella.[22]

With progress stalled in Castile, Isabella had little reason for complaint when Ferdinand rushed off to help his father, who had followed his victory in Catalonia with an attempt at recovering the borderlands of Roussillon and Cerdagne from France. She urged Ferdinand on, even writing to Barcelona's city council that she herself would go to Roussillon to help her seventy-four-year-old father-in-law, 'considering his age'. The queen's *élan* helped win her supporters in the Catalan port city, which wrote back thanking her for her enthusiasm. When Ferdinand arrived to help rescue his father from the besieged city of Perpignan, the French army melted away. 'This is the start of his emperorship over [the whole of] Spain,' wrote one admirer,[23] echoing the belief that he would soon rule both Castile and Aragon.

The chaos in Castile grew with 'deaths, robberies, arsons, insults, uprisings, armed challenges, rapes, mobs and damage that are carried out in daily abundance', according to Pulgar. In southern Andalusia a virtual civil war had broken out as nobles fought each other for power and similar battles were being fought across the country. 'There is no more Castile [to fight over]. If there was, then there would be even more war.' Pulgar saw little hope for the future and, like other Castilians, prayed for someone to deliver his country. 'If God does not miraculously decide to rebuild this ruined temple [of Castile], don't hope for any other solution, but rather [fear] that things will get much worse.' Rumours of terrible omens continued to spread. Two wolves had run through the streets of Seville, it was said, with one making its way into the church of Santa Catalina and drooling spittle all over the priest's robes before being chased out and killed with spears. It could mean no good.[24]

Palencia blamed the king's weakness and Pacheco's meddling for the chaos. He told Isabella as much when he travelled to Salamanca to inform her and the archbishop about the chaotic situation in Seville, where nobody seemed in full control of Castile's biggest city. 'She understood the gravity of the situation,' he reported. But he was shocked when she announced she was ready to go to Seville without Ferdinand and sort out the city's problems herself. 'I did not hide from her the many difficulties and obstacles that her plan would encounter, chiefly that a woman was not appropriate for the manly action required under such circumstances,' he said.[25] He was not ready to accept an emerging truth, that Isabella felt no need to rely on her husband and was fully prepared to act on her own.

Things came to a head, meanwhile, between the devious Alarcón and the irascible Friar Alonso de Burgos. Alarcón's arrogance had found an equal and opposing force in Burgos's uncontrollable temper. Meetings involving the two men quickly turned into shouting matches. 'The palace was aflame with rivalries and mutterings by one side or another,' reported Palencia. They were brought before Isabella, where they got into such a violent argument that they began beating each other with their sticks. 'They were hitting each other so furiously that it was impossible to separate them,' reported Palencia. Isabella and her ladies had to shout for help and soon her manservants came rushing in to separate the sorcerer and the friar. Isabella was furious. 'She gave vent to her rage by banning Friar Alonso from her chamber for several days and ordering that Alarcón be thrown out of the palace,' said Palencia. The archbishop was upset but obliged to accept.[26]

Palencia's descriptions of Isabella revealed the way he, the archbishop and many others now saw the relationship between the princess and her husband. He called Isabella 'wife of the Prince Ferdinand and legitimate heiress to these kingdoms'. She was, in other words, wife first and heiress second. In the absence of Ferdinand, they expected her to take the advice of other men. Ferdinand does not seem to have been so concerned. The royal family of Aragon had a long tradition of women, especially wives, filling in for absent kings and serving as their deputies, or 'lieutenant generals', in one of their several kingdoms. As a young man he had watched his formidable, self-confident mother Juana Enríquez wield power successfully as her husband's 'queen lieutenant' in troublesome Catalonia. He must already have realised that Isabella was equally capable of managing her affairs without him. As if to confirm his confidence in their arrangement, a cryptic message had arrived from his wife over the summer. 'The Castile business is now in the hands of the princes,' it said. Ferdinand was, however, in no hurry to go back. He planned to wait until Christmas, but in late November news reached him of radical changes.[27]

While Ferdinand was away, Isabella's situation in Castile slowly began to improve. The city of Aranda de Duero declared for her and she spent time there as negotiations progressed with a new leading player, Andrés de Cabrera, one of Enrique's senior officials and the man who had been given charge of the *alcázares* – or fortresses – in Madrid and Segovia. This gave him control of the royal jewels and treasury, first kept in Madrid and then moved to Segovia early in 1471 in a lengthy mule train. Cabrera's wife Beatriz de Bobadilla had been one of those ladies-in-waiting who abandoned Isabella as soon as she made it clear she was about to marry Ferdinand. But their friendship went back many years, and she became the conduit through which Isabella now managed an extraordinary triumph, striking against Pacheco and showing that she could seize an opportunity when she saw one. Cabrera and Pacheco had fallen out after Enrique first had Madrid's *alcázar* transferred into the latter's power and then ordered that the same happen in Segovia. Pacheco then encouraged Segovia's old Christians to attack the city's *conversos*, apparently as a way of loosening Cabrera's grip on the city. This would sow chaos and force Cabrera, himself a *converso*, to take sides. But Pacheco's attempt to use the seething resentment of old Christians as a tool for seizing control of the royal treasury back-fired, with Cabrera winning the day and forcing Pacheco to flee the city in May 1473.[28]

This confrontation between two of Enrique's senior counsellors suited Isabella, who had been wooing Cabrera for the better part of a year, with her negotiator Alfonso de Quintanilla riding over the mountains separating Segovia and her base in Alcalá de Henares thirty-six times. In mid-June he signed an agreement pledging to keep the city (and the royal treasure) under his personal control if Isabella and Enrique agreed to meet there and talk about reconcilia-tion. He also made an explicit pledge of support to Isabella herself. If Enrique did not appear then he would 'serve and follow her with this city, its *alcázar* and all else that I am able to'. Isabella had, in effect, just gained control of Castile's valuable royal treasure.[29] Enrique had little choice. He could lose the treasure and face a fresh rebellion from an important sector of the nobility or play along.

Three days after Christmas 1473, Isabella rode across the freez-ing *meseta* from Aranda de Duero towards Segovia with Beatriz de Bobadilla. It was a long, tiring and cold ride. It had taken months of negotiating, and a few more adhesions to Isabella's cause, but the following day she finally met her half-brother for the first time in almost five years. Isabella found Enrique overjoyed to see her as he once more proved his dislike of conflict. 'After lunch he went to see her in a chamber where he ordered that she be served with the finest things that he has here, and there was great joy with the Lady. They spoke at length,' reported the archbishop of Toledo in a letter to Juan the Great. 'Another day he came to see her and they dined with great service and pleasure, and the lady Princess danced and he sang before her, and they enjoyed themselves long into the night, and there was impatience for the Prince to arrive; and the next day he took her around the city so that all could see her, taking her reign. This news is spreading joy across the whole kingdom.' It was New Year's Eve, 1473, and for the first time in seven years ordinary people learned that Castile's royal family was at peace with itself.[30]

The following day Ferdinand, who was staying near by, was invited into the city, and was amazed by the reception. It was his first ever meeting with the king. There had been 'good fellowship and understanding', he boasted to the councils of Valencia and Barcelona. 'Everyone was terribly pleased,' wrote the archbishop. 'The lord Prince danced in his [the king's] presence, which caused such delight that it would take too long to explain.'[31] The early days of 1474 invited Castilians to imagine, once more, that their future was peace, not civil war.

Isabella and her husband had received advice on how to deal with Enrique, starting with his taste buds. 'When he is with his close advisers and with music, let him be and don't attempt to do anything with him,' read the instructions from one of her father-in-law's allies, Vázquez de Acuña. 'And when he comes out, they should have his food ready, *almojábana* cakes filled with soft cheese, butter and cheeses from Buitrago, *buñuelo* cakes (full of cream or *cabello de ángel*), pastries and similar foods, and with that they will have him as they want.' Early in the new year the three of them rode through the streets of Segovia together before going to an Epiphany feast at the Cabrera household, where a Milanese merchant was impressed to find a woman, Beatriz de Bobadilla, in charge. The seating was carefully arranged by rank, with Enrique placed on a slightly higher platform than Isabella and Ferdinand. When the feast was over they went off to a separate room to listen to music.[32]

A confusing period of negotiations, during which Isabella appeared to be about to regain the position of heiress, saw the archbishop of Toledo finally break with the princess and her husband. 'The archbishop was not in the slightest bit happy with the [two] princes, as the cardinal [Mendoza] had come to serve them and they gave him anything he wanted in such a way that he was known to govern over them,' reported one letter-writer. Then in October,

Pacheco died, leaving a void that proved impossible to fill. Enrique IV had lost his right-hand man and friend. 'He was sadder about this than he ever had been for anything else,' one observer reported. Others were delighted at his passing. 'What gluttony and hunger you had in this world for accumulating lands!' wrote del Castillo. Isabella saw an historic change in the configuration of power and wrote to Ferdinand, who had left again for Aragon. 'The queen and others who write to me, are urging me to go there as fast as possible,' he told his father in a letter from Zaragoza in November.[33]

Palencia blamed the grandiose and powerful alchemist Alarcón for the archbishop's increasingly erratic behaviour, especially after he teamed up with another trickster called Beato whom he claimed to have seen float above the ground. The two men duped young girls into taking part in mysterious initiation ceremonies, Palencia claimed. 'The prelate's faith in him meant that he added lies to lies, increasing the archbishop's dementia,' he reported.[34]

Soon even Pacheco's death would seem a relatively minor event. Enrique's failing health was not helped by his sadness. The king took to the forests near Madrid to hunt, at ease once more with wild animals and nature. But he was visibly exhausted. He had been suffering intense stomach pains, provoking rumours of poison.[35] By 11 December 1474, he was in bed at Madrid's Alcázar fortress and it became increasingly clear that the king was dying. His confessors reportedly leaned in close, waiting for him to pronounce the name of his heiress – but he either did not say or, out of fear for their lives, they later refused to broadcast his words. According to one version of his death, he begged the doctors for more time. 'Won't your knowledge allow me to live two more hours?' he asked. 'No,' they replied. Half an hour later he passed away.

On paper, at least, the crown now belonged to little Juana, still referred to by doubters as 'the queen's daughter' rather than 'the princess'. The ceremony in front of Cardinal Albi at the Lozoya Valley had made that perfectly clear. Enrique's oversized, dishevelled corpse was carried off on rough wooden boards, with no attempt made to embalm him. Even in death he somehow avoided the royal pomp that he so disliked during his life. The ever spiteful Palencia mocked his modest funeral as 'miserable and abject'. The body, dug up for inspection in the twentieth century, was buried in his everyday clothes and leather gaiters. The unusually broad hip bones and large, rounded skull confirm the physical oddness of a gentle king whose hatred of conflict and excessive kindness had, cruelly, made him a terrible ruler. Among all the turmoil and complaining, however, Castile's economy had boomed and civil war had been avoided for the eight previous years. Isabella had watched and learned. She did not share Enrique's emollient spirit or weakness for half-measures. Nor did she plan to make the same mistakes.[36]

Queen

Plaza Mayor, Segovia, 13 December 1474

Isabella was a picture of grief. The day after her half-brother's death she was the chief mourner at Segovia's cathedral, then just opposite the Alcázar, as the city marked the passing of a king who had ruled for twenty years. She had donned the strict black outfit of mourning. Some later claimed that she wept. Isabella may, indeed, have spilt a few tears of genuine sorrow. She and her half-brother had always enjoyed one another's company, even if there had been few opportunities to do so. Her later memories of being treated cruelly in his house centred on Queen Juana, not on Enrique himself. 'She was upset and saddened, and with good reason, because she not only esteemed him as her brother, but also considered him like a father,' reported one observer.[1]

The sadness did not last. Nor did the mourning rags. An open-sided wooden stage had been hastily erected in the city's Plaza Mayor. The following day, after a return visit to the cathedral, Isabella appeared on it in full, regal glory. Palencia claimed that she had changed after leaving the cathedral, swapping the black for 'a rich outfit, adorned with glittering jewels of gold and precious stones that heightened her magnificent beauty'. She had clearly dressed for maximum impact, to create the awe she now needed to inspire. There, in front of a crowd of Segovians braving the December cold, she was proclaimed queen regnant of Castile. She swore to protect her people, respect the church and make her kingdoms prosper. She also pledged to 'respect the privileges and freedoms that the *hidalgos*, cities and other places enjoy' while maintaining her kingdoms undivided and her people free from the yoke of others. Isabella's bold plans for Castile were already being dressed up in her favoured language of tradition.

Trumpets, bugles and other instruments rang out as drums were banged loudly.[2] Pennants and flags were hoisted to cries of 'Castile! Castile! Castile! For our queen and lady, Queen Isabella, and for King Ferdinand as her legitimate husband!' It was then that Isabella truly shocked some onlookers. She processed through the streets in her robes, preceded by something few could have imagined. 'Before her went a single gentleman, Gutierre de Cárdenas, who held in his right-hand a bare sword held by the point, with the hilt upwards, in the Spanish fashion, so that all, including those furthest away, could see that she who approached could punish the guilty on Royal authority,' Palencia reported. 'Some of those in the crowd muttered that they had never seen such a thing.'[3]

The eager crowd of onlookers must also have commented on the paucity of Grandees and bishops attending such a momentous event. Apart from Andrés de Cabrera – the man who controlled the Alcázar and royal treasure – and her own staff, few of these were present. The amazement quickly turned to grumbling among traditionalists. No woman had ever assumed, yet alone dared to display, such absolute authority or the symbols of violent intent. That Isabella did this while married, thereby ignoring her husband's masculine authority, was even worse. 'It seemed to them a terrible thing for a woman to show off the attributes that belong to her husband,'[4] said Palencia, who shared their concerns. Others muttered about 'certain laws that avowed women had no right to carry justice', Valera confirmed.

There was another, even bigger problem. Isabella was not the real heiress to Enrique's kingdoms. That honour lay with Juana la Beltraneja – the twelve-year-old girl whom he had declared, just four years earlier, to be his 'natural daughter'. Evidence about his dying wishes, however untrustworthy and partial the sources, only points to Juana as the chosen one. 'On his death-bed the father [Enrique] called to him a considerable number of Grandees and men of all classes and, with them present, ordered that his final wish was that he be succeeded in all his kingdoms by his daughter,' Portugal's King Afonso V claimed in a letter to France's Louis XI six weeks later. 'Having first confessed . . . he told me that he considered his only daughter to be his legitimate, natural and universal heiress and successor in these kingdoms and lands of Castile and León,'⁵ Enrique's royal secretary Juan de Oviedo would write four months later.

Isabella had received news of Enrique's death from a knight called Rodrigo de Ulloa, who rode through the freezing December night from Madrid to Segovia. He had requested, on behalf of Enrique's *junta* of nobles, that she do nothing. She should not declare herself queen, but first let a decision be made about who was the rightful monarch. But Enrique had been sick for a long time and Isabella must have had her plan ready. She would move first and fast, forcing Enrique's nobles and anyone who thought Juana la Beltraneja was the rightful heiress on to the back foot. (Indeed, she seems to have moved with such unseemly haste that her paid-for chroniclers felt obliged to invent the scene of her mourning her brother in the cathedral – an event that only happens several days later in Segovia's municipal records.) After the ceremony in Segovia, Isabella wrote to Castile's cities as if there had been nothing untoward in the oaths and pledges she had just received. 'Recognising the allegiance and loyalty that these kingdoms of mine and that city [of Segovia] owe me as their queen and natural mistress and as the sister and legitimate, universal heiress to my brother the king, they swore obedience to me and pledged fidelity in the usual solemn ceremonies required by the laws of my kingdom,'⁶ she wrote. It all sounded straightforward.

She now demanded that other cities do the same. 'I order you to raise flags for me, recognising me as your Queen and natural mistress and also to the high and mighty prince, King Ferdinand . . . as my legitimate husband,' she said. The message was clear in its reference to Ferdinand. He was king consort. She was the legitimate, rightful ruler. That is what the people in Segovia had proclaimed. The news she sent out came with a threat. In her letters she ordered both the cities and the commanders of fortresses in them to send representatives to swear allegiance to her. 'Otherwise you will fall foul of the penalties contained in our laws,'[7] she added.

Isabella was a usurper. Her proclamation was a pre-emptive strike against the rightful heiress which made civil war inevitable. Despite the tension and chaos during his reign, Enrique had devoted much of his energy to avoiding war, but Isabella must have seen that this was now inescapable and knew that she needed to move quickly to establish her authority over as much of the country as possible. An unstable Castile would, once more, become a prize in the wider game of European politics as its neighbours – France, Portugal and Aragon – sought to control the demographic heart and economic powerhouse of Iberia. The absence of Grandees and senior churchmen at Isabella's proclamation was a sign of weakness, and Juana la Beltraneja was now in the hands of Pacheco's son, Diego López Pacheco, who had taken over as head of the family. He had inherited his father's taste for mischief and was already reinforcing his castles and fortresses.[8] Isabella's rival was still too young to exercise her own authority.

No absence in Segovia was quite as glaring as that of Isabella's husband. Ferdinand was in Zaragoza, trying to help correct a disastrous Aragonese campaign against the French in Roussillon. Palencia, who would hear the details of Isabella's proclamation second-hand, was with him, lobbying for one of his clients – the Duke of Medina Sidonia – who wanted to be the new master of the Santiago order. Isabella's proclamation of herself as ruler and her husband as consort put her on collision course with those who assumed that he, not she, would rule Castile. Among them was the mighty and troublesome archbishop of Toledo, who continued to complain that Isabella mistreated him.[9] Five years earlier she had used her self-proclaimed independence to choose a husband. Now the usurper queen had to make sure her husband stayed loyal, that the Grandees, bishops and cities backed her and that her independence did not suddenly disappear.

And King!

Zaragoza, 14 December 1474

Gonzalo Albornoz threw himself at Ferdinand's feet in his palace in Zaragoza, took his right hand and delivered the dramatic news. 'Today I kiss this hand one hundred and one times, because it is now that of my king and master,' he said.[1] Ferdinand was shocked by the abrupt, theatrical appearance of the Castilian gentleman, who still showed signs of having ridden hard from Madrid. 'So, does that mean the king is dead?' he asked. 'The letters will inform you of that,' said Albornoz, handing over the message given to him by his master, the archbishop of Toledo. Alfonso de Palencia was present to witness the scene and said that Ferdinand reacted with a mixture of sadness and relief at the death of a man he viewed as his, and his father's, rival.

Ferdinand was annoyed, however, that the messenger bearing such historic news had come from the archbishop rather than from his wife. 'He expressed to me his surprise that he had not received a letter from the queen on such an important matter,' commented Palencia. Ferdinand had to wait three days before receiving a letter from Isabella. Palencia reported its tepid contents: 'The presence of the Prince would not be useless, but he must do whatever he thinks best given the circumstances, because she does not know well enough the state of things in Aragon.' It was a half-hearted invitation to join her, or so it seemed to those in Zaragoza, though it also took into account the possibility that Ferdinand might have to save his own future kingdom first, before attending to hers. Isabella knew that the

French were pressing hard and that the situation in Roussillon was going from bad to worse. Once her letter had arrived, he gave his final instructions about what should be done to save Roussillon and set out slowly through the pouring winter rain for Segovia.[2]

In the snake's nest that was the Castilian succession, Ferdinand was a major rival to his wife. On one hand he could claim to be *de facto* ruler, if he believed his wife's sex made it impossible for her to govern. Castilian history, his counsellors insisted, showed that that was a husband's job. Isabella had herself already recognised that he could also make a direct claim of his own, on the grounds that he was now one of the senior surviving males in the Trastámara family, though she placed him immediately behind herself in the line of succession. Others saw Aragon's King Juan the Great as the senior Trastámara male and proper heir, with his son able to govern in his name. Either way, a long list of people now expected Ferdinand to govern Castile. It included his own father, the archbishop of Toledo and Palencia. The latter already looked upon the events in Segovia with deep suspicion. Isabella was receiving 'bad advice from her counsellors who, from the very first days of their marriage, had been plotting so that the queen should enjoy first place in the government of the kingdom', he sniffed. He was crystal clear about what he himself thought ought to be happening. 'Upon his death *don* Enrique . . . was succeeded in the kingdoms of Castile and Leon by the prince of Aragon, *don* Ferdinand, according to his hereditary rights as husband of the queen, *doña* Isabella,' he stated.[3]

Ferdinand appeared to concur, even if the wedding agreements he had signed said something very different. Her tardiness in writing to him had already upset the young prince. Some of those surrounding Ferdinand were even more disturbed, especially when they heard that the royal sword had been held before Isabella as she processed through Segovia. 'We were sorry to hear about it and certain that it would cause future rivalries,' said Palencia. Ferdinand's own counsellor, Alfonso de Cavallería, warned Juan the Great that the problem threatened to snowball. 'The first thing you should do is intervene with his highness [Ferdinand] and the queen, his wife, so that they should love [the idea of] agreement and union between them and the benefits that this will bring. You should condemn and denounce the discord and differences between them and the unfortunate damage that might result.'⁴ That discord had been sown long ago, but had been suppressed by the young couple's fight for survival in their first few years together. Now that the prize was within reach, it blew to the surface.

Three days later at Calatayud, on the road to Castile, Isabella's messengers brought him a longer letter, and full details of the Segovia ceremonies. Palencia claims Ferdinand expressed shock on reading confirmation that his wife had processed through the city's streets with the upside-down royal sword before her, attributing to herself the right to mete out violent justice. 'I want Alfonso de Cavallería, as an expert in laws, and you Palencia, who has read so much history, to tell me whether in the past there has been a precedent of a queen who has ordered that she be preceded by the symbol of punishment of their vassals. We all know that [this right] belongs to kings, but I do not know of any woman who has ever usurped this manly attribute. Perhaps I am ignorant because I have seen little and read much less.' Palencia told Ferdinand that Isabella had acted against Castilian tradition. 'The young king expressed his astonishment, time and again, at such unheard of events,'⁵ Palencia insisted, worrying that this would provide the Grandees with ammunition to cause trouble.

Not everyone thought like Palencia. Martín de Córdoba, a distinguished Augustinian friar, disagreed strongly. In a book he wrote to guide Isabella in the exercise of authority, *The Garden of Noble Ladies*, he claimed that it was ignorant or old-fashioned to 'believe it evil when some kingdom or other polity falls to a woman's government . . . I, as I will declare, hold the contrary opinion.' There had been plenty of learned women, including princesses and saints, in the past 'especially in letters. So why is it that now, in this our century, women do not give themselves to the study of liberal arts and other sciences; rather it appears to be prohibited?'⁶

Ferdinand did not spend Christmas with his wife. He progressed slowly through the bitter cold towards Segovia, building up a large retinue as he went. By Christmas Day he had made it only as far as Almazán, a town in the power of the Mendozas. He seemed both determined to impress and in need of time to think through the new situation. Palencia poured poison into his ear. 'Most of that [Christmas] day he spent secretly talking to me, given that the way events had gone made him pay greater attention to my repeated warnings about . . . the perfidious advice being given by the queen's adulators,' he said.[7]

Archbishop Carrillo also stirred the pot of marital strife. He had already reached Segovia, demanding the best rooms in the palace and swearing allegiance to Isabella. But he made little secret of the fact that his plan was to follow the king, not the queen. Palencia blamed Cardinal Mendoza, the archbishop's great rival and now becoming one of Isabella's main advisers, while 'various of the principal knights continually encouraged the petulance that they had begun to introduce into the Queen's womanly spirit'. As Ferdinand made his way towards Segovia, the cardinal and his brothers had already signed up to a confederation of nobles who pledged to protect Isabella's supposed right to the throne. They would support 'the queen, our mistress doña Isabella, as queen and natural mistress of these kingdoms, and King don Ferdinand, her legitimate husband, our master'. Once more, they put him in second place as consort. The Mendoza clan placed itself under Isabella's command, telling her that 'Your Highness must order us to do whatever best serves you.' Palencia explained that fear of the Aragonese yoke had spread rapidly through the Castilian court. 'Those ideas moved the queen who, after all, is only a woman, and quickly caused others who had previously been against the queen's arrogance and high-handedness to change their minds,' he said.[8]

The Aragonese, meanwhile, openly rejoiced at what some saw as a bloodless takeover of Castile, referring to it as 'our happy succession in those our [new] kingdoms'. The city of Barcelona, for example, wrote to congratulate Isabella, but put her second behind her husband, with Enrique's heirs given as 'the king [Ferdinand] and you'. In other correspondence Aragonese officials failed to mention Isabella at all, while talking about Ferdinand as 'successor to the kingdom of Castile'. His father announced that Castile 'has been passed to the illustrious prince'.[9]

It took Ferdinand a further week to reach Turégano – just two *leguas*, or riding hours, from Segovia. It was New Year's Eve, and Segovia was busy celebrating the change of year. Ferdinand was asked to wait before entering the city. In the meantime, a stream of senior nobles left Segovia to visit him. On 2 January 1475, Ferdinand made his formal entry. Those watching could be forgiven for believing that the relationship between Isabella and Ferdinand was perfectly harmonious. She, and the city, laid on a stunning reception. The nobles who had assembled in Segovia waited for him outside the walls. He wore a long black cloak, to mourn Enrique, which was ceremoniously removed to reveal a shiny outfit embroidered in gold and lined with the fur of pine martens. A canopy was held above him as he walked to Segovia's San Martín gate and there swore to respect the privileges and rights of the city. A torchlight procession then led him through the dusk to the cathedral to pray and swear his oaths. It was only then that he went to see Isabella, who waited in the outer courtyard of the Alcázar.[10] Much had changed since they last saw one another, eight months earlier. Now, instead of confronting adversity together, they had to confront one another. Castile, and the nobles gathered in Segovia, wanted to know how they planned to govern a kingdom that Isabella had claimed as hers.

While courtiers on both side schemed and argued, Isabella and Ferdinand kept their heads. The latter thought that a generous dose of husbandly love would soften his wife up. He told those who thought he was being too gentle with her to wait. 'He replied that he was confident of overcoming the situation with patience and that he was sure of triumphing by assiduously satisfying the demands of conjugal love, which would undoubtedly soften the harsh intransigence that wicked men had placed in the queen's heart,' recorded Palencia. After the feast that followed Ferdinand's proclamation as king, the young couple slipped away.[11]

Palencia was so disgusted that he marched off, cursing Isabella's pride. Even the archbishop of Toledo, now fully under Alarcón's spell, seemed to him to have gone mad. In fact, the situation was resolved with ease. Ferdinand accepted that the archbishop, a pro-male traditionalist, and Mendoza, an Isabella supporter, should be the arbiters. The two rivals did their job efficiently. Within two weeks a document was drawn up and signed. It did not differ greatly from the original marriage accord signed at Cervera in 1469, though it made some concessions to Ferdinand. As 'legitimate successor and proprietor of these kingdoms', Isabella would receive the pledges of loyalty, name officials (though both could name *corregidores*, the representatives of royal power in the cities), give grants and sign off on Castile's accounts, with money first going to cover administration costs. Ferdinand's name would go first on their joint documents and coins, but her shield had precedence. Both could administer justice, jointly or apart. Pulgar claimed that Isabella won her husband over by pointing out that, if he insisted that only men could inherit the crown, he was putting their own daughter Isabella – still their only child – in a situation where she, too, would be prevented from ruling. He also claimed that the two monarchs realised that much of the advice they were receiving was self-interested and that they had already decided not to let the Grandees divide them. A key understanding, mostly stuck to over the years, underpinned their power-sharing alliance: they would never, even when apart, override each other's decisions.[12] A unique alliance was being formed between two people who were not just husband and wife but also political partners representing their own different interests. All would depend on how this compact worked in practice, and how they both behaved.

The agreement was a victory for the Castilians over those who wanted Isabella to remain in the background while Ferdinand governed. But that does not mean Ferdinand was dissatisfied. He had not sought the full unity of their two dynasties' kingdoms but hoped, among other things, to gain advantage for his family's crown of Aragon and, crucially, for his own offspring. One of his most immediate aims had been to raise a Castilian army that could ride to the rescue of his father – and his own future kingdom – in Roussillon. Within three days the Castilians had pledged to send 2,000 lancers. He also, according to Pulgar, had full confidence in Isabella's ability to govern without him.[13]

The young monarchs could feel satisfied with their achievements in this first month. Isabella's old supporters had mostly stayed loyal. The Mendozas had joined them, along with other nobles who declared their loyalty in the weeks after Isabella's rapid proclamation.[14] But the Pacheco family and many other senior nobles had not offered support. More importantly, Juana la Beltraneja had a rightful claim to the throne. She was too young to act for herself, but it was only a question of time before someone took up her cause.

Clouds of War

Segovia, March 1475

The archbishop of Toledo was furious. He may have taken the best rooms in Segovia and played an important part in drawing up the agreement between Isabella and Ferdinand on how they would rule, but the new situation jarred. Isabella was not being nearly nice enough to him. In fact, he thought, she was being downright rude. He had spent years working for the cause of Aragon and had played a crucial role in bringing Ferdinand to Isabella's side. The princess and her husband had sworn to obey him and not to appoint anyone without consulting him first. Even though his loyalty had wavered towards the end of Enrique IV's reign, he thought that he had every right to expect to be the new royal *privado* – heir to the likes of Juan Pacheco and Álvaro de Luna, who had run Castile for most of the previous half-century. But Isabella did not want a *privado*. Nor did Ferdinand. Instead, Isabella's dislike of the archbishop and his madcap court of sorcerers and frauds grew daily. 'All one heard were his frequent complaints about the ingratitude the queen showed by giving preference to absolute enemies over certain friends,' wrote Palencia.[1]

Isabella was pleased with herself. Her husband had signed a contract that kept Castilians happy. Her strategy, already evident at her wedding to Ferdinand, of acting boldly and forcing others to deal with a *fait accompli* appeared to be paying off. A sufficient number of nobles had come round to her cause to make her usurper's coup an established fact – at least for the moment. Dislodging Isabella would now require a considerable amount of force and money. A new era was dawning, she felt, where the dubious royal authority of her brother would give way to something far more potent – an authoritarian, semi-absolutist monarchy in which the new queen and her husband could rule with minimum interference from the nobles, the church or anybody else. The Grandees and other oligarchs were needed to help govern her kingdoms and maintain the existing social order and its hierarchies, but they must know their position. Ferdinand was her greatest ally in this strategy, though this was far from being the tradition of Aragon, with its complex power-sharing between the crown and its various kingdoms and cities. He had already shown his frustration with that arrangement, angering the burghers of both Zaragoza and Valencia with summary executions carried out without consulting local authorities. In Castile he, too, agreed that a stronger, more authoritarian monarchy that concentrated power in the royal court was best. Among the cheerleaders for Isabella's firm hand and new style of government was Friar Torquemada, the influential prior whose Santa Cruz monastery sat just outside Segovia's walls. In a memorandum to her outlining Castile's ills, he would call on her to correct the numerous errors of government in a kingdom which was being run by 'inefficient' and 'avaricious' officials, where the church was often up for sale and where Jews and Moors were not kept in their place. But many of the great feudal magnates differed utterly in their view, seeing themselves as rightful co-participants in the government of the kingdom. If Isabella thought they would accept the change without a fight, then she was wrong. The grandiose, proud and warlike archbishop of Toledo harboured extravagant fantasies of eternal life and limitless wealth. He could hardly be expected to accept diminished status as a secondary player in Castilian politics.[2]

Archbishop Carrillo fumed, none too quietly. He demanded seven of the most important posts at court for himself and his family. He developed a growing hatred of Isabella and kept trying to tell Ferdinand how marvellous and clever his sorcerer Alarcón was. 'He was supposed to be devoted to the king and a firm backer of his cause,' said Palencia. 'But he gave space in his heart to the virulent hatred inspired by perfidious Alarcón.' The archbishop's support for Isabella stretched back to those first days after her brother Alfonso's death and it was he who had led her mule to the historic meeting with Enrique at the Guisando bulls. Perhaps she knew him too well and had tired of his moods, eccentricities and misogyny. Perhaps she mistrusted him after their recent falling-outs. Either way, this was not a moment for pushing away one of the most powerful men in the kingdom. Isabella's early triumph was built on fragile foundations. It badly needed consolidation.[3]

Isabella and Ferdinand, fuelled by impetuous audacity, spent the first weeks of her reign celebrating their early success with youthful exuberance. The latter wrote upbeat letters to Aragon, making out that the whole kingdom was behind them and that it was just a matter of time before the Castilian army appeared on the horizon and scared off the French. Isabella seemed remarkably unaware of exactly how big a threat they posed to a number of important people. These included the kings of Portugal and France, now faced with an alliance between the two halves of Spain that boosted their might on the frontiers of both countries. Those who had gained most from Enrique's weak kingship also felt threatened – especially the Pacheco family. Last, but not least, was a twelve-year-old girl who had been sworn in as heiress by the country's nobility and was already in the Pacheco family's power.[4]

Ferdinand's recent triumph in Perpignan suggested that the combined might of Castile and Aragon had created a new, powerful player in Europe. Threatening letters were written to the Portuguese king warning him that he would feel the wrath of both crowns if he declared his support for the cause of his niece, Juana la Beltraneja. But reality bit quickly and devastatingly into the young couple's fantasy of a newly potent Castilian–Aragonese alliance that would make other European monarchs tremble. In February the Catalans informed them that, unless 'the power of Castile was awakened', Perpignan would soon have to be handed back to the French. Early in March Ferdinand was forced to tell them that the royal exchequer was empty and Castile itself too impoverished to help. On 10 March 1475, Perpignan fell.[5] Catalonia was convinced that it was only a matter of time before it, too, ended up under the French yoke. It was an enormous blow to Isabella and her husband, just three months after she had claimed the crown.

Only a combination of naivety and hubris can explain why Isabella and her counsellors failed to spot the speed with which a potentially devastating alliance was being built by her enemies and some whom she thought of as friends. Just two weeks after Isabella had proclaimed herself queen, and before Ferdinand had even made it to Segovia, the king of Portugal had begun urging others to recognise the 'clear right' of the woman Enrique had declared to be his legal heir, Juana la Beltraneja. 'We consider that his daughter, our niece doña Juana, is queen and that her honour and condition is now, more than ever, in our hands and that we are obliged to help her as much as is possible, seeing how she was sworn in and approved as the true and legitimate successor to those kingdoms,' he wrote to Rodrigo Ponce de León, Marquess of Cadiz. The marquess was one of two nobles (the other was the Duke of Medina Sidonia) who fought for personal control of wealthy Seville and its surroundings, an area where royal authority had effectively lapsed long before. 'We are sure of the loyalty that all her subjects are now obliged to show her and that they should recognise and obey her, *and nobody else*, as queen, especially and above all because at the time of his passing away, in the presence of several of the Grandees of his kingdom who were there, the king her father pronounced her to be the true heir and successor to his kingdom and, as his legitimate and natural daughter, telling them to obey her,'[6] the Portuguese king now claimed.

A far different dynamic to that imagined by Isabella and her husband was beginning to reshape Europe. The ambitious Louis XI, also known as 'the universal spider' because of the way he spun his web across the continent, had found himself confronted by a series of alliances between his neighbours in Aragon, England, Burgundy and Brittany. Castile's new alliance with Aragon could have been expected to corner him further, but his reconquest of Perpignan proved that this so-called Great Western Alliance was built on sand, and soon all the other members had signed peace deals with him. Isabella looked increasingly isolated and Afonso V now decided that Castile was, in the right circumstances, Portugal's for the taking. The excuse was already there, as Isabella's claim to the throne was, at best, tenuous. Afonso's insistence that Enrique had pronounced Juana la Beltraneja heiress on his death-bed was almost certainly false, and could not be reinforced with documentary proof, but it was hardly the most substantial part of a very clear claim.[7] All he needed was sufficient support both abroad and within Castile itself.

That support was already taking shape. Afonso V, by now nick-named 'the African' after expanding Portugal's lands in modern-day Morocco to Tangiers and Asilah, had started sounding out both Castilian nobles and the French king almost as soon Isabella declared herself queen. The most powerful noble in the land, López Pacheco, had not travelled to Segovia to kiss the hands of the new monarchs. He also had possession of the rightful heiress. He soon began plotting with Afonso but, cleverly, also lobbied Isabella and Ferdinand for control of the Santiago military order, making it look as though he might still be won over. While the second most power-ful noble, the archbishop of Toledo, remained by the new queen's side, López Pacheco's scheming with King Afonso remained insuf-ficient. Archbishop Carrillo knew this and, his pride hurt, decided to prove it by storming off. Juan the Great sent an envoy with instructions to win him back. 'This gentleman told him about the numerous times that the king had exhorted and charged his son to remember how only the archbishop of Toledo, with his authority, courage, great prudence and power, has maintained him and the queen his wife in Castile,' Zurita reported. But the archbishop now claimed to have intercepted a letter showing that people at Isabella's court were plotting to murder him. The young monarchs, especially

Isabella, did not treat him or his people with the respect they were due, he insisted. An alarmed Juan the Great tried to arrange a personal meeting with Toledo,[8] not knowing that the archbishop had been in secret negotiations with Afonso for a while. López Pacheco was the match-maker.

A third senior grandee, Álvaro de Stúñiga, added further weight to the alliance against Isabella. The young queen might have won him over, but he wanted to hold on to the dukedom of Arévalo[9] which had been gifted to him by Enrique after Isabella's mother was ejected from the town where she had spent the sweetest days of her childhood. That was an open sore for Isabella. Stúñiga was, quite simply, her enemy. She was happy for it to stay that way. One day, she hoped, revenge would be hers.

Loyal Castilians lobbied the Portuguese king, warning him against his fickle allies. The Pachecos, Toledo and Stúñiga 'were the [same] people who had broadcast throughout Spain and abroad that she [la Beltraneja] had no right to inherit Enrique's kingdoms nor could be his real daughter because of the impotency he suffered from', Fernando del Pulgar pointed out in a letter. He also reminded Afonso that, before Enrique's death, the Portuguese king had pursued a marriage with Isabella while turning down several opportunities to marry La Beltraneja precisely because he doubted her legitimacy. But Juana la Beltraneja had already been moved to Trujillo, in the frontier region of Cáceres. On 1 May, at a ceremony in which Afonso sent Baron Biltri to represent him, they became formally engaged – allowing the Portuguese king, according to an outraged Palencia, to start calling her 'my wife' and himself 'King of Castile and León'.[10] Soon Portuguese soldiers were massing at the frontier. It would be war.

13

Under Attack

Valladolid, 3 April 1475

Isabella appeared on a big hackney pony in elaborate trappings, its rump covered with a colourful skirt and the mane, breast strap, bridle and overcheck decorated with small silver plates and flowers shaped out of gold. She wore a crown and a dazzling brocade dress and was accompanied by fourteen ladies, all wearing tabards that were half of grey-brown velvet and half of green brocade. The women of Valladolid hung from windows, determined to catch a glimpse of their magnificently turned-out new monarch and her retinue as they prepared for a celebratory week of jousting and partying in the city. 'The queen and all her ladies came, she so richly dressed and hatted and her ladies with such diverse, gallant and rich clothes of the kind that women of this kingdom have never been seen wearing to fiestas,' said one chronicler.[1] Isabella had claimed the throne just fourteen weeks earlier and had, among other reasons, come to Valladolid to marshal support against her rival, Juana la Beltraneja, and the king of Portugal. One of the best ways to assert her splendour and authority was by showing off her wardrobe and jewels. The more dazzling, magnificent and regal she seemed, the better for her reputation as it spread by word of mouth across the country. This was a lesson, like so many, that Isabella had learned from the failings of her half-brother Enrique IV. Where he was scorned as sloppy, humble and unregal, she would be magnificent, admired and feared. 'She was sometimes accused of the vice of showing too much pomp,' one of her own chroniclers admits. 'But we should understand that there are no other ceremonies in this world quite as extreme as those required by the royal condition . . . which, as it is uniquely superior, must make an effort to show itself above all others, given that it enjoys divine authority on earth.'

The woman who rode through the famously muddy streets of Valladolid was twenty-three years old, and in the early stages of a fresh pregnancy from those first nights when she had been reunited with Ferdinand in Segovia. 'This queen was of medium height, well put together in her person and the proportion of her limbs, very pale and blonde,' reported Fernando del Pulgar, the new chronicler who arrived at court with the Mendozas. 'The eyes were between green and blue, her look is honest and graceful, her features well arranged and her face beautiful and full of joy. She was very measured in her bodily movements; she didn't drink wine; she was a very good woman who liked to be surrounded by good, elderly women of fine lineage.' A portrait believed to be of her as a young queen, painted by an anonymous Flemish-style artist in the first decade of her reign, highlights those green-blue eyes and the light auburn hair. It also shows her wearing the heavy jewellery that she liked to don on her public outings. A large gold chain is decorated with green emeralds and fat pearls, while the jeweller has reproduced her sheaf-of-arrows motif several times in different sizes, using elaborately worked fingers of gold with pearls at their tips.[2] More emeralds, pearls and large, plum-coloured balass rubies decorate the large brooches used to pin strips of white silk to her cloth-of-gold dress. A thick Moorish-style *axorca* gold bracelet is encrusted with even more precious stones. Isabella still has a young girl's unlined face, and the narrow plucked eyebrows of the time, though a slight hardening of the jawline – which would become pronounced later on in life – can just be detected.

Isabella was already her own woman, confident in her beliefs and decision-making. 'She enjoyed talking to religious people who lived honestly, from whom she frequently sought advice, and she would listen to them and to the other lawyers around her, but mostly she made up her mind by following her own ideas,' said Pulgar. 'She wanted her instructions and orders to be carried out to the letter . . . She was firm in her intentions, changing her mind only with great difficulty.'³ She was not, in other words, a woman who liked to be crossed. Nor was she used to obeying, though it was probably in Valladolid where she now became close to Friar Hernando de Talavera.

As queen, Isabella made sure that others knew their place was below her – not just figuratively but also literally by sitting or standing on platforms that raised her above them in public. That explains her surprise when she suddenly found herself forced to kneel, accepting a position of inferiority. It was Friar Talavera, her new confessor, who insisted that she drop to her knees. Previous confessors, whom she had the power to appoint and replace, had never dared order such a thing. 'We should both be on our knees,' the queen protested. 'No, my lady, I must be seated while your Highness kneels, because this is God's tribunal and I am his representative,' Talavera replied. Isabella was impressed. 'This is the confessor that I have been looking for,' she said afterwards. This story was first recounted in a history of the Jeronymites, Isabella's favourite monastic order along with the observant Franciscans, and is possibly apocryphal, but it reflects the truth of her relationship with the devout, honest priests whom she chose as confessors and, later, as bishops, archbishops and administrators. These were men who might lecture her about God and morals, including her own, but they did not actively seek political power or personal wealth. They respected her regal power in ways that, say, the grumpy and scheming Archbishop Carrillo of Toledo had never done, while also demanding absolute respect for their role as men of God. It was the sort of clean, clear division that Isabella liked. It was also a world in which each man, and woman, knew their place. And Talavera had clear, unbending and traditional ideas on exactly what each person's place was.

Talavera was a learned *converso*, from a new Christian family, who had been a professor at Salamanca University. The austere, reed-thin friar famously toyed with his food, eating as little as possible and adding just a few drops of wine to his cup of water. He also wore a cilice hairshirt under his friar's habit and 'practised what he preached and always preached what he himself practised' according to a contemporary in the royal court. As prior of the Santa María del Prado monastery near Valladolid he was an eminence within his order and a senior churchman in Castile. Talavera became not just Isabella's confessor but also one of her most valued officials, placed in charge of large, complex projects like church reform, peace negotiations, raising church money for the crusade against the Moors and the recovery of royal lands and rents given away by King Enrique. Famed as a preacher and winner of converts, he belonged to a school that frowned on forced conversions – a moot point for a *converso*, since many Jews had converted under pressure of violence at the end of the previous century.[4] He preached not just obedience but love and charity. When Isabella's conscience was troubled, it was Talavera whom she turned to. Indeed, Talavera appeared to have more influence over Isabella – whatever that meant to a woman not famed for changing her mind – than anyone apart from Ferdinand. He held her to the highest standards, demanding that she be exemplary in all things.

When she or Ferdinand slipped in their personal morality, Talavera would be sure to tell them off. Few people, if any, dared confront Isabella in such a forthright manner. She liked that, even if Ferdinand did not. But Talavera also had competition from other priors. In Segovia, Tomás de Torquemada had only to climb the steep hill from his Santa Cruz monastery beside the River Eresma to find the royal family. Isabella lavished money on his monastery, which was soon emblazoned with her sheaf-of-arrows symbols and became known as Santa Cruz la Real ('the Royal') as a result. The Dominicans – founded in Spain in the thirteenth century, with Santa Cruz as the first monastery – were famed pursuers of heretics and, like the Franciscans, had long been involved in stirring up hatred against Jews and *conversos*. Chief among them was Alfonso Hojeda, prior of a Dominican monastery in Seville. When Talavera's advice or methods seemed too bland, Isabella could always turn to these men, with their unbending dogma, suspicious nature and liking for harsh measures, using fear, punishment and, where necessary, torture. Torquemada was quite explicit about how much of a danger Jews and Muslims posed to Spain. In the memorandum 'of the things which the monarchs must remedy' that he felt bold enough to send Isabella and her husband, he urged them to pursue heretics among the *conversos* and separate Jews and Muslims from Christians.[5]

Talavera now publicly scolded the coquettish noblewomen of Valladolid after they had excitedly embraced the festive, fashion-conscious spirit of their young queen and ignored the local bishop when he threatened to excommunicate them for wearing ruffs and primitive farthings or bustles that exaggerated their hips. 'They even make themselves up and dress during Lent just as they do outside it and go like that to funerals, as if they were weddings or christenings,' he protested. His complaints fitted perfectly within his general view of women as flighty and morally fragile, 'being, as you are, naturally weak and thin in understanding and in body'.[6]

The pious prior could be equally damning about men – as individuals, rather than collectively – and even felt free to chastise Isabella's husband Ferdinand when he thought he was not paying enough attention to his wife. 'A lot more substance is owed in your love and honouring of your most excellent and worthy wife,' he said, while also telling him to spend less time on games.[7] Isabella's husband ignored him, and remained an enthusiast for games of all kinds.

Ferdinand's reputation was mixed. On the one hand he was considered wise and experienced beyond his age, the result of a late childhood spent running from one battle zone to another. But he was also a keen partier and womaniser with several illegitimate children. 'This king was of medium height, well proportioned, with the features of his face well composed, laughing eyes and straight black hair,' wrote Pulgar.

He was very restrained in both his drinking and eating and in the way he moved, because neither rage nor pleasure appeared to alter him . . . He was naturally inclined towards doing justice, but also towards clemency and took pity on those miserable people who he saw were suffering. And his special gift was that whoever spoke to him wanted to love and serve him because he communicated in such a friendly way. He took good counsel, especially that of his wife the queen because he knew she was so very capable . . . He liked all kinds of games, with balls, boards or at chess, and spent somewhat more time than he should playing them; and although he loved his wife the queen greatly, he also gave himself to other women.

They were, in other words, a couple who understood one another perfectly when it came to government, though Isabella struggled to cope with Ferdinand's sexual wandering. All that self-confidence in government was underpinned by a layer of insecurity which, in turn, revealed a passion for her husband that went beyond what might have been expected of a politically motivated marriage. 'She loved after such a fashion, so solicitous and vigilant in jealousy, that if she felt that he looked on any lady of court with a betrayal of desire, she would very discreetly procure ways and means to dismiss that person from her household,' wrote Lucio Marineo, one of several Italian humanists drawn to her court. This was something she tried to control in public, but others agreed that she 'watched jealously over him beyond all measure'. In later years, indeed, her daughters would vow not to fall into the same bouts of destructive jealousy that Isabella was clearly unable to control. 'My lady the queen . . . was equally jealous,' one of them would later remark. 'But time cured her Highness of it, as I hope to God it will for me.'[8]

Valladolid was a place of special memories. Isabella and Ferdinand installed themselves once more in Juan de Vivero's palace – the same house where they had celebrated their wedding night. They had come here from Medina del Campo – another of the major towns of

Old Castile (the part that lay north of the Guadarrama and Gredos mountain ranges) that they now controlled – as they began a nomadic lifestyle that would continue for decades. Indeed, one of the most striking sights for ordinary Castilians during Isabella's reign was the royal court in motion. Her account books would soon show large outlays on *acémilas*, the pack beasts laden with bundles and chests which trudged behind them in long trains over the coming years as they criss-crossed Castile in almost perpetual motion. Isabella's court moved so often, indeed, that a quarter of its spending went on transport. Travel was uncomfortable and lodgings sometimes basic, with households obliged to give over half their space (and furniture) to the court. The royal family moved on horses and mules, or were carried on litters borne by animals or men. Padded mule saddles held together with golden nails and covered in silk cushions and blankets were ordered up for little Isabella and the other children to come as they, too, wandered through their parents' lands. Crossing Castile's mountain ranges and long, broad rivers brought moments of danger as they climbed up slippery mountain passes or waded through fast-flowing water. With so many people travelling with the court, provisions were sometimes hard to find as the towns and villages they passed through were pressed into providing sustenance. Isabella's *gallinero*, the man charged with sourcing chickens for the royal table (Isabella had been recommended to eat fruit in the morning and vegetables in the afternoons, but poultry was the most common dish), was deemed 'worse than a kite for the villages and peasants of the area he visits'.[9] Even the most basic logistics could go wrong in a country where the land was not always productive and water could be scarce. A black slave and two yeomen even died of thirst on one trip to visit Isabella's mother at Arévalo.[10]

Isabella believed that a monarch should be seen by her people and, even when the court was on a longer stay in a city or castle, was rarely shy of jumping on a horse with a smaller entourage and riding for days to put out political fires as they erupted in different corners of her kingdom. Even pregnancy did not stop her. With their joint monarchy, indeed, they soon found that they could douse two blazes at once, by the simple ruse of splitting up. If this worked it was because their political relationship rested on a single, essential element – trust.

The jousts in Valladolid were held in an atmosphere of feverish excitement. 'As the king and queen were so young and at the very start of their reign, many wanted to show their grandeur or display their magnificence by spending as much as they could,' one chronicler explained. The Duke of Alba was allowed to joust only twice after falling, fully armoured, from his horse and knocking himself out while practising. He made up for it by throwing the best party, which ended as the sun rose over the city. Alba also bought, and gave away, so much silk and brocade to the ladies that a short-term scarcity in Castile sent the price rocketing. He drained his personal exchequer, providing mummery and more partying all week long as Valladolid went into a dizzying frenzy of jousting and revelry. Alba had already captured the spirit of the new, changing times, returning the all-important castle of La Mota in Medina del Campo to royal hands.[11] It had been one of the many possessions that Enrique had handed over to nobles as he tried to buy their support.

Everyone knew that the Portuguese were readying an army, but a devil-may-care attitude gripped the young court. 'The king of Portugal and his supporters were held in little esteem, with the king and queen deriding the things he might do to them,' reported a local chronicler. 'They passed those days full of high spirits and careless of fear.' Other Spaniards were more worried, seeing omens that a ferocious war was about to start. A group of Portuguese bulls had escaped from their herdsman, waded across the River Guadiana and attacked some Spanish bulls, according to one story. These had lowered their horns and charged in response, with the heavy beasts clashing on the Spanish side of the river before the Portuguese bulls trotted back and began calmly grazing again. Word also spread of an aerial battle between flocks of magpies and thrushes in Andalusia, considered another harbinger of violence. A stern Palencia accused Isabella and her husband of partying when they should have been readying for war. 'Ferdinand and Isabella wasted a lot of time in Valladolid, which would have caused them great harm had the enemy not also dallied for days,' he said.[12]

The people of Valladolid scratched their heads, and tried to recall if they had encountered anything like it. This was a wealthy city, home to a thriving silver trade and surrounded by fertile land, but they had not seen such a show of grandeur for more than half a century. 'And as there were many foreigners in Valladolid, the names of the monarchs rang out across the whole world. It seemed as if they were not like any previous monarchs of Castile but, rather, that Caesar had returned to earth in all his magnificence and grandeur,' wrote the local chronicler. The obligation to impress was augmented by the presence of ambassadors from France, England, Brittany and Burgundy – all eager to measure up the new queen and her husband.[13]

Jousters competed for glory both in the tiltyard and in the magnificence of their clothes, horses and servants' uniforms. Horses were dressed in blankets woven from gold thread and trimmed in marten's fur.[14] The warrior-like thrill of the tiltyard – where torches had to be brought after contestants insisted on carrying on after dark – was accompanied by its necessary counterpart of courtly love, with jousters dedicating their efforts to their favourite ladies. They also competed to produce the wittiest or cleverest mottoes and slogans to impress them. Ferdinand knew how to play the knight's role and, on one later occasion, publicly devoted his jousting to Isabella in the following terms. 'Any prison or pain / that I suffer is just / because I suffer for love / of the greatest and best / in the world and the most beautiful.' But this time, with the losses in Aragon and the expected Portuguese invasion troubling him, he was deliberately sombre. He was a fine horseman and keen jouster, but the motto he chose showed that he and Isabella were aware that this was an interlude before greater trials. 'Like a forge I suffer in silence because of the times in which I find myself,'[15] it read. Portugal lay just eighty miles away.

The Portuguese king, reputedly flush with gold from his adventures in Africa after conquering Tangiers and sending explorers and navigators to open up trade routes further south, was gathering an army that made the 2,000 men Castile had planned, but failed, to send to Aragon look feeble. At least 10,000 footsoldiers and 5,000 cavalry were on their way. His ambassador Ruy de Sousa travelled to Valladolid and delivered a demand that Isabella and Ferdinand leave the country. He received a curt 'no' as an answer, along with a reminder that those nobles who now backed La Beltraneja were the same ones who had first claimed she was illegitimate. The archbishop of Toledo remained of crucial importance. If he could be brought back to their side, then the balance of power would shift dramatically. Isabella and Ferdinand now began moving separately. Isabella set out from Segovia, riding south over the rugged mountain passes that separated Old and New Castile, to see the archbishop in his main palace in Alcalá de Henares.[16] By now, however, it was clear that his anger was chiefly directed at her. 'It was agreed that the queen, who is the one he is unhappiest with, should go to him,' Ferdinand told his father.[17] But the archbishop threatened to leave Alcalá if Isabella appeared. 'He sent to disabuse her of the idea and to say that he would not see her,' Zurita recorded. 'And that his aim was for them to leave him alone in his retirement.'[18] Instead Isabella, who was pregnant, spurred her horse on to the city of Toledo, the largest in New Castile, whose support she wanted to guarantee in a region dominated by two hostile lords – López Pacheco and the archbishop. 'She was well received,' noted Pulgar.[19] 'She was there several days organising the things needed for the defence of that city, of the cities in Andalusia and Extremadura and all that region.'

With Toledo firmly in the hands of her followers, she set out back towards Valladolid on 28 May and rode so hard that, three days later, she lost her baby and had to stop in Avila to recover. By now she had signed a new document that gave her husband sweeping powers. The deal so carefully worked out at Cervera and then reiterated in Segovia had been brushed aside by circumstance. 'You must know', she wrote in an open letter,

> that for the good governance, custody and defence of these kingdoms and lands of mine, it may be best for the king my lord and myself to separate with each one going in their own direction to different parts of these kingdoms. So I am giving the said king, my lord, power so that wherever he goes in those kingdoms and lands, he can, on his own and without me being there, order, do, instruct and provide whatever he considers best to be of service to himself and to me and to the custody and defence of those kingdoms and lands.

He was now allowed to administer towns, cities and forts, hand out grants and *mercedes* – mostly gifts of income from royal taxes – and appoint officials. 'With the present [letter] I assign to him all powers, however great or small, that I have and which belong to me as heiress and legitimate successor – which I am – to these kingdoms and lands.'[20] With the Portuguese army massing on the border,[21] few were inclined to protest. A unique dual monarchy was being installed, which rested not just on trust and intimacy but also on mutual respect for their abilities.

Isabella's husband could occasionally suffer – or, at least, look as though he was suffering – from that staple of both courtly and real romance, the pangs of unrequited love. After Isabella had left, he reprimanded her for not writing to him frequently enough: 'So many messengers have come without letters, and it cannot be for lack of paper or for not knowing how to write, but out of lack of love and haughtiness. You are in Toledo and we are travelling here through villages, though one day we will return to our first love. But if your ladyship does not wish to be responsible for homicide, you must write and let me know how you are.'[22]

Portugal's King Afonso crossed and recrossed the border with his army in a leisurely fashion, reaching Plasencia by 29 May when he was personally present at a second espousal ceremony with Juana la Beltraneja. Palencia claimed that his arrival angered many of the townsfolk, who blamed Leonor Pimentel – the bold and self-assured wife of the city's master, Álvaro de Stúñiga – for being placed on La Beltraneja's side of the civil war. He also claimed that hatred of La Beltraneja's mother – the dowager Queen Juana, who was also King Afonso's sister – ran rife. If women were 'the perdition of Spain', he sighed, now 'her daughter was the spark that lit a vast blaze'.[23]

There was no attempt to complete or consummate the marriage between uncle and niece but both now used the titles that were proclaimed to the world on a stage raised in Plasencia. They were the king and queen of Castile, León and Portugal. The country's cities, towns and fortresses soon received a second set of letters, this time signed by Juana. They reminded the recipients that Enrique had declared her to be his true daughter. 'During his lifetime he always wrote and swore, both in public and in private to all those prelates and grandees who asked about it and to many other trust-worthy people that he knew me to be his true daughter,' she wrote. In both canon and civil law, she said, there could be no doubt. That much was true. More dubiously, she also claimed that Enrique had repeated this to his confessor, the Jeronymite prior Juan de Mazuelo, on his death-bed, naming her as heiress. Her accusations that Isabella and Ferdinand had poisoned Enrique can be similarly ignored.[24] Cities, towns and fortresses were once more ordered to pay homage to a new queen – only this time she was called Juana. The usurper Isabella should be dealt with harshly, she insisted. 'You must all rise and join, serving, helping and ensuring that this abominable, detest-able action be punished.'

The Portuguese king now made a strategic mistake by heading straight for the heartland of Castile when an attack on the south, where unstable Seville was an important prize, would have provided a relatively simple victory. To the north, the city of Burgos – where his supporters held the castle – might have been another good objective. It was one of the main gateways of Old Castile and was on the path that the King of France, who had pledged to add his troops to those of Portugal (in what he hoped would be a two-way division of the booty to be obtained in both Castile and Aragon), would probably take. But Afonso headed for Arévalo, taking La Beltraneja with him and hoping that her presence would generate the enthusiasm of loyal – or legalistic – Castilians wherever they went. López Pacheco joined him with 500 men, but soon had to travel east back to his own lands in the southern *meseta* of New Castile to quell pro-Isabella rebellions and attacks from neighbouring Aragon. Ferdinand boasted that he could easily deal with the threat. 'Within a few days I will have brought together such a force that there will be no reason to fear the King of Portugal,' he wrote to his father from Valladolid in mid-May.[25]

In geographical terms Isabella's party now controlled most of Old Castile, in the north, with important exceptions like Toro, Arévalo and, especially, the fortress at Burgos. In a civil war where the main strategic aim was to win possession of cities, these sometimes found themselves opposed by their own fortresses or even by individual commanders in control of turrets, gateways, bridges or anywhere else sufficiently fortified to lock themselves away and use thick, high walls to their advantage. So it was that while the town of Toro and the fortress at Burgos sided with La Beltraneja, the fortress at Toro and the city of Burgos sided with Isabella. Support also stretched north from there, via the Basques, to the French border and the sea, while the north-western region of Galicia mostly stood aside as local nobles fought their own petty battles. Andalusia was also in a volatile state of disarray as nobles there squabbled among themselves. The lands bordering the northern half of Portugal were now mostly backing La Beltraneja. New Castile, dominated by López Pacheco and the archbishop of Toledo, was a distinct problem for Isabella, with the city of Toledo her most important possession. But

the Portuguese king chose to stay in Old Castile, moving his army
north to the relatively safe haven of Toro as Isabella and Ferdinand
gathered armies on either side of him.[26]

Three days before Ferdinand set off towards Toro to do battle
against King Afonso, he wrote a will. It displayed absolute trust
in Isabella, asking her to care for his bastard children Alfonso (his
favourite and a future archbishop of Zaragoza) and Juana and their
mothers. 'I trust that your royal highness will look after them as well
as, or better than, I myself would,' he said. The will also contained
a sincere declaration of love from Isabella's twenty-three-year-old
husband, who asked to be buried beside her. 'This is so that, just as
we have had a singular love and marriage in this world, so we will
not be separated in death,' he said.[27]

An extraordinary section of the will reveals just how far he and
Isabella had already travelled in their ambition for a united Spain.
Ferdinand wrote that his daughter, the four-year-old Isabella, should
be his heiress, despite Aragonese laws that blocked women from ruling.

> I appoint my dear and beloved daughter Princess Isabella as my
> universal heir in all my goods and lands. In particular, I make her
> my heir and legitimate successor in the kingdoms of Aragon and
> Sicily, regardless of any laws, charters, instructions or customs of
> those kingdoms that state that a daughter cannot succeed. I beg
> the king, my lord [and father], to cancel and annul those laws in
> this case. And as soon as I can, I myself will cancel and annul
> those laws in this case. I do not do this out of ambition . . . but
> because of the great profit that our kingdoms would gain from it
> and so that, in this union with Castile and León, one royal person
> be lord and monarch of all of them.[28]

The will was remarkable not only for its explicit request that Juan
the Great break Aragon's long traditions (unlike in Castile, and
despite occasional debate, it had long been established practice that

the heir to the Aragonese crown be male) and accept a woman as heir should his son die, but also for the scale of Isabella and Ferdinand's ambition. They now consciously sought, through their offspring, to bring together Castile and Aragon under a single crown in order to create, in effect, Spain. With that, Ferdinand set off for Toro with his army of Basques, mountain folk and excited nobles. Isabella gave them a final, morale-boosting harangue.[29] It was time to do battle.

14

Though I Am Just a Woman

Tordesillas, June–August 1475

Isabella was finding war, and the challenges it presented, stimulating. It was also hard physical work, especially in a country of rugged mountain ranges and poor roads like Castile, where coordinating her forces meant continually climbing on and off mules or horses and riding for days at a time. She had lost her baby as she travelled back towards Ferdinand from Toledo and was now resting for a month in Avila. Even from her sickbed, however, Isabella could not stop herself from taking an active part in events. She had written again to loyal nobles around the country, ordering them to make war on La Beltraneja's supporters. 'You can freely wound or kill them without suffering punishment of any kind, and capture and imprison people on your own authority,' she said.[1] The war was to include, if necessary, the razing of buildings, burning of crops, destruction of food and wine stores and chopping down of olive or fruit trees. All this, she told them, was permitted because it was a 'just war'.

Her reaction surprised some, who thought she would leave warfare to her husband. It was during these troubled early days of her reign that commentators began to attribute to her certain manly qualities. This was the only way they could find to explain such a dynamic, warlike and assertive spirit in a woman. 'When the queen saw how, in such a short space of her reign, they no longer allowed her to impart justice in the way that she so liked and as she realised that wickedness was spreading more avidly than ever, she took upon her own soul, more like a vigorous man than a woman, the weight of correcting matters,' wrote an anonymous chronicler who seems to have been present as she gathered her armies.[2] It was a sign that Isabella had stepped outside the limits of traditional womanly behaviour, provoking both perplexity and admiration. Castilians were waking up to her forceful personality and firm hand – obliging them to rethink exactly what a woman or, at least, a queen might be capable of. For the moment it was easiest to think, quite simply, that she was behaving like a man.

Isabella moved north from Avila towards Tordesillas with the large army she had gathered there and from neighbouring Segovia. Isabella's own *batalla*, or regiment, of 1,500 men, led by senior members of her household, carried her flag with her personal symbol that many would have seen for the first time, the sheaf of arrows. It was now July 1475 and only a month after the loss of her baby, but Isabella was vigorously, excitedly involved in war preparations. Along the way, she met up with the Duke of Alba and his private army. She was delighted to see he had primitive *lombarda* cannon for attacking walled fortresses along with some 8,000 foot-soldiers and 1,200 cavalry. These she took to Tordesillas, along with troops raised by other nobles. The reunion between the two spouses was spectacular, because of the number of troops each brought with them. Some 28,000 men met at Tordesillas on 12 July, forming a classic feudal host that was a hotch-potch of forces. They ranged from *peones*, inexperienced footsoldiers on day wages who made up the bulk of the forces, to well-armed cavalry *lanças*, elaborately armoured mounted nobles and *hombres de armas*, or men-at-arms. The greatest Grandees and churchmen brought personal armies of more than 1,000 horsemen apiece, plus accompanying footsoldiers. Isabella's chief counsellor, Cardinal Mendoza, led a force of 500 lancers of his own. Dressed in their finest cloaks and jewels, the Grandees competed to outdo each other in both firepower and fashion. Alfonso de Fonseca, *señor* of Coca, was deemed to have outdressed the rest with an Italian cape dripping with pearls and precious stones, while his horse was caparisoned to match. The city militias arrived, as did the bold Basques and the rustic men from the towering mountain ranges that loomed above the Cantabrian coastline, often in family groups. Some of those present had, quite recently, been at war with one another and there was a lingering mistrust of the nobles among the militias. The latter saw them – not without reason – as a group of unreliable schemers. The army had to wait another ten days while last-minute negotiations were carried out to ensure the presence of several Grandees, including Beltrán de la Cueva – none other than the alleged father of Isabella's rival, La Beltraneja. There were now some thirty-five different *batallas*, and 'so many tents and provisions that it seemed like the whole world was there'. Isabella herself wanted to move with the army to Toro, but eventually it was decided that Ferdinand would lead this mass of troops west towards the Portuguese king's army while she stayed with the reserves twenty-one miles away in Tordesillas. It was one of those occasions in which Isabella bent to the opinion that this was not really women's work.[3]

News reached them on 16 July that Zamora, only twenty miles further west along the broad River Duero from Toro, had also declared for La Beltraneja and her Portuguese fiancé. Isabella and Ferdinand were struck by the enormity of Zamora's decision to back their enemy since this now gave King Afonso's army a clear path to and from the Portuguese border, making him extremely difficult to dislodge. Their large army moved sluggishly and ran into resistance the very same day it left Tordesillas, with a small river fort on an island in the River Duero refusing to surrender. Ferdinand's men attacked, with the young king himself at the forefront and the hardy Basques doing much of the close-up fighting. A hail of missiles and arrows rained on the fort from the Duke of Alba's siege machines and twice the defenders raised a flag asking to talk, but Ferdinand refused and they were eventually dragged from its walls. Those not immediately lanced to death by a furious group of Basques seeking revenge for relatives killed in combat were hung from the walls. 'Nobody who was there had ever seen so many people hung together,' said the anonymous chronicler. 'That night they were stripped by some of the poorer men and they were left [hanging] there for many days which, given the heat, was an appalling thing to witness and, with them naked, it seemed like hell itself.'[4]

It was a small and particularly vicious triumph, but Isabella was overjoyed. Military victories, it soon became obvious, thrilled her tremendously. They were not only a source of glorious revenge, but also proof that God was on her side. The arrival of the Count of Benavente with 800 well-armed cavalry lifted Isabella's spirits further and she immediately sent them on to Ferdinand. Benavente's own horse, its armour covered with long black-and-white spikes, was a spectacle that one onlooker compared to a giant porcupine.[5] 'No one dared approach that horse in battle, as, even on its own, it could do so much damage,' said the anonymous chronicler.

Ferdinand had set off full of confidence, ready to storm Toro or lure the Portuguese into an open battle. The fall of Zamora, however, made him change his mind. It was too close to Toro and meant that the Portuguese and La Beltraneja's other supporters could easily harry his men. Instead, Ferdinand issued a personal demand for man-to-man combat with King Afonso. Neither man seems to have taken the idea seriously, but honour codes obliged them to pretend by negotiating conditions. Afonso demanded that Isabella be handed over to him in exchange for Juana la Beltraneja while the duel was being fought. Ferdinand refused and the whole affair ended in farce when a Portuguese royal herald was attacked by the uncontrollable Friar Alonso de Burgos who, enraged by the sight of him carrying the royal symbols of Castile and forgetting the norms of chivalry and diplomatic immunity, knocked him off his mule. It was such an affront that Ferdinand had to load the poor messenger with personal gifts to recompense him. To the fury of the Basques and the men from the northern mountains, Ferdinand eventually decided to turn back. The angry northerners, fuelled by strong wine, stormed into his camp, claiming that the king must be being held captive by cowardly or treasonous nobles. Ferdinand had to calm the mutiny personally before giving the order for this vast army – which had required Isabella to raid the treasure kept at Segovia's *alcázar* and hand over their daughter Isabella to Cabrera and his wife Beatriz de Bobadilla as surety[6] – to turn back to Tordesillas.

The troops returned in a thunderous mood, but no one was as angry as Isabella. She left Tordesillas at the head of a small cavalry force of her own as soon as she saw the first soldiers returning. The livid queen rode frantically backwards and forwards to stop what she thought must be a routed army in retreat. 'She ordered that the first horses to appear be turned back at lance-point, saying words that seemed more to come from an energetic man than a frightened woman,' the anonymous chronicler said. When Ferdinand and the nobles appeared, she delivered a furious, public dressing down. 'All that night the queen spoke to the Grandees in words charged with great rage and irritation, complaining about them and their inadequate assistance and bad advice, as one does when impassioned, and likewise, with great daring, she spoke frankly to the king about it all,' said the chronicler. Isabella was so enraged that the council meeting at which they had planned to debate the matter that night had to be postponed. She was still boiling when they met the following day. The chronicler who passed on – or, possibly, invented – her speech as it was recalled by those present had her spit sarcasm at the assembled men. 'Even if women lack the discretion for knowledge, the energy for daring and sometimes the language for speaking, I have found that we do have eyes to see with,' she said. 'And what is certain is that I saw such a huge force leave Tordesillas that I myself, as a woman, would have dared take on any challenge in the world with it.'[7]

'What sort of danger could they possibly meet that would take away the sense of daring and commitment that usually grows in the hearts of men?' she asked.

Because if there were danger, it would be better to take it, like medicine, and for it to be over in an hour rather than have to suffer a prolonged illness . . . And if you tell me that women, as they don't put themselves in danger, shouldn't talk about this because the people who always talk most bravely are those who don't place themselves in battle, I will answer that I don't see who else could be risking more, given that I offer the king my lord, whom I love more than myself or anything else in the world, and I offer so many fine gentlemen and people and so much wealth that, if lost, would also be lost to this kingdom.[8]

'Although I am just a weak woman, I would find out whether fortune was on my side, or not, before fleeing the enemy without putting it to the test,' she added. 'From now on we should lose ourselves to fury rather than allow moderation to triumph, because war needs the counsel of the brave rather than that of *letrados* [university-trained lawyers]; things are only achieved by action.' And with that she apologised, as a woman, for daring to be so frank, but declared that she felt much better for saying it.[9]

The nobles were left speechless, not daring to answer their sovereign. Only the king himself replied, claiming they had been right to retreat but had probably not explained their reasons well enough. Afonso had many well-armed men, he said, and the Portuguese were good fighters. He also had the town walls, turrets and gateways of Toro. Ferdinand insisted that he would have defeated him in open warfare, but that trying to dislodge him from such a well-defended town which could be reinforced from Zamora was pointless. Wisdom, in this case, was better than valour. 'We mustn't fall into traps, but rather be lords of the open country,' he said.

In wars where there is not [good] counsel, the fury that takes hold of one's head later falls at one's feet; time and effort are what win victory. Madness, in my world, must be lashed down . . . If things are looked upon lightly, then the falls are heavy – as we have all seen and read – and if we did not test our luck [this time], well we hope it will be on our side in more equal contests, because it is obvious that in this instance, even if we had had faith in victory, we know it was impossible and would not have come.[10]

Those present were left with little doubt that behind Isabella's normally calm and regal façade lay a strong, uncompromising and, when roused, passionately demanding character. Some nobles were clearly worried that they had pledged allegiance to a war-crazed queen. The chronicler, reflecting this opinion, had Ferdinand publicly rebuke his wife with barbed words. 'The person who is able to keep you content has yet to be born,' he said.[11]

15

The Turning Point

Burgos, December 1475–February 1476

Despite the freezing January weather, there were dances and children sang as Isabella rode into the city of Burgos. The young queen had ridden for six days through snowstorms and biting winds, but the journey was worth it. She was here to oversee one of the first major victories in her war against Juana la Beltraneja and her supporters. The city's fortress had given up the unequal fight after nine months under siege. Many of its defenders were wounded, others were long dead. Food was running scarce and siege machines were slowly battering down the fortress's thick walls. Isabella herself, now accompanied almost everywhere by Cardinal Mendoza, oversaw the final negotiations that brought the surrender of those inside. The glory of victory was hers alone to savour, as Ferdinand was busy elsewhere. By 2 February 1476, she was able to walk through the half-destroyed interior of the fortress, the loyal people of Burgos following along behind her.[1]

By taking possession of the fortress Isabella had secured one of the principal cities of Castile and done much to block the path of the king of France if he stuck to his pledge to join the battle against her. This was a wealthy, busy city that wore its reputation for experiencing 'ten months of winter, and two of hell' lightly.[2] Burgos's dark, narrow streets bustled with activity and its well-travelled wool traders were among the most worldly people in Castile. No monarch could hope to control the kingdom without the city's help.

It had become a slow-moving, diffuse war, with the two major armies occasionally manoeuvring, but mostly not engaging. Cities, towns and fortresses held out for one or other side – and both success and failure were measured by the capture, or loss, of these strategic outposts. The young monarchs had set new objectives after the troops that turned back from Toro marched off angrily and chaotically for home. The Burgos fortress was a priority and Ferdinand's illegitimate half-brother Alfonso of Aragon – already famous for his capture of the Catalan castle of Ampurdán – appeared with skilled siege engineers at the end of November 1475. His know-how, tactics and hardware brought a quick victory. Tunnelling under the castle to cut its water supply was the most effective measure. The defenders gave up ten days later, requesting the customary two-month period of grace to either be rescued or surrender. Her brother-in-law's presence was part of Isabella's reward for her alliance with Aragon, whose experienced soldiers were also harrying López Pacheco's properties in New Castile.[3] If ever there was a moment to reflect on the rightness of her choice of husband, and ally, this was it.

Isabella played an important part in the military manoeuvres that won her the Burgos fortress by preventing the Portuguese army from coming to its rescue. 'Since she knew that the King of Portugal was awaiting more people in Peñafiel in order to carry out the rescue [of the Burgos fortress], she ordered that the footsoldiers and cavalry with her be distributed across various spots near Peñafiel and that they should harry the King of Portugal on all sides, cutting his supplies,' Pulgar reported. Isabella's troops kept the Portuguese king busy and he eventually turned back to Zamora, leaving those in the fortress at Burgos with no hope of succour.[4]

Isabella continued to shadow the Portuguese king, now moving herself to Valladolid to be closer to the latter's base at Zamora. 'In this war they were always careful that either the king, the queen or, on their orders, their captains were as close to the King of Portugal as was possible,' said Pulgar. The methods used for winning over fortresses and towns were not always orthodox. The contest at Valencia de Don Juan, for example, was won when the Isabella-supporting Juan de Robles hurled his Juana-supporting brother-in-law, the Duke of Valencia, off the walls of his own castle.[5] This unchivalrous act of murder went without punishment, prompting observers to assume that the perpetrator must have sought the permission of the young monarchs first. Both Isabella and King Afonso used dirty tricks, secretly trying to create or buy up turncoats. When Isabella heard that the *alcaide*, or captain, of the fortress in the city of León had been in negotiations with La Beltraneja's supporters, she rode swiftly off to the city herself. In a face-to-face confrontation outside the fortress walls, she forbade the *alcaide* from going back inside until control had been handed over to a replacement she had brought with her. 'You must not move from my side until I have control of the fortress,' she instructed him.[6]

She also oversaw potentially crucial negotiations with her own secret supporters in the pro-Juana cities of Zamora and Toro. These finally bore fruit at Zamora in December. Isabella's supporters were prepared to open the city gates secretly so that it could be stormed. She immediately sent for Ferdinand and set about raising an extra 2,000 *lanzas* to add to the army of more than 4,000 cavalry that was already prepared. She told Ferdinand to fake illness and then steal out of Burgos without anyone knowing. He was able to leave his brother in charge and ride secretly away, meeting Isabella in Valladolid. Two clandestine Isabella supporters who were senior officers in Zamora, Francisco de Valdés and Pedro de Mazariegos, were prepared to let him cross a fortified bridge which was under their command and led straight into the city. It was a golden opportunity to capture La Beltraneja, but someone tipped the Portuguese king off and he sent his men to storm the bridge. When that failed, Archbishop Carrillo – one of Portugal's principal Castilian allies – warned that they were in imminent danger. 'I know the king and queen of Sicily,' he said, refusing to refer to Isabella as queen of Castile. 'Either one of them will arrive here soon, or they will send such a force that they will push back the people you have ready to fight . . . And it is not advisable to fight in the streets of Zamora, where all of the neighbours are our enemies.'[7] The Portuguese king realised that there was no time to waste and ordered his troops to evacuate the city and head for Toro before the Isabelline army arrived. By the time Ferdinand reached the city, Zamora was already theirs, though the pro-Juana fortress garrison locked its gates and vowed to hold on until it was reconquered once more. The fact that the people of Zamora supported Isabella was a further sign of the natural confluence of interests between the queen and city-folk. The latter wanted to shake off the yoke of the bullying nobles, while Isabella wanted to augment royal control in every way she could. In Burgos, this confluence of interests had been even more apparent. Before agreeing to the surrender, Isabella signed a document promising the city that the fortress would remain under royal command and would not be returned to the Stúñiga family that had held it for four generations and which had long been at the forefront of rebellions against established royal authority.[8]

These were two important victories, but they did not tilt the balance of the war definitively. In fact, the scales began to move in the opposite direction as two large new armies prepared to invade Castile from abroad in the spring of 1476. In France, Louis had been busy with the English over the previous summer, but he had won that war and was now ready to take on Castile.[9] In Portugal, meanwhile, the king's son João was preparing a new army to come to his father's aid. Together they presented a considerable threat to Isabella's still weak grasp on Castile's crown.

Isabella busied herself once more raising troops while Ferdinand prepared to do battle with the Portuguese reinforcements. 'It is well known that the prince of Portugal is gathering troops to enter these kingdoms and that is why the king, my lord, wants to wait for him rather than leave Zamora,'[10] she wrote to her father-in-law from

Valladolid on 30 December 1475. 'From this town I myself am gathering as many people as I can so that I can send them to the king if necessary and so that I can supply whatever else is needed.' Isabella and Ferdinand were establishing a military relationship that, once more, was based on intelligent division of labour and would last them through more than one war. Ferdinand led the army while Isabella raised troops, looked after the reserves and acted as the army's quartermaster general, keeping it armed and fed. Wider strategy on how to pursue the war was agreed jointly and, when necessary, Isabella would also manoeuvre with a small army of her own.

A second opportunity to catch La Beltraneja and her Portuguese fiancé almost came at Toro, thanks to a deal similar to that struck with Isabella's secret supporters in Zamora. Spies in Ferdinand's army informed the Portuguese about the plot however, and when the time came the town's gates were not opened. The Isabelline conspirators were, instead, caught, tortured and hanged. Ferdinand was then unable to prevent Prince João crossing the frontier and making it to Toro on 8 February 1476. The Portuguese army was now big enough to risk open battle and Isabella, who had moved near by to Tordesillas, continued to raise troops as a full-frontal confrontation loomed. Her father-in-law Juan the Great counselled prudence, urging them to avoid direct battle and concentrate, instead, on winning over the Grandees who were on Juana's side. Perhaps he was thinking of Pedro de Stúñiga, who tried to persuade Isabella that his father, the Count of Plasencia, was too old to make decisions and had chosen to follow La Beltraneja on the instructions of his stepmother, Leonor Pimentel. Pedro had stayed loyal to Isabella in what appeared to be a family strategy to play on both sides. If Isabella could forgive her father, Pedro now told her, he would switch sides with the rest of the family. Isabella found it notoriously difficult to forgive people, Pulgar observed, and in this case she was dealing with the man whose family had taken possession of her mother's lands in Arévalo. Sense, however, prevailed. Isabella acquiesced and the Stúñigas gave up the title of counts of Arévalo.[11] It was the first major transfer of loyalty towards her among the enemy Grandees, and the whole family, including Leonor Pimentel, became important allies.[12]

By this stage, King Afonso had told Isabella that he could be bought off, though the price would be high. He wanted Toro, Zamora and the ancient kingdom of Galicia, the Castilian lands that stretched from Portugal's northern boundary to the Cantabrian Sea. Others would have seen this as a tempting offer. If a French army invaded while they were still fighting the Portuguese, Isabella and Ferdinand's forces could well be overwhelmed. But neither had come this far only to start giving away lands that had belonged to Castile for centuries. 'The queen, on hearing the Portuguese king's demands, replied that . . . she would rather put it all in the hands of God so that he decided what should be done with them than, during her lifetime, permit a single battlement to be taken,' wrote Pulgar.[13]

The Portuguese king and his son now set off with their army from Toro towards nearby Zamora. Their aim was to besiege the city and relieve the fortress, which was still in the hands of their supporters. But when Isabella sent part of her army to menace his supply lines, the Portuguese king decided he was too exposed and set out back towards Toro. After a late start, Ferdinand began to chase them. He eventually caught up with the enemy an hour's march from Toro at a place known as Peleagonzalo. The Castilian troops harassed the rearguard, forcing the Portuguese army to turn and take a stand. Ferdinand's exhausted troops had ridden hard, leaving many of his footsoldiers behind. There was debate about whether they were really prepared for a set-piece battle, but eventually the order to attack was given. Among the reasons Ferdinand later gave for attacking was: 'Faith in the justice that I and my very dear and very beloved wife the Queen have in these kingdoms'. It was already late in the day and, though Ferdinand's forces captured the Portuguese king's royal pennant and drove the centre and one wing of his army back to Toro, the other wing – commanded by Prince João – stood firm and beat off its enemies. Ferdinand's men chased those who fled, including the archbishop of Toledo's men, back to the bridge into Toro where there was close fighting. 'The figure of the archbishop, so large in the previous battles that he took part in, was now reduced to very little,' commented his former friend Palencia.[14] The latter claimed, on no discernible grounds, that the Portuguese had lost 500 men to just five on Ferdinand's side. But the lengthening shadows, impending rainstorm, lack of footsoldiers and his troops' undisciplined desire to stop and loot anything the Portuguese left behind meant this could never be a full rout. Keeping control of his troops became increasingly difficult and Ferdinand, at one stage, found himself riding with just three men. At night-time both sides withdrew, and both would later claim victory, though this belonged, narrowly, to the Castilians. The Portuguese king was said to have hidden himself at the fortress in Castronuño, not far from Toro, with his panicked men unsure of his whereabouts until the morning. 'We were in the field, and in control of it, for three or four hours, and then I returned back here to Zamora victorious, arriving at one o'clock in the morning,' Ferdinand claimed when he wrote to his father.[15]

Isabella waited nervously in Tordesillas, on the far side of Toro. It was a rainy and – for the queen – very long night. The next morning a messenger arrived from Ferdinand, announcing victory. 'I must inform you that news has arrived this hour that yesterday, on Friday the first day of this month [of March 1476] . . . the king won and the adversary and his men were scattered,' she immediately wrote in a letter to be sent urgently around her kingdoms. That night she set out, barefoot, to walk to the monastery of San Pablo in the company of the town's clergy to give thanks. 'It is impossible to describe the queen's delight,' said Palencia. A few days later she joined her husband in Zamora, where the defenders of the city's fortress soon also surrendered. It was neither a great nor an absolute victory – but it proved decisive. In a world where military victories were seen as proof of God's approval, it could also be taken as a sign that Isabella's claim to the crown was not just valid but divinely sanctioned. A usurper's claim, in other words, could be made good by the blood of her opponents. Isabella made sure that her slanted version of what had happened – that the battle had been an outright defeat of her enemies – was spread quickly. She needed not just victory on the battlefield, but also to win the war of propaganda and persuade Castilians that this was proof that God had chosen her to rule over them. Celebrations were organised around her kingdoms, while a new church and monastery in Toledo would become monuments to the victory.[16]

This triumph was accompanied, almost immediately, by further fine news. The Basques had halted a French invasion, turning it into a siege of the fortress at Fuenterrabía, just across the mouth of the River Bidasoa from France. Louis XI had, crucially, waited to see whether Charles the Bold, the Duke of Burgundy, would respect a peace treaty, or attack him. That had allowed Isabella and Ferdinand to secure three important victories – at Burgos, Zamora and Peleagonzalo – which freed them up to help the Basques organise their defence of the relatively narrow Castilian frontier with France. The siege of Fuenterrabía was lifted after two months, and although King Afonso later travelled to France to try to persuade Louis XI to invade again, the latter was no longer interested. Isabella and her supporters had, in effect, seen off the threat from outside Castile. That, undoubtedly, was a relief. But this was also a civil war, and it would not be over until enemies like López Pacheco and the archbishop of Toledo recognised Isabella as queen. And after decades of weak rule chaotic Castile itself had yet to be tamed.[17]

Degrading the Grandees

Madrigal de Las Altas Torres, 6 May 1476

The origins of the argument between husband and wife were simple enough. With the Portuguese army in disarray and victory in sight, Ferdinand needed to take a break in order to help fight the French on his father's borders. Isabella was clearly unhappy about this, but if she was to be left in command of the army, then she would at least give the orders. Ferdinand had organised a ceasefire at the besieged pro-Beltraneja town of Cantalapiedra for while he was away, but an impatient Isabella now decided otherwise. One of Juan the Great's agents at the royal court was there when the plans were suddenly, and controversially, changed overnight. As he waited to see Ferdinand, the agent was surprised to hear the strident and bellicose Friar Alfonso de Burgos, one of Isabella's closest advisers, loudly informing a group of people that the queen had decided the siege must continue. 'The queen knows that by taking Cantalapiedra the king of Portugal will be destroyed,' Burgos said. 'And so the monarchs do not want any of it [the agreement] carried out, but instead that the siege continue, and the fighting go on until it is taken.' Isabella was a bigger risk-taker than Ferdinand and had found an ally in their siege-master, his half-brother Alfonso of Aragon. The latter stormed into Ferdinand's rooms, insisting he would not aban-don Cantalapiedra until it had fallen. An angry Ferdinand found a sudden need to go hawking with some of the 120 falconers that the couple employed. Isabella, meanwhile, shut herself up in her rooms, refusing to receive people. She had imposed her will, but at a price to her usually smooth relationship with her husband.[1] It was, perhaps, also a glimpse of who normally won their arguments – even when they were out of sight.

Isabella had yet to sign a peace, but it already looked very much as if she had won a war. Burgos and Zamora were hers. The French invasion had only inched its way into her lands before being stopped by the Basques, and the Portuguese had been forced into an ignominious retreat outside Toro. Ninety years earlier, Castile had been humiliated on the battlefield by Portugal at Aljubarrota. Now revenge, a God-given gift, had come her way. King Afonso V of Portugal left Castile on 13 June 1476, taking Juana la Beltraneja with him, but leaving his troops garrisoned in Toro and neighbouring forts.[2] Isabella was in a strong position to start negotiating a peace deal, but was much too ambitious for that. Already she was seeing her reign in historic, messianic terms as that of the woman who would return to Castile the greatness it deserved, making it feared and respected by others. She wanted a clear-cut, absolute victory, rather than some ambiguous peace which might leave cities like Toro or Zamora being squabbled over for decades to come. That meant evicting the Portuguese definitively and quashing the pro-Juana Grandees.

Soon after Afonso left, Isabella ordered an assault on Toro itself. Her captains had told her that there were now only 300 Portuguese troops in the city. This was a chance for her to achieve what Ferdinand had failed to do when he had turned his enormous feudal host back from Toro, to her immense fury, a year earlier. An attack was launched, but the city walls were high enough and thick enough for the Portuguese to see off the Castilians, who retired with their dead and injured after four hours of fighting.[3] Isabella had tasted defeat, but remained determined to take both Toro and Cantalapiedra at the first opportunity.

Isabella also needed to impose her authority on two, often rival, focuses of non-royal power – the cities and the nobles. Among the latter, the Grandees remained a political power with huge wealth and even greater self-regard. An Italian visitor was startled to find them 'living splendidly, in great luxury . . . they have abundant tables and ensure that they are served with such ceremony and reverence as if they were, each one of them, a king . . . In a word, they make sure they are adored.'[4] Yet the Grandees and other nobles were self-interested and fickle, making them faster to jump ship and easier to manipulate than the cities. The Stúñigas had been among the first of La Beltraneja's supporters to swap sides. But her rival's two main backers were López Pacheco and the archbishop of Toledo. If Isabella could either win them over or defeat them, Castile would be hers. The Pacheco clan was one of the most powerful families in the land and Isabella decided to divide and rule, offering pardons to some in order to weaken López Pacheco himself. The first to come over was his cousin Juan Téllez Girón, Count of Urueña, who had sworn loyalty to Isabella by May 1476. Girón's brother Rodrigo, head of the Calatrava military order (one of the big three military orders, along with Santiago and Alcántara), followed later that month.[5]

She was not so generous with López Pacheco himself or with the archbishop, whom she clearly saw as in need of serious, public reprimand. They at first thought they could negotiate, ensuring they kept much of their power while transferring allegiance to her. That was the way things had been done under Enrique IV, when their families had swapped sides continuously – often receiving rewards in the form of more lands for doing so. But Isabella would have none of that. When they refused a straight surrender, she ordered an all-out attack on them and their possessions. Whereas her husband had concentrated on persuading López Pacheco's men to turn against their leader, presumably using the usual mixture of bribery and threats, Isabella preferred the blunter instrument of war. 'You may make war and do as much trouble and damage to the said Marquess of Villena [López Pacheco] and the others . . . whom you can freely kill or wound, without punishment, and arrest people on your own authority and throw them in jail,' she informed her followers in Murcia. 'I will not receive them [into my service] until they give up all that they have taken and occupied from the crown in this kingdom of mine.' Her husband could use subtlety; Isabella wanted them crushed.[6]

López Pacheco soon realised that he was on the losing side and formally recognised Isabella as queen. 'He promised to serve them in public and private from then on with complete faithfulness and loyalty, be it against the Portuguese king, his niece [La Beltraneja], the French, their allies or anyone else,' recorded Zurita. He also pledged to raise the pennants of Isabella and Ferdinand in all his towns and castles and swear to their daughter, the *infanta* Isabella, as legitimate heiress. Isabella pardoned him, but also punished. He was to lose control or possession of many of his properties (especially those which had already been taken from him by force). The Pacheco clan was still one of the great families of Castile, but the damage to its power and prestige was enormous.[7] It was no longer a threat to the monarchy. With this exemplary punishment, Isabella struck a death-blow to the *privado* system that had worked so well for Álvaro de Luna and for López Pacheco's father, Juan. Future power would be both more diffuse, exercised by a larger body of lesser officials, and more concentrated in the hands of the monarchs they served.

The man who had expected to be Isabella's *privado*, the surly Archbishop Carrillo, also eventually gave up. He did so less magnanimously and, true to character, grumbling about his lot and the respect he was due. Juan the Great tried to intercede on behalf of his old friend, but Ferdinand warned him off, saying that Isabella would not brook interference. She had been infuriated by the archbishop's constant duplicity and obstinacy. The sixty-six-year-old churchman was as curmudgeonly as ever, but in September 1476 he finally recognised Isabella's authority. He was pardoned, but he also agreed to allow the monarchs to review which properties and other gifts given to his family by Enrique IV must be handed back to the crown. The archbishop went on to sign a crucial document in which he recognised that Enrique IV had died 'without leaving legitimate sons or daughters', thereby confirming that La Beltraneja had lost her last major supporter in Castile. Isabella shunned the archbishop completely, stinging his pride further and provoking complaints that she was not respecting her part of the bargain.[8]

In mid-September, a shepherd who lived in Toro informed one of Isabella's captains that he regularly took his sheep in and out through the high, rough terrain that protected one side of it and never encountered a Portuguese sentry when he did so. The Portuguese obviously thought the ground there was too difficult for an assault, allowing the shepherd to lead seventy of Isabella's men secretly into the city. They opened the gates and the Portuguese soldiers fled to Cantalapiedra after first making sure that María Sarmiento, the widow of the man who had originally declared the town's support for Juana la Beltraneja, had locked herself inside its fortress with her men. A pleased Isabella was thus able to enter the town that her husband had failed to capture, while ordering the siege of the fortress to start. The capable Alfonso of Aragon was on hand to take charge of that and Isabella herself, according to Palencia, liked to sneak through the trenches and tunnels to the fortress walls in order to see how the siege was progressing as it was bombarded with large cannon balls and peppered with fire from catapults. 'Doña Isabella . . . often went into the [waterless] moat to watch the fighting,' he said.[9] Soon a message came to her from María Sarmiento, asking to be forgiven her late husband's sins and offering to surrender this and three other fortresses in her family's power. A month after the attack, Toro was wholly in Isabella's hands.

As Isabella rushed from one side of her kingdoms to another, one journey in particular was suddenly so urgent that in early December 1476 she was prepared to ride through the slippery, snowy mountain passes into New Castile. A few weeks earlier the master of the Santiago military order, Rodrigo Manrique, had died. He had been a highly capable ally, defeating López Pacheco and the archbishop of Toledo in a battle for the fortress in the order's town of Uclés. His death left a highly important position open – one that was traditionally filled, with permission from the pope and the monarch, by a vote among the thirteen knights who formed the order's council. Whoever controlled the order – in Pacheco's hands during Enrique IV's time – controlled its vast lands and the income from them. Isabella took direct possession of the order's headquarters in the town's monastery and forced the council, where the two main candidates looked set to make war on each another, to accept her husband Ferdinand as temporary administrator. He could sort out the order's internal problems first and then, if necessary, help appoint a new master. Tellingly, López Pacheco was one of those who acquiesced. The major, non-royal *señorio* lands of New Castile – belonging to the military orders, Pacheco's family and the archbishop – were now obedient to her commands.[10]

Isabella's authority was becoming unquestionable and in order to prove that things had changed she and Ferdinand, who had joined her again, moved on to the region's biggest city, Toledo. As the former capital of Christian, Visigothic Spain, Toledo held great symbolic importance. Perched on a steep, granite hill surrounded on three sides by the looping River Tagus, the city was famous for the gold, silver and jewels hidden inside large, heavy chests in its cathedral – and for the numerous priests who clambered up and down its steep streets. It remained one of the most important cities in Castile, with a population of some 30,000 people squeezed inside its walls. 'In Spain Toledo is rich, Seville is big, Santiago [de Compostela] is strong and León beautiful,' was a ditty picked up by the German traveller Hieronymus Münzer a few years later. Toledo conserved the walls and some of the gates built by the Moors before it was taken by the Christians, in one of the most significant moments of the *Reconquista*, in 1085. The sovereigns organised a brilliant formal entry designed to provoke awe and prove that even here, in one of the most divided and troublesome cities in Isabella's kingdoms, it was they who ultimately governed all. Isabella ordered the city's authorities to dress up in their best and most colourful silks. Some had to dust off very old finery, but they were there waiting for Isabella and

Ferdinand with a broad silk canopy as the couple rode up to the city's Visagra gate. 'The noise of the trumpets and drums and people, in their joy, was such that it seemed that heaven and earth shone with heartfelt joy,' reported one witness, Bachiller Palma.[11] As trumpets pealed and drums were banged, a young woman awaited them at the door of the Santa María cathedral, Spain's senior church and resting place of many of its greatest kings. She wore a golden crown on her head to show that she represented the mother of Christ.[12] It was the last Friday of January 1477, but the clouds parted and the sun shone. Isabella's jewels, which were both adornment and a statement of power, dazzled dutifully.

Two days later Isabella returned to the imposing Gothic cathedral, deemed the most beautiful in Spain, wearing a jewel-studded gold crown and a necklace of dark rubies that, according to legend, had once belonged to King Solomon. Before them, along a nave that Münzer measured at 200 paces, were carried Ferdinand's battlefield trophies from Toro – the pendants of Portugal's King Afonso and his standard-bearer's armour. These were hung above the grave of King Juan I as a sign that Castilian honour had been restored after his historic defeat at Aljubarrota in 1385. 'And so the fall and dishonour of King Juan was avenged,' remarked Palma.[13] The message was clear and simple. Isabella was restoring Castile to rightful glory – however imaginary that past glory might be. She would right the wrongs done to her ancestors, never mind how many centuries had gone by.

The spectacle in Toledo was typical of Isabella's embrace of any and every kind of propaganda as a way of driving this message home. This turned modest victories into great feats, acts of usurpation into statements of legitimacy and humdrum government into magisterial acts of royal wisdom. A usurper to the crown, after all, needed to persuade everyone that she was no such thing. Isabella excelled especially in her use of the written word, though this did not require her to put pen to paper herself, since the royal chroniclers who acted as paid-for publicists had long been on hand for that. But she was the first Spanish monarch to have access to the printing press, which reached Castile in the same year that she claimed the crown. This technological leap offered previously unknown opportunities for social and intellectual control. It allowed her to reshape the past, spin the present and produce a narrative of her life and reign that would last long into the future.

The press was quickly put into use to broadcast the results of her first great law-making events, when she gathered together the Cortes in Madrigal in 1476 and then, four years later, in Toledo. These were important events at which she and Ferdinand stamped their authority on the kingdom and set in motion their quasi-absolutist government. The *procuradores* from the seventeen cities represented at the Cortes were too weak to resist Isabella and her husband, though the young monarchs were still keen to win their favour as a balance against the nobility. At both Madrigal and Toledo, they imposed their will, raising money, reforming their exchequer and extending the tentacles of royal power deep into Castile's cities, villages and countryside through wider use of the often brutal Hermandad police force. The queen appointed chroniclers to write up versions of these meetings that would impress her new subjects. These ignored the fact that at Madrigal, for example, royal-appointed *procuradores* were fraudulently drafted in to represent the pro-Beltraneja cities of Madrid, Córdoba and Toro. Nor did they broadcast the news that, at the Toledo meeting, Isabella's decision to reward her faithful backer Cabrera with lands belonging to Segovia had provoked public protests in that city. Instead, the chroniclers presented these meetings as moments of great national consensus, epitomised at Madrigal by the ceremonious swearing in of the monarchs' daughter Isabella as heir to the throne. The meetings, they made out, were proof that the entire kingdom was now behind Isabella and backed the new style of government.[14]

Isabella sought not just legitimacy but also fame. In the mindset of the time, it was only saints, successful kings, famous knights and the great figures of romance fiction – including Merlin and Arthur – who lived in the popular imagination for anything greater than their lifetimes. Isabella, like many monarchs, was determined to be one of them.

It was via her chroniclers that Isabella did most to project her propaganda into the future writing of history. There was nothing new about such 'royal' chroniclers, who ranged from the respectably erudite to sensationalist scoundrels who 'would rather relate what is bizarre and extraordinary than what is true . . . in their belief that their story will be regarded as inconsequential if they do not tell of things that are larger-than-life', according to the poet Fernán Péréz de Guzmán. Isabella hiked their wages by 60 per cent and encouraged creative competition to see who would produce the most useful work.[15]

Those who disappointed, like the cantankerous and self-opinionated Palencia, were eventually sidelined. Those who toed the line had jobs for life, board and lodging, access to documents, the ear of the monarch and guarantees of being published. There was only one price to pay. Their version of events had to be approved by Isabella or her officials. 'I will go to your highness in accordance with the order you have sent me, and I will bring you what is written to this point, so that you can have it examined,' the man who took over from Palencia, Hernando de Pulgar, assured her. Others read their work out aloud over the royal dinner table, while officials commented and corrected. It was not just the facts of her own reign that Isabella was keen to massage. Spanish history itself had to be shaped, or reshaped, to fit a narrative of lost glory followed by the renewal of Castile under her messianic leadership and that of her husband. Thus it was that Diego de Valera's *Short History of Spain* (*Crónica Abreviada de España*), which included a ruthless character assassination of Enrique IV, became one of the first popular Spanish histories – with eight reprints between 1482 and 1500. Valera, who had served both Isabella's father and Enrique, knew full well that his task was to be, as another of the queen's chroniclers put it, 'an earthly evangelist' who would make her 'immortal'. Of the chroniclers and historians whom she and Ferdinand hired, however, none quite equalled Giovanni Nanni, whose 'Commentaries' invented a whole line of ancient Spanish kings based on entirely fictitious texts.[16] The royal family, nevertheless, quickly adopted them as proof of the monarchs' (and Spain's) long pedigree.

Some historians believe that an entire royal department, or workshop, was set up to refine the dark arts of spin and propaganda, approving their carefully polished products before they went to press.[17] It is more likely, however, that Isabella's desire for royal control of information became a natural reflex for her authoritarian administration. Some chronicles were kept in the royal archive for decades before being heavily edited and published.

Isabella's first visit to Toledo not only achieved her aim of broadcasting this new narrative for Castile, but also brought the final pacification of the city. Officials were ordered to disband the armed guilds and rival leagues that had long been the source of bloody rivalries which periodically erupted into gang warfare, rioting and pillaging. 'All the citizens were accomplices to wrongdoings and crimes, and the people's hearts were perverted,' said Palencia. Different factions had taken it in turns to run the city or be forced into exile and fight to get back. 'In punishment for I don't know what sins, this great city receives such great trials and can expect to receive even worse,' Pulgar had written after one round of bloodletting. Isabella left behind her a message to those who thought the squabbling and fighting could continue: Juan de Córdoba, a city official in charge of a fortified bridge that passed high over the River Tagus, was hanged for disobedience.[18]

While royal authority had been weak in the heartlands of Castile under Enrique IV, it had been almost non-existent on some outer fringes of the kingdom, like distant Galicia, in the green and rainy north-west, and the borderlands with Portugal in Extremadura. Local nobles spent much of their time squabbling over land, offering only cursory acknowledgement to royal authority or siding directly with Portugal. That was anathema to Isabella. She wanted no weakness, half-measures or turning of blind eyes, showing her disgust by confiscating all property belonging to Fernando de Pareja, a key Galician noble who had backed the Portuguese king. In Extremadura, Isabella decided that the last rebels needed dealing with personally. As in Galicia, personal ambition and alliances with Portugal had overlapped, creating a dense thicket of thorny, interconnected problems. Her council warned her not to go, claiming that she would have few places to hide if things went wrong. 'They said that neither the king nor the queen should go to those parts of Extremadura until the lands were pacified,' Pulgar reported. Isabella's reply was typically decisive and belligerent. 'To continually hear how the Portuguese, as our adversaries, and [some] Castilians, as [local] tyrants, wage war in those parts and to suffer this in silence would not be the behaviour of a good monarch, because monarchs who wish to govern must also work . . . It seems to me that the king my Lord should go to those *comarcas* on the other side of the mountain passes [that is, to Cantalapiedra and the last few small fortresses holding out near Toro] and I should go to Extremadura, so that we can deal with both of these things.' So Isabella set out anyway, taking draconian decisions where necessary. Where she decided that local nobles were untrustworthy, she simply ordered that their forts or hill-towers be pulled down. In the cities, she found the best strategy was to ally with the major families. In Cáceres she famously settled a dispute between two families who claimed control of the city by lottery, giving the winners life-long tenure.[19]

The most important challenge left was now Andalusia, one of the youngest regions of the kingdom, reconquered from the Moors in a process that began early in the thirteenth century and home to almost a fifth of Castile's population. It was a frontier region, with its south-eastern border stretching along the limits of the Moorish kingdom of Granada. It was also fertile and wealthy. Not only was Seville Christian Spain's biggest city, but both Córdoba and Jaen were among the largest in the land. Two nobles, the Duke of Medina Sidonia and the Marquess of Cadiz, continued to dispute power in and around Seville. The former had nominally backed Isabella's claim to the crown, but they were more interested in their own rivalry and played little part in the civil war. Once again, some counsellors thought Andalusia was far too big a task for Isabella to tackle on her own. 'Some criticised the queen for going there before don Ferdinand, and predicted that a woman would not have sufficient resolve to deal with such grave matters, despite her abilities,' wrote Palencia. But they had said much the same about Extremadura and Isabella's successes had stoked her natural audacity. She set off, once more, without her husband.[20]

Rough Justice

Seville, July 1477–October 1478

The people of Seville were truly sorry. Now many of the city's senior men, those who had not yet fled, stood before Isabella and begged for clemency. The queen sat impassively above them on a raised throne covered in gold cloth in one of the great rooms of the Royal Alcázar, the impressive fortress built by the Moors before the city had been captured more than two centuries earlier. The high clergy and senior officials sat in rows below Isabella as she prepared to hear the scared *sevillanos* make their excuses. The bishop of Cadiz, Alfonso de Solís, spoke on their behalf, admitting that they had indulged in murder, violence and robbery during Enrique IV's reign, and afterwards, while the civil war dragged on during the first years of her reign. They were now glad that Isabella had arrived in July 1477 in order to impose order. The public executions of the worst offenders and the number of people who had fled before they could be caught were all proof of that. They just wished, they told her, that she would be less severe.[1]

'These gentlemen and peoples of your city come here before your royal highness to inform you that there was as much joy when you arrived in these parts, as there is now terror and horror caused by the great rigour with which your ministers are executing justice, which has converted all their pleasure into sadness, all their joy into fear and all their delight into anguish,' he said. Solís admitted that the law had sometimes been made a fool of in previous decades, but placed the blame on the constant warring in the city between the Duke of

Medina Sidonia and the Marquess of Cadiz and their followers. 'We cannot deny that, in those dissolute times, some killings, robberies, violent attacks and other excesses were committed by many people of this city and its lands, which were caused by the malice of the times and not dealt with by the king's justice: and there are so many of these that we think there must be few homes in Seville that are free of sin, either by committing or covering it up,' the bishop admitted. 'But if at that time [the city] was about to lose itself through the lack of justice, now it is lost and fallen because of the great rigour of your judges and ministers: about which these people now appeal for your royal highness's clemency and compassion, and with the tears and sobbing that you now hear they humble themselves before you . . . and ask that your royal stomach take pity on their pains, their exile, their poverty and their anguish and the trials that they suffer continuously, staying away from their homes out of fear of your justice.' The bishop added a short lecture on the unchristian nature of excessive punishment. 'Too much rigour in justice creates fear, fear creates upheaval and upheaval causes despair and sin,' he said. 'Excellent queen, taking the gentle doctrine of our Saviour and of saintly and good kings, moderate your justice and spill your mercy and tenderness on our land.'[2]

Isabella does not seem to have been overly impressed, nor did she think this was a time for 'gentle doctrine'. She had known Seville would be a tough city to tame (a German visitor called its inhabitants 'rude, cheating and avaricious . . . but clever') and had spent considerable time softening it up before her arrival. The tool she used for this was one that had only just fallen into her hands – the local militias known as the Hermandades, or brotherhoods. These policed roads and rural areas, but also raised money and men at time of war. Brotherhoods from individual cities (and their hinterlands) that backed Isabella had also sent militia units to help fight against Juana's supporters. But now she shaped them into something very different – a nationwide network of police and magistrates that could become a tool for the imposition of royal authority. Previously the Hermandades could act only in the countryside or in villages of under fifty inhabitants. Now the Holy Brotherhood, as its nation-wide network was called, could decide for itself what sorts of crimes it could tackle, almost wherever they were committed. It was also available to raise a national army, either to defend the monarch or to attack her enemies. Isabella was adapting an old Castilian institution, but the uses she wanted to put it to meant a huge expansion in her power over the lives of her subjects. This was the way she would change things, taking existing institutions and – often in the name of history and tradition – turning them into something both harder and sharper, trampling over customs and acquired rights if necessary, but appealing always to God and the greatness or purity of Castile.[3] In the Hermandades, Isabella now had a crucial weapon that could be used to impose justice or, if she ever chose, tyranny.

Membership was obligatory for all cities, and the crown had its own magistrates in each provincial brotherhood, which brought together the cities, towns and hamlets in each province. Some cities were clearly reluctant to join, seeing a threat both to their independence and, via the taxes needed to fund the brotherhoods, to their purses. Seville was one of them. In the months before Isabella's arrival, several royal officials, including Palencia, who was appointed attorney general of the nationwide Holy Brotherhood, had been sent to make sure one was established in the city. The city's strongman, the Duke of Medina Sidonia, reacted so angrily to the idea that he threatened to kill Isabella's emissaries, two of whom hid. 'He threatened Juan Rejón with the gallows, and Pedro del Algaba with cutting his throat,' reported Palencia.[4] When the city authorities finally agreed to set up their Hermandad, they were characteristically lackadaisical about it. Isabella wrote angrily, ordering them to stop dragging their feet. 'We ordered you to set up the Hermandad in your city, its lands and the towns and hamlets of its archbishopric . . . to bring an end to the robberies, break-ins, deaths and other wickedness and damage done in my kingdoms . . . and so that the roads were safe,' she wrote. 'Now I have been informed that, however you have organised the said Hermandad, it has not been done as fully as it should have been

... The failure to carry this out with diligence in the service of God, myself and in the general interest and carrying out of justice in that city amazes me ... so I order all of you to organise the Hermandad as you have been instructed, without delay or any further excuses.'[5]

The nationwide Holy Brotherhood was meant to last for two years. It eventually lasted for twenty-two. The justice it meted out was often rough. A Burgundian traveller was astonished to discover that the Hermandad preferred to execute people with lances or arrows rather than with the rope. 'In Spain it is not usual to hang people; they tie wrongdoers who deserve death to a post and put a white paper target on their heart. Then the justices order that the best archers available shoot at them until they die; and if the wrongdoer knows that a friend of his is a specially good bowman then he asks the justices for him to shoot the arrows, in order to die as quickly as possible ... And if they do not kill them this way, they lay them on the ground with their head on a block and cut it off with an axe.'[6] Other travellers were surprised to find that a tall stone column with four arms at the top stood on the outskirts of many towns – permanently ready to hang people or display those executed by some other form. On his five months of travels Münzer twice came across the macabre sight of corpses dangling from these columns. 'On leaving Almería we saw a column made of stones, with six Italian Christians hung from it by their feet, for sodomy,' he wrote. A similar punishment had been meted out, for the same crime, in Madrid. 'Two men were hanging, with their testicles tied to their necks,' he said.[7]

Isabella had first appeared outside Seville on 25 July on a boat that brought her downstream towards the twelve-sided Tower of Gold, whose façade of lime mortar mixed with straw glistened in the summer sunlight. It had been built 250 years earlier as a Moorish watchtower and was attached to the city's Alcázar fortress by its own wall. A Gothic cathedral was being erected where the city's main mosque had stood. Bits of this survived, including the slim minaret that was now known as La Giralda, and the Courtyard of Oranges, with its cypresses, palms, lemon, orange and citron trees. As the queen rode into the city, Seville's citizens watched and, according to Palencia, wondered what tricks they could play on her to prevent effective rule and prolong the anarchy in which they thrived. This may have been the moment when, observing the finery in which the Duchess of Medina Sidonia had dressed herself in an unwise attempt to outshine the queen, Isabella complained that the people of Seville did not seem to love her very much. 'They don't seem very keen to see the Queen in Seville and Andalusia, as they already have so many [queens] of their own,' she told Medina Sidonia, apparently referring to his wife. 'No, there is only one in Castile and Andalusia, which is yourself. After God comes your majesty,' the duke replied nervously.[8]

Like other visitors, Isabella must have been impressed by the city, with its wide streets, its gardens and occasional palaces belonging to the local nobility. 'The impression caused by the streets full of people and the magnificence of the Royal Alcázar . . . made her confess that she had never before imagined that the city would be so grand,' reported Palencia, who was there.[9] The Alcázar was wondrous, full of the best decorative masonry, stucco latticework and colourful ceramics from the city's five centuries under Moorish rulers. One of Isabella's predecessors, Pedro the Cruel, had been so enchanted by the palace that he had lavished money on it, enlarging the original building with the help of *mudéjar* artisans. Water was channelled through rooms, baths and patios were decorated with marble and gold, while a dense orchard of orange trees provided the scent of blossom in late spring and a refuge of cool shade in the summer months. Friezes in Gothic and Kufic script were a further reminder of the sometimes fragile coexistence of Christians and Muslims over seven centuries. A popular legend surrounding the Patio de las Doncellas, or Courtyard of the Maidens, claimed that the Moorish rulers had once demanded an annual tribute of one hundred Christian virgins.

Seville lay in a fertile plain alongside the wide, navigable River Guadalquivir, whose waters rose and fell with the tide. 'It was the biggest plain that I saw in Spain, fertile in olive oil, with unbeatable wines and all kinds of fruits,' reported Münzer, who was impressed by the way fresh water was transported around a city that, having looked down on it from the Giralda, he declared to be twice the size of Nuremberg. 'It has an aqueduct with 390 arches . . . And this water is of great use for watering its gardens, cleaning its squares and houses and for other purposes.' The olives were the size of plums, he added, and – with the vines of Jerez a short distance away – the wine was better even than the sweet, fortified white *malvasia* of Italy.[10]

According to Palencia, who had made Seville his adopted home, almost all the Grandees in Andalusia were now opposed to Isabella, seeing a threat to their traditional stranglehold on the cities. Medina Sidonia was one of those who 'now preferred, like the other nobles, a victory by the Portuguese king, before seeing the supreme [royal] authority – grown in arrogance since the battle of Zamora – determined to exact revenge on those nobles who had held public titles'.[11] The nobles wrote off Isabella's campaign against them as an ill-advised example of 'feminine resolve', while Palencia himself accused her of madness for thinking she could evict the local strongmen from their cities. Those who doubted Isabella's fortitude were in for a rude shock. Seville had been a city of loose laws and, occasionally, of direct lawlessness. The opportunities for getting away with everything from robbery to murder – sometimes in the names of the Grandees themselves – had been plentiful. 'There were so many gangs that it was not safe to go out at night,' Münzer was told. The city's gravediggers reputedly doubled up as thuggish burglars and 'would enter homes at night in masks and take away all the gold, crockery and anything else they could find. There wasn't a single safe place in the city.'[12] The list of those seeking justice in Seville was long. To clear up the back-log, Isabella ordered that all complaints be resolved in three sessions and punishment, where relevant, meted out immediately. Petitioners came to her in person at weekly Friday hearings where she sat on her throne and despatched cases as fast as she could. Death sentences were handed down and carried out. Property was taken and handed back to the rightful owners. For the first two months of her stay she imposed draconian measures, and some 4,000 people fled to Portugal or the Moorish kingdom of Granada. 'The excessive severity brought about the flight not just of murderers, paid assassins and robbers, but also of their friends and accomplices,' said Palencia.[13] It was not just Seville, however, that felt the weight of Isabella's strict justice, or the harsh discipline imposed by the Holy Brotherhood. 'She was very determined that justice should be carried out, so much so that she was accused of applying more rigour than clemency; and that was something that she did to rectify the great corruption and criminality that she found in the kingdom when she came to the throne,' explained her chief apologist, Fernando del Pulgar.[14]

Far from loving their queen, the people of Seville grumbled. Gangs of city youths fought with the youngsters of the court, whom they called *ganseros*, or goose-herds, because of the flocks they had charge of. These hit back by labelling the local youths *jaboneros*, or soap-boys, because of their excessive and supposedly effeminate use of soap. This was a tradition handed to them by the Moors and which was kept going by the people of Triana, where a factory with huge vats of boiling olive oil, lye, lime and ashes produced the hard, white Castell soap that was exported to England, Flanders and elsewhere.[15] Medina Sidonia became a focus for the discontents, but by 10 September – with Ferdinand and his troops on their way – he had agreed to hand over control of the Alcázar and the city's other strategically important points to Isabella.[16]

Isabella eventually declared a general pardon for all but the most serious crimes, including treason, murder, *lèse-majesté* and rape, shortly before Ferdinand arrived on 13 September 1477. Fewer people than expected turned out to see his arrival – which the acerbic Palencia ascribed to the fact that this coincided with the city's siesta. Palencia himself had frantically lobbied Ferdinand to travel to Seville and correct what he saw as Isabella's errors. 'All Andalusians had placed their hope on his arrival ever since . . . they had found out just how little use to them a woman's government was,' he wrote.[17] But when Ferdinand finally arrived, he was soon persuaded that his wife had been right. Those *sevillanos* who thought there would be a softening of royal justice were furious, now complaining that he was dominated by his wife. Even Palencia began moaning that what little good was being done was due to Isabella, not Ferdinand. In one incident between soap-boys and goose-herds, stones were thrown and insults shouted against Ferdinand. Rumours then spread that the Duke of Medina Sidonia had been involved and had been locked up. As angry *sevillanos* prepared to riot, several hundred mounted royal cavalry chargers were brought out to guard the palace door. But Isabella's ferocious rule in Seville soon produced a second major victory that brought wild Andalusia further under the royal yoke. The Duke of Medina Sidonia's rival – the Marquess of Cadiz – slipped secretly into Seville in August, begged forgiveness for having opposed his monarchs and gave them control of Jerez and other strategically important fortified outposts.

Isabella celebrated by boarding a boat on the wide, murky Guadalquivir and sailing down to its mouth fifty-five miles away with the aim of fulfilling an unrealised dream. They reached the flat, scrubby wetlands and sandy Atlantic beaches at the mouth of the river 'to the great pleasure of the queen who, before she arrived, had wanted to see the ocean and, even, meant to sail out to the open sea, but was stopped by fears about seasickness and the suspicion that she might be pregnant', reported Palencia.[18] Medina Sidonia and Cadiz now vied with each other for the approval of the young monarchs, with the former handing back five more fortified places to the crown. A similar deal was struck in Córdoba, a city that was considered to be either the second or third largest (after Seville and, perhaps, Toledo) in Isabella's kingdoms, where the factions led by Álvaro de Aguilar and the Count of Cabra had long been fighting for control. Rioting had broken out in the city a few years earlier, during Enrique's reign, after a *converso* woman accidentally threw water out of a window on to a passing procession bearing a statue of the Virgin Mary. A local blacksmith claimed it had been urine, provoking two days of violence, as the mob murdered, raped, stole and burned *conversos* out of their homes.[19]

Ferdinand, meanwhile, travelled to Madrid to ensure a further three-year extension of the Holy Brotherhood. A bored Isabella was 'determined to do something useful', according to Palencia, and busied herself mopping up some of the last resistance in Andalusia. This included the conquest of the rebel fortress at Utrera, on a hill-top eighteen miles from Seville. Isabella's own personal guard led the attack. Several were killed or wounded and when the garrison finally surrendered, Isabella showed little mercy. Conscripts were allowed to go free, but others were hanged or decapitated on the queen's orders and their bodies strung up along a road outside Seville 'to serve as a lesson to the multitude'. By now even Palencia had little choice but to agree that Isabella was gaining a reputation for quashing opponents on her own. 'The queen's talent for dealing with the insolence of rebels during her husband's absence was properly proven,' he said.[20]

By now court poets, when not encumbering Isabella with masculine attributes to explain her ascendancy over them, had turned instead to the forlorn language of courtly love – a rare outlet for men to express inferiority to or fear of a woman.

> Help me, I am dying
> and everybody knows
> that you are the cure
> for this, my fierce torment,

wrote one, who found himself either struck dumb or babbling incoherently before her.

> If I wish to speak, I dare not,
> if I try to stay silent, I cannot.
> Like a fearful child
> before a stern father
> I am overcome by fear of you.
> Just as clemency is begged for
> by those condemned for crime

So with great reverence
before your presence
My every sense trembles,

he said. Fear, admiration and loyalty were difficult to express, especially as they came together. 'It is worth noting', wrote another, apparently surprised, court poet, 'that fear and love can exist together.'[21] Isabella did not seem to mind. These were, after all, exactly the emotions that a successful sovereign was meant to provoke. Faced with the famous question later posed by Machiavelli, about whether it was better to be loved than feared or feared than loved, Isabella had clearly reached the conclusion that, while it was obviously better to enjoy both, being feared was the most useful of the two.

Isabella's long stay in Seville was not all about the rigours of imparting justice or forcing fractious nobles to accept their authority. Ferdinand had arrived on 13 September 1477. Popular obsession with the queen's pregnancies was such that one letter-writer to Isabella claimed, just two days after Ferdinand's arrival, that she must be pregnant already. He was not far off. Years had passed since her last pregnancy, and she had sought the advice of a Jewish doctor, Lorenzo Badoç. Ferdinand would put this new pregnancy down, in part, to his help. Now everyone was waiting to see what would happen, a full eight years after she had given birth to Isabella. 'One single hope for the future shone brightly in the hearts of Castilians, the long-desired delivery of Queen Isabella's child,' wrote Palencia, who said Isabella hoped for a son. Ferdinand, conscious that he would soon be king of Aragon, also prayed hard for a son – but he worried more about his wife. 'As the pregnancy looked as if it might run the danger of a miscarriage, the king was especially anguished, moved by his indescribable love for his wife, preferring above all outcomes that she should emerge safely from the experience.' Others might have put the birth of a male heir first. Perhaps Ferdinand was frightened by the size of Isabella's expanding womb and the dangers that pregnancy and childbirth brought to her. A rumour spread that he had ordered the beheading of a man who had joked that the Queen would 'either give birth or explode'.[22]

18

Adiós Beltraneja

Seville, 30 June 1478

Amidwife from Seville, known as 'La Herradera', delivered the child in the queen's rooms in the Alcázar, in front of a clutch of city officials. She may have had the 'thin hands and long fingers' that were deemed necessary for her profession. It was 30 June 1478, exactly nine months and seventeen days after Ferdinand's arrival. This time it was a son, named Juan. Nine days later a grand procession wound its way through the city's streets to the Santa María la Mayor cathedral. The baby boy was carried by his governess, while bishops and Grandees walked or rode alongside to the sound of trumpets, pipes and sackbuts. Crosses from the city's churches were paraded in front of them.[1] A cardinal and the papal nuncio were on hand to oversee the baptism of a boy apparently destined to become one of the most powerful kings in Europe. Joy – and relief – spread quickly across both Castile and Aragon.

The child was named after his two grandfathers, though some warned that Castile's previous King Juans had brought bad fortune. He was greeted with predictions of messianic glory, as if he was a cross between John the Baptist and the long-awaited Lion King of legend. 'The queen has paid off the debt of providing this kingdom with a male heir,' observed Pulgar, who now decided that the birth was final proof that God had chosen Isabella above both of her brothers to raise Spain back to glory. 'He chose not from the tribe of Alfonso nor, because he rejected the tabernacle of God, from Enrique. He chose instead the tribe of Elisabeth [meaning Isabella], which he loved.'² The reaction was, in part, explained by the fact that Spain now had a prince whose expected destiny, as future king of both Castile and Aragon, was to rule most of Iberia – from the Atlantic ports of western Castile to the Mediterranean coast of Catalonia and Valencia. 'This is the union of kingdoms,' wrote the enthusiastic councillors of Barcelona.³ A writer from Toledo was so delighted that he thought he knew exactly what effect the birth must have had on Isabella. 'The queen, our lady, was very pleased that she was now free from the danger inherent in childbirth and for the birth of the *señor* prince because, as the words from the New Testament say: "Women, when they give birth, are sad; but once they give birth to a son, they forget the anguish because of the pleasure it gives them, since the newborn is both man and prince." '⁴ Isabella may, or may not, have experienced the anguish, but she must have felt that this auspicious birth crowned the glory of her first few successful years as queen. Castile was, barring a few troublesome spots, under her control. Isabella was a traditionalist and had no interest in changing the rules of inheritance to favour women, or balance their rights against those of men. She ruled Castile as queen, with help from her husband, but that rule was clearly enhanced by the existence of a male heir who could avoid future bickering about women sitting on thrones. Now she must make sure that the heir had something stable, pure, wholesome and grand to inherit.

Isabella did not reappear in public for a month, when she put on a silk dress studded with pearls and rode a white horse, its saddle decorated in gold, to church while little Juan was carried by his governess, once more, on a mule. The only event to spoil the celebrations was an eclipse which blotted out the sun so thoroughly that the stars came out. 'It was the worst anyone could remember,' reported the chronicler Andrés Bernáldez. Isabella's subjects were Christians, but they were also deeply superstitious and some must have muttered about harbingers of bad luck. In Aragon, Juan the Great fretted about leaving his precious grandson in Castile. Two generations of Castilian kings had been captured and groomed by *privados* in their infancy, turning them into weak pawns. The king of Aragon did not want Isabella's officials doing the same to little Juan. The great families who now clustered around his mother, vying for positions and participating in the baptism service were proof that the danger still existed. 'As soon as possible and as cautiously as you can, move him to my kingdoms and believe me that the health of your estate and deeds depends on it,' he told Ferdinand. The increasingly ancient Aragonese king also appeared to stick to his belief that Ferdinand, not Isabella, was the true monarch of Castile – and assumed that an heir would inherit the kingdom's crown only once both parents were dead.[5] He was wrong on both counts.

Isabella was not about to hand her precious son over to anyone else. Juan, instead, was installed with his wet nurse María de Guzmán in Isabella's court. With her baby son settled safely close to her, she could turn once more to affairs of state. Castile was still, at least nominally, at war with Portugal. A few obstinate outposts of pro-Beltraneja rebellion remained – especially in Extremadura. One of the most important figures there was a bastard daughter of Juan Pacheco, the Countess of Medellín, who had inherited her father's thirst for power and, thanks to a legend about her locking up her young son in a castle tower for five years, his reputation for ruthlessness.[6]

In October 1478 Isabella moved away from Seville towards the frontier, initially with her husband, as they plotted their own attacks on Portugal. By Christmas they were in one of Isabella's favourite places, the sanctuary at Guadalupe. Hieronymus Münzer would arrive here as he rode south from Salamanca towards Seville through country that he described as 'mountainous, full of wild beasts, with sudden, steep-sided valleys, in the middle of which, as if in the centre of a circle, the monastery lies beside the little

River Guadalupejo.' Nestled against well-watered mountains and looking out over a plain, Guadalupe was surrounded by vines and olive trees which, to Münzer's surprise, were still populated by singing birds in January. Visitors had taken to leaving exotic gifts as thanks for answered prayers. A Portuguese king had brought a crocodile skin, while an enormous turtle shell and an elephant tusk had also come from Africa. With its 200 priests and monks, gardens, kitchens, hospital, smithy, sewing and cobblers work-shops, the monastery was a small town in itself. 'The queen loves this monastery, and when she is here says that she is in paradise,' noted Münzer.[7] 'She attends all the prayers in her splendid private oratory above the choir.'

Isabella was still here when she and Ferdinand finally settled the peace with France on 10 January 1479, gaining an explicit promise not to side with Portugal while leaving the future of the contested lands with Aragon (Roussillon and Cerdagne) up in the air. This was an example of Ferdinand putting Castile first, presumably to the chagrin of his aged father. It was here, too, that the archbishop of Toledo finally accepted a humiliating peace deal. The inveterate schemer had been encouraging Afonso V of Portugal to launch a fresh invasion. Several Grandees had also pledged to back the Portuguese king if he took his relationship with La Beltraneja further by finalising a marriage which, otherwise, would be easily undone. 'They would do this if I were married and completely tied to her,' Afonso admitted. But Isabella and Ferdinand struck first, occupying the archbishop's fortresses and taking away almost all his temporal powers.[8] Castile's biggest troublemaker, the last of a generation of swaggering Grandees, was now out of the way. A new Portuguese invasion, launched with the support of the Countess of Medellín — mistress of an impressive castle overlooking the River Guadiana — and a handful of other nobles in Extremadura was short lived. A single battle, on the banks of the River Albuera on 24 February, was enough to end Portuguese dreams of conquest and annexation.[9]

The new year had barely got off to a start before news that was both tragic and historic arrived from Barcelona. Juan the Great had died on 20 January 1479, at the grand old age of eighty. Ferdinand was now king of Aragon. The couple toyed with the idea of entitling themselves 'kings of Spain', but instead opted to add all their new kingdoms to the already long list, including those – like the dukedom of Athens – that reflected Aragon's once mighty Mediterranean empire. That also meant that they were respecting Aragon's traditional composition as a mosaic of kingdoms under one crown, rather than as a more unified Castilian-type state. The mighty alliance between the two great Spanish kingdoms had become a domestic reality in Isabella's nomadic home – and her new-born son was heir to it all. A new and powerful, if loose-knit, political entity known simply as 'Spain' was being born.

With his French alliance in tatters and his army defeated, the Portuguese king finally recognised that his Castilian endeavour had been a disaster. The peace, it soon became apparent, was to be negotiated by two women. Isabella's Portuguese aunt, the *infanta* Beatriz of Braganza – who was also sister-in-law to the Portuguese king – made the first approach. She and the king's son and heir, João, had lobbied hard for peace and she now urged Isabella to meet her in the frontier town of Alcántara, so that they could start talks.[10] Isabella went without Ferdinand and waited as her sickly aunt was carried slowly towards the border. Aware that she had the upper hand, Castile's emboldened queen demanded proposals in writing before they met. Isabella now had to consider what price she was prepared to pay in order to rid her – and her descendants – of the stigma of her dubious claim to the throne, of which La Beltraneja was such a painful reminder. Isabella saw her victories at war as proof that 'divine providence chose to demonstrate the justice of my cause',[11] but that was no guarantee that La Beltraneja might not reappear with a husband and an army some time in the future. Aside from peace, Isabella had a single obsessive objective. She wanted La Beltraneja erased as a rival for ever.

Isabella and her aunt talked over three days, their conversations stretching long into the night.[12] Beatriz began by demanding a pardon for La Beltraneja's Castilian supporters and an agreement that Castile would pay the expenses of war. She also proposed the engagement of little Prince Juan and La Beltraneja while demanding that Isabella publicly recognise her rival's right to be called princess.[13] A parallel engagement would see the queen's daughter Isabella betrothed to Prince Afonso, the four-year-old son of João, Portugal's crown prince. Both girls would live as semi-prisoners in a frontier castle, watched over by Beatriz, until the peace conditions were met.[14] But Isabella wanted La Beltraneja under much tighter control than that. In fact, she wanted her handed over – either to await marriage or to be sent straight into a convent as a cloistered nun, which was another form of prison. 'The queen insisted strongly that she enter a Castilian convent,' according to an official report on proceedings that carefully ignored the question of La Beltraneja's paternity by referring to her as 'the daughter of the queen [Juana]'. She might consider a marriage deal, but would rather go back to war than recognise La Beltraneja's right to any sort of Castilian title of her own – whether as *infanta* or princess. 'Giving her that title is to confess that she is the daughter of a king and a queen. And the queen [Isabella] thinks that . . . this in itself is sufficient reason to stop talking about peace,' her officials observed.

Isabella's principal aim was prevent Juana from retaining the slightest hint of legitimacy in her claim to the crown that she herself had now so successfully won by force of arms. This was what she most fretted about during the negotiations. She certainly did not want to pay the war costs, but was prepared to share them. And she might pardon the nobles who had backed Portugal but, rather sneakily, asked to be provided with a list first. The Portuguese king then kept Beatriz waiting for further instructions, until Isabella's patience snapped. 'I take these next few days as a deadline to know your decision and your will on whether you want war or peace,' she said.[15] 'I place before you all the deaths, robberies, fires, wickedness and damage that are caused by war; and if these are even worse than they have been so far, well that will be your fault, for having given up on making peace.'

The negotiations were tough, lasting six months.[16] Isabella was grateful to her aunt, whose heart was genuinely for peace,[17] and blamed King Afonso for all the delays. She stayed waiting for her aunt's replies, first in Alcántara and then in Trujillo, and ignored warnings that rebel outposts in Mérida, Medellín and elsewhere placed her in personal danger. 'I have decided to stay here until we win this war, or reach a peace,' she said, according to Pulgar.[18] Instead, she busied herself issuing daily instructions about how to besiege the same places. Isabella eventually appointed representatives to negotiate a deal with two separate but intimately connected parts – a peace treaty and an agreement on the question of what to do with La Beltraneja. She continued to oversee obsessively the negotiations about the latter's future, scribbling angrily on the margins of official documents wherever she saw La Beltraneja being treated too benevolently. The final agreement was generous to Portugal, but relentlessly hard on La Beltraneja. Both monarchies agreed to drop their claims on the other, while Castile also recognised Portugal's possessions of the Azores, Cape Verde, Madeira and its growing list of west African properties, including Portuguese Guinea, the valuable mineral trading port of Mina de Oro (today Elmina in Ghana), and undertook not to explore further south than Cape Bojador, a point on the African coast just south of the Canary Islands. The latter islands were the only significant lands in or along the Atlantic, where both nations were now competing in exploration and conquest, that the Portuguese recognised as belonging to Castile. Portugal also received financial recompense via the enormous dowry that accompanied little Isabella's engagement to Prince Afonso, which sealed the peace deal by tying the royal families together in future generations.[19]

Isabella was generous, too, to those rebels – like the Countess of Medellín – who had stuck with Portugal to the bitter end. They were pardoned. 'As your queen and natural lady, who does not recognise any superior in the temporal world, I pardon . . . all things, whatever their nature or gravity, that they committed against the king my lord and myself after the death of my brother, the king don Enrique,'[20] she pledged. Isabella was naturally given to flexing her power and to vengeance against her enemies. But she had other priorities. If this was the part of the price of lasting peace and the end of La Beltraneja as a challenger, so be it.

The final agreement, at first sight, gave the impression that Portugal had forced Castile into accepting humiliating conditions. Isabella both paid off the losing side and agreed not to drive home her advantages, instead respecting Portugal's borders and gifting it as yet undiscovered lands in Africa. In return, she insisted that La Beltraneja either accept an engagement to her infant son (which he could renege on at fourteen, if he wanted) and spend more than a decade in semi-confinement while she waited for him, or take a nun's vows and entered a cloistered Portuguese convent. The eighteen-year-old chose the lesser evil of life in a convent, though she would prove a rebellious nun who occasionally escaped – initially with the excuse of fleeing an epidemic – to the palace of the Countess of Abrantes. Isabella also ensured that her rival could not flee to a third country. 'If Juana was free to leave Portugal we would end up at war with whichever place she went to,' Isabella argued.[21] She was prepared to make a sacrifice of her own to ensure that La Beltraneja was sidelined for ever. Her own ten-year-old daughter Isabella would live in *tercería* – basically as a privileged, carefully cared-for captive and guarantee that the peace terms would be met – in the Portuguese town of Moura for more than two years. On 4 September 1479, with Ferdinand still not present, Isabella (now seven months pregnant with a daughter, to be named Juana) approved an agreement that settled the dispute with Portugal, but gave her little else except the final political annihilation of La Beltraneja.

She moved on to Toledo, where Isabella gave birth to Juana in November 1479, though she typically managed to make sure that childbirth did not interrupt business. Ferdinand had spent the previous four months in his new kingdoms in Aragon and appeared in Toledo with an elephant that had been given to him by visitors from Cyprus.[22] He and his wife were now both solidly in charge of their realms and able to celebrate, eleven years after their marriage, the achievement of jointly ruling over most of Spain. Ferdinand gave himself over to partying and received a rare reprimand from his wife. Isabella was in the last few weeks of her pregnancy and obviously thought he should devote more time to government.[23] In a world where officials could expect to labour for only six hours a day,[24] Isabella herself was already proving to be a hard-working monarch and had called a gathering of the Cortes in Toledo for just a month after Juana's birth. When not riding off to visit the far-flung corners of her lands, she held open courts on Tuesdays and Fridays, where petitioners could come directly to her and Ferdinand. Her interest in the minutiae of government, especially at her exchequer, was a sign of a controlling, somewhat obsessive nature. A tight rein was kept on spending, with her household never accounting for more than 15 per cent of income and Isabella herself[25] chastising officials when the food bill grew too large. Debts troubled her and, even on her death-bed, she would fret about what she owed.

It was at the Toledo Cortes that Isabella first set about unifying Castile's laws in a single collection of volumes, and her concern for the efficient administration of justice would also see two permanent courts set up in Valladolid and, much later, Granada. Above all, though, it was her clever choice of officials that allowed her to build a newly efficient central administration. A dozen of these officials, mostly from the new class of university-trained *letrados*, became her most important advisers and sat on the royal council – with the occasional Grandee or bishop also in attendance. Many were *conversos*. The most loyal officials often came from her days as a princess and were kept close by through the early decades of her reign. They included the round, ruddy-faced and thickly bearded Gutierre de Cárdenas – the man who had held her sword when she first made her bid for power – and the small but cheerful Chacón, who had filled her head with stories of Joan of Arc as a child. The latter would be succeeded by the equally loyal Cabrera. The two men ran a court of anywhere between 400 and 1,000 people (which was larger than her husband's). Isabella's central corps of household officials and priests doubled to 430 and she kept a book with the names of men they thought could be useful, referring to it when she and Ferdinand had to choose candidates for official posts.[26] With the only challenger to her throne safely dealt with, these men could now turn their energies to tightening her control over Castile.

It was not until late 1480, however, that her rival finally donned her nun's habit, and on 11 January 1481 the younger Isabella was transported across the border. Her mother had fretted over visiting rights during the treaty negotiations, and asked for a clause that would allow the girl to be temporarily swapped for another of her children, but had effectively given her daughter away for the next twenty-eight months in order to ensure her own security as queen and that of her son as heir.[27] Once La Beltraneja had chosen the Santa Clara order's convent in Coimbra (one of only five convents that Isabella deemed safe enough, because they were 'said to be the most cloistered ones'), the queen sent ambassadors to check that she really was there. In his rose-tinted version of events, Isabella's faithful Pulgar makes it look as though they went to reassure La Beltraneja that she could change her mind and wait to marry Juan if she preferred. But the truth of her situation was contained in a chilling phrase uttered by the ambassadors. 'You are now tied,' they said. Isabella would continue to fret over her rival's status for years to come, harrying popes to make sure she stayed in her convent and reminding each new Portuguese king about the terms of their agreement – to which would eventually be added a further stipulation, that La Beltraneja be prevented from ever marrying. Just as she had once urged her supporters to 'make war with fire and blood, taking, devastating and destroying' the towns that backed her rival, so she would go on to ensure that her annihilation of La Beltraneja was absolute.[28]

With La Beltraneja safely cloistered, Isabella was able to follow her husband into Aragon. Seven years had gone by since she made her bold bid for the crown. Now it was securely hers. The civil war had left her with little time for her husband's kingdom. But now they moved east, crossing the frontier and bearing with them little Juan. The young prince was sworn in as heir by the Aragonese court that April, replacing his elder sister. Isabella also had her first encounter with one of the Aragonese crown's greatest cities, Barcelona – with which she had carried on her own love affair, at a distance, since marrying Ferdinand. The plague had hit both the city and Catalonia hard, halving the population and allowing the city of Valencia to over-take it as the principal trading post on the Mediterranean. Barcelona's recent squabbles with Juan the Great had drained its resources further. The once great city surrounded by grand monasteries was 'almost dead compared to how it had been before', said Münzer, while the Italian diplomat and writer Andrea Navagero found its streets surprisingly empty and not a single vessel in its famous ship-yard.[29] Relations with Ferdinand had also not always been easy and the city's councillors saw Isabella as a crucial ally in their dealings with their new king. The queen did her best to mitigate what she saw as the weak point of the Aragonese crown – its constant obligation to strike deals with the Cortes of its individual kingdoms. It was a system that she naturally mistrusted because it was too resistant to royal power and, she thought, encouraged rebellion. 'Aragon isn't ours. It must be reconquered,' she would reportedly say in a fit of pique with its heel-dragging Cortes.[30] Ferdinand's kingdoms also had their own separate laws, with the German traveller Nicholas von Popplau amazed to hear that in Catalonia lords preserved the right to sleep with their vassals' wives on their wedding nights – 'which is most unChristian'.[31]

Isabella had, however, exchanged frequent letters with Barcelona's authorities and pledged to be their 'advocate and protector'. The feeling of joy was mutual as, breaking with custom, city officials met her outside the Sant Antoni gate before she processed through its underpopulated streets and squares under a scarlet *palio* or canopy. From an elaborate stage, a child representing the city's patron saint, Eulalia, begged her to help Barcelona recover from the effects of the ruinous war it had fought with Ferdinand's father. 'The queen was received in that city with the greatest glory and celebrations ever seen for a monarch in the past, with the Catalans wanting to stand out above others,' said Zurita.[32] A fountain squirting jets of wine kept many city folk happy. Three hundred burning torches lit Isabella's way as she was accompanied to a nearby monastery at the end of the lavish ceremonies. This did not mean, however, that she enjoyed the same powers in Aragon as her husband had in Castile. Ferdinand would go on to name her as his 'other me' and the 'co-regent, governor [and] administrator' of his lands, but these were powers that she rarely exercised.[33]

When they travelled back to Castile in November 1481, the Barcelona council's representative Juan Bernardo Marimón went with them. Isabella was now pregnant with twins and Marimón deemed her 'a little bit tired by the road and the pregnancy',[34] but her spirits picked up when they visited the little prince. 'I was delighted to see him, and the queen seemed even more so to be showing him to me,' he said. They spent Lent and Easter in Medina del Campo, the trading town that Isabella enjoyed so much, watching the religious processions and counting the troops who began to gather there for a campaign against the Moors of Granada. In May its huge central plaza and neighbouring streets filled up with merchants and buyers from around Iberia and other parts of Europe, trading everything from wool, cloth, silk and sewing materials to spices, shoes, weapons and books. Isabella also found herself increasingly busy dealing with a problem that had come to her attention during her stay in Seville. Castile might be safe, but it was not yet pure.

19

The Inquisition – Populism and Purity

Seville, Winter 1480

Isabella had already warned Seville's municipal authorities to prepare a sufficient supply of shackles and chains, as well as making sure there was enough space in dungeons, jails and elsewhere for the expected wave of new prisoners in the city. Now there were also guards on the gates of Seville to catch those trying to escape a previously unknown kind of terror brought by a new kind of religious tribunal that she and her husband had invented – the royal-led, or state, Inquisition. 'If you find any examples of such people who leave or want to abandon the places where they live in order to leave our kingdoms, do not protect or defend them, but rather arrest them,' she ordered. Seville had already suffered the ravages both of Isabella's overly harsh system of justice and of the plague. But this was the biggest exodus yet. Many of the merchants' houses along Genova street, as well as some near the Minjohar gate and in the San Bernardo parish or other areas where the so-called new Christians, or *conversos*, lived were empty. As many as 3,000 homes were abandoned, with one observer excitedly claiming that the city was 'almost uninhabited'.[1]

During her time in Seville Isabella had heard vivid stories about how people from the *converso* families that had converted from Judaism over the previous century were secretly and obstinately holding on to their old faith. The Dominican prior Alonso de Hojeda had been especially vociferous, repeating many of the slanders that had been poured into the ears of previous Castilian monarchs. Groups of secret Jews were holding their clandestine meetings right there in the city, under her royal nose, he insisted. They continued to light candles and dress in clean clothes on the Sabbath, refused to eat pork and prepared for death by turning in their bed to face the wall. They also secretly buried their dead in Christian soil but according to Jewish rites. 'I have been told,' wrote Isabella, 'that there are certain graveyards beside the monasteries of St Bernard, the Holy Trinity and St Augustine in which the *conversos* of the city used to bury their dead, and that they were buried with Jewish rites and ceremonies, seeking out virgin land, in Jewish clothing, with their arms laid straight and not in a cross, insulting and casting opprobrium on our ancient Catholic faith.' If that was true, as she obviously believed, then measures would have to be taken and the dead dug up. 'Proceed according to law . . . If you decide that these yards and graves should be confiscated and given to my treasury, it is my desire that the prior and friars of St Dominic of Porta-Coeli, of the Order of Preachers, should be given the yard of St Bernard, with all the stones and brick from the tombs therein,' she said.[2] The rotting corpses and bones of the dead heretics could be publicly burned.

There can be little doubt that a small number of secret Jews continued to practise their faith clandestinely. Many more had not yet shed all their family traditions or been properly taught the rules and codes of the new religion. In previous decades, however, any sensible inquiry had always concluded that cases of 'judaisers' (the catch-all term for those who observed some form of Jewish ritual or customs) were few and far between.[3] A significant number of *conversos* still remained subtly but recognisably different in their linguistic tics, culinary practices and other cultural habits. Many still lived in or near the old Jewish neighbourhoods, especially in big cities with large *converso* populations, and were sometimes talked about, even by themselves, as a distinct 'nation', 'race' or 'breed' within Spain. Some had close relatives who were still Jews. But that did not make them heretics. Some *converso* families — especially the elites — had intermarried with old Christians. Others had entered high-profile professions as notaries, judges, priests or public officials. Indeed, by the end of the fifteenth century most of the noble families of Castile and Aragon had Jewish blood running through their veins. Some felt pride in that. 'Is there any more noble a people than the Jews?' mused Diego de Valera, a *converso* who was also one of Isabella's most loyal chroniclers.[4] Even Isabella's husband, Ferdinand, was rumoured to have Jewish blood,[5] allegedly via a mysterious Jewish great-great-grandmother from Guadalcanal, near Seville, called doña Paloma. And many of their senior officials, like Andrés de Cabrera or Isabella's outspoken confessor Alonso de Burgos, were also from new Christian families. The vast majority of *conversos* — whose numbers are hard to assess, but accounted for up to one in fifteen Spaniards — were properly integrated into the Catholic church, not least because they were spurned by the Jews. They may not all have followed the church's rules to the letter, but at a time of widespread ignorance about proper Christian behaviour, few people did. Radical friars and embittered rivals continued to whip up popular hatred, however, and outbreaks of violence were increasingly frequent. The conflict between old and new Christians had become a major social problem, at least in the cities. Yet where previous monarchs had spotted the economic envy or racial prejudice that drove *converso*-haters, Isabella saw serious reasons for concern. 'We couldn't have done anything less, given the things they told us in Andalusia,' Ferdinand would explain later.[6]

The church had long had a mechanism for dealing with heresy. Papal or 'medieval' inquisitions could be, and had been, activated by the pope whenever necessary in a particular bishopric or entire country. One had long existed in Aragon, with the master general of the Dominicans naming the inquisitors, though it was low-key and was not very interested in *conversos*. The pope's nuncio in Castile, Nicolò Franco, had arrived in 1475 with instructions to use the traditional inquisition to find out if the *conversos* really were a problem, but Isabella sought something more robust and severe. She wanted a state-backed inquisition, with royal appointees in charge, so that she could throw both the church's moral might and the violence of the state against this threat to Spain's Christian purity. Pope Sixtus IV signed a bull allowing Isabella and her husband to appoint inquisitors that was dated 1478. It sat unused until September 1480, when she and Ferdinand appointed the first two inquisitors and ordered them to seek out heretics in Seville.[7]

The choice of city was by no means random. At the end of the previous century Seville had boasted what was almost certainly the world's largest city population of Jews, with twenty-three synagogues and up to 35,000 people in its Jewish quarter. The pogroms that spread across Spain in 1391 had seen the worst massacre of all in Seville, with up to 4,000 people murdered.[8] 'They killed a multitude,' reported a well-informed Jewish source.[9] 'Many of the Jews in Spain left the faith of Moses, and especially in Seville, where most of them abandoned their self-respect,' another Jewish writer, who saw conversion as cowardice, confirmed.[10] As a result Seville was now home to the biggest group of *conversos* in Castile, who accounted for well over a third of the city's population.[11] The Spanish Inquisition, as it would be known, made them its first target.

Isabella's old confessor from Segovia, the Dominican prior Tomás de Torquemada, whose 'heart and soul were alight with inspiration . . . to pursue the depraved heresy', had long been trying to persuade her that this new form of inquisition was necessary. Already, at the beginning of her reign, he had warned her against heretics and had been explicit about the need to keep Christians away from the corrupting influence of Jews and Moors, wanting them forced into ghettos – a measure that Isabella also adopted in 1480.[12] 'Your royal highness should threaten punishments if the Jews and Moors are not moved apart so that they do not live among Christians, and order that they wear their identifying symbols,' he urged her in a memorandum he is thought to have written in 1478.[13] They were ideas he had been whispering into her ear ever since they first met when she was a teenage girl in Segovia. 'She swore to him in the name of our Lord that, if God handed her the royal state, she would order proceedings against the crime of heresy and that it should be the main task,' Zurita said.[14] But opposition came from Isabella's trusted confessor, Talavera, who thought any failings among the *conversos* were down to poor teaching, and from senior churchmen like Cardinal Mendoza, who merely disliked the idea of state control over a religious matter.[15]

Isabella stood back while Talavera tried to rectify this through preaching, but her patience snapped when she was shown a manuscript written by a judaising *converso* who argued for a syncretic religion mixing the best of Christianity with the best of Judaism. This, he said, would avoid the idolatry and corruption of the established church. A furious Isabella took it to Talavera in Valladolid. 'It was your royal hand that brought it to me in this, our monastery,' he said in his own written answer to the manuscript.[16] The author's claim to speak for all *conversos* was an obvious falsehood, but he had put into writing what a small number of them must have thought. It was the most obvious proof that heresy really existed — however limited in extent — and Talavera scribbled a rapid, angry response to it, damning the author while also taking pre-emptive swipes at the new state inquisition that now looked inevitable. 'This detestable and most horrible of all crimes is reserved for ecclesiastical jurisdiction,' he claimed. Isabella took no notice.

The fiercely anti-semitic[17] chronicler Andrés Bernáldez, who was a parish priest in the nearby town of Palacios as well as chaplain to the archbishop of Seville, listed the *conversos*' crimes as running from observing Passover to seducing nuns. 'The *conversos* observed the faith very badly,' he said.[18]

The habits of their common people were exactly the same as those of the stinking Jews, as a result of the continued contact between them. They were just as greedy and gluttonous, never losing the Jewish customs of eating revolting food, and stews or awful dishes of onions and garlic, of things fried in oil, and they cooked their meat in oil, or they poured oil on it instead of lard and pig fat in order to avoid the lard; and this mixture of oil and meat produces a horrible stench; and as a result their houses and doorways stank of that disgusting food; and they themselves also had the smell of Jews about them. And they observed the Passover and Saturdays as best they could; they sent oil for the lamps to the synagogue; they had Jews who secretly preached to them in ther homes, especially and very clandestinely to the women.

Bernáldez watched the Inquisition's introduction with approval. 'The King and Queen were made aware of all this,' he reported. They had asked the bishop of Cadiz to look into the problem with the help of the radical Hojeda, who belonged to the same Dominican order as Torquemada. The report that came back was, predictably, full of dark warnings of terrible heresy. 'Given that this could in no way be tolerated, nor resolved without an inquisition into it, they denounced the situation at great length to their highnesses, informing them of how, who and where the Jewish ceremonies were performed and which powerful people were involved along with a large part of the [population of the] city of Seville,' Benáldez reported.[19]

Isabella's inquisitors, then, were clearly expected to find evidence of heresy. While making sure that they were installed in proper living quarters she also wrote warning the city's *asistente* (as Seville's version of the *corregidor* – the royal overseer in the cities whose power Isabella was busy increasing as she extended her reach deeper into Castilian society – was called) to watch out for the trouble and unrest which, she supposed, their arrival might provoke. 'If anyone does [create trouble], arrest them and confiscate their property and goods,' Isabella instructed. The inquisitors took just days to provoke tumult, making a show of authority by pursuing the most prominent *conversos* first. 'By different ways and means they knew within a very few days the truth about this wickedly depraved heresy and they began to arrest men and women from among the most guilty, and they put them in San Pablo [monastery]; and then they arrested some of the most respected and wealthiest of them,' Bernáldez said. With such a large number of *conversos* considered suspect, the jails quickly filled up and, as an overflow, the inquisitors had to borrow the castle across the River Guadalquivir in Triana, transporting the prisoners across the elaborate pontoon-style bridge called the Puente de Barcas.[20]

Sevillanos soon became used to the smoke and smell of the Inquisition fires, which burned their first victims on 6 February 1481, on a bonfire overlooked by four plaster statues of the prophets. 'At the first burning, they brought six men and women out into [the Plaza de] Tablada and burned them: and Friar Alonso [Hojeda], a jealous defender of the faith of Jesus Christ and the person who worked hardest to bring the inquisition to Seville, preached there,' Bernáldez reported. 'In the first few days they burned three of the most important and richest men in the city.' The victims included Pedro Fernández Benadeba, the *mayordomo* of the city's cathedral, and a respected, learned judge called Juan Fernández Abolasia. 'Neither their wealth nor favours could help them,' said Bernáldez, who noted that three *converso* priests and four monks were also among those burned over the next eight years.[21]

The first two inquisitors, the Dominican friars Juan de San Martín and Miguel de Morillo, were not as high ranking as the pope might have expected for such an important role, but they were accompanied, at least to begin with, by Juan Ruíz de Medina, the prior of the large collegiate church in Isabella's beloved Medina del Campo, who would rise rapidly through the ranks of both royal and ecclesiastical officialdom. Their powers were extraordinary. By January 1481, just three months after starting, they felt free to threaten one of the city's strongmen, the Marquess of Cadiz, for protecting *conversos* who had fled to his lands. The marquess must originally have thought of them as two lowly friars, but their warning to him was another blow to the status of the Grandees, as – either by design or through useful coincidence – this new, royal-backed Inquisition also served Isabella and Ferdinand's wider, authoritarian aim of wresting power from them. 'We warn you that we will act against you and others in every possible way . . . as a defender, protector, receiver and coverer-up of heresy,' they said.[22]

Those who 'confessed' and repented, the so-called *reconciliados*, might be let off with fines, but only after public humiliation at the crowded open-air *auto de fe* ceremonies. Up to 500 *reconciliados* at a time were paraded through the city's streets in their rag-like gowns and tall, conical *sanbenito* hats. 'The inquisitors would take people out of prison and put *sanbenitos* on them – with red crosses in front and behind – and they had to walk around in those *sanbenitos* for a long time,' said Bernáldez.[23] Those who escaped Seville often ended up being condemned in their absence and their possessions handed over to the royal treasury – which received a considerable boost from the flood of fines and confiscated property. The church itself could not spill human blood, so the guilty were handed over to the so-called 'secular arm', the civil authorities who carried out the executions either by fire or by garrotting. The latter was the 'lucky' fate of those who confessed on their way to execution. It was the church, however, that promoted death by burning – a concept alien to Castile's common law. The logic was that this was doing the victims a favour, as punishment on earth might save them from eternal damnation after death.[24]

In time the fires came to incinerate not just the living but the already dead, like those in Seville's graveyards about whom Isabella had written to her inquisitors. These were dug up and their bones thrown on to the fires. Their offspring were notified and invited to defend them, but they mostly declined. They only risked being prosecuted themselves. Even then, their children often found themselves forced to pay fines for the supposed crimes of their deceased, disinterred and carbonised forebears – including those who had died up to seventy years before. Later instructions to inquisitors in the city were quite clear. 'While concentrating on those who are alive, one should not neglect those deemed to have died as Jewish heretics, who should be exhumed so they can be burned and so that the tax collectors can deal with their goods according to the relevant laws,' proclaimed the instructions, signed by Torquemada, who was made inquisitor general in 1483 and became its driving spirit. Among those to receive property taken from Seville's *conversos* was Torquemada's own servant, Martín de Escalada, who was gifted the houses taken from Juan Pinto, 'the Deaf Man'. The burning of the already dead was accompanied by great ceremony. Effigies were made, dressed in Jewish burial clothes and individually denounced at one of the great *auto de fe* gatherings before being pronounced guilty and tossed into the flames with the bones. Four hundred of the dead were condemned and ritually burned at a single sitting in Toledo.[25]

Palencia, who was also from a *converso* family, put the numbers who were in some way dealt with by Seville's Inquisition in its early years at 16,000 – or half the city's *converso* population, and one in six of its inhabitants. Like many, he seemed anxious to distance himself by showing support for the Inquisition, blaming some of his fellow *conversos* for daring to rise above their station. 'Extraordinarily enriched by strange arts, proud and aspiring with insolent arrogance to public office, men of lowly extraction had bought themselves the status of gentlemen with money, against the rules and using the vilest trickery,'[26] he wrote. Their other crime, in other words, was to be successful newcomers into the Christian community, using the quick wit and adaptability of the outsider to their advantage as soon as they had converted and had access to the privileges and tricks of the dominant, Christian majority.

With the Seville inquisitors so rapidly and efficiently 'proving' that judaising was widespread, it was inevitable that the Inquisition should soon extend its reach to other cities in Andalusia and across both Castile and Aragon – making it one of the first shared projects of the new Spain being created by Isabella and Ferdinand. The forced confessions of Seville's supposed secret Jews helped to convince them that heresy had become an epidemic. 'From their confessions . . . the [secret] Jews in Córdoba, Toledo, Burgos, Valencia, Segovia and the whole of Spain were found out about,' said Bernáldez. The Inquisition thus became a self-perpetuating, self-fulfilling machine. By extracting false confessions from those it tortured or tyrannised, it created such a huge number of heretics that it was quickly assumed that many of the *conversos* really must be secret Jews. And the more that *conversos* saw there was no escape beyond confession, the more inquisitors were furnished with proof. To affirm one's innocence, as the proudest and most devout *conversos* did, was a risky strategy that could end up in the torture chamber. If the wealthy, the privileged and even ordained members of the church were unable to defend themselves, then the lowly craftsmen and tradesmen who made up most of the *converso* population must have fared even worse. Anonymity was guaranteed to those who denounced suspected judaisers, meaning that the accused could often do little to defend themselves. An Inquisition document from 150 years later lays out its sweeping approach to suspicious behaviour that good Christians should immediately denounce:

> If you know of or have heard of anyone who keeps the Sabbath, observing the Law of Moses, wearing clean white shirts and other best clothes, and putting out clean table-clothes and clean sheets on the beds on feast days, in honour of the said Sabbath, without lighting lights from Friday evening onwards . . . Or who have eaten meat during Lent and other days prohibited by the Holy Mother Church. Or who have done the great fast, which they call the fast of pardon, remaining barefooted. Or if they say Jewish prayers and at night beg forgiveness of each other, with parents placing their hand on children's heads without making the sign

of the cross or saying anything but: 'Be blessed by God, and by Me' . . . Or if any woman spends the forty days after childbirth without entering church. Of if they circumcise their children at birth, or give them Jewish names. Or if after baptism they wash the places where the oil and chrism were put. Or if when someone is on their death bed, they turn to the wall to die, or wash the dead body with warm water, shaving their beard, armpits and other parts of their body.[27]

With anonymity guaranteed, the Inquisition became a conduit for private revenge and popular hatred. Old Christians no longer needed to riot or attack the neighbourhoods of the *conversos*, who were also derided as *marranos*, or pigs. They could simply make up stories. The Inquisition was, in that respect, an efficient way of maintaining public order (something Isabella was keen on, as *sevillanos* knew only too well), if only by transferring the blame – and punishment – on to the victims. Even some Jews, who looked down on the *conversos* as traitors, joined the game, volunteering as witnesses – false or other-wise – against those whose families had shunned their own faith or who, quite simply, were personal enemies. A Jewish doctor was among the witnesses in a case in Soria, telling the inquisitors that one of the accused had called none other than the chief inquisitor Tomás de Torquemada 'a dog . . . and cruel heretic'.[28] Jews came under intense pressure. 'Proclamations were issued in all the synagogues that every man or woman who knew anything about the *marranos*' conduct was required to inform on them, regardless of whether their offence had been a minor or major one,' wrote a Jewish historian who spoke to those in exile.[29] Isabella herself moved to quash some of the false testimony given against *conversos* in Toledo, ordering arrests and torture.[30]

A Jewish writer saw greed behind many of the denunciations, whether by old Christians, fellow *conversos* or Jews. 'If a woman longed for the silver and gold vessels of her neighbour or of a woman who shared the same building with her, and the woman refused to hand them over, she [the other woman] was denounced,' he wrote.[31] A second Jewish author agreed. 'There were at that time some *conversos* who delivered their own brothers into the cruel monster's power. Poverty was the spur and the reason for most of their evil acts. Many poor *conversos* went to the houses of their richer brothers to ask for a loan of fifty or one hundred crusados for their need. If any refused them, they accused him of Judaising.'[32] Two *conversos* from Huesca, Simon de Santángel and his wife, were famously burned at Lleida after being denounced by their own son.

Where inquisitors were not sure of guilt, or wished to force a defendant to testify, torture was encouraged. A document instructing torturers is most eloquent. It gives a step-by-step guide to using the rack to stretch limbs to breaking point, advising the torturer to take his time and offer the victim a chance to speak in between each step.[33] Victims were to be tied to the rack with separate ropes around each limb that could also be tightened, stopping the flow of blood. 'You must understand that these steps in the torture are designed to inflict the greatest possible pain on the prisoner in order to get a confession by applying it to the most sensitive areas and going from limb to limb,' the anonymous author explained. 'You may apply whatever is most effective. I am just writing down what I have done.' It was easier to confess than to resist.

As suspicious behaviour often revolved around household habits in the kitchen and elsewhere, many more women than men were arrested.[34] When a thirty-two-year-old spice merchant's wife called Marina González was visited on her sickbed by an Inquisition notary in her home town of Almagro she admitted to following certain Jewish customs and rituals, blamed her two brothers-in-law and begged for pardon. 'From now onwards [I pledge] to live and die and end my days in the Holy Catholic Faith for the rest of my life,' she said. But when she was arrested again and taken before the Toledo tribunal by the city Inquisition's special jailer, Pedro González, 'the Snub-Nosed', the court decided she should be tortured to discover whether she had stuck to her pledge.[35] Her lawyers pointed out that she never rested on the Sabbath, owned a statue of St Catherine, ate pork, killed fowls by strangling them and ate 'all other christian foods, without distinction'. Marina González lived, dressed and spoke like a good Christian woman 'hearing mass and taking holy communion and following the church's fasts', they declared, and they complained that the allegations were all vague, with no dates or places. 'And though she wears little skirts made of red cloth . . . your reverences did not forbid such a thing unless it was of scarlet.'[36]

Marina González was given a chance to confess, but insisted on her innocence and was sent to the torture chamber.

She was stripped of her little old skirts and placed on the rack, with cords tied tightly around her arms and legs and a cord holding her head tight . . . and with a jar which contained around three pints, they started to administer the water and once they had poured a pint [into her mouth and nose], the Licenciate [Fernando de Mazuecos, the inquisitor] asked whether she had done anything wrong; and she said 'no'. They continued to pour the water and then she said that she would tell them the truth; but she did not say anything. [So] they gave her more water and she said that, if they stopped, she would tell them the truth. But she did not say anything at all. His Reverence ordered that she be given more water until that three-pint jug was emptied and she never said a thing.

Occasionally they untied her head, allowing her to sit up and inviting her to talk. She at first refused, but eventually accused a neighbour of observing Jewish fasts. Taken back to prison, Marina González refused to eat, and this was her final mistake. She was found guilty of trying 'to kill herself in prison in order to avoid confessing to her errors'. She was placed on a wooden scaffold in the city's Plaza Zocodover, while the judgment was read out loud. 'We declare her a heretic and relapsed apostate,' the court decided. 'And having incurred the sentence of major excommunication and confiscation and loss of her goods, we must remit her to the justice of the secular arm [the civil authorities, answerable to the crown, who carried out the punishments].' That meant death.[37]

Seville's *conversos* reacted angrily to the Inquisition's high-handedness, clamouring for proper justice and demanding that Isabella and Ferdinand intervene. The *conversos* mostly considered themselves to be – and were – proper Christians, at least as good as those who had no Jewish blood.

All Christians were, in theory, on an equal footing before God and they could not understand why the Inquisition's victims were 'only those converted to the faith who came from Jewish lineage, and not others'. Heresy of other kinds was not rife in Spain, but ordinary Spaniards were hardly good, observant Christians. 'Of 300 people, you will barely find 30 who know what they are meant to know,' wrote a Dominican friar sixty years later, pointing out that the rich were as likely to be ignorant as the poor. Secrecy and torture distorted the judicial process, the *conversos* complained, while those who erred in their faith should be reasoned with, not burned. 'They said it was inhuman and cruel to throw into the fire anyone who pronounced the name of Christ, who confessed that they were Christian and wished to live as a Christian,' said Pulgar.[38]

Men like Pulgar, who clearly saw the hand of 'the Christian queen' at work, could see that it was wrong to punish the majority for the sins of a few. 'You should treat the few relapsed people in one way, but treat the majority differently,' he said.[39] Pulgar could also see that the *conversos*' lapses, where they existed, often reflected those of old Christians. With few good examples to follow, it was not surprising if some *conversos* were not observing church doctrine properly: 'Given that the old ones are such bad Christians, the new ones are [also] bad,' he wrote. 'To burn them all because of this would be the cruellest of things.'

As Rome was deluged with complaints from the Seville *conversos*, the pope reversed his decision on the royal nature of the Inquisition, claiming he had been bamboozled into signing a document he did not fully understand. 'I have been informed that many people have been unfairly and deliberately jailed, without proper observance of the law; they have been subjected to terrifying torture, unjustly declared to be heretics and had their goods snatched away from them,' he wrote,[40] after Ferdinand had reformed the old Aragonese Inquisition along the Castilian model so that he could name his own inquisitors there. 'The Inquisition has for some time been moved not by zeal for the faith and the salvation of souls, but by lust for wealth, and many true and faithful Christians, on the testimony of enemies, rivals, slaves and other lower and even less proper persons, have without any legitimate proof been thrust into secular prisons, tortured and condemned as relapsed heretics, deprived of their goods and property and handed over to the secular arm to be executed, to the peril of souls,' the pope went on. It had become, in other words, a form of terror. Sixtus believed that the Inquisition had run wild because he had ceded the naming of inquisitors to Isabella and Ferdinand. As a result, the royal Inquisition launched in Seville was temporarily suppressed in January 1482 while Sixtus withdrew the sovereigns' right to name inquisitors, took away the anonymity of the accusers and allowed appeals to Rome. But Isabella and her husband were not prepared to give up such a potent tool. Ferdinand answered the pope with an angry letter insisting that 'we are determined never to let anyone hold this office [of inquisitor] against our will'.[41] And Sixtus soon backtracked. First the original inquisitors were allowed to continue in Seville, then he permitted the Inquisition's extension across Castile with the original rules sought by Isabella and Ferdinand.[42]

A papal bull sent to Isabella in February 1483 leaves little doubt about her personal backing for the tribunal. In the letter, Pope Sixtus IV tries to calm her fears that the Inquisition will be viewed by outsiders as a mere money-making operation, designed to strip *conversos* of their wealth and enrich the crown. 'The doubts you seem to have about whether we think that, by taking measures to proceed so severely against those perfidious people who, under Christian disguise, blaspheme and, with Jewish insidiousness, crucify Christ . . . that you are motivated more by ambition and a desire for worldly goods than for defence of the faith and Catholic truth or fear of God; you should know that we have never entertained the slightest suspicion that this might be the case.'[43] She had written to the pope, then, because she was worried about her image, not about the institution. By setting it up, Isabella insisted, she was merely doing the right thing by God. It was not the first time, and certainly would not be the last, that she deposited responsibility for her actions in Him.

Isabella's enthusiasm for the Inquisition becomes even clearer in two letters she wrote to a different pope ten years after it had been founded – when its mortal victims were well above a thousand people. By this stage senior churchmen like Juan Arias Dávila,[44] the *converso* bishop of Segovia, found their families under attack and were fighting a rearguard action in Rome – where a different pope, Innocent VIII, was fretting about the Spanish monarchs' power over the Inquisition. 'You can imagine how disturbed I was at seeing the effect on your holiness's spirit of the information provided by a bishop whose journey to that court [of Rome] obviously has not just been in order to hide the truth in the cases affecting his parents and family, but mainly to impede and create problems for the Holy Office of the Inquisition, defaming its ministers,' Isabella wrote in one letter.[45] Under the terms of the Inquisition's foundation such cases should not be heard in Rome, she averred. When the first letter failed to provoke the desired reaction, she composed a furious, handwritten follow-up, insisting that the Inquisition's powers did not diminish the pope's authority. 'It would be more damaging to your pre-eminence, honour and fame – given that this heretical crime is widely known to exist in these kingdoms – if the judicial investigation into it was in some way impeded or led off course,' she wrote. 'The truth about this business cannot be discovered over there [in Rome]. . . Your holiness should listen to those who say they are motivated only by zeal in the elevation of our Catholic faith . . . rather than to those who mouth and create heresy, who attempt to undo the Inquisition and are opposed to it, like the Bishop of Segovia and others.' Isabella was clearly upset, and her handwritten letter was full of angry crossings out. She ended up by apologising if she had gone too far in her words, but said she thought it her duty, however 'poorly reasoned and in bad handwriting' her arguments were. The Inquisition was something she felt strongly about and the personal power she and her husband wielded over it was important because that way it could be kept on course. A significant portion of her Christian subjects were now the target of a cruel and often arbitrary persecution, but she remained convinced that she was doing God's work.

The most convincing proof that the *conversos* were not secret Jews comes from Spain's real Jews. Those who had held on to their faith were disgusted by those who had not and were now 'inadvertently our enemies'.[46] 'They follow the laws of the gentiles willingly,' observed one downcast Jew, not long after the original conversions.[47] By Isabella's days they routinely referred to them as *meshumadim*, or willing converts, rather than *anusim*, or forced converts, with Isaac Abravanel, one of the prominent Jews of Isabella's day, calling the vast majority of them 'sinners' and 'criminals'.[48] In fact the eager embrace of both Christianity and anti-Jewishness by some suggests that many had the fervour of new converts.[49] 'They and their descendants after them, sought to be like complete Gentiles . . . imbued with the new faith,' he wrote. But Abravanel was also aware that this would not help them in the eyes of some Christians who 'will call them Jews, and by the name of Israel they will be known against their will and they will be considered Jews and accused of Judaising in secret and by fire they will be burned because of this'.[50] Another Jewish writer saw the Inquisition as God's way of punishing the *conversos* for abandoning one faith without fully embracing another, and the fact that most victims took the softer option of repenting and being killed by a garrotte while holding on to the cross rather than on the stake as proof that very few were real Jews.[51]

The two communities – where they still existed as such – lived near to one another, with inevitable overlaps in business and through blood ties. The bishop of Segovia had a sister living with him who was Jewish, and a prominent Jewish family in Aragon, the de la Cavallerias, had split after several brothers converted, while two did not.

Ironically, the Inquisition itself seems to have sparked a new, if very small, crypto-Jewish movement among those who now felt orphaned in their Christianity, though not all Jews were welcoming, with some claiming they had forfeited a right to return. These crypto-Jewish 'returners' eventually accounted for perhaps one in 200 *conversos*.[52]

It was race, as much as religion, that made the *conversos* suspect. Perhaps the most telling description of them, at least by their enemies, was as Castile's 'fourth [ethnic] type' (presumably after the Castilians, Galicians and Basques), but while the latter three were all 'natural' Castilians, the *converso* 'nation' was not – it remained an outsider people infiltrated into Christian ranks.[53]

Further proof of the racial enmity underpinning the Inquisition and other religious measures approved of by Isabella came with the slow spread of 'purity of blood' rules. These banned *conversos* from elite institutions, monastic orders and other places, purely on the basis of their Jewish blood. Mixing *converso* blood (or culture) with that of old Christians, the logic went, would make later generations more prone to heresy. A college at the university in Salamanca was the first to ban them just as the Inquisition was starting its work in around 1482, followed by another in Valladolid. Torquemada banned all *conversos* from a Dominican monastery that he founded in Avila, and – although these rules were often policed laxly – the Jeronymite order, which owned Isabella's favourite monastery at Guadalupe, also banned them in 1493. Isabella reportedly 'heard [this news] with pleasure', and was happy to see the Inquisition also apply an adapted version of these blood rules by punishing the offspring of its victims. Among the royal orders she passed was one banning the children and grandchildren of Seville's *reconciliados* from holding public or royal offices in 1501.[54]

Although they were bending to both popular prejudice and the fantasies of radical friars, Isabella and Ferdinand were the true founders of the Inquisition. It was they who had complained to the pope about the false converts in their kingdoms and asked permission to appoint inquisitors 'to tear such a pernicious sect out by the roots'. In Castile Ferdinand was often seen as the instigator, while in Aragon the blame was often laid on Isabella. Perhaps, given the unpleasantness of an exercise that combined elements of both religious and ethnic cleansing, it was easier in each kingdom to shift blame to the sovereign's partner. In fact they saw eye to eye on the matter, with Isabella keeping a close, protective watch over the welfare of her inquisitors, and ensuring that they received generous incomes.[55]

The queen's quest for religious purity did not end there, and the Seville Inquisition soon had a dramatic aftermath in the city. Several thousand Jews had clung on to their religion, despite the violence occasionally unleashed on them and in the face of increasing social hostility. Jews had been an important part of Seville's society for centuries. Now Isabella decided that they should be expelled from almost the whole of Andalusia, on the grounds that they were a moral danger to the *conversos* and encouraged them to judaise. In an extraordinary extension of its powers to cover a religious group outside the Christian church, the Inquisition was to oversee the process. On 1 January, 1483, it issued instructions for Jews to leave the bishoprics of Seville, Córdoba and Cadiz.[56] Some 5,000 people would move over the ensuing months. 'They went mostly to Toledo and old Castile,'[57] reported Isaac ibn Farradj, whose parents left for Medina del Campo. It was the first expulsion ever ordered in Castile. It would not be the last.

20

Crusade

Zahara de la Sierra, 27 December 1481

Isabella was now used to victory, so news of a defeat on the Granada frontier must have shocked her. Two days after Christmas 1481 a group of Moors rode out of the kingdom of Granada and, in a stealthy night-time attack, scaled the walls of the fortress at Zahara de la Sierra, a small town perched high on a steep, rocky outcrop on the northern edge of the Grazalema mountains. They slew most of the garrison, took the townsfolk captive and installed their own force of well-armed and well-supplied archers and horsemen, effectively pushing the kingdom's borders back into Christian territory.[1]

Isabella could have viewed this as just another minor setback on a 600-mile frontier where skirmishing, smuggling, raiding and trading had long been the norm. The kingdom of Granada still occupied an area not much smaller than modern Belgium. A long time had gone by without any dramatic changes in the frontier and Isabella herself had been careful to keep the peace with the Moors while she dealt with Portugal and Juana la Beltraneja. A second war front would have been too debilitating. But the loss of Zahara was a reminder that, even before her reign started, she had sworn to expel the Moors from Spain. That ambition had been written down quite clearly in the first marriage contract with Ferdinand, signed at Cervera in 1469.[2] She and her husband reacted to the loss of Zahara with equanimity. 'We were angry and upset . . . [but] it can also be said that we were pleased by what happened because it offers us the opportunity to get speedily to work on what we were already planning . . . to make war on the Moors on all fronts in such a way that, God willing, we hope to recover not just the lost town but also others, in order to [better] serve Our Lord and spread his holy faith,' they wrote in a letter to the Andalusian city of Seville.[3] Those plans were still vague and their initial reaction was chaotic, but Isabella and her husband needed to keep the militarised followers who had helped her win the throne busy and away from mischief. A war against the Moors would help them do that.

During the civil war, Isabella and Ferdinand had agreed two separate peace treaties with the Kingdom of Granada in order to keep their southern frontier quiet and, while in Seville, had begun negotiating the next treaty. The man with whom their emissaries negotiated was neither scared nor intimidated by the might of his Christian neighbours. Abū al-Hasan 'Alī ben Saad, known to Christians as Muley Hasan, was a vigorous and successful king. His kingdom was wealthy, densely populated, fertile, warlike, backed by fellow Muslims on the north coast of Africa and, crucially, proud of its religion. With generations of Muslim forebears buried in the often rich soil of a broad and occasionally mountainous strip of southern Spain, the Moors did not like to harbour feelings of inferiority to their northern neighbours, however powerful they were. Muley Hasan's Nasrid dynasty had, despite bloodthirsty infighting, ruled from the magnificent surroundings of the hilltop Alhambra palace complex they had built in Granada for far longer than the Trastámaras had run Castile. It was true that the Nasrid kingdom was nominally a vassal state to Castile, but that was a fluctuating relationship, with the demands for monetary tribute often ignored.[4]

Muley Hasan was a suitably fearsome representative of seven centuries' worth of Muslim leaders who had both proved capable warriors and, in previous centuries, overseen an intellectual flowering that made their Christian neighbours seem like not just religious infidels but cultural heathens. An anonymous Arabic chronicler summed up the monarch's virtues like this: 'He enforced the rule of religious precepts, worked to better the state of the castles and greatly improved the army; which meant that the Christians feared him and signed peace treaties, covering both land and sea. Wealth multiplied, food supplies increased and prices fell, with public security spread across all the lands of Andalusia and a general state of wellbeing,' he said.[5] That, at least, is how Muley Hasan had started his reign a decade before Isabella came to throne. He had a reputation for ruthlessness, having dethroned his father (who, in turn, had grabbed power by murdering his own uncle), and for being merciless with his enemies.[6]

Trouble came, according to the anonymous Arabic chronicler, when he began to enjoy his wealth and success excessively. 'The king devoted himself to pleasure, giving himself up to passions and enjoying himself with female singers and dancing girls. Immersed in leisure and carefreeness, he destroyed the army, getting rid of a large number of brave knights. And at the same time he overwhelmed the countryside with public levies and the ꝣocos [town and city markets] with taxes.'[7] But his worst sin was to have fallen for Isabel de Solís, a Christian slave-girl who swept floors in the rooms of one of the daughters Muley Hasan had with his aristocratic wife Fatima. Isabel had been captured during a cross-border raid when she was no older than twelve and, converted to Islam, became known as Zoraya.[8] 'This [king] had the habit of trying to bed all the women of his household,' wrote Hernando de Baeza, an Arabic-speaking frontiersman who would become a close friend and translator to the king's son Mohammed ben Abū al-Hasan 'Alī, known to the Christians as Boabdil.[9] A pageboy acted as secret intermediary, but one night after Zoraya left the king's room the queen's ladies set a trap and 'waited for her to return, then beat her continuously and almost to death with their slippers'. Muley Hasan's furious reply was to install her as his new queen, and turn his back on Fatima. 'From then on he lived with her and she was considered queen and he never again spoke to or saw his wife,' explained Baeza. The extensive Alhambra complex of palaces was easily big enough for the two royal families to coexist without meeting. Fatima and her children were moved into rooms near the Courtyard of the Lions, while Muley Hasan took Zoraya, who soon produced two sons, into his home in the imposing Comares palace, with its impressive tower and rooms looking onto the glassy sheet of water and marble floors of the Court of Myrtles. Converts to Islam provoked the same kind of suspicion as the *conversos* in Christian Spain – especially those, like the family of powerful *alguacil mayor* of Granada, Abulcacim Venegas, who rose to positions of importance. Zoraya would forever be referred to as *romía*, a name originally referring to people who had lived under Roman law.[10]

If Isabella had not forgotten the pledges made at Cervera, some of her nobles proved themselves even keener to strike back after the loss of Zahara. Cross-border rivalries were not just between kingdoms, but between the lords who controlled either side of the frontier. The modest Moorish victory was soon answered with a daring raid into the heart of the Granada kingdom by an army raised by the Marquess of Cadiz. This secretly made its way to within thirty-five miles of the kingdom's great capital city and surprised the sleepy garrison at the strategically important town of Alhama late in February 1483. As the town was both well fortified and perched high on a cliff above a bend in the River Alhama, its inhabitants had assumed it was unassailable and had dropped their guard. A group of the marquess's troops scaled the walls early one morning and knocked a hole through them to let other troops in, with fierce hand-to-hand fighting as the townsfolk hastily threw up barriers in the streets. An angry Muley Hasan appeared with his own army, but found himself having to besiege a solidly fortified town of the kind that he himself so liked to build or maintain. The Christian occupiers hurled the stinking, rotten bodies of those Muslims who had died during the assault over the town's walls, where hungry dogs tore at the corpses.[11] Hasan was outraged and his best archers picked the animals off from a distance.

Isabella and Ferdinand, who were in Medina del Campo, received the news twelve days later and immediately ordered that reinforcements be sent. 'Knowing just how useful and advantageous holding and sustaining that town is to us for the conquest of the kingdom of Granada, which we propose to pursue with all our might, we are sending as many horsemen as possible to the frontier,' they told the Seville city council, while instructing it to gather troops and artillery.[12] Ferdinand himself would soon be on his way, they added. Christian and Moorish troops began moving towards Alhama in their tens of thousands. A few weeks later Hasan was confronted by a fresh Christian army of up to 40,000 led by Cadiz's long-term rival, the Duke of Medina Sidonia, who had come to reinforce the garrison. Hasan was forced to withdraw and Ferdinand himself arrived soon afterwards, resupplying the town and leaving a fresh garrison.[13] A delighted Isabella was able to relish a new phenomenon that could help bind her unruly kingdoms together and that was already apparent in the collaboration between Cadiz and Medina Sidonia. A crusade against Spain's Muslim lands made her bothersome Grandees forget their squabbling and united her still-bruised and fractured kingdom around a single, joint cause. She immediately ordered that Alhama's three main mosques be turned into churches, sending crosses, silver plate, ornaments and books needed for Christian worship to be carried out where, just weeks earlier, Muslims had prayed. It was her contribution to a piece of freelance daring that restarted the seven centuries' old drive to oust the Muslims from their oldest stronghold in western Europe. Not only had the conquerors left the stinking bodies of their enemies to rot outside the city walls, but she had now planted the cross of Jesus Christ in the heart of the Muslim kingdom.

Alhama was a great feat of arms, but it was also a problem. Isabella's counsellors warned her that the town could become a liability, as supplying and holding it required a huge effort, with a vast mule train of some 5,000 animals obliged to wend its way through enemy territory every two to three months. It was as if they were trying to conquer the kingdom of Granada from its centre, rather than from frontiers backed by an infinite stretch of Christian land. 'It is difficult to begin the task in the middle of the kingdom as this makes it both laborious and expensive to sustain what has been won,' Diego de Valera wrote, urging the monarchs to start by capturing the Mediterranean ports, which could receive reinforcements of mercenaries and 'holy warriors' from north Africa. The best thing she could do would be to order that Alhama be razed to the ground and left as a pile of useless rubble. Isabella was not happy. 'She knew only too well how in all wars the amount of spending and work grew, but said that she and the king had decided to go ahead with the conquest of Granada with the budget that they had,' reported Pulgar. 'Given that this town [Alhama] was the first that had been won, she felt that abandoning it would see them accused of weakness.'[14] And so she and Ferdinand set about not only resupplying Alhama but also attacking the Moors elsewhere.

Ferdinand proposed they target Loja – a strongly fortified town in the Genil Valley that was a key post on the way to Alhama and, ultimately, to the city of Granada. Isabella was heavily pregnant with twins, but must also have taken part in the war councils in Córdoba that agreed on the Loja plan. Soon she was writing to distant corners of her realms, as far away as the Basque country, for troops to take part in the expedition. There was little more that she could do. The day before her husband was due to depart, she gave birth to her fourth child, a baby girl called María. In what may have been Isabella's most painful birthing experience yet, the little girl's twin was stillborn a day and a half later. And then her husband left, on his way to a new and different kind of war while, according to Pulgar, Isabella continued to oversee it all from a safe distance.[15]

Isabella and Ferdinand had already discovered in Alhama that defence was far easier than attack. If they had captured the town, it was due to the surprise nature of that attack. But now the Moors were waiting for them. The building and defence of thick, high-walled towns, castles, forts and other buildings had been one of the main – and most effective – military strategies for centuries. In the absence of surprise, the effort required by the attackers in men, arms, supplies and rations was many times greater than that of the defenders, who would stock up with supplies and drive their cattle inside. The frontiersmen who manned Loja were seasoned fighters and Muley Hasan had already spread the word to north Africa, seeking volunteers to defend Islam against the Christian infidel. Ferdinand had no great experience as a field commander in this kind of warfare and neither he nor Isabella had the strategic or logistical know-how to mount a major siege in enemy territory. Ferdinand misjudged his positions, his supplies and the fighting prowess of his opponents. He squeezed his troops into a camp that was both too small and too exposed, lying in a dip between olive groves and open country that was within range of Loja's guns. He also failed to prevent reinforcements entering the town, doubling its garrison. In an error directly attributable to Isabella as the person in charge of supplies, bread ran out in the besiegers' camp after two days and there were no ovens to cook more. The skilled Moorish commander in Loja struck repeatedly at Ferdinand's troops, riding out daily to harry them before retreating back behind the solid city walls. One of the most prominent victims was the young master of the Calatrava order, Rodrigo Téllez Girón, who died after two javelins pierced his armour. Chaos grew and morale plummeted. After just five days Ferdinand ordered his men to abandon camp (some, seeing the chaos, already had) and a disordered retreat saw many of the supplies left behind.[16]

Loja was a lesson in failure and Isabella, whose main task was to oversee the supplies, shared the blame. 'She was deeply upset, both because of the hugely diligent work she had put into provisioning that camp and because of the boost in morale for the Moors at seeing themselves so quickly relieved of a task that they had not looked forward to,' reported Pulgar.[17] But Isabella had learned much since she publicly castigated Ferdinand and his troops for returning empty-handed from Toro seven years earlier and now 'no one could know from her words or her actions the great sorrow that she felt'. Instead, she immediately vowed to keep working in order to send her husband back to Loja with an even stronger and better-organised army.

Isabella could not know that, while she was angrily digesting the defeat at Loja, the seeds of future success were being sown in the Alhambra palace. The growing tension between Muley Hasan and Fatima's sons, led by Boabdil, had exploded. 'The same day of the victory news reached the ears of those in Loja that two of emir Muley Hasan's sons, Mohammed [Boabdil] and Yusuf, had fled from fear of their father,' the anonymous Arabic chronicler said. Fatima had been won over by Muley Hasan's enemies, led by the Abencerrajes – a once-powerful clan that had fallen from favour. Legend has it that they were seeking revenge because thirty-six of the clan's leading members had had their throats cut after Hasan tricked them into meeting him in a room by the Patio of the Lions, which later became known as the Salón de los Abencerrajes.[18]

There had been omens that Muley Hasan's luck might change. The people of Granada recalled with horror how a military parade he had ordered in 1478 had been washed out by rain accompanied by lightning and thunder. The storms had washed tree trunks into the River Darro and these had jammed against a bridge to form a dam that, in turn, provoked a terrible flood. The city's leather artisans, silk traders, tailors and other merchants had seen their goods and livelihoods float away. The sight of a comet upset those given to superstition even more. It was not, however, Isabella and her husband who were to prove Muley's downfall. Boabdil and his brother Yusuf had scaled down the walls of the Alhambra at night – throwing a thin cord down to a group of waiting Abencerrajes knights who attached a rope to it that was hauled up and tied around a column. They fled to the towns of Guadix and Almería, respectively, where the people rebelled in their favour. Six months later the people of Granada and of the walled Albaicín district – which lay just across the steep valley of the River Darro – also rose for Boabdil, and after a failed attempt to win the city back Hasan had to withdraw to Málaga with his own brother, Zagal.[19] The infighting was a relief to Isabella and Ferdinand, whose campaign had got off to such a poor start. They now concentrated on maintaining their only new possession, Alhama. As Isabella had said, its loss would have made the Christian army look weak – even more so after it had been so thoroughly shamed at Loja.

As Isabella and her husband and their nobles thought of ways to press forward again the following year, the example of Alhama – with its elements of daring and surprise – remained high in their minds. It was quickly transformed into a legendary feat of arms, not least because many who took part returned rich with pillaged goods. Perhaps that is why the campaign against Granada in 1483 started off with an attempt to sneak through the treacherous, rugged hills of the Axarquía of Málaga – a region of broken, arduous terrain, steep hillsides, jagged outcrops and deep ravines. It was an improbable route to take and some experienced local guides warned strongly against it, but that may have made the plan seem even more like the adventurous march on Alhama. Whatever the reasons, a group of nobles led by the Marquess of Cadiz and the Master of the Santiago order, Alfonso de Cárdenas, set out with some 3,000 mostly mounted men into the steep, silk-producing valleys north of Málaga. With Ferdinand off dealing with the last few rebels in Galicia and Isabella several days' ride away in Madrid, the queen either could not, or did not want to, stop them.[20]

They rode for a day and night through the tricky terrain only to find the hamlets and villages they wanted to attack ready and waiting for them, with the villagers ensconced in fortified towers or hidden away in the harsh, craggy sierras. Small groups launched surprise guerrilla-style attacks, their knowledge of the terrain allowing them to pick the best ambush spots. The exhausted riders were outwitted and quickly forced to turn back. They began a chaotic retreat via an alternative route close to Málaga – the most important of Granada's port cities, which most had never set eyes on before. But that allowed Muley Hasan's brother Zagal to join the rout with his men and, as night fell, the Christian troops became lost in the steep valleys and dried-up riverbeds. The anonymous Muslim chronicler celebrated what was, initially, the victory of a few poorly armed farmers over what was meant to be a well-organised force led by some of Castile's most senior nobles.[21] 'They had barely arrived in that part of the countryside when the local people began to call out [to one another] and a group of men came together and, on foot and without the aid of cavalry, closed the route forward and fought the Christians along the gullies, gorges and through the rough terrain, inflicting a terrible massacre,' he wrote.[22] The Christians 'ran into dangerous mountain passes like fools, just as flies and moths fly into fire'. Spears and rocks rained down on them as they lay trapped in ravines or on narrow valley floors in single file – unable even to turn their horses around. The fleet-footed Moors skipped along above them, hurling down their rustic weapons, howling, lighting fires and made more terrifying by the fact that they were largely invisible and seemed far more numerous than they really were.

Cadiz eventually abandoned his men and was led out of the dangerous countryside by his personal guides. Some 2,000 or more men were lost, more than half as captives. Among those left behind were two of his brothers and three nephews.[23] Ferdinand later concluded it had taken fewer than a hundred mounted Moorish soldiers, with the help of the local country folk, to destroy the expedition. Bernáldez blamed greed. 'It seems that our Lord allowed this to happen because most of them went with the intention of looting and pillaging rather than serving God,' he wrote.[24] Instead they found themselves locked up in Málaga's *alcázar*, known as the Alcazaba, where those without wealthy relatives to pay ransoms could expect to remain for years. Isabella was upset, but that did not stop her from also refusing to allow richer families to buy their relatives' freedom. That went against tradition and must have shocked some people, but she argued that it would simply provide Granada with resources to use against her. Pulgar wrote to the Count of Cifuentes, one of those captured, telling him to be patient. 'News about what the queen is doing, or wants to do, you will hear just as accurately from the

Moors there as from the Christians here, which is why I won't write them down here,' he said.[25]

Isabella herself remained remarkably dispassionate. The expedition had been put together by the nobles, not by the monarchs, and those who died had done so in the service of God. 'I have heard at great length about what happened with the Moors; about which I am greatly displeased,' she said. 'Yet as this is nothing new in warfare, and such events lie in the hands of Our Lord, we cannot do more than thank him for it.' But many senior officials had been lost and she ordered the city authorities in Seville to allow sons or other relatives automatically to take over the positions held by those who were dead or captive. The task of filling the more important jobs would have to wait for Ferdinand's return from Galicia, 'because the presence of his highness is necessary so that we can together decide with the authority and proper consultation required by law'.[26]

The Nasrid royal family, once more, quickly proved its talent for turning dramatic success into disaster. The victory near Málaga had belonged to his father's faction, so now Boabdil felt obliged to seek his own triumph, riding out of the Alhambra at the head of a raiding force in April 1483. One of his pennants snapped as it hit the arch above the gate of Elvira, sending shivers down the spines of those inclined to suspicion. When a loose arrow shot from the city walls killed a fox as it darted through his troops, it was seen as a second bad omen. Boabdil now committed the same mistake as the Christians, riding ill-prepared across the border in an attempt to seize the town of Lucena – which was commanded by the inexperienced but clever nineteen-year-old noble Diego Fernández de Córdoba. The latter was able to keep Boabdil's force of up to 10,000 men busy long enough for reinforcements to arrive. These surprised Boabdil's men as they sat down to eat.[27] The Moors were quickly scattered, with almost half of them captured or killed. 'It was, in truth, a shameful defeat,' the anonymous Arab chronicler wrote. 'But the most shameful thing was that the emir [Boabdil] himself was captured.'[28] He was wearing a patterned red silk coat and a central-European-style helmet engraved with intricate latticed motifs. Fortune had come to Isabella's aid.

With Boabdil in Christian hands, the Moors turned once more to his father as king, while his mother fled to distant Almería, which remained loyal to her son. But Isabella and Ferdinand knew they had been handed a gift. They handled Boabdil with exquisite care, making sure his captors treated him as royally as possible, though Isabella could not help gloating over the victory after she received three of Boabdil's pennants as a present.[29] 'Our lady the queen was very pleased with the three pennants and Moorish trumpets that you sent and, even more, with the description of the battle,' Cardinal Mendoza wrote to the wife of one of the victorious commanders at Lucena.[30] Tales of military triumph, as ever, pleased her greatly. When a smaller Moorish raid went wrong at Lopera later in 1483 Isabella showed her joy with an annual gift to the victor's wife of the clothes that she herself wore on the date of the battle. Negotiations with Boabdil's mother produced a peace deal in which Boabdil exchanged his freedom for the status of vassal and ally. A two-year peace treaty was signed, but he had to promise to make war on his own father. He also agreed to leave his small son, Ahmed, in Isabella's hands as surety. Ahmed, believed to be aged around two years old and known by the diminutive *infantico* – or little prince – may have been a captive, but it was he who captured Isabella's heart whenever she visited him at his castle lodgings.[31]

Boabdil was now their ally, but he controlled only a small part of the kingdom. Isabella and Ferdinand realised that the derring-do spirit of Alhama would no longer work. The division within the kingdom of Granada weakened their enemy and Alhama was a valuable outpost from which to disrupt Moorish movements, but there was no substitute for the methodical process of medieval warfare – the patient besieging of walled towns, forts and castles. Open, battlefield warfare was – just as it had been in the civil war – an unlikely event, but the kingdom of Granada could perhaps be slowly shrunk by picking off the castles and towns along its fringes, while burning crops and destroying orchards. Technology, in the form of improved artillery, was making that easier and – in Burgos and elsewhere during the civil war – the Spanish monarchs had some experience of siege warfare. But the civil war had also shown that the process could be painfully slow. Sieges in enemy territory required a huge logistical effort and Isabella began to make herself an expert in exactly that. With the disaster of Axarquía now compensated for by the capture of Boabdil, Ferdinand embarked on a classic raid into Granada territory. His aim was to resupply Alhama, raze as much farmland as possible, burning crops and chopping down orchards to reduce the Moor's own supplies of food and, along the way, take the modest town and fortress at Tájara. The success of Ferdinand's army would depend as much on logistical prowess and the building of siege contraptions as on the hand-to-hand combat or archery of fighting men. Carpenters built huge shields and screens that were pushed up close to the fortress's walls. The defenders reacted by hurling down burning wads of flax and hemp soaked in oil and tar. The weight of the relatively large attacking force, which now included Swiss mercenaries, was such that the Tájara fortress was taken relatively quickly – and Ferdinand ordered it be razed to the ground.[32]

Although Zahara was also retaken, Isabella and Ferdinand were left with an unimpressive booty from the costly season's fighting in 1483. They had held on to Alhama and taken Tájara, but had little more to show in terms of conquered territory. That reduced their ability to reward those who had fought with gifts of new lands and, in turn, to bind closer to them the potentially rebellious aristocrats with promises of future wealth to be gained in Granada. Boabdil's capture had been due to luck and his own rashness. At one stage Granada's rulers had thought they might now sign the usual kind of peace deal, offering to pay 'great quantities of gold' in annual tributes. Ferdinand wrote to Isabella, who had travelled north to Vitoria, to ask her opinion. She was firm. Not only would she not condone a ceasefire, but she also wanted to prevent Granada from receiving

Isabella used jewellery to express power and provoke awe. The thick, bejewelled gold necklace in this portrait, bearing her symbol of a bundle of arrows, suggests that it is an early representation of the young queen, painted as Mary Magdalene.

© *The National Gallery, London*

Isabella refused to let others choose her husband. By opting for Ferdinand of Aragon, she brought the two largest kingdoms in Iberia together, though her own Castilian kingdoms were much more powerful.

Royal Collection Trust © Her Majesty Queen Elizabeth II, 2016 / Bridgeman Images

Isabella and Ferdinand formed a formidable partnership based on mutual respect for each other's abilities as monarchs of Castile. *Convento Agustinas, Madrigal, Avila / Bridgeman Images*

Isabella was both aware of the power of propaganda and keen to portray herself as a pious woman and instrument of God. *© Getty Images*

A small band of clever churchmen, often strict and pious friars like Francisco Jiménez de Cisneros, became important advisors and powerful administrators.
Ministery of Education and Science, Madrid, Spain / Index / Bridgeman Images

Tomás de Torquemada (top, centre), architect of both the Spanish Inquisition and the expulsion of Spain's Jews, helped persuade Isabella and her husband to pursue an aggressive policy of Christian purification.
© Getty Images

Margaret of Austria travelled from her home in Burgundy to Spain to marry Isabella's son and heir to the throne, Prince Juan. *Metropolitan Museum of Art, New York, USA / Bridgeman Images*

Isabella's daughter Juana was both rebellious and, ultimately, unable to match her mother's ability to impose her will on a world run by men. She went down in history as Juana 'The Mad'. *© Getty Images*

Philip the Handsome, Duke of Burgundy, was the husband chosen for Juana, as Isabella used her daughters to create a network of alliances across Europe. © *Getty Images*

It took Christopher Columbus seven years of lobbying at Isabella's court before he was given permission, and funding, to sail into the unknown in search of the east coast of Asia.

money or provisions from those trying to buy back the freedom of relatives caught in the foolhardy Axarquía raid. 'She wrote saying that, were it up to her, the Moors would not get their ceasefire,' said Pulgar.[33] She also ordered that the frontiers be closely watched to stem the flow of cattle, cloth or oil being sent as ransom payments. 'The queen did not allow provisions, great or small, to be taken to the Moors to pay the ransom of any Christians,' Pulgar added. On the Christian side of the only loosely demarcated frontier the so-called *alfaqueques*, whose profession was to negotiate the payment of ransoms on both sides, found their task much harder.[34] Isabella's crusade had started, and she was not going to stop – even if that meant Christian captives would have to suffer in the stockades of Málaga's thick-walled Alcazaba.

By the following spring it had become clear that Isabella was the motor behind this crusade. The royal family had spent Christmas 1483 in the north, making plans for the following year. But Aragon had its problems – notably its traditional rivalry with the French over Roussillon. Ferdinand decided that this was his priority. Isabella, however, travelled south to Córdoba to prepare for that year's campaign in Granada. If her husband could not organise it, then she would do so herself. She was an admirer of Joan of Arc, whose chronicle sat on her bookshelf with an anonymous dedication urging her to fight the 'damned sect' of Muslims[35] and reminding her that the Frenchwoman had also restored the crown to great-ness, though Isabella had no intention of leading troops into battle herself. She had plenty of willing field commanders for that. But generals need a commander-in-chief to set their objectives and raise their troops. And Isabella was more than happy to fill that role if her husband thought he had better things to do.

They Smote Us Town by Town

Córdoba, May 1484

Isabella bade goodbye to her husband at Tarazona, a town in the north-west corner of Aragon, at the end of March 1484. She had been implacable about resuming the Granada War and Ferdinand agreed to join her again once he had settled affairs in Aragon.[1] Her trip south took her past Las Navas de Tolosa, the spot where a great victory over the Moors had been won in 1212 when the combined armies of Castile, Aragon and Navarre engaged the Moors in an open battle that saw more than 30,000 men in the field. Among those with her was Cardinal Mendoza, an old-style aristocratic clergyman-warrior who was ready to lead her troops if Ferdinand did not appear on time. The long train of horses and mules had first wound their way along the canyon of the Despeñaperros River with its bare quartzite walls – where a shepherd had famously led the Christian armies to the surprise attack at Las Navas de Tolosa. From there they crossed over the top of the Sierra Morena and then ambled gently down its southern slopes. Isabella moved on to Córdoba, which was dominated by a vast old mosque with 365 horseshoe arches resting on hundreds of columns of jasper, marble and granite. It had been consecrated as a Christian place of worship 250 years earlier, but the cathedral still occupied only a fraction of the space inside.

Córdoba, like Seville, was a place where Isabella could appreciate the sophistication of those she now came to conquer. Her home here was in the *alcázar*, close to the former mosque and overlooking the broad River Guadalquivir and a long, sixteen-span bridge with its thick buttresses – a reminder that, before the Muslims or Visigoths had held the city, Spain had been part of the Roman empire. Noisy mills churned up the river water. The splashing and creaking of the mill wheels spoiled the queen's sleep and, reputedly, she soon ordered them to be halted at night. This had been one of the most troublesome cities during the days of weak royal power, with *conversos* and old Christians clashing regularly and a handful of local nobles scrapping for control. Much of the former were falling victim to the Inquisition, with its voluminous archives housed in one of the *alcázar* towers; but, with the business of crusade at hand, the city's attention now turned to legitimate war-making.

Isabella had written to Seville, demanding it raise troops for the upcoming campaign. She did not just want horsemen, archers and footsoldiers, calculating that technicians, engineers and labourers were as important as fighting men for the task ahead. Her soldiers were as likely to need to build roads and bridges for her artillery to cross – or chop down fruit trees and wreck crops – as they were to shoot an arrow, hurl a lance or handle a sword. So it was that more than half of the 8,400 men she wanted from Seville were to come equipped not just with arms but with tools. Isabella gave detailed orders: '2,500 must bring, apart from their arms, a sickle each. And 500 should bring an axe for cutting wood, and 2,000 a large saw.' A further 100 were to be stonemasons, also with their tools.[2] All this needed paying for and a fresh source of financing came from the Crusade Bulls that would now be signed every three years or so by the Pope. These allowed the widespread sale of indulgences by the church – a means of buying escape from punishment for some sins – to help fund the war.

Isabella studied the latest developments in artillery, hiring French and German experts who gave her instructions on which guns and munitions to buy. While the civil war army that had fought against Portugal had just four *lombarderos*, or master-gunners, the new crusading force would eventually boast ninety-one.[3] She had also ordered that a fleet patrol the Mediterranean to prevent reinforcements and supplies reaching the Granada coast from Africa. It was only now, late in May, that Ferdinand, having settled his affairs in Aragon, appeared. He led the troops against the town of Álora, set up on a rocky crag. The town was well fortified, and the defenders had not thought it necessary to evacuate their women and children. Pulgar accused them of having turned soft. 'The Moors live under the thumbs of their women,' he said. 'Tender love of their children turns them into cowards and, since they seek so boastfully to have offspring, their houses were stuffed full of helpless beings.' The army had been preceded by Isabella's carefully recruited labourers and road-builders, who created paths for the artillery that slowly pounded away at the towers and battlements of Álora's castle. The Moors fired back with long hand-held *espingarda* guns and hurled poisoned javelins at the attackers, but watched impotently as their defences crumbled away under the bombardment. Isabella had also realised that front-line medicine could save lives and boost morale, and sent with the army what came to be known as 'the queen's hospital' – large tents and a team of primitive surgeons. It would become a custom. 'The queen would always send six large tents along with the bedding needed for the sick and wounded; and she sent surgeons and doctors and medicines and people to serve them and said that the costs did not matter, because she would pay,' explained Pulgar.[4]

It took just a week before the battered defenders came out to parley, agreeing to abandon the fortified town in exchange for their lives and the price of the cereals stored there. As always, one of the conquerors' first actions was to consecrate the town's mosque as a church. A satisfied Ferdinand ordered the walls repaired and the town garrisoned, then prepared to return to Isabella with his troops. But she would have none of it. She had prepared for a longer campaign. Mule trains had been readied and vast quantities of barley and flour bought. Some 800 mules were delivering weekly supplies and were expected to do so for a full seven weeks.[5] As Palencia recounted, 'The queen, who worked daily sending money and people, and pack animals and supplies, and equipment for that war, having heard that the king was thinking of leaving the war and returning with his host from the Moorish lands, sent to tell the King that – if he wished – he should continue laying waste to the Vega or should besiege some other town, since there was still enough of the summer left to be able to do so.' Ferdinand did exactly that, his troops rampaging through the fertile Vega of Granada, destroying the orchards, storehouses and well-watered fields that had helped fill Muslim stomachs for centuries. As Ferdinand's army returned, Isabella wrote daily letters to ensure that supplies reached a similar expedition led by the Duke of Medina Sidonia.[6]

The monarchs wintered in Seville, a city now at the heart of the war effort but devastated by the expulsion of its Jews, the persecution of its *conversos* and occasional outbreaks of the plague. They were back in one of Isabella's favourite spots – the Royal Alcázar – which brought back happy memories of the procreation and birth of little Juan. But members of her household soon began to die from the plague and Isabella fled with her family to healthier climes. The outbreak was so severe that, when she sent Ferdinand off to war again early the next year, she banned *sevillanos* from joining him.[7] 'I order that nobody from the city of Seville or from those places around it and in its archbishopric where there is plague be so bold as to go to the king's camp,' she wrote.[8] They were now settling into a pattern of warfare. Winters were for rest, planning and even for giving birth – with her fourth daughter, and final child, Catherine of Aragon born in the break after the 1485 campaign. Fighting could start again in the spring, with fresh troops and supplies. On each expedition the weight of artillery and the importance of road-makers, bridge-builders and labourers increased as the heavy cannon were dragged through the alternately arid and rain-drenched landscapes of Andalusia so that ferocious bombardments could be unleashed on Moorish towns and castles. That spring, as he set off towards spectacular Ronda – a strategic town that straddled a deep canyon north of Málaga – Ferdinand was followed by an artillery force drawn by 1,500 carts.[9]

Double-dealing, the use of Moorish allies and plain good luck all came to their aid. But the keys to success were the ever more refined siege techniques and supply trains that Isabella ensured arrived regularly at the camps where more than 10,000 hungry soldiers were gathered. Isabella herself watched from a prudent distance, worrying constantly about whether her resupply programme would perform properly. A pivotal victory came when, after a short two-week siege and bombardment, a secret deal was done with some of the senior families in Ronda. All those who had battled for control of Spain's southern Mediterranean coastline, from the native Iberians to the Phoenicians, Greeks, Carthaginians, Romans and Muslims, had established themselves here. A whole swathe of towns fell with it, as the Moors decided it was better to accept the status of *mudéjares* – Muslims in Christian Spain – than fight to the death or be captured and enslaved.[10]

Isabella and Ferdinand were changing the parameters of warfare. As the artillery guns they used became heavier and more numerous – along with the increasing number of road-builders available to flatten valleys, carve roadways out of hillsides or build bridges across river beds – so the great defensive bastions of medieval military strategy, the castle and the city wall, slowly crumbled before them. It was no longer necessary to concentrate on blocking routes in and out of towns while waiting for the besieged to starve. This new sort of army, in which artillery and infantry replaced knights and their mounted followers as the most important elements, saw fear of Isabella and Ferdinand's troops spread as – according to one Muslim poet – they 'smote us, town by town, / Bringing many large cannons they demolished the impregnable walls of the towns.'[11] The royal arsenal would soon have some 180 big and medium guns and several foundries to supply them. 'Towns and fortresses . . . which once could have held out for at least a year and fallen only by starvation, now fell in a month,' remarked Bernáldez.[12] Thousands of cannon balls made of iron or stone were hurled at walls that had previously been thought impenetrable. The largest were carved out of 150-pound lumps of rock. Some of the worst damage was done, however, by fireballs made of hemp, pitch, sulphur and gunpowder, which spewed flames as they fell, raining fire across a wide area.[13] Defenders who tried to patch up the damage would then find themselves subjected to intense fire from smaller cannon, from bowmen or from the long-barrelled, hand-held *espingarda* guns, which gradually became more numerous in the army's ranks.

A typical assault, described by Pulgar, saw the town of Setenil taken in just three days. 'Setting up his big *lombarda* guns, the king ordered them fired at the two great towers at the entrance gates. These fired as directed until, in three days, they had reduced the walls to great heaps of rubble. The *cerbatanas* and *pasabolantes* and *ribadoquines* [all smaller artillery pieces] hit the town's houses, killing men, women and children and destroying homes. Such was the terror the firearms inspired and the carnage and ruin inflicted on the Moors that they could not endure it.'[14] Breached walls then allowed the artillery to start targeting and flattening the houses inside or shooting fireballs at them. Little surprise, then, that many towns did not even wait for the bombardment to start – and instead sued for peace while the guns were being set up before them. The traditional rag-bag Castilian 'host' of conscripts, regional Hermandad militias, feudal lords' armies, mercenaries, technicians and well-organised groups from the military orders were gradually marshalled into disciplined units of around 800 men. At the core of it was what would eventually become Europe's largest standing army.[15]

Granada's own civil war spluttered on, weakening the enemy further. Muley Hasan was ousted by his brother Zagal before dying in 1485, and Boabdil remained rebellious and unreliable. Isabella and Ferdinand aided him in his civil war and at one stage he appeared in Murcia, being fêted by his Christian allies. By 1486 the Albaicín district, on a hill opposite the Alhambra palace complex, had rebelled in his favour and was being bombarded with cannon and catapults from the other side of the Darro Valley. But then he allied with his uncle Zagal and took charge of the defence of Loja, the scene of Ferdinand's embarrassing first attempt at besieging a walled town. 'Now you are going to suffer a defeat similar to the one you have already suffered here,' his *mudéjar* interpreter, Abrahim de Robledo, threatened. But the hapless Boabdil lost the town almost immediately as the walls collapsed under intense cannon-fire and fireballs set houses ablaze. He was captured once more, becoming Isabella and Ferdinand's vassal again – and his uncle's enemy.[16]

By this stage news of Isabella's crusade had spread across Europe. Volunteers appeared from far and wide, including the English aristocrat known as Lord Scales, believed to be Edward IV's brother-in-law, Edward Woodville, with more than a hundred English archers and footsoldiers armed with axes and lances. They were deemed to have turned the final battle over Loja, though Scales himself lost two teeth after being hit by a rock and worried that his looks had been spoiled. Ferdinand told him to be proud of a crusader's injury that made him 'more beautiful than deformed', and Isabella showered him with 2,000 *doblas'* worth of gifts, including 'a very rich bed, and two tents, and six big, beautiful mules and four horses'. Scales amused Isabella when she arrived at the freshly conquered town of Íllora by greeting her dressed in white, with a plumed hat, his chestnut horse wearing a long blue silk skirt, accompanied by a similarly attired retinue. Scales made his horse perform vigorous dressage jumps for the onlookers, who obviously approved of this eccentric display of aristocratic pomp.[17]

Isabella's morale-boosting visit to Íllora was designed, in part, to thank the volunteers who had arrived from across Europe. The surrendering Moors had just left the city and Isabella – accompanied by her ladies-in-waiting and eldest daughter Isabella, now aged fifteen – was greeted by a loud band of trumpets, sackbuts, shawms and drums. The army of Castile awaited her, dipping its flags as she rode past on a mule dressed in rich scarlet and gold cloth. She herself wore a Moorish-style dress with a black brockade hat – an unsubtle homage to the land her armies and her husband were conquering. Ferdinand, who also carried a curved Moorish scimitar-style sword, greeted them by kissing his wife on her cheek and his daughter on the mouth.[18]

Isabella now followed just a few steps behind the conquering army. At Moclín, which was taken in 1486, eighteen heavy *lombarda* guns kept up a permanent barrage 'so fast, day and night, that there was never a moment when the reverberation of one gun or another was not heard'.[19] Eventually a fireball landed on the town's stock of gunpowder, producing a rapid victory that saved Isabella's army from being peppered by gunshots from the town walls. While Ferdinand then went off to lay waste to the farmland of the Vega of Granada in the summer of 1486, Isabella moved to the conquered town and soon found herself also negotiating the surrender of nearby Montefrío. As in other places, the inhabitants gave up without a fight, leaving with their possessions for the city of Granada itself.[20]

God Save King Boabdil!

Málaga, 1487

The Granada War had already dominated the affairs of Castile, and Isabella's time and energy, for several years, but the biggest tests lay ahead. In 1487 she and Ferdinand decided to besiege Granada's second biggest city, Málaga. It was a huge, well-fortified port, needing a greater amount of military muscle than Isabella had ever put together before. A great army of 53,000 men, including 13,000 on horseback, was assembled and marched first on the town of Vélez-Málaga in early April. Zagal also raised an army and set out for Vélez-Málaga, with Isabella suddenly panicking that she had not recruited enough men. It was now, however, that her strategy of dividing the Nasrid royal family by turning Boabdil into a vassal paid off.[1] She and Ferdinand had even sent Christian troops to reinforce Boabdil after he had reappeared beside the Alhambra, taking control of the Albaicín district the previous autumn. 'The enemy helped the master of the Albaicín [Boabdil] with all sorts of supplies: men, guns, powder, animal feed, cereals, animals, gold and silver,' wrote the anonymous Muslim chronicler after fighting had erupted across the narrow Darro Valley.[2] 'With that the enemy achieved what it sought, that infighting would break out.'[3]

A nervous Zagal had made the people of Granada swear not to rise against him while he led his troops towards Vélez-Málaga, but no sooner had he gone than an elderly Moor locked himself inside one of the city's towers and climbed the stairs to the top. He removed his headpiece, tied it to a lance and started to shout: 'God save King

Boabdil!'⁴ The latter was soon in control of the city. News reached Zagal at two o'clock in the morning as he camped near Vélez-Málaga and, with his way back to Granada now blocked, he set off east towards his strongholds of Baza and Guadix. The inhabitants of Vélez-Málaga, presented with the sight of their king riding away from them while Ferdinand lined up his mighty guns, took just ten days to surrender. Boabdil, meanwhile, thanked Isabella for her help by sending her a Christian captive from Úbeda along with a gold chalice and various exotic scents. He also wrote to explain that he had slit the throats of some of his father's most important supporters in the city, and asked Isabella to remind Ferdinand to send him more reinforcements.⁵ 'You should know that we have killed four of the enemy captains,' he told her. 'Perhaps God will make sure this happens to all the enemies who are left.'⁶ Ferdinand sent him 3,000 Christian troops and orders were issued to Christian frontier commanders to help Boabdil make war on his uncle wherever possible. Boabdil later returned the favour by attacking a Muslim force sent by his uncle to reinforce Málaga.⁷

Isabella and Ferdinand might have expected an easy handover of Málaga, where a wealthy and spoiled merchant class lived off the sea-trade between Granada and north Africa. But it was also the most important point of connection with the kingdom's supporters on the southern side of the Mediterranean. 'The city was a magnificent emporium for the profits of all vessels that docked there and the main point of support for the people of Granada,' said Palencia.⁸ Arab, Egyptian, Tunisian, Numidian (Berber) and Sitifensian (Kabyle) vessels weighed anchor there, supplying the kingdom of Granada with men, horses and money that had been gathered from across north Africa. Málaga also had a large force of Gomeres – a tribe of warlike Berbers who, motivated by religion, money or both, provided fighters determined to save the kingdom of Granada from the Christian onslaught. With the backing of Zagal, these helped an experienced commander called Hamete Zegri take control. Among the keenest to hold out were the small population of converts from

Christianity – afraid of their future fate as apostates – and the wild *monfíes* bandits from the countryside who had vowed to fight to the death. That made the siege which started in May 1487 a far more complex affair than anything Isabella and Ferdinand had embarked on before.[9]

Isabella's supply task was eased by the fact that goods, especially artillery, could now be delivered by boat, but the fierce spring rainstorms made the tracks muddy and the sea choppy. This time the monarchs had drawn their forces from further afield as foreign volunteers sought the mystique of successful crusaders and Aragonese nobles joined their ranks, bringing their own men. The Holy Roman Emperor Maximilian sent two ships' worth of artillery, though he almost certainly charged them for the assistance.[10]

Isabella and Ferdinand's men, most of whom had never seen Málaga before, were awed by its size and defences. Pulgar was one of those who realised that this was like no other city they had come across before. 'It is situated on a flat piece of land at the foot of a long slope, and is surrounded by a round wall, fortified with many thick towers, at a close distance from one another; and it has a thick outer barrier, where there are also many turrets. And on one side of the city, where the slope begins to rise, is the *alcázar* – known as the *alcazaba* – surrounded by two walls in which we were able to count up to 32 thick towers of wondrous height and cleverly built. And along the walls there are up to 80 other medium-sized and small turrets close to one another,' he wrote. From there two more walls protected a road that led straight up the steep slope to the top of the hill, where the Gibralfaro castle sat, overlooking the areas where any attack might come from. Some of Isabella and Ferdinand's advisers thought a siege would be too risky – that Málaga could be slowly strangled from afar now that all the neighbouring towns and castles were occupied. Others hot-headedly urged a direct assault. But even taking strategic positions around the city was difficult, as hilltops were fought over at close quarters and the Moors proved themselves to be highly motivated fighters.

Ferdinand's own tent, poorly placed on a hilltop, had to be moved back out of sight after the Moors picked it out and began to target it with cannonfire.[11]

In the end it was Isabella who, according to Pulgar, took the final decision to carry on with a classic siege of attrition and avoid a frontal attack. A massive ditch was dug around the city, with palisades erected as a further obstacle to anyone trying to ride out and fight. The idea was to starve the defenders out, while bombarding them with the growing mass of artillery. Walls and fences were built to give the attackers cover. Tunnels were dug to get close to the city walls. Siege machinery, much of it built on site, began to populate the plain around Málaga. Huge towers, designed to be rolled towards the walls so that troops could scale them, were built, along with elaborate fireproof mobile protective shelters. Attacks launched against breaches in the walls caused by bombardment, however, were always beaten back. And Zagri's men often rode out, bypassing the palisades and eager to do battle with their besiegers. Groups of Moors dug away outside the walls to create their own defensive barriers or to find the tunnels being dug by the Christians. All those who stepped within firing range could expect to be harassed by archers or gunners. The siege dragged on and, unlike others, it brought a high cost in human lives. The besiegers were losing thirty men a day, while the Moorish defenders suffered even more heavily – with around fifty a day dying. Those inside the city lived in equal terror of the Christian army and of the ruthless Gomeres, and anyone who dared to suggest negotiating risked execution for treasonable cowardice. As the numbers of injured and wounded grew, so did the size of Isabella's hospital. By the end of the siege it had expanded from the original six tents to two large pavilion tents and a further fifteen smaller ones. Isabella found her army was running out of gunpowder and sent ships to Valencia and Sicily to seek supplies, while a begging letter also went to the king of Portugal. But the sea was her best support. It meant that Isabella could ship in food and gunpowder relatively easily, landing it at a dock set up within sight of the city walls – presumably exasperating the defenders as they themselves began to run short.[12]

On days when, because of the stormy weather at sea and the water-logged, slippery tracks, supplies did not reach the camp, the rumour mill churned and there was loose talk of retreat. With her soldiers suffering, Isabella decided to join them on the front line. Her visits to recently conquered towns had, in the past, boosted morale quickly and, despite the obvious dangers of a place where dozens of her men were dying in the daily skirmishing, she moved to Málaga in May. She set up her camp at a safe distance on a hill overlooking the city. She came accompanied by her own court, including Cardinal Mendoza and her eldest daughter Isabella, along with singers, musicians and her own artists, whose task was to immortalise the siege in paint. 'She was welcomed with great joy, as her coming brought lightness to their toil and they put greater effort into their work,' said Pulgar.[13]

Isabella wanted to see, in person, how the siege was going, whether her provisions were sufficient and to quash rumours that fear of the plague might provoke an order to lift the siege. Ferdinand evidently needed Isabella to stiffen spines, and hoped that her presence would weaken them among the defenders so that 'the Moors could see for themselves that it was both his will and hers that the siege should continue and that it would not be lifted until the city was taken'. There was some grumbling that war was men's work and that, even though she had been at Íllora the previous year, the queen should not be there, but overall Isabella's impact on the besieging forces was electrifying. 'Most were happy, because the queen was loved and feared by everyone,' reported the Marquess of Cadiz's chronicler. Soldierly pride meant many were itching to show her what they could do. 'Everyone in the camp thought that, with the coming of the queen, they should strike at the Moors,' said Bernáldez. But while her presence may have emboldened her own men it did nothing to weaken the resolve of the defenders. 'As people from Spain . . . they came out valiantly to fight,' he said admiringly, while also recognising the common 'Spanishness' of Moors and Christians.[14]

'And they never once mentioned negotiations, but fought to defend their city, causing as much damage as they could while themselves receiving much harm and many deaths.'

Within the city walls zealous holy men preached the creed of resistance to the death, while the Gomeres enforced discipline and sent out raiding parties. One of the most ardent Gomeres was Abrahen Algerbí, a fiery preacher who had travelled from the island of Djerba in modern-day Tunisia. He soon found a gang of followers who were seduced by his warlike tone, invocations of the Prophet and conviction that victory could be obtained. Algerbí led a daring mission to reinforce Málaga with 400 of his followers, catching the besiegers unaware at night, jumping the wooden palisade they had erected and wading through the sea towards the city. Some 200 of his men made it into the city but Algerbí himself remained outside, ostentatiously sinking to his knees and praying. The astonished besiegers detained him and took him to see the Marquess of Cadiz. Algerbí claimed to be a holy man with a secret message for Isabella and Ferdinand explaining to them how to take the city. He was sent to the royal enclosure but Isabella ordered that he be kept waiting outside their tents until Ferdinand woke up. When Algerbí saw two people approaching who looked, to him, like the king and queen he produced a small sword that he had been hiding inside his cloak and slashed at them. He had attacked the wrong people. Isabella's lady-in-waiting Beatriz de Bobadilla and Álvaro de Portugal, whom he had mistaken for the sovereigns, were reportedly saved by the fact that Algerbí tripped over a tent rope.[15] The man's end was, according to Palencia, gruesome. He was stabbed to death by the guards and then his body was taken to a catapult and hurled over the city walls into Málaga, presumably splattering on to a rooftop or into a city street.

As conditions inside the city worsened, Málaga's military commanders requisitioned most food, leaving many of the Jews trapped inside the city to die of starvation. Soon donkeys, horses and rats were being eaten. Yet even as starvation set in, the fighters rallied to the cause of their holy war. In a last great display of foolhardy bravery, they broke out of the city and launched a suicidal attack that saw several of their best commanders killed or wounded. The commander of the surviving Gomeres then took his troops into the Alcazaba and suggested to the city's inhabitants that it was time for them to negotiate. As the inhabitants of Málaga starved, Isabella and Ferdinand met representatives of the fourteen main groups in the city. The representatives demanded that – as in the towns that had given way with less of a fight – they be allowed to go free, even if they had to abandon all their possessions. The demand came with a threat if it was turned down. 'They would hang from the city's battlements the 500 Christian men and women whom they were holding captive and, after placing the elderly, women and children in the [safety of] the *alcazaba*, would set fire to the city and would come out ready to die and kill Christians, so that the king and queen's victory was bloody,' reported Pulgar.[16] 'That way the events at Málaga would be known to all living people and would perdure throughout all the ages of mankind.' But Isabella and her husband were no longer interested in negotiating. That option was available only to those who declined to fight. And if they killed the Christian captives, they could expect each and every inhabitant of the city to have their throat cut. 'They can go to the devil,' replied Ferdinand.[17]

When the final surrender came, the thousands of surviving Moors were pushed into the same corral where the 500 Christian captives had been held while their future was decided. They, or their relatives, could buy their freedom at thirty gold *doblas*, or some 13,000 *maravedís**, per head – though they would then have to leave immediately for north Africa. Those who could not pay ransoms became slaves. Several of the most fanatical defenders, including some converts from Christianity, were excepted from the agreement. And those *conversos* who had installed themselves in the city after fleeing from the Inquisition in Seville and elsewhere now found themselves back in its grasp. Many were burned. A dozen Christian traitors found in

* For a table on relative monetary values, coinage and the prices of both everyday and extraordinary items see Appendix, pages 489–90.

the city were given the most painful death, tied to posts and stabbed with sharpened canes until they bled to death.[18]

Málaga was a city in ruins, its streets impregnated with the stench of rotting corpses. From behind its battered walls there now emerged a train of 500 wretched-looking people, their legs still shackled to metal chains. A cross was paraded before them. Isabella had ordered that a large tent be set up with an altar inside it, so that these Christian captives – many of whom had been there since the disastrous Axarquía raid – could be ceremonially released from their shackles, clothed and blessed. Isabella and Ferdinand refused to enter the city until it had been cleansed of corpses and the stink had subsided. Then they processed to the main mosque, already consecrated as a church, to give thanks and complete the ritual expulsion of Islam from a city that had been Muslim for more than seven centuries.[19]

The haul of 11,000 prisoners from Málaga was so huge that Isabella had to issue letters ordering the people of Seville to take them into their houses. Payment for their upkeep came from the sale of slaves and from ransoms. 'I order you to use the money received for the Moors who were sold in this city to pay those people who have had those same Moors [in their houses] for the days that they had them there,' she told the city authorities. The prisoners were divided into three groups.[20] One was given to the *caballeros*, captains and *hidalgos* who had taken part in the campaign, while another was used for swaps with Christians held in north Africa. The final, and largest, group went to Isabella and her husband, and were sold off to boost an exchequer exhausted by war costs.

Moors also made good gifts. One hundred of the warlike Gomeres were sent to the pope. The queen of Naples received fifty Moorish girls from Isabella, and the queen of Portugal a further thirty. 'And the queen also made a gift of a large quantity of Moorish women to some of the [great] ladies of her kingdom, while others remained in her own palace,' commented Pulgar. The fate of the 450 Jewish inhabitants of Málaga was resolved by the Jewish community in

Castile, which paid 22,000 *doblas,* or around 8 million *maravedís,* for their freedom.[21]

Isabella and Ferdinand retained strict control over the Málaga booty. 'Nothing was lost that was worth money, all of which went to the king and queen,' remarked the author of a chronicle about the Marquess of Cadiz. Isabella distributed 3,000 captives among the nobles and troop commanders, allowing her to write off the debts she had run up with many of them.[22] 'This seemed fine to everyone, especially to the marquess, because it enabled them to avoid the shame of not being able to pay what they owed,' explained the marquess's chronicler, almost certainly glossing over the inevitable squabbling about war booty. 'And that is why the Moors went into the monarch's exchequer.'

It was an historic victory. The ancient kingdom of Granada had lost its main port and second city. Some of its most determined and toughest fighters had been blasted and starved into submission. And the remaining territory in Muslim hands was divided into opposing halves – with Boabdil and Zagal sworn enemies. The upper hand in that battle now lay with Boabdil, who was also Isabella and Ferdinand's vassal. They could now concentrate all their firepower on Zagal and his lands to the east. A fragment of a new treaty with Boabdil, which survives among the records of Isabella's secretary Hernando de Zafra, shows that he had promised to help them. 'The said King Boabdil, their vassal, will truly and faithfully help their royal highnesses and their people against the said Moors with all his might. And the king of Granada is obliged to hand over the city of Granada and its forces, as and when he can.'[23] He, in return, would be granted many of the lands they now planned to take from Zagal, as well as the return of his son Ahmed, who was currently in the fortress at Moclín, under the watchful eye of Hernando de Baeza's employer, Martín de Alarcón. Under the terms of this treaty, the inhabitants of El Albaicín – who had long proved the most open to a settlement with the Christians – would receive a ten-year peace deal that allowed them to maintain their mosques and way of life, or to move freely to north Africa. And the most important of them were also allowed privileges – including the right to sell their possessions to Christians. 'If I break this agreement . . . the king and queen, my lords, will not be obliged to keep to any of the agreements contained here,' Boabdil added.[24] The Granada War, Isabella may have been tempted to think, was all but over.

Boabdil was increasingly dependent on Isabella and Ferdinand but, given that the lands he was to receive in exchange for Granada were so obviously inferior in size and importance, he was also in no great hurry to see the treaty through to its logical conclusion. 'The Queen sent this Moorish king money every month for his own upkeep and that of those who were with him,' Pulgar explained.[25] At one stage Boabdil wrote a grovelling letter of thanks in reply to one from Isabella, exhausting his list of adjectives to praise the 'glorious, magnificent, excellent, generous, famous, illustrious, noble, virtuous, charitable and honourable' queen of Castile. 'We have also received your help and gifts with your sergeant, the gentleman Guzmán, and with my servants and gentlemen. We accept them with many thanks . . . we are at your service; we will sacrifice our people and our lives for your honour . . . we do not have any other aid, apart from that of God, other than from your household and your royal majesty. To maintain ourselves in this capital, dear princes of sultans, we need many things and there is no other source of money or anything else of any use that is not the house of your royal majesty. May God prevent your royal highness from stopping to help or forgetting us.'[26]

For the next two years Isabella and Ferdinand switched the focus of the war to the eastern borders of Granada, where the city of Almería – once the Muslim kingdom's greatest port and capital of a major silk-producing zone – and bastions such as Baza and Guadix were the key to unlocking a region with easy, well-used sailing routes to and from north Africa. Zagal proved a wily foe and the men of this region were famed fighters, with Palencia claiming that the children of Baza were 'trained from childhood in the arts of war and forcibly dedicated to it in their constant fighting with the frontier Christians'.[27] In the first year they captured large stretches of territory, but failed to dislodge Zagal and his commanders from the most important towns and cities, who fought off the attackers with, among other things, cauldrons of boiling oil.[28]

As the summer of 1489 drew to an end, Isabella grew increasingly worried. The fighting season was meant to come to a close soon, yet the siege of Baza was dragging into its sixth month and morale was plummeting. Couriers rode post, swapping horses as they tired in the heat, taking just ten hours to transport messages to her. With the besiegers themselves talking of giving up, Isabella, once more, urged them to fight on. Her message to them was straightforward. 'If they agree to continue the siege of that city, as at the beginning all had agreed on, then she, with the help of God, would order that they were supplied with people, money, provisions and all that was necessary until the city fell,' reported Pulgar.[29] But she had to use threats to recruit more men from Seville and, as some of Ferdinand's troops began to abandon him, she hurriedly issued instructions to imprison deserters. Poor harvests and bad weather, meanwhile, disrupted her supply chains. 'There has been and is a great lack of goods in the camp,' she wrote, as she ordered extra supplies be sent along the muddy, slow roads to Baza. These had to be delivered 'before the water washes away the roads and makes it more difficult to transport things'.[30]

Zagal's men continued to hold out, however, and Isabella now decided it was time that she herself visited the front, arriving with her ladies and led by an escort of gentlemen – including a Genoese sailor called Christopher Columbus – and musicians. Her favourite daughter Isabella, by now a young lady herself and inseparable from her mother, rode with them.[31]

In the atmosphere of religious crusade and increasing royal authority, dissent or criticism of a war that was draining Castile's exchequer was dangerous, if not impossible. Direct criticism of Isabella or the war was either rarely made or done in secret or, at the least, almost never recorded on paper. Whereas court wits and popular poets had laughed at her predecessor, they now kept their tongues carefully guarded. The Hermandad and the Inquisition helped to set the new tone of controlled conformity. One of the few who publicly dared to criticise her in his satirical rhyming *coplas* was the poet Fernando de Vera, who soon found himself sentenced to death.[32] In the office of a friendly *escribano* – or notary – in Jerez, Vera read his barbed poetry to a small group, who presumably laughed heartily at his bitter critique of the queen. He painted Castilians as sheep who were being regularly 'fleeced' by Isabella. 'You have shorn so much wool that, if you felt like it, you could make a blanket to cover the whole of Spain,' he declaimed. 'Either you are trying to fool us, or just think we are stupid.' Vera was voicing the widespread anger at the burden of war taxes, especially in the cities. When news of his treasonous humour reached local authorities in the city, however, the *escribano* and others were arrested. Vera fled on a galleon to the Canary Islands and was handed a death sentence in his absence, while the man who had tipped him off was caught and executed. It was not until six years later that Isabella and Ferdinand, thanks to Vera's family connections, commuted the death sentence to galley service.

Pulgar claimed that the king's counsellors, who wanted him to give up on the siege, were too scared to say so in public – because the queen would not approve. They hoped that, by bringing Isabella to Baza, they could make her realise how difficult the situation was. 'Given the constant efforts of the queen to provide the camp with men, money and supplies, but not having achieved the expected fruit after all that time, they didn't dare counsel the king publicly as they did in private. They begged the queen to come to the camp so that she could see the constant fighting and the daily toll of deaths and injuries . . . and by seeing herself what she heard in reports, she would agree to up camp, leaving garrisons at points near to the city,' he reported.[33] Others worried that the presence of so many women would 'weaken the entire garrison'.[34]

Isabella's arrival, however, had the opposite effect. Tired, bored troops suddenly shook off six months of tedium and growing apathy. The impact on the Moors was even greater. They watched from the town's towers and walls as Isabella's noisy party arrived to the musical accompaniment of slide-trumpets, clarions, Italian trumpets, shawms, sackbuts, oboe-like *dulzainas* and drums. Over years of warfare, Isabella's frightening reputation as a fierce and implacable enemy had grown to such an extent that her mere presence was enough to shatter the resistance of Baza's Moors. Whereas, two and a half years earlier, the defenders of Málaga had blithely ignored her presence, Pulgar now swore that the queen's arrival silenced the Moors' guns for ever. 'We don't know whether it was because they thought the queen was coming to set up her own camp until the city was taken or for some other idea that they imagined, but it was amazing to see the sudden change in their attitude . . . As we were there and saw it, we can testify before God and the men who [also] saw it, that after the day in which the Queen entered the camp it seemed as if all the rigours of the battle, of the cruel spirits, of the enemy's wicked intentions, ended,' said Pulgar. 'The arrow and *espingarda* shots, and of all kinds of artillery, which just an hour earlier never ceased to fly from one side to the other, was not seen or heard again, nor were armed skirmishes repeated or the daily battles that had become the custom.'[35]

Negotiations were soon started and the city's commander was given permission to consult with Zagal in Guadix. Terms were reached quickly, with Zagal giving up all his territory – including Baza, Guadix and Almería – in exchange for considerable personal rights and *mudéjar* status (similar to the ancient Muslim communities of Old Castile) for his people.[36] There was little left for Isabella and Ferdinand to conquer now except for the city of Granada and the land around it, which was – at least in theory – due to be handed over under the terms of their treaties with Boabdil.

Isabella and Ferdinand proclaimed the end of the war. They had captured the major ports of Málaga and Almería and defeated Zagal. Boabdil, now the ruler of (almost) all that remained of Granada, was their vassal. On 8 January 1490, they wrote to Seville. 'After much effort, work and expense, it has pleased Our Lord in his mercy, to bring the war with the Kingdom of Granada to an end,' they said. 'King Boabdil, who currently holds the city of Granada, has agreed to hand over to us and our people the said city. We have sent our messengers to him and a reply and agreement on this will take no more than 20 days.'[37] More than seven centuries of Muslim rule in Spain was over. Or so, mistakenly, they thought.

23

The Tudors

Medina del Campo, 14 March 1489

Isabella waited for the English envoys in the grandest room of her palace at Medina del Campo. A cloth-of-gold canopy had been erected above where she now sat with Ferdinand as the awestruck ambassadors were brought in a torchlight procession through the sharp, early-evening chill of the streets of the great wool and textile trading town of the *meseta*. Isabella's war against the Moors was heading towards a triumphant climax, as English volunteers like Lord Scales must have informed King Henry VII. Unlike the English king's nascent Tudor dynasty, there were no longer any rivals to the crown that Isabella had definitively secured with Juana la Beltraneja's forced retirement into a convent. Isabella was determined to avoid a repeat of the kind of embarrassment she had suffered during a previous English ambassador's visit to her court early in 1477. On that occasion, early in the civil war, a scaffold that had been erected for the envoy, Thomas Langton, collapsed mid-speech – though the phlegmatic ambassador had picked himself up and continued as if nothing had happened.[1]

A court that was mostly either on the move or at war was not a place for daily displays of grandeur and luxury – or for the expense that came with that. But, when it was needed, Isabella ensured that her Castilian court gained a reputation for flamboyant hospitality. It was a sure way to transmit the message that this was a wealthy and powerful monarchy, able to compete in magnificence with other European courts. Her great crusade against the Moors of Granada had already enhanced Castile's standing across Christendom but, now that it was almost over, she and Ferdinand were starting to look beyond the frontiers of their joint realms towards other countries that might become allies. Henry VII had sent his ambassadors here to negotiate just such an alliance, which would be cemented by an engagement between Isabella's three-year-old (and fourth) daughter, Catherine of Aragon, and the English king's own two-year-old son and heir, Prince Arthur. She wanted them to go home impressed. The ambassadors Dr Thomas Savage, a future archbishop of York, and Sir Richard Nanfan were astonished by the hospitality they received.[2] 'People speak of the honour done to ambassadors in England; certainly it is not to be compared to the honour which is done to the ambassadors in the kingdom of Castile, and especially in the time of this noble king and queen,' wrote their herald, Roger Machado.[3]

Just as Isabella had known when to shed the black robes of mourning and dazzle the people of Segovia with her brilliant, regal robes, so she now also indulged in blatant power-dressing. A starstruck Machado reported that the queen wore a cloth-of-gold robe covered by 'a riding hood of black velvet, all slashed in large holes, so as to show under the said velvet the cloth of gold in which she was dressed'. The hood was decorated with finger-sized, oblong-shaped blocks of gold thread encrusted with jewels 'so rich that no one has ever seen the like'. A white leather girdle with a pouch – which Machado saw as an odd, manly touch – was decorated with a 'balass ruby [from Persia] the size of a tennis ball, five rich diamonds and other precious stones the size of a bean'.[4]

The queen's jewellery spoke even more eloquently of wealth and power.

She wore on her neck a rich gold necklace composed entirely of white and red roses, each rose being adorned with a large jewel. Besides this she had two ribbons suspended on each side of her breast, adorned with large diamonds, balass and other rubies, pearls, and various other jewels of great value to the number of a hundred or more. Over all this dress she wore a short cloak of fine crimson satin furred with ermine, very handsome in appearance and very brilliant. It was thrown on [nonchalantly] cross-wise over her left side. Her head was uncovered, excepting only a little *coiffe de plaisance* at the back of her head without anything else.[5]

Isabella would have been pleased to know that Machado was minutely noting down all he saw – and all she wore during the feasts, jousts, bullfights and dances celebrated over the next two weeks – in order to report back to Henry VII. He even produced an estimate for the value of the jewellery she was wearing – some 200,000 crowns of gold. Isabella's family and ladies-in-waiting were also magnificently attired, but no one was allowed to outshine the queen. Strict sumptuary laws regulated everything from the use of silk and brocades to the gold- or silver-plating of swords and spurs by anyone outside the royal family. The report included descriptions of the elaborate ceremonials at feasts and, crucially, the seating arrangements at formal events which showed (by whoever was closest to the sovereigns – with Cardinal Mendoza always near to Isabella) where power in the court lay.

France had long been a Castilian ally, but Isabella was ready to change that, especially as her husband's kingdom of Aragon was continually fighting the French on its borders. England, whose monarchs had long styled themselves kings of France (and who still maintained sovereignty over the area around Calais) was a perfect ally. The ambassadors were, like much of Europe, intrigued by the relationship between Isabella and Ferdinand. It was now that the herald Machado produced his convoluted explanation of how Castile could be ruled jointly by the royal couple. 'Perhaps some may blame me that I speak of "monarchs" [in the plural], and some people may be astonished, and say, "How! Are there two monarchs in Castile?"' observed the herald Machado. 'No [I say], but I write "monarchs" because the king is king on account of the queen, by right of marriage, and because they call themselves "monarchs", and superscribe their letters "From the King and Queen", for she is the heiress [of the throne].'⁶

The journey to Medina del Campo, a sprawling walled town overlooked by an imposing castle, had been long and arduous. The stormy, dangerous Bay of Biscay had twice driven the English emissaries back to Southampton with a blast of wind toppling their ship over sideways so that it took in 'so much water that she was quite under water and all on one side for a while, with the great sail almost entirely steeped in the sea'. They had sheltered in the port town of Laredo while snowstorms painted the Cantabrian *cordillera* above them white and blocked the roads. When they finally set out across the mountains and sought somewhere to stay the night they found themselves confronted by an irascible Spanish landlady who ordered them back into the cold for being 'so bold as to come into her house without her leave'. After being bawled out as 'great devils' and 'bawdy villains' she allowed them back in and they spent an uncomfortable night before rising early and fleeing to Medina del Campo, where Isabella had arranged cosy lodgings hung with fine tapestries.⁷

Isabella's first encounter with the Englishmen was as carefully stage-managed as each of the meetings that would follow over the next seventeen days. A gaggle of Grandees, bishops and 'great persons' accompanied the starstruck ambassadors from their lodgings as they travelled towards the palace. Isabella and Ferdinand sat on separate bench seats. 'The Queen was accompanied by thirty-seven great ladies and maidens of noble blood all richly dressed in the fashion of the country, and in cloth of gold with several other rich [materials] which would be too tedious for me to relate,' observed Machado. There was formal hand-kissing and speech-making, though the English visitors failed to understand the mangled Latin of the ancient Diego de Muros, bishop of Ciudad Rodrigo, who spoke on behalf of the Spanish sovereigns. 'The good bishop was so old, and had lost all his teeth, that what he said could only with great difficulty be heard,' said Machado.[8] It was not until two o'clock in the morning that they were finally led off back to their quarters, with the promise of another meeting the following day.

The next day's meeting was more businesslike. Isabella's quest to have children and, especially, to produce an heir, had been fraught – and had been interrupted by the rigours of her nomadic lifestyle and commitment to planning for and provisioning her armies. But she now had an heir, Juan, and four daughters. While she had longed for a boy, and showed particular devotion to little Juan, she could not be faulted for her attentiveness to her daughters. These she kept close, raising them according to a set of criteria that were at once strict and conservative on personal morality and public image, while groundbreaking and progressive in terms of education. Their training, in Latin, the lives of saints, music and proper religious behaviour, imparted by foreign tutors who had drunk deeply from Italian humanism, was not completely altruistic. Her daughters were also political assets, as she would show the following year by marrying the eldest – Isabella – into the Portuguese royal family. Her other daughters held out the promise of three more alliances sealed by marriage. 'If your highness gives us two or three more daughters in 20 years' time you will have the pleasure of seeing your children and grandchildren on all the thrones of Europe,' a prescient Pulgar had told her.[9]

Henry VII was deeply excited by the thought of his heir marrying the daughter of such a formidable woman, even claiming that he would be willing to give up half of his kingdom if Catherine was like her mother.[10] The founder of the Tudor dynasty needed the match more than Isabella and Ferdinand. His crown was still precarious, with threats both from within and from abroad. Little Catherine offered not just an ally on France's southern flank, but one with influence in Rome and whose approval of his son's suitability as a husband provided a valuable display of confidence. The commitment, in any case, would never be considered cast-iron. Such engagements could be, and frequently were, broken when a better bidder appeared.

Isabella was in no hurry for the wedding treaty to be closed. She planned, instead, to woo the ambassadors slowly, continuing the display of magnificence that had started the previous evening. On this occasion, Machado reported, Isabella was dressed 'in a rich woven cloth of gold, and above it, as before, a hood of black velvet, and above that a line of beaten gold strewed with red and white roses of beaten gold, each rose being adorned with rich jewels. She had on her neck a rich necklace decorated with large rubies and carbuncles, and of great value.' Now it was time to start showing off her family. Ten-year-old Juan and eighteen-year-old Isabella – accompanied by four maids – were ushered in, with Catherine kept tantalisingly out of sight for the moment. 'The prince was dressed in a robe of rich crimson velvet, furred with ermine, and on his head a black hat after the French fashion with a *cornette* of purple very narrow all like the branch of a tree,' wrote Machado. 'And the Infanta was dressed in a kirtle of cloth of gold, and over it a robe in the fashion of the country with a long train of very rich green velvet. She wore a head-dress made of gold thread and black silk in the form of a net, all adorned with pearls and other precious stones.' Hands were kissed, more speeches made, and a viewing of little Catherine promised for later.[11]

On the Sunday, four days later, they were invited to the royal chapel for compline, the evening prayers, before withdrawing to a large salon, where there was music and young members of the court were already dancing. The younger Isabella performed with one of their Portuguese dance teachers. Machado wrote:

Princess donna Isabella . . . came very handsomely and richly dressed and sat down beside the King her father at his right hand side, at a little distance from him. Certainly it was a rich sight to see the Queen and her daughter [so] dressed, and twenty-six ladies and maidens all daughters of great noblemen, most of them dressed in cloth of gold, velvet, and silk, very handsomely. The Queen was all dressed in cloth of gold, she wore a head-dress of gold thread, and a fine necklace adorned with huge pearls, and large and very fine diamonds in the centre. Then the sovereigns commanded the princess their daughter to dance. And she immediately rose and went and took a young lady who was Portuguese . . . This young lady was very gorgeously dressed and danced with her.[12]

At the jousting, a few days later, Machado found Queen Isabella wearing a Spanish mantilla 'all spangled with lozenges of crimson and black velvet, and on each lozenge was a large pearl . . . [and] a rich balass ruby the size of a beechnut . . . no man ever saw anything equal to it'.[13] Two rubies 'the size of a pigeon's egg' and a large pearl worth 12,000 crowns hung as pendants from her head-dress. Machado was overwhelmed. 'So rich was the dress she wore that day that there is no man who can well imagine what could be the value of it,' he said.

A casual, but obviously stage-managed, encounter with Catherine and Isabella's third daughter, six-year-old María, followed soon afterwards. Isabella and Ferdinand, together with the elder three children, took the ambassadors into a gallery hung with their best tapestries (many of which must have travelled with them on mule trains) where they encountered the separate 'junior' court built around the youngest children. 'The Queen was very richly dressed. And all her daughters were similarly dressed, and the said two daughters, the Infanta donna Maria, and the Infanta donna Catherine, princess of England, had fourteen maidens . . . all of them dressed in cloth of gold, and all of them daughters of noblemen,' reported Machado. 'The eldest of them was not more than fourteen years old.' Catherine was too young to dance, but little María took the floor with 'a young lady of her age and size, and led her to dance'. There was no mention of the female court midget whom Isabella had hired to entertain her daughters.

The following day the ambassadors witnessed what was already a quintessential part of Spanish royal fiestas, the bullfight. This was a mounted affair, with riders attacking the bulls with lances. It was a gory spectacle that Isabella disliked, not out of concern for the bull but because men sometimes died. One of the few things she was squeamish about was the unnecessary loss of Christian blood.[14] The ambassadors also saw mock skirmishes and running with dogs 'in the way they fought with the Saracens [that is, the Moors]'. Machado spent much of his time watching Isabella, who had little Catherine with her, marvelling at how affectionate and attentive she was. 'It was beautiful to see how the queen held up her youngest daughter,' he noted.[15]

Two days later, on 27 March, the Treaty of Medina del Campo was signed. England and Spain were allies, with France now discarded.[16] The ambassadors stayed a few days longer in Medina, heavy with gifts for themselves – including a Spanish war-horse, a smaller Moorish 'jennet' horse, a pair of mules, yards of silk and sixty marks of silver each. First, however, they rode out of Medina for 'about two bow-shots', accompanying Isabella and her family as the peripatetic court took off again, accompanied by more than a hundred nobles, knights, bishops and 'squires'. Ferdinand and Juan rode ahead, while Isabella led her own group of daughters, ladies and maids-in-waiting. Perhaps, as she rode across the *meseta*, Isabella felt a warm glow of revenge, recalling just how offensive France's ambassadors had been when they came to seek her own hand in marriage. Since then she had stuck to her opinion that France was 'abhorrent to our Castilian nation'. Her husband must have been even more delighted to have Castile definitively on his side in Aragon's long-running feud with the French.

24

Granada Falls

Moclín, May 1490

The twelve shiny Castilian *doblas* that Isabella handed to Juan were a mark that her son and heir, who was about to turn twelve, was growing up and ready to ride to war. The heavy gold coins were for Juan to give away at the religious service to mark his new status as a *caballero*, or knight. That had been confirmed at a solemn ceremony by the Acequia Gorda – one of the main channels of a complex irrigation network built and maintained by Granada's Moors – as Juan rode with her husband while he prepared to lay waste to the agricultural land around the city in May 1490. There the young prince had been formally knighted and handed his chain mail, dagger, helmet and campaign boots. Juan could now ride with his father and learn about war from him, though he was not expected to fight in the front line. Until now Isabella had overseen her son's upbringing and education and would continue as his 'tutor, carer and legitimate administrator' for another two years, but her work with him was mostly done.[1]

She must have felt proud, not just of her son but of the legacy she was preparing for him as future sovereign of a united Spain. Isabella had taken an unprecedentedly firm grip on the crown. Her unique alliance with Ferdinand had created a dual monarchy that not only spanned most of the Iberian peninsula but had enlarged its territory further in Granada while also proving to be Christendom's most effective defender in its continuing battle with expansionist Islam. A parallel battle to purify Castile by imposing order and justice, chasing down supposed heretics among the *conversos* and reforming the church was already under way – though there was much more to do. Juan would be the heir to all that. Little wonder that, as messianic predictions continued to sweep through Iberia,[2] many saw him as the promised Lion King – the man who would finish the task started by his parents and drive the Muslim heresy out of north Africa and, eventually, out of the Holy Land itself.[3] In three years' time, too, Juan would be old enough to marry, give Isabella grandchildren and ensure the continuity of her work for generations to come.

This was not the only major family event of the year. A few weeks earlier her eldest daughter Isabella had finally married the heir to the crown of Portugal – the now fifteen-year-old Prince Afonso, whose father João II had inherited the throne shortly after the end of the war with Isabella in 1481. The marriage fulfilled the terms of the Alcáçovas Treaty that had brought the civil war to an end, cementing a lasting peace with Portugal and keeping Juana la Beltraneja – who still obstinately signed letters as 'I, the Queen'[4] – firmly in her place. The partying in Seville for her daughter's proxy 'wedding by powers' (when Portuguese representatives came to confirm the final terms of marriage) that spring and her eventual send-off for the full wedding ceremony in Portugal had lasted fifteen days. Isabella had purchased an impressive trousseau and spent freely on the celebrations. There was jousting, mummery and tilting at the ring, with young Juan performing both on the stage and in the tiltyard. Her daughter's husband was five years her junior, but the younger Isabella had, from the ages of ten to twelve, spent two years with him when they had been confined together in Portugal under the terms of the peace treaty that ended their war. The partying in Seville was, in part, the celebration of a kingdom on the rise which was provoking admiration, respect and fear in other parts of Europe. Isabella's personal reputation was also soaring. Two years had gone by since the fall of Málaga and, though the war was still not finished, it was only a matter of time before her crusade to oust the Moors was over.[5]

Isabella rode from Moclín, where she had been enjoying the company of Boabdil's little son Ahmed *el infantico*, back towards Córdoba in June of 1490. Granada itself, the most populous city in the peninsula, was not yet hers. Boabdil had proved as unreliable an ally to the Spanish monarchs as he had been to his own father and uncle. They had expected him to accept the gift of the region based on Baza and Guadix in exchange for the keys to the Alhambra and the city. Yet magnificent Granada, the symbol of centuries of Muslim history, was a difficult prize to give up. Not only was Boabdil reluctant to hand over the palace complex that his Nasrid dynasty had so lovingly built, he was also aware that the city-folk and thousands of refugees who had flocked there over the previous half-dozen years were not ready to accept what, for them, was the end of history – the surrender of a place whose soil held the remains of thirty generations of forebears. Rather than give up Granada, Boabdil now made war again.[6]

The monarchs were not in a hurry. As hostilities broke out again in May 1490 Zagal himself was pressed into service, willingly turning against his rebellious nephew. One of the cleverer pieces of trickery of that summer's campaign saw his men take a fortified tower by pretending to be driving cattle and Christian captives towards Granada. They asked for shelter in the tower and, once the doors were unlocked, stormed in and captured those manning it – who were then sent running off to the city of Granada. It was not until April the following year, however, that the campaign to take the city itself received the money, men and might it needed. Isabella, never quite as patient as her husband, took extreme measures, issuing a wide-ranging call-up as she sought overwhelming force. She also knew that this siege might last and one of her most important decisions was to construct something far more solid than the usual siege camp of tents and roughly made huts. The Santa Fe camp, set up outside Granada, was a small fortified town in itself, attached to a much larger camp of tents surrounded by ditches and barriers, with buildings that were designed to remain standing after the war. In the space of just a few months a square, white-walled town appeared within sight of Granada, with towers and other defences that would enable it to operate through the winter. It was a symbol of her determination and sent a message to those in the city that Isabella, Ferdinand and their armies were here to stay. Isabella was so proud of her little improvised city that she had a tapestry made of the scene and sent to the court in Portugal. Just as at Málaga, she could no longer bear to be away from the action. She moved to Santa Fe in early July, two months after her husband had begun setting up the siege.[7] Again, her front-line hospital came with her and one of her ladies, Juana de Mendoza, was put in charge of supplying it.

As at any military camp, daily life in Santa Fe mixed occasional moments of danger and heroism with long spells of boredom and frustration punctuated by infighting, self-inflicted accidents and even desertions. On the night of 14 July 1491, Isabella and her second daughter Juana had not yet moved into a proper house and were still sleeping in the spacious tent that the Marquess of Cadiz had lent them. It was a large, Moorish-style *alfaneque* campaign tent, another element of Arab culture that had been effortlessly taken up by Christian Spaniards, and was the most luxurious in the whole camp. 'The Queen ordered one of her maids to move a candle that was preventing her from sleeping from one end of the tent to the other,' wrote Bernáldez. 'Either something fell on the candle, or the flame [somehow] reached the tent itself, which caught fire and began to erupt into flames.' The blaze immediately spread through the tents and primitive thatched huts near by. 'When the Queen noticed, she fled to the tent of the king, who was asleep, to warn him, and they rode off together on horses,' said Bernáldez.[8]

As her children also ran from the fire and men started fighting the flames, the Marquess of Cadiz rode out with his men to form a defensive line in case the camp was under attack. Isabella was clear about what had happened. 'The queen said that she only harboured one opinion, which was that the fire had been started by mistake, by one of her own ladies,' said Bernáldez.[9] Silk curtains, priceless tapestries and bedding had all gone up in flames. One version of the story has Isabella herself grabbing her secret documents before rushing out with them in her arms, the *infanta* Juana – her second daughter – behind her.[10] The monarchs now speeded up the construction of the buildings at Santa Fe, though Isabella and Juana would have to wait some time before their house was ready in a camp where, in the space of just a few months, historic decisions that would affect the future of Castile, Spain and as yet undiscovered parts of the world would be taken.

Sieges are dull, and only the idea that an epic moment in the history of Christendom was being written kept spirits high. Inside the camp, poets and priests turned the almost daily brushes with the enemy into heroic feats of chivalry magnified in their greatness by the glorious prize that awaited. The defenders, meanwhile, sallied out to raid the Christian camps and supply trains and were so successful that the city ended up with an abundance of cheap meat. But each raid cost the lives of some of those who, with little to lose, were prepared to fight almost to the last. And with no reinforcements, the dwindling numbers of soldiers available to defend the city became at least as much of a problem as the lack of food that had brought Málaga to its knees. Only a tenth of the original mounted fighting men were left after eight months.[11] Many fled across the Sierra Nevada and into the impenetrable, steep-sided valleys and sierras of the nearby Alpujarra region, a route that also allowed provisions of oil, cereals, animal feed and dried fruits to reach the besieged city.

Isabella herself seems to have sparked the biggest battle between defenders and besiegers, after asking that she be taken closer to Granada so that she could study the city better. Accompanied by Ferdinand, Juan and Juana, she rode into the hamlet of La Zubia, which was little more than a collection of huts. There she dismounted and climbed up to the second storey of a house to look out at Granada and, perched above it, the rust-red walls of the Alhambra complex. Such a risky outing by almost the entire royal family required the company of a large force of cavalry and footsoldiers, who spread out in a defensive formation in front of La Zubia. The Moors may have realised that the monarchs were close or simply decided that a force that size was a threat to the city. Either way, a similar-sized force soon rode out from Granada, towing cannon behind them. Isabella and her daughter, tradition has it, spent much of the ensuing battle on their knees praying, though Isabella's appetite for chivalric tales suggests that she might have preferred to be watching her knights in action. Whatever her vantage point, she would have seen up to 600 of Granada's defenders die that day as 'not a single Christian knight there failed to plunge his lance into a Moor'. The Christians claimed victory and Isabella vowed to build a convent on the spot she had watched from. A group of besiegers were then captured as they tried to ambush those who went to gather up the dead and injured. This time the Moors used the sophisticated network of irrigation channels in the fields outside the city to flood the land and trap them.[12]

As winter closed in, Isabella's decision to build a town from which they could besiege Granada seemed increasingly sensible. The siege had started in April 1491. It was still going in November as the nights shortened, temperatures dropped closer to freezing and the white blanket covering the Sierra Nevada spread wider and lower down the mountainside. 'Winter arrived, with the snow that had fallen on the mountains cutting off communications with the Alpujarra,' explained the anonymous Muslim chronicler. 'That produced such a shortage of foodstuffs in the markets of Granada that many began to suffer hunger and the number of beggars increased dramatically.' With the besiegers now controlling the fertile lands outside the city walls, the Muslims were unable to sow their fields and it became clear that their supplies would be even more meagre the following year.[13]

Hernando de Baeza describes a scene in which Boabdil, warned that the Christians were preparing an all-out assault on the city, prepare for a definitive battle by taking his army into the field in front of Granada. The king donned his armour and asked his mother Fatima for her blessing. He then went through his normal pre-battle ritual of kissing the women and children of his household, including his sister, his wife and one of his smaller sons and asked them to forgive any grievances they held against him. When his frightened mother demanded to know what was happening, Boabdil explained that this might be the final battle, with all involved fighting to the death. Her reply was to scold him. 'So, my son, who will look after your sad mother, wife, sister and children, relatives and servants as well as this city and all the other places that you rule over? How will you explain to God that you left them so poorly protected, giving the order that we must all die by the sword or end up as captives? Think carefully about what you are doing.'[14]

'My lady, it is far better to die once than to die many times while still alive,' Boabdil replied.

'That would be true, my son, if only you died and the rest of us were saved and the city freed,' the weeping mother retorted.[15] 'But such a huge loss would not be a task well done.' Baeza must have heard this version of the story from the Moorish king himself, though nothing is known about the battle that followed, if there was one. Either way, the story illustrates the problem faced by Boabdil. He must now decide whether Muslim Granada should die fighting, or seek favourable terms for surrender.

As supplies ran short in the frozen city, a group of senior Granadans went to see Boabdil. 'None of our Muslim brothers who live on the [north] coast of Africa have come to help us, despite the requests that we have sent,' they reminded him.[16] 'In the meantime our enemies have erected buildings which they live in and from which they can attack us. As their strength grows, ours diminishes. They receive aid from their lands, and we have no aid at all. Winter has started and that means that the enemy forces have been dispersed, are much weaker and have suspended their attacks on us. If we negotiate with the enemy now, they will accept our proposals and agree to our demands. But if we wait until spring, their army will come together again and, on account of our weakness and lack of provisions, they will no longer be ready to accept our demands.' Boabdil listened carefully and acquiesced. In fact, he had been negotiating since September, keeping the talks secret in case the people of Granada turned on him. The constant delivery of messages and gifts to the captive Prince Ahmed in Moclín provided an excuse for the negotiators to ride back and forth from the city. The negotiations contained, as always, two elements: the terms for the general population, and those for the negotiators themselves and the other elite families of the city. 'I ask for very little,' wrote one of them, Abulcacim el-Muleh.[17] 'Please ask their majesties if I can have the fish market, with all the rights that go with it, and if not the shoemaker's square and rights over the slaughter of cattle.' He also wanted 10,000 *castellanos* (the gold coin valued at 465 *maravedís*) each for himself and another negotiator, Aben Comixa, as well as 30,000 for Boabdil. In the meantime, Isabella and Ferdinand answered their requests for the expensive cloth that they were used to dressing in. There was olive, red and purple cloth from Florence, thick black, green and blue silks, crimson from London, green and black velvets, brocades and other materials ordered up for the jackets, dresses, gowns, cloaks, hats, hoods and leggings of Granada's proud aristocracy. These were probably delivered by the translator Baeza or by their chief negotiator Hernando de Zafra, who made frequent visits to the Alhambra before an agreement was finally signed at Santa Fe on 25 November 1491.[18] Boabdil promised to hand over the city at the beginning of January, on condition that Granada's Moors would enjoy almost exactly the same rights as the old *mudéjar* communities of Castile – and that both he and the city's elites receive preferential treatment.

A Granada poet remembered the moment – and the whole war – with shame, recalling that their hopes of rescue by fellow Muslims from north Africa had been dashed.[19]

The Christians attacked us from all sides in a vast torrent, company after company
Smiting us with zeal and resolution like locusts in the multitude of their cavalry and weapons.

Nevertheless, for a long time we withstood their armies and killed
group after group of them,

Though their horsemen increased at every moment, whereas
ours were in a state of diminution and scarcity,

Hence, when we became weak, they camped in our territory and
smote us, town by town,

Bringing many large cannons they demolished the impregnable
walls of the towns,

Attacking them energetically during the siege for many months
and days; with zeal and determination.

So when our cavalry and foot soldiers had perished and we
observed that no rescue was forthcoming from our brethren,

And when our victuals had diminished and our lot had become
hard indeed, we complied, against our will, with their demands,
out of fear of disgrace . . .

The Moors had decided to surrender the city because 'for lack of
victuals, they ate horse and dogs and cats', an English chronicler
noted approvingly, before adding a colourful, if inaccurate, description of the exotic booty yielded up to Isabella and her husband.[20]
'In one of the halls where the king and queen of Granada lived, the
walls of the hall and chamber were of marble, crystal and jasper, set
with precious stones, and more over there was found great and innu-
merable riches.' France sent an ambassador to watch the handover
and several Italians also travelled to witness the momentous event.[21]
Isabella's crusade was over – at least on Castilian soil, for her ambitions also extended to north Africa – and the marriage pledges made
at Cervera, when she was just a seventeen-year-old bride-to-be and
potential future ruler of Castile, had been met. Christendom's frontiers, shrinking elsewhere, had been extended to the south. It was, by
the measures of her time, an epic achievement.

Handover

Granada, 2 January 1492

Isabella had always liked the Arab style of dress, but the gowns, cloaks and slippers that she wore for comfort or warmth were mostly kept for the intimacy of her own rooms. On this historic day, 2 January 1492, however, she deliberately chose to dress up for public display *a la morisca* – in the Moorish style.[1] She had picked out a silk and brocade *aljuba*, with its tight, buttoned-up upper top, long sleeves and knee-length skirt. Her husband, children and many of the nobles who accompanied them as they prepared to ride into Granada, were also dressed in *aljubas* and loose, pinafore-style *marlota* cloaks that tied at the back. This was a day for triumphant celebration, and an excuse to forget the dark mourning clothes that they had worn since news arrived that her daughter Isabella had been widowed when her young husband, Prince Afonso of Portugal, fell from his horse after just eight months of marriage.

Boabdil rode out of the Alhambra on a mule, accompanied by fifty of his retainers, his head held high but his face reflecting the tragedy of defeat. When he encountered Isabella, the two monarchs performed a simple, pre-established ritual in which Boabdil would play the humble defeated king and Isabella the magnanimous victor. Boabdil doffed his hat, took one foot out of a stirrup and grabbed the pommel of his saddle as if he was about to dismount and kiss her hand. Isabella, who was riding with her son Juan, signalled that this was not necessary and he should stay in his saddle. 'She spoke to him . . . and consoled him and offered her friendship and help, and he thanked her greatly and replied that there was nothing in the world that he wanted for himself, but that those he wished things for were his mother, the queen, and the princes who were his brothers,' wrote one observer. Isabella followed the form agreed in negotiations during which Boabdil and his mother had insisted, and she had personally agreed, that he avoid the humiliation of having to kiss their hands.[2]

In the meantime, Isabella awaited the appearance of the 400 captive Christians who had been held inside the Alhambra. Just as at Málaga, they appeared in their chains, following three crosses and a statue of the Virgin Mary as they intoned the psalm Benedictus Dominus Deus Israel. 'The queen received them with great reverence and ordered that they be taken to the fortress at Santa Fe,' said Bernardo del Roi, a Venetian who had come to witness the great moment. There were tears as, trudging past the assembled army, some prisoners were recognised by their own relatives. At the same time, the Christians handed their most important captive, the *infantico* Prince Ahmed – now about nine years old – back to the mother he had not seen for most of his young life.[3] This formed part of the surrender deal. With Granada in their hands, Isabella and Ferdinand no longer needed him – though Isabella would try not to lose contact with the child whose education she had overseen from afar and to whom she felt such strong, almost maternal, ties.

By now the entire Christian army was paraded in front of the city, on land across the River Genil. From there Isabella looked up at the walls of the Alhambra palace and saw a cross being raised on one of its most impressive towers, the Tower of Comares. Alongside it appeared the flag of St James – also called 'the Moorslayer', because of a legend that he had miraculously led a ninth-century Christian army to victory over the Muslims at Clavijo, northern Spain – and the royal flags of Isabella and Ferdinand. 'Granada! Granada! For King Ferdinand and Queen Isabella!' the soldiers shouted. 'When the Queen saw the cross, the members of her chapel began to sing the Te Deum Laudamus. The joy was such that everyone wept,' wrote one chronicler. Trumpets were blown and cannon fired as the city's inhabitants started their new life as *mudéjares*, Muslim subjects of Castile's Christian queen.[4] None of Isabella's forebears had been so powerful – though this was just the start of what would become a momentous year for Spain and Christendom.

A formal handing over of the keys to the city followed, with these passing through the hands of Prince Juan as the future king eventually destined to rule over the city.[5] With that, Boabdil went on his way, heading to the lands in the Alpujarra – the steep, south-facing foothills of the Sierra Nevada – that had been given to him as recompense for surrendering his kingdom. Legend has it that he stopped to weep and view the city that his forebears had ruled for two and a half centuries for one last time from a spot that became known as the Pass of the Moor's Sigh. By the time Washington Irving, the nineteenth-century American writer who romanticised the fall of Granada, arrived here the hill leading up to the pass was referred to as 'La Cuesta de las Lágrimas', the Slope of Tears. Irving recorded a tale in which Boabdil's mother Fatima ticked him off. 'You do well to weep as a woman over what you could not defend as a man,' she said.

Isabella did not yet dare enter the city itself. In fact, the surrender agreement explicitly banned the Christian army from entering Granada to begin with, though its walls, gates and turrets would have to be occupied, thereby ensuring military control of the city. Boabdil's negotiators had begged that the Christian takeover should be done gradually, starting with the Alcazaba and the rest of the Alhambra – which could be entered through its eastern gates without passing through the city itself. 'You should by no means enter or leave the city by any other route,' one of Boabdil's negotiators told them.[6]

The original agreement with Boabdil had foreseen the entry of Christian troops into Granada on 6 January. But five days before that he had sent word that he was about to lose control of the city. Some 500 Muslim hostages from its best families, who had agreed to be held at Santa Fe until the handover was completed, had left on 1 January, but the sight of them going aroused the ire of those opposed to surrender. 'So the Moorish king sent a message to our king and queen and agreed that the very same night they would secretly send someone to take it [the Alhambra] over, because just as soon as the Moors saw that the Christians had taken it, they would lower their heads, but that if they were seen coming to the city to take it over during the day that would provoke trouble and danger,' an eyewitness named Cifuentes wrote.[7]

Within an hour, Gutierre de Cárdenas – the same, loyal official who had carried the sword of royal justice before Isabella on the day she proclaimed herself queen – was ordered to prepare his men to move out at night towards the Alhambra. 'He left at midnight, with a number of officials, people who were standing guard and footsoldiers, *espingardero* gunmen, lancers and bowmen,' explained Cifuentes, who joined the expedition.[8] They were then taken secretly, on a route avoiding the best-known roads and paths, to the open countryside by the Alixares part of the Alhambra, out of sight in the eastern angle of the Alhambra mount. A gate was opened, and they were able to enter the palace complex without the city's populace noticing. 'We entered just as day was breaking,'[9] said Cifuentes. Most were stunned by what they saw. 'Granada is the most wonderful and amazing thing in the world in its grandeur, strength and beauty, with the [Royal Alcázar] palace in Seville seeming like little more than a thatched cottage beside the Alhambra,' the letter-writer Cifuentes said.[10] 'This palace is so huge that the biggest section of it is larger than the entire palace in Seville,' agreed the Venetian del Roi, who had accompanied the expedition.

Boabdil had waited for them in his rooms at the Comares Tower. The senior Castilian nobles, having kissed his hands, were handed the keys to the Alhambra's gates and asked to sign a document showing that this had been done. Boabdil and his men then left through one of the gates into the city, while Christian soldiers took up positions along the walls and in the towers. An altar was erected and, amid tears, the soldiers and some of the Christian captives who had been held in the Alhambra celebrated mass in the elaborate surroundings of the palaces built so lovingly by generations of Nasrid kings. By the end of the day the Count of Tendilla had installed himself in the Alhambra with a force of 6,000 men, while Boabdil rode out of the city to meet Isabella and Ferdinand and leave for ever.[11]

Isabella and Ferdinand then returned to Santa Fe, staying faithful to their promise not to march boastfully through the city and making sure their troops entered the Alhambra via its back gates.[12] It is difficult to believe, however, that in the following days they did not also surreptitiously visit the Alhambra to view their long-desired prize. The palace complex that they discovered now, or on their return visits, was both bigger and far more colourfully decorated than it would eventually become after centuries of Christian neglect and vandalism added to the ravages of time and nature. 'I don't think there is anything to equal it in the whole of Europe,' wrote Münzer. 'Everything is so superb, magnificent and exquisitely built that one might think oneself in paradise.' Previous Muslim rulers had failed to maintain some of the numerous palaces and gardens of the enormous hilltop complex, but the impression was still of overwhelming splendour. The marble, mosaics and silver lamps of the Royal Great Mosque, for example, had won the praise of Muslim poets and the palaces that have since disappeared included that of the Abencerrajes and the one, adorned with silk furnishings, that was soon occupied by the man who would stay to run the city, the Count of Tendilla.[13]

Isabella was used to the Royal Alcázar in Seville, but must still have been impressed by the subtle play between ornamental intricacy and architectural simplicity in the Nasrid palaces. This was meant to be a place of contemplation. 'Enter with composure, speak thoughtfully, be short on words and leave in peace,' read one piece of Arabic script. Glistening marble was everywhere, inside and outside, in columns and on the floors in great big fifteen-foot-long slabs. Crystalline water moved gently through manicured gardens of lemon trees and myrtles and into palace bedrooms through a system of pipes and channels the likes of which Münzer had never seen before. 'And a bath house – oh what a marvel! – with a vaulted roof.' The baths had rooms for hot, warm and cold water.[14]

Ceilings were painted in vivid colours. 'All the palaces and annexes have superb coffered ceilings made of gold, lapis lazuli, ivory and cypress, in such a variety of styles that one cannot begin to explain or write about them,' said Münzer. The *muqarna* ceilings of interlaced stucco or cedar had honeycombed designs which seemed to float above the heads of those who walked below them.[15] Even the stone creatures guarding a fountain in the Court of the Lions were brightly painted. The night sky of stars was mirrored in the glassy surfaces of courtyard pools, while the white marble slabs in the Court of the Myrtles glowed softly under the moon, radiating a soft, dreamlike light.[16]

The Generalife gardens would become one of Isabella's favourite places. Münzer recalled 'a truly royal and famous garden, with springs, pools and charming little channels of water', while another visitor saw it as a place to 'enjoy a life, in repose and tranquillity'. A gushing waterfall fell ten *braças*, or arm-lengths, into a tank, splashing those who came close with cooling droplets of water. Rabbits hopped among the myrtles and water was everywhere, brought in over an aqueduct and cleverly distributed by pipes and channels. These flowed off towards the Alhambra and were also cut into the steps and stone banisters that ran down an outside staircase called the Escalera de Agua. The game here was to wait for a group of people to walk down the steps, then switch the flow of water so that it flooded over their feet and hands. A similar trick could be played in a patio orchard that could be silently flooded so that, according to one Italian visitor, 'whoever is in it, without knowing how, sees the water rise beneath his feet, so that he gets all soaked and then the water disappears without anyone coming into sight'.[17]

Isabella and Ferdinand had not only captured the greatest piece of Islamic architecture in Europe, but their status across the continent was now unassailable. Christendom had, at last, struck back at Muslim encroachment and could start to hope that its fortunes were finally changing. European witnesses to the final days of the siege wrote excited accounts back to their home countries.[18] Christopher Columbus, who had been pursuing Castilian support for his own projects, was among them. 'That January by strength of arms I saw the flags of your royal majesties placed atop the towers of the Alhambra,' he would remind them a few months later. 'And I saw the Moorish king leave through the city's gates.' England's Henry VII ordered a special Te Deum sung at St Paul's cathedral in London and Rodrigo Borgia led the celebrations in Rome, where there were bullfights and processions.

Isabella and Ferdinand had been generous in victory. If the surrender negotiations were not arduous it was, in large part, because they gave Boabdil virtually everything he asked for. He himself received control of much of the Alpujarra, with the right to sell that back to Isabella and Ferdinand whenever he wanted. He also received 30,000 gold *castellanos* and was allowed to hold on to the lands and mills that he had inherited from his father, while his wife, mother and sister were all also allowed to keep their lands. They had the right to leave, whenever they wished, taking their goods with them on two large Genoese carracks that Isabella would pay for from her exchequer and which would take them to Alexandria, Tunis or anywhere else they wished to go. They were allowed to take their weapons with them to the Alpujarra, but not those that used powder. Before leaving, Boabdil had ordered that the bones of his forebears be dug up from the Alhambra cemetery, sending them off to a new burial site in Muslim lands in the Alpujarra. But he did not last long. Within a year he and his family were busy selling their possessions and preparing to accept the free shipping to Africa. Eventually he sent envoys to Isabella and Ferdinand, offering to sell his lands. Boabdil's wife Moraima died in August 1493, after an illness that had slowed down the departure plans. Boabdil, his mother, family members and many of his officials embarked for north Africa in October. 'All of them, the king and his companions, boarded the vessels they had been loaned and were respectfully and honourably treated by the Christians,' remarked the anonymous Muslim chronicler. 'At the end of their sea journey they landed in Melilla, on the coast of north Africa, from where they continued to Fez.' Boabdil installed himself in Fez, building his family Andalusian style *alcázares* to live in. Within a century, some members of his once magnificent family would be reduced to begging.[19]

Isabella was upset by the departure of the *infantico* Ahmed. 'The king's departure has given us much pleasure, but that of his son the *infantico* saddens us greatly,' she wrote, regretting that she had not tried harder to stop the boy – whom she had wanted to convert to Christianity – from leaving with his father.[20] 'Wherever he goes we must always keep up with him, visiting with the excuse of seeing his father and sending him something.' Baeza, the translator, would be a good person to carry the messages, she believed.

Isabella had offered increasingly generous terms to most of the towns captured as the Granada campaign progressed. In the early stages those who fought against her armies would not only be forced to live outside the walls of their town or fortress but would also lose their land and properties. Where there was no resistance, they were allowed to hold on to them. Those who fought hardest, especially in Málaga, received the worst possible punishment of either captivity or, if they could not buy their way out of that, slavery. From 1488 onwards, however, even those who had fought were allowed to keep their lands – a formula that made it easier to persuade them to surrender. They were even offered money in exchange for their Christian captives and allowed to keep their horses and bladed weapons (but not firearms). If they later rebelled, as some did, confiscation was automatic. And confiscation was, eventually, followed by repopulation with Christians brought in from elsewhere in the kingdom.[21]

Granada and the Alpujarra received the best settlement of all. Isabella had negotiated several of the previous surrenders, but she and Ferdinand obviously realised that they were facing exceptional circumstances. Granada had been overcrowded, short of supplies and without support. But this was not the moment to humiliate a defeated people whom she would have to govern. Up to 100,000 people, including many refugees from previously conquered areas, were packed into the city or living in the valleys of the Alpujarra. It would have been impossible to keep them all captive, and ruinous to expel them. A more prolonged war would have cost more lives, many of them Christian. Just policing Granada, a large, dense city of steep, narrow roads and alleys, was a daunting task. More than seven centuries of history, Muslim pride and the sense of humiliation that came with being governed by a supposedly inferior faith could not be wished away. The best Isabella could hope for, to begin with, was to occupy the Alhambra and other strongpoints in the city that she now saw as the jewel in her crown, trusting that the inhabitants would police themselves using their own long-standing local institutions. Much the same had been done with Almería and with the town of Purchena in 1489.[22]

And so she and Ferdinand accepted the terms of Granada's negotiators, almost to the letter.[23] The latter wanted to keep their properties, their laws and their religion. They wanted to be able to call worshippers to prayer from the city's minarets and be judged by the same officials and the same laws that they were used to.[24] And they would be excepted from Castile's rules about wearing distinguishing marks on their clothes to show that they were *mudéjares*. Revenge and compensation, for war damages or Christian slaves sold in Africa, were out of the question. Christians could not enter their houses without permission and, if one did, he could be killed without punishment. Even those former Christians who had converted to Islam, the so-called *elches*, had to be left in peace.

The kingdom's Jews were to be given the same conditions and the Christian converts to Judaism, probably including former *conversos* who had fled to Granada, were to be allowed to leave the country peacefully without being pursued by the Inquisition. The Moors themselves could sell their goods and properties at market prices and move to the Muslim lands of north Africa while conserving the right to return for a few years. And they were to be allowed to trade freely with both Africa and the rest of Castile.

Isabella's negotiators cut short the handover time, bringing it forward from March to January. And the period in which Moors could freely leave for north Africa was reduced from five years to three. Only a handful of demands were deemed unacceptable. The right to kill Christians who entered their homes without permission was turned into a royal pledge to pursue any Christians who did so. And legal issues between Christians and Moors were not to be tried only by the Moorish judges, as they had wanted, but by tribunals that included Christian judges as well. They could keep their swords, knives and bows but, as had happened elsewhere, firearms were banned. A few clauses were made deliberately vague, such as the one permitting the call to prayer, which took out any reference to this being done 'with voices'. But the negotiations also saw some demands fulfilled in terms that were even more generous than might have been expected. Isabella and Ferdinand, for example, pledged to leave the income and endowments of the mosques and their religions 'now and for ever'.[25] And the rules against Christians seeking revenge were extended to war booty and the mistreatment of slaves and captives.

Some of the clauses added to the agreement reflect Isabella and Ferdinand's awareness that, at least numerically, their soldiers would be vastly outnumbered in the city, while others sought to prevent Christians from inadvertently sparking rebellion. The 500 hostages from the city's best families remained in their power as surety while the Christians installed themselves in the Alhambra and the Alcazaba fortress, repairing damage to walls and defences. Other clauses protected Muslims against forced conversion or extra taxes. 'No Moor or Mooress will be forced to become Christian,' the final document pledged.[26] That promise was extended to the *elche* converts to Islam from Christianity and to the children of the *romías*, women like Boabdil's stepmother Zoraya who had been born Christian. Minor alterations also foresaw the potential problems of Moors and Christians living together in the city. Granada's sophisticated water-distribution system, which brought fresh water into the heart of the city, was to be respected. Neither Christians nor Moors could cut it off, or wash their clothes in it.

Isabella was remaining true to the history of Castile and the traditions of the three cultures. A kingdom whose biggest non-Christian group had long been the Jews now had a large population of *mudéjar* Muslims – up from 25,000 before the war to perhaps some 200,000 people, though some 100,000 had either left or were about to. Adding in the numerous *mudéjar* communities from Ferdinand's Aragonese lands, the Muslim population they jointly ruled over was now almost 300,000 people – or one in twenty Spaniards.[27]

Some saw this, however, as merely a way of keeping Granada's Moors quiet and peaceful while other measures were subtly applied to persuade them to abandon the country. 'The agreement is very beneficial to the Moors, but when things have reached such an honourable and beneficial end it is right to finish them off by whatever means,' said the letter-writer Cifuentes. 'Now that the monarchs have Granada, which is what they wanted, they can apply cunning to the remaining task and, the Moors being as they are, make them leave the city without breaking the agreements.'[28]

These new Castilian Muslims may, however, have felt they had little to fear after signing such a generous surrender. There was no reason to believe that Isabella might change Spain's ancient rules respecting the rights of religious minorities. But then they did not know what was about to happen to Castile's Jews.

26

Expulsion of the Jews

Santa Fe, 1492

The queen listened to the well-heeled supplicants, men whom she knew well from their years at court as loyal officials and royal collaborators. First among them was don Isaac Abravanel, his throat sore from begging and reasoning with all those who would hear him out. His exact words to Isabella are not recorded, but perhaps they matched those he used with Ferdinand. 'Why do you act in this way against your subjects? Impose strong taxes on us – a man from the house of Israel will make presents of gold and silver and of all that he has for the land of his birth.'[1] But Isabella would not bend to money. The Jews of Spain, whose roots stretched back beyond the arrival of Christianity, must convert or leave the land they had inhabited for at least ten centuries.

Isabella remained firm, claiming that this was God's work. 'Do you believe this comes from me? It is the Lord who has put this idea into the king's heart,' she told the group of eminent Jews before her, including some who had been among her most important supporters during her bid for the throne.[2] 'The king's heart is in the hands of the Lord, like the waters of a river. He directs them wherever he wants.' Isabella, according to this version of events, was placing the blame on the shoulders of others. One of those was her husband who, as a mortal, could be challenged. But the other was God, whose word was absolute. What she did not say was how God's message had arrived in their court and changed centuries of royal policy in Castile. It was, however, an effective way of telling Abravanel and the country's senior Jews to give up any attempt to stave off expulsion. We do not know whether the idea was more Isabella's or Ferdinand's. One of the advantages of a dual monarchy was that, whenever it was politically useful, responsibility or blame could be transferred to one's partner. But Isabella was there again when the Jewish leaders tried, once more, to dissuade Ferdinand from carrying out the measure. 'We worked hard, but without success,' said Abravanel. 'It was the queen who stood behind him and hardened his resolve to carry out the [expulsion] decree.'³

A sixteenth-century Spanish historian added a twist to this story by bringing in one of the most feared men in Spain, the inquisitor general Tomás de Torquemada. The seventy-two-year-old inquisitor reacted angrily to the sight of Isabella, whom he had known since she was a teenage girl, and her husband wavering before this group of senior Jews, some whom the couple knew well. He appeared bearing a crucifix and said: 'Judas once sold the son of God for 30 pieces of silver: your majesties are thinking of selling him a second time for 30,000: well, *señores*, here he is, sell him!'⁴ They did not dare. The story is probably false, but it reflects well the intimate connection between two infamous inventions overseen by Isabella – the Spanish Inquisition and the expulsion of the Jews. The victims of this purge were only too aware of Torquemada's menacing presence, and his influence on Isabella. 'In Spain there was a priest who had tremendous hatred for the Jews and the rule is that whoever afflicts the Jews becomes a leader by doing so,' observed Solomon ibn Verga, who sought exile in Portugal.⁵ 'He was the confessor to the queen, and he instigated the queen to force the Jews to convert. If they would not, they were to be put to the sword.'

Spain's Jews sometimes claimed to be descended from the original tribe of Judah which was expelled from Jerusalem and its lands by the Babylonian king Nebuchadnezzar six centuries before Christ. In fact, they probably first arrived in appreciable numbers in the first century after Christ, following the sacking of Jerusalem and when Hispania was still part of the Roman empire. Several centuries of intermarriage made them ethnically indistinguishable from other hispano-romans, and they went on to live through centuries of religious change. The Visigoth kings who took over when the Roman empire crumbled converted to Christianity in the sixth and seventh centuries and seemed set on persecuting them. Then the Muslims swept across the Iberian peninsula early in the eighth century, initially tolerating the presence of religious minorities and sometimes using Jews to garrison forts and town castles. Over the centuries the Jews, like the Christian minority, became thoroughly arabised, in both their language and many of their habits. Many probably converted to Islam – as did an estimated 80 per cent of the Christian population. Some rose to positions of importance, and strong communities flourished in numerous cities. One city, Lucena, was essentially Jewish. Great philosophers and scientists like Maimonides, whose *Guide for the Perplexed* tried to resolve the conflicts between faith and reason, emerged from their ranks. When religious fanaticism swept through the Muslim kingdoms with the arrival of the Berber *almohades* and their fundamentalist caliphate in the twelfth century, many were either forced to convert or fled to the Christian north. Maimonides himself, who wrote his first version of the *Guide for the Perplexed* in Arabic, feigned conversion before leaving for the more relaxed environment of Cairo and becoming doctor to the sultan. Spain's Muslim kingdoms were far more culturally advanced than the Christian north, and the Jews brought this cultural wealth across the frontier with them. They were crucial to the so-called School of Translators – a broad movement based around flourishing Toledo that began to translate into Latin and Spanish many of the Arabic texts found in the libraries of the recently conquered city. These included translations or adaptations of lost Greek works as well as scientific tracts that drew on Persian and Indian sources, which helped Europe recover knowledge lost during the intellectually drab days of what some would later call the Dark Ages. A Jewish golden age saw the city of Toledo – a cultural and economic powerhouse – become their principal city. A handful put their wealth to the service of the *Reconquista*, as the slow Christian march southwards was called, with the great victory at Las Navas de Tolosa part-financed by a loan from Joseph ibn Salomon ibn Shoshan.[6] Numbers are hard to assess accurately but, as the end of the fourteenth century approached and the population hit a peak, Spain had boasted the world's largest Jewish community.[7] In Castile it may have accounted for up to 250,000 people, or as many as one in fifteen Castilians.

The coexistence of Christianity, Judaism and Islam made Spain almost unique. One of Isabella's predecessors, Fernando III 'the Saint', had termed himself 'king of the three religions' in the first half of the thirteenth century and the writing on his tomb in Seville – which Isabella must have visited – was in the four languages of Spanish, Latin, Arabic and Hebrew.[8] The latter declares him conqueror of Sepharad, the name the Jews had given to the Iberian peninsula. But tolerance had its ups and downs. In reality, this coexistence included sporadic outbursts of inter-religious and social violence, alongside great cultural enrichment.

Yet Spain was an anachronism. While Jews were contributing to a cultural renaissance that would help Europe awaken from a period of relative intellectual slumber, they were being persecuted across the rest of the continent. England expelled them in 1290, while France had had five separate expulsions by 1394. In parts of the German-speaking world there had been terrible pogroms earlier in the fifteenth century. And in just the half-dozen years leading up to 1492 Jews had been forced out of the Swiss city of Geneva, Italian territories like Perugia, Parma and Milan and German areas like Würzburg and Heilbronn (with Pomerania and Mecklenburg following suit in 1492).[9] Only eight years earlier the German traveller Nicholas von Popplau had been amazed and appalled by the presence of Muslims and Jews across both Castile and Aragon. 'Some condemn the King of Poland because he allows various religions to live in his lands, while the lands of Spain are inhabited by baptised and converted Jews and also by infidel Moors,' he said.[10] He could see only one possible explanation for the presence of Jews. 'The queen is the protector of the Jews, and is herself the daughter of a Jewess,' he declared. He was right on the former claim, for Jews were under royal protection, though not on the latter.

Vital to the survival of the Jews in Christian Spain was the protection offered by monarchs in both Castile and Aragon. These allowed them to live by their own laws, with their own courts that could even order death sentences on the so-called *malsin* – Jews who denigrated or libelled their own community. One Castilian monarch, Alfonso X, had said they should 'live in captivity for ever as a reminder to all men of those from their line who crucified our Lord Jesus Christ'.[11] They paid special taxes directly to their royal patrons. This was both tribute and protection money. The latter was needed to keep them safe from the violence of mobs who chose to believe the standard lies and legends about the Jews – that they ritually murdered Christian children, or had plotted with the Muslims to enable the eighth-century conquest of Toledo. Their professions were as mixed and varied as those of Christians,[12] but their elites sometimes worked directly for the monarch, including as tax collectors and doctors. 'The Jews were beloved in Spain by monarchs, intellectuals and other social classes – with the exception of the common people and the monks,' observed Solomon ibn Verga.[13] That made them vulnerable, and badly in need of a monarch's protection.

Slowly, however, intolerance – both official and unofficial – had spread. In the thirteenth century the Jews lost the right to own farming land, pushing them into the cities. Among other urban professions they found there was that of money-lenders, with the monarchy setting interest rates at 33 per cent in Castile and 20 per cent in Aragon. The vast majority, however, worked at other things – as artisans, say, or traders.[14] Tax collectors and financiers are easy to hate. So, too, are religious minorities. At times of political or economic crisis, the Jews found themselves the victims of popular rage, though anyone who attacked them risked the wrath of the monarch – or, occasionally, of the Grandees and other nobles – under whose protection they lived. Isabella herself was quite clear about that status. 'All the Jews in my kingdoms are mine and are under my protection and safe-keeping and it falls to me to defend, protect and provide them with justice,'[15] she proclaimed in 1477. She repeated the instructions in Seville that same year. 'I take under my safekeeping, protection and royal defence the said Jews in the said *aljamas* [their city-based local communities, or ghettos] and each one of them, their persons and goods are assured by me against each and every person, whatever their position . . . and I order that they shall not be wounded or enchained, nor that [anyone] allow them to be injured, killed or wounded.'[16]

The Jews were at their most vulnerable during economic or other crises and when royal protection weakened. A political vacuum caused by the death of King Juan I in 1390 had allowed the masses, their anger and prejudice whipped up by populist preachers, to unleash the onslaught that led to the mass forced conversions of the following year. Juan had been succeeded by the eleven-year-old Enrique III. 'There was a lack of fear of the king, because of his young age,' observed the then chancellor, López de Ayala. 'It was all robbery and greed, it seemed, more than [religious] devotion.'[17] By the time a second round of conversions, under less duress, occurred in 1414, their numbers were vastly reduced – with perhaps only 50,000 or so left. On that occasion a supposedly saintly friar, Vicente Ferrer, had toured Spain. Ferrer may have preached non-violence, but he was often accompanied by an intimidating mob and he felt free to force himself on the Jews, preaching in their synagogues. It was he who turned Toledo's Ibn Shoshan synagogue into a church, which still stands today, called Santa María la Blanca.[18] The white-walled synagogue was itself already a monument to Spain's complex cultural intermixing, with its horseshoe arches, white walls, brick columns and ornate capitals.[19]

While the Jewish elites in Spain boasted about their superiority in 'lineage, wealth, virtues and wisdom' over other Jews, a growing sense of pessimism began to spread. Some rabbis had fled, while others became prominent converts. A breakdown in the Jews' intellectual traditions brought a growth in wild mysticism but, at the same time, despair that the messiah had still not come. The great Jewish communities were soon a shadow of their former selves. By 1424 Barcelona had found it unnecessary to designate a Jewish quarter. Toledo's once magnificent Jewish neighbourhood is thought to have contained just forty households by 1492. In Burgos, where the former Solomon Halevi went on to become the city's bishop as Paul of Burgos, those who refused to change found that the converts turned against them. 'The Jews who have recently become Christians oppress and do much harm,'[20] they complained. But in some smaller places Jews still outnumbered Christians. In the town of Maqueda, near Toledo, there were five Jews to every Christian. Crucially, they were also no longer economically important – jointly contributing just one *maravedí* for every 300 that entered the royal coffers.[21]

By the time Isabella came to the throne, the remaining Jews – mostly firmer in their beliefs and toughened by almost a century of Christian aggression – had adapted to their reduced weight within Castile and Spain. They still had their own courts, paid their special taxes and had a sort of parliament of their own in Castile, with the monarch naming a *rab mayor* or chief justice to lead them.[22] Communities survived in more than 200 cities, towns and villages – where their populations typically varied from 1 to 10 per cent of each place.[23] There were some 80,000 Jews in Castile, or one for almost every fifty Christians, and another 10,000 in Aragon, or about one for every 100 of Ferdinand's subjects in mainland Spain.[24] With their numbers so vastly reduced, the Jews had also become a far more discreet presence and so less bothersome for those seeking hate figures or scapegoats for social or economic ills. Popular racial hatred, indeed, was now focused on their blood relatives, the *conversos*. Isabella was, initially, an active protector. From Seville, in 1477, she had issued instructions to protect the 'good Jewish men' of the frontier castle of Huete in a financial dispute with their Christian neighbours. She also sent a stern warning to the people of Trujillo when they turned on the local *aljama* that same year. 'I order that each and every one of you from now on do not permit . . . anyone from that city or from outside it to bully or oppress these Jews . . . [nor] that they order them to clean out their stables or wash their tubs . . . nor should they billet ruffians or prostitutes or any other person in their houses against their will.'[25]

Even in 1490, just two years before the expulsion, Isabella was busy fulfilling her royal role as protector-in-chief of the Jews. 'By canon law and according to the laws of these kingdoms of ours, the Jews are suffered and tolerated and we order you to suffer and tolerate their living in our kingdoms as our subjects,' she warned the burghers of Bilbao after they had refused to allow Jews to stay overnight in the city, forcing their traders into insecure accommodation in the countryside.[26]

There were a handful of important Jews, too, close to Isabella in the court. Yucé Abranel was in charge of cattle taxes in Plasencia. Samuel Abulafia had been one of Isabella's chief administrators for provisioning troops during the Granada War. Abraham Seneor, the *rab mayor*, had become chief treasurer of the Hermandades.[27] He was also one of just seven men on Isabella's council, which had grown in importance as it administered – with the help of the royal secretaries – the new powers that Isabella concentrated in her court. Isaac Abravanel, who had previously served in the Portuguese court, lamented that his own successful court career had meant that 'all the days that I was in the courts and palaces of kings occupied in their service I had no opportunity for study and I did not know a book and spent in vanity my time and my years in confusion to acquire wealth and honour'.[28] Prominent Jews were still being protected or sponsored by Grandees, aristocrats or bishops, with the bishop of Salamanca taking under his wing the talented astronomer Abraham Zacuto, who invented a copper astrolabe that allowed sailors to create better nautical tables – as the great Portuguese and Spanish navigators would eventually discover.[29] More intimately, Isabella had turned to the Jewish doctor Lorenzo Badoç when she found herself struggling to produce male offspring. The monarchs freely expressed their immense gratitude to Badoç after the birth of Prince Juan; and among the rumours about Ferdinand's own parents were that they had engendered him while both holding palm fronds in their hands – on the advice of a Jewish woman.[30]

If the Jews belonged to the queen, so did the rules governing them and she could change these at will. Measures forcing them to live apart in their own *aljamas* or to wear distinguishing marks had been passed earlier in the century but not applied. Now, as Isabella began thinking about unleashing the Inquisition on the *conversos*, she also decided to be stricter with 'her' Jews.[31] Among those egging her on was the severe and austere Tomás de Torquemada – who shunned meat and continued to wear a simple friar's habit despite the personal wealth that came with his status as one of Isabella's senior churchmen.

It was Torquemada who had urged her to drive Jews and Moors into their own separate neighbourhoods.[32] The 1480 meeting of the Cortes in Toledo ordered just that, pushing the Jews into city ghettos, often behind walls.[33] In some places this was a huge task, involving major changes to a city's layout. In an operation that took longer than the projected two years, Jews had to be moved in, Christians moved out, walls built and thoroughfares cut. The aim was to avoid 'confusion and damage to our holy faith', according to Isabella and her husband. But it was also a way of tightening the noose.[34] Those who wanted greater freedom could always choose apostasy. Jews were already expected to wear coloured badges on their right shoulder and, in an order issued two years previously, were banned from wearing silk or gold and silver jewellery because otherwise some might be taken 'for churchmen or lawyers of great estate'.[35]

The Inquisition brought with it further demonisation. If its task was to eradicate Judaism from the hearts of the new Christians, how logical it now seemed to view the Jews as a cancer in the body of Spain. That was certainly the conclusion that the first inquisitors, and Isabella, had reached when they expelled the Jews from much of Andalusia, nine years earlier, in 1483.[36] Isabella had wanted the measure to serve as a warning to Jews elsewhere to stop them tempting people from *converso* families back into the fold. 'The Jews from those *aljamas* were ordered to leave because of the wicked heresy,' she and her husband explained.[37] 'We thought that would be enough to stop those of other towns and cities in our kingdoms and *señorial* lands from doing the same.'

Expulsion, then, was intimately linked to the Inquisition and, especially, to the zealous friars and priests who served it. It was Torquemada, as inquisitor general, who signed the first expulsion order in 1492 – beating Isabella and Ferdinand to it by eleven days – though this was restricted to the Jews of the bishopric of Girona.[38] 'It was agreed with the sovereigns that I would send this letter in which I order each and every Jew and Jewess, whatever their age . . . to leave the city, its bishopric and all its towns and villages, with their sons and daughters, family members and servants, and not come back,' he wrote.[39] The Inquisition had discovered that the presence of Jews was one of the main causes of heresy, he argued, and 'if the principal cause is not removed' things would get worse.

This was a clear, if mostly false, statement. But it was the logic of the times, and one that Isabella fully shared. In the fifteenth-century imagination nations were often seen like bodies, with the monarchs as their head. But bodies could also fall sick and purging was one way of curing them. Torquemada was careful to state that Isabella and her husband agreed with him. And just eleven days later, on 31 March 1492, they both signed the wider expulsion order, whose language coincided so closely with that of Torquemada's that it is difficult not to see his hand in it.[40] In this case, however, the order was far more dramatic, sweeping and devastating.

Isabella and Ferdinand stated that the 1480 order to isolate the Jews inside their own ghettos had not achieved its principal aim – of restricting communication between Jews and Christians and so preventing judaising. 'It has been shown that great damage is done to Christians by the contact, conversations and activities that they share with the Jews, who always try – by whatever means they can find – to subvert and snatch faithful Christians away from our holy Catholic faith,' they said.[41] The innocent were tainted with the same guilt. 'When some grave and horrific crime is committed by some members of a group, it is sufficient reason to dissolve and annihilate that group,' they added. Isabella and her husband then stated that they had thought expelling the worst offenders from Andalusia would be enough. But they had been wrong. 'So . . . after much deliberation, we have agreed to order all Jews and Jewesses to leave our lands and never come back,' they said.[42]

The order was absolute, though the intention was also to provoke a fresh round of conversions. It covered Jews of all ages, anywhere in their kingdoms. 'We command that . . . if they do not obey and do as they are told or are found in our kingdoms or lands – or come here in any way at all – their goods be confiscated and given to our exchequer and that the death sentence be applied.'[43]

Although the justification for all this was religious, the Inquisition also served to fan the flames of racial intolerance by, among other things, the repetition of long-standing slurs. The allegations circulating around Europe which claimed that Jews carried out the ritual killing of Christian children were absurd, but in 1491 the Inquisition claimed to have discovered a real case. For some unexplained reason the Inquisition jail in Segovia was holding a Jewish cobbler called Yucé Franco. This was already an abuse of its power, since its remit did not include Jews, but torturers obtained a strange confession. Franco told them that he had taken part in the crucifixion of a Christian child in the town of La Guardia, near Toledo, on an Easter Friday some fifteen years earlier.[44] The child's blood and part of its heart had then been mixed with a consecrated host and witchcraft employed in an attempt to provoke the plague. Ten years later, a Burgundian traveller would be told a revised version of the apocryphal story. 'Eight or ten people, pretending to be Christians, secretly stole a seven-year-old child and took him to a mountain and crucified him in a cave like Jesus Christ . . . Then they jabbed a lance in between his ribs . . . But the child, before his death, spoke so wisely that they saw that clearly it was the holy spirit speaking on his behalf. They took him down from the cross and, when they had taken out his heart, they buried his body, then they burned his heart to ashes.'[45]

The child was never named, no parents came forward, a body was never found and the case was heard in Avila rather than Toledo itself – almost certainly so that Torquemada could oversee it. Yet the cobbler Franco, another Jew and three *conversos* were declared guilty of ritual child-murder and burned at the stake after an *auto de fe* on 16 November 1491. It was a sign of just how far the Inquisition's power, paranoia and ability to conjure up imagined crimes had developed.[46] For those seeking the expulsion of the Jews the timing was perfect. Here were Jews consorting with *conversos* to carry out the most evil of acts. The outrage the case provoked, both in Isabella's court and in the streets of Spain's cities, must have been considerable. It can only have helped the queen make up her mind.

The Vale of Tears

*The Santa María monastery at
Guadalupe, 15 June 1492*

Isabella must have looked with satisfaction on the scene that unfolded in the chapel of her favourite monastery at Guadalupe. The man before her was both a close ally and a Jew, but that was about to change. Abraham Seneor was one of the dozen men who made up her most trusted group of counsellors – the people whom she consulted frequently and leaned on for support. They included her beloved friar Hernando de Talavera, two cardinals and the loyal administrators Cabrera, Chacón and Gutierre de Cárdenas. Now, Seneor and his family were about to become Christians. Isabella was there, together with her husband, in the Gothic and *mudéjar* surroundings of Guadalupe to act as a godmother. The holy water was poured on them. The eighty-year-old Seneor changed his name to Fernando Pérez Coronel, while his brother-in-law Meir Melamed, Castile's chief tax collector, and his two sons took the same surname.[1] Iberia's population of Jews – still the world's biggest when those in Spain and neighbouring Portugal were combined – was reduced accordingly.[2]

The sixteenth-century Jewish historian Elijah Capsali, a Jew from Crete whose uncle had been chief rabbi in the Ottoman empire, claimed that Seneor and Melamed had been left with little choice, with Isabella insisting that she needed the services of both men. 'I have heard it rumoured that Queen Isabella had sworn that if Don Abraham Seneor did not convert, she would wipe out all the communities, and that Don Abraham did what he did in order to save the

Jews, but not from his own heart,' he wrote after meeting exiles who eventually found safety in Ottoman lands.[3]

That was wrong. In fact, Seneor had been an Isabella ally ever since he and Cabrera had held the city of Segovia for her against Enrique IV's *privado*, Juan Pacheco. Their action, which included bringing about a temporary reconciliation with her half-brother, had been crucial to her future success. And both had stayed loyal. Seneor, a wealthy man, had financed Isabella and the later campaign against Granada to the tune of almost 2 million *maravedís*. He went on to become both *rab mayor* – the royal-appointed head of Castile's Jews – and treasurer to the Hermandad General. He was one of the richest men in Spain and his family was sufficiently grand for it to be exempted from the rules banning Jews from wearing silk and crimson. Already, some in the Jewish community disliked Seneor's family intensely. He was certainly not above using dirty tricks, accusing the *converso* Juan de Talavera of witchcraft – a matter for the Inquisition – after the latter accused him of overcharging and creaming off part of the taxes paid by Spain's Jews.[4] Other Jews were less charitable about the conversion, with an elderly rabbi from Málaga, Abraham Bokrat HaLevy, angrily denouncing Melamed's change of heart. 'He was named Meir ["he who gives light"], but there is no light in him at all . . . His name is in reality the thickest of darkness.'[5]

Another writer from a leading Aragonese family of Jews saw Seneor, Melamed and a group of converted rabbis as traitors who, worse still, dragged some of the less well-educated along with them. 'People who did not understand what they should do followed these leaders who had used their wisdom to do evil, and they too left the fold,' he lamented.[6] Yet while Seneor and other prominent members of the Jewish elite converted and continued their lives almost as before, it seems that most Jews did not.[7] They had good reasons not to. Their families had survived the pogroms of a hundred years earlier. They had been courageous and convinced enough to stick to their faith. They had also witnessed the Catholic church's suspicious, violent attitude to its own converts. The charred corpses on the Inquisition bonfires were proof of that. 'The Jews despaired and all feared greatly,' reported Abravanel.[8] 'Each said to the other, "Let us strengthen one another in our faith and the Torah of our God, against the enemy who blasphemes and wishes to destroy us. If he lets us live, we shall live, and if he kills us, we shall die, but we will not desecrate our covenant and we will not retreat." '[9]

The last Jewish Passover celebrations in Spain began two days after the expulsion decree was signed. Those who received the news before Passover started were thrown into shock, dressing in sack-cloth and ashes on the first day and refusing to eat or drink. 'Even those who did eat, did so with the bitterness of the bitter herbs in their mouths,' reported Capsali.[10] Others watched with alarm as their own distant relatives, now *conversos*, joined the movement to expel them. In Aragon, the de la Cavallerias looked on aghast as a cousin bearing their surname led the charge against them. 'Alfonso [de la Cavalleria] thought evil of God's nation, he and a group of his friends . . . conspired to wipe out the name of Israel from the land,' wrote one chronicler.[11]

So it was that the Jews began to pack those few belongings they were allowed to take with them. Rabbis who stayed true to their religion tried to stiffen spines, preaching to them as they went. 'Their rabbis . . . encouraged them and gave them vain hopes, tell-ing them that they should realise that this was God's will, that he wanted to free them from slavery and take them to the Promised Land; and that as he led them out they would see God perform many miracles for them, and that he would ensure they left Spain rich and with great honour.'[12] They also recalled a previous great exodus in the history of the Jews, when they had been forced out of Egypt. 'A mighty torrent of people left: the old and the young, men and women . . . travelled in search of a safe haven,'[13] said Capsali. But such safe havens were few and far between. The Ottoman empire, normally accessible only after journeying through less hospitable lands, welcomed them as, initially, did the kingdom of Naples and

Portugal (though further expulsion awaited them from both these places). Some, too, ended up in the lands of the Egyptian Mamluk sultans or in the kingdom of Fez.[14]

In the edict expelling the Jews, Isabella and Ferdinand had both guaranteed their physical safety and placed severe restrictions on them. 'So that the said Jews and Jewesses, during the period up to the end of July, can organise themselves, their goods and their wealth in the best way possible, we hereby take them under our royal protection,' they said.[15] 'They may sell, barter or transfer all their movable and immoveable goods, and dispose of them freely until the end of July; and during that period, no harm, injury or wickedness can be done to them or their goods . . . They may take their possessions and wealth out by sea or land, as long as they do not take gold, silver, coins or other things banned by the laws of our kingdoms.' While the guarantees were only partially respected, the restrictions seem to have been applied rigorously.

The Jews were now easy targets for everything from fraudulent business deals to robbery and murder. Isabella acted to protect them where individual cases reached her, but the expulsion order brought mass abuse. Hatred was freely expressed. 'The Jews were bad and disbelievers,' said Bernáldez. They had mistreated Jesus Christ, and now were receiving their just reward. 'With malice they persecuted and killed him; and, having made that mistake, they never repented,' he added.[16]

Isabella's promises of protection must now have seemed, at best, half-hearted to those who, out of greed or hatred, fell on the weak and desperate Jews of Spain. Property was sold, where it could be, at knock-down prices. Even Bernáldez, who approved of the expulsion, admired the courage with which the Jews set out – and reported on how Isabella's Christian subjects mistreated them. 'Young and old showed great strength and hope in a prosperous end,' he said. 'But all suffered terrible things; the Christians here acquired a great quantity of their goods, fine houses and estates for very little money, and even though they begged, they could not find people prepared to buy them, exchanging a house for an ass or some vines for a small amount of cloth, since they could not take gold or silver.'[17] A vineyard in Santa Olalla worth 10,000 *maravedís* was swapped for a donkey worth just 300, while a house in the same town was sold for a tenth of its real worth.[18]

The roads towards Portugal, via Zamora, Badajoz, Benavente, Alcántara or Ciudad Rodrigo, were soon busy with refugees. Checkpoints were set up to make sure they weren't carrying gold or silver. Swallowing the precious metals was the only way of smuggling them. 'In the places where they were searched, and in the ports and frontiers, the women especially swallowed more, with people swallowing up to 30 ducats at a time,' said Bernáldez. Weddings were hurriedly celebrated to ensure that girls did not travel as single women.[19]

Processions of Jews crossed the frontiers of Portugal and Navarre, or travelled north to the Atlantic port of Laredo or south to embark in Málaga or Cadiz. Aragonese Jews – for, like the Inquisition, this was one of the first measures to truly cover the joint kingdoms of Isabella and Ferdinand – mostly headed for Mediterranean ports.[20] Robbery and death, at sea or on the land, were not uncommon 'at the hands of Christians as much as Moors', Bernáldez observed.[21] Some lost their willpower at the last minute. 'Tens of thousands of Jews converted, and this even included some who were leaving or who had left the country, as they saw what a terrible fate awaited them in their travels,' reported Capsali.[22]

The initial expulsion was by no means the end of their trials. The lucky ones travelled straight to the Ottoman empire or to the few Jewish refuges in Provence and the papal lands at Avignon.[23] Some did not survive the journey. 'Those who left by sea found that there was not enough food, and a great number attacked them each day. In some cases, the sailors on the ships tricked them and sold them as slaves,' reported one exile.[24] 'A number were thrown into the sea with the excuse that they were sick [with the plague].' One shipload was dumped on shore, miles from the nearest settlement, after an epidemic broke out in their boat. On land they were also treated as plague-carriers or kept at a distance because they had appeared in such huge numbers that local people feared for their own food supplies.[25]

Those who reached north Africa and the kingdom of Fez (covering much of the northern part of modern-day Morocco) found themselves in a shanty town that soon burned down, or were attacked by mobs.[26] The founder of the Wattasid dynasty in Fez, King Abu Abd Allah al-Sheikh Mohammed ibn Yahya, however, proved generous, at least in spirit. He 'accepted the Spanish Jews in all his kingdom and received them with great favour', and, after some difficult years, a flourishing community grew up in the city of Fez, in Tlemcen (in modern Algeria) and in Ksar el-Kebir 'and we built spacious and artistically decorated houses with attics, and . . . beautifully built synagogues', according to a literary rabbi from Zamora, Abraham Saba.[27]

Navarre also came under pressure and expelled its Jews in 1498 – so that within six years of the expulsion many either found themselves on the move again or heading home in despair, ready to convert. The worst stories came from Fez, perhaps reflecting the prejudices of Christian writers. 'The Moors appeared and stripped them naked to their bare skin,' said Bernáldez, who dealt with many of those who fled back to Spain.[28] 'They threw themselves upon the women with force, and killed the men, and slit them open up the middle, looking for gold in their abdomens, because they knew that they swallowed it.' Mouths were forced open and hands thrust down trousers or up orifices amid tales of abuse of women and young men.

In Portugal, King João II at first thought of closing his frontiers to the Castilian Jews, but seems to have decided he was better off extorting money from them. His counsellors warned against allowing Spain's Jews into the country, pointing to France and England, where Jews had been expelled many years before and 'where the [Christian] faith is now flourishing and perfect'.[29] In the end, he declared that 600 wealthy 'households' would be allowed to settle, but the rest would have to leave after eight months or be enslaved.

The refugees had to pay an entry tax of around 2,900 *maravedís* a head – roughly equivalent to the annual salary of, for example, the municipal doctor in an important town like Medina del Campo. Charges on goods taken across the frontier were as high as 30 per cent. With more than 25,000 refugees (and possibly a lot more) flooding in, this was good business. Officials watched closely on both sides of the border, either preventing money from leaving Castile or taking it off those who arrived in Portugal. Refugee camps of hastily built shacks sprang up on the Portuguese side, as many towns refused to let the Jews in.[30] King João had to write to Évora, on the road to Lisbon, reminding it that he had not banned Castilian Jews from entering the town. 'We have not ordered you to act in this manner, but have only ordered those places on the borders not to receive Jews from parts of Castile where they are dying [of the plague]. We order you to let into the town those Jews that are not from such areas,' he wrote.[31] Epidemics, meanwhile, spread through the crowded, unsanitary camps and many died.

The wealthy 600 households were spread across the country and continued to be taxed separately. Saba moved to modest Guimarães – twenty-five miles from the border – with his wife and two married sons, taking at least part of his library of several hundred books with him. Portugal's population of almost 1 million was suddenly boosted by around 3 per cent – and its Jewish population doubled. In towns like Santarém, south of Lisbon, the Castilians suddenly accounted for almost a quarter of the whole population.[32]

Within eight months, the vast majority of these Jews – excepting the 600 families – were put on boats heading for the Portuguese-held ports of Tangiers and Arzilla, on their way to the kingdom of Fez. Even Portugal's royal historian, Damião de Góis, admitted there was widespread abuse on the ships. 'In addition to treating them badly, they deliberately strayed off course in order to vex them and sell them meat, water and wine at whatever price they saw fit. They humiliated the Jews and dishonoured their wives and daughters,' he reported.[33] In one of the cruellest moves, João ordered the kidnapping of some

2,000 children whose parents had stayed, apparently without paying the appropriate tax. These were sent to populate the island of São Tomé – off the west coast of Africa – where many would die and which Saba would call 'the Snakes Islands'. They included one of Aravanel's grandsons, who had been smuggled into the country with a wet nurse after his father heard rumours that there were plans to kidnap him in Castile in order to pressure his wealthy family to convert.[34] Solomon ibn Verga, himself a refugee, told the story of a woman who had six children snatched from her and pleaded with the king as he left mass one day, throwing herself in front of his horse. 'Let her be, for she is like a bitch whose pups have been taken away!' he allegedly responded.[35]

Judah ben Jacob Hayyat, a teacher of law who was then in his forties, embarked from Lisbon after being expelled, only to find himself captured by a Basque boat and sailed back to Málaga, where Spanish priests came on board to preach to them daily. 'When they realised the devotion and the tenacity with which we clung to our God, the bishop placed an interdict upon them that they give us no bread, and no water, and no provisions whatsoever . . . Thereupon close to one hundred souls apostatised in one day . . . Then my dear innocent wife, peace be unto her, expired of hunger and thirst; also maidens and young men, the old and the young, altogether fifty souls.'[36]

Others returned home to Spain, preferring baptism to the suffering they found elsewhere. Hunger, sickness, despair and the decimation of their families drove them back, willing to accept any conditions. Priests like Bernáldez in the frontier and port towns through which they returned found themselves continually baptising returnees. 'Here in Los Palacios they provided one hundred new souls [to Christ], whom I baptised, including some rabbis,' he wrote. 'There was no end to the people crossing the frontier in Castile to turn Christian.'[37] Those returning from Fez came barefoot, hungry, lice-ridden and full of stories about the calamities they had experienced. 'It was painful to see them,' he admitted.

Bernáldez personally baptised ten rabbis on their return.[38] In November 1492 Isabella and Ferdinand signed a document allowing returnees to buy back property they had sold, at the same price.[39] 'Many . . . converted more out of necessity than out of faith, and returned to Castile poor and dishonoured,' reported one Portuguese writer.[40] At least one Castilian town, Torrelaguna, saw half its Jews return as converts. Among those to move back was Isabella's former tax collector Samuel Abulafia, who had been converted in Portugal, and much of his family. He returned in 1499 and – despite a fourteen-month period in the Inquisition's dungeons ten years later and a second arrest in 1534 – had a successful second career under the name of Diego Gómez. Isabella and Ferdinand tried to protect the returnees. But they were going back to a world of intolerance and some ran the same gauntlet of muggings, murder and robberies that they had experienced abroad, this time at the hands of their old neighbours in the home towns to which they returned.[41]

The question of exactly how many Jews left, how many returned and how many converted remains unresolved. 'Of the rabbis of Spain and their leaders, very few were willing to sanctify God's name by dying for Him, or were willing to endure any other punishment,' wrote Abraham ben Solomon.[42] He especially blamed Seneor and his family, because 'the masses looked towards them, and because of them the masses sinned'.[43]

The hatred felt towards Isabella, the woman who had not so long before declared that 'all the Jews in my kingdoms are mine',[44] was resounding. She 'deserved to be known as Jezebel because of the way she did evil in the eyes of God', declared Capsali. 'Isabella had always hated the Jews,' he added. 'In this, she was spurred on by the priests, who had persuaded her to hate the Jews passionately.'[45] In this version a bullying Isabella was blamed for the expulsion, with her husband little more than someone she pushed around. 'Queen Isabella was thus clearly superior to him, and whatever she wished was done,' wrote Capsali.

But there was also fatalism among the people she had exiled. If they had been expelled it was, ultimately, because God wanted to punish them. 'God decided that the time had come for the Jews to leave Spain,' wrote Capsali. 'And once such a decision was reached, nothing could prevent it, for all is written in the book.'[46] Solomon ibn Verga spelt out a long list of sins for which they were being punished – including eating and drinking with Christians, coveting their women and money and the conceit that had made them feel superior and want 'to be lords over non-Jews'.[47]

If Isabella's aim had been to push the last Jews into peaceful conversion, she mostly failed. In fact, the expulsion appears to have ended up being almost as terrible as the pogroms unleashed by uncontrolled mobs a century earlier. It was further proof that the modern, power-hungry monarchy that she was busy building could be at least as cruel as the unwieldy medieval order that was being gradually overturned. In Isabella's mind, expelling the Jews was just another step in the process of constructing a religiously pure, homogeneous and ordered society – and one that would be a shining example, rather than an exception, to Europe and Christendom. The price, in terms of human suffering and lives lost, did not trouble her greatly.[48]

The Race to Asia

Santa Fe, 17 April 1492

Isabella must have smiled once more at the sight of the eccentric, entertaining Italian sailor who had come to sell her his dreams. Christopher Columbus was difficult to miss. Tall, flamboyantly dressed and full of the kind of bubbling, voluble self-confidence that hides deeper insecurities, he had been in and out of her court over seven years, hawking his extravagant plans for a journey into the unknown – heading west across an Atlantic Ocean that was still known simply as the 'Ocean Sea'. On the occasions that they met, he addressed the queen in an accent that reportedly owed much to the lisp of southern Andalusia, but presumably with the sometimes awkward phrasing of a man for whom Castilian Spanish was merely his third or fourth language. Conversations with him were difficult to forget. He had first sat before her as the rain poured down during those damp, muddy January days of 1486 at Alcalá de Henares in the weeks after her youngest daughter Catherine of Aragon was born. On that occasion in the archbishop of Toledo's palace he had started his painfully long and drawn-out campaign of persuasion and seduction. This involved showing her maps of the known world, telling stories of secret, westerly routes to the spice-, gold-, silver- and pearl-producing lands of Asia and explaining how his venture would help Isabella and her husband to send a final crusade to recover Jerusalem and the holy lands. Like many people he believed in the millenarian fantasies like that of the Last World Emperor, who was meant to retake these lands and convert the world to Christianity before engaging in a final battle with the Antichrist. Isabella and Ferdinand, Columbus was suggesting, could do at least part of that task. He was amusing, but difficult to take seriously.[1]

'He explained his ideas, to which they did not give much credit, and reasoned with them, saying that what he told them was true and he showed them a *mapa mundi*,' recounted Bernáldez.[2] The idea was, if not mad, then impossible. That was what a committee of experts in the Castilian court, led by Isabella's trusty friar Hernando de Talavera, eventually decided after Columbus had pestered the itinerant court for much of the next two years.[3] The wise men, salty sailors and careerist lawyers who were asked to study his plans now or in later years almost all shook their heads in suspicious wonder at his extravagant ambition to sail into the unknown. What Columbus was saying 'could not possibly be true', they said. And they had good reasons for thinking so.

The Genoese-born sailor had later insinuated himself into Isabella's small, colourful party as she rode grandiosely into the siege camp at Baza in 1489 before seemingly frightening the besieged Moors into submission. At some stage in their meetings over these years he talked about the Great Khan – the king of kings from the mysterious east, made famous by Marco Polo – and the legend of how he had begged for Christian preachers to be sent to enlighten his people. It was a request that had been ignored, he pointed out, but that Isabella and Ferdinand could make good by sending him on his own daring route towards Asia via the west. Isabella had not read Marco Polo – or certainly did not own a copy of his work at the end of her life – but she was familiar with the writings of that fraudulent armchair traveller Sir John Mandeville. She owned two copies of the latter's so-called *Travels* and may have been familiar with a popular treatise on oriental history that served as one of Mandeville's sources, *The Flower of Histories of the East* by the Armenian monk and noble Hayton of Corycus.[4]

But Columbus – a man with influential friends in Seville – was relentless, even boorish and mono-thematic. He had planted a seed in Isabella's mind and refused to accept that it would not eventually sprout and grow. Now Columbus was back at her court in the camp at Santa Fe, as Isabella reflected on the enormity of Castile's victory over the kingdom of Granada and the daunting task of administering her newly conquered lands and their Muslim population. The Genoese-born adventurer with a strong mystical streak and a mysterious seafaring past in Portugal and elsewhere argued that his bold project suited the greatness of crusading monarchs who had 'thrown the Jews out of all your lands and kingdoms',[5] were proven 'enemies of the sect of Mohammed' and, thanks to the Inquisition, were relentless pursuers of heresy. If they sent him to find a new route to the lands of India then he could discover how their people might be 'converted to our holy faith' while also claiming them, and the wealth they contained, for Castile. These were, indeed, remarkable times. Less than four months had passed since the fall of Granada and the expulsion order was barely two weeks old. If ever Isabella and her husband were going to fall for his ambitious and courageous project, he must have thought, this was the moment.

It is not clear exactly where Columbus, already an experienced sailor whose previous travels had taken in almost all of the western edge of the known world from Iceland to Africa's Gold Coast, first came across the notion that Asia could be found by sailing west. It was generally agreed that the earth was a sphere, so the idea was not ridiculous, but there was disagreement over the size of the earth's circumference (some more recent guesses by people Columbus trusted made it far too small). And information about what lay on the other side of the Atlantic was based on legend, fantasy, rumour, conjecture and what little evidence overland travellers and the ocean currents – as they conveyed flotsam and jetsam – could provide.

Those who imagined a clear sea from Europe to Asia could give no good reason why that should be the case, though it was equally hard to argue that it was not. The unknown was just that, unknown. Where some saw an open ocean, others saw a distant, undiscovered continent – the legendary Antipodes – which would block the way. Still more imagined that islands known variously as Antillia, Brasil, St Brendan or Isle of the Seven Cities lay along the way. Foremost among the believers in an open route was a Florentine cosmographer called Paolo del Pozzo Toscanelli, whom Columbus sought out as he mulled over the idea of sailing west. The Florentine replied enthusiastically, believing him to have the backing of Portugal, where Columbus had lived and married Felipa Perestrello – the daughter of one of the explorers who discovered, and became lord of, the island of Porto Santo, near Madeira. Toscanelli sent him a map he had drawn showing 'the short distance from here to the Indies, where the spicelands start, which is a shorter path than that via Guinea [Africa]'. Toscanelli enthused not just about the journey but also about the riches that could be found there. He placed Cathay, the China of Marco Polo, only 5,200 nautical miles away.[6] 'This country is worth seeking,' he wrote, claiming to have met Chinese visitors to Rome many years earlier. 'Not only because great wealth may be obtained from it, gold and silver, all sorts of gems, and spices, which never reach us; but also on account of its learned men, philosophers, and expert astrologers, and by what skill and art so powerful and magnificent a province is governed, as well as how their wars are conducted.' Cipango, modern-day Japan, was thought to be much closer, at 3,000 nautical miles. 'You should know that the temples and royal palaces are covered in pure gold,' he said. 'And it can be safely reached.' But Columbus managed to shorten even this distance by using his own observations at sea and the calculations of the tenth-century Arab cosmographer al-Farghani, or 'Alfraganus', to shrink the size of the globe even further. The distance to Japan, he thought, was just 2,400 nautical miles, or a quarter of the true figure.[7]

He had previously, in 1484, sought the backing of Portugal, a country which already had an impressive record of navigation and discovery in west Africa and the Atlantic, having claimed the Azores and Madeira. Portuguese sailors were on their way to discovering the eastward route towards Asia around the southern horn of

Africa, with Diogo Cão already sailing south past the mouth of the River Congo to the coast of modern-day Angola. In 1488 King João invited Columbus back to Lisbon. In his letter the Portuguese king used some of the grand new titles – such as Lord of Guinea (as the newly discovered regions of west Africa were called) and King 'on both sides of the sea of Africa' – that served as reminders of his own country's recent successes and of its rivalry with Isabella's Castile. Columbus was there in December 1488 when Bartolomeu Dias returned from rounding Africa's southern tip at the Cape of Good Hope for the first time – though he had failed to reach India and its lucrative spice markets.[8] Columbus's admiring, intelligent and cultured younger brother Bartolomé – himself a skilled map-maker – appears to have accompanied Dias on the trip.

A committee of Portuguese wise men, including the eminent Jewish cosmographer Joseph Vizinho, decided that Columbus's fixation with Cipango and its alleged proximity was, at best, unrealistic. Columbus had then despatched his brother to England to seek the backing of King Henry VII – who allegedly showed some interest after Bartolomé painted him a map modelled on Toscanelli's – and to try his luck in France.[9] Meanwhile, after years of lobbying among those closest to Isabella and Ferdinand, news reached him late in 1491 that he was being given one last opportunity to persuade them. Isabella and her husband were preparing for the inevitable fall of Granada. It was a good time to strike again. The euphoria of the moment, and the proof that great, historic tasks could be brought to a successful end, might make them more open to Columbus's ambitious, if fantastical-sounding, project.

The key that unlocked Isabella's door this time was a former confessor, the Franciscan friar Juan Pérez, who was now at the friary at La Rábida, on the south-west corner of Castile. Built on a rocky outcrop overlooking the spot where the rivers Odiel and Tinto join just before spilling their waters into the Atlantic on Spain's southern coast, this was a religious community famed among mariners. It looked out over the apparently endless ocean that Columbus wished to sail, its cloisters lined with horseshoe *mudéjar* arches and its friars keen chart-makers and collectors of both maps and sailors' stories. Inside its thick walls, the friars knew all the tales about what might lie beyond the horizon. The friary of Observant Franciscans had long been one of Columbus's refuges, and it was Pérez who recommended the Genoese sailor and adventurer to Isabella once more. He and another senior friar, the astrologer Antonio de Marchena, had been among Columbus's few constant supporters and the Italian had even lived with them when his money ran out.[10] This time the queen wrote back speedily, encouraging Friar Pérez to hire a mule and travel to Santa Fe to see her. She asked him to tell Columbus 'to expect a positive reply'.[11] Soon afterwards a similar invitation was extended to Columbus himself, including a generous sum of money so that he could dress appropriately for court.

Columbus was a seducer, as tenacious in his pursuit of people as of new places. Over the years he would study Isabella and her court, thinking up different ways to impress her.[12] The Italian mariner adopted a mixture of gallantry, boldness and religious conviction, knowing that she was open to the flirtatious, if carefully circumscribed, games of courtly love and chivalry. A later letter to Isabella is full of sensual praise for the woman who holds 'the keys' to his desire and to whom he boasts of 'the scent' and 'taste' of his goodwill while also flattering her as the recipient of a God-given 'spirit of understanding' (of him).[13] Columbus's proposals, too, contained plenty of the stuff of the legends that Isabella found so exciting – of brave men going off on remarkable adventures, fearless and absolute in their belief that God was behind them. There was nothing false about this, since Columbus's own personal ambitions were framed in exactly the same social and chivalric codes. This son of a Genoese weaver turned innkeeper sought, above all, glory and rank. In the socially strict framework of Castilian society it was not easy to scale the upper heights, which were reserved for the nobility or – under Isabella – the earnest priests and lettered men emerging from her universities. But there were several examples of explorers who had catapulted themselves into the highest echelons of society by virtue of their finds. Columbus's own father-in-law, Bartolomeu Perestrello, had performed exactly that trick by 'discovering' Porto Santo for Portugal and becoming its governor.[14] The Norman explorer Jean de Béthencourt had declared himself King of the Canary Islands. The discovery and conquest of new lands – especially islands – was also a colourful part of chivalric romances like the popular Catalan novel *Tirant lo Blanc*, which sat on Isabella's bookshelf. This included a character who was King of the Canary Islands, and in Cervantes's later Don Quixote the knight-errant hero promises his sidekick Sancho Panza that he, too, will become lord of an island.

Columbus was an avid reader, but he was not a university man. The chronicler Bernáldez called him 'a man of great ingenuity but little education'.[15] His knowledge was extensive but hotch-potch, gleaned from experience and his vast but uncritical reading of the science, myth, rumour and legend contained in the works of philosophers, historians, astrologers, travellers and geographers from ancient Greece, medieval Europe and the Arab world. These books, once he had made his mind up, were selectively raided for proof that he was right. He and Isabella were, in this respect, a perfect match. They were equally enamoured of bold action, divine justification and, in moments of weakness, romantic folly. It is hard, indeed, not to see something of Don Quixote in him – a knight errant bent on glory or death, with Isabella as his Dulcinea. And if that was not enough, he added a touch of messianic Spanish glory to the adventure. 'All the profits from this enterprise of mine should be spent on the conquest of Jerusalem,'[16] he added. This would be, he meant, just an extension of Isabella and Ferdinand's crusading successes.

By the time he met Isabella again at Santa Fe, Columbus's campaign to find Castilian backing was already seven years old. He had worked on the prosperous Genoese and Florentine trading and banking communities of Andalusia, drawn close to the friars in La Rábida and become friendly with Grandees like Medina Sidonia and the Duke of Medinaceli. None of these people were able to give him official patronage, but they did form a valuable chorus of supporters who helped change the mood at court. Columbus seduced not just the men who surrounded Isabella and Ferdinand, but also the women. He appears to have sung the praises of the *miel rosada*, a medicinal syrup made from honey and rose water, produced by Prince Juan's governess Juana de la Torre[17] – who would make it for him to take on his journeys – and may also have targeted the influential Beatriz de Bobadilla, one of Isabella's closest ladies-in-waiting and wife of her long-time ally Andrés Cabrera. A later poet would claim that 'Bobadilla had been the main reason' for Columbus winning Isabella's backing (though he could have been referring to one of her relatives).[18]

Columbus had as fine a sense of self-publicity and propaganda as Isabella. The story of exactly how he gained permission – and financing – to sail was written by the man himself, as was much else about him. It is coloured by the grandstanding and self-justification that he so frequently indulged in, but the core of it is true. Columbus recalled his triumphant visit to the royal court in a typically vivid and dramatic manner. He had been seated, once more, before a committee of experts. Perhaps this was a moment when he chose to explain, as he noted in the margin of one of his books, how he himself had already come across strange peoples from the western ocean who had been carried by strong currents on to the shores of Europe. 'Men from Cathay came east. We have seen many interesting things and, above all, in Galway, in Ireland, a man and a woman who had been blown by storms in their boats in the most amazing way.' He almost certainly introduced the arguments of writers and scientists like Toscanelli, Pierre d'Aylli, Pope Pius II – who claimed that all oceans were navigable and so most lands were accessible – and al-Farghani.[19] Again, however, the experts chose not to believe his claims that the Ocean Sea was relatively small or that Asia lay within sailing distance on the other side of it. Not even the alternative of finding the mythical Antilles islands or the Antipodes could persuade them.[20] 'There was, once more, much debate, with information from philosophers, astrologers and cosmographers . . . and all agreed that this was madness and vanity, and at each step they laughed at and scorned the idea,' his editor Bartolomé de Las Casas, who often paraphrased Columbus's own words, reported in his *History of the Indies*.[21] 'The state of disbelief and disdain about what Columbus offered was such that it all collapsed, with the sovereigns ordering him to leave promptly.' Las Casas blamed Talavera – who was, once more, the man tasked with counselling Isabella against backing the journey – and others who, allegedly, were incapable of understanding the project. But the committee was also put off by the arrogance of the Genoese adventurer. After all, this foreigner was demanding an extraordinary set of Castilian titles. He wanted the title of admiral, just like the admiral of Castile – a powerful and lucrative hereditary position that belonged to Ferdinand's maternal family, the Enríquez – as well as those of *virrey*, or viceroy, and governor in perpetuity, with his children to succeed him.[22] As had happened earlier in Portugal, Columbus's quest for grandeur overrode his thirst for adventure and, at first, stymied his chances of achieving either. Isabella had listened to her advisers and concurred that the idea was too eccentric, the risks too great and the demands too high.

Columbus packed his bags once more. He had already been peddling his dreams around Europe for almost a decade and, as he rode off, the indefatigable mariner immediately began thinking of where to find the right backer. His brother Bartolomé was already trying to do exactly that in England and France.[23] But as Columbus began to reconsider his plans, Isabella also had a dramatic change of heart. In Santa Fe, she ordered that a messenger be sent to catch up with Columbus. The Italian had left an hour or so earlier, but was in no hurry. He had been on the road for just two hours when he heard the sound of a horse's hoofs behind him and the messenger told him to stop.[24] The queen, he was informed, had changed her mind.

A momentous decision had been made, though no one realised then quite how important it was. There is no record of why Isabella changed her mind. Responsibility has variously been attributed to her ladies-in-waiting, Columbus's many friends in her entourage and Ferdinand and his advisers. The project certainly fitted the spirit of the time. It also came in the context of the growing rivalry between Spain and Portugal for territorial expansion, trade and colonies. Spain, or rather Castile, was losing that battle. The world's oldest surviving terrestrial globe, made the following year in Nuremberg by Martin Behaim, shows Portugal's chequered flag sprouting from numerous spots along the eastern Atlantic while only one flag, perched atop the Canary Islands, bears the lions and castles of Castile. The papacy had given Portugal's claims its seal of approval, erecting a further barrier to Castile which Isabella formally recognised in the peace treaty signed at Alcáçovas in 1479 that put an end to Juana la Beltraneja's claim to the throne.[25]

Above all, though, Columbus's plan was cheap. The Genoese sailor needed just three ships and ninety sailors.[26] A small investment from the royal coffers offered up a potentially unlimited amount of gold, trade in spices and other goods or – following the Canary Islands model – slaves, plantations of sugar and other crops. That was especially tempting after the war in Granada had both emptied the royal exchequer and left it without an important source of tribute paid by the Moorish kingdom. In the end it may have been Luis Santángel – a Valencia *converso* who was one of Ferdinand's senior financial officers – who finally persuaded Isabella to call Columbus back. The chances of success were low, but any losses were manageable. The overall budget was a mere 2 million *maravedís* – described by one historian as 'perhaps the annual income of a middling provincial aristocrat'[27] – of which the crown would directly raise just over half. The rest would be paid in kind by the port of Palos, which owed fine-money that it could pay off by providing vessels for the trip, and by Columbus himself and others via a banking syndicate that relied partly on a Florentine merchant and financier in Seville, Giannotto Berardi.[28] Isabella and Ferdinand had 1.14 million *maravedís* forwarded by Santángel against funds to be raised via the sales of indulgences permitted by a Crusade Bull in Extremadura.²⁹ This was an abusive use of money meant for crusading against infidels, but it also fitted Columbus's belief that this was a divinely inspired venture designed to augment both the glory and reach of Christendom. Isabella, too, felt obliged to continue her crusade to enlarge Christendom after the fall of Granada and this was a cheap way to attempt that. 'There was no certainty about what Columbus said,' recalled one royal official. 'In the end, it was done at very little cost.'³⁰

The task of finalising the details was now handed over to Talavera, Prince Juan's tutor friar Diego de Deza (another future inquisitor general) and Ferdinand's chamberlain Juan Cabrero. Columbus showed the same tenacity when negotiating the terms and conditions of his trip as he had when pursuing royal backing. Others may have ridiculed his demand to be admiral, viceroy and governor general – but that is what the 'Capitulaciones de Santa Fe', the document signed by Isabella and her husband on 17 April 1492, awarded him. The 'Capitulaciones' signal that the monarchs knew this was an extraordinary expedition. But the terms were also vague, giving Columbus grandiose titles without detailing exactly what they meant. In the end it was Talavera who now recommended signing the final document. 'You should order this be done, even if it means spending something, because of the huge profit and honour that would come from the discovery of the said Indies,' he said.³¹

These were extraordinary things for Isabella, who drew as much power as she could towards the monarchy, to give away. Historians cannot agree on whether she and Ferdinand simply thought that this was a *merced* – a royal privilege or gift of crown income that could be given, but also taken away – or a binding contract. Perhaps they did not pay much attention. They were, after all, giving away rights to lands that most people thought did not exist and which, should Columbus discover the east coast of Asia, might already be under the sovereignty of some powerful monarch like the Great Khan. It was just as likely that Columbus would disappear over the horizon and fail to return or come back empty-handed. Isabella may be forgiven for not arguing too hard with a man to whom she was giving relatively little money and who was prepared to take such obviously extreme risks in her name (for this was Castile's enterprise, not Aragon's). Indeed, the text of the 'Capitulaciones' looks suspiciously as if it had been drawn up by Columbus himself and only lightly edited by royal officials. Ferdinand later explained quite explicitly why it was that Columbus obtained such generous terms and why they seemed so unthinkable later on. 'These days it is very easy to discover [new lands],' he wrote, twenty years afterwards. '[People] don't think about how, at that time, there was no real hope that anything at all would be discovered.'[32]

The available models of territorial expansion and naval exploration for Isabella were those that she herself had already overseen in the Canary Islands, along with Portugal's extensive experience along the coast of Africa and deeper into the Atlantic. The Canary Islands, wrested away from the indigenous peoples who had sometimes fought solely with sticks and stones, were an example of true colonies – faraway lands incorporated into the crown of Castile and occupied by its own people. The islands were used for cultivating sugar cane and its ports were safe points from which to trade or explore the rest of the Atlantic Ocean. Madeira and the Azores served a similar role for Portugal, while its trading posts along the African coast from Ceuta to Cape Verde and the Gold Coast were major sources of slaves and gold. Aragon had a different, and longer, tradition of empire in the Mediterranean – where its twelfth- and thirteenth-century lands had stretched to Sicily, Naples and even Athens – which provided Columbus with examples of the titles of viceroy or governor that he coveted.[33]

Isabella had been energetic in her pursuit of the Canary Islands, which lay 650 miles to the south of Spain and just seventy miles off the west coast of Africa. For historical reasons the Herrera-Pereza family were the feudal lords of four of these – Lanzarote, Fuerteventura, La Gomera and Hierro – and had been given the right of conquest over the more heavily populated islands of Tenerife, Gran Canaria and La Palma. But her council, once consulted, quickly came up with a formula that would allow her to take back the right of conquest over the islands that the Herrera-Perezas had not yet managed to invade. The family was paid compensation, and the right returned to the crown.[34]

The conquest of the island of Gran Canaria was a prolonged and bloody affair. Starting in 1478, it took five years, with the defeated natives either eventually allying with Castile or, more dramatically, and possibly apocryphally, hurling themselves to their deaths into a deep gully.[35] 'Their main weapons were stones, and whatever left their hands landed exactly where they wanted it to,' said Bernáldez. 'Their bravery made up for everything,' wrote another chronicler.[36] Isabella had received one of the Canary chieftains, Tenesor Semidán, who was baptised and became an ally.[37] He would visit her more than once, as Isabella tried to carry out a process of evangelisation among the islanders. The methods used were cruel, bringing about the virtual destruction of their society, with those that remained quickly adapting to Castilian models and their chiefs, like some Moorish or Jewish converts, receiving special attention and privileges. 'We have many advantages [over those on the other islands], as we [have learned to] speak [Spanish] and are accepted as Castilians,' said one.[38] Higher estimates claim that up to 85 per cent of the more than 60,000 islanders were killed or exiled, often after being lured on to boats with trickery.[39] The conquest of the other Canary Islands also proved hard, slow work, with neither Tenerife nor La Palma wholly in Isabella's hands before Columbus set off on his quixotic adventure.

Gran Canaria was, then, the only real model that Isabella had of the conquest of populated Atlantic islands before Columbus set sail, with conversions as one of its main aims. The principle that only those who fought against Isabella's armies, or rose against the crown's authority, could be enslaved did little to stop widespread trafficking in the Canary Islands' indigenous *guanches* and other peoples. They were forced to work at anything from cutting sugar cane and cleaning floors to prostituting their bodies. Canary slaves were fetching between 8,000 and 10,000 *maravedís* a head in Seville, Valencia, Barcelona, Lisbon and as far away as Venice.[40] Münzer came across a group of seventy-three Canary islanders, fourteen of whose number had died on the crossing, in a slave-trader's house. They were 'very dark, but not black . . . well proportioned, with long, strong arms and legs'.[41] Isabella did her best to protect those who had peacefully converted to Christianity. 'We have been told that some people have brought . . . Canary islanders, who are Christians, and others who are on the path to conversion to our Holy Faith and they want to divide them up and sell them as slaves,' she and her husband wrote to the authorities in Palos in 1477 after Gomerans began to appear in local slave markets.[42] 'Such a thing would be a poor example and cause for none of them at all to convert to our Holy Catholic Faith, which is something we seek to remedy.' The following year an angry Isabella wrote to those leading the Gran Canaria conquest, demanding that the same slaves from La Gomera, who had sailed back to the islands with the expeditionary force, be put in boats and sent back to their homes, rather than kept on Gran Canaria. 'I ordered them to be returned and given their freedom,' she said.[43] '[But] you have not taken or sent them to their own homes on the island of Gomera, as I had instructed.' Her insistence did not seem to carry much weight. Twenty years later she was still receiving complaints from Canary Island slaves, or from the so-called *procurador de los pobres* – a sort of public ombudsman for the poor – complaining about the rapacious settlers. A native woman from La Palma, called Beatriz, was among those to complain, claiming her Christian status had been ignored when she was sold to a man called Bachiller de Herrera in Seville. 'She says he beat her so much that she was close to death,' the court stated.

The Canary Islands had, in the imagination of Castilians, once belonged to their Visigothic kings, and Isabella's stated aim was 'to submit them to the crown and to expel, with God's favour, all superstition and heresy that are practised there and in other infidel islands by the Canarians and other pagans'.⁴⁴ This, then, she saw not just as reconquest but also as a religious crusade, just like the war against the Moors of Granada. Usefully, this also meant that it could be financed the same way — with the help of the pope and the sale of the indulgences offered in the Crusade Bulls he had issued.⁴⁵ But its people were not like the Moors, deemed rather to be religious innocents. It was also, in terms of financing, a precedent that could be followed for Columbus.

Columbus's daring, foolhardy project did not go down well among the seamen of Palos who were ordered to provide both boats and crews. 'It was publicly known and said that there was no land in those parts because Portugal had gone looking for it many times,' one of them, Bartolomé Colín, recalled later. 'Many wise men of the sea said that going to the west . . . even if you sailed for two years, you would never find land,' added another, Martín González. Indeed, local anger about being picked as the port that should provide the vessels and seamen was such that even the man who had rented his mule to Friar Pérez, so that he could see Isabella, found himself being blamed. 'Many people mocked the admiral and his business of going to discover the said islands, and they laughed about it, and even blamed this witness because I had provided the mule,' said the beast's owner, Juan Rodríguez Cabezudo. Friar Pérez had to twist many arms and convince many hardened sailors before the small fleet could be gathered.⁴⁶

In such an open-ended, risky expedition as that proposed by Columbus, Isabella probably did not have a particular objective beyond increasing her wealth, her power and, if possible, the reach of Christianity. There were no colonisers or priests sent with Columbus on his first voyage, so it is safe to say that she saw it as pure exploration, looking for 'islands and mainland'. The royal instructions included orders to avoid Portugal's gold trading station at La Mina, in present-day Ghana, and to respect existing treaties giving Portugal rights of conquest over Fez, possession of its Atlantic islands and trading priorities with the west African lands known as Guinea. A document signed by the monarchs as a passport for Columbus if he fell into foreign hands made it clear what he was expected to find. 'We send the nobleman Christopher Columbus with three caravels [in fact they were two caravels, *La Pinta* and *La Niña*, and a larger, sturdier *nao* called *Santa María*] over the ocean sea toward the region of India,' it read. Columbus even hired an oriental translator to go with him.[47]

Isabella herself may have given Columbus little thought after he had left Santa Fe that May. She could be forgiven for being more interested in the conquest of the Canaries. In the previous five months she had brought Spain's crusade against the Moors to an end and taken the dramatic step of expelling the Jews. The fortunes of the three vessels that left from Palos – within sight of the La Rábida friary – on 3 August 1492 were unlikely to worry her excessively.[48]

Columbus set off first for the Canary Islands, where he resupplied his ships and, it was rumoured, spent a few passionate days with the cruel, tyrannical and widowed mistress of the island of Gomera, another Beatriz de Bobadilla (a niece to Isabella's lady-in-waiting, she had allegedly ended up in the far-flung island after a jealous Isabella married her off to its feudal lord, Hernán Peraza, to keep her away from Ferdinand). He sailed west into the empty ocean from the port of San Sebastián on La Gomera on 6 September 1492. Most explorers heading into the unknown chose to sail into the wind, thereby ensuring that they could simply turn around in order to be blown back home. Instead, Columbus sought out the following wind that he knew blew at these latitudes. Those who watched his sails disappear over the horizon, and the queen who was sending him on his way, must have wondered if he would ever find a way back.[49]

29

Partying Women

Barcelona, 1492

It was a new comic twist to the noble sport of jousting, and those who sat looking out to sea with Isabella after the lengthy feasting with her French guests at the great *lonja* trading house in Barcelona laughed uproariously. 'This is how it was done: A man stood in the prow of a rowing boat with a lance at the ready and an oblong shield which he used to protect himself against the other jouster,' explained one of Prince Juan's pages, Gonzalo Fernández de Oviedo. 'Each boat had twenty oarsmen . . . and the two boats with the jousters would pick up as much speed as possible and when they clashed the jousters sometimes ended up in the water with their shields, which provoked great laughter.' The party at the great, domed hall where the city's merchants met daily to sign their deals and talk to their bankers had been just one of several festive interludes while the French ambassadors were tying up a peace agreement that would see Cerdagne and Roussillon return to Spanish hands. Several feasts involving all the royal family, the court, their visitors and the great and good of the city had ended in dancing, bullfights and games.

Hernando de Talavera, the austere Jeronymite friar who 'preached what he practised', was not pleased. Isabella did not usually disagree with Talavera, nor was she used to being scolded, either in public or in private. But that is what her confessor, now archbishop of Granada, had done and she was determined to persuade him that his biting criticism of her behaviour during the partying that had accompanied the arrival of a French embassy was wrong. 'We did nothing new, nor did we think that we had done anything untoward,' she wrote back.[1]

That is not what Talavera had heard. In Isabella's court, men and women normally ate separately, yet this time they had been allowed to sit together. His anger extended to Isabella's dancing, the way her ladies-in-waiting were led off by the French visitors and the gory bullfights laid on for them as entertainment. 'I won't criticise the gifts and prizes, though for those to be considered good they ought to be moderate. Nor the spending on clothes and new dresses, even though, where it is excessive, blame must be attached,' he had sniffed.[2] 'What I think most offended God in so many and diverse ways were the dances – especially those involving someone who should not dance – which only a miracle can prevent from being sinful . . . and, even more, the licentiousness of mixing French gentlemen with Castilian ladies during the dinner and that they were allowed to lead them around however they wished.'

'And what should I say about the bulls?' Talavera asked. 'They are, without doubt, a prohibited spectacle . . . Without any kind of profit for the soul, body, for honour or income,' he declared. Talavera had obviously disapproved, too, of the partying and bullfights in Seville two years earlier with which the queen had marked her daughter Isabella's marriage to her Portuguese husband. He now chose to remind Isabella that all that partying had been for nothing, given that Prince Afonso had died just eight months after the wedding. It was a low blow, and Isabella responded with unusual, if controlled, anger.

She cared deeply about her moral reputation and Talavera's criticisms meant that it was being questioned. 'They must have told you that I danced there, but that is wrong. It did not even pass through my mind,' she insisted. Spending on clothes had been minimal, though she had been unable to resist ordering up a new dress for herself. 'Neither I nor my ladies wore new clothes,' she said. 'I only had one dress made, and that was silk . . . and as plain as possible.'[3]

She admitted that the men had worn costly costumes, but that had been done against her instructions.

Isabella cared not just about her own reputation, but also about that of her ladies-in-waiting – who were meant to reflect her own image of virtuous femininity. Through her propagandists, she held up her supposedly wicked sister-in-law Queen Juana, whose Portuguese ladies had created such uproar, as an example of everything a queen should not be. 'As for leading the girls off, which I read in your letter, I did not hear anything at all about them being taken off, and I still have not,' she told Talavera. This had by no means been the first time that the rule about segregated eating had been relaxed in order to entertain visitors. 'Eating at table with the French is an old custom and one that they themselves usually follow,' she explained. 'Whenever they are here and their main people eat with the monarchs the others sit at the tables in the salon of the ladies and gentlemen. That is how they always are, as they never place the women apart on their own. This was also done [by us] with the Burgundians, the English and the Portuguese.'[4]

The only justifiable complaint was, she said, about the bullfighting. 'With the bulls I felt the same as you, even though it was not quite so bad. But afterwards I decided with all my determination never to watch them again in my life,' she said, though Isabella recognised that she could not ban a tradition enjoyed by, among others, her own husband.[5] Her concern was not for the animals, but for the men who were gored. Isabella did not stick to her pledge, and later rued the fact. The following year she saw two men and three horses gored to death in a bull-run at Arévalo and responded by introducing a new rule to make the bulls less dangerous by covering up the points of their horns.[6] 'She ordered that the bulls' horns be covered with others from dead animals and stuck on . . . in such a way that the tips of the [newly-added] horns pointed backwards,' recalled Oviedo. The result was as if the bull's horns had suddenly grown longer, but curled inwards like a goat's, so that they could be used to batter runners, but not to impale them.

Isabella was a strict mistress of her own household, where women were expected to behave themselves or, at the very least, be discreet about misbehaviour. Scandal, above all, was to be avoided. 'She detested bad women,' Pulgar explained.[7] Normally the two sexes were kept rigorously separate. 'In her palace she oversaw the upbringing of noble young ladies, the daughters of Grandees . . . investing great diligence in the supervision of them and the other palace women,' said Pulgar.[8] They normally ate apart from the men, and Isabella acted like a mother superior, making sure the girls in her care were closely chaperoned. Male officials and doctors had to wait outside Isabella's quarters until all her daughters, and the ladies-in-waiting who slept there, were dressed and ready.[9] The ladies-in-waiting were, in part, there to provide a shield. 'In the absence of the king, until now she always slept in the common dormitory of certain young ladies and maidens of her household. Now she sleeps in the company of her daughters and other honourable women in order not to give root to gossip that could blemish her reputation for conjugal fidelity.'[10] An English envoy whose host disappeared to eat with his wife noted that similar rules often applied outside the royal palace. 'It is not the custom in this country that women ever come and eat in company with strangers,' he explained.[11]

Isabella's ladies followed their mistress's daily routine, where long and intense sessions of administration were punctuated with meals and regular visits to the chapel. In the chapel the cultural and material wealth of musical instruments, choristers, incense, priests' robes, altar cloths and sparkling gold and silver ornaments provided a welcome change of atmosphere. The ritual sounds, sights and smells of her daily services were an invigorating feast for the senses that contrasted with the relatively drab world outside. Isabella's chapel was a place to meditate not just on spiritual affairs, but also on the Christian ideology that drove many of her political choices. 'Even though she spent night and day at work on the large and arduous tasks of government, it seemed as though her life was more one of contemplation than of action,' said one Italian at her court, who noted that she rarely missed the daily services.[12] Yet it would be a mistake to see her court as a cloistered, convent-like place reserved only for the prim and the pious. There was fun, too. Dwarfs, dancing girls and musicians entertained her court in the evenings and at meals. There were board games, cards, singing and dancing. Acrobats were also popular, with one of them astounding wedding guests by standing on a tightrope to juggle balls, swords and bells before hanging 'by the teeth, most marvellously'. And in the intimacy of the queen's quarters, her ladies played with pet cats and rabbits, while dressing up their little lapdogs with bells and collars. For literature they had heart-fluttering sentimental novels and the sung troubadour romances of knights and damsels.[13] The queen's household was overseen by her 'milk sister' Clara Alvarnáez, whose mother had been one of Isabella's wet nurses in Madrigal. Isabella mixed young noble girls with well-bred older women in her group of a dozen ladies-in-waiting, while matchmaking the former to suitable partners became one of her favourite pastimes.[14] Her ladies helped to manage the hospital for the poor that travelled with the queen – an item of royal charity that also served to augment Isabella's popularity as she traversed her realms. The ladies were meant to be a reflection of Isabella herself – well behaved but providing a dazzling chorus of finery when she needed to put on a show of pomp. Like Isabella, they were expected to remain well turned out, clean and sweet-smelling. Apart from the soaps and perfumes available to them, a resident tooth-cleaner was on hand and there were slave-girls for hairwashing.

The restricted contact between the sexes meant that, on the occasions when the separation was relaxed, the court went into a frenzy of courtly love. The Spanish courtiers' ability to exaggerate their love interest involved everything from limpid adoration to swooning, and the elderly Spanish Duke of Alba, who later accompanied Catherine of Aragon to England, had to be carried out of a feast after fainting at the sight of one English lady.[15] A Burgundian who passed through the Castilian court was amazed to see one young woman at a banquet simultaneously playing along three apparently besotted suitors. 'She spoke to one who remained on his knees, with his head uncovered, for an hour and a half; she was a quarter of an hour with the second and a full hour with the third. She would talk to one, while throwing glances at another and keeping her hand on the shoulder of the third. That way she kept all three happy; because, given that they did not see them often, they show great delight at being with the women with whom they are in love,' he explained. The Burgundians were shocked and wanted to know why the woman toyed with them like that. 'We do as we want while we are waiting to marry, treating them like this,' she replied. 'Because once we are married they lock us up in a room in a castle. That is how they get their revenge on us for having such a good time when we were single.'[16] Talavera would have approved. A woman's wedding day, he said, was 'the day in which you lost your freedom'. Married women were meant to stay at home since 'they are made to be shut up and busy in their homes, while the male is made to move around and deal with the things outside it'. Like Eve, he thought, women were inherently foolish and easily led astray. 'It is natural for them to easily believe in bad things.' Isabella was so determined to protect them from temptation that when an unfortunate young man called Diego Osorio was found outside their window armed with a rope and, presumably, a desire to scale into their rooms, he was immediately sentenced to death.[17]

Isabella's daughters were the other great torch-bearers of her reputation. The *infantas* were expected to spin, sew, weave and embroider, since even queens should take pride in sewing a husband's shirt.[18] Isabella's propagandists and hagiographers, understandably, praised the virtues of her daughters, who were deemed pure, honourable, loving and properly submissive to their husbands. Clumsiness and lasciviousness were their 'enemies', according to one contemporary.[19] More importantly, they were also extremely well educated. Isabella had little formal education herself but soon realised its value, teaching herself Latin – the language of high culture and of the mass – as an adult. She called a talented woman Latinist, Beatriz Galindo, nicknamed 'La Latina', to court to give her lessons and kept her there to teach her daughters, while also hiring Italian humanists as their tutors.[20] Juana 'answered instantly in Latin to any question she was asked, just like the princes who travel from one land to another. The English say the same thing of Catherine, Juana's sister. And the whole world has similar praise for the [other] two sisters,' said the contemporary humanist Luis Vives. Even the Dutch humanist Erasmus was impressed, though fawning to royalty was one of his specialities. Catherine was 'well instructed – not merely in comparison with her own sex', he commented after meeting her.[21] 'And is no less to be respected for her piety than her erudition.'

Isabella had a library full of devotional works, the lives of saints and pious manuals instructing her on how best to bring up her daughters.[22] The latter were written by friars or other religious men with no experience of raising children of any kind. They often saw women as naturally afflicted by a series of vices. They were envious, grasping gossip-mongers in constant danger of the most terrible feminine weakness of all – the 'madness of love'.[23] And when women strayed, the world trembled. 'Disordered love is a sin that occurs especially among women, which in turn causes discord, deaths, scandals, wars, the loss of goods . . . and, what is worse, the perdition of the most tragic souls to the abomination of carnal sin,' Alfonso Martínez de Toledo, known as the archpriest of Talavera, wrote in his *Reprobation of Wordly Love*. 'Love is foolishness, madness, deranged and a waste of time,' he added. 'Lust together with shameless, dishonest love is . . . counsellor to the twisted Satan, mortal enemy of human salvation.' One of the most influential of these works was the *Carro de las Damas*, or *Book of Women*, by the Franciscan monk Francesc Eiximenis. He was less radical in his assessment of women's 'natural' faults, but still believed they needed a firm hand when they misbehaved. 'Punish them and wound them on the back with some switch,' he advised.[24] Self-control and discretion were the distinguishing qualities of well-brought-up girls, who were meant to carry rosaries and spend part of each day praying. They should also learn to avoid non-Christians, refusing food from them and staying away from Jewish or Muslim men.

Isabella consciously cultivated an image of virtue and feminine modesty, creating a public persona which was both majestic and impassive. As with many a fellow teetotaller, self-control was paramount. 'She was measured and contained in her bodily movements; she did not drink wine,' reported Pulgar. This rendered her difficult to read and frightening, while also making her moments of public warmth or joy seem that much more endearing. But life on what her English counterparts would have called 'the queen's side' of the court was not just about primers, prayers and needlework. Her daughters learned falconry, horse-riding and hunting. There were dancing lessons with Portuguese teachers and musical instruments of all kinds to be learned. Songs were sung at dinner and stories of chivalry – Isabella's favourites – were told out loud.[25] Legends from the magical, mysterious world of Merlin and Lancelot also sat on her shelves,[26] though these would be condemned by one male contemporary as 'based on lust, love and boasting . . . causing weak-breasted women to fall into libidinous errors and commit sins they would not otherwise commit'.[27] The archpriest of Hita's ribald *Libro de Buen Amor* (The Book of Good Love), with its brazen women and earthy sexuality, was also on her bookshelf. Perhaps, behind closed doors and in the entirely feminine world of her private court, the scatalogical references to sexual organs, pubic hair and bodily functions in some of the bawdier songs in the *Cancionero de Palacio* (Palace Songbook) were allowed. There was no lack of well-paid musicians to sing them.[28]

Such bawdiness was certainly not for public display. And the thought of French knights wandering off with her carefully controlled ladies-in-waiting during the partying in Barcelona cannot have pleased Isabella. Talavera's complaints did not go unheeded. As she awaited the arrival of her future daughter-in-law Margaret of Austria, with her court of Burgundians, Isabella issued instructions to avoid the 'familiarity, common treatment and informal communication used by queens and princesses in Austria, Burgundy and France'. She ordered, instead, that the visitors be welcomed with 'gravity . . . as was the [common] usage in Spain'.[29]

30

A Hellish Night

The Old Royal Palace, Barcelona, 7 December 1492

At midday on a grey, overcast December day in 1492, after a morning of listening to pleas from his Catalan subjects, Ferdinand began to walk down the steep stone staircase that fanned out from the corner of what was already considered the 'old' royal palace in Barcelona. He must have briefly glimpsed a peasant farmer called Juan de Canyamars as the man appeared from a chapel beside the main doorway and then stepped aside to let the king, who was wearing a favourite heavy gold chain, sweep past. As Ferdinand took the first two steps, Canyamars pushed his way through the king's entourage, came up behind him, pulled a large, machete-like farmer's knife out from under his coat and lunged at his neck. The knife entered the base of the left-hand side of the king's neck, though his collarbone and the thick loops of his chain deflected part of the blow. Those with Ferdinand reached for their own knives and swords, and soon both men were on the ground and bleeding from their wounds. Ferdinand was rushed back inside, blood issuing from a two-inch-deep gash.[1]

Isabella was in a separate palace that gave on to the beach and the Mediterranean Sea. When news arrived of the attack, she automatically assumed that some kind of coup was under way. She wanted to run straight to Ferdinand, but her mind instantly turned to the consequences of regicide. She ordered that boats be brought up so that her fourteen-year-old son Juan could be rowed out to sea. If her husband died, Juan would become king of Aragon. That made him the next target for any plotters. Her Castilian courtiers armed themselves and stood by, ready to repel any attempt to kidnap the child.[2] Rumours flew around the city – about Moors or Navarrans or others who might want Ferdinand dead – and the mob grew restless.

Isabella had never felt such fear. 'My soul could not have felt it more if it had left my body. It is impossible to exaggerate, or even express, what I felt; and should death want him again, I pray to God that it would not be in the same way,' she wrote to Friar Talavera. Ferdinand would not initially allow her to go to him, as he was preparing for death with his priests. 'He wrote to me because he did not want me to come while he was confessing,' Isabella said. Pere Carbonell, a chronicler who worked in the neighbouring Archive of Aragon, ran into the palace to see what was going on, but found the doors to the great hall locked with the king inside. 'Some said the king was injured; others that his throat had been cut with a sword,' he recalled. 'I thought I would faint when I heard that, but I recovered my strength . . . there was so much pushing and shoving that I was unable to see him.'

Ferdinand's bulky gold chain had 'prevented [Canyamars] cutting off his head with a single slice', but he still appeared to have suffered a mortal blow, according to Peter Martyr d'Anghiera, an Italian humanist whom Isabella had hired to run the court's school for young noblemen.[3] Anghiera reported that 'a battalion' of doctors and surgeons had appeared to save the king's life. These cleaned the wound, removing hair and fragments of bone before sewing it up with seven stitches.[4] 'The doctors are not sure whether the king will survive, or not,' he said afterwards. Isabella feared she would now lose the man she loved with a jealous passion and with whom she had reached a pinnacle of glory. Their unique partnership, and the future fruits that it might bring, hung by a very fine thread. 'We count the days and live between fear and hope,' wrote Anghiera the following day, as the court prepared to mourn.[5] In Barcelona and across his kingdoms, people prayed for Ferdinand's recovery, vowing to perform extravagant acts of gratitude if he survived.

The next evening hopes were raised as Ferdinand began to show the first signs of recovery, but a week later he was back in danger again, collapsing as an infection took hold. His tongue swelled, his heart beat frantically and his face turned red.[6] 'It was a hellish night,' Isabella recalled. 'The wound was so big that, according to Dr Guadalupe, you could put four fingers inside,' though her squeamish side prevented her from checking that for herself. 'I was not brave enough to look.' One courtier suggested that her suffering 'seemed greater than the king's'.

Barcelona was gripped, once more, by fear. Churches filled up. 'There was more demand for confession than was ever seen in Easter Week, and all without anybody issuing instructions,' Isabella wrote to Talavera. By Christmas Day 1492 – although weak – Ferdinand was out of danger. He still could not leave the palace, but showed himself at a window to reassure those below that he was recovering.[7] 'God behaved with such mercy that it seems he measured the site [of the knife-blow] precisely to avoid danger in such a way that it missed his tendons, the neck-bone and all the dangerous parts,' Isabella told Talavera. Soon Isabella was preparing to ride with her husband to a different house where he could rest better. 'He is up and walking about outdoors and tomorrow, if God wills, he will ride to the other house that we are moving into. The pleasure of seeing him up is as great as the original sadness was, so that we all now feel revived,' she declared.

Isabella was not the only person to see divine intervention in Ferdinand's survival. There could be little more providential than being saved by the golden chain of God-ordained royal authority. His surviving the attack, indeed, only added to the couple's reputation as God's chosen servants, destined to restore Christianity's authority even beyond their own frontiers. Those who had vowed to give thanks and make pilgrimages if he recovered now kept their word. Catalonia's holy mountain, the serrated rocky outcrop known as Montserrat, saw the faithful clambering up its steep, dangerous sides – some barefoot or on their knees. Isabella and her children, too, made the trip up the mountain's steep, winding tracks, walking at least part of the way, to give thanks. 'All sorts of people are making pilgrimages up mountains, through valleys or along the coast to any place where there is a sanctuary,' reported Anghiera.[8]

Fears of a plot were soon dampened. Canyamars had acted on his own. The farmer from a village near Barcelona was mad and delusional. He had been convinced that if he killed Ferdinand, the crown would be his. He was tortured to extract the truth of a wider plot, but stuck to his story.[9] 'No evidence could be found, or suspicion raised, that anyone else knew about this except for the person who did it,' Isabella reported. He had been visited by either the holy spirit or the devil almost twenty years earlier, he said, and told he would be king. Isabella's prime concern was that the attacker refused to confess his sins to a priest before death, thereby placing his soul at risk, and she sent her own friars to persuade him. Canyamars finally gave way. 'And on deciding to confess, beforehand, he realised that he had done wrong and said that it was as if he was waking from a dream, that he had not been himself. And he said the same thing after confessing, apologising to the king and to me,' Isabella told Talavera. The royal council had condemned him to death and only Isabella's intervention prevented him being handed over to the mob for lynching. She insisted, as an act of clemency, that he be killed by drowning.[10] He was paraded through the city in a cart, then drowned (though some reports claim he was garrotted) and butchered. 'They cut off the right hand with which he had done the deed, and the feet he used to get there and plucked out the eye he had used to see it with and the heart with which he had thought it up,' a local historian said a century later.[11]

Isabella wondered whether the attack on Ferdinand meant that she was being punished for her own sins, though she did not enumerate them and she asked her confessor, in a rare display of remorse, to draw up a list of those she may have committed while seeking power. 'That was one of the things that hurt most, to see the king suffering what should have happened to me, without him deserving to pay for me,' she wrote. 'That nearly killed me.'

A New World

The Atlantic Ocean, 14 February 1493

Five months after setting sail, Christopher Columbus doubted whether he would see Europe or the queen who had sent him on his journey ever again. As he battled fierce Atlantic storms and worried about his ship sinking hundreds of miles from land, he made a special plan to ensure that news of his journey reached Isabella and her husband. He knew well that a discovery does not exist if the discoverer perishes without telling anyone. That is why, according to his own account, he wrote out a long document explaining all that had happened since he left La Gomera. The document was then wrapped tightly in a waxed cloth and sealed inside a wax tablet before being put in the equivalent of a glass bottle – a wooden barrel that was tossed overboard. A well-made barrel was the object most likely to survive if the ship and its crew went to the bottom of the ocean. A note inside the barrel offered a reward of 1,000 ducats to whoever delivered it, with the seal intact, to Isabella and Ferdinand.[1] 'I placed a similarly packaged message at the highest point of the poop deck, so that if the ship sank, the barrel would float off on the waves and be at Fortune's mercy,' he explained later. If found, history would record the fact that he had indeed discovered new lands. The barrel was never found, or the money claimed, but the letter would have been very similar to the one which, by a more orthodox route, found its way into Isabella's hands the following month during the family's long stay in Barcelona.[2] It had been sent overland from Lisbon and contained a dramatic declaration: 'I come from the Indies with the fleet that your Highnesses gave me, which I reached 33 days after leaving your kingdoms.'³ This was, Columbus told her, the greatest moment of Isabella's reign so far. 'That everlasting God who has handed your Highnesses so many victories has now given you the greatest victory ever delivered to any monarch until now.'

Columbus's letter promised 'as much gold as you need' and 'slaves without number' while the 'whole of Christendom must hold great celebrations . . . for the discovery of such a multitude of peoples so concentrated together who, with very little effort, can be converted to our Holy Faith'. Isabella must have found perfectly reasonable his claim that Castile's great prize came from God, who had 'decided that I should find gold, mines, spices and countless people willing to become Christians'. Columbus had not, of course, found India – having bumped, instead, into the islands of the Caribbean. Nor had he found any gold mines or, as he told Isabella and her husband, islands populated entirely by women. But he had crossed what we now know as the Atlantic Ocean, and the news that there were other lands – and other peoples – far away to the west was stunning. One of the boldest, or most foolhardy, pieces of navigation in history had ended in triumph for Castile. It was an extraordinary letter and, for Isabella, doubly so. She was not just one of the first people in Christendom to hear of these distant, exotic lands that Columbus described so gushingly in his letter. She also knew that they now belonged to her.

———

From Columbus's dramatic and colourful descriptions, Isabella could be forgiven for thinking that she was now queen of something akin to the Garden of Eden. 'The islands are so fertile that, even were I capable of describing it all, it would still be difficult to believe; the climate is very temperate, the trees, fruit trees and grasses are beautiful, though very different to our own, and the rivers and ports are many and extremely good,' she read. 'The islands are well populated with the finest people in the world, who are without wickedness or pretence. All of them, whether men or women, go about as naked as the day their mothers gave birth to them.' One of the islands he had found, and called Hispaniola, he thought must be bigger than Spain itself, while a second one, which he christened Juana (and then Cuba), he deemed larger than Britain. 'This sea [the Caribbean] is the sweetest in the world for sailing with little danger for *naos* and other ships,' Isabella read.[4]

Columbus appears to have used a shipboard log to write a much longer and more complete narrative of the journey that reached Isabella later. It remained, nevertheless, a subjective and biased report intended to persuade Isabella and her husband that their money had been well spent and that further investment would provide even greater gains. The original was lost, but some of Columbus's own words survive in a version provided by Las Casas, a contemporary who became the first historian of what was soon called 'the Indies'. He used Columbus's narrative to compose an account known as the *Diary of the First Voyage*[5] and to write his own *History of the Indies*. Other original sections of Columbus's writing can be found in the much later *Histories of the Admiral*, attributed to his son Hernando.[6] 'As well as writing down each night the events of that day and, during the day, logging the night's navigation, I plan to draw up a new chart, in which I shall include all the sea and landmasses of the Ocean Sea in their places,' Columbus wrote in an introduction addressed to Isabella and her husband. 'Above all it is important that I should renounce sleep and concentrate instead on navigation, which will require a great amount of work.'

Isabella learned that Columbus, who commanded his tiny fleet from the sixty-foot *Santa María*, had begun to lie to his own crew almost immediately, since he was worried they would mutiny if they knew how far from Europe they were sailing. He pretended that each day they had covered a shorter distance than they really had 'so that if the voyage stretched out they would not be overcome by fear or dismay'. After ten days on the open sea, they saw a bolt of fire fall into the ocean, upsetting superstitious crew members 'who began to imagine they were signs that we had taken the wrong course'.[7] With no sight of land, they became anxious, muttering that the winds would never blow them back to Spain.

They made good daily distances. On 10 October, more than a month after setting out, Columbus calculated that they had sailed 62.5 leagues, but told the crew it was only 46. In the Mediterranean Sea, or along the Atlantic seaboard routes, it was rare for sailors to go for long periods without seeing land and by now there was a restless, almost mutinous, air on his ships, but he made it clear that he would not turn back. 'His aim, and that of the monarchs, was to discover the Indies via the western sea and they had chosen to accompany him,' said Las Casas.[8] 'He would continue until, with God's grace, he found them.' On the following day, the miracle happened. They began to spot tree trunks and branches, as well as the remains of artefacts that had obviously been shaped by human hands, floating around them.[9] At ten o'clock that night Columbus thought he saw a flame in the far distance. 'It was like a wax candle rising and falling,' he said.[10] He secretly called over Isabella's overseer Rodrigo Sánchez de Segovia, one of the men she had sent to keep an independent eye on the expedition. But while another royal official called Pedro Gutiérrez thought he could also see the light, Sánchez de Segovia did not, and they decided not to tell the crew. It would not have been the first time that a sighting of land had proved false. Columbus later claimed for himself the 10,000 maravedís prize that Isabella had promised to give the first person who spotted land, though that honour probably goes to Juan Rodríguez de Bermejo, also known as Rodrigo de Triana, the lookout on the speedier *Pinta*, who made the first confirmed sighting after his vessel forged ahead overnight.[11]

They approached the island sighted from the *Pinta* slowly, spotting naked people on shore. Columbus had himself rowed ashore, accompanied by a group of armed men and the royal standards he would use to claim the island for Isabella's Castile and Christendom.

As the banners bearing Castile's castles and Christ's cross were planted on this new, exotic land, Columbus appeared to believe that the green vegetation, plentiful streams and strange fruits that they could spot were a sign that he was close to Asia. In fact, he had probably reached San Salvador or Watling Island, lying on the eastern side of the Bahamas.[12]

Isabella's new subjects were, she read, mostly good natured, innocent and simple. They had gathered eagerly around the strangely hirsute and overdressed newcomers, with their pale skins and beards. 'Since they were so friendly and seeing that they were people who would be best converted to our holy faith through love rather than by force, I gave them some red bonnets and glass beads which they hung around their necks and many other things of little value, all of which pleased them greatly and they were so easily won over that it was marvellous,' wrote Columbus. 'They brought us parrots and balls of cotton thread and darts and many other things, which they exchanged for the things that we gave to them, like glass beads and little bells.'

Columbus was impressed by the people he referred to as 'Indians', though they were mostly Taíno, a people of Arawak descent who were spread across the islands of the Caribbean and modern-day Florida.[13] They were well built, 'with handsome bodies and fine features' – though the fact that he saw very few old people suggests that they did not live very long. Broad faces with 'beautiful eyes' were daubed with different colours – charcoal black, white, red or whatever they could find. Some painted their entire bodies. Their natural skin colour was a yellowish shade of brown and Isabella was told that they reminded her sailors of the native *guanche* Canary Islanders who had visited her at court, though the Taíno were slightly lighter-skinned. Some, indeed, were deemed 'so fair that if they wore clothes and stayed out of the sun and wind they would almost be as white as people in Spain'.

Isabella read that the Taíno hair was so thick, straight and black that it reminded Columbus of a horse's tail and he would soon find that it was worn in varying styles on different islands. Some men cut it short, with a few long trails of hair down their back. Others wore it long at the back and cut straight across a fringe that reached down to their eyebrows, or allowed it to grow 'as long as the women in Castile' and gathered it up in a net held together with colourful parrot feathers. All went about in different degrees of nakedness, without any sense of shame, though some wore small loincloths or larger strips of cotton tied around their waists. Columbus was impressed not just by their physique and apparent innocence, but by their sailing skills – especially the way they handled dug-out canoes that fitted up to forty men. Bows, arrows and primitive clubs were the only weapons they carried, though some bore the marks of cuts and blows received during fighting.

Isabella must have been delighted by Columbus's belief that it would be easy to conquer, convert and persuade these people to guide him to sources of gold. They had never seen swords such as those Columbus showed them, which 'they held by the sharp edge, cutting themselves', Isabella read. Their innocence extended to religion, and she was told that 'they would easily become Christians, as it seemed that they did not follow any sect at all'. Columbus pledged to take half a dozen of them back with him to show Isabella and her husband, though he did not initially say whether he planned to do this by persuading or imprisoning them.

Her new subjects had little gold adornments hanging from their noses and 'from their gestures I understood that on the southern side of the island there was a king with large pots full of it'. Columbus genuinely believed that he had bumped into the outlying islands of Asia, and dreamed of reaching Japan. As they sailed on to other islands, natives continued to appear on the beaches, or swam out to their three boats, while the exotic tropical vegetation, dazzling fish and apparently perfect harbours continued to amaze the visitors. As Isabella read on, Columbus's description of this earthly paradise grew in both passion and colour. 'These islands are very green and fertile with sweet air and there may be many other things that I don't know about them, but I do not want to stop here because I wish to explore many more islands in order to find gold,' he said. Even the fish, which in Isabella's world mostly came in tones of silver, grey, brown or pink, were dazzling, 'with the most wonderful colours in the world, blues, yellows, reds and all sorts of colours arranged in a thousand ways . . . so exquisite that no man can fail to wonder at them'.

The queen also learned that, on Friday, 19 October he had sighted an island that he named after her, Isabella (having already named another one Ferrandina, after Ferdinand, and two others San Salvador and Santa María of the Conception).[14] 'I have named a westerly cape here, Cabo Hermoso [Cape Beautiful]. And beautiful it is, indeed,' he said, before lamenting that it would take him fifty years to explore these new lands. Again, he was entranced by what he understood to be stories of magnificently wealthy monarchs. 'The people I am carrying with me say there is a king here, who is lord of all the islands of this area and wears on his own body large amounts of gold . . . I cannot stop to see everything, as I could not do so in fewer than fifty years and I want to explore and discover as much as I can before returning to your Highnesses, if God wills it, in April.'

Isabella may have sensed, however, that for all the beauty and charming naivety of the people, Columbus had been suffering from growing frustration. He had erected crosses on the islands he found, claiming them for her Castile and Christ. But he had not yet found proof that this was the Asia he had promised to discover, nor had he found any appreciable quantities of the gold, spices or other goods that might make him, and Castile, wealthy. 'I am still resolved to find the mainland and the city of Quisay [in China] and present your letters to the Great Khan, asking him for a reply and bringing it back to you,' he wrote in his diary on 21 October.

When he reached Cuba – which he hoped might be Japan – his anxiety and inability to understand the natives allowed his fertile imagination to interpret their words and gestures in the most optimistic, and unrealistic, fashion – even imagining that he had been told the Great Khan's ships came here, taking just ten days to sail from Asia. 'They said large ships and merchants and such things came from the south-east,' he added. 'And I also understood that, far off, there were people with just one eye and others with dog's noses who ate men and that, when they captured one, they slit his throat and drank the blood and cut off his penis.'

Columbus's delight at the naivety of the people did not stop him from kidnapping five of the more trusting men who came aboard his ship, the *Santa María*, or ordering his men to seize seven women from a house they raided. If Isabella and Ferdinand wanted converts to Christianity, he said, then this was the best way to start. The captives could learn Spanish and the customs of Castile, be instructed in the faith and return as interpreters. 'These people have no sect of their own and are not idolators,' he wrote. 'They are very meek, with no knowledge of evil or killing or of taking other people captive,' he insisted. They also believed that Columbus and his men were messengers from God and so were 'ready to recite any prayer that we say to them and to make the sign of the cross'. Isabella and her husband should 'set about making them Christians, which I think will not take long, with numerous peoples converting to our Holy Faith as great lands, riches and all these peoples are won for Spain'.

Columbus squabbled with his crew and Martín Alonso Pinzón, captain of *La Pinta*, who sailed off separately for more than a month. Isabella's new 'admiral', meanwhile continued exploring and singing the praises of the places and peoples he encountered. She learned, for example, that even for a seasoned sailor, the islands of the Caribbean offered incomparable harbours. 'I have sailed the sea for 23 years, barely leaving it for any time worth counting, and I have seen both the Levant and the west . . . and have gone on the northern route to England and south to Guinea, but in none of those places are the ports as perfectly formed [as here],' he wrote after encountering yet another bay surrounded by dense green vegetation and fed by crystal-clear river water.

Isabella was told that these new lands were 'as much yours as Castile itself' and that their inhabitants would be easy to control and even easier to put to work. 'With the people I have with me, who are not many, I could run through all these islands without trouble,' she read. 'I have seen three of our sailors step ashore and watched a multitude of these Indians run away, even though nobody wanted to do them any harm. They carry no arms, go naked and have no skill with weapons . . . and will be easily persuaded to obey orders, sowing seeds or whatever else is needed, building towns and being taught to wear clothes and learn our customs.'

Disaster had struck on Christmas Day, 1492. On a calm night, Columbus went to his bunk while a junior seaman took the helm. A gentle current sucked the ship, the *Santa María*,[15] silently on to sand or rocks off the island which the Indians who lived there called 'Heiti'[16] (Hispaniola, now home to the Dominican Republic and Haiti) with Columbus waking to the sound of a juddering rudder and panicking crew. They abandoned ship and Columbus threw himself on the mercy of a local chief called Guacanagari who 'showed great sadness at our adversity and shed tears, immediately sending everyone from his village in many big canoes, so that we and they could unload the decks'. Isabella's new subjects behaved with a natural generosity which, had they been aware of their new status in the eyes of their Castilian visitors, might have been less forthcoming. 'Nowhere in Castile would our things have been so well looked after . . . I swear to your Highnesses that there are no better people on earth. They love others as they love themselves, talk in the sweetest tones in the world, are gentle and always smiling.' They might wander around stark naked, but he was quick to assure his prudish queen that this did not mean there was anything untoward about the behaviour of the men towards the women, or vice versa, which remained 'honourable'.

Trinkets were traded for local goods, but what most impressed the natives was Columbus's firepower. When he ordered a lombard and a long-barrelled *espingarda* gun to be fired, the watching Indians fell to the ground in surprise and shock. 'So many good things happened that this disaster turned out to be a great thing,' the document that Columbus had prepared for Isabella read. 'Because it is true to say that if I had not run aground I would have sailed off without anchoring here.' Divine intervention was a theme that chimed perfectly with Isabella's beliefs. He had not initially planned to leave a colony behind him but now he decided to build a wooden fort, depositing a small garrison of thirty-nine men inside it.[17] 'I trust in God that on my intended return from Castile, a ton of gold will have been found by those who had to be left behind and that they will have discovered the gold mine and the spices,' he said, adding that there would be such an abundance of wealth that Isabella and Ferdinand could within three years recover for Christendom the Church of the Holy Sepulchre in Jerusalem, and Jesus' empty tomb. This was a reminder of his extravagant request, undoubtedly designed to flatter Isabella's crusading spirit, that any money generated by his expedition should go towards helping them conquer Jerusalem. 'Your Highnesses laughed and said you liked the idea and that this was already one of your desires,' he wrote.

On 4 January 1493, he weighed anchor and, in a light breeze, set sail for Europe, leaving behind his small garrison at the makeshift settlement he had christened La Navidad – including an Englishman known as Tallarte de Lajes and an Irishman known as Guillermo Ires (William Irish).[18] He left them with a year's supply of biscuit and wine, some of his artillery and goods that they were instructed to use to barter for gold. His orders to this first European colony in the Caribbean included the stipulation that they should be kind and solicitous to the natives, paying special respect to their chief Guacanagari. A list of prohibitions included avoiding any kind of violence, thievery or confrontation with their hosts and, above all, that they should be careful not to 'insult or harm the women in a way that might provoke offence or provide a bad example to the

Indians and besmirch the reputation of Christians'.[19] Two days later he linked up once more with Pinzón, who reacted furiously to the news that thirty-nine of the men he had helped recruit in Palos had been left behind.

Spain's colonisation of the Americas had started, ushering in a new period of European expansion to the west. Christendom was on the rise again and what would later develop into 'Western civilisation' was embarking on a sudden spurt of growth. The impact of that ripples into the present day. It was an accidental beginning, caused by the ground-ing of the *Santa María*, since Isabella had not ordered any potential colonists to go with him. But now that Columbus had planted her flag on several islands in the Caribbean, Isabella was the queen of places and peoples that she had never seen. The queen of Castile had just expelled one group of subjects. Now she was incorporating others, and had to decide exactly how her new peoples should be treated.

Technological progress cannot explain the dramatic and history-changing success of Isabella's Atlantic venture. Quadrants, astrolabes, latitude tables and portolan charts were either mistrusted, used wrongly or inaccurate. Navigators like Columbus still relied on the stars, the sun, compasses, defective tables and their own experience or intuition. Nor were their ships a vast improvement on previous models, though the addition of triangular sails meant the caravels could sail much closer to the wind.[20] Luck and the *Reconquista*, however, had placed Isabella's Castile at the gateway to a system of fixed winds and ocean currents that made the return journey to the Americas possible. These had long been taking her ships south to the Canary Islands. It was from there that Columbus had picked up the north-east trade winds as they swooped towards the equator and then swung west towards the Americas and the Caribbean. Those winds, in turn, helped set up a huge circular current – the north Atlantic gyre – which ran clockwise around the ocean. This turned north as it neared the Americas and east again by mainland north America, where prevailing westerly winds had helped blow Columbus's vessels back towards home.

In simple terms, Isabella's new admiral had discovered that a great wheel of winds and currents could carry a ship from Castile to the Caribbean and back to Europe. When the *Reconquista* gave their country Palos and a stretch of south-facing Atlantic coast in the mid-thirteenth century, Castilian sailors gained access to this circular system. Nobody knew how far it reached or how it really worked, but Portuguese sailors were already returning home from Africa by first sailing deep into the Atlantic to pick up the right currents and winds in a manoeuvre they called the *volta do mar largo*, or long sea turn.[21] It took a large dose of courage, however, to imagine that those same winds and currents would take a sailing ship to the other side of the Atlantic and, especially, back again. Only someone with the considerable navigational skills of Christopher Columbus, a large dose of self-belief and a lively imagination would even have thought of embarking on such a venture.

Isabella's Castile also made its giant leap across the ocean because it was a cornered culture with nowhere else to go. Christendom was blocked to the east and, for various reasons, plans to conquer parts of north Africa had never worked out. Even with that in mind, however, the venture appears little short of mad. Perhaps the best explanation for why it happened at all is the ambitious nature of the personalities involved – especially Isabella and Columbus. The queen believed strongly in a chivalric ideal that elevated adventure into a moral virtue, thereby encouraging high risks.[22] So did Columbus. A century later, the Castilian writer Miguel de Cervantes would create the famously honour-crazed Don Quixote of La Mancha, whose only interests – reflecting the values of Isabella's time – were glory and fame. It was Isabella's embrace of competitive adventure and the reckless pursuit of glory that allowed this breakthrough to happen under her flag. The impact of this bold Castilian voyage into the unknown on the next five centuries of world history would be spectacular – tilting the balance away from the more sophisticated east towards a west that would eventually use it as a springboard for global dominance.

Indians, Parrots and Hammocks

Palos de la Frontera, 15 March 1493

*L*a Niña rode a rising tide as it sailed past the Saltés Bar into the calm waters of the Odiel and Tinto estuary at midday on 15 March 1493. It had sat offshore overnight and the friars at La Rábida must have watched its arrival excitedly from their privileged viewpoint just inland. News of Columbus's return to Europe with the men from the local ports of Palos and Moguer may already have reached them, as fierce storms had driven him first to a safe harbour in the Azores and then on to Lisbon on 4 March, where his exotic cargo of natives, birds, animals and tropical foods had attracted the envious attention of King João II, known as 'the Perfect Prince'. From there[1] he had written that first historic letter to Isabella and her husband, announcing their 'greatest victory'.

In fact, Columbus was not the first person to send Isabella news of the Americas, or to make the return crossing to Europe. That honour lay with Pinzón, whose *La Pinta* caravel had become separated from *La Niña* when they ran into a storm on 14 February. He landed at Bayona, in Galicia, and some four days later wrote to Isabella and Ferdinand of his arrival, rested for two weeks and then sailed to Palos, entering the port later on the same day as Columbus but rushing off to a house in nearby Moguer so as to avoid meeting the man with whom he had fallen out so badly during the voyage. Pinzón's letter reached Isabella's court some two weeks before she heard from Columbus, though it does not survive. Nor did Pinzón himself, who was very sick. Within days he had been taken in by the friars at La Rábida, but they failed to cure him.[2] By the time Isabella wrote asking him to come to court, he had died.

Columbus remained true to character. He was boastful and flamboyant, aware that it was important to broadcast and exaggerate his triumph as loudly as possible. But he was also mistrustful, resentful and insecure – knowing that he had failed to find any gold mines and that many people still did not believe he had found the Indies. In a later, written vision of his exploits he reminded Isabella and her husband of the disbelief his plans had provoked originally. 'I was in your court so long . . . against the advice of so many of the principal people in your household, all of whom were against me, making fun of this idea [of mine] which, I hope, will prove to be the greatest honour to Christianity that has ever been seen.'[3] On their arrival in Palos, he and his crew had gone straight to the Convent of Santa Clara to fulfil a promise that the ship's crew would give thanks there for their safe return. He then processed through nearby Seville, his Taíno 'Indians', multi-coloured parrots and Caribbean trinkets on full display. The same show would be put on at numerous places as he travelled towards Barcelona to see Isabella and Ferdinand. He had previously planned to go by sea, but eventually chose a triumphant march through Castile that might enhance his reputation even further, setting out on 9 April on a trip that took thirteen days.[4]

Bartolomé de Las Casas, then an eight-year-old boy, was taken by his father to see the Indians in the house where they stayed in Seville, near San Nicolás church. 'He left Seville taking the Indians with him, there being seven of them because the others had died,' Las Casas reported. 'He took beautiful, bright green parrots and *guayças* [*guaízas*], which were masks carved from fishbones, worn like pearls, and strings of them that displayed admirable artisanship . . . with lots of fine gold and other things that had never been seen or heard of in Spain.'[5] The tiny *guaíza* masks, also carved out of seashells, were a small but significant sign that Isabella's new peoples were somewhat more sophisticated than her 'admiral' had imagined.[6]

Columbus had been careful to broadcast his arrival as widely as possible. Within a week of landing, for example, city councillors in Córdoba were excitedly debating the news and looking forward to him passing through the city. In a letter signed jointly with her husband on 30 March, Isabella had sounded anxious, excited and exasperated. Seeing ahead of them a potential race against Portugal to colonise the new lands, made worse by the fact that he had stopped first in Lisbon, she and Ferdinand had ordered him to appear before them as soon as possible. 'As we desire that what you have started should, with God's help, be continued and taken forward, we wish . . . that you put as much speed as possible into your coming here, so that there is time to provide all that is needed; and as summer is already upon us and in order not to waste time before returning, see if you can start organising in Seville and other places for your return to the land that you have found,' they wrote. He was to write them instructions, telling them what needed doing so that he could set off back to the Americas just as soon as he had returned from his trip to Barcelona. That very same day they signed a royal order banning anyone else from sailing to the Indies without their permission. 'You should know that we have recently brought about the discovery of some islands and mainland in the part of the Ocean Sea that is the part of the Indies,' they said, apparently believing Columbus's claim to have sailed to Asia. 'Some people could be tempted to go to the said Indies and trade there and bring back merchandise and other things, but that is something which we do not want done without our licence and special orders.'[7] The letter was to be read aloud in town squares across the land.

Columbus was slowed down by the crowds that greeted him wherever he went. 'It wasn't just that everyone came out to watch in the places that he passed through, but that other places far off this route were emptied out as the road was packed with people wanting to see [him] or with others who were rushing ahead to the towns to receive him,' said Las Casas.[8] They marvelled at the parrots, the small rabbit-like hutias and the wild turkeys. But most of all they came to gawk at what everybody assumed were 'Indians'.

It was, in part, a freak show, but it was also an amazing display of colour and novelty, lighting up the grey life of Spain's often harsh interior. The cultural, sensual and aesthetic world of most Europeans was at best narrow and predictable. Few knew more than the dull certainties of their town or village and the palette of colours offered by the changing seasons and the local countryside. Spaniards were not extravagant dressers – or so Italian visitors thought – though costume varied from region to region, with people's geographical origins recognisable by their clothes and Isabella ordering her costumers to confect outfits in the style of the regions she was visiting. 'One day she would appear in Galicia as a Galician and the next in Vizcaya as a Vizcayan,' a Spanish historian wrote a century later.[9] But mostly this was a world of repetitive experiences and restricted social and sensual input. The smells, sounds and images of churches or religious processions and encounters with Moors or Jews were the most exotic experiences that the vast majority of Spaniards who lived outside the major trading cities could hope to experience.

Isabella finally set eyes on her new subjects – so effusively described in Columbus's letters – at the end of April. It is not entirely clear whether her meeting with them took place in Barcelona itself, or at the monastery of San Jerónimo of Murtra in nearby Badalona. Once again, crowds took to the streets to see Columbus and his menagerie of animals and human beings. 'The people barely fitted into the streets, wanting to admire the person who was said to have discovered another world,' said Las Casas.[10]

Isabella and Ferdinand were equally thrilled, according to Francisco López de Gómara, who wrote sixty years later:

He showed the monarchs the gold and other things that he had brought from the other world; and they and those with them were amazed to see that all of it, except the gold, was as new to them as the land it came from. They praised the parrots for their beautiful colours: some very green, others very colourful, others yellow, with thirty different varieties of colour; and few of them looked anything like birds brought from other parts. The hutias and rabbits were very small, with rats' ears and tails. They tried the *ají* spice, which burned their tongues, and the *batatas* [sweet potatoes], which are sweet root crops and the wild turkeys, which are better than ducks or hens. They were amazed that there was no wheat there, and that they made bread from their corn.

Canoes, tobacco, pineapples and hammocks were among the exotic items that Columbus was able to describe or place before Isabella and her husband, who were appalled to hear his reports of cannibalism.[11] But it was the native Taíno who really astonished them. 'What they most stared at were the men, who wore gold rings in their ears and noses, and were neither white, nor black, nor brown, but rather jaundiced-looking or like the colour of stewed quince. Six of the Indians were baptised, as the others did not make it to the court,' he said. Isabella, Ferdinand and their son Juan were the godparents.[12]

In Isabella's mind the desired destiny for Jews, Moors and Indians was the same – that they be converted to the true faith of Christianity. But while Jews and Moors had to be convinced, cajoled, threatened or – if they resisted – expelled, the indigenous peoples of the Caribbean posed a different sort of problem. They neither resided in mainland Castile nor had they ever heard of Christianity. They were not, in that sense, heretics or infidels, though had Columbus spent more time with them or learned their languages he might have realised that they had their own religions.[13] And that raised the question of the proper way to treat them.

A more pressing problem for Isabella, however, was Portugal. João II's special ambassador arrived even before Columbus, complaining about a possible breach of the 1479 Alcáçovas agreement that had sealed the end of the war over the Castilian crown. Isabella and Ferdinand's spies in Lisbon soon discovered that the

Portuguese king was already plotting to send boats south and west from the Canary Islands, to lands that he might more easily claim under the terms of that treaty. They, in turn, sent an ambassador to Lisbon within days of Columbus's arrival in Barcelona to demand that Portugal stay out of the new territories and stick to the areas accorded to it in and around Africa. They also ordered the Duke of Medina Sidonia to have boats ready to attack any Portuguese ships that might set sail. More importantly, a bout of frantic activity by their ambassadors in Rome saw the pope issue two briefs and a bull in the space of just two days at the beginning of May in which he confirmed that the islands found by Columbus belonged to Castile, as would those found on future expeditions. Just as Portugal had managed to persuade the pope to give it rights over much of west Africa, so Castile now secured for itself whatever it could find across an ocean that was still not known as the Atlantic.[14] The papal permits also made clear that one of the tasks expected of Isabella's explorers was to convert the natives of the new lands to Christianity.

Reports of the new lands added to Isabella's crown soon spread across the rest of Europe. Within a handful of days of Columbus's arrival, the find was being recorded in Siena, Italy, along with rumours of abundant gold.[15] A famous letter that Columbus allegedly wrote to Santángel was published in Barcelona at the time of this arrival, with three editions selling out. It was translated into Latin and published in Rome a few months later with other editions printed that same year in Paris, Antwerp and Basle. It was one of the printing press's first international bestsellers and added further to the burgeoning prestige of Isabella's Castile, after the previous year's conquest of Granada.[16] The letter was rewritten previously by somebody else and there is evidence that this was done on the instructions of Isabella and her husband, who were only too aware of its potential for boosting their image.[17] Among other things, the letter passed on to readers titillating rumours about the presence of cannibals, Amazonian-style women who lived without men and monkey-like people 'born with tails', while admitting that Columbus himself had 'so far found no human monstrosities, as many expected, but on the contrary the whole population is very well formed, nor are they negroes as in Guinea, but their hair is flowing'.

It warned, however, that not all were peaceful. 'An island which is the second one encountered on entering the Indies is populated by people who are deemed ferocious by those on all the other islands and who eat human flesh,' Columbus, or whoever re-edited his letter, wrote. 'They are the ones who have relations with the women from Matinino, which is the first island of all, where there are no men at all. The latter do not follow women's customs, but use the bows and arrows . . . made of cane and they armour themselves with metal plates.'

The letter also informed readers of the rich pickings that awaited Castile, since one sailor had managed to swap a lace for 'gold weighing as much as two and a half *castellanos*' (or 1,200 *maravedis*) with the guileless Indians, 'while others exchanged things of even less value'. It also explained that the different groups of Taíno that Columbus had found shared similar languages and customs – enough for them to understand each other as they skilfully navigated from island to island. 'They have a subtle intelligence and it is wonderful how the men here who know how to sail those seas explain everything.' The natives Columbus had kidnapped were, the letter said, still convinced that he was divine and the people he met had often 'run from house to house and to nearby villages, shouting in loud voices: "Come! Come to see the people from heaven!" '

Isabella and Ferdinand's fame increased as the document circulated through Europe, with the letter insisting that the discovery would reap vast riches for them. 'With a little bit of help from their Highnesses I will give them as much gold as they need; and also all the spices and cotton that their Highnesses order me to ship . . . and as many slaves as they order,' it said. The islands would produce countless valuable delicacies, including mastic, rhubarb and cinnamon, to further increase their wealth and standing, he insisted. 'Our Redeemer gave this great victory to our illustrious king and queen and to their famous kingdoms for this great deed, and the whole of Christendom should celebrate . . . that so many peoples will have embraced our faith and, after that, for the great wealth that not just Spain but all Christians must gain here.'

News of the discovery, then, was racing across the continent. Mariners, traders, monarchs and adventurers were all intrigued. The Iberian peninsula was now the focus of European maritime exploration and expansion, as Spain reached west and Portugal headed south and east around Africa's Cape of Good Hope. But Italians also played a vital role, especially through their trading communities in Spain. Another Italian sailor called Amerigo Vespucci, for example, was among those to hear the news in Seville. He would soon become a friend and collaborator of Columbus. A Venetian sailor and maritime engineer called Giovanni, or John, Cabot also heard the news in Spain. Cabot was working on a port project near Valencia, eastern Spain, and would soon move to Seville to begin work on a bridge to replace the Puente de Barcas – the pontoon that provided a link to Triana across the River Guadalquivir.[18] Like Vespucci, whose Christian name eventually provided the new continent's name, he also became determined to start exploring the western Atlantic on his own. He would eventually find backing from England's Henry VII, with the Spanish ambassador sending back worried reports about 'a man like Columbus . . . [pursuing] another undertaking like that of the Indies'. It was only several years after Columbus's return, however, that Cabot finally sailed north and west from Bristol with just a single ship and no royal money to discover an inhospitable-looking Newfoundland draped in fog, with banks of cod so thick that they could be scooped up in baskets.

Isabella and her husband were in a hurry. Whereas Columbus's first voyage had been financed with little money and represented a blind bet on the unknown, they now had a concrete purpose – to claim for themselves lands that, even with Columbus's limited exploration, they already knew were extensive (Columbus's descriptions of Hispaniola as larger than Spain, and Cuba as bigger than Great Britain were wrong, but the latter alone was still larger than Aragon's Spanish lands). A race had begun and, having started in the lead, they were determined to win it. The Canary Islands, so recently conquered, provided an administrative and legal model. The days of feudal-style expansion, with conquered lands becoming personal fiefs of the conquerors, were over. Any new lands found by Columbus, and their peoples, would belong firmly to the Castilian crown or, in other words, to Isabella. Columbus could have his extraordinary set of titles – of admiral, viceroy and governor – but he remained their servant.[19] As early as 7 May 1493 they ordered a royal accountant called Gómez Tello to prepare to join Columbus on a second trip 'to receive in our name all that, in whatever way, belongs to us'.[20] Another royal bureaucrat, Juan Rodríguez de Fonseca, was given joint responsibility, with Columbus, for organising the expedition – while the latter's thirst for nobility was partly quenched with formal recognition of a quartered coat of arms that he could now boast as his own and that would include 'golden isles on waves in the sea'. On 23 May Columbus and Fonseca were told to scour the ports in and around Seville and Cadiz for suitable vessels that could be bought or chartered – and armed – for the trip.[21]

This time their expedition was to include soldiers, settlers, judges, priests and all the paraphernalia of colonisation. Skilled technicians in irrigation, animal husbandry and mining were hired. Isabella and Ferdinand ordered taxes and customs dues dropped on goods bought for the new journey. Penalties were decreed for those refusing goods to Columbus and his men. Provisions had to be bought in the great fair at Medina del Campo and as far north as the sailing ports of Vizcaya. The monarchs wanted strict control over the fleet of seventeen vessels and 1,200 to 1,500 men and women, with royal accountants to track cargoes and crews, both outgoing and on the return. All was to be carefully controlled and logged by the expanding royal bureaucracy, with copies sent to Isabella and her husband. A special customs shed was to be organised in Cadiz to receive the bounty sent home, though this was still a royal monopoly with Columbus due to receive an eighth share of the profits. The trip was to have two aims. The first was to colonise and extract gold or whatever other wealth could be found, mined or harvested, and the second was to win souls. 'Treat the Indians well and lovingly, without upsetting them in any way,' was the clear instruction. A senior Catalan friar, Bernat Boïl, was to lead the attempt at capturing converts. Special customs sheds in Cadiz were to house the expected treasures.[22]

Only 15,000 gold ducats (or 5.625 million *maravedís*) could be found directly, by raiding funds from the Hermandad. This was almost three times the entire budget for the first voyage but it was still insufficient.[23] Royal officials cast around for liquidity and their gaze soon came to rest on a new source of income reaching the royal coffers – the goods confiscated from the Jews whose expulsion had been completed the previous August, just a week after Columbus set sail on his first voyage.[24] Envoys were sent out to points along or near the border with Portugal where tens of thousands of Jews crossing the frontier had been searched by zealous local officials who confiscated their gold, silver and other things they were banned from taking with them. Almost 2 million *maravedís* – enough to have financed the first voyage – had been confiscated from financiers like Rabi Efraim and Bienveniste de Calahorra before they joined the forced exodus, as well as a sum at least twice as much as that which was still owed to them by various debtors. Among the objects taken from Jews and used to raise funds were those made of gold or silver – including coins, rings, jewels, toothpicks, thread, clasps, buckles, cups and spoons. An accompanying haul of silk cloths, shawls, blankets, three Torah covers and at least twenty Torahs also appears to have been sold off to raise funds. Isabella and her husband also wanted the 580 gold pieces found in a mysterious leather bag, apparently abandoned by a group of expelled Jews in Zamora, to be tracked down and its contents handed over.[25]

Much of this went into the funding pot for Columbus's second voyage. Spain's outcast Jews, whose fate Columbus himself had linked with his first expedition, thus provided more than 5 million *maravedís* – or funding for five of the seventeen vessels. It was as much as Isabella and her husband had been able to raise from their own funds, via the Hermandad. The rest they took as loans. But money was tight and this time the outlay was large, with costs including the arming of 230 soldiers with armour, guns, crossbows and short lances. Cows, bricks, mortar, plants and quantities of oats, barley, rye and wheat were loaded before the fleet left from Cadiz to the sound of drums, trumpets and broadsides fired by some visiting Venetian vessels recently arrived from England. Calves, goats, sheep, pigs, chickens, wood, sugar and seeds that were to be introduced into the islands were picked up in the Canaries, where they were cheaper and the animals would not need so many days' feed after they set sail from El Hierro on 13 October. Many of those who sailed on the trip would have to wait one, two or more years for full payment.[26]

This was 'the fleet that we have ordered be prepared for sending to the islands and mainland that we have in the region of the Indies and those [lands] that will be discovered there', wrote Isabella and Ferdinand.[27] A separate, defensive fleet of Basque ships was also on hand in case the Portuguese decided to set out on their own.

Columbus made the second crossing much more quickly than the first, taking just twenty-one days to reach (and discover) the island of Dominica. The fleet then sailed slowly towards Hispaniola and the settlement at La Navidad, discovering other islands along the way, including Guadalupe – where leg bones and skulls hanging in the doorways of some houses appeared to provide proof of cannibalism. They followed the arc of the Antilles as far as Puerto Rico,[28] with Columbus feeling his way towards Hispaniola and eager to push on to La Navidad in order to meet up with Rodrigo de Escobedo, the man he had left in charge. Columbus had ordered de Escobedo to keep for him the 'four large houses and five small ones'[29] that Guacanagari had given him as a present.

They reached Hispaniola on 22 November and, although the native people were still friendly and willing to barter, the discovery of the decomposed bodies of two unidentifiable men, one with his arms tied to a plank of wood, provoked a growing sense of nervousness. When the following day they found a corpse with a beard – something they had never seen on any of the natives – they knew that at least some of the Spaniards were dead. Messengers from Guacanagari claimed that all the Spaniards had disappeared, some dying from illness while others had trekked inland with a group of women. When Columbus finally reached La Navidad, all he found were the charred remains of the settlement and some old clothes.[30] The local people now blamed two other island chiefs, Caonabo and Mayreni, for the massacre, which had taken place just a month earlier. The Spaniards' greed and pursuit of women had, they said, provoked Caonabo's attack. A weeping Guacanagari at first claimed he had been injured by the attackers and then, after visiting Columbus on his flagship, helped some of the women picked up on other islands to escape and disappeared with them. Columbus's vision of the indigenous peoples cowed by his technology and convinced of the heavenly origins of their visitors lay in tatters. More importantly, he had lost the men who were meant to have gathered information that would allow him to start exploring for gold – though it seems they had found little of it, as nothing was discovered when Columbus ordered a search of the settlement's well (where he had ordered any gold finds to be secretly stored).[31]

This time, however, he had Isabella and Ferdinand's troops.[32] If the natives could not be persuaded by good words and gifts into co-operating, or if they actively resisted, force could now be used.

33

Dividing Up the World

Barcelona and Tordesillas,
5 September 1493 to 7 June 1494

Isabella needed a map. A line had to be drawn in the ocean, dividing the world in two. New lands found on one side of this north–south line would belong to her and Castile.[1] Those on the other half belonged to her rivals from Portugal. She also needed a record of the lands found so far to share with her officials and, if necessary, other captains she might choose to despatch west across the Atlantic. 'The sea chart that you must make for me, once it is ready, you may send later; and, in order to serve me well, give great urgency to your departure so that, with God's grace, this may happen without delay as, you will understand, this will benefit the whole enterprise,' she had written to Columbus from Barcelona in September 1493, shortly before he set out on the second voyage. 'And write to tell us all that there is to know from over there.'

Columbus had argued for, and thought he had obtained, a dividing line that was a hundred leagues from Portugal's Cape Verde islands – but Isabella that the matter was still open to negotiation.[2] 'Nothing has been decided with the envoys here, although I believe their King will come to see reason in the matter,' she said, unaware that Portugal's João II was determined to strike a much tougher deal. A year later she was still worrying about dividing lines, apparently because she also wanted one in the east – a project that proved impossible. 'We should like you, if possible, to play a part in the negotiations . . . See whether your brother or anyone else you have with you can master the question. Brief them very fully orally, in writing and perhaps with a map, and send them back to us with the next fleet,' she wrote.[3]

Isabella was clear, too, that these new lands belonged to her and Castile alone, rather than to her husband's Aragonese kingdoms. 'The discovery and conquest was paid for by these kingdoms of mine and their people,' she wrote at the end of her life. 'And that is why the profit from them is something to be dealt with and negotiated in my kingdoms of Castile and León and why everything that comes from them must be brought here, both from the lands that have been discovered so far and from those to be discovered in the future.'[4] Even she could not know, however, just how extensive those 'lands to be discovered' would eventually prove to be.

In Christopher Columbus Isabella had found a magnificent explorer, and a disastrous administrator. But Columbus had his titles – as admiral, viceroy and governor – and, as such, was almost a monarch in his new lands. He was still intent on proving that he had discovered a gold-laden arcadia on the eastern edge of Asia. Once he had found La Navidad in ruins and after his ally Guacanagari had run off, he set sail again, seeking a spot closer to the supposed source of gold in the Cibao region of the island where he might build a proper town. Eventually he picked a windswept harbour beside the mouth of the River Bajibonico. Here he would build a town named after Isabella herself, La Isabela. First, however, he sent one of his captains on a forty-five-day round-the-island journey to chart the coastline – thereby obeying Isabella's instructions to provide her with a map.[5]

Columbus was in a hurry to explore further and, crucially, find a source of gold. He needed to disembark his people and send some of the fleet home. His descriptions of the site of La Isabela were idyllic – close to fresh water, well protected by the jungle, with fields that could be easily cultivated and a huge harbour. They were also exaggerated. The harbour was exposed to strong northerly winds, vessels often had to anchor more than half a mile from shore and drinking water was a full mile away. La Isabela would turn out to be a poor emplacement, but, rather than think about geography, Columbus based his choice on his conviction that this was a good place from which to hunt for gold mines.[6]

The colonisers set about the construction of the first European town in the Americas with verve, using good local stone for the public buildings. Among the most important buildings was the combined customs house and armoury that would house Isabella's officials – and symbolise her rule over this lush, verdant spot. A church that Isabella would fill up with statues and silver ornaments sent from Spain, as well as an altar cloth from her own collection, was built in under a month. A governor's house known as the Royal Palace and a hospital were also at the top of the list of new public buildings. They sounded grand, but were almost certainly modest in size. At the same time Isabella's bureaucracy at home had set about establishing the system and institutions that could both govern and manage the profits that her new lands were expected to deliver. That profit was meant to come, above all, from gold. Columbus despatched an expedition of twenty men into the interior, convinced that they were just three or four days' march from where he imagined the gold mines were. They returned without finding any mines, but with samples of gold provided by local Indians and reports that the precious metal could be found by sifting in rivers.[7]

On 4 February 1494, Columbus sent most of the fleet – twelve of seventeen vessels plus 300 or more men – back to Spain. The fleet was captained by Antonio de Torres, who was given written instructions about what to tell Isabella and Ferdinand when he arrived. The truth was that Columbus had little to boast about. For many of his men, the grand adventure had already turned sour. Sickness, hard work and scarce supplies made life on Hispaniola miserable. 'On top of all these hardships was the anguish and sadness of realising that they were so far away from their homeland and so far from finding a quick solution to their problems while also seeing themselves cheated of the gold and riches which they had promised themselves,' said Las Casas.

With La Navidad destroyed and its inhabitants dead, Columbus had been forced to start the process of reconnoitring Hispaniola – which was almost as big as mainland Portugal – from scratch. He had little more to show Isabella and her husband than his charts, some tropical fruits, his colourful accounts and a small amount of gold. The vessels made the return crossing without trouble, reaching Cadiz on 7 March. An excited Isabella and Ferdinand immediately ordered Torres to travel to Medina del Campo to see them.[8]

Columbus's instructions about what Torres was to say to Isabella and her husband see him desperate to paint a rosy picture of what – to all effects – was a disaster. Torres told her that many of the men had fallen sick, others were refusing to obey orders and they were desperate for food, wine and medicines from home. The supposedly fertile land was not producing what they wanted, gold was, he claimed, easy to find yet – mysteriously – he had been unable to obtain any. And the peace-loving natives were turning out to be much more warlike than he had thought, especially those led by a chieftain called Caonabo. He needed more men, more supplies and specialists in sifting[9] for gold in rivers, as he had failed to find any mines.[10] He had nothing to pay for them except for the one export good that was sure to find an easy market – slaves.

Torres informed Isabella and her husband, however, that success was assured. La Isabela was well positioned, he claimed, and lay in a rich region where the rivers were full of gold and mines could not be far away, while spices were clearly set to prove another lucrative source of income. 'Tell their Highnesses that I wanted to send them a far greater amount of the gold to be found here, and would have done so had most of our people here not suddenly fallen ill,' Columbus had written in his instructions, adding that his men also risked being attacked if they did not go out in force. 'These are the reasons why the fleet has not waited and they are only being sent samples.'[11]

With his men ill, Columbus wanted Isabella and her husband to know that he was having trouble constructing a well-defended settlement and, though the local indigenous people seemed completely peaceful, he dared not drop his guard. 'The other men who remained here [after the first voyage], though they were few, failed to take proper precautions,' Torres was to tell the monarchs. 'Yet [the Indians] would never have dared attack them had they seen that they were properly prepared.' He put the illnesses that now smote the men and women with him down to the change of air and water. They missed their normal diet of fresh meat, bread and wine and he asked for honey, sugar, raisins and almonds to be sent to help restore their strength. He also hoped that the gold he was sending would be enough for a local Seville merchant to pay – or provide an advance for – two caravels laden with wine, wheat and other goods.[12]

There was barely anything else to send back. The attempts at farming and self-sufficiency had, so far, failed. Sugar cane, which had proved an important crop in the Canaries and Azores, looked promising, but would take time. In the meantime, the colony was costing more than it produced. That left just one form of trade that was both easy and lucrative – in human beings. Columbus justified his decision to send back slaves by claiming that the people he had caught were cannibals and so were fair game. 'In these ships are being sent some cannibals – men, women, boys and girls – who their Highnesses can order to be placed in the power of people with whom they can best learn our language, teaching them also other skills,' Torres was to tell Isabella and her husband. 'They will learn more quickly over there than here, and will become better interpreters.' At first sight, then, his main interest was in giving his captives an immersion course in Spanish or preventing them from eating other people, but his letters to Spain revealed deeper, financial needs. 'The more we send over there the better. And their Highnesses could be served in the following way: that given how bad the need here is for cattle and for working animals in order to sustain the people who will eventually be here . . . their Highnesses can award licences and permits for a sufficient number of caravels to come every year, bringing the cattle and other goods so that the country areas can be populated and the land worked,' he said. 'These things could be paid for in slaves taken from among these cannibals, who are so wild and well built and with a good understanding of things, that we think they will be finer than any other slaves once they are freed from their inhumanity, which they will lose as soon as they leave their own lands. And there could be many of them . . . with their Highnesses receiving their dues over there.'[13] Isabella, in other words, could make a lot of money out of the relatively simple business of capturing people and sending them to Europe as slaves. He initially preferred not to enslave any of the friendly Taíno of Hispaniola who were 'your Highnesses' vassals', saying that he would rather capture slaves from the rival Carib people who lived on the islands and, he reported, were cannibals.[14]

Isabella and Ferdinand's reply to his missive was, mostly, to reassure him that he appeared to be making correct decisions and to agree to his requests. This included the trade in slaves, though approval came with a rejoinder that revealed some doubts. 'Explain to him what has happened with the cannibals who came here,' they wrote in their reply, presumably referring to debate over the issue of whether this slavery was legitimate or not. 'That this is very good, and he should continue doing it, but that he should try, wherever possible, to convert them to our holy Catholic faith there, as well as doing the same with those [the Taíno] on the islands where he is now.'[15]

Isabella's own state of confusion about slavery is apparent in the contradictory instructions she and Ferdinand now issued. On 12 April 1495, they wrote to Seville saying that the slaves due to arrive with Torres 'would best be sold there in Andalusia', but four days later suspended the same sale until Columbus had explained their status (presumably to establish whether they were war prisoners, cannibals or simple captives) so that 'we can consult with lawyers, theologians and canon law experts whether they can be sold with a clear conscience'. A later instruction to pay ship's captain Juan de Lezano's salary in slaves suggests that at least some were acceptable, even if there were also eventually instructions to send others home.[16]

Details of the slavery debate in Castile are scant, but can be easily guessed at. Papal bulls issued earlier in the century to the Portuguese as they set about conquering parts of north Africa had given wide-ranging slavery rights that justified forcing Muslims, idolators and cannibals into slavery. This was not so strange. In the continuing warring between Christians and Muslims, slavery was already considered – by both sides – an acceptable destiny for the captured. Isabella herself had Muslim slaves serving in her court, including as seamstresses and as attendants to her daughters. Isabella's own accounts show her ordering up clothes for a dozen slaves, while her letters see her buying one slave because 'she is a good jam-maker' and ordering that her other slaves be well fed but 'given things to do to stop them getting lazy'.[17] Two decades later the Flemish illustrator Christopher Weiditz drew pictures of Muslim slaves in Spain with iron chains on their legs and waists. The free rein given to the Portuguese responded, in part, to growing Christian fears that the battle against Islam, with the seizure of Constantinople and later Turkish expansion through Greece, Bulgaria and Serbia, was being lost. The papal bulls sanctioning the campaign did not discriminate between Berber and other Muslims in the north and sub-Saharan black Africans who had their own 'pagan' religions, perhaps because Islam was already spreading south into the gold-rich empire of Mali and elsewhere. 'We grant that you and your successors as Kings of Portugal . . . will have in perpetuity, the right to invade, conquer, seize, subject and reduce into perpetual slavery the saracens, pagans and other infidels and enemies of Christ, whoever they are and wherever their kingdoms are,' one papal bull stated. Another referred specifically to 'Guineans [west Africans] and other negroes, captured by force or bought . . . with legitimate contracts'.[18] It urged the settlers to 'wage continuous war against the gentile and pagan peoples who exist there and who are profoundly influenced by the repugnant Mohammed'. It is not surprising that the Portuguese, initially seeking gold and spices as well as a route around Africa to India, took this as approval for both colonisation and the lucrative business of commercial slavery. Up until 1481, several popes reiterated those same rights.

Yet the papacy's position was not entirely clear. Instructions given to the bishop of the Canary Islands, for example, banned the enslavement of Christian converts among the *guanches* and other indigenous people or of those who, thanks to peace agreements, were in a position to be converted – even if they were still pagans. As a result, Isabella herself tried to restrict slavery on the islands.[19] In simple terms, then, the debate was about whether Isabella's new subjects could be treated like black Africans, and automatically turned into slaves, or whether they should be treated like any non-belligerent *guanches* in the Canaries ought to have been – as potential Christians who could not be enslaved. Isabella's own confusion on the matter suggests that she was being presented with both sides of the argument. Talavera probably defended the milder set of rules, while Columbus himself – and his fellow colonists – were the main promoters of the harsher approach already being applied in Africa.

Isabella's viceroy and governor continued to display his incapacity for man management. He had long been accustomed to lying disdainfully to his crews. Now he found many of those serving under him either lazy, reluctant to obey or so aghast at his manner that they wanted to go straight home or were openly rebellious. In any case, he himself seemed far more interested in sailing to discover still more lands – partly because he needed to find gold or some source of wealth beyond slaves, but also because this was his genuine passion and talent. Those he left in charge were not always good at their jobs and he fell out spectacularly with almost all those he appointed, switching from admiring praise to virulent hatred in a short space of time. Already in 1493 he was complaining that the cavalrymen brought from Granada were lazy and refused to loan their horses when they themselves were sick. Isabella and Ferdinand promised to investigate his gripes and saw no reason to blame their new admiral and viceroy for these problems. More importantly, they soon sent him a small fleet of three vessels with provisions, captained by his brother Bartolomé – who had failed to arrive back from France in time to join Columbus's second trip.[20]

The news that reached Isabella and Ferdinand was, inevitably, already out of date. Columbus's problems continued to pile up. Soon after Torres had left, two-thirds of La Isabela (mainly made of wood and straw huts built by the men for themselves) went up in flames. Then a mutiny led by Bernal Díaz de Pisa saw a group of men try to seize control of the remaining fleet of five vessels, forcing Columbus to arrest them and move all the naval weapons on to a single ship guarded by men he trusted. His son Hernando blamed a combination of greed, laziness and sickness. 'Many on that journey had thought that all they had to do was touch dry land to be able to load up with gold and return wealthy, even though gold, wherever it is found, is never retrieved without effort, industry and time. As events did not unfold the way they had hoped, they were unhappy and worn out by the building of the new town and exhausted by the sicknesses of this new land,' Hernando wrote in his own *History of the Admiral*. The real root of the rebellion, however, was that many more men – including Díaz de Pisa himself – had wanted to sail home with Torres but were refused permission.[21]

Columbus then set off to look for the Cibao mines himself with an army of 400 men, ready to do battle with Caonabo if necessary, and built an inland fort. The Indians alternately fled or were welcoming, and were almost always ready to bargain away their (normally small) gold pieces. Gold fever among the men was such that many hid what they obtained, with Columbus meting out punishments that included cutting off the perpetrators' ears or noses. Some 3,000 *castellanos*' worth of gold was obtained this way, but no mines were discovered. In La Isabela he forced the gentlemen adventurers who had come with him to perform many of the same manual tasks as the common soldiers and workmen, arguing that all hands were needed. This contravened the norms of Castile's class system, or so the *hidalgos* and other privileged gentlemen thought. Discontent grew and Columbus considered sending back most of the men, maintaining a colony of just 300. The greedy garrison at his inland fort, Santo Tomás, soon began stealing gold from local Indians and word came that Caonabo was preparing to attack again. Columbus did not worry, not least because the Indians tended to flee in panic at the sight of horses, previously unknown to them and seemingly huge and frightening, but sent a force inland with instructions to capture Caonabo. Then he sailed off with three ships to explore the coastline of Cuba, which he now decided was part of mainland Asia.[22]

In Cuba, too, the 'Indians' were welcoming, rowing out in their canoes to offer gifts to the men on what, for them, were enormous boats. But they said there was no gold on the island, suggesting that there might be some on another island five days' sailing (for them) away. Columbus had already heard of this island, which he called Jamaica, and sailed on. The indigenous people of Jamaica were not nearly as welcoming and attacked Columbus's men, but were easily put to flight with the help of a small cannon and one of the admiral's dogs. By mid-May 1494, however, Columbus realised that there was no gold or other precious metals to be had and so turned back. Stopping off again in Cuba he met a local chief who informed him, somewhat confusingly, that although it was 'infinite', he was sailing along the coast of an island. But he clung to his fantasies and when one of his men bumped into a man in long white robes, Columbus wondered if he had not been the famous Prester John – the mythical ruler of a lost but wealthy Christian kingdom believed to be somewhere in Asia. Columbus continued to sail along the coast of Cuba and, having just failed to reach its westerly tip, he turned back, making all his men swear an oath saying that it was mainland. His desperation was such that he also threatened to whip or cut out the tongue of anyone who later declared otherwise.[23]

Torres had arrived back in Spain with Columbus's charts in time to help Isabella and Ferdinand close their agreement with Portugal over the demarcation line separating their spheres of exploration and sovereignty. It was not the right moment to pick another fight with Portugal. Growing tension with France, an increasingly aggressive Turkish presence in the Mediterranean and the raids of Berber pirates were already trouble enough. The Portuguese king wanted the line, running between the poles, as far west as possible to increase his chances of finding new lands. He had claimed that it needed to be pushed from 100 to 370 leagues west of Cape Verde so that his vessels could have room for manoeuvre on the return trip from Africa, as they sailed west to pick up the winds and currents that would push them back to the Iberian peninsula. This division of the globe meant that Spain could not sail or explore around Africa or sail east to Asia, while the Portuguese could not cross beyond the 370-league line. But the map Torres had brought back appeared to prove the lands that Columbus had discovered to be a full 750 leagues away.[24] Isabella must have been convinced that all the new lands to be discovered would fall comfortably across the line and so would belong to Castile. She certainly could not have known that, far to the south of Columbus, the American continent stretched out east, with large parts of modern-day Brazil lying on the Portuguese side. The Treaty of Tordesillas was signed on 7 June 1494, ensuring peace with Portugal and allowing the Columbus adventure to continue unimpeded.

Isabella now turned to making sure her new lands were properly supplied. This had been her special area of expertise during the Granada War, and Columbus's man in Seville, the Florentine Giannotto Berardi (who described himself as a trader in 'merchandise, male slaves and female slaves'),[25] now wrote directly to her proposing that she offer to maintain each new colonist for two years, giving them time to become self-sufficient. She should also allow vessels to set out freely from Hispaniola to explore other islands, but these should carry one of Isabella's officials, he said, to take note of the goods obtained, with strict control of all merchandise so that she could receive her share. 'This way the population of the island will increase and others will be discovered and explorers, officials, miners and other skilled workers will go seeking their fortune, which will be good for your highness,' he said. It would also help avoid a rush to come home, he added, from people who were owed salaries. 'It seems to me that your highness cannot better explore the islands more cheaply, without offending the Indians and ensuring there is no harm to the trade from these islands. I hope that within six months your highness will have received so much from your fifth share that your officials will be able to cover the ten or twelve *cuentos* [ten to twelve million *maravedís* of salary] that must be paid to people, and they will feel happy and that it has been fruitful.'[26] It was a sign that Isabella was prepared to break Columbus's monopoly, but also reflected fears that he had already died and would not return from his exploratory trip to Cuba and Jamaica.[27]

As the frequency of contact with her new colonies increased, Isabella began to receive worrying news. The Spaniards had not just disrupted the lives of the indigenous people on Hispaniola, but were fast destroying the ancient lifestyle of peoples who were ill prepared for their strange and increasingly aggressive demands. The Taíno were abandoning their crops as they fled or were captured and that meant less food for everybody, including the colonists. Malnutrition had become widespread and many of the settlers were unable to fight off the illnesses that ravaged their ranks, killing half of them. Columbus handed command of the settlements on Hispaniola to his brothers Bartolomé and Diego, who proved unpopular. Some of the senior men claimed seniority and both friar Boïl and the commander of the inland fort, Pedro Margarit, had abandoned Hispaniola in September 1494, sailing home with many of the lancers who were the backbone of Columbus's tiny army. The garrison of the inland fort then ran wild, stealing women from the Indians.[28] 'They would not stop their abuses, snatching away island women in sight of their fathers, brothers and husbands; given over to stealing and thievery, they had altered the spirit of the natives,' reported Las Casas. 'They meted out beatings and the rod, not just on common people, but also on the principal, noble men.'[29] When Columbus arrived back he was told a group of local chiefs had formed an alliance to fight against Isabella's colonists. Columbus took with him his most formidable weapons, twenty attack dogs which (like his horses) provoked absolute panic among the Indians. He soon made a shocking discovery – the Indians had destroyed their food supplies and stopped planting in the belief that this would force the Spaniards to leave. As he advanced through the island, he found Indians dying of starvation. He easily defeated the alliance, capturing more than a thousand people and imposing a tax – to be paid in gold – on the rest, though this also failed to produce significant quantities of the treasured metal. The conquest came at a terrible price, with contemporaries estimating that at least 50,000 natives died from wounds, starvation or illness as a simple and relatively harmonious way of life was chaotically and violently disrupted.[30]

Only the return of Torres, with four vessels full of provisions and fresh men, allowed the colony to regain some form of stability. Torres also brought letters from Isabella and Ferdinand in which they suggested that, with the division of the New World with Portugal now settled, a regular service with at least one vessel travelling in each direction every month could now start. They also issued instructions ordering all those on the islands (they made no reference to any mainland) to obey Columbus's orders 'as if we in person had commanded it, or face the punishment that he orders on our behalf'.[31] Columbus feared that Boïl and Margarit, on arriving in Spain, would destroy the promising and sometimes idyllic picture he had painted of the lands he had found, so he sent Torres back again. He also sent 400 slaves, a quarter of the 1,600 Indians that he was holding captive after his confrontations with the alliance. These were mostly local Taíno, rather than the supposedly cannibalistic Caribs that he had originally promised. The colonists were allowed to pick personal slaves from the rest while those left over (some 400, presumably weaker or older) went free. Most of the men who had travelled to Cuba with Columbus now agreed that the oath he had made them swear – declaring it to be a mainland continent – was false, with an adventurous and learned abbot from Lucerne who had joined them using his own knowledge of cartography to dispute Columbus's claim. 'For that reason the admiral has not let him come to Spain with us,' wrote Michele de Cuneo, one of those who had been on the Cuba exploration. Columbus also prevented the gold sifters from returning home, hoping they could still be of use.[32]

Boïl and Margarit had reached Spain in November 1494, giving Isabella and Ferdinand a very different picture of the Indies to that provided by Columbus. 'They dampened the monarchs' hope of finding wealth in the Indies, saying that it was a deceit, and that there was scarcely any gold in the island [Hispaniola] and that the expenses were high and never repayable and many other things against this business and the hopes that the monarchs had placed in the Admiral,' wrote Las Casas. 'This was not least because they had not returned in ships that were laden with gold.' Also, since Columbus had not reappeared from his exploratory trip to Cuba and Jamaica at the time Boïl and Margarit set off on the return voyage, it was conveniently assumed that he had died. It was only when Torres reappeared with a fleet in April 1495 that they realised he was still alive. Torres brought slaves (a quarter of whom had died on the journey) and Columbus's own written claims of having discovered the mainland in Cuba. An anonymous report sent to Isabella suggested that cotton might be an appropriate and lucrative crop.[33]

It was time, Isabella and her husband realised, to change tack. They sent one of their senior officials, Juan Aguado, with the next fleet, giving him extensive powers to investigate Columbus.[34] They also issued orders allowing others to sail independently of Columbus and the royal payroll to explore, settle and trade in the new lands.[35] 'Anyone who wishes to go to live in the said island of Hispaniola without a salary can go freely, without paying for the right, and have for himself and his heirs the houses they build, lands they work and fields they plant . . . giving them a year's maintenance . . . and keeping a third part of the gold they find or obtain,' they wrote. Aguado had originally formed part of the second expedition, going home early, so he must have been aware of the gap separating reality from the descriptions Columbus was sending home. Aguado's return to Hispaniola was greeted with joy by almost everyone except the Columbus family.[36] Aguado and Christopher Columbus locked horns and both decided to return to Spain, but a hurricane ripped through the fleet in La Isabela's poorly protected harbour, sinking the four ships that Aguado had brought as well as two others. This bought Columbus precious time because one of his men who had fled after a fight with Bartolomé's servants had ended up crossing the island to the south coast before bringing back hopeful news. The man, Miguel Díaz, had become the ardently beloved guest of a female chieftain who had shown him sources of gold around the River Hayna – producing examples of what was clearly better quality gold than they had seen elsewhere. Díaz returned with the news and was pardoned for his fight with Bartolomé's man. Columbus had by now realised that La Isabela, exposed on the north coast, was a poor port and sent Díaz back to found a settlement, the future capital of the Dominican Republic, Santo Domingo. He himself, meanwhile, prepared the remaining two vessels for a return trip to Spain. The journey took him three months, but Columbus finally made it back to Cadiz in June 1496.[37]

Isabella's new admiral had returned determined to defeat the naysayers who claimed his voyages were a waste of time and money. He dressed in one of Isabella's favourite male outfits, the habit of a Franciscan friar. He also clothed himself in a heady mix of messianic religiosity, self-interested interpretations of the scriptures, scholarly wisdom, history and myth. In addition he brought with him a fist-sized piece of gold, or gold ore, handed to him by a local chieftain.[38] Caonabo, the chieftain who had wiped out the first settlement at La Navidad, travelled with Columbus, along with his brother and thirty other Taíno. Caonabo had died on the journey, but a few months later Isabella met his brother, who had been given the name Diego. He wore a gold chain of 600 castellanos, or some 2,760 grams.[39] Isabella soon found herself bombarded with memoranda defending Columbus's projects and insisting on his personal rights as admiral, governor, viceroy and discoverer. Much of his energy went on ensuring recognition that all this could be passed on to his descendants, cementing their position among the highest families of the land, while he also made vague threats about taking his family back to Genoa. His extravagant financial claims, calculated at up to a quarter of the wealth extracted from the Indies, were secondary. Glory, self-justification and rank were what most preoccupied him.[40] Nor was he above the odd resentful reference to the sovereigns' original disbelief in his project. 'Their Highnesses gave me the right and powers of conquest and to reach, thanks to Our Lord God, this entailed estate, though it is true that, after I came to propose this enterprise in their kingdoms, they took a long time before giving me the means to put it into practice,' he wrote in the document in which he laid down the terms by which his titles should be passed on.[41]

Isabella continued to receive complaints from him about how certain people at her court had begun 'to criticise and belittle the enterprise that had started there, because I had not sent ships full of gold, without taking into account the short period of time that had passed or what I had said about other difficulties'. That was why he had come to see her and Ferdinand to explain 'about the different peoples I had seen and how so many souls could be saved, bringing with me the obedience of the people of the island of Hispaniola, who agreed to pay tribute and have you as their sovereigns and masters'.[42]

He reminded Isabella of all those other great monarchs and emperors – from Solomon to Nero – who had searched in vain for the oriental lands that he was now convinced he had found. Isabella's Castile, he was telling her, had achieved something that previous great civilisations – Roman, Greek and Egyptian – had failed to do. 'Not that this was good enough to stop some people who felt like it from criticising the enterprise,' he wrote. 'Nor did it help to say that I had never read before of any Princes of Castile who had ever conquered territory outside it . . . or to point out how the Kings of

Portugal have had the heart to persist in Guinea [west Africa] and its discovery.'[43]

Isabella and Ferdinand had by now realised that the open-ended project they had started when they sent Columbus off on his first voyage had vast potential, not least because it seemed obvious that there were new lands still to discover. They were grateful to him, aware of his exceptional talents as a navigator, and not that worried about the complaints they were receiving. 'Your Highnesses' reply was to laugh and say that I should not worry about anything because you gave no credence or respect to those who spoke badly to you about this enterprise,' he recalled.[44] That did not mean he was the right person to continue leading this remarkable expansion of Isabella's domains.

34

A New Continent

Sanlúcar de Barrameda, Late May 1498

The convicts who clambered aboard Columbus's boats in Sanlúcar de Barrameda, at the mouth of the Guadalquivir River, in the final week of May 1498 were proof that the gold-rush fever that had accompanied previous voyages to Isabella's new overseas possessions had dimmed. Isabella and Ferdinand had offered reduced sentences to convicts who joined his fleet, in order to find men prepared to go to a place whose reputation diminished with every returning shipload of disgruntled colonists. This time there had been less of a rush to send Columbus back, too, and he had spent part of his two years in Spain thinking up new and extravagant plans, which he sent to Isabella and her husband, for sailing to Calcutta or launching a crusade against Mecca.[1] They can have done little to boost her confidence in the Genoese adventurer, whom she nevertheless continued to treat with kindness. She had written to him on separate business, calling him 'a very special and faithful servant of mine' and thanking him for his advice and 'the goodwill and love with which you give it to us, as we have always found with you in all the ways you have served me'.[2]

Columbus split his fleet in two. Five ships carried supplies directly to Hispaniola, where Bartolomé was governing in his absence. He himself led an exploratory squadron further south, sailing on the same latitude as Sierra Leone – where the Portuguese had found gold – in the belief that land along the same parallel was often similar. There were also rumours (which he claimed to have heard from Portugal's João II) that another continent lay to the south of the islands he had found. 'May Our Lord guide me and allow me to be of service to him and to the king and the queen, our lords, and to the honour of all Christians, as I believe that this route has never been sailed by anyone, and that this sea is completely unknown,' he wrote. Columbus was right in the latter judgement. It began as another gruelling voyage. They spent eight days becalmed in the doldrums in boiling heat. He then sailed west for as long as he dared without spotting land, but eventually decided to head further north towards the islands he knew. Amazingly, he was right for the second time about the existence of unknown lands across this stretch of unnavigated water. When he finally saw three hills on the horizon and reached an island that he named Trinidad, at the south of the curve of the islands that would be known as the Antilles, he also sailed into the waters flowing out from the vast River Orinoco on the north coast of what is now Venezuela. He was at first perplexed by the presence of this deluge of fresh water, which created fierce currents. Then he realised that such a spate could have been collected only by a land mass of considerable size, even though this did not fit his expected location of Asia. 'I believe that this is a very large continent that nobody before me has known about,' he wrote in his diary as he sailed off, effectively noting down the European discovery of South America. But he was not sure and, although his men became the first Europeans to set foot on the new continent when they went ashore on the Paria peninsula, he soon set off north for Hispaniola, while vowing to return at a later date. He could not know just how large this land mass would prove – or how much land it would eventually yield for Spain. By now Columbus had gone almost blind from staring out to sea with squinting, bloodshot eyes and relied on his sailors and pilots to inform him of all they saw.[3]

Columbus was now on something more than a mere voyage of exploration and colonisation. A sea captain's life could be solitary and more so if one was accustomed to keeping secrets from one's crew or constantly falling out with trusted aides. In moments of great strain he turned to higher forces. The great sailor increasingly saw himself as an agent of God, specially chosen to help spread

Christianity and recover Jerusalem.[4] Isabella and Ferdinand's Spain, he declared, had been chosen to fulfil the predictions of Christendom's revival with the Old Testament prophet Isaiah long ago proclaiming 'that it was from Spain that the Holy Name would be spread'.[5] He continued to fret about gold and spices, but with his position among Castile's nobility now cemented he appeared more interested in his prominent role in God's projects than in the annoying administrative details of governing a colony. 'I do not suffer these hardships in order to find wealth or treasure for myself since I know that all that is done in these times is vain except for that which is for the honour and service of God, which does not mean amassing riches, magnificence or the many other things that we use in this world, to which we are more attached than those things that can save our souls,' he wrote. He began to imagine, too, that he was close to discovering the Garden of Eden, traditionally considered to be somewhere in the east.[6]

Few of those who travelled with Columbus shared his messianic vision, romantic ideals or occasionally delusional nature. This was driven home as soon as he returned to Hispaniola, where he found the colonists in revolt. The man Columbus had appointed mayor of La Isabela, Francisco Roldán, had rebelled and persuaded fellow colonists that Columbus and his brothers – who were, after all, foreigners – were deliberately preventing them from returning to Spain. He set up a free-wheeling alternative settlement in Jaragua where 'each had whatever women they wanted, taken by force from their husbands, and they also took girls from their parents to serve as maids, washerwomen and as many other Indians as they desired to serve them', according to Las Casas.[7]

Columbus now sent a fleet of five vessels back to Spain with 600 Indian slaves on board – even though Isabella and her husband had obviously not finished consulting canon law experts on the rights and wrongs of the slavery issue. He also wrote to them claiming that the rebels were a threat to their sovereignty. 'This Roldán and his men and their supporters had a way of forcing everyone to join them, promising them no work, a free rein, lots to eat, women and, above all, the freedom to do whatever they pleased,' he told them.[8]

Isabella and Ferdinand were asked both to ensure a constant supply of fresh men and to provide a handful of trustworthy friars to improve the settlers' morals. 'Of our people there, neither the good nor the bad have fewer than two or three Indians to serve them, dogs to hunt for them and, though one should not say so, women who are so beautiful that it is a wonder,' they were informed.[9] The men had expected gold and spices simply to fall into their hands. 'They were so blinded by greed that they did not think that, if there was gold, it would be down mines like other metals, or that the spices were on trees, and that they would have to dig for the gold while the spices would have to be gathered and cured . . . all of which I made clear to them in Seville.'[10] But the reality of life in Columbus's colony was far worse than even the hardiest settlers could have expected and the death rate in the semi-ruined La Isabela was terrible. Syphilis was rife, with up to 30 per cent of the colony suffering. The disease would be yet another, if unwanted, novelty introduced into Europe by Isabella's returning colonisers.[11] Smallpox, typhus, measles and cholera would travel in the opposite direction, to devastating effect.

Columbus began to panic about the messages reaching Isabella and her husband. He accused Roldán's faction of telling lies and appealed to Isabella's lowest instincts by blaming the *converso* colonists and their Jewish blood for the rebellion.[12] 'This would never have happened had a *converso* not hatched the plan, because the *conversos* are enemies of your Highness's prosperity and of all Christians,' he wrote. 'They say that most of those with this Roldán are from their ranks.'[13]

Isabella was hearing a very different story from other sources. Returning colonists rioted in front of her, denouncing the Indian project as a monument to Columbus's deluded vanity. Already Isabella and Ferdinand were licensing other explorers, with the first arriving in May 1499.[14] And even before Columbus set sail on his third journey, he had astonished them by reacting violently to a visit by a royal official, Jimeno de Briviesca, whom he attacked, 'giving him many kicks and tearing at his hair'. Las Casas admitted that the admiral had gone too far. 'In my opinion, that was the main reason, above all the other complaints and rumours against him . . . that the highly indignant sovereigns decided to take away his governorship, sending the *comendador* Francisco de Bobadilla to govern that island and those lands,' he wrote.[15]

In May 1499 Isabella and Ferdinand signed documents appointing Bobadilla – whose original task had been simply to investigate the Roldán rebellion – as governor, ordering that he take back some of the slaves with him. Even then, though, Isabella and Ferdinand hesitated, and Bobadilla had to wait a year before he was given permission to set out. Perhaps they hoped that Columbus, who was much closer to Isabella than to Ferdinand, would resolve the problems himself or, with his undoubted navigational skills, discover new lands that would provide the wealth they had been promised.[16]

Bobadilla sailed into Santo Domingo in August 1500, accompanied by just nineteen of the freed Indian slaves. The limp bodies of two men swung from scaffolds on either side of the river mouth. He soon discovered that seven men had been hanged for rebellion that week and a further five were awaiting their turn, while the Columbus brothers had set out on expeditions to track down more rebels. Bobadilla announced that he had come with orders to pay all outstanding salaries – a move guaranteed to win the colonists' support. Columbus returned to Santo Domingo from his expedition in September, was interrogated by Bobadilla, arrested and sent home. 'As I was awaiting, confident and happy, for ships that would take me to your mighty presence with great news of gold and victory, I was taken prisoner and thrown with my two brothers into a ship, weighed down with chains, stripped naked and treated very badly,' Columbus recalled bitterly in a later letter to Isabella and Ferdinand.[17] Columbus allegedly turned down an offer to have his chains removed, because he wanted to wear them on his arrival as proof of how he was being maltreated. In the meantime

Bobadilla formally interrogated twenty-two witnesses, asking them if Columbus had tried to organise armed resistance, planned to hand the colony over to a foreign power or deliberately stopped Indians being christened so that they could be enslaved.[18]

Isabella must have been shocked by the contents of Bobadilla's report. The witnesses claimed that Columbus often refused to give priests permission to baptise the Indians because he wanted them as slaves. He also refused to allow the pregnant girlfriends of several colonists to be baptised, thereby preventing mixed marriages – apparently on the instructions of Isabella and Ferdinand. None of that had stopped the colonists cohabiting with Indian women, seeking out the daughters of local chieftains or *caciques*, thereby winning themselves powerful allies.[19] Men were hanged for thievery or disobedience. One man escaped the noose only to have his ears and nose cut off instead. A woman who spoke badly of Columbus had her tongue cut out and another was lashed to a donkey and whipped because she was thought to be pregnant.

Bobadilla's finding that Columbus had also slowed down the number of baptisms shows that expediency had trumped ethics in the slavery debate. Some of the raids made against the Indians appeared to have no other purpose than to capture them, which also went against the more restrictive versions of what was acceptable. Moreover Columbus saw fit to enslave Indians who had failed to pay him the tribute he demanded, using trickery and false promises of an amnesty to capture them. The greatest quantity of slaves were on Hispaniola itself, where he was able to demand one or two from each colonist in 1499 in order to send them to Castile. Colonist Juan Vallés could not quite remember, just a year later, whether he had handed over three or four – suggesting that he had many more than that. Columbus had seen the Portuguese selling black Africans in Cape Verde for 8,000 *maravedís* a head and thought the people he was sending for sale would fetch at least 5,000. He dreamed of selling 4,000 of them. It was a lucrative and easy trade, as long as they did not die on the way to Europe, which often happened to begin with. Columbus thought it best that they be given meagre rations. They ate little, he said, and 'if they ate too much, would fall ill'.[20]

Isabella's patience finally broke when she found out that Columbus was giving away slaves to his own colonists. 'What power does my admiral have to give any of my vassals away?' she allegedly asked. Yet Bobadilla's miserable cargo of nineteen returnees was a fraction of the 1,500 slaves who had been shipped by 1500 and an investigation had to be launched into their whereabouts. But in 1501 Isabella and Ferdinand continued issuing permits for cannibals to be enslaved.[21] Isabella repeated them two years later, saying that cannibals who refused to surrender and reform could be 'captured and brought to these my kingdoms . . . and sold . . . paying us the part which belongs to us'.[22] Instructions were, however, issued to end enslavement of the Taíno of Hispaniola, because there were no cannibals on the island. This was confirmed in 1501, when Isabella wrote to her new governor Nicolás de Ovando: 'You will try to ensure that the Indians are well treated and can move safely everywhere and that no one will exercise violence against them or steal from them, nor inflict any other damage or wickedness.' Indians were now to be treated 'as our good subjects and vassals', she insisted. 'If from hereon anyone harms them or forcibly takes something from them, they should tell you because you will punish them [the perpetrators] in such a way that no one will ever again dare to do them any harm.'[23]

The indigenous people of Hispaniola, however, must have felt that little had changed, as a forced-labour system called the *encomienda*, in which the Indians effectively paid a Spanish *encomendero* for their 'protection' in either work or goods, was introduced.[24] A decade later, the firebrand friar Antonio Montesinos summed up the situation in an angry sermon preached in Santo Domingo:

Tell me: with what right and justice do you keep these Indians in such cruel and terrible servitude? On what authority have you waged such hateful wars against these people who were peacefully and gently in this land, waging so many of them, with unheard of deaths and damage? Why do you keep them so oppressed and exhausted, without giving them [proper] food or curing them of the illnesses they contract because of the excessive work you give them so that they die or, better said, you kill them in order to obtain gold every day? And how careful are you to ensure that they are taught [church] doctrine, learn about God their creator, are baptised, and go to mass, observing holidays and Sundays?[25]

In time, the slavery problem disappeared by the worst possible means. The decimation of the local population by war, famine and sickness was such that soon there were not enough inhabitants to work the land. Swine flu appears to have wiped out a quarter of the population of Hispaniola in the two years after Columbus returned on his second voyage, and within fifty years there would be fewer than 500 Indians on Hispaniola, down from 100,000.[26] By then slavery had long been going into the Caribbean, rather than out of it, with the traffic of Africans to the islands. Isabella's administration issued the first licence to transport African slaves to the Indies, as a way of replacing the disappearing native population, in 1501, just nine years after Columbus's first voyage. It was the start of an enormous forced movement of African people into the Americas that would last for centuries.

After his undignified arrival home as a prisoner, Columbus was taken before Isabella and Ferdinand in Granada. They had been upset by the treatment meted out to him and had ordered his release and payment of 2,000 ducats so that he could prepare himself for court. His son Hernando, or whoever wrote in his name, later claimed that Isabella and Ferdinand welcomed him with 'joyous faces and sweet words'. Columbus began a letter-writing campaign, managing to have some of his letters delivered to court before Bobadilla's report, which had travelled in the same fleet.[27]

One of these letters went to Juana de la Torre, Prince Juan's nurse, who could be counted on to relay its contents to Isabella – his real target. The queen, he said, had been the decisive benefactor of his voyages of discovery, above Ferdinand. 'Everyone reacted with disbelief but [Our Lord] gave to my lady the Queen the spirit of understanding and great strength, and made her the heiress of all [those lands] as his dear and beloved daughter. I went to take possession of all this in her royal name. Those who had shown their ignorance then tried to cover it up by talking instead about problems and expenses. And yet, despite this, her Highness gave her approval and maintained it in every way.'[28]

Columbus's wild mysticism was matched by false modesty, claiming that he had set out on his third voyage only in order to please Isabella. 'I would love to bid farewell to this business, if I could do so in way that was honest towards my Queen. The strength of the Lord and of her Highness made me continue,' he wrote.[29] In an attempt to gain the moral high ground, he also painted a savage picture of his own colonists as traffickers of young girls. 'Today when so much gold is being discovered there are arguments over how best to make profit, by going to steal or by going to the mines: a woman can be had for one hundred *castellanos*, as much as for a small holding: that is quite common and there are plenty of merchants on the lookout for girls of nine or ten years old, which is currently the most expensive group.'

Those who had arrested him had ulterior motives, he insisted to Isabella, via Juana de la Torre.[30] 'It is a great dishonour that a judge has been sent to investigate me, especially as he knows that by sending a damning report, he himself can take over the government.' Tough measures had been needed, he said, because of the rough nature of the colony and because the Indians – whose peaceful nature and innocence he had previously praised – were so warlike. 'I should be judged as a Captain who left Spain to conquer the Indies and numerous, warlike peoples with customs and beliefs that are opposed to ours . . . and where by divine right I have established the sovereignty of the King and Queen over a new world; so that Spain, which was once reputed to be a poor kingdom, is now among the richest.' It was a very different picture to the earthly paradise of his earliest letters.

'When I finally thought that I had earned a rest and could reap my rewards, I was suddenly made prisoner and brought here in chains, to my great dishonour. The charges against me were brought out of sheer malice,' Columbus wrote in a separate letter, believed to have gone to Castile's main council, the Consejo de Castilla.[31] He had abandoned his wife and children to serve Isabella's Castile, he said, and 'now at the end of my life I find myself stripped of my honour and estate for no reason at all'.

Isabella and her husband did not need much persuading that Columbus had been shabbily treated by Bobadilla. 'Such grateful princes could not allow that the admiral be treated badly, and so they ordered that he come to them with all the rents and rights that he kept here but which had been sequestered when he was detained. But they never again allowed him to take charge of the government [of the islands],' wrote Prince Juan's page Oviedo, who went on to become another early historian of the Indies. Isabella and Ferdinand ordered that Columbus's share of trade profits be restored along with his property. Bobadilla, who was replaced ten months later, was instructed to return samples of gold ore that he had taken from Columbus and repay him for any he had sold.[32]

Late in 1501, Isabella received another letter from Columbus, this time addressed to her alone, in which he donned the mantle of a chivalrous knight writing to his lady. 'Most Christian Queen. I am your Highness's loyal servant. The keys to my free will I handed to you in Barcelona. And if you sample it, you will find its scent and taste has grown and there is no little pleasure to be had from it. I think only of your contentment . . . I gave you my devotion in Barcelona in its entirety, with all my soul and honour and estate. Friar Juan Pérez [at La Rábida friary] and the nurse [Juana de la Torre] will both confirm that this is true. And I am ever more firm in my dedication to you.'

By now Isabella was beginning to suffer long bouts of illness, and Columbus saw her weaker control as one cause of the mounting problems.

> The other matters that your Highness must deal with, along with your poor health, mean that the government of this affair is not being carried out so perfectly. That saddens me for two reasons: first, because of the Jerusalem business, which I beg your Highness not to ignore, or to think that I spoke of it just to impress; the other is my fear that this whole business may escape from us. I beg your Highness not to consider me anything other than your most loyal servant in all this, and that I do not lie when I say that I put all my effort into bringing you peace of mind, and joy, and to augment your great dominion.[33]

Isabella did not take his offer to recapture Jerusalem for Christianity too seriously, but was prepared to send him back to the New World – under very strict conditions, which included not stopping in Hispaniola, where the new governor Nicolás de Ovando had arrived in a mighty fleet of thirty-two vessels. Las Casas had sailed with Ovando and found the colonists in a good mood since they had now discovered a reasonable quantity of gold,[34] while an Indian 'uprising' offered an excuse to take more slaves.

Columbus eventually embarked on his fourth and final voyage in April 1502 with a relatively discreet squadron of four vessels and his brother Bartolomé and his thirteen-year-old son Hernando with him. By this time other explorers, including Amerigo Vespucci, had been sailing to the Indies and widening the area of discovery with growing evidence of a continent to the south of the islands that Columbus had discovered in the Antilles. Columbus's mission on this occasion was to find a channel that would take him towards Asia. He ignored Isabella's instructions to stay away from Hispaniola's main port at Santo Domingo and was turned back.[35] 'The reply was to tell me that, on orders from over there, I could not pass or try to land,' he wrote in what was probably his last letter to Isabella. 'The hearts of those with me sank out of fear that I would take them far away, where, they said, there would be no remedy to any dangers that might befall them.'[36] Columbus felt the humiliation keenly, especially after his ships had been caught out of port by a storm that he had predicted would arrive. His four vessels and his sickly son survived, but an outgoing fleet heading back to Castile that ignored his warnings lost nineteen vessels. Some 200,000 gold *castellanos* (the largest haul of gold yet, worth 100 million *maravedís*, which included a single, huge piece found in a riverbed that was believed worth 3,600 *pesos de oro*, or more than 1.5 million *maravedís* alone) went to the bottom along with 500 men. His nemesis Francisco de Bobadilla and the former rebel Francisco Roldán were among those who drowned. 'Neither man nor boy survived, with no one found either alive or dead,' reported Las Casas, adding that the mud and straw buildings that made up much of Santo Domingo had also been flattened.[37] 'It was as if an army of devils had been let loose from hell.'

Columbus sailed on to central America and modern-day Honduras, where he received news that another sea (the Pacific Ocean) was just nine days' march away, but decided not to seek it out, being more interested in gold and channels that would take him further towards Asia. His attempts to set up new colonies failed and, after being chased off by Indians in modern-day Panama, he eventually found himself stranded in a remote corner of Jamaica.[38] It was from here that Columbus wrote that final letter to Isabella, claiming to have heard of new gold mines while also reflecting on his failure to achieve one of his main aims – to become wealthy. 'Today I do not even own a roof tile in Castile; if I want to eat or sleep somewhere, I must go to a tavern or inn, and often I cannot even pay for that,' he claimed.[39] Columbus also reprimanded Isabella and her husband. 'Until now I have been treated as a foreigner. I was in your royal court for seven years, and everyone I spoke to about this enterprise treated it as a joke. Now even tailors are asking [permission] to make discoveries. And they obtain it, though it is to be believed that they are really going to steal, by which they do great damage to my honour and to this whole business.'[40] He added a final lament, demanding that the monarchs act to restore his honour.

> I came to serve you when I was 28 years old and now I do not have a single hair that has not turned white. I am sick in body and have spent my final years in this, but all was taken away from me and my brothers and was sold, including the clothes on our backs, without us being heard or seen in court and to my great dishonour. I must believe that this was not done by your Royal command. The restoration of my honour and of the damage done to me along with the punishment of those who are to blame would make your Royal Name ring out loud once more.

We do not know how Isabella, a person to whom honour (meaning her reputation and the respect due to her) was also very important, reacted – but time was running out. Only after two of his men had managed to paddle a canoe to Hispaniola was Columbus able to leave Jamaica, though by then he had been stranded for a full year. It was June 1504. He would return to Castile later in the year with his reputation in tatters, sick, indebted and soon to die. Neither he, nor Isabella, could have known what a huge impact his voyages – and their mutual love of grand adventure – would have on the world.

35

Borgia Weddings

The Vatican Palace, 12 June 1493

While Isabella tried to impose strict morals on her court, her church and Castile's growing territories, a new pope was flouting the most elementary rules of good conduct in a brazen fashion which angered and exasperated her. The new pope was a Spaniard, none other than Rodrigo Borgia, the wily, powerful cardinal who had helped Isabella while she jostled for position as her half-brother's heir in Castile. The sixty-one-year-old had been elected in August 1492, taking the name Alexander VI, and news soon filtered back to Isabella that he had brought his own, special form of nepotism and notoriously loose understanding of personal morality to the Vatican palace. The most scandalous event of all was the wedding procession led through the palace's sumptuously decorated rooms in June 1493 by the pope's daughter, the thirteen-year-old Lucrezia Borgia. Famous for her hazel eyes, slender neck and calf-length mane of blonde hair, Lucrezia had inherited both her father's poise and his pouty mouth. Male contemporaries also commented on an 'admirably proportioned' bust. A black servant girl carried her bridal train and behind them walked more than a hundred of Rome's greatest ladies dressed in their full wedding finery.[1] Much of the chatter would have been in Catalan or Spanish, the languages that the huge Borgia clan and their friends had brought with them to Rome. At their head was the dark-haired, vivacious nineteen-year-old Giulia Farnese, also referred to as Giulia Bella, 'the beautiful Giulia', or, less flatteringly, as 'the pope's concubine'.

Thus it was that a pope's bastard-born daughter was being married into one of Italy's most powerful families, the Sforzas of Milan, while his concubine acted as first lady and a large brood of similarly bastard-born children looked on. Chief among them was the immature, spoiled and ruthlessly ambitious Cesare. He was the eldest of the four children born to Vannozza dei Cattanei, at least some of whom had since been been legitimised. Although he was still only eighteen years old, and not yet ordained, Cesare was already being lined up by his father for a cardinal's hat.[2]

Lucrezia was led into the Sala Reale, or Great Hall, where her father sat in papal magnificence on a throne surrounded by velvet hangings and tapestries. Her brother Juan Borgia, who held the Spanish title of Duke of Gandía, escorted Lucrezia into the room, where she and the bridegroom, the twenty-six-year-old Giovanni Sforza, knelt on cushions before the pope. A third brother, twelve-year-old Jofre, presumably stood near by. Borgia's master of ceremonies Johannes Burchard was disapproving of the gaggle of women who followed – most of whom forgot to genuflect to the pope. The vows were made, a ring was placed on Lucrezia's finger and the partying began. 'Valets and squires served two hundred dishes of sweets, marzipan, candied fruits and various sorts of wines,' Burchard reported. 'At the end the guests threw large quantities of the sweets to the people outside.'[3] In Spain, a disapproving Isabella would soon hear rumours that the party had been lewd and rowdy, with guests lobbing sweetmeats into the cleavages of the younger women. 'Each cardinal has a young lady beside him. The meal went on until long after midnight, with bawdy comedies and tragedies which made everyone laugh,' Burchard recorded. 'Many other things are being said, but I am not reporting them because they are not true, and if they were true they would, in any case, be unbelievable.' This mysterious, throwaway last line was a reminder that Rome lived off scandal and gossip as much as religion, and that the Borgia pope himself was central to many of the city's favourite scurrilous tales. 'Alexander VI could be moved by anger and other passions but principally by his excessive desire to magnify his children, whom he loved to distraction,' wrote the Italian historian Francesco Guicciardini, who was twenty years old when the pope died. 'Many popes had had children before but had usually hidden this sin by describing them as nephews; he was the first to present them openly to the world.'[4]

Four years earlier, the then fifteen-year-old Giulia had married a member of the powerful Orsini family. The wedding festivities had been hosted by Rodrigo Borgia, then fifty-eight years old and not yet pope but still – according to one observer – 'tall with a medium complexion, neither dark nor fair. He has dark eyes and a full mouth, his health is excellent and he has enormous energy. He is unusually eloquent and blessed with innate good manners, which never leave him.' Giulia was either impressed, manipulated or merely calculating.[5] Either way, she soon became the powerful cardinal's lover. Borgia considered this a highly satisfactory arrangement and gave her the kind of prominence that made her role as his 'concubine' obvious to all. He even had her face painted on a fresco depicting the Virgin Mary and baby Jesus above his bedroom door in the Vatican. It was the kind of thing that made Isabella furious.

Borgia made no attempt to separate his private life and ambitions from those of the papacy. When he proposed creating an unprecedented thirteen new cardinals in September 1493, there was outrage among the existing cardinals. One of his nominees was Cesare and another was Alessandro Farnese, Giulia's brother. 'Such discord has never been seen,' the Mantuan ambassador wrote.[6] Borgia, in turn, reportedly declared that he would 'show them who was Pope, and that at Christmas he would make more cardinals, whether they liked it or not'.

Isabella must have heard the details of Lucrezia's wedding party from her own ambassadors, who had arrived in Rome a week before – with the new pope countering attempts to cancel the Corpus Christi procession on account of the terrible rains because he badly wanted to impress the Spanish ambassadors. Their masters, after all, were vital to his personal and political ambitions. Reminders of the power now being exercised by Isabella and Ferdinand were everywhere, including just outside the walls of Rome at the gate that led to the Via Appia, where a tented camp of refugee Spanish Jews had sprung up (which would soon be blamed for an outbreak of plague).[7]

Although Borgia's election was seen as further proof of Isabella and Ferdinand's growing might – with a torchlit, festive procession of 4,000 Roman nobles and their children shouting 'Spain! Spain!' as they walked through the city's streets – the queen deplored the scandalous behaviour of the Borgia family and disapproved strongly of the papal offspring. Most of all, however, she hated that this Spanish pope was so shameless. It was perfectly normal for Popes to have children, but usually they were discreet. For Isabella, the avoidance of public scandal involving those in power was just as important as correct behaviour itself.

She had tried to prevent Borgia from handing the title of archbishop of Valencia to the teenaged Cesare. The new pope's ambitious plans in Spain for his son Juan, Duke of Gandía (a duchy near Valencia), irritated her too. When she heard that he also planned to make Cesare a cardinal Isabella was livid, calling in the papal nuncio, Francisco Desprats, for a private meeting.

> She said that . . . if on occasions she referred to things that your holiness did, to be sure that it was not out of bad will, but with great love, but that she was obliged to speak out by some of the things she had heard about your holiness, which cause her, on your holiness's behalf, great displeasure and disgust . . . and she specified to me the parties that were held for the engagement of doña Lucrezia and the creation of cardinals, naming the Cardinal of Valencia [Cesare] . . . and she asked that I write on her behalf, begging your holiness not to show such warmth towards the duke [of Gandía] and his brothers.

The nuncio had replied to Isabella by revealing to her some of the more scandalous behaviour of the recently deceased popes Innocent

VIII and Sixtus IV. 'I told her not to be so disgusted by your holiness's things, that she should not think they were the kind of things that provoke unfortunate consequences, and that it seemed her majesty hadn't been so interested in discovering the lifestyle of the other popes who came before your holiness,' he said. The scabrous details he revealed – probably including Innocent's nepotism towards his own bastard children or the half-dozen Sixtus nephews who became cardinals, as well as the latter's allegedly uncontrollable passion for beautiful young men, 'proved how much more dignified your holiness's behaviour was than theirs'.[8]

Political advantage was, however, more important to Isabella than the behaviour of the Borgias. The ambitious Rodrigo Borgia saw himself as a *pontifex imperator*,[9] a pope-emperor, and was determined to strengthen the papal states. He played the neighbouring Italian kingdoms off against one another and trod a fine line between support for the conflicting ambitions of the young French king, Charles VIII, and of the powerful new monarchs in Spain, all of whom had their eyes set on the large southern kingdom of Naples, which was ruled by a bastard line of the Aragonese royal family.

Borgia read Isabella and Ferdinand well. He realised that the Spanish sovereigns were far more concerned about dividing up the New World, reforming the church at home and containing France than they were about his own family's infamous behaviour. He had been quick to issue bulls giving them rights over the New World shortly after Columbus's first voyage. He also conceded on church reform, giving them a large degree of control over a process that was of utmost importance to Isabella. They, in turn, accepted Cesare as archbishop and arranged a match between one of Ferdinand's cousins, María Enríquez, and his other son Juan. *Realpolitik* was evidently more important to Isabella than the moral stench emanating from Rome.[10]

Since gaining the upper hand in the Hundred Years War against England some sixty years earlier, France had become the dominant nation in Europe. The newly potent Spain was now a challenger for that role, but Isabella and her husband first needed to recover from the expense and effort of the Granada campaign. In January 1493 they had signed a non-aggression pact with Charles VIII, pledging not to oppose his attempts to take control of Naples in exchange for the return to the Aragonese crown of the borderlands of Roussillon and Cerdagne.[11] Their agreement fell apart a year later after King Ferrante of Naples died, ending forty-six years of rule, and the French announced plans to invade Italy. By September 1494, the twenty-four-year-old Charles had an army of 50,000 men in the north of Italy and four months later Borgia was forced to open the gates of Rome to him.[12]

This was a step too far for Isabella and, especially, for her husband. Ferdinand now also formally made a claim to the throne of Naples – which needed his help if it was to survive the French onslaught. Isabella and her husband sent a modest army of 2,000 men and 300 light horses. They were led by a distinguished veteran from the Granada War, Gonzalo de Córdoba, soon to become one of the major military figures in Europe and dubbed 'the Great Captain'. The following month Charles reached Naples and expected the pope to proclaim him king. But by March 1495 a wider Spanish-led, anti-French league that was backed by Borgia had been formed.[13] This was Isabella and Ferdinand's first major military venture outside Iberia, and a sign that a newly self-confident Spain felt it could use its muscle well beyond its own borders (though Sicily and Sardinia had long been, and remained, Aragonese possessions).[14] An anonymous note was pinned to the doors of the pope's Sant'Angelo castle in Rome warning the Spaniards that 'the day would come when they would all die by the knife'.[15] Charles VIII reportedly vowed to 'cut the chain [of the league], even if it was stronger than diamonds'. A contest for domination of Italy and, by extension, for the role of Europe's greatest power had started.

All the Thrones of Europe

Almazán, July 1496

In Almazán, the fortified town on the River Duero near the Aragonese frontier where Isabella was setting up a separate, independent household for her heir Prince Juan, the queen sat down with a special code sheet that transformed words into groups of Latin numerals and laboriously wrote out a secret message to her ambassador in England, the *converso* Rodrigo de Puebla. He was to insist that Henry VII join an alliance against France that already included the pope, Spain and the German lands ruled over by the Holy Roman Emperor Maximilian. 'The King of France assembles as great an army as he can,' she wrote on 10 July 1496. 'Considering the weakness of Italy, there is no doubt that he will conquer it very soon if the King of England, and the King and Queen of Spain, do not henceforth assist it effectually . . . you must request him, in all our names, to send succour without delay, and not permit the Church to be trampled on. You must speak not only to the King, but to all Britons,' she added. In return she offered not just to finalise the wedding between her daughter Catherine and Arthur, Prince of Wales, but also to help the Tudor king see off the threat posed by Perkin Warbeck – the pretend Duke of York whom Isabella called 'the boy in Scotland'. 'We are strong enough to assist him,' she said.[1]

Isabella had received a letter from Warbeck in September 1493, in which he claimed to be one of the two missing sons of Edward IV, the so-called Princes in the Tower. His elder brother – who would have become King Edward V – had been murdered, he claimed, but the man who had been ordered to kill him discreetly had found it impossible and had, instead, kept him hidden. After a wandering childhood he had received pledges of support in France, Denmark and Scotland as well as from the Emperor Maximilian. 'Many of the chief personages in England, whose indignation has been roused by the iniquitous conduct of the usurper, Henry Richmond [Henry VII], have done the same in secret,' he had told Isabella. 'I hope Queen Isabella, who is not only my relative, but also the most just and pious of Princesses, will have pity on me, and intercede on my behalf.'[2]

Isabella did not swallow his story, but still worried about just how resilient the new Tudor dynasty that her daughter was marrying into would prove. Her stock of four marriageable daughters was, once more, proving a precious resource that promised, as Pulgar had already put it, to see her 'children and grandchildren on all the thrones of Europe'. Catherine of Aragon had long been engaged to Henry VII's eldest son Arthur (giving rise, some claim, to an English nursery song about how 'the King of Spain's daughter came to visit me, and all for the sake of my little nut tree'), but the match still had to be finalised and it now became one of the building blocks of the wider alliance against France.[3] In July 1496 Isabella heard that Henry's ambassadors in Rome had agreed that he should join the anti-French league.[4] 'If it be so, and he really has joined [the league], you must strongly urge the affair of the matrimonial alliance . . . to uphold and aid one another in matters affecting our states against all persons whatsoever,' she wrote in late August. She moved quickly to bind the English king closer, and Catherine's future was formally settled in an agreement signed in London on 1 October 1496.[5] She would marry when Arthur, who had just celebrated his tenth birthday, turned fourteen.

A second daughter, Juana, also served to buttress the alliance. She was already engaged to Philip of Burgundy, lord of an extensive and important stretch of land on the North Sea and, as Maximilian's son, heir to his Habsburg father's German lands. Juana was due to leave in the summer of 1496 and Isabella found herself busy preparing the great fleet that would accompany her sixteen-year-old daughter, and a trousseau that needed ninety-six mules to carry it, north to Flanders.[6]

Isabella's belief that the alliance needed England urgently was, it turned out, misplaced. The Great Captain was already close to inflicting defeat on the French army in the kingdom of Naples. The lessons learned in Granada, including the use of artillery to overcome castles, had been refined and improved on with Italian help and the discovery that lightly armed but mobile troops could defeat the heavily armoured, cumbersome French cavalry. Spain's control of the sea and its diplomatic activity in Italy and elsewhere helped to isolate Charles VIII. This was the first great Spanish victory at the start of more than a century of warring as France's domination of continental Europe weakened and Spain's increased. By the end of the year, Borgia would show his appreciation, awarding Isabella and Ferdinand the title of 'Catholic Monarchs' in acknowledgement of their conquest of Granada, the expulsion of the Jews, their promise to fight the Turks and, crucially, their opposition to France's Italian ambitions.[7] It was a recognition of power, not piety.

With both Juana and Catherine already engaged, Isabella turned her attention to her other daughters. Her children proved to be as intense and obstinate about their spouses as their own, famously jealous, mother. The short marriage of her eldest daughter Isabella to Prince Afonso, heir to Portugal's throne, had set the pattern. Although this was a political union, they fell passionately in love, lust or both. She was twenty, he was just fifteen, and their marriage ended dramatically after just eight months with Afonso's sudden death in July 1491. Like the tragic heroines of the first Spanish sentimental novels that the new printing presses in Burgos and other cities were beginning to produce – including the popular *Treatise on the Loves of Arnalte and Lucenda*, which was dedicated to the queen's ladies, who must have been the novels' most avid readers – the young Isabella reacted dramatically.[8] She cut off her magnificent reddish-blonde hair and dressed in the habit of a Poor Clare nun. 'She does not want to know another man,' reported Peter Martyr d'Anghiera.[9] Food became a challenge and, like her sister Catherine, she appears have suffered some kind of eating disorder – suggesting a perfectionist nature and, perhaps, a demanding mother. Fasting and vigils had left her 'thinner than a dried-out tree' and she had vowed to mourn for the rest of her life, becoming obstinate and panicky whenever the subjects of marriage or childbirth were raised.[10] But Isabella refused her request to enter a convent. Their daughters were a crucial part of her foreign policy and she and Ferdinand needed the younger Isabella to continue their dynastic alliances. 'Her parents try to persuade her, they plead and beg that she procreates and gives them grandchildren,' said Anghiera.[11] 'But she has been surprisingly firm in refusing a second marriage. Such is her modesty and chasteness that she has not eaten at table again since her husband's death . . . She flushes and gets nervous whenever the conversation turns to marriage.' Isabella herself admitted that they were having trouble with their eldest daughter. 'We have to tell you that the princess, our daughter, is very determined not to marry,' she wrote to her ambassador in London on 18 August 1496.[12]

One Italian visitor was surprised to see the queen's daughter 'wearing a widow's habit', though it seems there was nothing extraordinary about a Spanish widow parading her sorrow in such an exaggerated fashion. 'Sometimes, when a Spaniard dies, on the day of the funeral, his widow or her closest relative . . . cries and wails throughout the funeral, pulling at her hair and shouting: "Dear God! Why have you taken from me this man, who was the greatest in the world?" ' reported one surprised visitor from northern Europe. 'And she continues with a thousand more words, all lost or mad; and if they do not do it themselves, they hire other women to do it for them, who show exactly the same emotions. It seems their pain is greater in appearance than in their hearts.'[13] The *infanta* Isabella, like her sisters, was also aware that a major part of their task was to produce children who could be heirs to their fathers and grandchildren to both Isabella and Ferdinand, so helping cement alliances with Spain. Her openly expressed fear of childbirth, a frequent cause of death among young women, might also have driven her desire to seek the safety of a convent.[14]

Her single-minded devotion to her deceased Portuguese husband eventually backfired. The Portuguese were so impressed that their new king Manuel, who had inherited the crown the previous year on the death of his cousin João II (and had been supported by Isabella, who moved to the frontier with troops in case he faced an armed challenge), now wanted her as his wife. Isabella offered him María, her third daughter, but Manuel insisted that only the younger Isabella would do, and she eventually found it impossible to resist her parents' insistence that she remarry. Among other things, she was told that a place at Manuel's side would allow her to exercise her religious zeal and promote the kind of reforms that her mother was already carrying out in Castile. What neither parent expected, however, was that she would make personal demands to Manuel before consenting. The younger Isabella had inherited her mother's prejudices and during her previous spell in Portugal she had, it seemed, felt deep shame at the sight of so many Inquisition suspects flooding freely into Portugal. She had also inherited her mother's obstinacy and insisted, in a letter to Manuel, that 'all those condemned over here [in Castile] who are presently in his realms and lordships'[15] be expelled before she set foot in Portugal again. Isabella and Ferdinand were forced to excuse and explain their daughter's behaviour. 'We were very upset with her for sending it [the letter] without telling us first, but she said that she sent it without informing us because she was worried that we would stop her,' they explained to Manuel.[16]

Isabella's excuses for her daughter's behaviour remain unconvincing. She herself was given to accusing Manuel of deliberately harbouring *conversos* and would write to him again in 1504 complaining about that. It is probable that her daughter was merely repeating her mother's complaints. The impact of all this on Portugal's religious minorities was devastating, as Manuel readily bowed to his fiancée's wishes. In November 1496 he expelled the Castilian *conversos*, though some families obtained papal absolution and were allowed to stay. The following month he ordered the expulsion or conversion of the Jews and, going even further than Isabella's Castile, added the expulsion of Muslims as well.[17] It was as though he was competing with Isabella to see who could be toughest. This was a double blow to those she had already forced out of Castile. 'A wind of terror swept the Hebrews and particularly those Jews who had come from Castile who lamented: "We have fled from the lion only to fall into the jaws of the bear," ' wrote one Jewish chronicler.[18] Given the choice between conversion and exile, most Jews again chose the latter. But Manuel was piqued by the suggestion that he might be less devout than his future mother-in-law and tried to outdo her. He ordered the confiscation of all Jewish books, many of which were burned.[19] 'They already took one Jew who loved his books and beat him severely with straps,' wrote Saba, the fugitive scholar from Zamora.[20] 'As I listened, I stood trembling, walking on with trepidation and fright, and I dug into the middle of a large olive tree which had extensive roots in the ground, and there I hid these books which I had written.'[21]

Manuel's real aim was forced conversion, rather than deportation, and just before Easter 1497 he increased the pressure by decreeing that Jewish children under the age of fourteen be taken from their families and forcibly baptised. When the child-snatching failed to break enough wills,[22] further force was used. 'I witnessed with my own eyes how Jews were dragged by the hair to the baptismal fonts; how a father, his head covered [with a prayer shawl] as a sign of his intense grief and with a broken heart, went to the baptismal font accompanied by his son, protesting,' reported the bishop of Lamego, a royal council member who was hardly a pro-Jewish witness.[23]

Those who resisted conversion and insisted on leaving were pushed into an encampment near the Estaus palace in Lisbon[24] and forcibly baptised. Some chose martyrdom, smashing Christian statues in the full knowledge that they would be put to death. Of the thousands there, only Saba and some forty men and women avoided baptism. 'They stripped me, and took away my sons and daughters,' he said. 'I was left with nothing. And I and the [forty] others were imprisoned and chained, and after six months the king ordered we be given one broken ship to take us to Arzilla.'[25]

There is no record of Isabella's reaction to all this, but she was unlikely to be upset about neighbouring Portugal replicating her own actions in Castile. If anything, it served to justify what she herself had already done. She and Ferdinand, perhaps worried that their new Muslim subjects in Granada would blame them for Portugal's expulsion order, were surprisingly sympathetic to Portugal's Moors. In April 1497 they acceded to a request for them to move to Spain. 'We order that you, your wives, children, men, servants and goods be permitted to come into our kingdoms and to be there as long as you wish,' they said. The result was a sudden boost in the *mudéjar* population of Castilian border towns.[26]

Though We Are Clerics . . .
We Are Still Flesh and Blood[1]

Seville, 1496

Santiago Guerra was just one of the many churchmen to be found in the small, windswept *meseta* town of Boadilla de Rioseco, forty miles from Valladolid. A long-established and wealthy Cistercian monastery, the Royal Monastery of Benavides, held sway here and those who wore religious habits enjoyed the privileges, status and security that came with them. Those privileges obviously did not include the right to attack and rape local women, but when Guerra did exactly that to a girl from the town's Cano family, the victim found it impossible to obtain justice from the bishopric of León.[2] Instead of being placed on trial, Guerra wandered around Boadilla de Rioseco armed and threatening to kill the girl's father, Pedro Cano. It was only after the family had appealed directly to the royal authority of Isabella and Ferdinand that a judicial investigation was finally opened.

It is not clear whether the case made its way to Isabella herself or was dealt with by her officials, but this was just one more example of a priest behaving as if he was above all laws. Among the many advantages that priests enjoyed, indeed, was a degree of protection against civil courts, and some recruits to the minor orders had joined purely to avoid trial or being pursued for their debts. These not only sought 'to escape punishment for their crimes', as Isabella herself put it in 1500, but even continued 'to perpetrate many and diverse crimes'. She eventually felt it necessary to demand that lower-order priests be banned from carrying arms in towns and cities and that bandits, blasphemers and murderers be stopped from joining their ranks.[3] Even otherwise honest priests thought they had the right to flout basic laws relating to women. In one case heard at a court in Seville, a woman called Marina Rodríguez complained that her lover, a priest at the city's cathedral called Juan Simón, had reached for his weapon when confronted by her husband. The cut to her husband's face was deep enough to 'slice through skin and flesh, losing a lot of blood', Marina told the court. Simón does not seem to have been punished, however, and when the husband died some time later, Marina publicly pardoned his attacker and, presumably, re-established herself as his official *manceba*, or mistress.[4]

The Spanish church was among the richest and most powerful in Christendom. Its income in Castile in 1492 was 50 per cent greater than that of the crown and, together with Portugal and Aragon, it provided one-third of the income of the papal treasury in Rome – more than France, England and Scotland combined. That wealth made it a magnet for the lazy, the ambitious and the venal, as well as for holy men and women. In the steep streets of Toledo, home to Castile's senior archbishopric, visitors were amazed both by the number of tonsured heads and by their owners' individual wealth. 'The cathedral has many chaplains [Münzer counted more than 100 in 1494] who earn 200 ducats a year, such that the masters of Toledo and of its women are the clergy, who have beautiful houses and can spend and conquer, giving themselves over to the highest living without anyone scolding them,' observed the Italian diplomat and writer Andrea Navagero later in the sixteenth century.[5] Positions could be, and frequently were, bought. Important bishoprics were bickered over by the Grandees and aristocracy, because they brought the same wealth and secular power as the great noble titles. Teenagers became bishops, bishops became political players and their bastard children were often raised to greatness.

Isabella disliked all this immensely. On the one hand the church, via the secular holdings of its great archbishops and bishops, was a rival source of power and a potential cause of trouble in much the same way as the Grandees were. On the other, she was outraged that so few monks, friars and nuns abided by the basic rules of poverty, chastity and obedience to their orders, and that so many priests lived openly with their concubines. Spain's nuns, the Italian professor at Salamanca Lucio Marineo Sículo tutted, often 'lived with great freedom and dissolutely' and, worse still, 'in contact with men'. At the convent of San Pedro de las Dueñas, where Isabella's half-brother had placed his lover Catalina de Sandoval as abbess, they reputedly enjoyed a 'dissolute and frenetic life'.[6]

The queen wanted order, discipline and decency restored by reforming the monasteries, the clergy and, if possible, the papacy itself so that all behaved more like people whose prime interests were God, souls and charity, rather than wealth, power and pleasure. There were plenty of good examples to follow too, especially in the observant monasteries that had sprung up over the previous century in an attempt to renew the original, disciplined spirit of the monastic orders.

Spain was no worse than elsewhere. In England, France and the German principalities of the Holy Roman Empire, corruption and simony were also prevalent. Redemption from sins, and avoidance of purgatory, could be and frequently were bought with money. No one could foresee the dramatic splits of sixteenth-century Christendom, but popular dismay with the church was there in rhymes, songs and satirical *coplas*. 'Whenever a friar dies, the rest go to sing, because one less means another ration to share out,' was one. The first stirrings of what would become a Protestant revolt against these excesses had already been seen in England, with the Lollards, and among the Czechs, with the emergence of the Hussites. Martin Luther had been born in a town in Saxony in 1483, just nine years into Isabella's long reign. He would lead the assault on a corrupt church where almost everything, including virtue, seemed up for sale, while Isabella's own daughter Catherine of Aragon would eventually help provoke Henry VIII's split with Rome by refusing to accept the nullity of her marriage.

At the same time as she battled the Moors, chased heretics and expelled Jews, Isabella insisted that the church cleanse itself of corruption and venality. She soon gave up with Rome as a source of reform. How could popes like Borgia or his predecessor Innocent VIII – who watched prostitutes dance naked and paraded their bastard children in public – demand chastity, or anything else, of ordinary priests, monks or nuns? Rome itself was full of the illegitimate children of cardinals, and envoys like Palencia had returned with their tales of decadent luxury, bacchanalian parties and old men in their underwear racing before the pope.[7] As with the Inquisition, reform was either carried out under the aegis of the Castilian crown, or would probably not be undertaken at all. And if that meant increasing royal power over the church, that also fitted Isabella's ambition for a centralising, more authoritarian monarchy.

Ironically, it was the dissolute, power-greedy and nepotistic Borgia who did most to help her. If Isabella and Ferdinand wanted powers to reform, they needed his permission. That gave him an extra bargaining chip as he manoeuvred for his own children's benefit and to keep the papal states protected from outside powers. In March 1493 he issued a bull allowing them to oversee a reform of the monasteries that, in simplistic terms, saw many of them forced into switching their allegiance from the less strict 'conventual' branch of their order to the 'observant' branch, which insisted on poverty, chastity and correct behaviour. Isabella also wanted nuns to be cloistered and greater devotion in all monasteries and convents to meditation, penitence and the mass. In the most exaggerated of cases, this was a change from good food, fine wine and the company of women to hairshirts and hard work. Of the three bishops who were to oversee the reform, one would always be at court so that Isabella and Ferdinand could watch over the process. This made it similar to the Inquisition and the Hermandad, or Holy Brotherhood, whose senior officials also moved with the court – reflecting Isabella's priorities about policing, religious repression and purifying reform. On the same day Borgia also formally handed Isabella and Ferdinand control of the wealthy and powerful military religious orders of Alcántara and Santiago, adding another important building block to Isabella's royal absolutism. She and Ferdinand had already grabbed control of the third big military order, Calatrava, though some in Rome deemed it 'illegal and monstrous' that a woman like Isabella might be given control of a masculine order. Borgia's backing was bought with a simple series of trade-offs, including allowing Cesare to become archbishop of Valencia.[8] Monastic reform, in other words, was exchanged for outrageously obvious papal nepotism.

A similar reform of the non-monastic clergy was also initiated. In this case it was mostly a problem of public morality, though Isabella and Ferdinand worked hard to appoint honest, learned bishops who would, in turn, appoint honest, qualified priests. 'No one without a university degree enters here,' Talavera said when he was made archbishop of Granada. The German Popplau had been shocked when he visited in 1484. 'The clergy, with only a few exceptions, do not even know how to speak Latin,' he said. Concubinage was a particular target, but so was dress – with priests ordered to make sure their tonsure was the right size, their hair not too long and their habits below the knee. A particular blight was the large number of clerics living openly with women. This had long been a tradition and official reaction had varied from tolerance to largely unenforceable intolerance. Punishment mostly fell on the women, who could be fined and forced to wear a red strip of cloth in their hair as public proof that they were not 'honourable'. But when the rules were publicly flouted by the clerics of Santo Domingo de la Calzada in 1490 and officials tried to punish their women, the boyfriends reacted by excommunicating the officials. Isabella had originally trusted the church to sort this problem out itself but imposed her own punishments when it became clear not only that clerics continued to live with women but – a particular worry for Isabella, for whom image was often as important as reality – also flaunted their scandalous behaviour. 'We have been informed that many clerics have had the audacity to take concubines openly and these publicly proclaim themselves to be their women, and that they do not fear the law,' Isabella and Ferdinand wrote as they tightened the rules again. Once more, it was the women who were to be punished, with banishment from their town or village or with 100 lashes and fines for reoffenders. These punishments were also extended to the mistresses of married men,[9] who were not allowed to flaunt relationships that challenged the established order.

Isabella's attitude to prostitution, however, was relaxed and she even handed out licences. All cities had their brothel districts. In Córdoba these were on cathedral land, and paid rent directly to the church as well as local taxes. In 1486 Isabella and Ferdinand awarded a licence to Alonso Yáñez Fajardo, sometimes described as a priest, 'so that he can establish brothels in all the conquered towns and places yet to be conquered' in the kingdom of Granada. Higher-class prostitutes, known as *encubiertas*, or hidden ones, were to be treated differently to public mistresses, especially as they conducted their business discreetly in private. Officials 'should not confiscate anything from any woman who is not a public prostitute. Those they call "the hidden ones" should not be fined or given a bad reputation, because that could cause scandal or other problems,' Córdoba's bylaw stated.[10] The priorities, then, were mostly to avoid social scandal and trouble, but also to protect the status of properly married women. Even Isabella's own court, so praised by her own propagandists, was suspect. 'How difficult it is to conserve virtue and honesty or avoid unfortunate disillusions in the court,' lamented Popplau.[11] One of Isabella's favourite poets, the allegedly womanising court preacher Friar Íñigo de Mendoza, admitted that it was all temptation. 'To flee the devil it is better to go to the stables than to the royal court,' he said.[12] He might have been referring to Enrique IV's court, but Isabella's reputation for expelling young ladies who interested her husband suggests that her 'reformed' court had its own not-so-secret life of clandestine trysts and sexual dalliance. One out of every seventeen children of nobles in the Extremadura region, for example, were bastards.

Isabella may have been strict and reasonably devout, but that did not mean she could impose her view of the church on her husband.[13] Ferdinand apparently saw no conflict between reforming the church and appointing his own bastard son Alfonso of Aragon (born the same year as his first legitimate child with Isabella) as archbishop of Zaragoza when he was just eight years old or, many years later, making him archbishop of Valencia.

Isabella would have liked to reform Rome itself, which many saw as the root of the church's ill-discipline and decline. But that would mean reforming Borgia. 'His own house was in such disarray that all the rest of Rome could have claimed to be a monastery full of monks and nuns in comparison to it,' said Zurita. The sermons of the firebrand puritan Italian preacher Girolamo Savonarola – who organised bonfires of vanities in Florence to burn sinful art, books and cosmetics, and who also savaged Borgia's papacy from the pulpit and was excommunicated – were on Isabella's bookshelf. One Spanish official even accused Borgia to his face of promoting Rome as a 'house of pleasure' rather than as the home of St Peter.[14]

Isabella could not press Borgia too far because the church was becoming an important source of income for her. When her beloved friar Talavera wrote a damning letter to a Spanish cardinal in Rome she censored his complaints about hypocrisy, scratching them out. 'You will have to pardon my great presumption for changing it, but I rubbed out the part where you mentioned hypocrisy, because I did not think Rome should be besmirched,' she explained to Talavera. With the excuse and considerable expense of the Granada War, they had received papal authority to raise extra money directly from, or via, Spain's wealthy church. Over time this source of income grew from a quarter of the money that reached Isabella's exchequer to account for up to 40 per cent. Every three years Isabella and Ferdinand would have to go back to the pope to ask for a renewal of the so-called Crusade Bulls by which they raised much of this. They continued to do this after the Granada War was over, by which time church money had become a bedrock of their funding. The money

Catherine of Aragon was the youngest of Isabella's four daughters – and was chosen to cement an alliance with England's new Tudor dynasty by marrying Henry VII's offspring. © *Getty Images*

Henry VII hoped that Catherine of Aragon would be as impressive a figure as her mother. © *Getty Images*

Elizabeth of York, Henry VII's wife, advised Isabella to make sure her daughter learned to drink wine, as English water was undrinkable.
De Agostini Picture Library / Bridgeman Images

Arthur, Prince of Wales, wrote love letters to Catherine of Aragon, his future bride, after Isabella and her family installed themselves in the Alhambra Palace complex in Granada.
Hever Castle Ltd, Kent, UK / Bridgeman Images

After Arthur died aged only fifteen, Catherine of Aragon married his younger brother, Henry VIII – depicted here as a young child. *Royal Collection Trust © Her Majesty Queen Elizabeth II, 2016 / Bridgeman Images*

The Spanish cardinal Rodrigo Borgia became Pope Alexander VI and angered Isabella with his scandalous behaviour and blatant nepotism.
Pictures from history / Bridgeman Images

Giulia Farnese, believed to be the model for this picture, became Rodrigo Borgia's lover – her face was painted on the wall of his bedchamber at the Vatican Palace.
Galleria Borghese, Rome, Italy / Bridgeman Images

Lucrezia Borgia, the Pope's daughter, had an opulent wedding at the Vatican.

CAES·BORGIA·VALENTINVS

The ambitious and ruthless Cesare Borgia was blamed for the murder of his brother Juan, Duke of Gandía, by the latter's Spanish wife.

Isabella's grandson, Charles V, inherited a vast empire from his grandparents.
Fitzwilliam Museum, University of Cambridge, UK / Bridgeman Images

Isabella's granddaughter, Mary Tudor, would become known as Bloody Mary after inheriting the crown of England.

Isabella's final years were marked by the pain of mourning the deaths of two of her children and one grandson. © *Patrimonio Nacional*

was used not just for fighting the Moors, helping the pope in Italy or sending fleets against the Turks.[15] It also helped fund Columbus's voyages and those of their daughters Juana and Catherine when they went to Flanders and England, respectively, to marry. Isabella was obviously anguished about this. She knew that the extra money was meant for crusading, and in her will, as she totted up the balance of wrongdoings that might be held against her when she sought to enter heaven, she asked that any misappropriated funds be paid back.[16]

On the other side of the balance, however, she could point to having achieved genuine reform in the monasteries and partial reform of the clergy (though, as Navagero witnessed in Toledo, the problems of concubines and wealth had obviously not been completely eradicated). By reforming in advance, Isabella can also be credited with helping prepare Spain to resist the impact of the Protestant Reformation in the sixteenth century. As a result, it remained an almost universally Roman Catholic country that would spread the faith through the Americas and to other Spanish lands like the Philippines. 'She had the great dishonesty and dissoluteness among the friars and nuns of her kingdom corrected and punished,' said her loyal propagandist Andrés Bernáldez,[17] though this was only partially true.

Isabella did not, however, achieve her full ambition for the Spanish church. The model she and Ferdinand really sought was that enjoyed by other monarchies in Europe who controlled the naming of bishops and archbishops. This they were given in Granada and the Indies, along with a share of the church's income there, though they pushed continually for the right to be extended and fought any attempt from Rome to appoint non-Spaniards as bishops. They did, however, bring change to the kind of men who became bishops. Alfonso Carrillo and Pedro González de Mendoza had been old-style Grandee-archbishops in the main see of Toledo, plucked from the ranks of the upper nobility and as interested in politics and their own glory as they were in the church itself. Isabella's new bishops were more modest, more learned and more devout. Middle-class men with university degrees and profound convictions were handed power, sometimes against their will. Among them were the two most influential churchmen of her reign, archbishops Hernando de Talavera of Granada and Francisco Jiménez de Cisneros of Toledo – both of them friars who had originally planned to follow a more humble life.[18] After her husband, these were the men who most influenced Isabella and the way she governed.

38

Juana's Fleet

Laredo, 22 August 1496

Queen Isabella was not accustomed to the sea, let alone to sleeping on a boat. But she had always felt a fascination for the ocean that, at the same time, terrified her. Now she was aboard ship in the well-protected northern port of Laredo, with her sixteen-year-old daughter Juana, listening to the water lap against the hull of a heavy Genoese carrack. This was a mother's attempt to calm her daughter's fears about travelling across the seas, allowing the young girl to get used to the rocking of waves and the creaking of timbers. Juana was about to set sail for Flanders, where she was due to marry Philip, Duke of Burgundy, whose lands included much of modern-day Holland, Belgium and Luxembourg. The pale-skinned, long-faced duke with orangey-auburn hair was known as 'the Handsome' and, as a son of the Habsburg Emperor Maximilian, also used the title Archduke of Austria. Isabella knew that, in the future, she would probably see little of her second daughter. With her chestnut hair, dark eyes and narrow face, Juana was more obviously cast in the mould of her father's family. Isabella had given her second daughter the nickname *suegra*, or 'mother-in-law', apparently because she looked so like Ferdinand's adored and legendary mother. Ferdinand joined this game, and also jokingly called his daughter 'mother'. Juana, like her two younger sisters Catherine and María, had not received as much maternal attention as Isabella had lavished on the older children, Isabella and Juan.[1] Now she was leaving home, and as her departure date of 22 August 1496 approached her mother was concerned.

A vast fleet of more than a hundred ships had gathered at Laredo. The towering green bulk of Mount Buciero and its cliffs protected the bay way off to the north, while Laredo itself was tucked into the western fold of a steep promontory created by an extinct, eroded volcano. At the quayside and anchored in the bay off the broad, sweeping beach the costly cargo of linens, clothes, jewels, silver and gold plate for Juana's trousseau had slowly been loaded. Isabella both oversaw it all and conducted affairs of state from a large, solid stone house on one of the steep streets running down to the port. The lengthy shopping list that Isabella approved included 200 thimbles, 10,000 sewing needles, 40,000 pins and 62 pairs of clog-like *chapines*. Four miles of silks, brocades, velvets, cottons and wool were ordered up for clothes and linens. Delicacies included green ginger, sugared fruits and quince jelly. Perfumes bore strange and sometimes Arabic-sounding names like *menjuí, estoraque, algalía, ámbar* and *almizque* (the latter, civet oil, came from caged African civets, with Münzer shown a 'furious and choleric' animal that had what looked like its testicle sack turned inside out and a small spoon thrust in to extract oil that made his hands 'smell of civet oil for several days').[2] Among the more exotic pieces of jewellery to travel with her were Juana's much loved three-inch-thick Moorish-style gold *axorca* bangles, which could be secretly scented.[3]

The royal fleet of forty-one vessels was led by two giant 1,000-ton Genoese-style carracks which were notoriously safe. Smaller carracks, swift caravels and small pinnaces with both oars and sails made up the rest of Juana's personal fleet.[45] Half of the 4,500 men manning the vessels were soldiers, mostly Basques, in charge of 600 artillery pieces and other guns, some made especially to protect the Spanish *infanta*.[6] An attendant merchant fleet, including two ships carrying iron to England, numbered more than sixty vessels. At least 200 people – including four slaves – formed Juana's household and the accompanying party of nobles was led by Ferdinand's cousin, Fadrique Enríquez, the admiral of Castile. It was an enormous expense for the crown.[7] The origins of Juana's goods show that *mudéjar* Muslims were still important as artisans, with her copper kitchen pots made by 'Ali, a Moor from Torrelaguna' while another Moor called Palafox made thirty-six chests and Mohammed Moferrez (a 'great Moorish master from Zaragoza') was charged with providing the new-fangled claviorgan or harpsichord (or both) that went with her.[8] All these were, of course, designed for showing off – including the 95 pounds of gold and 256 pounds of silver used to create jewels, plate and chapel ornaments.[9] Isabella was accustomed to displaying wealth and power at home. Now she was determined to put on a similar show abroad. If Spain was to become a major European power, it had to impress.

The stormy Bay of Biscay and the English Channel were terrifying for non-sailors, but Isabella's worries were not just about the natural hazards of the sea. What, she wondered, would happen if her daughter's vessel was attacked by the French as it travelled around Brittany and squeezed through the English Channel? The worry was real, for the marriage with Philip was part of the concerted attempt to create an anti-French alliance that would be further bolstered by a match between his sister, Margaret of Austria, and Isabella's son Juan. Tension with France had reached such a state that Isabella was in Laredo without her husband, who had rushed off to Catalonia to deal with the French threat there.[10] She would not see him for almost three months.

When she wrote to England's King Henry VII, via her ambassadors, three days before Juana set out, it was as a mother rather than as a stateswoman. 'Tell the king of England, my cousin, about the departure of my daughter . . . because they have orders from me, if the need arises, to put in to any harbour or land belonging to the king of England. Because of the trust that we have in him, I believe that my children will be treated by his subjects in the same way as his children would be treated in my kingdoms,' she wrote.[11] If the fickle Atlantic weather drove them into an English port, she meant, she hoped that he would treat Juana as he would his own daughter.

Isabella may have been seeking her own solace by spending the two nights before Juana's departure with her lively, intelligent and creative daughter – for her own mother, Isabella of Portugal, had died at the old house in Arévalo just a week before. She had long been a depressive recluse, but her daughter had continued to visit whenever her duties allowed. On 22 August, after two nights on the carrack, Isabella waved her daughter off. 'The queen bade farewell with many tears, thinking that they might never see one another again,' the chronicler Alonso de Santa Cruz reported. 'Last night at midnight the armada set sail, the weather, thanks to God, being favourable,' Isabella wrote as Juana's fleet disappeared over the horizon. 'May it please Him very quickly to bring it to the desired haven, as He has the power to do.'[12]

Isabella moved on to Burgos, where she spent several days in a state of anxiety. 'She was distressed about her daughter, in deep need of news of her. As she had gone into the mouth of hell [at sea], she worried that she would be struck by some storm or be unable to pass the Flanders banks,' wrote Santa Cruz. 'For that reason she kept men of the sea around her, so that they could tell her what winds were blowing, in order to calm her.' In a fresh letter to her ambassador in England she now asked Henry VII to send boats to Juana's rescue if she was attacked at sea 'by any who want to do harm'. The safe conduct she sought from Henry VII proved necessary after the English Channel lived up to its stormy reputation, with the fleet forced to put in for several days at Portland. The Flanders banks also wrought damage. A heavy Spanish *nao* was lost and the huge Genoese carrack carrying most of Juana's trousseau grounded and sank, taking with it the jewels of many of the Grandees and other nobles travelling with her.[13]

Juana reached Flanders on 8 September 1496. The sea turned out to be the least of her worries. Her huge retinue was surprised to find that no one of equivalent rank awaited them. Neither Philip nor his father Maximilian was in Flanders, and it was another month before she met her husband and married him. Juana was joining one of the most flamboyant courts in Europe and one that set fashions and standards of display for the rest of the continent. Philip's courtiers had laughed at the poor dress sense of Isabella's ambassador, Francisco de Rojas, when he played Prince Juan's part in the engagement ceremony to Margaret of Austria. Rojas was one of the men Isabella had raised from a relatively lowly status to become a favourite envoy. He had to partially undress and climb into Margaret's bed, revealing torn crimson tights held together by a leather strap around his thigh. The Spaniard's austere dress sense – a reflection of the moralistic type of human-ism embraced by Isabella's court – clashed with the hedonistic style favoured by the courts in both Burgundy and France. The Spaniards who accompanied the *infanta* were shocked by the loose morals and easy spending. Burgundians, the word came back, 'honour drinking well more than living well'. A particu-larly cantankerous Castilian ambassador, Gutierre Gómez de Fuensalida, later observed that Juana 'should no longer counten-ance these people, since they have no manners at all'.[14]

Maximilian was not the most reliable of allies, partly because he was often short of money. One of Isabella's ambassadors called him 'slow to take decisions, and with a penchant for contradicting people; who never wants what is proposed to him, even if it is for his good; and with a reputation for generosity, but not very much [as] he is so poor that to get 100 florins from him people have to insist for 100 days'.[15] But Isabella and Ferdinand knew that the best counterweight to France's muscle and ambition was an alli-ance between themselves, the Habsburgs and the Tudors.

Messengers, meanwhile, carried descriptions of the Burgundian court's luxurious and novel style back to Spain. Rumours quickly spread that Isabella was preparing rooms for her future daughter-in-law Margaret in Spain that would be almost identical to those draped in gold cloth *à la nouvelle mode* that the Spaniards saw when she eventually received her new sister-in-law.[16] While Juana and the chief nobles with her now impressed the Burgundians with their clothes and jewellery, the latter were disappointed with the rest of the party. 'Their followers were too thinly wrapped and spent very little,' recorded the chronicler Jean Molinet.[17] 'For they are sober in eating and drinking.' Philip then dismissed most of Juana's Spanish court, leaving her lonely and powerless. Among those permitted to stay were her four slave-girls, though this later provoked another culture clash as they bathed her and washed her hair so much that her culturally obtuse husband eventually worried for her health. Isabella did her best to stop Philip from leaving her daughter without Spanish staff, sending a bishop to Flanders with instructions 'to ensure that the persons that the archduchess took with her for her service are not removed from her household'. She also lobbied for Juana to be given control of her own income, following the Spanish fashion, rather than having to squeeze money out of her husband's accountants. It did not work. Philip was neither caring nor faithful and was often absent. Fuensalida found him to have 'a good heart, but [he] is changeable and under the influence of counsellors who intoxicate him with a dissolute lifestyle, taking him from banquet to banquet and from lady to lady'. Many of those counsellors were radically pro-French and disapproving of a marriage designed to weaken the Valois monarchs of France. Juana herself soon discovered that she had inherited her mother's propensity for passionate, possessive love. 'This passion is not found only in me,' she admitted later. But if her mother had been 'equally jealous', she said, time had eventually cured her of it and she hoped that the same would happen to her.[18]

To make things worse, the Spaniards found the change of climate unbearable. They had arrived so late in the summer that it was now impossible to make the return trip, taking Margaret of Austria with them to marry Juan, until the spring. The cold, damp weather of the Zeeland coast, combined with the unfamiliar food and an outbreak of the plague, meant that many did not survive a terrible winter. Their fingers froze and the storms sweeping in from the North Sea left them shivering and vulnerable. 'Whether from the change of air, or of diet, or because of the skimpiness of their clothes, which were unable to resist the agonising cold, the plague got to them and some three to four thousand of them finished their days,' recorded Molinet.[19] Around half of the Spanish party died and some 75,000 *maravedís* was spent just on burying them. Not surprisingly, many of the Spaniards who had been due to stay with Juana now begged to be taken home. Abandoned to her fate, she could – at least initially – do little to bring Isabella's kingdoms closer to Burgundy or help promote Spain's interests against those of France. Philip was not very involved in administering his own lands, leaving that work to his counsellors. Partying and hunting interested him more. 'He was neither ambitious nor greedy and was not given to work, preferring others to take it from him and govern,' reported Zurita. Philip often agreed with Juana when they were together alone, she told an ambassador, 'because she knows that he loves her'. But as he shared everything that she said with his former tutor, the pro-French archbishop of Besançon, she also learned to hold back from telling Philip 'certain things that she believed should be said to him and that should be done'.[20]

Isabella's son-in-law, then, was a disappointment. He showed few signs of turning pro-Spanish and, indeed, created more problems for Isabella than he solved. She had lost a daughter and gained very little in return. She now hoped that the other part of their agreement with the Habsburgs – the marriage between her son Juan and Philip's sister Margaret – would produce happier results.

Twice Married, But a Virgin
When She Died

Burgos, March 1497

Welcoming candles burned in the windows of houses and 1,500 flaming torches, mounted on stands, lit the streets of Burgos. Once more, Isabella had chosen dusk as the most dramatic moment for an important meeting and night was falling as the cavalcade bringing her daughter-in-law Margaret of Austria entered the city. Isabella waited for her by the inner door of the palace, wearing a cloth-of-gold brocade gown, a gold-decorated crimson scarf and black mantilla – an outfit that was copied for both Catherine and María. The encounter was elaborately stage-managed. When Margaret tried to kneel and kiss the queen's hand, Isabella raised her gently up. 'The queen's reception of her was quite a sight,' the Venetian ambassador observed. 'Kissing and hugging many times, she took her with her.'[1]

A tiered stage had been set up in the palace's grand hall, with the royal family carefully arranged by rank. Isabella and Ferdinand sat at the top, with their daughters a step below them and Ferdinand's illegitimate daughter, also called Juana, another step further down. The latter seems to have been born before his marriage, though at least two other illegitimate daughters, both of them nuns called María who spent most of their lives together in a convent in Madrigal de Las Altas Torres, had come later. 'In her youth she was praised as the most beautiful girl in Spain,' reported a visitor who saw Juana marry a Grandee, the Condestable de Castilla (with whom she already had a child) many years later. The choreographed pomp in Burgos, with sixty of Isabella's ladies queuing for almost an hour to kiss the new princess's hand, impressed the Venetian ambassador – who praised the fine clothes of the '*damisele . . . nubile*'. Margaret brought with her not just the sophistication of Burgundy but also that of the similarly hedonistic French court, where she had once been betrothed to Charles VIII. She dazzled the audience with a glamorous French-style dress of gold brocade and crimson lined in ermine, topped off by a black felt hat and accompanied by large pearls. 'Since she was so very beautiful and very pale, the gold and precious stones she was wearing seemed even more rich,' reported Santa Cruz.[2] 'And her ladies were much the same, all dressed according to their customs.'

Isabella's anxiety about Margaret's sea journey to Spain had been almost as bad as that which she had felt on Juana's departure. Once again, her fear proved legitimate. Margaret was energetic and intelligent, with a wry sense of humour. This was, after the collapse of her long-term engagement to France's Charles VIII, her second attempt at marrying. When the fleet taking her to Spain, which also had to put into English ports, was battered by storms in the Bay of Biscay, she jotted down her own witty epitaph. 'Here lies Margot, the willing bride, / Twice married – but a virgin when she died.'[3] News of her arrival at Santander reached Isabella in Burgos early in March 1497. A large group of nobles set out across the Cantabrian mountains to greet the princess-to-be and bring her to court. Margaret's party had little idea about Spain and its rugged geography, bringing with them the four-wheeled carriages that were used in north-west Europe. These soon fell foul of Spain's steep mountains and muddy spring tracks. 'They are for flat terrain,' sniffed the prince's page, Gonzalo Fernández de Oviedo, many years later.[4]

The boy whom Margaret had come to marry was Isabella's most special child and had always been adored and spoiled by his mother. 'My angel', Isabella routinely called him, even when scolding him.[5] For most of his life she had taken charge of his expenses, education and household officials. His *ama*, or nurse, Juana de la Torre, the woman who had made Columbus his *miel rosada*, was clearly the boy's favourite. Juan became so attached to her that he considered her 'like a mother',[6] missed her when she was away and, more confusingly, once dipped his pen into ink and, in scrawly handwriting, said he expected to marry her.[7] 'My *ama*, what sadness you gave me with your departure; I don't know how you did not suffer great anguish at leaving me like this, because you know the loneliness that I will feel without you,' he wrote. 'I beg you, my *ama*, that for love of me you return, because you should have me – and nobody else – as your husband.' It was not until he was eleven (in 1489) that his household was separated out from Isabella's own accounts, but, by the time of his marriage, he had his own court and palace at Almazán.[8]

Like all Isabella's children, Juan had a peripatetic childhood. As a small boy he had been carried in a litter by servants as the court moved from place to place. Later he had learned how to perch on a mule – something his younger sister Catherine was doing at the age of six. Large, padded children's saddles – with crossed poles attached so they could be lifted on and off or carried by bearers – were covered in silk cushions and blankets. The endless journeys traipsing along trails, tracks and old Roman ways, wading rivers or scrambling up mountain passes, meant that all Isabella's children became practised riders at an early age. Juana's mule had stumbled and was washed downstream as the family waded across the River Tagus at Aranjuez in 1494. A frightened Isabella began shouting for help as Juana clung bravely to her saddle while her mule tried to swim, and, when rescued by a stableboy, she was 'red as a rose' and 'with great spirit'. All were equally accustomed to spending the night in palaces big and small, as well as village houses or large (sometimes Arab-style) tents pitched in the open. That did not mean that they were used to discomfort. Ermine, rabbit, hare, otters and martens were all sacrificed to keep the royal children warmly wrapped. Juan's accounts show him going through at least fifty-five pairs of shoes and a similar number of high, soft *borceguí* boots each year.[9] But Juan's liking of his clothes, and his habit of holding on to them rather than giving them away to retainers, angered Isabella, who stepped in to educate him about proper royal generosity.

'The queen was told that the prince was becoming tight-fisted,' reported Oviedo. 'As a prudent and magnanimous queen, she wondered how to free her son from this defect and make him more generous . . . because it is a great defect if a king does not know how to gratify those who love and serve him.' One day she asked the prince's chamberlain, Juan de Calatayud, what had happened to a suit of clothing that the prince should have given away. 'My lady, it is in the prince's chamber. He has not given it away, nor does he generally give away anything that your highness has bought him,' came the reply.

'It would have been better for him to give it away, because princes should not have the trunks in their chambers stuffed full of clothes,' said Isabella. 'From now on, you must make sure that, every year on the last day of June [the prince's birthday], you bring before me all the doublets, tunics, capes, other clothes, hats and harnesses, and all the trappings of horses, mules and ponies, in other words all the personal apparel of the prince – except the tights and footwear.' At his next birthday all his clothes were laid out and an inventory made. Isabella called Juan to see her and, with the list in her hands, scolded him gently: 'My angel . . . princes should not be like second-hand rag merchants, nor have their trunks full of personal clothes and attire. From now on, on this day of the year and in front of me, I want you to share all this out between your servants.'[10] Isabella, of course, already did much the same with her own clothes.

Bullfights, hawking, ball games, music, mummery, fireworks and chess were among the entertainments provided for Juan. Perhaps as he gripped in his hand the chess figure of the queen – newly powerful after rule changes that allowed her to move diagonally across the board – he thought of his mother, who some historians see as a model for the change. Isabella's main concern, as always, was education. Once he had reached school age by turning seven, a Dominican tutor, Diego de Deza, trotted along behind him, filling his head with Latin, grammar, ethics, reading and musical tuition.[11] Seven years old was, according to one manual, the age at which young royalty should start 'reading, writing, learning the Latin language, and then playing instruments, dancing, swimming, firing bows and crossbows, fencing, board games, ball games and other things that prudent and well-trained men can do'.[12] As he grew older, Juan was drawn closer to both parents, learning by proximity about royal decision-making, war and justice. By the age of fourteen he was a wealthy man in his own right, accumulating lands that paid rents and taxes – and the responsibilities that went with them. In 1496, shortly before they waved goodbye to Juana, Isabella and her husband had formally given him the title enjoyed by the heirs to the crown, prince of Asturias.[13] 'By ancient custom in these our kingdoms . . . when there is an eldest son to be heir to the kingdoms, when he leaves tutorship and comes of age, the sovereign used to give them a household and principality to have and to govern,' they wrote.

Juan was the third of Isabella's children to marry and, like his sisters and mother, he quickly turned a marriage of political convenience into a passionate, ardent relationship. The couple married on 19 March 1497, but it was still Lent – a time of church restrictions – and they were forced to wait two weeks before being allowed to consummate the marriage. In the meantime, the celebrations were dampened by the death of a young noble who fell under his own horse during an energetic game of *cañas*, with some seeing a bad omen for the couple. The blonde, fair-skinned Margaret impressed the southern Europeans who saw something superior and desirable in her pale complexion. 'You would think you were contemplating Venus . . . unspoiled by make-up or artfulness,' wrote Anghiera, though it is difficult to imagine a product of the French and Burgundian courts being quite so unadorned.[14]

Juan and Margaret took to one another immediately. Some, indeed, worried about the obviously intense sexual attraction between the young couple, with court physicians concerned about the amount of time they spent in bed together.[15] They fretted that the prince, whose long history of illness saw him regularly fed tortoise meat to deal with stomach pains, was too young and weak for such exertions. 'A prisoner to his love for the lady, our young prince is once more too pale,' wrote Anghiera, who accompanied Juan as he rode down streets carpeted in thyme and other herbs on his royal entry into Salamanca on 28 September.[16] 'The king's doctors have advised the queen to separate Margaret from the prince's side from time to time, giving them rest, arguing that such frequent copulation is a danger.' Isabella did not listen. 'Time and again they tell her to observe how thin he is getting and what poor bearing he has and they warn the queen that, in their judgement, this might soften his marrows and weaken his stomach. They don't achieve anything,' said Anghiera.

Isabella's reply may have reflected her own experience of both sex and marriage. 'The queen says that it is not right for man to separate what God has joined,' reported Anghiera, who worried that Isabella was transferring her husband's natural robustness on to her obviously weaker son and blamed a bland diet of 'chicken and other weak food' for his sickly nature. 'The prince has patently been weak from birth . . . They advise her [Isabella] not to trust in the example of her husband, whom nature gifted an admirable robustness as soon as he emerged from his mother's womb, repeatedly telling her that a great difference exists between father and son,' he said.[17] On matters of state Isabella was obliged, at the very least, to seem as though she was listening to advice. When it came to her children, however, she clearly felt that the decisions were hers to take alone. 'The queen will not listen to anyone and clings obstinately to her womanly decision,' said Anghiera in mid-June, after the family had gathered in Medina del Campo while the younger Isabella prepared for her return to Portugal, this time as queen consort. 'She has turned into something that we would never have expected in her. I have always proclaimed her to be a very reliable woman. I wouldn't like to call her obstinately rebellious; [but] she is overconfident.'

Isabella and Ferdinand had other things to think about. The younger Isabella had to be seen off in proper style, and a series of festivities and ceremonies had been organised for early October in the border town of Valencia de Alcántara. From there she was due to cross into Portugal. The family split, with Isabella, Ferdinand and their daughters moving on to the frontier while Juan stayed in Salamanca – one of his personal *señorios*, where some 3,000 students at Spain's greatest university made up about a sixth of the population. He had been showing signs of exhaustion and soon took to his bed with fever. 'In the full effervescence of pleasure, Prince Juan reached the end of his journey exhausted,' wrote Bernáldez, who was among those who thought the prince was overexerting himself with his playful wife. Despite his weakness, he had continued with his favourite pastimes, which by now appeared mostly to be hawking and crawling into bed with Margaret. He may also have been suffering from smallpox (he had already had a bout in 1488) or consumption. It probably had not helped that, shortly after his marriage, a horse he was riding through the streets of Burgos after attending mass with Margaret bolted, dumping him in a water channel and 'putting him in grave danger'. He had to be fished out by a senior knight, the Adelantado de Cazorla, Hurtado de Mendoza.[18]

Juan's illness worsened at a worrying rate. He stayed as a guest of his former tutor, Friar Diego de Deza, who was now bishop of Salamanca. Isabella must have read with terrible concern a letter from Deza that reached her on the Portuguese frontier. It was dated 29 September and warned that the prince's condition was serious.

> It is the world's worst burden to see his appetite so poor and his highness barely able to help himself. If this illness had come upon

him at a time when your highnesses did not have to be absent, you would be the remedy, because your highnesses' presence helps him a lot, and he is more obedient to the doctors and receives more support and happiness. I beg your royal highnesses to say what should be done with the prince in this state; and if by doing this I am serving your royal highnesses poorly, I beg your forgiveness. I am exhausted and do not know what it is best.

Ferdinand galloped back to Salamanca and appears to have arrived in time to give his dying son some comfort. Bernáldez's version of his last words to his son, which were probably invented, reflect the drama and tragedy of the day: 'Beloved son, be patient because you are being called by God, who is the greatest of all kings, whose kingdoms are far greater and better than those you have or awaited . . . Prepare your heart to receive death, which all of us are obliged to do just once, with the hope that you will be forever immortal and will live in glory.'

Isabella did not see her son before his death, at the age of twenty, at the bishop's palace in Salamanca on 4 October 1497. His short, passionate marriage had lasted less than six months.[19] 'This death left his mother and father disconsolate, as it did Margaret, his wife . . . who was pregnant,' reported Bernáldez.[20] The death was a personal tragedy for Isabella, and a political drama with echoes that reached far beyond the country's frontiers. A Jewish songwriter in north Africa, almost certainly one of those expelled five years earlier, imagined the drama of Isabella's failure to make it to her son's death-bed. 'Where were you, my mother, my unfortunate mother? Pleading with God in heaven . . . But you were too late, mother – the sentence had already been handed down.'[21] It was, above all, a moment for intimate family grief. The day after his son's death, Ferdinand set out to see Isabella. He may have delivered the news of their son's death personally. 'He gave his soul to our lord with such devotion,' Ferdinand wrote in a letter shortly before he set out.[22] 'May thanks be given for everything, and now I must leave and take the road along which the Queen will come, because it seems to me that, for such news, I should be with her.'

Her son's death brought a quick, painful end to Isabella's joy at the second marriage of her favourite daughter. 'And so they went from the happiness of the wedding to the tears, crying and mourning for the Prince – all in one week,' said Bernáldez.[23] Isabella's public reaction of maintaining a serene and unflappable regal exterior was noted by Anghiera, who found it unconvincing. 'The sovereigns try to hide their deep sorrow. But we can see that, inside, their spirits are dejected,' he wrote.[24] Isabella and Ferdinand found support in a marriage that had lost none of its complicity. 'When they are in public, they do not stop looking at each other, which is when the feelings that they hide inside become obvious,' said Anghiera. Isabella's only reference to her own suffering comes in a later letter, signed jointly with Ferdinand, in which they take some consolation from the fact that Juan was able to confess and receive the last rites. 'Such a Catholic end as the one he managed gives us great consolation, but such a great loss cannot but cause us great distress.'

The coffin was laid out under a canopy in Salamanca's cathedral. So many candles were placed around it that wax had to be brought in from surrounding cities. Strict instructions were issued by Salamanca's authorities. No one was to wear gold, silver, silk or colourful clothes but 'only black cloth of grief and sorrow'. Pipes, tambourines, drums and fiddles were banned from weddings and baptisms. The *corregidor* also took advantage of the situation to insist that the local *mudéjares* wear not only mourning clothes, but also the blue half-moons on their shoulders that were meant to mark them out as Muslims.[25] The most devoted mourner, according to Oviedo, was Prince Juan's dark-brown and white lurcher, Bruto. 'He lay down on the ground, by the head of the tomb, and no matter how many times they moved him from there, he always returned to the same spot,' wrote Oviedo. 'Eventually, seeing him insist on accompanying the royal corpse, they put down a cushion for him to lie on, and he was there – day and night – as long as the body was there, and they gave him food and water, and after he went off to urinate, he always returned to the same place.' Both Ferdinand and Isabella's younger daughters, María and Catherine, were so amazed by the lurcher – who perfectly mimicked the dogs included on so many royal tombs as a symbol of loyalty – that the queen insisted on adopting it. 'And that is why, from then on, the queen always had that dog near to her chambers,' recalled Oviedo. Bruto joined Hector, Isabella's other favourite dog, who lived like royalty, and they devoured half a sheep between them every day.[26]

The body was moved to Avila as Spain continued to mourn. 'How fast the horrendous face of fortune has changed,' wrote Anghiera. 'All that was previously joy is now converted to tears.' Isabella, Ferdinand, their family, the court, nobles and many people around the country dressed in black or wore white tunics as a sign of respect.[27] Black flags hung from the gateways of cities and towns as Spaniards mourned the young man whose destiny, now frustrated, had been to unite them all. In the southern city of Córdoba local authorities closed dance schools, banned parties, stopped barbers from shaving people, prohibited the wearing of silk and brocade for a year and ordered people to stop adorning their horses with colourful trappings, 'on pain of 50 lashes'.[28]

Isabella diverted her grief by devoting herself to looking after the widowed Margaret. Her concern was driven by genuine affection for her daughter-in-law, but she was also hoping that the child in Margaret's womb might prove to be a replacement male heir. 'Our devotion to the princess only grows, as she tries hard and so sensibly, just as [the person] she is, and we will work to console her and to make her happy as if she had lost nothing,' the sovereigns wrote on 8 December, from Alcalá de Henares. 'She is healthy with her pregnancy, thank God, and we hope that – by His mercy – the fruit that emerges from her will be consolation and repair for our woes. We care and will care for the princess just as if her husband were still alive, for we hold her in that place and love for ever.'[29]

Amid the breast-beating over Juan's death, the idea that Spain's crusade would extend to Jerusalem re-emerged. 'He was feared at the same time by the Jerusalemites, the Turks and the Moors, because he was the enemy of all Christ's foes,' the epitaph on Juan's tomb read. An anonymous poet, or copyist, in the Aragonese town of Daroca, wrote down a simple poem of national grief. 'Never will there be another like him, nor by searching could we ever find one, even if we looked from here to Germany,' he said. The same poet wept for Margaret, but hoped that she would 'bring us consolation' with a new heir. It was not to be. After seven months of pregnancy Margaret miscarried a baby girl. 'Instead of bearing the much desired offspring, she offered us a dead child,' reported Anghiera bluntly. Bartolomé de Las Casas, the chronicler of the Indies, was kinder in his description, saying that Isabella had reacted with dignity and concern for her daughter-in-law. 'The sovereigns showed great patience and, as prudent and spirited princes, consoled all [of Spain's] peoples in writing,' he reported.[30] Margaret spent several months with them before returning home in March 1500.[31] Another short, childless marriage, to the Duke of Savoy, awaited her – though she would refuse to marry again after losing her second husband, eventually becoming one of the most powerful women in Europe as regent of the Netherlands.

A distraught Isabella now placed her hopes for a male heir on her eldest daughter Isabella, who was also pregnant. This was, potentially, an even more dramatic union. If it was a boy, he would inherit not just the crowns of Castile and Aragon, but that of Portugal as well, bringing the entire Iberian peninsula together under one monarch. Isabella travelled to Zaragoza to give birth to a baby son on 23 August 1498. Her prediction that childbirth would kill her was proved tragically correct and an hour later she died. 'She foresaw her death, the death that she had so often announced would come with the birth. That is why, before the day of the postpartum arrived, she made sure that the final communion was well prepared and continually made priests come to her so that she could confess.

And if, by mistake, she made some error she would plead, weeping on her knees, to be given absolution,' reported Anghiera in one of his letters.[32]

Anghiera counted up the blows to Isabella's morale: the attempt on Ferdinand's life, Juan's death and Margaret's miscarriage had already left her battling with accumulated fright and grief. 'A fourth wound was now inflicted on our sovereigns with the death in childbirth of your Queen Isabella, our wise heiress and, in the qualities of her soul, a wondrous copy of her mother,' wrote Anghiera to the Portuguese archbishop of Braga.[33] He contrasted her physique with that of the now thickset Isabella: 'The mother was large, while the daughter was so consumed by her thinness that she did not have the strength to resist the birth . . . Scarcely had the child emerged from her uterus than the mother's spirit was extinguished . . . Despite this, let's fix it so that this tragic tale ends with a [more] musical refrain. There is compensation for so much misfortune, an important lightener to such deep pain: she gave birth to a son.' Isabella and Ferdinand, in other words, had a new male heir. But the psychological blow of such dramatic losses began to show, with Isabella's health declining, and it seemed as if the glories of her reign could no longer quite compensate for the pain of personal bereavement.

The younger Isabella had ordered that if she gave birth to a girl, the child should be named Ana, and if it was a boy, he should be Miguel.[34] Anghiera was among those who immediately saw the potential in a little boy who stood to inherit in Castile, Aragon and Portugal. 'If he lives, he will have such great kingdoms,' he wrote. Queen Isabella, struck with grief at the loss of two children in less than a year, grasped at this straw of hope. Little Miguel now carried on his tiny shoulders all the hopes for the future, including for her own personal happiness, of a woman who felt far safer depositing her legacy in the male sex than in her own.

The Third Knife-Thrust of Pain

Granada, July 1499 to September 1500

The cavalcade traipsed slowly south through the summer heat across the flat, ferrous-soiled plain of La Mancha, with its windmills and herds of sheep, a chain of pack-horses and mules strung out in its wake. Towns and villages along the way must have been thrilled, frightened or both at hosting Isabella's demanding Castilian court, which brought colour and excitement but exhausted local provisions. Towards the end of June 1499, Isabella encountered the undulating olive groves of Andalusia; and, a few days later, the vast bulk of the Sierra Nevada mountain range reared up through the summer haze. As they closed in on Granada, the city of 200 mosques, she eventually spied the rust-red walls and towers of the Alhambra, perched high on their rocky spur. Her peripatetic life, which had seen her spend twenty of the previous twenty-five Christmases in different places, was coming to an end. The Alhambra, which she reached on 2 July 1499, was about to become much more than a cherished reward for finishing a centuries-long crusade. It was now her home – a place that, barring a few short expeditions elsewhere, she would alternate with Seville's Royal Alcázar for the next two and a half years.[1]

It was a suitable resting place for a visibly tired queen. Anghiera considered Granada Spain's most beautiful city and the land around it among the most fertile in Iberia, full of market gardens and orchards of figs, cherries, oranges, lemons, apples and pears. 'The atmosphere is pure and healthy; it boasts not just mountains but also an extensive plain; it has wonderful orchards, and its gardens compete with those of Hesperides,' he said. Münzer had visited five years earlier, when Muslims still outnumbered Christians by four to one. 'I believe there is no greater city in Europe,' he declared. For a northern European this was an exotic world of pomegranates, saffron, artichokes, almonds, raisins, wild palms, olives and fresh trout. Goats and, for the Christians, pigs provided plentiful meat, along with wild boar, deer and partridge. Münzer had estimated the population of the city at a little over 50,000 people, though its narrow, well-organised streets contained empty houses for many more. 'They almost all have [running] water and cisterns,' he said. 'Pipes and aqueducts are of two types: one for clear drinking water; the other to take away dirt, excrement, etc . . . There are channels in every street for dirty water, so that those houses which, because of their inconvenient position, do not have pipes, can throw their dirt into the channels at night.' Around the main mosque he found – apart from the standard washing facilities – urinals and blocks of squatting toilets that fed straight into an underground sewer. On Fridays 'the shouting from the towers of the mosques was hard to believe' as the faithful were called to prayer, with more than 2,000 people packed into the main mosque. He also recalled the early-morning calls to prayer and the veiled women in long white robes of silk, cotton or wool.[2]

Isabella herself may have seen somewhat less of the city, though her pride at having conquered it was evident. Monarchs were not expected to spend their time among the city people, especially if they were Muslims and defeated enemies who posed a threat. She would have remained mostly in the Alhambra, carrying out her daily administrative duties, saying her prayers and enjoying the peaceful sophistication of Nasrid architecture and the carefully tended beauty of the Generalife gardens. Her view of the city was from on top, looking down from the Alhambra, occasionally from the belvedere called Ain dar Aisha – the eye of Aisha's room.[3]

By the time Isabella had installed herself in the Alhambra, the call to prayer was no longer being shouted out. The words 'There is no God but Allah, and Mohammed is his messenger' were unacceptable to Christian kings and, indeed, had been expressly prohibited by Rome in the fourteenth century – though it was up to individual monarchs and local lords to apply the rule in Europe. One Muslim visitor saw it as part of a gradual erosion of traditional rights after the fall of Granada, with 'even the call to prayer from the minarets being suspended'. Instead, Granada's mosques used long horns to remind the faithful that it was time to pray. Even that, however, was a daily reminder to Isabella that, although Granada was hers, it was still a mostly Muslim city.[4]

The journey cannot have been easy for Isabella, who was now often sick. Anghiera put this down to the tragic deaths of Juan and Isabella, her two most adored children. 'We are with the queen who, because of her grief at the death of the daughter who, being so discreet and good, was her favourite, is [now] sick in bed,' he had written eight months before she set out for Granada. Little Miguel, the tiny new jewel in Isabella's crown, travelled with them, along with her two remaining unmarried daughters, María and Catherine. The boy's father had been happy to leave him in Isabella's care and her mood was both lightened by Miguel's presence and darkened by his fragility. 'He was born weak, fragile and sickly,' warned Anghiera, who was nevertheless relieved that an heir was at hand. 'With the child's birth, whatever his state of health, all debate over primogeniture is over.' Isabella fretted over the small, precious boy who had been sworn in as heir to her crown by the Cortes early in 1499.[5]

Grief did not, however, mean that Isabella could afford to stop thinking about international politics and the alliances needed to safeguard an inheritance which, after the deaths of Juan and the younger Isabella, was losing solidity. Two attempts at tying Portugal close through marriage had been stymied by fate with the deaths of Isabella and, previously, of her first husband, Prince Afonso. Now they sought to re-establish the alliance. Fortunately they had a deep

stock of daughters. Within nine months of the younger Isabella's
death, the Spanish sovereigns were negotiating with her widower
husband, the Portuguese king Manuel, to take their third daughter María as his new bride. Once again religious conditions were
laid down before the marriage in October 1500. This time it was
the Portuguese king who decided to set terms, as he competed with
Isabella over the issue of religious purity.[6] Just as Isabella's family
had bullied him over heretics during the negotiations for his first
marriage, so Manuel now added his own demands to his second
marriage. Isabella and Ferdinand, he insisted, must swear that they
would destroy all mosques and ban Muslim prayers. 'Mosques will
be torn down and we will not consent that in our kingdoms and
lands there are ordained houses for the Moors to pray in,' Isabella
promised in a handwritten document given to Manuel's ambassador which claimed, nevertheless, that they were already committed
to this.[7] Castile's own *mudéjar* Muslims, had they found out, would
have shaken their heads with bewilderment. The horns calling the
faithful to prayer, after all, still blared out over Granada and visitors found plenty of mosques in Ferdinand's kingdoms.[8] Münzer
had come across the shouted call to prayer in several places. Manuel
later claimed that his demands had been far tougher, including 'not
just that orders be given to destroy the mosques of the Moors in the
kingdom of Castile but that their small children also be taken from
the parents and baptised as Christians'.[9] Isabella may even have felt
a pang of competitive envy. Manuel, after all, was claiming to be a
better Christian monarch than she and, with God taking away her
favourite children, she might have wondered whether she was doing
enough to please Him.

Isabella kept Miguel close by, watching carefully over the little
boy who brought innocent joy to an otherwise gloomy household
where the normally colourful velvet, silks, cottons, wools and linens
that she ordered from north Africa and Europe now mostly arrived
in a single colour – the black of mourning. Little Miguel was sworn
in as heir to the crown of Castile but remained sickly. Isabella fretted

over him, but he died in July 1500, just twenty-two months old. It was yet another terrible blow. His death took away both her main source of consolation for her other recent losses and her final hope of a male heir. The next in line to the thrones of Castile and Aragon was the weak and unhappy Juana. It was, perhaps, the greatest of all the tragedies in her life. Bernáldez called it 'the third knife-thrust of pain to pierce the Queen's heart' after the deaths of Juan and the younger Isabella. Isabella plunged deeper into despair. 'The death of the *infante* Miguel has profoundly cast down both grandparents. They have evidently been unable to bear with equanimity so many strokes of fate,' wrote Anghiera. 'They dissimulate and present themselves in public with smiling, calm countenances, but everyone can see the darkness. It is not hard to guess what they are feeling inside.'[10] A portrait painted by Juan de Flandes suggests that, in Isabella's case, the darkness was overwhelming. Painted around her fiftieth year, it shows a wan, aged-looking woman, with an expression that is at once placid and pained, as if she has accepted the permanent martyrdom of bereavement and suffering. It was, perhaps, a role that constant reflection on the suffering and passion of Christ had already prepared her for and into which she slipped easily. Finely plucked eyebrows make her face seem even more pallid, while the still gloriously coloured reddish-auburn hair is mostly hidden under a bonnet and a gauze veil. The queen herself was ill and sliding into depression, the same problem that had afflicted her mother. 'From then on, she lived without joy,' recorded one chronicler.[11]

When María left for Portugal in September 1500, Isabella and Ferdinand could no longer gather the energy or enthusiasm for the elaborate send-offs they had given to Isabella and Juana. The rules of mourning, in any case, would have prevented major festivities. This time, after she had married by proxy in Granada, they simply rode out the short distance to Santa Fe with María and her court of fifty-two Spaniards, stayed with her there for a week and then waved her goodbye. Only one child, Catherine of Aragon, remained in the queen's house.

41

The Dirty Tiber

Rome, June 1497

Isabella already felt contempt for the pope's gaggle of illegitimate offspring, but when she heard that the bloated corpse of his murdered son Juan Borgia had been pulled out of Rome's filthy River Tiber on 16 June 1497, she must have thought that the family's reputation could fall no further. The 'haughty, cruel and unreasonable' Juan was also a Spanish nobleman, holding the title of Duke of Gandía, and had left a son and pregnant wife in Spain when called back to Rome by his father the previous year. The twenty-one-year-old duke had last been seen two nights earlier when he dined with his brother Cesare at their mother's house near San Pietro in Vincoli. As they trotted back Juan told his brother he had private business to attend to and, accompanied by his groom, he rode off. The pope was informed the following morning that his son had not returned home, but shrugged it off. 'He persuaded himself that the duke had been delayed at a party at the house of some girl,' reported Burchard, his master of ceremonies.[1] 'And that he would not leave this house until later in the day.'

Search parties were sent out on the Friday, finding Juan's wounded groom – who was unable to speak – and his horse. The same day a timber merchant called Giorgio Schiavo told of a scene he had witnessed two nights earlier when he had stayed on his barge to watch over a cargo of wood. Shortly after midnight he had seen two shifty-looking men emerge on foot from an alley beside the hospital of Schiavoni at San Girolamo. They walked along the river road, looking around them suspiciously to see if they were being watched before returning to the alley. Two other men appeared and carried out the same inspection, also returning to the alley. 'A rider on a white horse appeared, with a corpse slung over the horse behind him, heads and arms on one side, feet on the other,' Burchard reported. 'The first two men were walking beside the rider in order to keep the corpse from slipping. The horse was ridden further along to the place where the sewer emptied into the river . . . the two men on foot then lifted the body, one taking the arms and the other the legs, and threw it into the Tiber with as much force as they were capable. The man on the horse asked if the operation had worked and they answered, "Yes, Lord." ' The corpse's coat had then floated to the surface, requiring them to hurl stones at it to make it sink. Juan's body was eventually fished out of the water near Santa Maria del Popolo.[2] He had been stabbed nine times before his throat was cut. The list of enemies and potential assassins was long, but the murder boded badly for the stability of Italy, whose fortunes were tied up with those of the papal brood. And with Italy now vital to Spain's foreign policy, Isabella and her husband must have fretted about who had murdered Juan Borgia, and why.

Fingers were immediately pointed at Lucrezia's husband Giovanni Sforza, who had good reasons for hating the Borgias, especially as the pope had decided that his daughter could find a better match. He was insisting that Sforza, whose first wife had died in childbirth, now publicly state that he was impotent and had been unable to consummate the marriage. Lucrezia had dutifully signed a document declaring that their three-year marriage had been 'without sexual relations or carnal knowledge'. It would have taken great courage to hold out against the Borgias, and Sforza had no stomach for a suggestion made by his uncle Ludovico that he should disprove the allegations by having sex with Lucrezia, or any other woman, in front of witnesses. The more exaggerated rumours in a city that routinely took speculation to lurid extremes included that 'the Duke of Gandía had had commerce with his [Sforza's] wife [Lucrezia]'.[3]

Even incest, it seems, was routine grist for a Roman rumour mill that churned out tattle about alleged sexual relations between Lucrezia and almost every man in her family, including her father. Sforza may have started these rumours himself, exacting a far more durable form of revenge on the family than mere murder. Either way, Lucrezia's separation was announced soon afterwards.

Another suspect was the youngest of the Borgia brothers, the 'lascivious-looking' fifteen-year-old Jofre, since his wife Sancha de Aragon was far more likely to have been one of Juan's many mistresses. In her home city of Naples, it was said, a guard had been placed at her bedroom door to block the flow of young men. A more general, but equally unproven, theory was that Juan had been murdered by his other brother Cesare, possibly in a row over Sancha – who was also meant to be Cesare's lover. This was certainly believed by María Enríquez, Juan's Castilian wife. She commissioned an altar cloth which depicted Cesare stabbing his brother to death.[4]

One reason for Rodrigo Borgia wanting to end his daughter's marriage was that he was now intent on building an alliance with Naples. In July 1498 Lucrezia remarried, this time to a member of the royal family of Naples, Sancha's seventeen-year-old brother Alfonso of Aragon. The pope also wanted Cesare to abandon the church and marry the current king of Naples's eldest daughter, Carlota. This was a step too far for Isabella and Ferdinand, who were seen to be behind the moves to block the marriage, even though they knew that stymieing Rodrigo Borgia's ambitions for his children was a dangerous strategy and that they risked being made to pay for it.

The confrontation was far more serious than it might seem, because the fickle Borgia now switched sides in the battle between France and Spain. Cesare duly renounced his cardinal's hat in August 1498 and headed for France, where King Louis XII, who was intent on regaining the ground lost by his predecessor in Italy, made sure he was immediately given a French dukedom. Isabella and Ferdinand were outraged, and the Venetian ambassador to their court reported that they refused even to pronounce Borgia's name, while saying 'very bad things' about Cesare, now known as the Duke of Valentinois.[5]

The Spanish ambassadors in Rome expressed horror at this confirmation of the papacy's new alliance with France. Allegations were hurled backwards and forwards during an audience in December 1498 when Borgia was accused of buying his election, while he in turn accused Isabella and Ferdinand of usurping a Castilian throne 'to which they had no title and against [good] conscience'. It was a rare reminder of Isabella's coup against La Beltraneja. The murder of Borgia's son Juan, her ambassadors retorted, had been divine punishment for the pope's scandalous behaviour. Borgia was furious. 'Your monarchs have been punished more by God, which is why they have no [male] descendants,' he said.[6] Isabella's son had died only the previous year and nothing could have been more calculated to wound her pride. A second meeting ended just as badly. 'After a long speech from the ambassadors a violent and abusive argument developed between them and the pope,' Burchard reported.[7] 'The Spaniards demanded that a notary be summoned. The pope replied that they could write up the minutes themselves later, but they could not do this in his presence. It is said that the ambassadors were demanding that the pope recall his son from France and restore him to his dignity as cardinal.' Borgia told them that if the murderous Cesare had been present in Rome 'he would have replied in the way they deserved'. A final meeting ended with threats to hurl the ambassadors into the Tiber and, according to the Venetian ambassador, with insults directed against Isabella because of her holier-than-thou attitude. 'The queen is not the chaste woman that she claims,' the pope said, though he did not elaborate on the theory. Rome's frightened Spanish population chose to remain indoors during the carnival celebrations the following February.[8]

The Borgia pact with France, meanwhile, grew stronger and Spain's monarchs wisely stepped back, securing a deal that gave them control over just Calabria and Apulia – which occupied the toe and the heel of Italy's 'boot' but were close to the Aragonese lands of Sicily and Sardinia. This foreign carve-up of the kingdom of Naples saw Machiavelli comment that 'thanks to foreign troops, Italy has been conquered by Charles VIII, pillaged by Louis XII [and] raped by Ferdinand of Spain'.[9]

As France flexed its muscles in Italy, Isabella continued to concentrate on securing England as an ally. Her daughter Catherine had long been engaged to Henry VII's eldest son Arthur, but an alliance would not be secure until the wedding took place. Isabella had remained nervous about the Warbeck affair, worrying that the impostor might unseat Henry VII. The English king knew of her concern and when Warbeck first fled and then was recaptured in 1498 he made sure her ambassador Rodrigo de Puebla was informed immediately. 'The same hour that he was arrested, the King of England sent one of his gentlemen of the bedchamber to bring me the news,' de Puebla wrote in an urgent despatch, saying that Warbeck was now in the Tower of London 'where he sees neither sun nor moon'. Later on, Henry VII interrogated Warbeck in person in front of de Puebla. 'I, and other persons here, believe his life will be very short,' the ambassador reported afterwards. When Warbeck and the simpleton Earl of Warwick, another potential claimant to the English throne, were both executed in November 1499 he wrote that there no longer remained 'a drop of doubtful royal blood' in England. The pretenders had been executed, in part, to calm Isabella's worries.[10]

English excitement at the tie-up with the now legendary crusading Spanish monarchs, a powerful ally against the old enemy in France, was enormous. Even Henry VII, notorious for his stinginess, was preparing to dig deep into his exchequer. As the son of an iron-willed woman, Margaret Beaufort, he was fascinated by the Spanish royal women, telling one visitor that he would give up half of his kingdom if Catherine was like her mother. Catherine exchanged formal love letters with Arthur in the Latin she had learned at Isabella's school for young ladies. 'I have read the most sweet letters of your highness lately given to me, from which I have easily perceived your most entire love towards me,' the thirteen-year-old Arthur replied in one letter that reached the Alhambra. 'Let your coming to me be hastened, that instead of being absent we may be present with each other, and the love conceived between us and the wished-for joys may reap their proper fruit.'[11] The final line was a reminder that Catherine's prime duty – apart from boosting Castile's standing in England – was to provide heirs to the shaky new Tudor dynasty. Isabella had raised cultured, intelligent and high-minded daughters, but their main role in life was still biological.

Henry VII's miserliness and greed were legendary, with de Puebla amazed by his officials' 'wonderful dexterity in getting hold of other people's money'. But his plans for Catherine's wedding were too grandiose for Isabella. 'Demonstrations of joy at the reception of my daughter are naturally agreeable to me. Nevertheless it would be more in accordance with my feelings . . . that the expenses should be moderate,' she wrote to her ambassador in London. 'We do not wish our daughter to be the cause of any loss to England. On the contrary, we desire that she should be the source of all kinds of happiness . . . We, therefore, beg the King, our brother, to moderate the expenses. Rejoicings may be held, but we ardently implore him that the substantial part of the festival should be his love; that the Princess should be treated by him and by the Queen as their true daughter.'[12] Once again, Isabella worried about whether the sea would swallow up one of her daughters, asking that Catherine be allowed to land at Southampton. This was because '. . . the most important consideration is the safety of the Princess, and . . . all say that Southampton is the safest harbour in England.' Any extra costs resulting from her daughter's journey from there to London could be kept to a minimum, Isabella added. 'The Princess and her companions will be accustomed, during her journey through Spain, to staying at inns and in small villages.'

Henry's wife, Elizabeth of York, wrote warmly to Isabella, recommending that her daughter learn to drink wine because English water was undrinkable. No effort was made to teach Catherine English even though her almoner, John Reveles, was one of several Englishmen at Isabella's court, along with the painter known as Maestre Anthony and a singer called Porris.[13] Catherine had been expected in England in September 1500, when her husband-to-be turned the marriageable age of fourteen, but Isabella was in no hurry to part with her last child and held her back another eight months. The queen had planned to travel to the north coast with her daughter, but eventually settled for a less ambitious send-off from Santa Fe, claiming that she would just slow the party down. Six young Spanish girls went with Catherine to fulfil an English request that she be accompanied by ladies who were 'gentle and beautiful or, at the least, by no means ugly'. Their sea journey turned into yet another nightmare crossing, with her vessel blown back to port in Laredo before reaching Plymouth and one fellow traveller deemed 'it was impossible not to be frightened' by the heavy waves they encountered on the second, successful attempt.[14]

Isabella's daughter took with her fond memories of Granada and its luxuries, using its symbol of the pomegranate fruit as her personal emblem. Her wedding to Arthur on 14 November 1501 was one of the most lavish events of the early Tudor period, though Sir Thomas More later wrote to Erasmus describing her entourage as 'hunchbacked, undersized, barefoot Pygmies from Ethiopia'.[15] Dressed in a white silk dress that was 'very large, both [in] the sleeves and also the body with many pleats' and with a silk veil bordered in gold, pearls and precious stones hanging down as far as her waist, she walked along the aisle of the old St Paul's Cathedral on a 350-foot-long raised wooden platform. Her hooped Spanish skirt drew gasps of astonishment (and her ladies also wore 'beneath their waists certain round hoops bearing out their gowns from their bodies after their country's manner'),[16] the farthingale being a novelty in England.

Once again, disaster struck quickly. The sickly prince died just five months later in the grey, rain-lashed and inhospitable surroundings of Ludlow castle in Shropshire. Catherine, who had also been ill, was transported back to London in a black-draped carriage sent by her mother-in-law. Still aged just sixteen, she was already a widow. Isabella soon found herself embroiled in a debate over the key mystery of Catherine's first marriage. Was she, or was she not, still a virgin? Years later a member of her Spanish household described the morning after her wedding night like this: 'Francisca de Cáceres, who was in charge of dressing and undressing [Catherine] and whom she liked and confided in a lot, was looking sad and telling the other ladies that nothing had passed between Prince Arthur and his wife, which surprised everyone and made them laugh at him.'[17] An English chronicler, however, claimed that Arthur had left their bedroom demanding beer and boasting: 'I have this Night been in the midst of Spain, which is a hot region, and that journey maketh me so dry, and if thou hadst been under that hot climate, thou wouldst have been drier than I.'[18] Catherine's Spanish governess eventually put Isabella's mind at rest, writing back to say that she 'remained as she was when she left'.

A special envoy was sent to England with instructions to demand that their grieving daughter be sent home, but this was just a negotiating tactic aimed at pushing the English king into agreeing to a new engagement to Arthur's ruddy-faced brother, Prince Henry, who was six years younger than Catherine.[19] Henry VII was in no hurry and, when Elizabeth of York died just ten months after Arthur while trying to compensate for his death by bearing another child, he came to the conclusion that young Catherine would make an excellent new bride for himself. Isabella was horrified. 'It would be a very terrible thing – one never before seen, and the mere mention of which offends the ears,' she proclaimed.[20] 'If anything be said to you about it, speak of it as a thing not to be endured,' Isabella instructed her ambassador. 'You must likewise say very decidedly that on no account would we allow it, or even hear it mentioned, in order that by these means the King of England may lose all hope of bringing it to pass, if he has any. For the conclusion of the betrothal of the Princess, our daughter, with the Prince of Wales, his son, would be rendered impossible if he were to nourish any such idea.'

As she played a game of brinkmanship with Henry VII, Isabella even sent instructions for Catherine to pack her bags so that she could join a Spanish fleet on its way back from Flanders. A panicked Henry VII then agreed to the marriage with his other son. The seventeen-year-old Catherine suddenly found any hopes she harboured about going home dashed, and was formally betrothed to the eleven-year-old Prince Henry at the bishop of Salisbury's palace on Fleet Street.[21] Her father wrote to the pope explaining, once more, that her parents considered her to be a virgin, even if the English were insisting that the papal dispensation allowing her to marry again should state otherwise. 'In one part [of the dispensation] it says that the marriage between our daughter, doña Catherine, and the now defunct Prince of Wales, was consummated, but the truth is that it was not and that the princess remained as whole as she was before the marriage, as is well known.' The English, he said, had added the consummation claim to prevent any future arguments over legitimacy.[22] Decades later, when Henry VIII wanted to divorce Catherine as he sought a male heir and a new wife in Anne Boleyn, this very same issue would be central to his decision to separate the Church of England from Rome.

In the meantime, Catherine was to live at Durham House – overlooking the Thames from the Strand – under the strict eye of the ghastly, domineering governess chosen for her by Isabella, Elvira Manuel.[23] Isabella received constant reports of her ill-health, eating problems and general unhappiness, while the avaricious Henry VII treated her like a piece of merchandise and quibbled over her allowance. Isabella had little time for those who thought she had condemned their daughter to misery. 'Some people believe the Princess of Wales should not accept what the King of England offers for her maintenance,' Isabella and Ferdinand wrote. 'They do not understand that she must accept whatever she is given.' Once more, one of Isabella's daughters showed a capacity for drama and self-harm, often refusing to eat. It cannot have helped that Catherine's Spanish doctors concluded 'that the cause of her sickness was that she was a virgin, having not [carnally] known Arthur, and that if she married someone who had skills with women, she would get better'.[24] She fasted so vigorously that Henry VII, in a letter written in his son's name, asked the pope to order her to eat. The missive sent back gave the Prince of Wales power to prevent Catherine from fasting. 'A wife does not have full power over her own body,' the pope said.[25] 'And the devotions and fasting of the wife, if they are thought to stand in the way of her physical health and the procreation of children . . . can be revoked and annulled by men . . . because the man is the leader of the woman . . . She may not, without your permission, observe these devotions and prayers, and fasting and abstinence and pilgrimage, or any other project of hers that would stand in the way of the procreation of children.' Isabella would have agreed.

42

We Germans Call
Them Rats

Granada–Zaragoza, 1499–1502

Antoine de Lalaing was disgusted. The young chamberlain to
Isabella's son-in-law, Philip the Handsome, was a curious traveller and talented chronicler of the things he saw. But his visit to
Zaragoza's Moorish quarter left him appalled. 'They carried out their
abominable sacrifice to Mohammed in a place they call the mosque,'
he reported.[1] 'As for their refusal to drink wine or eat pig, we have
had vivid experiences of that from when we were put up in their
houses; because they made sure the plates where we had eaten bacon
and the pans where they had been cooked and the glasses in which we
had drunk wine were all cleaned, along with the parts of the house
where we had trodden.'[2] Lalaing seemed to admire the disciplined
way Spanish Muslims went to the mosque, washing themselves and
baring their feet, but the overall impression was of an alien people
with foreign habits living in the heart of Christendom. The German
traveller Popplau had been even more damning when he encountered Muslims in Christian Spain earlier during Isabella's reign. 'We
Germans call them rats,' he said.[3]

Lalaing's amazement had long been echoed by other visitors to
Spain. Hieronymus Münzer had visited Granada in 1494, when
Muslims still outnumbered Christians by at least four to one,
and after seeing more than 2,000 people in the main mosque, he

concluded that the city's Muslim inhabitants were 'truly devout'.[4] Some visitors may have respected Isabella's Muslims for their religious observance, but Spain was becoming increasingly unusual in western Europe. Even Portugal had now expelled its Moors. If Isabella needed a reminder of that, she had only to recall the negotiations over her daughter María's marriage to King Manuel – and his insistence on the destruction of Castile's mosques. Such destruction evidently had not happened by the time Isabella moved into the Alhambra in July 1499.[5] The horn blasts calling the faithful to prayer echoed across the valley of the River Darro and reverberated through the Alhambra itself. For the first time, Isabella was living in a city dominated by another religion. It is unlikely that she enjoyed the sensation.

Isabella's current home in the Alhambra was living proof of the artistic and architectural wealth that her country owed to its past and current Muslim population, and she was determined to conserve at least some of it. She loved the comfort and luxury of the palaces left behind by Moorish rulers, including Seville's Royal Alcázar, often choosing it as her home on those occasions when she remained in one place for a long time. She spent generously on restoration works at the Alhambra and other Moorish or *mudéjar* palaces. Her enthusiasm was shared by Ferdinand, who also cosseted the towering, fortified eleventh-century Moorish playground palace outside Zaragoza known as the Aljafería. Originally called al-Qasr al-Surur, or the Palace of Joy, it had been modelled on the desert castles built in modern-day Syria and Jordan by the eighth-century Umayyad dynasty. Here the elaborate, intersecting Moorish arches, the delicate geometrical ceiling paintings and plasterwork and decorative brickwork were fused with the couple's symbols, the sheaf of arrows and the yoke, by the *mudéjar* craftsmen hired to renovate it. Indeed, this love of 'islamised' *mudéjar* royal palaces made Isabella's royal buildings – often aped by the nobles – markedly different to the Gothic styles triumphing elsewhere in Europe.[6]

Even before the conquest of Granada, Castile's small population of *mudéjar* Muslims (which accounted for just 25,000 people, against 4 million Castilians) was well known for its skills in the building trade. *Mudéjares* were, among other things, valued carpenters, plasterers, bricklayers and ceramicists. But this was an unevenly spread and powerless group, with the 150 local communities – or *aljamas* – in Isabella's kingdoms varying hugely in size, importance and isolation.[7] Hornachos, an otherwise unremarkable town in Extremadura, was unique in being almost entirely *mudéjar* – an island of Islam in an ocean of Christianity. It alone accounted for a tenth of the Muslim population of Castile outside the kingdom of Granada, with some 2,500 Muslims on lands belonging to the mighty religious military order of Santiago, which protected them. Visitors in 1494 found 'no church or hermitage in the town or on its lands, because they are all Moors – the only exception was a small chapel in the fortress where the *comendador* and his men heard mass'.[8] Apart from that, *mudéjares* were most frequently seen in the small *morerías* of cities in Old Castile. Avila and its neighbouring villages boasted some 1,500 *mudéjares*, and the three separate *aljama* communities into which they were split for administrative purposes accounted for almost 10 per cent of the population. They played an important part in local celebrations, with their sword dances and mummery adding folkloric exoticism to the festivities for Isabella's proclamation as queen. Arévalo, where Isabella spent her early years, had more than 600 Muslims – an unusually large number – who occupied half a dozen streets and, from the taxes they paid, were wealthy by the mostly modest *mudéjar* standards.[9]

Borders are almost always porous and centuries of both trade and warfare, with its exchanges of hostages and raided goods, had seen the southern towns and cities close to the old Andalusian frontier naturally assume a certain degree of cultural blending. Neither side, for example, had minded occasionally hiring mercenaries from the opposite religion. The legendary Christian knight Rodrigo Díaz de Vivar, better known as El Cid Campeador, had hired himself out to the Moors in the eleventh century, and both Granada's ruler Boabdil and his uncle Zagal had fought for Isabella and Ferdinand when peace treaties obliged them to. The borders with the kingdom of Granada had often been unmarked, and those unfamiliar with the terrain who found themselves in 'enemy' territory were frequently escorted back in a courteous fashion. Towns on either side of the frontier appointed so-called *rastreros* to sort out, usually jointly, frontier crimes, and the *alfaqueque* negotiators from both sides travelled back and forth paying ransom and freeing hostages.[10]

The fusion between Christian and Muslim culture was there in everything from dress to building methods, decorations and the sweet pastries that emerged from the kitchens of certain nobles who made sure they had Moorish chefs.[11] There were even courtesy visits by knights from the opposing sides. Moorish knights from nearby Cambil must have looked with astonishment at the high jinks during fiestas in Jaen (just twenty miles away) when invited to witness a group fight between 150 apparently drunken Christians who beat each other over the head with dried courgettes. There was also ritual ridiculing of Muslims, with at least one game of *cañas* – one side dressed up as Moors, with fake beards, and the other as Christians – ending with a public ceremony to 'baptise' the Prophet Mohammed in Jaen's public fountain.[12]

Isabella herself was no stranger to the cultural crossovers that came with Spain's uneasy history of religious cohabitation and competition. She and her ladies frequently wore items of Moorish dress, especially in the intimacy of her chambers. These included loose-fitting shirts, or *alcandoras*, with decorative trimmings and Arab letters sewn into them in gold or black thread. The thin cotton or silk veiled headdresses known as *almaizares* and *alharemes* which protected them from the sun and wind as they zig-zagged across the country on their mules were also Moorish in origin. Isabella can be seen wearing one in the reliefs in the lower choir stalls of

Toledo's cathedral, in a scene representing the surrender of the town of Vélez Blanco.[13] Other garments she or her ladies used included pinafore-style *marlotas* and big, billowing hooded cloaks as a protective outer layer. Even the baggy leggings so typical of Granada's Muslim women, the so-called *calzas moras*, were worn in the privacy of their chambers. And, of course, the soft leather *borceguíes* and other Moorish leather goods were always present, from decorated cushion covers to the embossed leather, or *guadamecí*, used to cover trunks, furniture and, sometimes, walls. A royal penchant for silk cushions, pillows and rugs was another piece of the court's Moorish inheritance. Isabella's menfolk learned to ride not just in the straight-legged, long-stirruped fashion common to Castile but also in the short-stirruped *a la jineta* style of the Moors.[14] She and Ferdinand had famously both dressed in Moorish fashion when they met at Íllora in June 1486, during the Granada War. Isabella wore 'a Moorish-style, embroidered, cochineal [deep red] cloak' while Ferdinand had put on the entire outfit, including a 'head-wrap and hat' and 'a very rich Moorish sword' which hung from his waist.[15]

Before the Granada War, the Moorish population of Spain was mostly in Ferdinand's lands, where they were also called Saracens. There were some 70,000 in the kingdom of Valencia alone.[16] 'He who has no Moors, has no money,' was a popular saying, reflecting the Moors' role as agricultural labourers.[17] 'In the country villages of Aragon the Saracens are more numerous than the Christians,' observed Popplau.[18] Even their surnames, reflecting birthplace or profession, were sometimes the same as those of their 'host' Christian community. The Aragonese Moors worked the land and, in some cases, traded with north Africa, where their religion gave some protection against the Barbary pirates. Like the Jews, the *mudéjares* were organised in their own communities, followed their own religious laws and had their own justice system. The appointment of the *alcalde mayor*, the head of the community in Castile, lay in Isabella's hands. Like the Jews, too, they were not full citizens of Castile, but were under the personal protection of Isabella herself – a minority which was tolerated, or 'suffered', by royal order and which paid for that protection in special taxes. Many of the rules governing their behaviour were similar to those enforced on the Jews and they were often written down in the same texts agreed at meetings of the Cortes. They could not intermarry, visit Christian prostitutes, hold public positions that gave them jurisdiction over Christians[19] or have them as servants or slaves.

Centuries of coexistence had produced well-rooted communities, but the passage of time meant the majority of those in the old *mudéjar* communities of Castile knew no Arabic and had lost the intellectual traditions that once made Spain a famous source of religious, philosophical and scientific wisdom in the Muslim world.[20] The Christian image of the 'wise Moor' – a man schooled in the superior scientific and philosophical knowledge of the Arab world and, so, worthy of consultation by Christian kings and nobles – had also faded. 'They have lost their riches and their schools of Arabic,' the Segovian *mudéjar* author Isa Gebir lamented in 1462 after translating the Koran and several law books into Spanish. This created real religious problems. 'Is it possible or not to express the venerable Koran in non-Arabic words in order that those who do not understand the Arabic language can understand it?' was a question that early in the sixteenth century reached the religious authorities in Cairo from Spanish Muslims, who were also unsure about the rules allowing them to stay on Christian soil. 'And is it permitted for the preacher of a community whose members do not understand Arabic to give the Friday sermon in Arabic and then explain it in the non-Arabic language?' The Koran's 'unsurpassable literary qualities are based on its wording and construction [in Arabic]. And this [specific quality] is lost when it is translated,' came one disheartening reply.[21]

Two major differences, apart from religion, separated Isabella's *mudéjares* from the Jews. They were too few and too poor to be a threat, but they were not alone. Geographically, they had the kingdom of Granada and the Muslim kingdoms of north Africa close to hand, meaning they had places of refuge near by and armed neighbours who could take umbrage on their behalf. In that sense, mistreating Castile's Muslims carried a higher price than mistreating its Jews – or even the Christian *conversos* who were being chased by Isabella's Inquisition. Isabella and Ferdinand had learned this early on, when *mudéjares* from Aragon travelled to the powerful Mamluk Egypt to complain that their minarets were being torn down, and that tit-for-tat measures should be taken against Christian temples in Jerusalem.[22] The Portuguese chronicler Damião de Góis was explicit about this being one reason why King Manuel, who snatched away the children of Jews, did not do the same to Muslim children.

> To punish our sins God has allowed the Muslims to occupy the greater part of Asia and Africa as well as significant parts of Europe, where they have established great empires, kingdoms and lordships in which many Christians live under their yoke in addition to the many they hold as prisoners. To these [Christians] it would have been very prejudicial if the children of the [Portuguese] Muslims had been seized because the latter would seek revenge against Christians living in Muslim lands . . . And this is why the Muslims were allowed to leave the realm with their children, unlike the Jews.[23]

This did not, of course, prevent Manuel later claiming that he had urged Isabella and Ferdinand to do exactly that. The threat that Castile's Muslims might persuade Christians to turn to Islam was never a major issue for Isabella or her Inquisition. Those who did change religion, the so-called *elches*, generally fled to the kingdom of Granada.

Like the Jews, however, the Muslims had been subjected to Isabella's increasingly strict demarcations. The 1480 meeting of the Cortes in Toledo, one of her first great opportunities to impose her view of society, had seen those Muslims who lived in Christian neighbourhoods forced into the so-called *morerías* and made to observe dress codes that marked them out as non-Christians.[24] Isabella liked order and this measure also fitted her underlying urge for social purity in Castile. She found no contradiction in bullying part of the Muslim community out of their old homes while also protecting it against the attacks of those whose intolerance was based on lesser principles of greed or simple spite. They had fewer rights, but she ensured that these were respected. Rules, in Isabella's clear-cut world, were there to be obeyed.

The fall of Granada, however, made a huge difference. Suddenly Castile's Muslim population had multiplied tenfold, with one in twenty people living in Isabella's lands now *mudéjares*. With the Jews expelled, rumours began to circulate that the *mudéjares* would be next. Some Christians refused to do business with them, fearing that they would not be around long enough to honour debts and fulfil bargains. Isabella and Ferdinand angrily denied it. 'Our will and desire is not, and has never been, to order the said Moors out of our kingdoms,' they insisted in December 1493, threatening to punish anyone who contradicted them or publicly argued for the *mudéjares* to be expelled.[25]

The war and the years after it saw the kingdom of Granada's Muslim population halve to around 150,000, and the long-term aim remained to turn Granada into a properly Christian kingdom with tax breaks, land and houses offered to settlers. By 1501 there were 40,000 Christians living in the new kingdom – almost a quarter of the population.[26] They were no saints. 'Most of the people who came to populate the city [of Granada] were men of war or adventurers and many were wholly given up to vice,'[27] reported Luis del Mármol Carvajal, a chronicler from later in the century. Prostitutes, outcasts and those who had failed to find fortune elsewhere were all drawn to the city of opportunity, where the rules were new and the pickings easy. They were 'the shit from other cities' or 'those who had nowhere else to draw their last breath'. Some nobles were rewarded, but land gifts were kept small or fractured so that they could not become bases from which to challenge royal power.[28]

Granada was Isabella's proudest achievement. Its pomegranate symbol, with green skin and gold pips, was added to the royal arms and its identity as a separate kingdom respected. She placed it fifth in her list of titles as queen, after Castile, León, Aragon and Sicily – though it was always one of her personal kingdoms, as part of the wider kingdom of Castile, rather than belonging to her husband's Aragonese crown. Representatives of the city also joined the sixteen other major cities that had a vote in Castile's Cortes.[29]

Isabella and Ferdinand demanded a large degree of control over the church in Granada. This, in part, was because rather than being a source of income it was a huge expense. Isabella had to go through the costly business of building churches – often by transforming mosques – equipping them with chalices, crosses, monstrances (to keep the host in) and, of course, priests. There were no ready-made congregations to pay for the upkeep, though the transfer of some income from mosques helped. Orders were issued for bells to be taken down from old frontier fortresses, where they would no longer be needed to sound the alarm about impending attacks, and smelted down to make even larger ones for churches. Other bells were ordered from as far away as England. Isabella paid for much of this herself and it cost her 9 million *maravedís* to fund places of worship in Granada, Málaga, Guadix and Almería in 1493 alone. In return she demanded and obtained from the pope almost complete control over church organisation and clerical appointments, though she respected the clergy's own superiority on doctrine and pastoral work. She and Ferdinand chose the candidates for bishoprics and many lesser posts. In a society in which the church had so much temporal, as well as spiritual, weight that was a considerable concentration of power. It gave her, too, wider control over the quality – and degree of abuse – of a church which was the moral and intellectual foundation of her crusade to purify Spain. It was an important precedent, and this so-called Patronato Real system was extended to other 'new' lands, including the Canary Islands, as well as becoming the model pursued in the Americas. Alexander VI, the Borgia pope, handed these powers over in 1488, helping to turn the queen's new kingdom of Granada into the perfect modern, Isabelline state – and a model for her nascent global empire. Borgia had good reasons for acceding to Isabella's demands. On the one hand, the whole exercise would cost Rome nothing. On the other, few places on earth were producing so many potential new converts to Christianity as the kingdom of Castile. Isabella's beloved Franciscans were charged with carrying out much of the work of capturing converts among the Muslims, and received lands and properties to set up friaries in Granada.[30]

A letter from Isabella to her bishops in 1501 showed her happily issuing instructions. 'I have been told that in many parish churches in your bishopric the Holy Sacrament [the communion wafer or, more strictly, the body of Christ] is not treated with the reverence and solemnity that it should be and that it is not kept in a silver box . . . and neither the cloths nor vessels on the altar are clean, nor are the lamps that should burn in front of the host being lit as they should be,' she wrote in a tone that brooked no argument. 'Knowing this I am sure you will change and improve things, as is your duty.'[31] It was, at the very least, bold for a monarch whose power was meant to be secular and who was also a woman to issue general instructions to priests about how to prepare for one of the most important parts of the liturgy.

Isabella never forgot that Muslims were religious infidels. A small tolerated minority is one thing. A large tolerated minority, as she had already shown with the Jews, is quite another. Her first instinct was to trust her spiritual guide, Friar Hernando de Talavera. Here was a good, holy man who could surely convert many Muslims. Sincere and incorruptible, he was an example of the kind of devout, well-behaved churchman whom Isabella wanted, and she chose Talavera to be her first archbishop of Granada. If he had persuaded a queen to kneel before him when she confessed, surely he could do the same to lowly Muslims. Talavera worked hard to win souls. His evangelists spoke Arabic, and translations of Christian prayers and psalms were distributed. He adapted local cultural customs and combined them with Christian ones. At Corpus Christi processions the Moorish *zambra* and other dances were incorporated (though, providing proof of Spanish Christianity's cultural permeability, these were already included in other places in Castile). Forcible conversion was out of the question. 'Jesus Christ never ordered that anybody be killed or bribed to observe his law, because he did not want forced obedience but rather that it be willing and free,' the Castilian writer Juan Manuel had observed 180 years earlier. Alfonso X, the Castilian monarch who would go down in history as 'the Wise', had come to a similar conclusion in his great thirteenth-century law book, the *Siete Partidas*. 'Christians work to lead Moors towards our faith and convert them through good words and reasoned preaching, not by force or bribery,' he wrote.[32]

Not only was this a Castilian tradition dating back centuries, but it was also reflected in the Granada peace deal. 'It is agreed and established that no Moor be forced to become a Christian,' this stated. Talavera had limited success, doing best in the Albaicín.[33] His advice to the converts was to go beyond mere observation of Christian rites. 'In order that your conversion does not upset born Christians, and so that they do not suspect that you still hold the Mohammedan sect in your hearts, it is advisable that you imitate the customs of good and honest Christians in their habits of dress, shaving, eating, preparing the table and cooked foods, making them the same way, and in the manner you walk, give and take things and, above all, in the way you talk, abandoning as far as possible the Arabic language, making it a forgotten thing,' he said in a circular that was printed and handed to new converts.[34]

In his advice to avoid upsetting old Christians, Talavera was probably thinking of the *conversos*, whose problems with the Inquisition had much to do with popular prejudice against the cultural customs of Jewish origin maintained by some families. He knew this from personal experience, for Talavera was from a *converso* family himself.

The fact that Talavera felt obliged to advise Granada's converts on their cultural behaviour shows just how giant a leap Isabella and her religious counsellors expected them to make. It was not just their religion they were meant to forget. Their language, food and daily customs were also expected to disappear. It is not surprising that only a limited number opted for the change, despite the gifts and other advantages that came with being a Christian. Yet Talavera was clear that forced conversions were out of the question. 'Bringing them into the holy faith by force is something that should never be done, especially among adults,' he wrote. It was a sin, he added, to baptise an adult who had not had at least eight months' preparation.[35]

The peace *capitulaciones* included a clause protecting the *elches*. 'It is established and agreed that if any Christian had become a [Muslim] Moor in the past, no one should be so bold as to abuse or insult them in anything and that, should this happen, they shall be punished by their royal highnesses,' they read. This phrase contradicted church laws which, at least according to the Inquisition's interpretation, stated that all apostates were punishable. Just as it had lobbied for the expulsion of the Jews, so the Inquisition now barged its heavy-booted way into the delicate issue of dealing with Granada's Muslims. For the first eight years of her rule over Granada, Isabella was happy to see her own royal laws (as contained in the *capitulaciones*) override the more rigorous and inflexible laws of the church. But the Inquisition was one of her most important innovations and something to which she was fully committed. Being nice to the *elches* had been a political necessity in the early days of her reign over Granada's Muslims. Several months after installing herself in the Alhambra, however, she was ready to change her mind. Perhaps the sound of the city's Muslims being called to prayer reminded her how people from other parts of Europe looked down on her kingdoms because they tolerated the presence of Islam.

The man who eventually changed Isabella's mind was the powerful archbishop of Toledo, Jiménez de Cisneros, who had followed the royal court to the city in November 1499, just before Isabella left the Alhambra for a six-month sojourn in Seville. Cisneros and Talavera were, in some ways, remarkably similar. The two friars were Isabella's favourites. Both had been her confessors and both had fought against being promoted to positions of authority, preferring the simple, spiritual life of the friary. On Isabella's insistence, however, they had been raised to the highest clerical positions. The ascetic, hairshirt-wearing Talavera famously locked up the city's prostitutes in his own palace during Lent, preaching to them for an hour a day and telling them that the devil used them like mules. Cisneros, who had given up his worldly goods to enter a friary at the age of forty-eight, also wore hairshirts, slept on the floor and had retired to a shambolic country hut before being sent to court as Isabella's confessor. Similarities between the two men ended there. In Cisneros, a future inquisitor general who had been named archbishop of Toledo after Mendoza's death (and allegedly had to be physically restrained from running away when Isabella surprised him with the appointment), Talavera had a natural foe. While the latter believed in slow conversion by *festina lente*, or making haste slowly, the former favoured *compelle intrare*, or compelling people to enter. But Cisneros was senior to Talavera and in his mind church law was supreme. Isabella's need for careful compromise had also disappeared and Talavera had had his chance. Cisneros's inquisitorial methods were now unleashed on those who had been promised royal protection. Granada's *elches* had, in short, been duped. So, too, had their fellow Muslims.[36]

The End of Islam?

El Albaicín, Granada, December 1499

The two men who pushed their way through the narrow streets of the Albaicín on their mules were already infamous as part of a new breed of Christian enforcers who were riding roughshod over the peace agreements signed eight years earlier. Cardinal Cisneros had been in the city for only a month or so, but already both the spirit and the letter of the peace agreements signed eight years earlier were being ignored. Men like the officer of justice, or *alguacil*, Velasco de Barrionuevo and his sidekick Salcedo were trying to oblige the *elche* converts to return to Christianity. This they did by exploiting a loophole in the peace *capitulaciones* that allowed for *elche* women and their children to be questioned 'in the presence of Christians and Moors'. Although Talavera was Granada's archbishop, Cisneros was free to stamp his own authority on the city. Not only was he Spain's senior churchman, but Isabella and Ferdinand had also appointed him inquisitor in the city. Tension rose as Cisneros's men began to baptise the *elches*' small children without their parents' permission, 'as the [ecclesiastical] law permits'. Barrionuevo's presence in the Albaicín now lit the fuse of rebellion. The accounts vary. In one Barrionuevo was trying to snatch a young girl to be forcibly baptised. In another he was hunting for two brothers after forcing his way into their mother's house.[1] Either way, the result was the same. 'Thinking that this would [eventually] happen to them all, they rebelled and killed the official who had gone to arrest one of them, and they barricaded their streets and brought out the arms that they had hidden away and they made new ones as well as they prepared to resist,' according to a contemporary account. Cisneros claimed that his men had simply been attacked while plodding along on their mules and that the Albaicín's iron forges had quickly turned out 500 lances, as if the rebellion had been carefully plotted in advance.[2]

It took Talavera and the Count of Tendilla, the two old men who had successfully administered the city and ensured a relatively harmonious coexistence between the Christian newcomers and the original inhabitants for the previous eight years, three days to calm the *mudéjares* of the Albaicín. Tendilla used troops and diplomacy, even depositing his wife and children as 'hostages' and guarantors of the peace. An amnesty was offered to all those who were baptised. Talavera's hagiographers have him serenely parading the cross while *mudéjares* kissed his robes – an unlikely scene, given the tension. Other reports suggest he was pelted with stones before turning back. Isabella and Ferdinand were furious to begin with, blaming the clumsiness of Cisneros – who appears to have fled to the safety of Santa Fe. 'He has never seen, and does not understand, the Moors,' wrote Ferdinand. 'Brains, not stringency', were needed, he fumed, with only those responsible for killing Barrionuevo to be punished – and, he belatedly insisted, no forced conversion 'as that is not a good thing'.[3]

Yet Cisneros's bull-headed approach worked. Amid fears that those who were baptised would be separated from the others, almost the entire edifice of Muslim Granada crumbled. To begin with the conversions were of individuals, but by the end entire parishes were created by first consecrating a mosque to turn it into a church and then through the baptism – one by one – of most of those who belonged to it. In Granada that meant up to 300 individual baptisms per priest per day. Many of the baptismal records survive today, with 9,100 of them in just three months up to February 1500. Thus those called Mohammed, Ahmed, Ali and Ibrahim found themselves renamed as, for example, Juan, Francisco, Alonso or Fernando. Women with names like Axa, Fatima, Omalfata or Marien were baptised, in turn, as María, Isabella, Catalina or Juana. The registers for the new parish of San Gregorio – previously the mosque of Gumalhara – reflect the full mix of Granadan Muslims, who included immigrant *mudéjares* from elsewhere in Castile and Aragon (including a Muzehed from Hornachos, who became Pedro), a list of twenty-six black Africans and a dozen people who were baptised in jail. Over a single week-end in January 1500, three priests baptised 806 people in the former mosque.[4] A relief in the choir stalls of Granada's cathedral shows Muslim women queueing up, their faces covered as if in shame, to be baptised.[5]

Some 35,000 people in and around the city were baptised in the space of a few months, giving rise to a new category of converts called *moriscos*. 'This conversion business is going very well and there are now none in this city who are not Christians and all the mosques are now churches,' wrote Cisneros in mid-January 1500. 'And exactly the same is happening in the towns and villages near by.'[6] This was clearly forced conversion. 'They embraced the faith and took baptism, but without their heart or only in a ceremonial fashion,' commented Bernáldez.[7] As such, it was also in contraven-tion of numerous papal edicts and the advice of theologians.

Cisneros was anything but apologetic. His view was simple: where Talavera's mealy-mouthed attempts at conversion had achieved little in eight years, he had sorted the entire problem out in a matter of months. Force was the best form of persuasion, and conversion preferable to the exile inflicted on the Jews. It was 'better not to allow them to go into exile. We would rather they were converts or captives, like these ones. Because as captives they can become better Christians, and the land will be safe for ever, and as they are so near the sea, and so close to over there [north Africa], and as there are so many of them, they could do a lot of harm if times changed,'[8] he said, pointing up the practical benefits of forced conversion as much as the religious ones.

Isabella and Ferdinand were confused about how to react. They went from rage with Cisneros for stirring up trouble to joy at the number of converts he was creating. An exhausted and depressed Talavera, meanwhile, wrote to Isabella asking her to come to Granada as soon as possible.[9] It was too late. Isabella and her husband rapidly became enthusiasts for the Cisneros method. 'My vote, and that of the queen, is that these Moors be baptised and if they are not real Christians, their children will be, and so will their grandchildren,' Ferdinand allegedly said.[10] Isabella knew that Talavera and Cisneros did not get on,[11] but she clearly now backed the latter. She returned from Seville in July 1500 and immediately set about increasing the number of clergymen in her new kingdom, which now had tens of thousands of fresh converts.[12]

Blame for this change of heart might also be attributed to the Scottish friar Duns Scotus, who had made his way from Dumfries via Northampton to Oxford in the thirteenth century. Scotus was a Franciscan philosopher theologian, whose ideas had been widely promulgated by one of the Spanish royal family's favourite thinkers, the same Francesc Eiximenis whose advice on the raising of young princesses – using both God and the rod – had so influenced Isabella's world.[13] 'I think that it would be religiously correct to oblige parents through threats and terror to receive baptism,' Scotus wrote.[14] 'Their descendants, if properly educated, will be true believers in the third or fourth generation.' The end, he meant, justified the means.[15] That other great authority, Thomas Aquinas, would have disagreed. 'By no means should people be forced to accept the Christian faith, because belief is voluntary,' he had said.[16] There was room, in other words, for choice, and Isabella had now chosen the harsher of the two options.

Isabella considered the conversion of 35,000 people a spectacular success. But it still represented only a quarter of the Muslims in the kingdom of Granada. Isabella and Ferdinand were clearly fearful that they might face widespread rebellion and they wrote to those in the hill country around Ronda, who had been given a similar deal to Granada, assuring them that they were by no means affected. 'We have been told that some of you are saying that our will is to force you to become Christians, but since our will is that no Moors become Christian through force . . . we promise on our faith and royal word that we will not consent or allow any Moor to be forcibly converted, that our main desire is for those Moors who are our vassals to live in security and justice,' they wrote, just as crowds of *moriscos* were being processed through the new churches in the city of Granada. In the mountainous Alpujarras, where Boabdil had originally gone, and in other Granada towns like Guájar, the Muslims saw the writing on the wall. They rebelled, provoking a three-month Alpujarra campaign in which they were slowly subdued. Their rebellion served Isabella's aims well, for once they were defeated she and Ferdinand were able to accuse them of breaking the terms of the *capitulaciones* and impose fresh, harsher conditions on them. Property was confiscated and Isabella ordered some of those captured during a rebellion at Nijar to be sent to her as slaves. Most importantly, they were now forced to convert.[17] Another important block of Moors, and a geographical area of the new kingdom, was thus artificially and violently 'normalised'.

Other rebellions eventually broke out elsewhere, requiring further campaigns – but producing similar results in terms of mass conversions. Lynch mobs in Castile prepared to attack smaller, older *mudéjar* communities, with Isabella explicitly defending the *aljama* in Arévalo in a letter that promised to punish any who attacked them. By May 1501 the flames of rebellion had been dowsed. Entire towns in the kingdom of Granada now decided it was more sensible to seek baptism than risk the consequences of a visit by Cisneros's officials.[18] Two months later, in July 1501, Isabella and Ferdinand banned the entry of any more Muslims into a kingdom of Granada that was now mostly populated by so-called *moriscos*, Muslim converts to Christianity who maintained many of their cultural habits, their dress and traditions. The order assumed that 'there are no infidels at all' left, but the monarchs added a clause giving any who might remain just three days to leave 'on pain of death and loss of all their possessions to our exchequer'.[19]

In September 1501, in an instruction which was both self-contradictory and breathtaking in its cynicism, Isabella demanded that no further conversions be carried out through force or bribery, while explicitly threatening those who did not 'voluntarily' receive baptism. 'They should be treated well,' she wrote. 'But if in the end they do not want to convert to our will, you can tell them that they must leave our kingdoms, because there is no reason why there should be any infidels in them.'[20] It was, in effect, an expulsion order similar to that issued against the Jews and it now helped push the last of Granada's population into forced baptism.

As if the message was not clear enough, Isabella signed a further order to help eradicate Islam. All copies of the Koran and other Islamic texts were to be burned. The instructions, issued jointly with Ferdinand, left no room for doubt. 'As you know, by the Grace of our Lord the Moors who lived in this kingdom have converted to our holy Catholic faith. And because in the time that this kingdom was populated by Moors they had many books of lies from their false sect, these must now be burned in a fire, so that no memory remains of them,' they wrote. In squares, markets and wherever else people gathered in the city and across the kingdom of Granada, criers announced that 'within thirty days from the day of the announcement they must take to you, our officers of the law, all books that are within your jurisdiction so that no single Koran or any other book from the Mohammedan sect remains'. These were to be burned in public 'and we order any person who possesses such books or who knows of their existence to give them to you within this time limit so that none are left, on pain of death and loss of all their goods for anyone who keeps a book and hides it'.[21] Some 5,000 books and scrolls – including delicate pieces of art with beautiful illuminations, perfumed pages and decorations of pearls or gold – were burned. Much of the rich literary and poetic tradition of the Nasrids was lost.[22] Only medical texts, some philosophy – both of which the Arabs were admired for – and a number of historical chronicles were excepted.[23]

The smoke and smell of burning holy literature, of paper and parchment, wafted up from the squares and through the narrow streets of Granada and other towns through the autumn of 1501. This act of purification by fire, reportedly held in the Plaza Mayor of Granada[24] and fuelled by the city's *madraẓa* school libraries, was the ultimate humiliation for the now secret Muslims in Isabella's newest kingdom. A ban on these new converts bearing arms suggested that Isabella knew that many, seeing no other option, were pretending and could resort to violence.[25] It also meant that, as with the *conversos*, these new Christians were already being treated differently to old Christians. Talavera soon pointed out that in the city's new churches many converts were displaying obvious disdain, as the *morisco* converts 'mingle or sit down with the women, while some lean against the altars or turn their backs to them, and others wander about during the sermon'. Threats of excommunication proved meaningless, so Isabella and Ferdinand imposed fines or ten-day prison sentences.

Four months later, in February 1502, Isabella and her husband took the next, brutally logical step. 'We have worked so hard in the said kingdom [of Granada] where all were infidels and now none are left,' Isabella was able to boast as they published another dramatic edict, this time ordering the ancient *mudéjar* communities scattered around the rest of Castile to leave. They were granted just two and a half months, until the end of April 1502, to make up their minds. 'Given that it pleased our Lord to expel in these times our enemy from that kingdom [of Granada] . . . so it is right to show our gratitude . . . by expelling from [all] our kingdoms [of Castile] the enemies of his holy name, and no longer permit in these kingdoms of ours people who follow such reprobate laws,' said the edict that she put her name to in the Royal Alcázar in Seville on 12 February that year, apparently unaware of the irony of signing such an edict in one of the wonders of Moorish architecture. Ferdinand's name was also on the document, though it did not cover the Muslims in his own lands since these were far too important to the economy of kingdoms like

Aragon and Valencia. The reasoning was exactly the same as that which had inspired both the expulsion of the Jews and the foundation of their royal Inquisition. 'Given that the biggest source of the corruption of Christians that we have seen in these kingdoms was by contact and communication with Jews, so it is that contact with the said Moors of our kingdoms is a great danger to the new converts.'[26]

While the expulsion rules for the Jews had been brutal, those for the Muslims were simply impossible. They were not allowed to go to Ferdinand's Aragonese kingdoms or to Navarre. They could only go to countries that Castile was not at war with. This excluded the Ottoman empire, north Africa and much of Europe, where they were unlikely to be welcomed anyway.[27] The lands of Mamluk Egypt – which included Jerusalem – were about the only possible destination. These lay at the other end of the Mediterranean, but the expulsion order said that Castile's Muslims could leave only from ports in Vizcaya, on the Atlantic coast of northern Spain. This was the furthest possible spot from their destination. They would have to sail along the dangerous northern coastline of Galicia (later to be known as the Coast of Death) and around Spain's own rugged and storm-lashed World's End, Finisterre. The journey would then have to follow Portugal's Atlantic seaboard to the fast-moving Strait of Gibraltar just to enter the western end of the Mediterranean Sea. Barbary pirates and other dangers remained along the lengthy crossing to the east of the Mediterranean.

Unsurprisingly, the remaining *mudéjares* now also converted. Conversion was not even mentioned as an option in the expulsion order, but they had no real choice. And so the ancient *mudéjar* communities were also baptised en masse, adding another 20,000 to 25,000 people to the list of converts. In her Spanish kingdoms alone, between Jews and Muslims, Isabella had gained some 150,000 souls for Christ, even if many were faking it. She had also drawn the curtain on seven centuries of coexistence between the three 'religions of the book' in Castile. It had taken her just a decade. Her puritanical revolution was almost complete. Even Machiavelli was amazed at this 'pious work of cruelty'. 'There could not have been a more pitiful or striking enterprise,' he said.

Isabella tightened the screw further later in the year. In September 1502, in a *pragmática* signed by her alone, she banned the new converts in the kingdoms of Castile and León from leaving them for the next two years.[28] They had been given an opportunity to leave, however false, and now they were Christians. She did not want them tempted back to their old faith. They could trade in Aragon or Portugal only with an official ninety-day permit. If they tried to sell their properties, these would be impounded by the crown with no compensation for either buyer or seller.

Isabella addressed one copy of the new law to her daughter Juana, now also her heiress, as well as to all her nobles and officials. 'I have been informed that some of them, falling for false counsel, have begun to sell up their possessions so that they can move to other kingdoms and across the sea. And given that I, as queen and lady, am the keeper of the [proper] service of God our Lord and his holy Catholic faith I feel obliged to take measures in order to ensure that the new converts remain in our faith, away from those people who might urge them to wander,' she said.[29]

Castile's old *mudéjares*, now *moriscos*, were also banned from the kingdom of Granada, where they could not even trade. This, she explained, was 'for certain reasons that have to do with the new converts in the said kingdom'.[30] It was as close as Isabella could come to publicly admitting that the *moriscos* of Granada were, in large part, still secret Muslims or, at the very least, bad Christians who had been converted by force.

Isabella's final exercise in purification was, for most of its victims, a farce. Islamic law, under a self-protection clause called the *taqiya*, allowed pretend conversion under extreme circumstances where there was no other option, and Christian contemporaries quickly realised what was happening. 'They said they were Christians but paid greater attention to the rites and ceremonies of the Mohammedan sect than to the rules of the Catholic Church, and they closed their ears to whatever the bishops, priests and other religious men preached,' Mármol Carvajal, who was born in Granada and spoke Arabic, wrote at the end of the sixteenth century. Soothsayers known as *jofores* told the unhappy converts that they would one day return to their original faith. Even a century later, Mármol reported, many – if not most – were closet Muslims. 'They hated the Roman Catholic yoke and secretly taught one another the rites and ceremonies of the Mohammedan sect . . . If they went to Mass on Sundays and feast days it was out of obedience and to avoid punishment,' he added. Muslim prayers were said in secret, especially on Friday, and artisans would continue working behind closed doors on Sundays. Confession was, for many, a farce and Mármol claimed that recently baptised children were 'secretly washed in hot water to take away the chrism and consecrated oil' before they were given Moorish names and the boys were circumcised. 'Brides who had been made to wear Catholic [Christian] clothes to receive the church's blessing were stripped when they returned home and dressed as Muslims, celebrating a Moorish wedding with Moorish instruments and food,' he wrote.[31]

Some were scandalised, seeing trouble being stored up for later. 'You will object, however, that they will continue to live with the same spirit of commitment to their Mohammed, as it is both logical and reasonable to suspect,' Anghiera wrote to Bernardino López de Carvajal, one of Borgia's Spanish cardinals in Rome.[32] Anghiera obviously thought this himself, but also believed that their children would be good Christians. But acting against Castile's Muslims brought another set of problems, for powerful countries on the southern and eastern side of the Mediterranean were soon rumoured to be preparing to take tit-for-tat measures against Christians in their lands. That explains why Anghiera found himself being sent as an envoy to Egypt, where the sultan was receiving angry complaints from those being forcibly converted in Spain.

44

The Sultan of Egypt

Venice, 2 October 1501

Isabella's growing status and Spain's position as Europe's emerging political power meant that the shockwaves from her boldest
and most controversial actions now reached distant peoples and
lands. So it was that she felt obliged to turn her attention to the man
whom she thought of as 'the sultan of Babylonia, Egypt and Syria
and Lord of the whole of Palestine', meaning the Mamluk sultan in
Cairo, Qansuh al-Ghuri. In October 1501 she and Ferdinand sent
Peter Martyr d'Anghiera to see the sultan with strict instructions
that he should deny the forced conversions: 'If he asks you anything
with respect to the conversions of the Moors in this kingdom saying
that this was forced or some grievance was committed to make them
convert to our holy Catholic faith, tell him that the truth is that no
[conversion] was done by force and never will be, because our holy
faith desires this not be done to anyone.'[1]

Anghiera travelled to Venice where he boarded a three-masted
galeazza, a huge trading vessel with 150 men handling fifty-foot-long
oars that typically needed seven or eight people on each one. The
vessel was part of a fleet of up to fourteen that made regular trips to
the Syrian port of Beirut and to his own destination of Alexandria,
from where he planned to travel to Cairo to see the sultan. 'It is said
that he is threatening all the Christians so that, rejecting the laws of
Christ, they embrace Mohammed,' Anghiera explained in a letter.
'The excuse is that the Granadans have abandoned Mohammed,
and have done so because they have been forced to with violence.'

The large Venetian *galeazze* usually took expensive cloth and other goods, returning with precious stones, perfumes ('which effeminate the men and produce wantonness') and Arab medicines to distribute around Europe. Anghiera was impressed by Venice's industry, its bustling port, busy dockyards and huge vessels, sailing off to trade in such far-off spots as Constantinople, Beirut, Alexandria, the Black Sea, the (Russian) Don River, London and the 'glacial ocean' in the north.[2]

Anghiera's trip to Cairo may have been triggered by an appeal for help sent to the Mamluk emperor by some Spanish *moriscos*, in the form of a *qasida*, a rhyming 105-line poem in Arabic, written in 1501. This explained, in tragic terms, the fall of Granada and the plight of the self-styled 'slaves who have remained in the land of exile, in Andalus in the west' on whose behalf the appeal is written. These included 'old men whose white hair' has been plucked out, women whose 'faces have been bared to the company of non-Arabs' (though the *morisco* women sketched by Christoph Weiditz two decades later still had their faces half hidden by veils, at least in public),[3] girls driven by priests into 'beds of shame' and others 'forced to eat pork' and other meat from animals that had not been ritually killed.[4] The poet had told the sultan that Isabella and her husband had 'converted us to Christianity by force, with harshness and severity, burning the books we had and mixing them with dung or filth, though each book was on the subject of our religion'. These had been 'cast into the fire with scorn and derision' while their names had been changed for Christian ones 'without our consent'.

Anghiera reached Alexandria early in January 1502, and was welcomed by the local consul from Barcelona. He was forced to wait for permission to travel up the Nile towards Cairo – which he called 'capital of this empire and previously of Babylonia' – in order to see the sultan. He wandered like a tourist, admiring the port and the water tanks filled by aqueducts from the Nile, but aware that the city's glory days were over. 'From looking at its ruins, I would say that Alexandria once had 100,000 houses or more,' he wrote. 'Now it barely has 4,000. Instead of being inhabited by people they are nests for pigeons and doves.' The sultan did not, at first, want to see him, something that Anghiera blamed on expelled Spanish Jews. 'Quite a few have sought refuge in these regions,' he explained. Anghiera sent two Franciscan friars to inform the sultan that these Jews had been expelled by Isabella and Ferdinand 'like a dangerous plague' and were 'enemies of peace and goodwill between sovereigns'. Anghiera was also warned that other north African kings had sent envoys to the sultan 'instigated by those expelled from Granada, with terrible complaints'.[5]

Isabella and Ferdinand's envoy was amazed that the relatively few Mamluks – originally soldier slaves imported from as far away as the Balkans and Georgia – managed to enforce their authority over the nomadic Arabs. 'These Arabs, in the judgement of all including the Mamluks, are noble and industrious, while the Mamluks are, in their great majority, ignoble mountain types mostly brought here by pirates,' he said. 'Every Mamluk has such power over the people that they can hit anyone they want with the wooden stick they carry, out of pure whim or with the feeblest of pretexts.' He was eventually taken before the sultan at sunrise at a palace that he compared to the Alhambra, through patios and past eunuchs guarding the doors to the harem. 'The sultan . . . was already aware of how powerful you are,' Isabella read in one of the reports he sent back. 'That is why, against the customs of his forebears, he allowed me to be on the carpets laid out in front of him in his half of the patio.' He was also let off some of the bowing and scraping normally required of ambassadors. The sultan was himself a Mamluk, allegedly from a former slave family from Scythia, at the eastern end of the Black Sea. His headpiece sprouted cloth horns that seemed absurd to Anghiera. 'I can only imagine that these barbarians have modelled these ridiculous horns on spring snails, as I have never seen anything else like it before,' he sniffed. But the sultan seems to have liked Anghiera, and treated him well – much to the fury of the court's Mauritanian and Numidian (Berber) ambassadors, who reminded everyone that Granada's Moors were being forcibly converted or expelled. Anghiera reported back that Isabella and Ferdinand's reputation was 'that you are tyrannical, violent sovereigns and lying perjurers'. The sultan, fearing that his presence might provoke a rebellion, eventually ordered Anghiera to sneak out of Cairo by night, but the latter sent his messenger back, reminding him that he represented the sovereigns of a vast swathe of land that stretched from 'the world's most distant shores . . . to the part of the kingdom of Naples that looks east over the Adriatic Sea' and so was not far from Egypt itself. A secret pre-dawn meeting then saw the sultan quizzing him, above all, about the forced conversions.[6]

'You complain that my Catholic sovereigns have taken the city of Granada from the Moors, along with other fortified cities . . . that they have not respected the religions of the conquered and that many thousands have been forced to become Christians; then you have threatened to make them regret their decision,' Anghiera replied. 'You should know the following: that the Catholic king and queen of Spain have sent me to ask favours on behalf of the inhabitants of Jerusalem, not to recount their own victories . . . They are [now] so powerful that they fear no man . . . From the [Atlantic] Ocean where the sun hides below the sea, to the Adriatic, to the Italy that overlooks his [the sultan's] lands, via the columns of Hercules [the Strait of Gibraltar], to Sicily, Calabria . . . and Apulia, all is subjected to my sovereigns.'[7] It was an impressive list, unthinkable in the years before Isabella had claimed her throne, and the sultan knew he should listen.

Anghiera insisted that the Granadans themselves had begged Isabella and Ferdinand to baptise them after rebelling and realising that, as the vanquished, they could be enslaved. 'Baptism! Baptism!' they had shouted, or so he claimed. 'Our religion openly demands that nobody dare use violence or threats to incite people to change religion,' he added. Proof of this, he said, were the thousands of Moors and Jews who had chosen to move to the sultan's kingdoms. 'Surely they would have been forced into baptism if our religion permitted it,' he said. He also reminded the sultan that tens of thousands of Muslims still lived in the kingdoms of Valencia and Aragon 'with no less freedom than Christians'. It was a useful reminder to the sultan that any persecution of Christians in his lands could still be answered with the persecution of the remaining Muslims in Spain. Anghiera predicted that the sultan would rue having allowed Spain's Jews to settle in his territory, and urged him to ignore their complaints. 'Why would you worry about them? They were eliminated from their kingdoms by my sovereigns like a poisonous pest,' he said. 'One day, if the Fates give you long life, you will realise what kind of men you have given protection to . . . and then you will admit how wise my sovereigns were precisely because they decided to get rid of such despicable and sickly animals.'[8]

His most persuasive arguments, however, were to do with power – for the Mamluks were as worried about Ottoman expansion as Christian Europe was (and with good reason, given that they had held off the Ottomans during a war a decade earlier but the latter would overrun the Mamluk lands within fifteen years). The Spaniards had helped him during the previous Ottoman war and a good sultan always had to be prepared for domestic rebellion. 'In the [Spanish] fleets anchored at Apulia and Calabria [in southern Italy] experienced troops are ready, and if any rebellion against you should erupt or war break out, they can come rushing here to your aid,' Anghiera promised. 'The mere news of our friendship, indeed, could be useful to you, given our power on land and at sea.'[9]

The strategy worked. 'The sultan is prepared to do everything I asked in your name,' Isabella read in a triumphant report sent home by Anghiera. He continued his tourism, wandering off to marvel at the pyramids – which he described as 'the monuments of ancient Egypt' – while documents were drawn up that reflected Isabella's long-standing concern for the remnants of the Christian community in the holy lands, pledging to protect those who were in the sultan's lands.[10] They included safeguards and reduced taxes for pilgrims as well as the right to restore Christian churches and monasteries in

Jerusalem, Bethlehem, Beirut 'and wherever else there are remnants of Christ's work'. Many of these buildings had been falling into ruin for centuries but could not be restored without permission. 'And now, you can do that,' Anghiera reported. Isabella and Ferdinand's joint lands stretched from the islands of the Caribbean to the southern point of Italy. Now their influence was also being felt further east and, most importantly to the queen, in the holiest of places as Arab Christians benefited from her power and protection. The sultan sent Anghiera off with gifts that included a sea-green linen tunic and matching silk robe, and a garment interwoven with gold thread, with Arabic letters embroidered on it and bordered with fur. The envoy sailed back up the Nile, convinced that Christians should set about retaking the Holy Land.[11]

Anghiera eventually travelled to Toledo to inform Isabella of his experiences.[12] 'I have dropped anchor in the securest of ports . . . before the Queen who, as you know, is the greatest of all the feminine sex; she not only emulates men, but in spirit, prudence and strength – not exactly a feminine quality – she matches the great heroes; she has received me four times, affably and with a serene and pleased look,' he wrote to a friend in September 1502. Isabella had obviously not lost her capacity to scare even her own servants, and Anghiera's paean to the queen may have had something to do with the fact that she obviously did not always find him entertaining. 'I have pleased her sublime ears by telling her new things,' he added. 'She finds me more agreeable than usual.'

45

Like a Wild Lioness

Ghent, February 1500

The ring that Isabella's oldest surviving daughter Juana now kept with her had been worn by the Virgin Mary when she gave birth to Jesus Christ, or so the monks at an abbey near Ghent had claimed before lending it to her as she herself prepared to give birth in the city.[1] The child in her womb was not the first of Isabella's grandchildren. That honour belonged to Leonor, born two years earlier in 1498. On that occasion Juana's father-in-law Maximilian had been making his way towards Brussels for the baptism, but turned around after a girl was announced. Her husband Philip had reacted in an equally high-handed manner. 'As this one is a girl, put her on the archduchess' estate [her expenses]; when God gives us a son, put him on mine,' he said.[2] This time Juana was praying for a son and Philip began preparing the carriages, jewels and other finery that would provide the pomp to accompany the birth of a boy. In February 1500 she finally gave birth to the much desired male heir, who would be christened Charles. Juana's normally thoughtless husband was delighted, gifting her an emerald embedded in a white-gold rose.[3]

Juana's status at Burgundy's court improved marginally, but she was unable to exert the kind of pro-Spanish pressure that Isabella had hoped for. The previous year Isabella had sent an ambassador to tick her daughter off, presumably for not doing more to fight for Spanish interests. 'She took it well, kissing your royal hands [metaphorically] for advising her on how to lead her life, and she thanked me a lot,' the ambassador, Friar Tomás de Matienzo, reported back. 'She told me that she was so weak and cast down that whenever she recalled how far away she was from your highness she could not stop weeping.' But she could exert very little influence over her husband. 'All those on the archduke's council . . . have the lady so scared that she cannot lift her head,' Matienzo added. A second ambassador, Gutierre Gómez de Fuensalida, urged her to fight for more power. 'It seemed to me that she should no longer countenance these people [the Burgundians], since they had no manners at all,' he reported back to Isabella and Ferdinand. The straight-talking and undiplomatic Fuensalida also, however, judged her to be far from the mentally unstable woman who was to go down in history as 'Juana the Mad'. 'I do not think that so much sense has been seen in anyone of so few years,' he reported. Another special Spanish envoy who met her at about the same time agreed, calling her 'very sensible and practical' but pointing out that 'nobody helps her'.⁴ There was little Isabella could do, however, beyond sending envoys to encourage her daughter.

After the death of little Miguel in July 1500, Isabella lobbied hard for Juana and her husband to travel to Spain in order to be sworn as heirs to the thrones of Castile and Aragon. Yet another pregnancy, and the machinations of Philip's pro-French advisers, saw the trip delayed. 'The gentlemen [around Philip] abhor this journey because their customs in all things are as different from Castilians as good is from evil,' observed Fuensalida, adding that Philip himself 'would rather go to hell than to Spain'. A protesting Juana was taken to Brussels to give birth after the city had offered 4,000 florins or more if the child was born there. On 18 July 1501, she delivered what could have been considered a double snub – the baby was a girl, and she was christened Isabella after her Spanish grandmother.⁵

Juana, whose devotion to her philandering husband was becoming legendary, found herself torn between her two duties – to Philip and to Isabella. 'The sovereigns are convinced that their daughter will agree only to follow her husband,' wrote Anghiera. The Italian humanist was himself playing a careful political game of patronage-seeking and could see that Philip might become Spain's ruler when Isabella died. He was careful, therefore, to stress Juana's devotion to Philip rather than the fact that she, not he, was the heir to Spain's crowns. 'She is lost in love for her spouse. Neither ambition for such kingdoms nor the love of her parents and other childhood companions would move her,' Anghiera wrote in one of his letters. 'Only attachment to the man, whom they say that she loves with such ardour, would draw her here [to Castile].'[6]

When Juana and Philip eventually set off in November,[7] it was without her three children, providing yet another reminder that even domestic power lay firmly in her husband's hands.[8] And if Isabella and Ferdinand had hoped this would be the moment when Philip abandoned a worrying pro-French stance, they were wrong. He announced Charles's engagement to Louis XII's daughter and also made sure they travelled overland, ignoring the vessels sent for them from Spain, in order to pass through Paris and Blois, where Louis and his wife Anne of Brittany awaited. Juana found herself constantly struggling to force French protocol not just to recognise her as an archduchess, but also to acknowledge her newly elevated rank as heiress to the crown of Castile. She even dressed up in Spanish clothes (a trick that her sister Catherine would likewise use at meetings with the French) to emphasise the fact.[9] Crossing the frontier into Castile at Fuenterrabía, in January 1502, the Burgundians had their prejudices confirmed immediately. They had to abandon their sophisticated carriages and wagons (one hundred of which had set out from Flanders) and ride mules through the icy mountain passes on to the *meseta*. One obstinate Burgundian noble insisted on keeping his carriage as they struggled through the Basque Country. 'Monseñor de Boussut managed to get his carriage across the mountains of Vizcaya, something unheard of in living memory. And as the peasants had never seen carriages in their country, they showed utter amazement,' reported Antoine de Lalaing, who accompanied the party. He may also have been as amazed by the ancient and unintelligible language of the Basques. 'It is the strangest I have ever heard,' an Italian visitor observed, remarking that the women rarely spoke anything else.[10] 'It has no words from Castilian or any other tongue.' Lalaing noted, too, that Alcalá de Henares, like Seville, was one of the few cities they passed through with paved roads 'in the manner of our own country'. Among other entertainments along the way, the Duke of Benavente showed off his pet camel.[11]

When they finally entered the city of Burgos, it was Philip's own squire who carried the ceremonial sword belonging to the heir to Castile's throne, suggesting that he saw himself as the future ruler. Party-loving Philip was also quick to enjoy Spanish customs. Bullfights were a particular favourite, as was dressing up in Moorish costume to take part in games of *cañas* involving more than 500 horsemen. Lalaing was impressed by Isabella and her fierce reputation. He considered her the prime mover behind everything from the marriage to Ferdinand and the war on Granada to Columbus's journey of exploration. 'I believe that this queen of Spain, called Isabella, has had no equal on this earth for 500 years,' he said. 'She is obeyed in all her kingdom, and no great Lord on receiving her orders, even if they come from her lowest servant, has ever dared to disobey; because [they know] she would punish those who disobey harshly in order to make them an example to others.'[12]

Isabella waited to receive their daughter and meet her son-in-law for the first time in Toledo, where the visitors did not appear until May. By then the plans for their reception had been spoiled by the news that Catherine of Aragon's young husband Arthur had died. Toledo ran out of black cloth and Isabella ensured that an elaborate show of mourning was put on. Above all, she wanted news of that to drift back to England in order to keep Henry VII on their side in their growing rivalry with France. Ferdinand was keen to woo Philip away from Louis and made sure it was Juana's husband who walked with him under a golden canopy after they met at the gates of Toledo rather than the heiress. It took Isabella to correct things, bringing Juana under the ceremonial canopy after she met them for a mass at the Marquess of Villena's Toledo house, where they were staying. 'The queen . . . embraced them both with much love, and took her daughter by the hand to her own chamber,' reported Lorenzo de Padilla, author of a later chronicle about Isabella's son-in-law Philip.[13]

More importantly, Castile's Cortes then swore allegiance to Juana as princess of Asturias (and heiress) and to Philip only as consort. Tension began to rise. An offended Philip expelled some of his most pro-Spanish followers and, when a gang of Castilians attacked three of his men, Isabella chose to pardon them. Illness, as ever, plagued both hosts and visitors. Philip and Juana abandoned Toledo in the middle of the night after Isabella, many in her court and some visitors fell ill. Two of their senior servants stayed and died.[14] Then Philip's pro-French chief adviser, the archbishop of Besançon, also died amid rumours that he had been poisoned.

As the Burgundian party moved on to Aragon, some of their pages celebrated St Luke's Day by ransacking a local mosque. Isabella travelled as far as Madrid before she was struck down by tertiary fevers. There were rumours that she was faking her illness in an attempt to force Philip and a now heavily pregnant Juana to stay in Spain. In fact she was increasingly ill and unable, for example, to receive an envoy from her other son-in-law, the Portuguese king Manuel. She would stay in Madrid, or in nearby Alcalá de Henares, for almost a year. Philip then huffed angrily in Madrid, itching to leave. 'The queen wanted to avoid him leaving, arguing that the princess's pregnancy was very advanced, and that she would not make it to his country before the birth,' reported Lalaing. 'The archduke said he had important affairs to attend to . . . as far as the princess's pregnancy was concerned, he was happy to go, and would willingly leave her with her [mother].' Isabella thought, mistakenly, that her daughter might be able to stop him leaving. 'Strengthen her so that she very vigorously impedes his departure,' she and Ferdinand ordered Villena, Juana's host in Toledo.[15]

Isabella tried to reason with Philip. Not only was he now planning to travel back through France, seen as enemy territory, but the journey would endanger his wife and the child she was carrying. 'The queen insists that he forget it . . . adding that Juana, his wife, who is close to giving birth would miscarry from sadness or even die – given her ardent love for her husband – if he abandoned her,' reported Anghiera. Isabella was increasingly desperate. She wanted Philip on their side and was either unaware, or refused to see, that Juana's marriage was not like her own. Philip had made it clear from the very start that this was no match of equals. Not only was he a man, but he was the ruler of lands with different interests and priorities to those of Spain. Above all he had a powerful and threatening neighbour in France. If he feared that Isabella meant to use her daughter to turn Flanders and his other lands into a weapon against France then he was right. As Philip rode off from Madrid on 19 December, poor Juana found herself squeezed in the middle, unable to satisfy either a demanding mother or an uncaring husband. The archduke left strict instructions about access to Juana's household in order to prevent Isabella taking control of it. Anghiera claimed that Philip was his wife's 'only preoccupation, delight, and devotion'. Juana obviously planned to give birth and, as soon as she could, follow her husband. But Isabella had other plans for her twenty-three-year-old heiress.[16]

———

With Philip gone, Isabella spent lavishly on members of Juana's household – including 1.7 million *maravedís* in cloth and silk gifts in a single day. She was, essentially, trying to buy the support of people who worked for, and owed their allegiance to, Juana's husband. She also began to enlarge and fill her daughter's household with her own appointees, thereby entering into direct competition with Philip. Isabella then did all she could to prevent, or stall, Juana's return to her husband in Flanders,[17] hoping that this might temper his tendency to support France. A new grandson, Fernando, was born in the bishop's palace at Alcalá de Henares in March 1503, but Isabella still refused to bow to the calls from both Philip and Juana for her daughter to leave Spain.

Isabella had long shown herself to have a powerful, intense and sometimes unbending personality. Her daughters each inherited much of that. Juana was increasingly powerless, both in her Flanders home and in Castile, but she could also be tough and rebellious. A bitter battle now raged between mother and daughter, as their obstinate natures clashed. Love, anger and illness became the prime ingredients of an explosive confrontation.

'The disposition of the lady princess is such that it should greatly pain not only those so affected and who love her so, but even strangers, because she sleeps poorly, eats little, and sometimes nothing. She is very sad and quite thin,' Isabella's doctors reported, after tending to Juana on 20 June 1503. 'Her sickness advances substantially. The cure is usually undertaken by love and entreaty or by fear. Yet she does not accept pleas or persuasion or anything else, and feels such anger and at times such sorrow from any slight force applied, that to attempt it is a great pity, and no one wants or dares to.'[18] The doctors warned that the battles with Juana were also taking a toll on Isabella's own health. 'The weight of all this often falls on the Queen,' the three doctors, called Soto, Julián and de la Reyna, wrote to Ferdinand in Barcelona. 'The life that the Queen is living with the princess is putting her health in great danger, as every day there is some incident.' The three doctors also asked Ferdinand to burn the letter, perhaps fearing that Juana would take revenge on them if she found it after inheriting the throne.

The two women travelled together towards Segovia in the summer of 1503 on what was presumed to be the beginning of Juana's journey home after eight months without her husband. Isabella had been wary of Philip's attempt to negotiate on the Spanish monarchs' behalf a peace treaty with France in Italy, even though she and Ferdinand had given him powers to do so. Via a cyphered letter to her ambassador in London, she now warned Henry VII not to trust Philip. 'Tell him [Henry VII] on our behalf that if he is called on to do anything concerning any deal that the archduke [Philip] may have struck on our behalf with the king of France, he ignore it unless it is accompanied by our signature,' she wrote. Philip fell ill in France (which can only have increased Juana's anxiety), then returned home to Flanders. 'The princess begged the queen her mother to give her permission to return to her husband,' reported the chronicler Padilla, but the sickly Isabella continued to stall her. Her daughter then pushed on alone to Medina del Campo, taking up residence in the city's La Mota fortress and sending secret instructions to a ship's captain to await her in Bilbao. Her plan was stymied when Isabella ordered that the mules carrying her goods be detained and gave the bishop of Córdoba, Juan Rodríguez de Fonseca, who was with Juana, orders to stop her.[19]

Isabella herself narrates the unseemly events that followed in a letter to Fuensalida. 'I ordered the bishop of Córdoba, who was with her, that if that [leaving] was what she wanted to do, he should under no circumstances allow it to happen and, in my name, should prevent her from doing something that everybody would view as bad and that would be so shameful for her and disobedient towards us,' she wrote. 'The said bishop ordered, on my behalf, that her pack animals were not led off. And when the Princess found out, she wanted to leave the fortress and go alone on foot through the mud to where the pack animals were. Then the bishop, to prevent her doing something so damaging to her authority and reputation in such a public place and within sight of the many locals and foreigners who were attending the fair, ordered that the fortress gates be closed.' Fonseca was confronted by a furious Juana at the outer gates. 'However hard he begged and pleaded, he could not get the princess to turn back,' reported Padilla. With further progress blocked, Juana remained obstinately in the open on the fortress's ramparts, between the inner and outer gates (Isabella and Ferdinand had built an outer wall to help protect it from cannonfire). She sent Fonseca off with her words still ringing in his ears and continued to rail against those blocking her way. She stayed on the outer rampart on one of the coldest nights of that winter, demanding all afternoon and until two o'clock the following morning that the gate be opened. A hatless Juana refused to return to her quarters. 'Instead, after everyone there had pleaded with her, she went into some kitchens that are beside the outer rampart and was there for four or five days.'[20]

Isabella tried to reason with her from a distance as messengers braved the icy weather, galloping backwards and forwards along the exposed sixty-mile route separating Segovia from Medina del Campo. 'Despite the letters I sent her, this did not change. Because of this I came here as fast as I could manage, doing longer stages than were good for my health,' Isabella wrote after being carried on a litter through the rain and cold to her rebellious daughter. It must have been a difficult, uncomfortable journey, however warmly wrapped she was in blankets and furs, with the litter jolting up and down as the mules or horses plodded along wet, wind-blown tracks. The royal party had to rest overnight twice along the way, as Isabella could move no faster than twenty-five miles in a day. When Isabella finally crossed the broad moat that surrounded the imposing La Mota fortress, Juana was still camped out in the rough outer kitchens. She doggedly refused to return to the warm, comfortable brick and stone palace that lay just a few yards away behind thick walls. 'She spoke to me with such awful words of disobedience, and so beyond what a daughter should say to a mother, that if I had not seen the state she was in I would not have put up with it for a moment,' said Isabella.[21]

Juana had convinced herself that her parents were trying to provoke a permanent break-up with her husband, and Isabella sought to reassure her, asking her 'very lovingly to return to her quarters and promising that once her father the king of Aragon came back, she would send her to her husband'. Mother and daughter then spent an awkward four months together, as Juana waited impatiently for an opportunity to leave, apparently consumed by the belief that all were plotting against her, while Isabella sought both to calm her and to cope with her own declining health.

Ferdinand had been in Roussillon, lifting a siege at Salses-le-Château near Perpignan that had followed a French invasion in September 1503 and strengthening his borders. To Isabella's relief, the French had left without presenting battle – she had begged Ferdinand to avoid spilling Christian blood, fasting and praying on the day when she had expected the battle to take place. By now Spain also had the upper hand in the kingdom of Naples, which effectively become the seventh kingdom in the power of the Aragonese monarchy in addition to Aragon, Valencia, Mallorca, Sicily, Sardinia and the principality of Catalonia. As the French counterattacked through Italy, two of the Borgias – the pope and Cesare – fell foul of the malaria that was sweeping through Rome. Cesare survived. His father, who had just appointed six more cardinals from his home region of Valencia, did not. Borgia's already sickly successor, Pius III, lasted just 26 days. Further Spanish victories and the new pope Julius II's desire to rid his states of foreign armies helped push all sides towards peace, with Naples now firmly in Spanish hands. It was further confirmation that the balance of power in Europe was tilting towards Spain. The puritanical nature of Isabella and Ferdinand's regime was felt in Naples immediately. Instructions were issued to track down *conversos* who had fled the Inquisition, to pursue homosexuals and to make sure Jews were expelled.[22]

With Ferdinand back and France on its heels, Juana was finally given permission to leave. She travelled to Laredo in March 1504 and was forced to wait another month for the weather to change. She bickered with the Spaniards on her staff, but her choice of the potentially dangerous sea route rather than a land trip through France suggests that, in this at least, she wished to please her mother.

Isabella was, by now, thinking about the future of Castile after her own death. The crown would have to pass into Juana's hands, though it seemed clear that this meant that Philip would be the effective ruler. But Isabella was still determined to influence events after her death if, as she now began to suspect, this was not far off. She and Ferdinand now proposed that Juana's eldest son Charles be sent to Spain to be brought up and made king of Naples. The bait for his father Philip was simple. Charles would stay in Spain, being educated to govern the vast kingdoms owned by the crowns of both Castile and Aragon (and, unlike his father, learning to speak Spanish). Philip, meanwhile, could govern the kingdom of Naples in his son's name and his counsellors would be given valuable estates there.[23]

Philip's love for his in-laws, and for Spain, seemed about as great as his feelings for Juana – which were now mutating from disregard to dislike. 'Neither her highness writes to the prince, nor the prince writes to her,' the Spanish ambassadors reported. For Isabella, whose relationship to Ferdinand was the bedrock of what she always viewed as a shared success, the news reaching her was heartbreaking. 'What you have told us about the discontent and lack of love between the prince and the princess weighs heavily on us . . . try as best as you can to make sure that there is love and reconciliation between them,' she and Ferdinand wrote to Fuensalida. Their envoys could do little. Juana's mistrust had extended to all those around her, barring her slaves. Philip now acted against them. 'Given that the princess wanted no other company apart from her slaves, who were already exhausted by the work they had and also because of the continual bathing and hairwashing which, according to the physicians, were doing her so much harm, the prince decided to take the slaves away,' the Spanish ambassadors at the court in Brussels reported.[24]

Over the next few days their argument turned louder and nastier, while all around – including Isabella and Ferdinand's ambassadors – looked on with shock at the meltdown of the marriage. Philip refused to visit her again until the slaves had been exchanged for some trusty elderly retainers, while Juana apparently threatened to execute the messenger who brought her his letter. After several days of arguments via unhappy messengers, Philip confronted her personally. 'I am not happy that you are accompanied by these slaves. Expel them, because I will not sleep in your chamber while they are still here,' he told her. Juana at first pretended to have got rid of them, then brought them back, and an enraged Philip ordered that all entrances to her rooms be barred except one. Juana then refused to eat, and when her husband came back from hunting and went to his own rooms, which were below hers, to sleep, she banged on the floor with a stick and harangued him. 'Talk to me, I want to know if you are there!' she shouted. A furious, sleep-deprived Philip went to confront her the following morning, finding his wife similarly exhausted and angry. Juana now threatened to starve herself to death unless her children and staff were returned. Philip said he could do that, but demanded to know why she refused to obey his instructions. 'If you don't do what I say, then I will leave you and you won't see me again until you do,' he threatened. 'I will let myself die rather than do any of the things that you demand,' she replied. 'Then do whatever you want,' he said before storming off. One report suggested that the argument had ended with Juana 'like a wild lioness' and Philip hitting her.[25]

Isabella's ambassadors in Brussels saw it as a disaster. 'The prince has gone to Flanders with the intention of never seeing the princess again unless she does what he asked her to do, which are things that her royal highness ought to do,' they reported.[26] By Isabella's own standards, her daughter and heiress was failing her. For more than two decades she had imposed royal will on Castile, slowly disciplining and purifying it while turning it into a respected and feared European power. She was now worried about how much of that would survive after her death.

46

The Final Judgement

Medina del Campo, July–November 1504

Isabella was no longer able to travel any great distance. In 1504 she and Ferdinand spent Easter and June in the convent a few hours away at Mejorada de Olmedo, but the rest of the time she stayed in Medina del Campo – first at the La Mota fortress and then in a simpler palace with three interior patios beside the large Plaza de San Antolín. Medina had long been one of her favourite places. She once reportedly proclaimed that, were she to have three sons, the first and second would be king and archbishop of Toledo while the third would be an *escribano*, notarising the deals struck during the international trading fairs that kept the town busy for a hundred days each year. The mouse-infested palace had not been used much since her father was raised there. But even large fortresses could rarely cope with extended occupation by the court before the filth became unbearable and it may have been more hygienic to move from La Mota after spending several months there with both her own people and Juana's. The smaller palace by the town square was undergoing extensive repairs, but Isabella now passed much of her day in bed and needed very little space of her own. A carpenter was called in to make windows so that fresh air could blow in off the vegetable plots and the small orchard behind the palace, while a special passageway was built as a short cut between her rooms and the chapel.[1] The carpenter also had to knock together traps to keep the palace mice away from the royal bed.

There was something safe and snug about these old Castilian towns, which had prospered so thoroughly through her reign. The past two or more decades of stability and steady population growth had finally allowed her kingdom's economy to expand vigorously. Many towns, indeed, had spilt out beyond their medieval walls and were developing large 'suburban' neighbourhoods beyond them. The bustle of people, the thick defensive walls, the growing wealth of trade and even the presence of skilled artisans and learned men – dressed in the cloth of the clergy or the finery of *escribanos* and financiers – were all enriching and reassuring.

Medina itself was a reminder of many of the things that had happened during her thirty years on the throne. She had first visited its great fair as a child on trips from Arévalo. Now the fair, which lasted for two stretches of fifty days, had grown so much that wood for stalls was running out. Isabella and her husband had issued orders to replant local woodland and dig ponds for visiting merchants to water their horses and mules. During her reign the town's streets had been paved, but two fires, in 1479 and 1491, had done terrible damage. Isabella had responded by suspending the tax on building wood and then ordered that high walls be built every few streets to block the progress of future fires.[2]

Among the smells wafting up through the new windows in her room – and towns like Medina were not famously salubrious in this respect – would have been the complex aromas of incense and spices, the warm scent of wax, tallow or pitch, the sharp tang of recently cured or tanned leathers and the earthiness of cattle, mules and horses. The conquest of Granada, ease of trade with Aragon, peace with Portugal and increasing access to the trade routes east of Italy had helped drive the fair's growth. Flemish merchants bought bulk orders of merino wool for their own textile industry, with up to 40,000 bales a year making their way to Bruges and Antwerp. They brought finished cloth and materials with them to sell, competing for trade with French silks and Syrian carpets. Medina del Campo was now considered one of the great trading fairs of Europe, comparable to those of Genoa, Lyon and Antwerp and a sophisticated banking centre was being developed, providing credit, foreign exchange and financing that helped attract merchants from Italy, France and elsewhere.[3] Trade with the Americas was still embryonic, but the extraction of gold and silver and the future exploitation of crops like sugar meant that Isabella had already ushered in a century of unprecedented growth in Medina del Campo and across Spain.

Isabella and Ferdinand had both fallen ill with fevers in July 1504. The king eventually shook his illness off, but Isabella had barely recovered when she was hit again by alternating fevers and chills.[4] By the end of September she was noticeably worse – and showed few signs of getting better.

Ferdinand wrote to his ambassador in Flanders on 26 September, telling him to warn Juana and Philip to prepare for the worst. 'Keep secret what I am about to tell you. No living person apart from the princess and the prince should know,' his letter started. 'I have not wanted to write about the illness and indisposition of the serene Queen, my very dear and much loved wife, before because I thought that our Lord would give her health . . . but given what has happened and her current state, I am very fearful . . . our Lord might take her.' Ferdinand wanted Juana and Philip, to whom he now mostly directed his words, to be ready to travel to Spain urgently. All preparations had to be secret, he emphasised, but they must react swiftly when the fateful day came and should avoid any route through France, since they risked being captured or detained by Louis XII.[5]

Ferdinand also tried to ensure that he held on to some of his power when his wife died, at least as an adviser to the man who would govern in Juana's name. 'I know what he and the princess need to do to keep peace and justice in these kingdoms and I know well the people who would be good to serve him,' he wrote. 'With my advice – so that they do not make mistakes – they will be better able to handle affairs and fill positions here.' Above all, he did not want them to appoint officials – especially foreigners – before they travelled. It was not a piece of advice that his son-in-law, and those surrounding him, showed much sign of wanting to follow. If Isabella died, they knew, Ferdinand would instantly lose his formal powers in Castile.

Isabella, meanwhile, was preparing to die. Just as she felt no need to retreat to one of her more glorious palaces at this crucial moment, so she now made it clear that, in death, she sought humility. In October 1504, as the sound of bartering drifted up from the plaza in the various languages of Spain and elsewhere in Europe, she completed her will. Isabella was fearful of very little and repentant of even less. But God and Judgement Day scared her. Wearing a crown did not guarantee a place in heaven, she knew, though it did enable her to set aside money so that 20,000 masses could be said in her name after her death. She also wanted to clothe 200 poor people and pay the ransoms for 200 Christian captives held in north Africa. All this would help when she faced 'that terrible judgement and strict examination, which is even more terrible for the powerful'.

Her last testament was a chance to amend errors, but also to reaffirm the rightfulness of her actions and her place in history. Isabella was now fifty-three years old. Her thirty-year reign had been replete with historic events, many the direct result of her own will and effort. She had, through her marriage, brought together most of Spain's kingdoms in a curious and unique form of shared monarchy. That meant that they might, one day, be fully united through her children or – more probably – her grandchildren. She had finished off a seven-century crusade, absorbing the kingdom of Granada into Castile, and had expanded Christendom even further, to those mysterious lands across the Atlantic Ocean. She had purged much of the corruption out of the church and had begun the work of centralising power and building a modern state, taming the uppity Grandees and crushing her rival, the rightful heiress Juana la Beltraneja.

Severity, even cruelty, had been present in many of these ventures. Jews and Moors had been expelled, ending centuries of religious tolerance or, as she preferred to see it, sufferance. A royal-led state inquisition sought heresy among those whose chief crime appeared to be their tainted blood and Jewish forebears. Even old Christians stood in fear of her heavy-handed justice. Yet the medieval world from which Europe was slowly emerging was already famous for its 'violent contrasts' and outbursts of public brutishness.[6] Excessive punishment was a far more efficient way to provoke the 'love and fear' that an effective monarch was expected to arouse than generosity, compromise or blandishments. The line between strong rule and tyranny was wafer thin, and there is no doubt that Isabella crossed it.

She had built a nascent European superpower. More remarkably she had done this as a woman, inverting the status quo without ever challenging it. Isabella had demanded the obedience of men, and had received it. As she looked through her will in the mouse-infested palace in Medina del Campo, it is perhaps not surprising that she should associate this almost miraculous set of achievements with her pleas to God. Her prayers had been answered – even if she had had to bear the tragic deaths of her favourite daughter, her son and her cherished infant grandson Miguel. But for someone who took her religion seriously and literally, suffering was an understandable, even virtuous, price to pay for doing God's will. That, to her, was the true meaning of the word 'passion'.

All this had been enough to fulfil her ambitions as queen, but she now had to ask herself whether it would also secure her entrance into heaven. She declared herself sick in body but not in mind, and determined to put her house in order since 'we must all die, but never know when or where that may happen'. Her will showed her still busy centralising power in the monarchy and tidying up her administration. Political expediency had forced her to buy support, giving away too many royal rents and lands, she admitted. Isabella listed the ones that she most regretted on a separate document and asked that they be returned to the crown. And where she had pawned off lands and income in order to fund her war in Granada, these must also be reclaimed, where possible, for the crown. Her long memory was both grateful and vengeful. She demanded that the lands of the marquessate of Villena, formerly held by the still wealthy Pacheco family, never be given away again. It was a way of punishing the family of Enrique IV's *valido*, and her own enemy, Juan Pacheco. But she also remembered long-term loyalists like the *converso* Andrés de Cabrera and Beatriz de Bobadilla, the couple who had helped her take control of Segovia at a crucial moment. They were to be rewarded 'for the loyalty they showed so that I could take possession of my kingdoms, as is well known'.

If there had been errors, she believed, these were few and far between. The Inquisition was a necessity. 'Always support the things that the Holy Inquisition does against the depraved heresy,' she urged her daughter Juana. Some of her officials, she admitted, had been overzealous, self-serving or corrupt – and they must be dealt with. Apart from that there seemed little worth repenting for.

Most of all, she wanted her debts paid off. They were to sell, or use, all her possessions – barring the jewels that were for Juana and the gold and silver for the church in Granada – to do this. But Ferdinand had a right of veto and could keep any jewels or other objects 'if, on setting eyes upon them, they bring to mind the special love that I always felt for him and if that memory allows him to live a holier and more just life, bearing in mind that we must all die and I will be waiting for him on the other side'.

She named Juana as her heiress, but obviously feared that Philip would govern instead and warned against bringing foreign officials to rule over Spaniards or their church. Her advice to Juana and Philip was a short lesson in her own attitude to effective government. They must, first of all, show loving respect to each other. This had been the bedrock of her own successful period as queen with Ferdinand as her partner. They should enforce the law, be just, tax effectively but fairly, listen to Ferdinand's advice, keep the Grandees and other nobility under control and avoid giving away royal rents or property.

They must make sure that the new lands across the Atlantic, and those still to be found, belonged to the crown of Castile – while allowing Ferdinand half of the crown's profits. And they should try to continue Spain's crusade, taking it across the Mediterranean into Africa. Finally, she must be buried in the Alhambra – a reaffirmation of her most important achievement – wearing the plain habit of the Franciscan order. Her burial was to be 'simple, without excess' (thirteen torches would, she thought as she sank automatically into the minutiae of administration, be more than enough). The money saved could go to the poor. If Ferdinand wanted to move her later so that they could lie together, that was fine.

The will that she finished in her rooms in the small palace at Medina del Campo was typical of Isabella. Humble before God, she remained proud, resolute and unrepentant before men. As queen, she had tried to carry out God's will. Only He could now judge whether, in fact, she had achieved that.

———

Monarchs on their death-beds must think, too, about their legacy. This was magnificent, yet fragile. In her will, Isabella had shown no concern about the expulsion of Jews or the forced conversion of Muslims, but the latter remained a recalcitrant and repressed minority. Unlike the *conversos*, many of the new *morisco* Christians were clearly pretending and, an Italian visitor would observe, were 'not well treated' by Isabella's other subjects. Sporadic rebellions would continue until some 250,000 *moriscos* were finally expelled just over a century later. The Inquisition, meanwhile, would continue to invent crimes, inflicting pain and death or simply ruining reputations, until it became a byword for the worst forms of paranoid and tyrannical state repression. Even her beloved Friar Talavera, that most upright of churchmen, would bear witness to this after her death as he himself was persecuted amid claims that his nieces criss-crossed the country on the backs of billy goats, drunk and practising sorcery. 'Certain people who are envious of his good works, in an attempt to pay good with bad, have tried to stain his holy and incorruptible life,' a furious pope eventually wrote. 'And as they cannot find anything bad to accuse him of, they have locked up his elderly sister and his nephews and other servants and officers, who – though Christians – were tortured and tormented in such a cruel fashion that nobody would be able to bear it.'[7] This was the Inquisition that Isabella had bequeathed to her country, and which would survive for another 300 years.

Isabella was unforgiving and, as those *conversos* who fought the Inquisition in Rome or people who dared criticise her in public found out, protest was not tolerated. In a regime that preferred justice to be excessive rather than fall short, only the brave or foolhardy raised their voices. Those Christians who had complained about the expulsion of the Jews, for example, also found themselves being pursued by the Inquisition. It is no surprise that, despite the relative absence of recorded protest during her life, not everyone was sad at the thought of her dying. They included a man whom she may have seen while in Medina, the town's future *corregidor* – or chief royal official – García Sarmiento. 'She oppressed the people,' he said after her death, perhaps thinking that this meant he would avoid punishment.[8] 'The queen is in hell. She and the King of Aragon with her [did] nothing more than steal and ruin these kingdoms, and she was very tyrannical.'

Isabella and Ferdinand had never made a formal attempt to unite their kingdoms, preferring to leave that to biology and the course of time. On their deaths, they had originally hoped, the combined kingdoms of Spain – barring Navarre – would pass into the hands of their heir. But that now looked unlikely. Aragon's traditions had always prevented the crown being passed to a woman, and they had no surviving sons. At best, it would go to one of Juana's sons. The eldest, Charles, was just four years old. At worst, it meant that some other branch of the Aragonese royal family would claim the crown on Ferdinand's death, or even that he would marry again and produce his own male offspring with rights over Aragon, but not over Castile. The unity of Spain was by no means assured.

All that, however, was down to fate. There was nothing Isabella could do to influence the future of Aragon – and so the joint project of Spain – after her death. Even the future of Castile looked uncertain. Superficially, Juana's position at the beginning of her reign was far stronger than Isabella's. She was not a usurper, nor was there any other challenger for the throne. Castile itself was under firm royal rule, meaning there were no *válidos* or *privados* – men like Pacheco or Luna, who governed in the monarch's name – with the power to bend events towards their own objectives. That should have allowed a simple handover of power from one queen to another. But Isabella knew that this would not be the case. She had cleverly bolstered her own position as a female monarch, via a well-negotiated and well-managed marital alliance with Ferdinand, but she had done nothing to promote the position of royal women beyond improving their education. As a traditionalist, she had no interest in changing the status quo and, indeed, would much have preferred to have a male heir.

Isabella had married her daughters off to foreign princes whose cultures were different to those of Castile. As such, she must share the blame for Juana's predicament. For, while Isabella was an equal to her husband, their daughter was the very junior partner in a marriage in which the husband expected to hold all the power, including over his wife's titular lands. That meant a foreigner was about to take control of Castile, for the first time since Isabella's English grandmother, Catherine of Lancaster, had been regent. Even then, though, the regency had been shared and the outcome was always set to be the return of a Castilian man to the throne. The idea of being ruled over by a northern European who might drain the country's resources to bolster his power in his own lands was unsettling.

The fact that Juana looked as though she would be blocked from power was, in itself, a measure of Isabella's own greatness. Her singular achievement was to be a successful, powerful female monarch in Europe. Even by male standards, however, she had been a remarkable ruler. Had it not been for her sex, indeed, some might have seen her as a candidate for the Last World Emperor, that mythical monarch who was expected to save Christendom. A decade later the Florentine ambassador to Spain, the historian Francesco Guicciardini, summed up her achievements and the wonder provoked by a woman's ability to make them happen. Under her guidance, he said, Castile had shed its poor reputation, expanded its lands and been reduced to obedience to its monarchy 'in such a way that Spain has been enlightened and has left behind its natural darkness'. To the ambassador's surprise, he found many people happy to attribute most of the success to Isabella rather than her husband. 'In all these memorable events the glory of the Queen was no less [than that of Ferdinand], but rather everyone agrees that the greater part of it all should be attributed to her, because the affairs of Castile were governed mostly through her authority and control. She oversaw the most important matters, and for the lesser ones it was never less useful to persuade her than it was to persuade her husband . . . She stands up in comparison to any great woman of any previous era.'[9]

Yet there is an irony to this groundbreaking achievement as a woman, for she herself would never have seen it in those terms. As a powerful European queen regnant Isabella was undoubtedly the first of that small group of similarly successful female monarchs, but she neither knew that others would follow nor would have valued the gender aspect of her accomplishment. In her own mind she had simply been God's chosen one – the person whom He had decided should be placed on the throne of Castile. For some reason, God had wanted her – a woman – to lead her country back to glory. That belief and an unshakeable sense of entitlement, grandeur and self-confidence had spurred her to take strong, firm decisions. It drove, initially, her dubious claim to the crown. Victory on the battlefield, another divine decision, had proved what she was already convinced was the truth – that she was no usurper. This was no convenient invention of her own, but a generally accepted test of the rightness of a claim.

If God's decisions were absolute, they were also clear-cut. Relativism and moral doubt were never part of Isabella's make-up. That explains the unflinching manner in which she ordered that the Jews be expelled, the *conversos* persecuted or the Muslims forcibly converted. Between them, and given that even the purest and most powerful *conversos* lived in fear of the Inquisition, these measures afflicted one-third of Castile's population. Indeed, in purely numerical terms – if we add in the priests, monks, friars and nuns affected by religious reform and those helped or pursued by the Hermandad police and a newly strict system of royal justice – the weight of her decisions must have been felt directly by a large part of Castile's population. That made her a real, concrete presence in ordinary lives – rather than the distant, if feared, figurehead of many a medieval monarchy.

This sense of moral conviction made her a woman of action rather than of thought. When doubt is banished, action is easier to pursue and objectives are more easily obtained. The profound reforms to Castile marked Spain's future and that of an empire that would soon stretch across large parts of the American continent and (within seventy years) as far away as the Philippines. Accidents of history allowed her legacy to survive more or less intact, with Ferdinand taking over the government of Castile after Philip's sudden death in 1506 (as Juana famously traversed the country accompanied by his corpse). Extracted wealth would flow east across the Atlantic for the next two centuries, funding a golden age of Spanish power and prosperity. A literary flowering led by Miguel de Cervantes and the playwright Lope de Vega also became part of the wealth eventually generated by a confident, global powerhouse.

Lying in her sick-bed in Medina del Campo, Isabella could intuit only a fraction of this. Her intimate thoughts, plastered over by the considerations of state and administrative minutiae of her will, are not available to us – though they were as likely to dwell on the already dead among her family and offspring as on the future of Castile. Of those she would be leaving behind, Ferdinand was the most obvious regret. He came from a much longer-lived family and she might have to wait many years for him to be laid beside her. He might also remarry and choose to be buried with someone else. Nor, finally, was there was any guarantee that her death would provide a release from her suffering, with purgatory a terrifying thought.

———

These, then, may have been some of her final concerns as the days drew shorter, the shimmering heat of the *meseta* summer became a distant memory and the sharpness of the central Castilian winter set in. As October rolled into November and the palace fires roared louder, a sudden slew of worries began to trouble her conscience. They were a mixture of things grand and small, earthly and heavenly – but she felt they needed dealing with. On 23 November, shortly after the traders had disappeared from Medina's squares and streets, she wrote an appendix to the main will. Some of the *alcabalas*, or sales taxes, that were her main source of income might be unfair, and needed looking at, she admitted. She had failed to complete the drawing up of a unifying law book, being either too busy or too ill, and urged her successors to do so. More importantly, because this would be a real sin, she was worried that she had abused the income given to her through the sale of Crusade Bulls. This was meant to be spent on crusading, but had also been used on the conquest of the Canary Islands and on Columbus's expeditions. Any wrongful spending should be reimbursed. Likewise, the spending of the military orders of Santiago, Alcántara and Calatrava was meant to be in God's cause. If that, too, had failed, it must be remedied. She was still not worried about the excesses of the Inquisition, but fretted that some of those reforming the monasteries for her had been overzealous. That would also need checking, she said.

On the whole, these were all personal matters of conscience between her and God. Politically and socially, she remained without regrets, except for one large doubt that appeared at the last minute.

She had conquered unknown lands across the ocean, winning new converts for Christianity. These people were her subjects, apportioned to her by the pope so that she could convert them. It was legitimate, now, to have doubts about whether this was what had really happened or whether they were simply being destroyed, enslaved or bled for gold, pearls or whatever riches could be taken from them. She now begged Ferdinand, Juana and Philip to make sure that this pattern was broken. 'That should be the main aim, and you should be diligent about it, and not permit that the Indians, neighbours and inhabitants of the said Indies and Mainland that have been, or will be, discovered, are abused . . . but are, rather, treated fairly and if any have been mistreated that you remedy it, making sure that [this treatment] does not go beyond what is spelt out and ordered in the papal grants conceded to us,' she wrote. Isabella, in other words, was concerned that, in this enterprise at least, she had failed to do right by God. She also suddenly remembered the dead in her wars and others who had died in her service,[10] ordering another 20,000 masses (the same number she had already ordered up for herself alone) to be said for them. Finally, she named Ferdinand as administrator in her kingdoms until Juana's arrival.[11]

Three days later, in the morning, Isabella's concerns about unfair taxation were formally aired when a document she had written two weeks earlier was read out at the royal court. Isabella was too ill to attend. That same day, Catherine of Aragon sat in her rooms at Durham House in Westminster and wrote two separate letters to her parents, demanding news. Juana had told her that they were both sick. She had not heard from Ferdinand 'since a year ago', she said. Catherine told Isabella that she could not 'be satisfied or cheerful'[12] until she saw a letter from her mother telling her that she had recovered.

It was too late. That morning, Isabella remained 'awake and with contrition' in her room as she received the sacraments from her confessor. It was typical that, on her death-bed, she reportedly refused to allow the priest to raise her clothes above her ankles as he anointed her. The end, she knew, was approaching and it was comforting to receive the last rites. The hard work of repentance and preparation for death was now mostly done. All that remained was the God who had overseen her great enterprise in Castile and into whose hands, the priest reminded her, she was now being delivered.

On hearing this, Isabella sighed heavily and crossed herself. Shortly before midday, the priest proclaimed to her that 'all is over'. The queen of Castile took a final, shallow breath and died – bringing an end to three decades of rule and thirty-five years of marriage to Ferdinand. 'Her passing is for us the deepest grief that could ever happen to us in this life, for we have lost the best and most excellent wife that a king ever had,' he said. It rained for weeks after her death.[13]

A Beam of Glory

Hispaniola, 1504

In 1504, while Isabella lay in her sickbed in Medina del Campo, an ambitious eighteen-year-old Castilian called Hernán Cortés reached the island of Hispaniola. This young, capable man from a modest family of *hidalgos* from Extremadura was a product of the newly self-confident and adventurous Castile created during Isabella's reign. He had grown up on tales of Caribbean escapades and decided to take advantage of his monarch's offer of free farming land for new arrivals. He was fortunate, also, to be a distant relative of the then governor, Nicolás de Ovando, and went on to become a keen participant in expeditions to conquer the as yet uncolonised parts of Cuba and Hispaniola. Reasonably well educated and with an obvious talent for leadership, Cortés rose rapidly through the colonial ranks and, early in 1519, he raised a force of 600 men and thirty-two horses before setting sail for the coast of what is now Mexico.

In the quarter of a century since Isabella had sent Columbus off on his first voyage of discovery, Spain's colonists had drained the Caribbean islands of the most easily available gold and its native population was being decimated by war, hunger and European diseases such as influenza and smallpox. All that was left, or so it seemed to many of the colonists, was the dull business of farming or the quest for fresh lands to conquer and exploit. Fortunately for Spain, there was no lack of these – nor of men like Cortés who, imbued with the bold and sometimes foolhardy Castilian spirit of adventure promoted by Isabella and Columbus, would become the so-called *conquistadore*s of Latin America.

Cortés was meant to trade and explore, but instead conquered an entire empire. Having scuttled his ships at Veracruz, he led his small band of men inland to the great city of Tenochtitlan, where the Aztec ruler Montezuma awaited. Cortés kidnapped the latter and, over the next few years, skilfully and daringly used the advantages of Castilian steel weapons, gunpowder, Aztec infighting and his own ruthless guile to subdue an empire that boasted a fighting force estimated at up to 300,000 men.

A decade later his feat inspired a distant cousin, Francisco Pizarro, to sail south along the Pacific coast and then strike inland – where, with even fewer men and horses, he overthrew the ancient Inca empire that had its centre in modern-day Peru. It took him just a few years to bring most of South America's largest empire – with a population of around 20 million – under the Spanish yoke. During that time Pizarro captured the emperor Atahualpa, extorted a huge ransom in gold for his release and then garrotted him anyway. Such were the cruel, if efficient, methods of Castile's new *conquistadores* – men who had assumed the triple objective of Isabella's colonial adventures: of seeking personal glory; of winning prestige and gold for Castile; and of delivering fresh souls for their Christian God. 'We came here to serve God and his Majesty, and also to get rich,' one of Cortés's men later admitted.[1] Anyone who opposed this divine mission could be treated with the disdain and violence reserved for an enemy of Christianity.

Eventually, it took just a few thousand Castilian soldiers to conquer lands and peoples that were many times bigger than Spain itself – and to start the process of creating a continuous stretch of Spanish-ruled land that ran from Florida and California to Chile and Argentina. Spanish explorers seeking the wealth of mythical civilisations such as El Dorado struck deep into North America, to modern-day North Carolina, Tennessee, Oklahoma, Texas and Kansas. To the south, only the indigenous peoples of Chile were able, initially, to stop their progress. By the middle of the sixteenth century, after a Spaniard called Bartolomé de Medina invented the so-called 'patio process' – using mercury amalgamation rather than laborious and inefficient smelting to extract silver from the ore found in Mexican and Peruvian mines – bullion fleets were delivering an average of 2 to 8 million ducats of silver to Castile every year. They continued to do so for an entire century. Castile, in return, shipped foodstuffs and other goods to the colonists who flocked to the Americas, bolstering the economy further.

The influx of silver had an impact far beyond Spain, with some blaming it for a long period of high inflation, while also boosting onward trade to silver-hungry China. More importantly, it added to Spain's status as the new political powerhouse of Europe, often in competition with France. Spain's rulers were rich. They were also ambitious and, as a result, profligate. Between them, Isabella's grandson and great-grandson – Charles I and Philip II – were to take Spain to the height of its glory in the sixteenth century. It was a giddying rise to global prominence. 'For a few fabulous decades Spain was to be greatest power on earth,' says the historian J. H. Elliott.[2] No Europe-centred culture had been so successful, in terms of the lands it controlled, since the Romans.

Yet, as we have seen, the future of Castile – and of Spain – had looked precarious on Isabella's death. Philip 'the Handsome' arrived to claim the Castilian throne in his wife Juana's name in April 1506, forcing Ferdinand to retire to his own kingdoms. Spain's union under a single crown – the result of Isabella's choice of the future king of Aragon as her husband – was broken. But fate soon fixed that. Philip died six months after reaching Spain, apparently after partying too hard with his delighted followers. Queen Juana, by now deemed mad, eventually installed herself in Tordesillas. Castile's nominal monarch was a tragic figure who lived for another forty-six years, but she had been side-lined by her husband and would be equally ignored by her father, Ferdinand, when he took over once more after Philip's death. The unique partnership between Isabella and her husband meant that theirs had always been a joint project, and Ferdinand's return provided continuity. The same principles that had driven the young couple during their early years in power thus remained in force from Isabella's accession in 1474 until Ferdinand's death in 1516, meaning that the project ran for four decades. In 1512, Ferdinand conducted a rapid annexation of Navarre, thereby putting the final piece of the jigsaw of contemporary Spain into place. Elsewhere, Ferdinand continued both the good and the bad. Exploration and trade with the Indies was built up, and systems of royal control put in place. The Inquisition continued to torture, repress and persecute. Slaves were shipped from continent to continent. Purity of blood rules, designed to exclude *converso* families from power or privilege, were extended. Yet by the time Ferdinand was laid to rest beside Isabella in Granada few doubted that Spain was the major power in Europe.[3]

Fate meant that their successor would be a man who had grown up in northern Europe and spoke no Spanish – Juana's son, Charles I. As Isabella had feared, the crown was now in the hands of someone 'of another nation and another tongue'. As the grandson of the rulers of Aragon, Castile, Burgundy and the Habsburg lands in and around Austria, Charles I was the lord of several large, but very different, parts of Europe. He soon followed his grandfather Maximilian, the archduke of Austria, into the role of Holy Roman Emperor – increasing his focus on northern Europe and provoking a short-lived rebellion in Castile, where the so-called *comuneros* demanded a return to the home rule and the 'secure liberty' of Isabella's time. Charles, they insisted, should follow the customs of 'Don Ferdinand and Doña Isabella, his grandparents'. Charles's election as Holy Roman Emperor – making him the leader of the German princes whose lands were loosely gathered together in the Holy Roman Empire – cast him more deeply into his role as the defender of Christianity against Islam and the Ottoman Turks. This was a cause which the crusading Castile that Isabella had taken to its peak of glory was happy to embrace, even if the king himself spent only sixteen of his forty years' rule in Spain.

The battle to stop Islam advancing further into Europe, which had seen the Ottomans besiege Vienna unsuccessfully in 1529, reached a maritime peak after the accession of Charles's son, Philip II, to the crown in 1556. An encounter in the Gulf of Corinth near Lepanto in 1571 saw some 250 Christian galleys led by Spain engage in one of the greatest sea battles of all time. The number of vessels on each side was even, but the Turkish fleet was defeated, with part of it sinking to the bottom of the sea. Ottoman expansion into Europe had reached its limit. Both the Ottomans and the Habsburgs then found enemies of their own religions – Protestants in Europe and Persians in Asia – to concentrate on. Isabella and Ferdinand's reform of the church had readied Spain for the battle against Protestantism, making it a principal bulwark of the Counter-Reformation. Internally, the all-seeing Inquisition that Isabella had so vigorously helped to invent squashed the merest hints of Protestantism in Spain.

On his abdication and retirement to a Spanish monastery in 1556, Charles's sprawling empire – really a disjointed set of territories – was split in two. His son, Philip II, was given Spain (including the Aragonese kingdoms that covered most of modern-day Italy) and the Netherlands, while Charles's brother Ferdinand received Austria and took over as Holy Roman Emperor. It was now that Spain became the proper centre of empire, increasingly focused on the New World, though it also began to settle the Philippines (which were named after Philip) and trade with them from Mexico. Castile's wealth also helped bring it another prize, with Portugal accepting Philip as its king in 1581. Philip's already impressive empire now included Portugal's territories in Brazil, Africa and Asia. England's Lord Chancellor, the philosopher Francis Bacon, observed that this was an empire (the world's first) made up of dominions on which 'the sun never sets . . . but ever shines upon one part or other of them: which, to say truly, is a beam of glory'.[4]

The king himself built an austere, massive monastery at El Escorial, on a hillside thirty miles from Madrid, where he fretted over the endless paperwork of his empire. He also launched bold attempts to invade England (where, as Queen Mary's husband, he had briefly been king consort when younger) with his doomed armada and tried to halt the spread of Protestantism in the Netherlands. Spain grew in power, but paid a price – devoting considerable resources to these projects and to the administration of empire. Debt-ridden and overstretched, it eventually proved incapable of holding on to its lands. Spain's European pre-eminence vanished just as quickly as it had emerged. Eventually the country found itself being left behind by other parts of Europe and constantly asking itself how it had wandered from the glorious path that Isabella and her husband had set out on.

It is easy to make the present day look as if it all depends on a particular moment or event in history – a trick that, among other things, ignores what else might have happened without that event. Yet the arrival of three Castilian boats in the Caribbean, with Christopher Columbus and his eighty-eight sailors on board, had an obvious and tangible impact on the world over the following centuries. Consider, for example, some simple assumptions about the 'native' produce and cultures of different countries. By the nineteenth century potatoes had come to occupy a third of Ireland's arable land, but this would never have happened – and nor would the country have suffered the famines that killed a million people and drove 2 million to emigrate – had potatoes not been brought back from the Americas. The North American indigenous peoples who roamed the plains on horses, occasionally chasing buffalo or fighting settlers, were able to do so because Columbus and the *conquistadores* who followed him had introduced horses into the American continent, and these soon ran wild. The list goes on. Tomatoes are a central part of the traditional Mediterranean diet in Italy, Spain and elsewhere, but were unknown in Europe until Castilian boats brought them from America. The master chocolatiers of Switzerland and Belgium would never have developed their famous goods without cacao – another product that began to travel to Europe on the same boats. Tobacco, the fashionable pastime – and then the scourge – of Western society was another import. Even Africa, which would embrace maize and manioc, eventually saw its agriculture transformed.

Amid this world-altering 'Columbine exchange' of plants, animals, diseases and technology, however, it is easy to forget that one of the most important exports to America was Christianity. The greatest beneficiary of the discovery of a new continent was western Christendom – that shared cultural, religious and political space that defined Europe and was the fifteenth-century home of Western civilisation. The beliefs and cultural assumptions of a small corner of Eurasia were thus extended to a vast new land mass and to many of the people there (or, at least, to those who survived the more lethal consequences of the European arrival). America, both north and south, was transformed – especially after explorers from Portugal, England, France and Holland joined the race for land on the American continent and in the Caribbean. That expansion brought not just extracted wealth to Europe but also, over time, a shift in the balance of growth and power towards the Atlantic and, eventually, across the ocean to north America – something that finally became apparent in the twentieth century. There was nothing inevitable about this. In terms of Eurasian history, fifteenth-century Spain and the rest of western Europe were peripheral in more than just the geographical sense. 'Western Europe occupied the outer edge of world maps at the time,' the historian Felipe Fernández-Armesto points out. 'Scholars in Persia or China, confident in the superiority of their own civilised traditions, thought Christendom hardly worth a mention in their studies of the world.'[5] The later rise of Western civilisation, in other words, is inexorably linked to those three small vessels and eighty-eight sailors who departed from Palos de la Frontera in 1492.

But what of Spain and its motor, Castile, after the death of its emblematic queen? When Miguel de Cervantes published his *Don Quijote de La Mancha* in 1605, a century after Isabella's death, he was not just launching what is now seen as the tradition of the modern novel. He was also telling a nostalgic – if embittered – story about the values that had helped propel Castile to greatness, but were now becoming hopelessly idealistic and impractical. Cervantes's foolish, book-crazed hero, Don Quixote, sets out on a comical and humiliating pursuit of knightly glory. He has been driven mad by excessive reading of chivalric romances and invents for himself an imaginary Spain in which opportunities for carrying out feats of gallantry appear constantly (even if that requires mistaking windmills for giants), and where these will be admired. He is wrong on both counts, but cannot see it. Crusading, chivalry and the strict orthodoxy that came with the Counter-Reformation in Spain were becoming old-fashioned or, at least, unsuited to the coming century. The Inquisition helped stifle intellectual debate and science. The Americas drew away population, while also making Spain overly reliant on its empire's extracted raw materials and protected market. Wars elsewhere in Europe were both a distraction and a long-term waste of money. Grandiose ideals – of defending Christianity against Islam, of protecting Roman Catholicism against heresy or maintaining lands elsewhere in Europe – pushed Spain deep into debt, while preventing it from turning its energies towards looking after itself. Cervantes, a proud veteran of the Lepanto sea battle, appeared to realise that his country had exhausted itself in the apparently noble and heroic defence of Christendom and in its love of adventure, allowing others to reap the benefits. It is difficult not to see Isabella's personal beliefs and priorities as one of the engines driving this dynamic. Cervantes's death in April 1616 coincided almost exactly with that of William Shakespeare, a writer whose plays reflected the rising pride and self-esteem of England – a country that went on to build the only European-based empire which, in geographical terms, can rival the Spanish empire that had begun to emerge under Isabella's rule.

Internally, Spain remained a fractious collection of kingdoms with different rules and obligations that were difficult to manage. By the time Diego Velázquez was painting the moustachioed nobles, lantern-jawed monarchs and exaggeratedly wide farthingale dresses of little Spanish princesses in the mid-seventeenth century, there was already a note of decadence and corruption in the world he was portraying. The aristocrats painted the following century by Francisco de Goya were part of a different but often disastrous class of administrators, who allowed Spain to fall further behind the major nations of Europe. His darker paintings, of monsters, war, insanity and human folly, revealed the underbelly of decay hidden by the finery of his Grandee patrons and the idealised, romantic rural scenes he had also painted for them.

Self-obsessed, quarrelsome and suspicious, Spain watched its empire disintegrate, taking much of its prestige and glory with it. The European possessions disappeared first, with half of the Netherlands declaring independence in 1580 and Portugal rebelling in 1640. The half of Italy that Spain still controlled was lost between 1713 and 1715, along with the remainder of the Spanish Netherlands (basically composed of Belgium and Luxembourg). Spain's territories in the Americas rose up a century later, quickly achieving independence. The last few outposts of empire – Cuba, Puerto Rico and the Philippines – were lost during a short war against the United States in the disastrous year of 1898. Some see this whole long decline reaching its nadir with a bloody civil war in the 1930s and the forty years of dictatorship under General Francisco Franco that followed. Others say that the centuries of decline have been exaggerated by historians in thrall to the black legend or afflicted by a dark and irrational sense of national pessimism. Either way, it was a sign of how desperate Spain had become for national heroes that Isabella would be held up by that regime as proof of the country's 'natural' virtues. The symbols that Isabella and Ferdinand invented, of the yoke and arrows, were appropriated by Spain's fascist-inspired Falange party and by Franco. A statue from that period still stands outside a foreign ministry building in Madrid, the plaque proclaiming Isabella to be 'the mother of America . . . whose brilliant efforts completed the geographical and spiritual fullness of the world'.

It was under Franco's dictatorship that the official campaign for Isabella to be beatified was launched in 1958, with the archbishopric of Valladolid starting work on the required report that was eventually sent to Rome in 1990.[6] There it gathers dust, amid controversy over whether she brought intolerance towards Christian converts in Spain along with genocide and economic plunder, rather than Christian love, to Latin America.

Over recent decades, following the return to democracy in the late 1970s, Spain has enjoyed another, more modest, period of growth and prosperity – enough to establish it in its rightful place as one of Europe's major countries, safely anchored (for the time being) in the European Union. That has also allowed it to shake off some prejudices and insecurities about the past, including Isabella's appropriation by Francoism. The time is now ripe, in other words, to look back at Isabella without first donning the coloured lenses of political prejudice or of purely twenty-first-century values.

She was, quite simply, the first great queen of Europe. In terms of the impact of her reign – and of her decisions – on the future course of world history, she is also the most important of those queens. She was the co-unifier of a country, Spain, and founder of an empire that eventually became one of the largest in Western history. The unity of Spain's varied kingdoms was initially both fragile and temporary, but it would eventually stick. By sending Columbus off on an extraordinary adventure of blind, chivalric daring, she helped to reverse the decline of western Christendom and to alter the course of global history in the second half of the millennium. Western civilisation owes a lot to Isabella's Castile, however much it now disapproves of her mistreatment of Jews, Muslims and *conversos*. Would any of this have happened without Isabella and her partner Ferdinand? Inevitably, much of it would have done. History is not purely, or even mostly, the result of a handful of decisions made by monarchs and other extraordinary individuals. But the world cannot reinvent, or undo, the chain of events that created the present. That is both good and bad for Isabella's reputation. Some, for example, now draw connecting lines between waterboarding by the US military and the techniques of the Inquisition. Latin America's history of economic inequality, violence and repression of indigenous peoples – not to mention the ravages of European disease – are as much a consequence of her decisions as the glory accrued to Spain.

It may be wiser to ask ourselves how Isabella herself saw, or would have seen, her life. In an era of individual ambition and the constant assertion of personal rights, we are now encouraged to judge ourselves in terms of everyday happiness. By that measure, Isabella ended her life as a failure. The sombre-looking portrait of her as she enters her fifties is ample proof of that. Those three knife-thrusts of pain – brought by the deaths of her beloved son Juan, her daughter Isabella and her small grandson Miguel – cast misery over her final years. Even in terms of affairs of state, she seemed already to be handing much of the decision-making to Ferdinand in those final years. The dramatic arguments with her daughter Juana on the battlements of La Mota fortress showed Isabella putting her waning energy into a fight that we are all destined to lose – the one to control events after our death. Jealousy and, possibly, depression were also her lot.

It would be wrong to take pity on her, though, for Isabella did not view life in terms of self-fulfilment or the quest for personal satisfaction. Of all the current measures of success, the only one she would have recognised would be the quest for fame – which she certainly achieved. Apart from that, hers was a world of duty, obedience and fear of God. That explains why, in her final days, she did not fret about the obvious cruelty of expelling the Jews, forcibly converting the Muslims or torturing the *conversos*. The aims – of pursuing heresy and purifying Castile – were clearly ones that her God must approve of. She would have thought of personal suffering as a potential route to atonement and salvation. Jesus Christ's violent, slow and painful death by crucifixion – his 'Passion' – was proof of that. She could not, therefore, have seen her own suffering as a sign of any sort of failure and may even have taken secret satisfaction in enduring it. Wherever else she looked, she can only have seen success. Castile was pure and prosperous, or a lot more so than when she came to the throne. Her people were secure. And, whatever her concerns about the treatment of the peoples of the Caribbean, heretics and infidels were being chased off, or converted, at home and elsewhere. Western Christendom was, at last, expanding. She had, in other words, not just stuck to her principles – or those dictated by God – but had imposed them elsewhere. That was what a monarch's power, however doubtful its origins in Isabella's case, were for. Pride was a sin, but in her final moments of fear about what awaited, that knowledge can only have provided consolation and confidence.

APPENDIX: MONETARY VALUES AND COINAGE

Castile used a number of different coins whose values varied slightly during Isabella's reign. Much like some modern-day Spaniards, who still price major items such as houses or cars in the long-disappeared *peseta* rather than in euros, Castilians used the old *maravedi* as the common pricing value for almost everything. Coins were then also given a value in *maravedis*.

The following table provides official values for Castilian coinage as well as equivalencies for coinage from the kingdoms of Aragon and from Granada. I have included examples of what money could buy, which are extracted from Isabella's own accounts books and elsewhere.

COINS AND MONETARY QUANTITITES	EQUIVALENT IN *MARAVEDIS*
1 *dinero granadino* (Granada)	3
1 *silver pesante granadino* (Granada)	30
1 *real*	31
1 *florin* (Aragon)	265
1 *corona*, or crown	328
1 *libra*, or pound (Valencia)	357
1 *doble*	365
1 *ducado*	375 or 420
1 *dobla ʒahen grandino* (Granada)	445
1 *castellano de oro*	485
1 *justo*	580
1 *cuento* (quantity, not coin)	1 million

ITEM	VALUE IN *MARAVEDIS*
1 kilo of sugar	55
1,000 dressmaking pins	62
A clothes brush	62

One day's work by an embroiderer	62
A small prayer book	77
A pair of *chapines* clogs	135
Two glasses from Valencia	280
A brass sink for hairwashing	310
Two hats (one cotton and one wool)	324
Twelve pairs of gloves	375
A barber's payment for pulling out a prince's tooth	485
A book in Latin by the philosopher Boethius	485
A mule's bridle	530
A *vihuela* (a type of viola)	1,125
One year's salary for a noble's page	3,000
One year's hire of a mule and muleteer	4,500
Seventy-two pairs each of soft *borcegui* boots and prince's shoes	7,812
An African or Canary Island slave	8–10,000
A mule	12,000
The ransom payment for a Muslim captive in the Granada War	13,000
The largest gold nugget reportedly found on Hispaniola (estimated)	1.5 million
Columbus's first voyage	2 million

NOTES

INTRODUCTION: EUROPE'S FIRST GREAT QUEEN

1 Alonso de Palencia, *Crónica de Enrique IV*, ed. A. Paz y Meliá, 4 vols, Madrid, Revista de Archivos, 1904–8, Década 2, Libro 10, Chapter 10.

2 Ibid.

3 Álvaro Fernández de Córdova Miralles, *La Corte de Isabel I. Ritos y ceremonias de una reina (1474–1504)*, Madrid, Dykinson, 2002, pp. 44–6.

4 Antoine de Lalaing, 'Relato del primer viaje de Felipe el Hermoso a España', in *Viajes de extranjeros por España y Portugal, desde los tiempos más remotos hasta fines del siglo XVI*, ed. J. García Mercadal, Madrid, 1952, pp. 482–3, 486.

5 See J. A. Maravall, *Estado moderno y mentalidad social (siglos XV a XVII)*, Madrid, Revista de Occident, 1972. See also Felipe Fernández-Armesto, *1492. El nacimiento de la modernidad*, Madrid, Debate, 2010.

6 Hugh Thomas, *Rivers of Gold: The Rise of the Spanish Empire from Columbus to Magellan*, Penguin, London, 2010, p.28.

7 Norman Davies, *Europe: A History*, Oxford, Oxford University Press, 1996, pp. 409–13. Eugene Thacker, *The Global Genome: Biotechnology, Politics and Culture*, Cambridge, MA, and London, MIT Press, 2006, p. 218. Angus MacKay, *Spain in the Middle Ages: From Frontier to Empire, 1000–1500*, London, Macmillan, 1977, p. 183. Richard Britnell, 'Land and Lordship: Common Themes and Regional Variations', in Richard Britnell and Ben Dodds (eds), *Agriculture and Rural Society after the Black Death: Common Themes*, Hatfield, University of Hertfordshire Press, 2008, pp. 149–67.

8 Peggy K. Liss, *Isabel the Queen: Life and Times*, Philadelphia, University of Pennsylvania Press, 2004, pp. 103–4.

9 Francisco Guicciardini in Jorge de Einghen et al., *Viajes por España de Jorge de Einghen, del Barón Leon de Rosmithal de Blatine, de Francisco Guicciardini y de Andrés Navajero; traducido, anotados y con un introducción por Antonio María Fabié*, Madrid, Librería de los Bibliófilos, 1889, pp. 211–12.

10 Palencia, *Crónica de Enrique IV*, Década 2, Libro 10, Chapter 10. MacKay, *Spain in the Middle Ages*, pp. 58–9.

11   Joseph Pérez, *Isabel y Fernando. Los Reyes Católicos*, San Sebastián, Nerea, 1997, p. 91. MacKay, *Spain in the Middle Ages*, pp. 58–9. Tarsicio de Azcona, *Isabel la Católica. Estudio crítico de su vida y su reinado*, Madrid, Biblioteca de Autores Cristianos, 1993, p. 243.

12   Perry Anderson, *Lineages of the Absolutist State*, New York and London, Verso, 2013, p. 62 (citing J. Vicens Vives, *Manual de historia economica de España*, pp. 11–12). Simon Barton, *A History of Spain*, London, Palgrave Macmillan, 2009, p. 93.

13   Miguel Ángel Motis Dolader, 'Las comunidades judías de la Corona de Aragón en el siglo XV', in Ángel Alcalá (ed.), *Judíos, sefarditas, conversos. La expulsión de 1492 y sus consecuencias. Ponencias del Congreso Internacional celebrado en Nueva York en noviembre de 1992*, Valladolid, Ambito, 1995, p. 45. Miguel Ángel Ladero Quesada, 'El número de judíos en la España de 1492', in Alcalá (ed.), *Judíos, sefarditas, conversos*, p. 171. Alexander Marx, 'The Expulsion of the Jews from Spain: Two New Accounts', *Jewish Quarterly Review*, vol. 20, no. 2, January 1908, pp. 246–7. Miguel Ángel Ladero Quesada, *La España de los Reyes Católicos*, Madrid, Alianza, 2014, p. 18.

14   Niccolò Machiavelli, *The Prince*, trans. George Bull, London, Penguin, 1999, Chapter 21.

15   James Gairdner, *Henry VII*, London, Macmillan, 1889, p. 166.

CHAPTER 1: NO MAN EVER HELD SUCH POWER

1   Fernán Pérez de Guzmán, *Crónica de Juan II*, in *Crónicas de los Reyes de Castilla*, vol. 2, ed. Cayetano Rosell, Madrid, Rivadeneyra, 1887, pp. 595, 606, 683. Navagero in Jorge de Einghen et al., *Viajes por España de Jorge de Einghen, del Barón Leon de Rosmithal de Blatine, de Francisco Guicciardini y de Andrés Navajero; traducido, anotados y con un introducción por Antonio María Fabié*, Madrid, Librería de los Bibliófilos, 1889, p. 322. Isabel Pastor Bodmer, *Grandeza y tragedia de un valido. La muerte de Don Álvaro de Luna. Estudios y documentos*, Madrid, Caja Madrid, 1992, vol. 1, p. 253. Casimiro González García, *Datos para la historia biográfica de Valladolid*, vol. 1, Valladolid, Maxtor, 2003, p. 820. Modesto Lafuente, *Historia general de España*, vol. 6, Barcelona, Montaner y Simón, 1888, p. 48. Juan Agapito y Revilla, *Las calles de Valladolid. Nomenclátor histórico. Datos para la historia biográfica de Valladolid*, Valladolid, Maxtor, 2004, pp. 336–9.

2   See Carrillo de Huete, *Crónica del halconero de Juan II*, ed. Juan de Mata Carriazo y Arroquia, Madrid, Espasa-Calpe, 1946.

3   Carmen Alicia Morales, *Isabel de Castilla. Una psicobiografía*, San Juan, Puerto Rico, Adoquín, 2013 (Kindle edn), loc. 4192. Luis Suárez Fernández,

Enrique IV de Castilla. La difamación como arma política, Barcelona, Ariel, 2001, p. 29. José-Luis Martín, *Enrique IV de Castilla. Rey de Navarra, Príncipe de Cataluña*, San Sebastián, Nerea, 2003, p. 222. María Isabel del Val Valdivieso, *Isabel I de Castilla (1451–1504)*, Madrid, Ediciones del Orto, 2005, p. 33. José Manuel Nieto Soria, 'El "poderío real absoluto" de Olmedo (1445) a Ocaña (1469). La monarquía como conflicto', *En la España Medieval*, no. 21, 1998, p. 208. Peggy K. Liss, *Isabel the Queen: Life and Times*, Philadelphia, University of Pennsylvania Press, 2004, pp. 13, 23, 105–9. Francisco de Paula Cañas Gálvez, *El itinerario de la corte de Juan II de Castilla (1418–1454)*, Madrid, Silex Ediciones, 2007, pp. 481–2.

4   Pérez de Guzmán, *Juan II*, p. 584.

5   Jorge Manrique, *El Cancionero*, Madrid, Pérez Dubrull, 1885, p. 27. Alonso de Palencia, *Crónica de Enrique IV*, ed. A. Paz y Meliá, 4 vols, Madrid, Revista de Archivos, 1904–8, Década 1, Libro 1, Chapter 10. Fernan Pérez de Guzmán, *Pen Portraits of Illustrious Castilians*, trans. Marie Gillette and Loretta Zehngut, Washington, DC, Catholic University Press, 2003, pp. xxvi, 56. Morales, *Psicobiografía*, locs 4025–38. Val Valdivieso, *Isabel*, p. 33.

6   Morales, *Psicobiografía*, locs 1847, 1871, 4189, 4259.

7   Pérez de Guzmán, *Juan II*, p. 654. Palencia, *Crónica de Enrique IV*, Década 1, Libro 1, Chapter 10.

CHAPTER 2: THE IMPOTENT

1   Hieronymus Münzer, *Viaje por España y Portugal (1494–1495)*, Madrid, Polifemo, 1991, p. 263. Emilio Maganto Pavón, 'Enrique IV de Castilla (1454–1474). Un singular enfermo urológico. Retrato morfológico y de la personalidad de Enrique IV "El Impotente" en las crónicas y escritos contemporáneos', *Archivos Españoles de Urología*, vol. 56, no. 3, 2003, pp. 211–20. Willem Ombelet and Johan Van Robays, 'History of Human Artificial Insemination', *Facts, Views & Vision*, 2010, pp. 1–5. Felipe Fernández-Armesto, *Ferdinand and Isabella*, New York, Dorset Press, 1991, p. 34.

2   Diego de Valera, *Memorial de diversas hazañas, crónica de Enrique IV*, in *Crónicas de los Reyes de Castilla*, vol. 3, Madrid, Rivadeneyra, 1878, Chapter 7. Gregorio Marañón, *Ensayo biológico sobre Enrique IV de Castilla y su tiempo*, Madrid, Boletín de la Real Academia 22, 1930.

3   Marañón, *Ensayo*, pp. 23–5.

4   Peggy K. Liss, *Isabel the Queen: Life and Times*, Philadelphia, University of Pennsylvania Press, 2004, p. 11.

5   Juan José Montalvo, *De la historia de Arévalo y de sus sexmos*, vol. 1, Valladolid, Imprenta Castellana, 1928, p. 12.

6   Ibid., pp. 221, 223. Popplau in Javier Liske, *Viajes de extranjeros por España y Portugal en los siglos XV, XVI y XVII*, Madrid, Medina, 1878, pp. 55–6. See also Francesc Eiximenis, *Carro de las donas. Valladolid, 1542 / adaptación del Llibre de les dones de Francesc Eiximenis O.F.M., realizada por el P. Carmona O.F.M.*, ed. Carmen Clausell Nácher, Madrid, Fundación Universitaria Española, 2007. Miguel Ángel Ladero Quesada, 'Los mudejares de Castilla en la Edada Media Baja', in *Historia. Instituciones. Documents*. No. 5, Seville, 1978, pp. 284–8.

7   Alfredo Alvar Ezquerra, *Isabel la Católica*, Madrid, Temas de Hoy, 2002, p. 191. Carmen Alicia Morales, *Isabel de Castilla. Una psicobiografía*, San Juan, Puerto Rico, Adoquín, 2013 (Kindle edn), locs 3955, 3954. Carmen Alicia Morales, 'Isabel de Barcelos. Su importancia en la niñez de Isabel de Castilla, Arévalo', *Cuadernos de Cultura y Patrimonio*, no. 14, for La Alhóndiga, Asociación de Cultura y Patrimonio, April 2012, pp. 71–98. Liss, *Isabel*, p. 13.

8   Liss, *Isabel*, p. 13.

9   Fernán Pérez de Guzmán, *Crónica de Juan II*, in *Crónicas de los Reyes de Castilla*, vol. 2, ed. Cayetano Rosell, Madrid, Rivadeneyra, 1887, p. 566.

10   Montalvo, *Arévalo*, vol. 1, pp. 56, 60, 62–3, 67.

11   Theresa Earenfight, 'Two Bodies, One Spirit: Isabel and Fernando's Construction of Monarchical Partnership', in Barbara F. Weissberger (ed.), *Queen Isabel I of Castile: Power, Patronage, Persona*, Woodbridge, Suffolk, Tamesis, 2008, p. 8. Barbara F. Weissberger, *Isabel Rules: Constructing Queenship, Wielding Power*, Minneapolis, University of Minnesota Press, 2003, pp. 32, 102–5. See also Miriam Shadis, *Berenguela of Castile (1180–1246) and Political Women in the High Middle Ages*, New York, Palgrave Macmillan, 2009.

12   Luis Suárez Fernández, *Enrique IV de Castilla. La difamación como arma política*, Barcelona, Ariel, 2001, p. 73.

13   Ibid., p. 24.

14   Marañón, *Ensayo*, p. 30. Diego Enríquez del Castillo, *Crónica del rey don Enrique el Quarto de este nombre*, ed. A. Sánchez Martín, Valladolid, Universidad de Valladolid, 1994, Chapter 13.

15   Barbara Weissberger, ' "¡A tierra, puto!": Alfonso de Palencia's Discourse of Effeminacy', in Josiah Blackmore and Gregory S. Hutcheson (eds), *Queer Iberia: Sexualities, Cultures, and Crossings from the Middle Ages to the Renaissance*, Durham, NC, and London, Duke University Press, 1999, p. 298.

16   Alonso de Palencia, *Crónica de Enrique IV*, ed. A. Paz y Meliá, 4 vols, Madrid, Revista de Archivos, 1904–8, Década 1, Libro 7, Chapter 3.

17 Castillo, *Crónica*, Chapter 1.

18 Ibid.

19 Maganto Pavón, 'Enrique IV', pp. 211–20.

20 Castillo, *Crónica*, Chapter 1.

21 Suárez, *Enrique IV*, p. 145.

22 Ibid., p. 161.

23 Ibid., pp. 178–81.

24 Castillo, *Crónica*, Chapter 64. Palencia, *Crónica de Enrique IV*, Década 1, Libro 7, Chapter 4.

25 Palencia, *Crónica de Enrique IV*, Década 1, Libro 3, Chapter 8.

26 Benzion Netanyahu, *The Origins of the Inquisition in Fifteenth Century Spain*, New York, New York Review Books, 2001, p. 824. Suárez, *Enrique IV*, p. 243.

27 Netanyahu, *Origins*, pp. 821–2.

28 Ibid., p. 1291 (citing Espina, *Fortalitium*, lib. III, fol. 163).

29 Ibid., pp. 800–3, 811.

30 Ibid., pp. 814–15.

31 Palencia, *Crónica de Enrique IV*, Década 1, Libro 9, Chapter 6. Suárez, *Enrique IV*, pp. 243–7.

32 Netanyahu, *Origins*, p. 742. Suárez, *Enrique IV*, p. 246.

33 Castillo, *Crónica*, Chapter 53. Netanyahu, *Origins*, p. 742.

34 Netanyahu, *Origins*, pp. 716, 738–40, 742. Suárez, *Enrique IV*, pp. 152, 242, 245, 277, 289.

35 Alvar Ezquerra, *Isabel la Católica*, p. 191 (citing *Colección diplomática*, pp. 630–9, no. CLXXXVII).

CHAPTER 3: THE QUEEN'S DAUGHTER

1 Lorenzo Galíndez de Carvajal, *Crónica de Enrique IV*, ed. Juan Torres Fontes, Murcia, Consejo Superior de Investigaciones Científicas, 1946, p. 144. Diego Enríquez del Castillo, *Crónica del rey don Enrique el Quarto de este nombre*, ed. A. Sánchez Martín, Valladolid, Universidad de Valladolid, 1994, Chapter 23.

2 Nicasio Salvador Miguel, 'Isabel, Infanta de Castilla, en la Corte de Enrique IV (1461–1467). Formación y entorno literario', *Actes del XX Congres Internacional de l'Associació Hispánica de Literatura Medieval*, Alacant, Intitui Interuniversitari de Filologia Valenciana 'Symposia Philologica', vol. 1, 2005, pp. 191–2.

3 Castillo, *Crónica*, Chapter 37.

4 Álvaro Fernández de Córdova Miralles, *La Corte de Isabel I. Ritos y ceremonias de una reina (1474–1504)*, Madrid, Dykinson, 2002, p. 61. Tarsicio de Azcona, *Isabel la Católica. Estudio crítico de su vida y su reinado*,

Madrid, Biblioteca de Autores Cristianos, 1993, p. 40. José Sánchez Herrero, 'Amantes, barraganas, compañeras, concubinas clericales', *Clío y Crímen*, no. 5, 2008, pp. 106–37.

5 Alonso de Palencia, *Crónica de Enrique IV*, ed. A. Paz y Meliá, 4 vols, Madrid, Revista de Archivos, 1904–8, Década 1, Libro 3, Chapter 10.

6 R. O. Jones, 'Isabel la Católica y el amor cortés', *Revista de literatura*, vol. 21, no. 41–2, 1962, pp. 55–64. Luis Suárez Fernández, *Enrique IV de Castilla. La difamación como arma política*, Barcelona, Ariel, 2001, pp. 206–7.

7 Castillo, *Crónica*, Chapters 34–6. Palencia, *Crónica de Enrique IV*, Década 1, Libro 5, Chapters 2 and 4. Suárez, *Enrique IV*, pp. 206, 345, 555.

8 Castillo, *Crónica*, Chapter 23. Palencia, *Crónica de Enrique IV*, Década 1, Libro 4, Chapters 2 and 6. Suárez, *Enrique IV*, p. 207.

9 Luis de Salazar, *Historia genealógica de la Casa de Lara, justificada con instrumentos y escritores de inviolable fe*, Madrid, Imprenta Real, for Mateo de Llanos y Guzmán, 1698, vol. 2, pp. 142–3.

10 Palencia, *Crónica de Enrique IV*, Década 1, Libro 5, Chapter 8.

11 Ibid., Libro 4, Chapter 2. Jorge Manrique, *El Cancionero*, Madrid, Pérez Dubrull, 1885, p. 184.

12 Carmen Alicia Morales, *Isabel de Castilla. Una psicobiografía*, San Juan, Puerto Rico, Adoquín, 2013 (Kindle edn), loc. 2454.

13 Azcona, *Isabel la Católica*, p. 41. Morales, *Psicobiografía*, loc. 2454.

14 Castillo, *Crónica*, Chapter 36. Morales, *Psicobiografía*, locs 2531–44. Azcona, *Isabel la Católica*, p. 41.

15 Castillo, *Crónica*, Chapter 38.

16 Peggy K. Liss, *Isabel the Queen: Life and Times*, Philadelphia, University of Pennsylvania Press, 2004, p. 36.

17 Castillo, *Crónica*, Chapter 38.

18 Ibid., Chapter 40.

19 Azcona, *Isabel la Católica*, p. 43.

20 Castillo, *Crónica*, Chapter 40. Azcona, *Isabel la Católica*, p. 45. Cesar Oliveiza Santos, *Las Cortes de Castilla y Leon y la crisis del Reino*, Valladolid, Cortes de Castilla y León, 1986, p. 110.

21 Alfredo Alvar Ezquerra, *Isabel la Católica*, Madrid, Temas de Hoy, 2002, p. 191. Salvador Miguel, 'Isabel, Infanta de Castilla, en la Corte de Enrique IV (1461–1467)', p. 159 (citing *Colección diplomática*, pp. 630–9). Azcona, *Isabel la Católica*, p. 45.

22 Castillo, *Crónica*, Chapter 39. See also Salvador Miguel, 'Isabel, Infanta de Castilla, en la Corte de Enrique IV (1461–1467)' and Fernan Pérez de Guzmán, *Pen Portraits of Illustrious Castillians*, trans. Marie Gillette and Loretta Zehngut, Washington, DC, Catholic University Press, 2003.

23 Azcona, *Isabel la Católica*, pp. 47–8.

24 Suárez, *Enrique IV*, p. 125.

25 Emilio Maganto Pavón, 'Enrique IV de Castilla (1454–1474). Un singular enfermo urológico. Retrato morfológico y de la personalidad de Enrique IV "El Impotente" en las crónicas y escritos contemporáneos', *Archivos Españoles de Urología*, vol. 56, no. 3, 2003, p. 249. Isabel Pastor Bodmer, *Grandeza y tragedia de un valido. La muerte de Don Álvaro de Luna. Estudios y documentos*, Madrid, Caja Madrid, 1992, vol. 2, p. 293. Suárez, *Enrique IV*, p. 125; Castillo, *Crónica*, Chapter 118.

26 *Memorias de don Enrique IV de Castilla. Contiene la colección diplomática del mismo rey compuesta y ordenada por la Real Academia de la Historia*, ed. Duque de Berwick y de Alba, Madrid, Fortanet, 1913, p. 331–2. Suárez, *Enrique IV*, p. 290.

CHAPTER 4: TWO KINGS, TWO BROTHERS

1 Diego Enríquez del Castillo, *Crónica del rey don Enrique el Quarto de este nombre*, ed. A. Sánchez Martín, Valladolid, Universidad de Valladolid, 1994, Chapter 74.

2 Alonso de Palencia, *Crónica de Enrique IV*, ed. A. Paz y Meliá, 4 vols, Madrid, Revista de Archivos, 1904–8, Década 1, Libro 7, Chapter 8. Castillo, *Crónica*, Chapter 74.

3 Luis Suárez Fernández, *Enrique IV de Castilla. La difamación como arma política*, Barcelona, Ariel, 2001, p. 33.

4 Palencia, *Crónica de Enrique IV*, Década 1, Libro 7, Chapter 8. Castillo, *Crónica*, Chapter 74.

5 Palencia, *Crónica de Enrique IV*, Década 1, Libro 7, Chapter 8.

6 James A. Brundage, *Law, Sex, and Christian Society in Medieval Europe*, Chicago, University of Chicago Press, 1987, pp. 357, 433.

7 Castillo, *Crónica*, Chapter 57. Suárez, *Enrique IV*, pp. 267, 275. Nicasio Salvador Miguel, 'Isabel, Infanta de Castilla, en la Corte de Enrique IV (1461–1467). Formación y entorno literario', *Actes del XX Congres Internacional de l'Associació Hispánica de Literatura Medieval*, Alacant, Institui Interuniversitari de Filologia Valenciana 'Symposia Philologica', vol. 1, 2005, p. 199.

8 Castillo, *Crónica*, Chapter 60. *Memorias de don Enrique IV de Castilla. Contiene la colección diplomática del mismo rey compuesta y ordenada por la Real Academia de la Historia*, ed. Duque de Berwick y de Alba, Madrid, Fortanet, 1913, pp. 302–3. Suárez, *Enrique IV*, pp. 275–6, 279–81.

9 Suárez, *Enrique IV*, pp. 271–4, 282–3.

10 Palencia, *Crónica de Enrique IV*, Década 1, Libro 4, Chapter 7. *Colección diplomática*, pp. 327–34. Suárez, *Enrique IV*, pp. 277–8, 289–90.

11 Castillo, *Crónica*, Chapter 65. *Colección diplomática*, p. 348. Suárez, *Enrique IV*, pp. 292–9, 302–3, 311–12.

12 Castillo, *Crónica*, Chapter 85. Suárez, *Enrique IV*, pp. 351–3.

13 Castillo, *Crónica*, Chapter 85. Suárez, *Enrique IV*, pp. 353–4, 358.

14 Suárez, *Enrique IV*, pp. 305–6, 359, 367, 370, 375.

15 Lorenzo Galíndez de Carvajal, *Crónica de Enrique IV*, ed. Juan Torres Fontes, Murcia, Consejo Superior de Investigaciones Científicas, 1946, Chapter 92. Suárez, *Enrique IV*, pp. 310, 374–5, 378, 380.

16 Suárez, *Enrique IV*, p. 380 (citing Duque de Berwick y Alba, *Documentos escogidos de la Casa de Alba*, pp. 8–9).

17 José Martínez Millán and María Paula Marçal Lourenço, *Las relaciones discretas entre las Monarquías Hispana y Portuguesa. Las Casas de las Reinas (siglos XV–XIX)*, Madrid, Polifemo, 2008, p. 139. Suárez, *Enrique IV*, pp. 382–3.

18 Palencia, *Crónica de Enrique IV*, Década 1, Libro 10, Chapter 9. Suárez, *Enrique IV*, pp. 386, 393.

19 Juan Torres Fontes (ed.), *Estudio de la 'Crónica de Enrique IV' del Dr. Galíndez de Carvajal*, Murcia, Sucesores de Nogués, 1946, p. 832. Suárez, *Enrique IV*, pp. 393–4.

CHAPTER 5: BULLS

1 Diego Enríquez del Castillo, *Crónica del rey don Enrique el Quarto de este nombre*, ed. A. Sánchez Martín, Valladolid, Universidad de Valladolid, 1994, Chapter 116. Tarsicio de Azcona, *Isabel la Católica. Estudio crítico de su vida y su reinado*, Madrid, Biblioteca de Autores Cristianos, 1993, pp. 141–2. Luis Suárez Fernández, *Los Reyes Católicos*, Barcelona, Ariel, 2004, p. 54.

2 Luis Suárez Fernández, *Enrique IV de Castilla. La difamación como arma política*, Barcelona, Ariel, 2001, p. 405.

3 *Memorias de don Enrique IV de Castilla. Contiene la colección diplomática del mismo rey compuesta y ordenada por la Real Academia de la Historia*, ed. Duque de Berwick y de Alba, Fortanet, Madrid, 1913, p. 567. Alonso de Palencia, *Crónica de Enrique IV*, ed. A. Paz y Meliá, 4 vols, Madrid, Revista de Archivos, 1904–8, Década 2, Libro 10, Chapter 2. Fernando del Pulgar, *Claros varones de Castilla y Letras*, Madrid, Jerónimo Ortega, 1789, titulo XX. Miguel Ángel Ladero Quesada, *La España de los Reyes Católicos*, Madrid, Alianza, 2014, p. 255. Suárez, *Los Reyes Católicos*, pp. 52–4.

4 Suárez, *Los Reyes Católicos*, p. 53.

5 Jerónimo Zurita, *Anales de Aragón*, ed. Ángel Canellas López et al., Zaragoza, Institución Fernando el Católico, at http://ifc.dpz.es/publicaciones/ver/id/2448, p. 19. Joseph Pérez (ed.), *La inquisición española. Nuevas visiones, nuevos horizontes*, Madrid, Siglo XXI, 1980, pp. 36–8.

6 Castillo, *Crónica*, Chapter 117. Palencia, *Crónica de Enrique IV*, Década 2, Libro 1, Chapter 3. Alfredo Alvar Ezquerra, *Isabel la Católica*, Madrid, Temas de Hoy, 2002, p. 47. Suárez, *Enrique IV*, pp. 399, 407–8.

7 Castillo, *Crónica*, Chapter 117. Azcona, *Isabel la Católica*, p. 159. Suárez, *Enrique IV*, pp. 395, 400.

8 Azcona, *Isabel la Católica*, p. 137 (citing Archivo Municipal Jerez de la Frontera, *Actas Capitulares de 1468*, fols 128v–137). Juan Torres Fontes, 'Dos fechas de España en Murcia', *Anales de la Universidad de Murcia*, vol. 6, 1946, pp. 646–8. Juan Torres Fontes (ed.), *Estudio de la 'Crónica de Enrique IV' del Dr. Galíndez de Carvajal*, Murcia, Sucesores de Nogués, 1946, p. 832.

9 Azcona, *Isabel la Católica*, pp. 136–9. Antonio de la Torre y del Cerro, *Cuentas de Gonzalo de Baeza, tesorero de Isabel la Católica*, 2 vols, Madrid, Consejo Superior de Investigaciones Científicas, 1956, vol. 1, p. 160. Torres Fontes, 'Dos Fechas', pp. 641, 646.

10 Suárez, *Enrique IV*, pp. 395, 400, 407. Azcona, *Isabel la Católica*, pp. 140–1.

11 Palencia, *Crónica de Enrique IV*, Década 2, Libro 1, Chapter 4. *Colección diplomática*, pp. 562, 564. Suárez, *Enrique IV*, pp. 402, 404.

12 *Colección diplomática*, pp. 561–6. Suárez, *Enrique IV*, pp. 402–3. José-Luis Martín, *Enrique IV de Castilla. Rey de Navarra, Príncipe de Cataluña*, San Sebastián, Nerea, 2003, p. 72.

13 *Colección diplomática*, p. 562. Suárez, *Enrique IV*, p. 404.

CHAPTER 6: CHOOSING FERDINAND

1 *Memorias de don Enrique IV de Castilla. Contiene la colección diplomática del mismo rey compuesta y ordenada por la Real Academia de la Historia*, ed. Duque de Berwick y de Alba, Madrid, Fortanet, 1913, pp. 573–8. Tarsicio de Azcona, *Isabel la Católica. Estudio crítico de su vida y su reinado*, Madrid, Biblioteca de Autores Cristianos, 1993, p. 152.

2 *Colección diplomática*, pp. 573–8. Azcona, *Isabel la Católica*, p. 152.

3 *Colección diplomática*, p. 575.

4 Ibid. Luis Suárez Fernández, *Enrique IV de Castilla. La difamación como arma política*, Barcelona, Ariel, 2001, pp. 408–9.

5 *Colección diplomática*, p. 578.

6 Ibid., pp. 573–8.

7 Alonso de Palencia, *Crónica de Enrique IV*, ed. A. Paz y Meliá, 4 vols, Madrid, Revista de Archivos, 1904–8, Década 2, Libro 1, Chapter 5. *Colección diplomática*, pp. 573–8. Azcona, *Isabel la Católica*, p. 152. Miguel Ángel Ladero Quesada, *Isabel I de Castilla. Siete ensayos sobre la reina, su entorno y sus empresas*, Madrid, Dykinson, 2012, p. 106.

8   Palencia, *Crónica de Enrique IV*, Década 2, Libro 1, Chapter 7. Azcona, *Isabel la Católica*, p. 153. Suárez, *Enrique IV*, p. 443.

9   Jaime Vicens Vives, *Historia crítica de la vida y reinado de Fernando II de Aragón*, Zaragoza, Institución Fernando el Católico, 2007, pp. 199, 202. Azcona, *Isabel la Católica*, pp. 155, 161–2. Suárez, *Enrique IV*, pp. 437, 447.

10   Archivo General de Simancas, PTR, LEG, 49, Doc. 40. Valladolid, Diego Enríquez del Castillo, *Crónica del rey don Enrique el Quarto de este nombre*, ed. A. Sánchez Martín, Valladolid, Universidad de Valladolid, 1994, Chapter 127. Palencia, *Crónica de Enrique IV*, Década 2, Libro 1, Chapter 7. *Coleccion diplomática*, p. 619. Suárez, *Enrique IV*, pp. 419–28, 440–9. Azcona, *Isabel la Católica*, pp. 140, 167.

11   Palencia, *Crónica de Enrique IV*, Década 2, Libro 1, Chapter 7. Azcona, *Isabel la Católica*, p. 154. Vicens Vives, *Fernando II*, p. 247. Suárez, *Enrique IV*, pp. 249, 418.

12   Palencia, *Crónica de Enrique IV*, Década 3, Libro 2, Chapter 1. Castillo, *Crónica*, Chapters 128, 131. Suárez, *Enrique IV*, p. 431.

13   Azcona, *Isabel la Católica*, pp. 161–2. Diego Clemencín, *Elogio a la reina Isabel la Católica e ilustraciones sobre varios asuntos de su reinado*, vol. 6, Madrid, Memorias de la Real Academia de la Historia, 1821, p. 577. María Isabel del Val Valdivieso, 'Isabel, *Infanta* and Princess of Castile', in David A. Boruchoff (ed.), *Isabel la Católica, Queen of Castile: Critical Essays*, New York and Basingstoke, Palgrave Macmillan, 2003, p. 49.

14   Archivo General de Simancas, PTR, LEG, 12, DOC. 28. Luis Suárez Fernández, *La Conquista del trono*, Madrid, Rialp, 1989, pp. 232–3. Azcona, *Isabel la Católica*, pp. 165–6. Vicens Vives, *Fernando II*, pp. 247–9. Suárez, *Enrique IV*, p. 432.

15   Clemencín, *Elogio*, p. 577. Vicens Vives, *Fernando II*, pp. 247–9. Peggy K. Liss, *Isabel the Queen: Life and Times*, Philadelphia, University of Pennsylvania Press, 2004, p. 64.

16   Clemencín, *Elogio*, p. 577.

17   Palencia, *Crónica de Enrique IV*, Década 2, Libro 1, Chapters 8–9. *Colección diplomática*, doc. 168, p. 608. Castillo, *Crónica*, Chapter 142. Azcona, *Isabel la Católica*, pp. 160, 166–8. Clemencín, *Elogio*, p. 577.

18   Palencia, *Crónica de Enrique IV*, Década 2, Libro 1, Chapter 9; Libro 2, Chapter 3. Castillo, *Crónica*, Chapter 131. Azcona, *Isabel la Católica*, p. 170. Del Val, 'Isabel, *Infanta* and Princess of Castile', p. 50.

19   Palencia, *Crónica de Enrique IV*, Década 2, Libro 2, Chapter 3. Azcona, *Isabel la Católica*, p. 169.

20   Palencia, *Crónica de Enrique IV*, Década 2, Libro 2, Chapter 3. *Colección diplomática*, doc. 168, p. 608. Suárez, *Enrique IV*, p. 443.

CHAPTER 7: MARRYING FERDINAND

1   Alonso de Palencia, *Crónica de Enrique IV*, ed. A. Paz y Meliá, 4 vols, Madrid, Revista de Archivos, 1904–8, Década 2, Libro 2, Chapter 3. Luis Suárez Fernández, *Enrique IV de Castilla. La difamación como arma política*, Barcelona, Ariel, 2001, p. 446. Tarsicio de Azcona, *Isabel la Católica, Estudio crítico de su vida y su reinado*, Madrid, Biblioteca de Autores Cristianos, 1993, p. 173.

2   Palencia, *Crónica de Enrique IV*, Década 2, Libro 2, Chapter 3. Suárez, *Enrique IV*, p. 446.

3   Palencia, *Crónica de Enrique IV*, Década 2, Libro 2, Chapter 3. Antonio Paz y Meliá, *El cronista Alonso de Palencia. Su vida y sus obras. Sus décadas y las crónicas contemporáneas*, Madrid, Hispanic Society of America, 1914, pp. 24, 91. Azcona, *Isabel la Católica*, p. 173 (citing Jaime Vicens Vives, *Historia crítica de la vida y reinado de Fernando II de Aragón*, Zaragoza, Institución Fernando el Católico, 2007, p. 259).

4   Azcona, *Isabel la Católica*, p. 171. *Memorias de don Enrique IV de Castilla. Contiene la colección diplomática del mismo rey compuesta y ordenada por la Real Academia de la Historia*, ed. Duque de Berwick y de Alba, Fortanet, Madrid, 1913, p. 606. John Edwards, *Isabel la Católica. Poder y fama*, Madrid, Marcial Pons, 2004, p. 22.

5   *Colección diplomática*, p. 607.

6   Ibid., p. 609.

7   Remedios Ruiz Benavent, *Palacio de don Gutierre de Cardenas en Ocaña*, Madrid, Editorial Visión Libros, 2006, p. 25. *Colección diplomática*, p. 610. Palencia, *Crónica de Enrique IV*, Década 2, Libro 2, Chapter 3. Suárez, *Enrique IV*, p. 447. Felipe Fernández-Armesto, *Ferdinand and Isabella*, New York, Dorset Press, 1991, p. 41.

8   Palencia, *Crónica de Enrique IV*, Década 2, Libro 2, Chapters 3 and 5. Azcona, *Isabel la Católica*, p. 174 (citing Simancas, PR 11–45).

9   Palencia, *Crónica de Enrique IV*, Década 2, Libro 2, Chapter 5. Vicente Rodríguez Valencia and Luis Suárez Férnandez, *Matrimonio y derecho sucesorio de Isabel la Católica*, Valladolid, Facultad de Teología de Oña, 1960, pp. 50–1. Azcona, *Isabel la Católica*, pp. 176, 179, 181–3.

10   *Colección diplomática*, p. 636.

CHAPTER 8: REBEL PRINCESS

1   *Memorias de don Enrique IV de Castilla. Contiene la colección diplomática del mismo rey compuesta y ordenada por la Real Academia de la Historia,*

ed. Duque de Berwick y de Alba, Madrid, Fortanet, 1913, p. 635. Diego Clemencín, *Elogio a la reina Isabel la Católica e ilustraciones sobre varios asuntos de su reinado*, vol. 6, Madrid, Memorias de la Real Academia de la Historia, 1821, p. 590. Diego de Valera, *Memorial de diversas hazañas, crónica de Enrique IV*, in *Crónicas de los Reyes de Castilla*, vol. 3, Madrid, Rivadeneyra, 1878, p. 54.

2   Alonso de Palencia, *Crónica de Enrique IV*, ed. A. Paz y Meliá, 4 vols, Madrid, Revista de Archivos, 1904–8, Década 2, Libro 2, Chapter 5. Jaime Vicens Vives, *Historia crítica de la vida y reinado de Fernando II de Aragón*, Zaragoza, Institución Fernando el Católico, 2007, pp. 263–4.

3   Tarsicio de Azcona, *Isabel la Católica. Estudio crítico de su vida y su reinado*, Madrid, Biblioteca de Autores Cristianos, 1993, p. 188.

4   Jerónimo Zurita, *Anales de Aragón*, ed. Ángel Canellas López et al., Zaragoza, Institución Fernando el Católico, at http://ifc.dpz.es/publicaciones/ver/id/2448, Libro 18, Chapter 26.

5   Fernando del Pulgar, *Claros varones de Castilla y Letras*, Madrid, Jerónimo Ortega, 1789, titulo XX. Kayoko Takimoto, 'De secretario a cronista real. Fernando de Pulgar, oficial real de la corona de Castilla del siglo XV', *Hiyoshi Review of the Humanities*, no. 23, 2008, pp. 351–77, at http://koara.lib.keio.ac.jp/xoonips/modules/xoonips/detail.php?koara_id=AN10065043–20080531–0351. See also José Rodríguez Molina, 'Poder político de los arzobispos de Toledo en el siglo XV', in Antonio Luis Cortés Peña, José Luis Betrán Moya and Eliseo Serrano (eds), *Religión y poder en la Edad Moderna*, Granada, Universidad de Granada, 2005.

6   Azcona, *Isabel la Católica*, p. 174.

7   Zurita, *Anales*, Libro 18, Chapters 27 and 30.

8   Antonio Paz y Meliá, *El cronista Alonso de Palencia. Su vida y sus obras. Sus décadas y las crónicas contemporáneas*, Madrid, Hispanic Society of America, 1914, p. 108. Vicens Vives, *Fernando II*, p. 273.

9   Paz, *Cronista*, p. 101. Azcona, *Isabel la Católica*, p. 187.

10   Azcona, *Isabel la Católica*, p. 177.

11   Paz, *Cronista*, pp. 93–4. Zurita, *Anales*, Libro 18, Chapters 26 and 27. Azcona, *Isabel la Católica*, pp. 200–1.

12   Zurita, *Anales*, Libro 18, Chapter 30. Vicens Vives, *Fernando II*, pp. 272, 278. Luis Suárez Fernández, *Enrique IV de Castilla. La difamación como arma política*, Barcelona, Ariel, 2001, p. 469. Azcona, *Isabel la Católica*, pp. 188–90.

13   Zurita, *Anales*, Libro 18, Chapter 30.

14 Diego Enríquez del Castillo, *Crónica del rey don Enrique el Quarto de este nombre*, ed. A. Sánchez Martín, Valladolid, Universidad de Valladolid, 1994, Chapter 144. Azcona, *Isabel la Católica*, p. 188.

15 Paz, *Cronista*, p. 108. Zurita, *Anales*, Libro 18, Chapter 31. Vicens Vives, *Fernando I*, p. 272. Azcona, *Isabel la Católica*, p. 191.

16 Palencia, *Crónica de Enrique IV*, Década 2, Libro 3, Chapter 2. *Colección diplomática*, p. 618. Paz, *Cronista*, pp. 108–10. Álvaro Fernández de Córdova Miralles, *La Corte de Isabel I. Ritos y ceremonias de una reina (1474–1504)*, Madrid, Dykinson, 2002, pp. 76, 150 (citing Gracia Dei, *Blasón General*, p. 18). Azcona, *Isabel la Católica*, pp. 190–1.

17 Palencia, *Crónica de Enrique IV*, Década 2, Libro 3, Chapter 3.

18 Zurita, *Anales*, Libro 18, Chapters 30 and 31. Palencia, *Crónica de Enrique IV*, Década 2, Libro 3, Chapters 2–4. Paz, *Cronista*, pp. 105–6. See also José-Luis Martín, *Enrique IV de Castilla. Rey de Navarra, Príncipe de Cataluña*, San Sebastián, Nerea, 2003.

19 Zurita, *Anales*, Libro 18, Chapter 31.

20 Ibid., Chapters 30 and 31. Azcona, *Isabel la Católica*, p. 193. Suárez, *Enrique IV*, p. 439.

21 *Colección diplomática*, p. 619.

22 Ibid. Vicens Vives, *Fernando II*, p. 281.

23 *Colección diplomática*, p. 619. Azcona, *Isabel la Católica*, p. 192. Vicens Vives, *Fernando II*, p. 283. Suárez, *Enrique IV*, p. 467.

24 Vicens Vives, *Fernando II*, pp. 288–9. Azcona, *Isabel la Católica*, p. 197.

25 Vicens Vives, *Fernando II*, pp. 289–90. Azcona, *Isabel la Católica*, p. 198. Suárez, *Enrique IV*, p. 472.

26 *Colección diplomática*, pp. 630, 638. Vicens Vives, *Fernando II*, p. 243.

27 *Colección diplomática*, pp. 630–6.

28 Ibid., pp. 633, 636.

29 Ibid., p. 639. Azcona, *Isabel la Católica*, p. 195n. Suárez, *Enrique IV*, p. 476.

CHAPTER 9: THE BORGIAS

1 Alonso de Palencia, *Crónica de Enrique IV*, ed. A. Paz y Meliá, 4 vols, Madrid, Revista de Archivos, 1904–8, Década 2, Libro 5, Chapter 2. Jaime Vicens Vives, *Historia crítica de la vida y reinado de Fernando II de Aragón*, Zaragoza, Institución Fernando el Católico, 2007, pp. 288–9.

2 Ludwig Pastor, *Historia de los Papas desde fines de la Edad Media*, Barcelona, Gustavo Gili, 1910, vol. 4, pp. 192–3. Christopher Hibbert, *The Borgias*, London, Constable, 2011, pp. 26, 40.

3 Pastor, *Papas*, pp. 192–5. Hibbert, *Borgias*, p. 29.

4   Palencia, *Crónica de Enrique IV*, Década 1, Libro 7, Chapters 2, 3, 4 and 8.

5   Ibid., Chapter 4. Vicens Vives, *Fernando II*, p. 311. Tarsicio de Azcona, *Isabel la Católica. Estudio crítico de su vida y su reinado*, Madrid, Biblioteca de Autores Cristianos, 1993, pp. 203–4.

6   Azcona, *Isabel la Católica*, p. 206. Luis Suárez Fernández, *Enrique IV de Castilla. La difamación como arma política*, Barcelona, Ariel, 2001, p. 502.

7   *Memorias de don Enrique IV de Castilla. Contiene la colección diplomática del mismo rey compuesta y ordenada por la Real Academia de la Historia*, ed. Duque de Berwick y de Alba, Madrid, Fortanet, 1913, p. 635–6.

8   Diego Enríquez del Castillo, *Crónica del rey don Enrique el Quarto de este nombre*, ed. A. Sánchez Martín, Valladolid, Universidad de Valladolid, 1994, Chapter 150. Azcona, *Isabel la Católica*, pp. 197, 198.

9   Palencia, *Crónica de Enrique IV*, Década 2, Libro 6, Chapter 2. Antonio Antelo Iglesias, 'Alfonso de Palencia. Historiografía y humanismo en la Castilla del siglo xv', *Espacio, Tiempo y Forma*, vol. 3, 1990, pp. 21–40.

10   Palencia, *Crónica de Enrique IV*, Década 2, Libro 2, Chapter 9; Libro 6, Chapter 2.

11   Ibid., Libro 2, Chapter 9. Jerónimo Zurita, *Anales de Aragón*, ed. Ángel Canellas López et al., Zaragoza, Institución Fernando el Católico, at http://ifc.dpz.es/publicaciones/ver/id/2448, Libro XVIII, Chapter 39. Vicens Vives, *Fernando II*, p. 317.

12   Azcona, *Isabel la Católica*, pp. 198–200.

13   Ibid., p. 208.

14   Vicens Vives, *Fernando II*, pp. 311, 312 (citing Miralles, *Dietari*, 370), 319.

15   Zurita, *Anales*, Libro 18, Chapter 40. Vicens Vives, *Fernando II*, pp. 313–15, 318. Azcona, *Isabel la Católica*, pp. 206–8.

16   Suárez, *Enrique IV*, pp. 500–1.

17   Álvaro Fernández de Córdova Miralles, *La Corte de Isabel I. Ritos y ceremonias de una reina (1474–1504)*, Madrid, Dykinson, 2002, p. 314.

18   Palencia, *Crónica de Enrique IV*, Década 2, Libro 7, Chapter 6. Vicens Vives, *Fernando II*, pp. 320–2. Suárez, *Enrique IV*, p. 501.

19   Paz, *Cronista*, p. 124. Vicens Vives, *Fernando II*, pp. 323–7.

20   Palencia, *Crónica de Enrique IV*, Década 2, Libro 7, Chapter 6.

21   Ibid. Ramón Gonzálvez Ruíz, 'Las bulas de la catedral de Toledo y la imprenta incunable castellana', *Toletum: Boletín de la Real Academia de Bellas Artes y Ciencias Históricas de Toledo*, no. 18, 1985, pp. 66–9.

22   *Colección diplomática*, p. 689. Vicens Vives, *Fernando II*, pp. 333, 337, 566–9. Suárez, *Enrique IV*, p. 505.

23   Andreu Alfonsello in Vicens Vives, *Fernando II*, p. 346. Vicens Vives, *Fernando II*, p. 341 and n.

24 Palencia, *Crónica de Enrique IV*, Década 2, Libro 6, Chapter 2; Libro 8, Chapter 5. Fernando del Pulgar, *Letras*, ed. J. Domínguez Bordona, Madrid, Espasa-Calpe, 1958, pp. 127–34. Diego Clemencín, *Elogio a la reina Isabel la Católica e ilustraciones sobre varios asuntos de su reinado*, vol. 6, Madrid, Memorias de la Real Academia de la Historia, 1821, pp. 124–35.

25 Palencia, *Crónica de Enrique IV*, Década 2, Libro 8, Chapter 5.

26 Ibid.

27 Vicens Vives, *Fernando II*, pp. 346, 358–9. Theresa Earenfight (ed.), *Queenship and Political Power in Medieval and Early Modern Spain*, Burlington, VT, Ashgate, 2005, pp. 47–9.

28 Castillo, *Crónica*, Chapters 161 and 163. *Colección diplomática*, p. 693. Suárez, *Enrique IV*, pp. 508, 518, 501. Vicens Vives, *Fernando II*, pp. 346, 359–62. Azcona, *Isabel la Católica*, pp. 219, 224.

29 *Colección diplomática*, pp. 693–7. Vicens Vives, *Fernando II*, pp. 362–4. Azcona, *Isabel la Católica*, p. 221.

30 Suárez, *Enrique IV*, pp. 511, 517, 519. Azcona, *Isabel la Católica*, pp. 223–4.

31 Paz, *Cronista*, pp. 156–7. Azcona, *Isabel la Católica*, p. 225.

32 Castillo, *Crónica*, Chapter 164. Azcona, *Isabel la Católica*, pp. 226 (citing Astato Milano, *Sforzesco Carteggio*, p. 656), 227.

33 Paz, *Cronista*, pp. 170–1. Castillo, *Crónica*, Chapter 166. Vicens Vives, *Fernando II*, pp. 336, 341–2, 389. Azcona, *Isabel la Católica*, pp. 234.

34 Palencia, *Crónica de Enrique IV*, Década 2, Libro 10, Chapter 2.

35 Suárez, *Enrique IV*, p. 527.

36 Palencia, *Crónica de Enrique IV*, Década 3, Libro 1, Chapter 1. Paz, *Cronista*, p. 171. Suárez, *Enrique IV*, pp. 527–8. Azcona, *Isabel la Católica*, p. 236.

CHAPTER 10: QUEEN

1 Alonso de Palencia, *Crónica de Enrique IV*, ed. A. Paz y Meliá, 4 vols, Madrid, Revista de Archivos, 1904–8, Década 2, Libro 10, Chapter 10. Juan Torres Fontes, *Don Pedro Fajardo, adelantado mayor del reino de Murcia*, Madrid, Consejo Superior de Investigaciones Científicas, 1953, pp. 237–8. Tarsicio de Azcona, *Isabel la Católica. Estudio crítico de su vida y su reinado*, Madrid, Biblioteca de Autores Cristianos, 1993, p. 243n.

2 Palencia, *Crónica de Enrique IV*, Década 2, Libro 10, Chapter 10.

3 Ibid. Azcona, *Isabel la Católica*, p. 244 (citing *Acta de Proclamacion*, and Grau, 'Así fue coronada Isabel la Católica', pp. 20–39, and Peñalosa, 'Conmemoración del IV centenario de los Reyes Católicos', pp. 333–51).

4 Palencia, *Crónica de Enrique IV*, Década 2, Libro 10, Chapter 10. Azcona, *Isabel la Católica*, p. 244.

5　Jaime Vicens Vives, *Historia crítica de la vida y reinado de Fernando II de Aragón*, Zaragoza, Institución Fernando el Católico, 2007, pp. 391–2.

6　Azcona, *Isabel la Católica*, pp. 241–2.

7　Ibid.

8　Azcona, *Isabel la Católica*, p. 244n (citing Peñalosa, 'Conmemoración del IV centenario de los Reyes Catolicos'). Palencia, *Crónica de Enrique IV*, Década 2, Libro 10, Chapter 10.

9　Palencia, *Crónica de Enrique IV*, Década 2, Libro 10, Chapter 10. Vicens Vives, *Fernando II*, pp. 388–90, 394.

CHAPTER 11: AND KING!

1　Alonso de Palencia, *Crónica de Enrique IV*, ed. A. Paz y Meliá, 4 vols, Madrid, Revista de Archivos, 1904–8, Década 3, Libro 1, Chapter 1.

2　Ibid.

3　Ibid., prologo and Chapter 1. Fernando del Pulgar, *Crónica de los Señores Reyes Católicos Don Fernando y Doña Isabel de Castilla y de Aragón*, in *Crónicas de los Reyes de Castilla*, vol. 3, ed. Cayetano Rosell, Madrid, Rivadeneyra, 1878, Part II, Chapter 2, p. 255. Jerónimo Zurita, *Anales de Aragón*, ed. Ángel Canellas López et al., Zaragoza, Institución Fernando el Católico, at http://ifc.dpz.es/publicaciones/ver/id/2448, Libro 19, Chapter 16.

4　*Memorias de don Enrique IV de Castilla. Contiene la colección diplomática del mismo rey compuesta y ordenada por la Real Academia de la Historia*, ed. Duque de Berwick y de Alba, Madrid, Fortanet, 1913, p. 705. Palencia, *Crónica de Enrique IV*, Década 3, Libro 1, Chapter 1. Jaime Vicens Vives, *Historia crítica de la vida y reinado de Fernando II de Aragón*, Zaragoza, Institución Fernando el Católico, 2007, pp. 396, 397 (citing BAH, Col. Salazar, a-7, 160).

5　Palencia, *Crónica de Enrique IV*, Década 3, Libro 1, Chapter 1.

6　Blas Sánchez Dueñas, 'Una particular visión de la mujer en el siglo XV: Jardín de Nobles Doncellas de Fray Martín de Córdoba', *Boletín de la Real Academia de Córdoba*, no. 141, 2001, p. 298.

7　Palencia, *Crónica de Enrique IV*, Década 3, Libro 1, Chapter 2.

8　*Colección diplomática*, p. 706. Palencia, *Crónica de Enrique IV*, Década 3, Libro 1, Chapters 2–4. Diego de Colmenares, *Historia de la insigne ciudad de Segovia y compendio de las historias de Castilla*, Segovia, 1984, vol. 2, pp. 380–1.

9　Vicens Vives, *Fernando II*, p. 396nn. Tarsicio de Azcona, *Isabel la Católica. Estudio crítico de su vida y su reinado*, Madrid, Biblioteca de Autores Cristianos, 1993, p. 246n.

10 Colmenares, *Historia de Segovia*, vol. 2, Chapter 35, p. 382. Vicens Vives, *Fernando II*, pp. 397–8 (citing Anon, *Crónica incompleta de los Reyes Católicos*, ed. Julio Puyol, Madrid, 1934, p. 133). Azcona, *Isabel la Católica*, p. 247.

11 Azcona, *Isabel la Católica*, pp. 246–7.

12 Pulgar, *Crónica*, Part 2, Chapter 2. Diego Dormer, *Discursos varios*, Zaragoza, Herederos de Diego Dormer, 1683, pp. 295–302. Palencia, *Crónica de Enrique IV*, Década 3, Libro 1, Chapters 4–5. Vicens Vives, *Fernando II*, pp. 401–2. Luis Suárez Fernández, *La conquista del trono*, Madrid, Rialp, 1989, p. 232.

13 Pulgar, *Crónica*, Part 2, Chapter 2. Vicens Vives, *Fernando II*, pp. 399, 407.

14 Vicens Vives, *Fernando II*, pp. 405–6.

CHAPTER 12: CLOUDS OF WAR

1 Alonso de Palencia, *Crónica de Enrique IV*, ed. A. Paz y Meliá, 4 vols, Madrid, Revista de Archivos, 1904–8, Década 3, Libro 1, Chapter 4.

2 Joseph Pérez (ed.), *La inquisición española. Nuevas visiones, nuevos horizontes*, Madrid, Siglo XXI, 1980, pp. 36–8. Perry Anderson, *Lineages of the Absolutist State*, New York and London, Verso, 2013, p. 63. Jaime Vicens Vives, *Historia crítica de la vida y reinado de Fernando II de Aragón*, Zaragoza, Institución Fernando el Católico, 2007, pp. 389, 407. Tarsicio de Azcona, *Isabel la Católica. Estudio crítico de su vid y su reinado*, Madrid, Biblioteca de Autores Cristianos, 1993, p. 268.

3 Palencia, *Crónica de Enrique IV*, Década 3, Libro 1, Chapter 4. Vicens Vives, *Fernando II*, pp. 408–9.

4 Jerónimo Zurita, *Anales de Aragón*, ed. Ángel Canellas López et al., Zaragoza, Institución Fernando el Católico, at http://ifc.dpz.es/publicaciones/ver/id/2448, Libro 19, Chapter 22. Vicens Vives, *Fernando II*, p. 406.

5 Fernando del Pulgar, *Letras*, ed. J. Domínguez Bordona, Madrid, Espasa-Calpe, 1958, no. 7, p. 181. Antonio Paz y Meliá, *El cronista Alonso de Palencia. Su vida y sus obras. Sus décadas y las crónicas contemporáneas*, Madrid, Hispanic Society of America, 1914, p. 176. Azcona, *Isabel la Católica*, p. 271. Vicens Vives, *Fernando II*, pp. 346 (citing F. Fita, *Los Reys d'Aragó y la Seu de Girona des de l'any 1462 fins al 1482. Col.lecció d'actes capitulars*, Barcelona, 1873, 1, 51), 406–8.

6 *Memorias de don Enrique IV de Castilla. Contiene la colección diplomática del mismo rey compuesta y ordenada por la Real Academia de la Historia*, ed. Duque de Berwick y de Alba, Madrid, Fortanet, 1913, pp. 709–10. Azcona, *Isabel la Católica*, p. 265.

7 Zurita, *Anales*, Libro 19, Chapter 18. Vicens Vives, *Fernando II*, pp. 409–12.

8   Zurita, *Anales*, Libro 19, Chapters 22 and 24. Fernando del Pulgar, *Crónica de los Señores Reyes Católicos Don Fernando y Doña Isabel de Castilla y de Aragón*, in *Crónicas de los Reyes de Castilla*, vol. 3, ed. Cayetano Rosell, Madrid, Rivadeneyra, 1878, Part 2, Chapter 5. Vicens Vives, *Fernando II*, pp. 408–9, 413. Azcona, *Isabel la Católica*, pp. 259, 265.

9   Zurita, *Anales*, Libro 19, Chapter 18.

10 Palencia, *Crónica de Enrique IV*, Década 3, Libro 2, Chapter 5. Pulgar, *Letras*, no. 7, p. 183. Pulgar, *Crónica*, Part 2, Chapter 14. Zurita, *Anales*, Libro 19, Chapters 18–19. Vicens Vives, *Fernando II*, p. 409.

CHAPTER 13: UNDER ATTACK

1   Anon, *Cronicón de Valladolid*, Valladolid, Princiano, 1984, pp. 92–4. Anon, *Crónica incompleta de los Reyes Católicos*, ed. Julio Puyol, Madrid, 1934, pp. 165–9. Carmen Parrilla, 'Un cronista olvidado. Juan de Flores, autor de la Crónica incompleta de los Reyes Católicos', in Alan Deyermond and Ian Macpherson (eds), *The Age of the Catholic Monarchs, 1474–1516*, Special Issue of *Bulletin of Hispanic Studies*, Liverpool, Liverpool University Press, 1989, pp. 123–33.

2   Fernando del Pulgar, *Crónica de los Señores Reyes Católicos Don Fernando y Doña Isabel de Castilla y de Aragón*, in *Crónicas de los Reyes de Castilla*, vol. 3, ed. Cayetano Rosell, Madrid, Rivadeneyra, 1878, Part 2, Chapter 24. Pedro Flor, 'Un retrato desconocido de Isabel la Católica', *Archivo Español de Arte*, vol. 86, no. 341, January–March 2012, pp. 1–14. Navagero in Jorge de Einghen et al., *Viajes por España de Jorge de Einghen, del Barón Leon de Rosmithal de Blatine, de Francisco Guicciardini y de Andrés Navajero; traducido, anotados y con un introducción por Antonio María Fabié*, Madrid, Librería de los Bibliófilos, 1889, p. 322.

3   Pulgar, *Crónica*, Part 2, Chapter 24.

4   Ramón Gonzálvez Ruíz, 'Las bulas de la catedral de Toledo y la imprenta incunable castellana', *Toletum*: *Boletín de la Real Academia de Bellas Artes y Ciencias Históricas de Toledo*, no. 18, 1985, pp. 100–5. Alonso Fernández de Madrid, *Fray Hernando de Talavera*, Granada, Archivium, 1992, p. 112.

5   John Edwards, *Ferdinand and Isabella*, Profiles in Power series, Harlow, Pearson Longman, 2005, pp. 103–4.

6   See Cécile Codet, 'Hablar de la mujer o hablar a la mujer en tiempos de los Reyes Católicos. Visiones contrastadas en tres tratados de Hernando de Talavera', *La Clé des Langues*, no. 2, 2010–11, pp. 1–18.

7   Alonso de Palencia, *Crónica de Enrique IV*, ed. A. Paz y Meliá, 4 vols, Madrid, Revista de Archivos, 1904–8, Década 3, Libro 2, Chapter 3. Tarsicio de Azcona, *Isabel la Católica. Estudio crítico de su vida y su reinado*, Madrid, Biblioteca de Autores Cristianos, 1993, pp. 260–2.

8 Pulgar, *Crónica*, Part 2, Chapters 3 and 24. Vicente Rodríguez Valencia, *Isabel la Católica en la opinión de españoles y extranjeros. Siglos XV al XX*, vol. 1: *Siglos XV al XVI*, Valladolid, Instituto 'Isabel la Católica' de Historia Eclesiástica, 1970, p. 20. Giles Tremlett, *Catherine of Aragon*, London, Faber & Faber, 2010, p. 60.

9 Gonzalo Fernández de Oviedo, *Libro de la Cámara Real del Príncipe don Juan e offiçios de su casa e seruiçio ordinario*, ed. Santiago Fabregat Barrios, Valencia, Universitat de Valencia, 2002, p. 178. Álvaro Fernández de Córdova Miralles, *La Corte de Isabel I. Ritos y ceremonias de una reina (1474–1504)*, Madrid, Dykinson, 2002, pp. 139–42.

10 Antonio de la Torre y del Cerro, *Cuentas de Gonzalo de Baeza, tesorero de Isabel la Católica*, 2 vols, Madrid, Consejo Superior de Investigaciones Científicas, 1956, vol. 2, pp. 50–2. Oviedo, *Cámara*, pp. 126, 129. Bethany Aram, *Juana the Mad: Sovereignty and Dynasty in Renaissance Europe*, Baltimore, Johns Hopkins University Press, 2005, p. 26. Córdova, *La Corte*, pp. 140, 411. Azcona, *Isabel la Católica*, p. 269.

11 *Crónica incompleta*, pp. 166, 168. *Cronicón de Valladolid*, pp. 92–4. Peggy K. Liss, *Isabel the Queen: Life and Times*, Philadelphia, University of Pennsylvania Press, 2004, p. 107. See also Georgina Olivetto, 'Un testimonio de la crónica de Enrique IV atribuida por Nicolás Antonio a Fernando del Pulgar', *Cuadernos de Historia de España*, vol. 82, 2008, pp. 55–98.

12 Palencia, *Crónica de Enrique IV*, Década 3, Libro 2, Chapters 2 and 8.

13 Ibid., Chapter 3. *Crónica incompleta*, p. 168. *Cronicón de Valladolid*, pp. 92–4. Navagero in Einghen, *Viajes*, p. 322. Córdova, *La Corte*, p. 333.

14 *Crónica incompleta*, p. 166.

15 Ibid. *Cronicón de Valladolid*, pp. 92–4. R. O. Jones, 'Isabel la Católica y el amor cortés', *Revista de literatura*, vol. 21, no. 41–2, 1962, pp. 55–64.

16 Palencia, *Crónica de Enrique IV*, Década 3, Libro 2, Chapter 1. Pulgar, *Crónica*, Part 2, Chapters 9–10. Jaime Vicens Vives, *Historia crítica de la vida y reinado de Fernando II de Aragón*, Zaragoza, Institución Fernando el Católico, 2007, pp. 414–16.

17 Antonio Paz y Meliá, *El cronista Alonso de Palencia. Su vida y sus obras. Sus décadas y las crónicas contemporáneas*, Madrid, Hispanic Society of America, 1914, doc. 82. Jerónimo Zurita, *Anales de Aragón*, ed. Ángel Canellas López et al., Zaragoza, Institución Fernando el Católico, at http://ifc.dpz.es/publicaciones/ver/id/2448, Libro 19, Chapter 24. Azcona, *Isabel la Católica*, p. 272. Vicens Vives, *Fernando II*, p. 415.

18 Zurita, *Anales*, Libro 19, Chapter 24. Pulgar, *Crónica*, Part 2, Chapter 13.

19 Pulgar, *Crónica*, Part 2, Chapters 10, 13 and 15. Palencia, *Crónica de Enrique IV*, Década 3, Libro 2, Chapter 4. Azcona, *Isabel la Católica*, pp. 272–4.

20 *Crónica incompleta*, p. 210n. Diego Dormer, *Discursos varios*, Zaragoza, Herederos de Diego Dormer, 1683, pp. 302–5. Azcona, *Isabel la Católica*, pp. 251, 274. Vicens Vives, *Fernando II*, p. 418. Liss, *Isabel*, pp. 204–5.

21 Azcona, *Isabel la Católica*, p. 266.

22 Tarsicio de Azcona, 'El Príncipe don Juan, heredero de los Reyes Católicos, en el V centenario de su nacimiento (1478–1497)', *Cuadernos de Investigación Histórica*, no. 7, 1983, p. 240.

23 Palencia, *Crónica de Enrique IV*, Década 3, Libro 2, Chapter 7. Fernando Villaseñor Sebastián, *La corte literaria de Juan de Zúñiga y Pimentel (Plasencia, 1459–1504 Guadalupe)*, Anales de Historia del Arte 2013, Vol. 23, Núm. Especial (II), pp. 581–594. Azcona, *Isabel la Católica*, pp. 267, 273.

24 Zurita, *Anales*, Libro 19, Chapter 27. Azcona, *Isabel la Católica*, pp. 267–9.

25 Paz, *Cronista*, p. 181. Palencia, *Crónica de Enrique IV*, Década 3, Libro 2, Chapters 3 and 10. Vicens Vives, *Fernando II*, pp. 411, 415.

26 Vicens Vives, *Fernando II*, pp. 418–19.

27 Ibid., pp. 419–21. El Duque de Berwick y de Alba, *Noticias históricas y genealógicas de los Estados de Montijo y Teba, según los documentos se sus archivos*, Madrid, Imprenta Alemana, 1915, pp. 232–4. Azcona, *Isabel la Católica*, pp. 276–7.

28 Azcona, 'El Príncipe don Juan', p. 241. Vicens Vives, *Fernando II*, p. 422.

29 *Crónica incompleta*, p. 211. Vicens Vives, *Fernando II*, p. 422.

CHAPTER 14: THOUGH I AM JUST A WOMAN

1 Juan Torres Fontes, *Don Pedro Fajardo, adelantado mayor del reino de Murcia*, Madrid, Consejo Superior de Investigaciones Científicas, 1953, pp. 132, 267. Jaime Vicens Vives, *Historia crítica de la vida y reinado de Fernando II de Aragón*, Zaragoza, Institución Fernando el Católico, 2007, p. 418. Tarsicio de Azcona, *Isabel la Católica. Estudio crítico de su vida y su reinado*, Madrid, Biblioteca de Autores Cristianos, 1993, pp. 273–4.

2 Anon, *Crónica incompleta de los Reyes Católicos*, ed. Julio Puyol, Madrid, 1934, p. 208.

3 Ibid., pp. 208–22. Vicens Vives, *Fernando II*, pp. 418, 423. Fernando del Pulgar, *Crónica de los Señores Reyes Católicos Don Fernando y Doña Isabel de Castilla y de Aragón*, in *Crónicas de los Reyes de Castilla*, vol. 3, ed. Cayetano Rosell, Madrid, Rivadeneyra, 1878, Part 2, Chapters 23 and 30. Azcona, *Isabel la Católica*, p. 275.

4 *Crónica incompleta*, pp. 212, 220, 223–4, 226. Pulgar, *Crónica*, Part 2, Chapter 21.

5 *Crónica incompleta*, pp. 225, 227.

6 Alonso de Palencia, *Crónica de Enrique IV*, ed. A. Paz y Meliá, 4 vols, Madrid, Revista de Archivos, 1904–8, Década 3, Libro 2, Chapters 3, 5, 6 and 10. *Crónica incompleta*, pp. 222–3, 232–7. Vicens Vives, *Fernando II*, pp. 417, 425.

7 *Crónica incompleta*, pp. 238–40.

8 Ibid., pp. 239–40.

9 Ibid., pp. 239–42. Peggy K. Liss, *Isabel the Queen: Life and Times*, Philadelphia, University of Pennsylvania Press, 2004, pp. 203, 297.

10 *Crónica incompleta*, pp. 243–4.

11 Ibid., p. 473. Vicens Vives, *Fernando II*, p. 426.

CHAPTER 15: THE TURNING POINT

1 Tarsicio de Azcona, *Isabel la Católica. Estudio crítico de su vida y su reinado*, Madrid, Biblioteca de Autores Cristianos, 1993, p. 281. Jaime Vicens Vives, *Historia crítica de la vida y reinado de Fernando II de Aragón*, Zaragoza, Institución Fernando el Católico, 2007, p. 435.

2 Navagero in Jorge de Einghen et al., *Viajes por España de Jorge de Einghen, del Barón Leon de Rosmithal de Blatine, de Francisco Guicciardini y de Andrés Navajero; traducido, anotados y con un introducción por Antonio María Fabié*, Madrid, Librería de los Bibliófilos, 1889, p. 331.

3 Fernando del Pulgar, *Crónica de los Señores Reyes Católicos Don Fernando y Doña Isabel de Castilla y de Aragón*, in *Crónicas de los Reyes de Castilla*, vol. 3, ed. Cayetano Rosell, Madrid, Rivadeneyra, 1878, Part 2, Chapters 25 and 30. Vicens Vives, *Fernando II*, pp. 429–32. Azcona, *Isabel la Católica*, p. 278.

4 Vicens Vives, *Fernando II*, p. 432. Pulgar, *Crónica*, Part 2, Chapters 30–1. Azcona, *Isabel la Católica*, p. 279.

5 Pulgar, *Crónica*, Part 2, Chapters 22 and 33. Vicens Vives, *Fernando II*, pp. 427–8.

6 Pulgar, *Crónica*, Part 2, Chapter 28.

7 Ibid., Chapter 34. Vicens Vives, *Fernando II*, p. 433.

8 Pulgar, *Crónica*, Part 2, Chapter 30. Azcona, *Isabel la Católica*, p. 281. Vicens Vives, *Fernando II*, p. 434.

9 Vicens Vives, *Fernando II*, p. 427.

10 Antonio Paz y Meliá, *El cronista Alonso de Palencia. Su vida y sus obras. Sus décadas y las crónicas contemporáneas*, Madrid, Hispanic Society of America, 1914, p. 208.

11 Pulgar, *Crónica*, Part 2, Chapter 36.

12 Ibid. Azcona, *Isabel la Católica*, p. 282.

13 Pulgar, *Crónica*, Part 2, Chapter 26. Azcona, *Isabel la Católica*, p. 283.

14 *Memorias de don Enrique IV de Castilla. Contiene la colección diplomática del mismo rey compuesta y ordenada por la Real Academia de la Historia*, ed. Duque de Berwick y de Alba, Madrid, Fortanet, 1913, p. 713. Alonso de Palencia, *Crónica de Enrique IV*, ed. A. Paz y Meliá, 4 vols, Madrid, Revista de Archivos, 1904–8, Década 3, Libro 25, Chapters 8–9. Pulgar, *Crónica*, Part 2, Chapter 65. Vicens Vives, *Fernando II*, p. 438–41.

15 *Colección diplomática*, p. 714. Palencia, *Crónica de Enrique IV*, Década 3, Libro 25, Chapters 8–9. Pulgar, *Crónica*, Part 2, Chapter 65.

16 Azcona, *Isabel la Católica*, pp. 284–5. Vicens Vives, *Fernando II*, p. 441.

17 Pulgar, *Crónica*, Part 2, Chapter 37. Vicens Vives, *Fernando II*, pp. 452–4. Modesto Sarasola, *Vizcaya y los Reyes Católicos*, Madrid, Consejo Superior de Investigaciones Científicas, Patronato Marcelino Menéndez Pelayo, 1950, p. 106.

CHAPTER 16: DEGRADING THE GRANDEES

1 Antonio Paz y Meliá, *El cronista Alonso de Palencia. Su vida y sus obras. Sus décadas y las crónicas contemporáneas*, Madrid, Hispanic Society of America, 1914, pp. 220, 227–9. Fernando del Pulgar, *Crónica de los Señores Reyes Católicos Don Fernando y Doña Isabel de Castilla y de Aragón*, in *Crónicas de los Reyes de Castilla*, vol. 3, ed. Cayetano Rosell, Madrid, Rivadeneyra, 1878, Part 2, Chapter 20. Tarsicio de Azcona, *Isabel la Católica. Estudio crítico de su vida y su reinado*, Madrid, Biblioteca de Autores Cristianos, 1993, pp. 305–6. Jaime Vicens Vives, *Historia crítica de la vida y reinado de Fernando II de Aragón*, Zaragoza, Institución Fernando el Católico, 2007, p. 446.

2 Pulgar, *Crónica*, Part 2, Chapters 56 and 58. Alonso de Palencia, *Crónica de Enrique IV*, ed. A. Paz y Meliá, 4 vols, Madrid, Revista de Archivos, 1904–8, Década 3, Libro 26, Chapters 2 and 10.

3 Pulgar, *Crónica*, Part 2, Chapter 58. Azcona, *Isabel la Católica*, pp. 304–5.

4 Guicciardini in Jorge de Einghen et al., *Viajes por España de Jorge de Einghen, del Barón Leon de Rosmithal de Blatine, de Francisco Guicciardini y de Andrés Navajero; traducido, anotados y con un introducción por Antonio María Fabié*, Madrid, Librería de los Bibliófilos, 1889, p. 201.

5 Jerónimo Zurita, *Anales de Aragón*, ed. Ángel Canellas López et al., Zaragoza, Institución Fernando el Católico, at http://ifc.dpz.es/publicaciones/ver/id/2448, Libro 19, Chapter 54. Juan Torres Fontes, *Don Pedro Fajardo, adelantado mayor del reino de Murcia*, Madrid, Consejo Superior de Investigaciones Científicas, 1953, doc. 41, p. 280. Azcona, *Isabel la Católica*, pp. 306–7.

6 Antonio de la Torre y del Cerro and Luis Suárez Fernández (eds), *Documentos referentes a las relaciones con Portugal durante el reinado de los Reyes Católicos*, Valladolid, Consejo Superior de Investigaciones Científicas, 1960–3, vol. 1, doc. 34, p. 100. Torres Fontes, *Don Pedro Fajardo*, p. 286. Azcona, *Isabel la Católica*, pp. 307, 319 (citing Gual, *La Forja*, pp. 263–8).

7 Zurita *Anales*, Libro 19, Chapter 54. Azcona, *Isabel la Católica*, p. 307.

8 Zurita, *Anales*, Libro 19, Chapters 58–9. Azcona, *Isabel la Católica*, pp. 307–8, 317.

9 Palencia, *Crónica de Enrique IV*, Década 3, Libro 27, Chapter 9. Pulgar, *Crónicas*, Part 2, Chapter 63, pp. 315–18.

10 Zurita, *Anales*, Libro 19, Chapter 48; Libro 20, Chapter 1. Azcona, *Isabel la Católica*, pp. 315–17.

11 Bachiller Palma, *Divina retribución sobre la caída de España en tiempo del noble rey Don Juan el Primero*, Madrid, Bibliófilos Españoles, 1879, p. 62. Azcona, *Isabel la Católica*, pp. 317–18. Simon Barton, *A History of Spain*, London, Palgrave Macmillan, 2009, p. 17. Hieronymus Münzer, *Viaje por España y Portugal (1494–1495)*, Madrid, Polifemo, 1991, pp. 247–9, 259. Miguel Ángel Ladero Quesada, *La España de los Reyes Católicos*, Madrid, Alianza, 2014, p. 25. Miguel Sobrino, *Catedrales. Las biografías desconocidas de los Grandes Templos de España*, Madrid, La Esfera de los Libros, 2009, p. 865.

12 Palma, *Divina retribución*, p. 63.

13 Ibid., pp. 63–5. Münzer, *Viaje*, p. 247.

14 Ana Isabel Carrasco Manchado, 'Discurso político propaganda en la corte de los Reyes Católicos (1474–1482)', doctoral thesis, Universidad Complutense de Madrid, 2000, at http://eprints.ucm.es/2525/, pp. 398, 949, 962–5, 1015. Richard L. Kagan, *Clio and the Crown: The Politics of History in Medieval and Early Modern Spain*, Baltimore, Johns Hopkins University Press, 2009 (Kindle edn), loc. 1054.

15 Kagan, *Clio*, locs 928, 1129.

16 Ibid., locs 312, 1045, 1089, 1116, 1185.

17 Ibid., loc. 1142. Pulgar, *Crónica*, Part 2, Chapter LXI. David A. Boruchoff, 'Historiography with License: Isabel, the Catholic Monarch and the Kingdom of God', in David A. Boruchoff (ed.), *Isabel la Católica, Queen of Castile: Critical Essays*, New York and Basingstoke, Palgrave Macmillan, 2003, p. 259.

18 Eloy Benito Ruano, *Toledo en el siglo XV. Vida política*, Madrid, Consejo Superior de Investigaciones Científicas, Escuela de Estudios Medievales, 1961, pp. 153–5, 293. Azcona, *Isabel la Católica*, p. 318. Ladero Quesada, *España*, p. 25.

19   Zurita, *Anales*, Libro 19, Chapter 54. Pulgar, *Crónica*, Part 2, Chapter 65.
     Palencia, *Crónica de Enrique IV*, Década 3, Libro 7, Chapter 27. Azcona,
     Isabel la Católica, p. 321. Ladero Quesada, *España*, p. 20.

20   Palencia, *Crónica de Enrique IV*, Década 3, Libro 27, Chapter 7. Azcona,
     Isabel la Católica, pp. 320–1. Vicens Vives, *Fernando II*, p. 485. Ladero
     Quesada, *España*, p. 25.

CHAPTER 17: ROUGH JUSTICE

1   Fernando del Pulgar, *Crónica de los Señores Reyes Católicos Don Fernando y
     Doña Isabel de Castilla y de Aragón*, in *Crónicas de los Reyes de Castilla*, vol. 3,
     ed. Cayetano Rosell, Madrid, Rivadeneyra, 1878, Part 2, Chapter 70.

2   Ibid.

3   Marvin Lunenfeld, *The Council of Santa Hermandad: A Study of the
     Pacification Forces of Ferdinand and Isabela*, Coral Gables, FL, University
     of Miami Press, 1970, pp. 29, 31, 35, 38–9. Tarsicio de Azcona, *Isabel
     la Católica. Estudio crítico de su vida y su reinado*, Madrid, Biblioteca de
     Autores Cristianos, 1993, pp. 304–5. Peggy K. Liss, *Isabel the Queen: Life
     and Times*, Philadelphia, University of Pennsylvania Press, 2004, p. 141.
     Popplau in Javier Liske, *Viajes de extranjeros por España y Portugal en los
     siglos XV, XVI y XVII*, Madrid, Medina, 1878.

4   Alonso de Palencia, *Crónica de Enrique IV*, ed. A. Paz y Meliá, 4 vols,
     Madrid, Revista de Archivos, 1904–8, Década 3, Libro 28, Chapter 6.
     Lunenfeld, *Hermandad*, pp. 10, 36, 38. Miguel Ángel Ladero Quesada, *La
     Hermandad de Castilla. Cuentas y memoriales, 1480–1498*, Madrid, Real
     Academia de la Historia, 2005, p. 20.

5   Diego Ortiz de Zúñiga, *Anales eclesiásticos y seculares de la muy noble y muy
     leal ciudad de Sevilla*, vol. 3, Madrid, Imprenta Real, 1796, p. 86.

6   Lalaing in Emilo García Rodríguez, 'Toledo y sus visitantes extranjeros
     hasta 1561', *Toletum: Boletín de la Real Academia de Bellas Artes y
     Ciencias Históricas de Toledo*, no. 1, 1955, p. 21. Lunenfeld, *Hermandad*,
     pp. 34, 39, 99.

7   Hieronymus Münzer, *Viaje por España y Portugal (1494–1495)*, Madrid,
     Polifemo, 1991, pp. 83, 279.

8   Fidel Fita, *Historia hebrea. Documentos y monumentos*, Boletín de la Real
     Academia de la Historia, tomo 16, Madrid, 1890, pp. 432–56. Pulgar,
     Crónica, Part 2, p. 70. Jaime Vicens Vives, *Historia crítica de la vida y
     reinado de Fernando II de Aragón*, Zaragoza, Institución Fernando el
     Católico, 2007, p. 486. Münzer, *Viaje*, p. 155. Lunenfeld, *Hermandad*,
     p. 38. Miguel Sobrino, *Catedrales. Las biografías desconocidas de los
     Grandes Templos de España*, Madrid, La Esfera de los Libros, 2009, p. 607.

9   Palencia, *Crónica de Enrique IV*, Década 3, Libro 29, Chapter 8. Navagero
     in Jorge de Einghen et al., *Viajes por España de Jorge de Einghen, del Barón
     Leon de Rosmithal de Blatine, de Francisco Guicciardini y de Andrés Navajero;
     traducido, anotados y con un introducción por Antonio María Fabié*, Madrid,
     Librería de los Bibliófilos, 1889, p. 265.

10   Münzer, *Viaje*, pp. 155, 157.

11   Palencia, *Crónica de Enrique IV*, Década 3, Libro 29, Chapter 7. Antonio
     Antelo Iglesias, 'Alfonso de Palencia. Historiografía y humanismo en la
     Castilla del siglo xv', *Espacio, Tiempo y Forma*, vol. 3, 1990, p. 25.

12   Münzer, *Viaje*, p. 157.

13   Palencia, *Crónica de Enrique IV*, Década 3, Libro 29, Chapter 9. Pulgar,
     Crónica, Part 2, Chapter 70.

14   Pulgar, *Crónica*, Part 2, Chapter 24.

15   Palencia, *Crónica de Enrique IV*, Década 3, Libro 29, Chapter 9. Marineo
     Sículo in Einghen, *Viajes*, p. 547.

16   Palencia, *Crónica de Enrique IV*, Década 3, Libro 29, Chapter 9. Azcona,
     Isabel la Católica, pp. 322–3. Vicens Vives, *Fernando II*, pp. 486, 489.

17   Palencia, *Crónica de Enrique IV*, Década 3, Libro 29, Chapters 9 and 30.
     Vicens Vives, *Fernando II*, p. 488.

18   Palencia, *Crónica de Enrique IV*, Década 3, Libro 30, Chapters 3–4. Vicens
     Vives, *Fernando II*, p. 490. Lunenfeld, *Hermandad*, p. 39.

19   Alonso de Palencia, *Cuarta década de Alonso de Palencia*, ed. J. López de
     Toro, Madrid, Real Academia de la Historia, 1974, vol. 2, Década 4, Libro
     32, Chapter 3. Azcona, *Isabel la Católica*, p. 332. Vicens Vives, *Fernando
     II*, p. 490. Miguel Ángel Ladero Quesada, *La España de los Reyes Católicos*,
     Madrid, Alianza, 2014, p. 25. Luis Suárez Fernández, *Enrique IV de Castilla.
     La difamación como arma política*, Barcelona, Ariel, 2001, p. 510.

20   Palencia, *Cuarta década*, Década 4, Libro 32, Chapter 6. Azcona, *Isabel la
     Católica*, p. 323.

21   R. O. Jones, 'Isabel la Católica y el amor cortés', *Revista de literatura*, vol.
     21, no. 41–2, 1962, pp. 55–64.

22   Palencia, *Cuarta década*, Década 4, Libro 32, Chapter 1. Fita, *Historia hebrea*,
     pp. 432–56. Luis Suárez Fernández, *Documentos acerca de la expulsión de los
     judíos*, Valladolid, Aldecoa, 1964, p. 14. Antonio de la Torre, 'Un médico
     de los Reyes Católicos', *Hispania*, no. 14, 1944, pp. 69–72. Azcona, *Isabel
     la Católica*, p. 329.

CHAPTER 18: ADIÓS BELTRANEJA

1   Andrés Bernáldez, *Historia de los Reyes Católicos don Fernando y doña Isabel*,
     in *Crónicas de los Reyes de Castilla*, ed. Cayetano Rosell, vol. 70, Madrid,

Biblioteca de Autores Españoles, 1878, Chapter 32. Tarsicio de Azcona, *Isabel la Católica. Estudio crítico de su vida y su reinado*, Madrid, Biblioteca de Autores Cristianos, 1993, p. 329. Álvaro Fernández de Córdova Miralles, *La Corte de Isabel I. Ritos y ceremonias de una reina (1474–1504)*, Madrid, Dykinson, 2002, p. 167.

2 Pulgar, *Claros Varones de Castilla y Letras*, Madrid, Jerónimo Ortega, 1789, Carta 9, pp. 198–9. Alonso de Palencia, *Cuarta década de Alonso de Palencia*, ed. J. López de Toro, Madrid, Real Academia de la Historia, 1974, vol. 2, Década 4, Libro 32, Chapter 1. Azcona, *Isabel la Católica*, p. 329. Tarsicio de Azcona, 'El Príncipe don Juan, heredero de los Reyes Católicos, en el V centenario de su nacimiento (1478–1497)', *Cuadernos de Investigación Histórica*, no. 7, 1983, pp. 220–1.

3 Azcona, *Isabel la Católica*, p. 330. Jaime Vicens Vives, *Historia crítica de la vida y reinado de Fernando II de Aragón*, Zaragoza, Institución Fernando el Católico, 2007, p. 489.

4 Bachiller Palma, *Divina retribución sobre la caída de España en tiempo del noble rey Don Juan el Primero*, Madrid, Bibliófilos Españoles, 1879, p. 72.

5 Bernáldez, *Historia de los Reyes Católicos*, Chapters 33–4. Azcona, *Isabel la Católica*, p. 331. Azcona, 'El Príncipe don Juan', pp. 240–1. Ángel Rodríguez Sánchez, 'La muerte del Príncipe de Asturias, Señor de Salamanca', *Revista de Estudios Extremeños*, vol. 57, no. 1, 2001, 23–48.

6 Azcona, *Isabel la Católica*, p. 333. Rodríguez Sánchez, 'La muerte', pp. 41–3.

7 Hieronymus Münzer, *Viaje por España y Portugal (1494–1495)*, Madrid, Polifemo, 1991, pp. 223, 227, 237. Azcona, *Isabel la Católica*, pp. 331–2.

8 Antonio de la Torre y del Cerro and Luis Suárez Fernández, *Documentos referentes a las relaciones con Portugal durante el reinado de los Reyes Católicos*, 3 vols, Valladolid, Consejo Superior de Investigaciones Científicas, 1960–3, vol. 1, p. 147; vol. 2, pp. 297–300. Azcona, *Isabel la Católica*, pp. 324–5. Vicens Vives, *Fernando II*, pp. 502–3.

9 Vicente Álvarez Palenzuela, *'Paz con Portugal'. La guerra civil castellana y el enfrentamiento con Portugal (1475–1479)*, Alicante, Biblioteca Virtual Miguel de Cervantes (consulted 27 November 2014).

10 Fernando del Pulgar, *Crónica de los Señores Reyes Católicos Don Fernando y Doña Isabel de Castilla y de Aragón*, in *Crónicas de los Reyes de Castilla*, vol. 3, ed. Cayetano Rosell, Madrid, Rivadeneyra, 1878, Part 2, Chapter 85.

11 Ibid., Chapter 89. Carlos G. Villacampa, *Grandezas de Guadalupe. Estudios sobre la historia y las bellas artes del gran monasterio extremeño*, Madrid, C. Vallinas, 1924, p. 45. Azcona, *Isabel la Católica*, p. 334.

12 De la Torre and Suárez, *Documentos Portugal*, vol. 1, p. 179n.

13 Ibid., p. 180.

14 See Álvarez Palenzuela, *La guerra civil castellana*.

15 De la Torre and Suárez, *Documentos Portugal*, vol. 1, pp. 179–85, 227, 239, 241.

16 Azcona, *Isabel la Católica*, pp. 334, 339–40.

17 De la Torre and Suárez, *Documentos Portugal*, vol. 1, pp. 184–5.

18 Pulgar, *Crónica*, Part 2, Chapter 90.

19 De la Torre and Suárez, *Documentos Portugal*, vol. 1, pp. 184–5, 238. Azcona, *Isabel la Católica*, pp. 340, 345. Álvaro Fernández de Córdova Miralles, *Alejandro VI y los Reyes Católicos. Relaciones político-eclesiásticas (1492–1503)*, Rome, Edizioni Università della Santa Croce, 2005, p. 465. See also Álvarez Palenzuela, *La guerra civil castellana*.

20 De la Torre and Suárez, *Documentos Portugal*, vol. 1, p. 383.

21 Ibid., pp. 218, 227, 239, 241. Azcona, *Isabel la Católica*, pp. 340–1, 346–8. Vicens Vives, *Fernando II*, p. 504.

22 Córdova, *La Corte*, p. 373. Antonio Rumeu de Armas, *Itinerario de los Reyes Católicos, 1474–1516*, Madrid, Instituto Jerónimo Zurita, Biblioteca Reyes Católicos, 1974, pp. 75–85.

23 Córdova, *La Corte*, p. 353.

24 Lu Ann Homza, *The Spanish Inquisition 1478–1614*, Indianapolis, Hackett, 2006, p. 75.

25 Córdova, *La Corte*, p. 139.

26 Ibid., pp. 63–5, 133–9, 369–70.

27 Bernáldez, *Historia de los Reyes Católicos*, Chapter 162. De la Torre and Suárez, *Documentos Portugal*, vol. 1, pp. 284–327, 361–4. Azcona, *Isabel la Católica*, pp. 341–5.

28 Pulgar, *Crónica*, Part 2, Chapter 92. De la Torre and Suárez, *Documentos Portugal*, vol. 1, p. 218. Azcona, *Isabel la Católica*, pp. 345–8.

29 Münzer, *Viaje*, p. 44. Navagero in Jorge de Einghen et al., *Viajes por España de Jorge de Einghen, del Barón Leon de Rosmithal de Blatine, de Francisco Guicciardini y de Andrés Navajero; traducido, anotados y con un introducción por Antonio María Fabié*, Madrid, Librería de los Bibliófilos, 1889, p. 240.

30 Miguel Ángel Ladero Quesada, *La España de los Reyes Catolicos*, Madrid, Alianza, 2014, p. 114. Angus MacKay, *Spain in the Middle Ages: From Frontier to Empire, 1000–1500*, London, Macmillan, 1977, pp. 180–1. Azcona, *Isabel la Católica*, p. 635.

31 See Popplau in Javier Liske, *Viajes de extranjeros por España y Portugal en los siglos XV, XVI y XVII*, Madrid, Medina, 1878.

32 Jerónimo Zurita, *Anales de Aragón*, ed. Ángel Canellas López et al., Zaragoza, Institución Fernando el Católico, at http://ifc.dpz.es/publicaciones/ver/id/2448, Libro 19, Chapter 41. Alfredo Chamorro Esteban, 'Ceremonial monárquico y rituales cívicos. Las visitas reales a

Barcelona desde el siglo XV hasta el XVII', doctoral thesis, University of Barcelona, 2013, pp. 179, 188, 214–18. Azcona, *Isabel la Católica*, p. 635.

33 Chamorro Esteban, 'Ceremonial monárquico y rituales cívicos', pp. 22, 27, 128, 234. Theresa Earenfight (ed.), *Queenship and Political Power in Medieval and Early Modern Spain*, Burlington, VT, Ashgate, 2005, pp. 48–9.

34 Azcona, *Isabel la Católica*, p. 636 (citing Madurell, *Legaciones*, p. 207).

CHAPTER 19: THE INQUISITION – POPULISM AND PURITY

1 Joaquín Guichot, *Historia de la Ciudad de Sevilla*, vol. 1, Seville, Imp. Gironés y Orduña, 1875, vol. 1, pp. 183–4. Norman Roth, in Norman Roth (ed.), *Medieval Jewish Civilization: An Encyclopedia*, New York, Routledge, 2003, p. 226. Fernando del Pulgar, *Crónica de los Señores Reyes Católicos Don Fernando y Doña Isabel de Castilla y de Aragón*, in *Crónicas de los Reyes de Castilla*, vol. 3, ed. Cayetano Rosell, Madrid, Rivadeneyra, 1878, Part 2, Chapter 120. Julio Caro Baroja, *Los judíos en la España moderna y contemporánea*, vol. 1, Madrid, Ediciones Istmo, 1978, p. 66.

2 Antonio Collantes de Terán Sánchez, *Sevilla en la Baja Edad Media*, Seville, Servicio de Publicaciones del Excmo. Ayuntamiento, 1977, p. 417. Henry Kamen, *La Inquisición Española. Mito e historia crítica*, Barcelona, Crítica, 2013, p. 447. Henry Kamen, *The Spanish Inquisition: A Historical Revision*, New Haven, Yale University Press, 1998, pp. 48, 354. Henry Charles Lea, *History of the Inquisition of Spain*, vol. 3, New York, Macmillan, 1906–7, pp. 83–4.

3 Benzion Netanyahu, *The Origins of the Inquisition in Fifteenth Century Spain*, New York, New York Review Books, 2001, p. 410. Kamen, *Inquisition*, pp. 43–7.

4 Haim Beinart, 'The Conversos Community of Fifteenth-Century Spain', in Richard Barnett (ed.), *The Sephardi Heritage: Essays on the History and Cultural Contribution of the Jews of Spain and Portugal*, vol. 1: *The Jews in Spain and Portugal Before and After the Expulsion of 1492*, London, Vallentine Mitchell, 1971, pp. 425–6. Benzion Netanyahu, *The Marranos of Spain: From the Late 14th to the Early 16th Century*, Ithaca, NY, Cornell University Press, 1999, pp. 186, 236. Netanyahu, *Origins*, pp. 410, 994–5. Kamen, *Inquisition*, pp. 38–40, 43–6.

5 Roth, *Medieval Jewish Civilization*, pp. 320, 150–1. David Raphael (ed.), *The Expulsion 1492 Chronicles: Medieval Chronicles Relating to the Expulsion of the Jews from Spain and Portugal*, North Hollywood, CA, Carmi House, 1992 (Kindle edn), locs 451–84, 548 (citing Elijah Capsali, *Seder Eliyahu Zuta*, vol. 1).

6   Kamen, *Inquisition*, p. 49.

7   Tarsicio de Azcona, *Isabel la Católica. Estudio crítico de su vida y su reinado*, Madrid, Biblioteca de Autores Cristianos, 1993, pp. 502, 509, 521. J. Valdeón Baruque, *Cristianos, judíos, musulmanes*, Barcelona, Crítica, 2006, p. 139. Lu Ann Homza, *The Spanish Inquisition 1478–1614*, Indianapolis, Hackett, 2006, p. 9. José Antonio Escudero, 'Los Reyes Católicos y el Establecimiento de la Inquisición', *Anuario de Estudios Atlánticos*, no. 50, 2004, pp. 375, 381–3. Marques in Hernando de Talavera, *Católica impugnación del herético libelo maldito y descomulgado que fue divulgado en la ciudad de Sevilla* (with Francisco Marquez Villanueva and Stefania Pastore), Córdoba, Almuzara, 2012, Introduction p. LIX.

8   Netanyahu, *Marranos*, pp. 240, 258–9.

9   Ibid., pp. 239, 259 (citing Crescas, *Letter to the Jews of Avignon*).

10 Raphael, loc. 2022 (citing Solomon ibn Verga, *Shevet Yehuda*).

11 Netanyahu, *Marranos*, pp. 240, 247, 255, 258, 259.

12 Jerónimo Zurita, *Anales de Aragón*, ed. Ángel Canellas López et al., Zaragoza, Institución Fernando el Católico, at http://ifc.dpz.es/publicaciones/ver/id/2448, Libro 19, Chapter 49.

13 Joseph Pérez (ed.), *La inquisición española. Nuevas visiones, nuevos horizontes*, Madrid, Siglo XXI, 1980, pp. 36–8.

14 Zurita, *Anales*, Libro 19, Chapter 49.

15 Pastore in Talavera, *Católica impugnación*, p. xxiii.

16 Ibid., p. 12.

17 Roth, *Medieval Jewish Civilization*, p. 226.

18 Andrés Bernáldez, *Historia de los Reyes Católicos don Fernando y doña Isabel*, in *Crónicas de los Reyes de Castilla*, ed. Cayetano Rosell, vol. 70, Madrid, Biblioteca de Autores Españoles, 1878, Chapter 43.

19 Ibid.

20 Ibid., chapters 43–4. Fidel Fita, 'Historia hebrea. Documentos y monumentos', *Boletín de la Real Academia de la Historia*, tomo 16, Madrid, 1890, pp. 450–1. Guichot, *Historia de la Ciudad de Sevilla*, vol. 1, pp. 169, 178, 183–4.

21 Bernáldez, *Historia de los Reyes Católicos*, Chapters 43–4.

22 José Antonio Escudero, *Estudios sobre la Inquisición*, Madrid, Marcial Pons, 2005, pp. 119–20, 376, 383–5.

23 Bernáldez, *Historia de los Reyes Católicos*, Chapters 43–4.

24 Pulgar, *Crónica*, Part 2, Chapter 120. Roth, *Medieval Jewish Civilization*, pp. 221, 226.

25 Bernardino Llorca, *Bulario Pontificio de la Inquisición española en su período constitucional (1478–1525), según los fondos del Archivo Histórico nacional*

de Madrid, Rome, Pontificia Università Gregoriana, 1949, pp. 63, 109, 110. Archivo General de Simancas, RGS, LEG, 148612, 7. Lea, *Spain*, vol. 1, p. 577 and vol. 3, pp. 81–4.

26 Valdeón, *Cristianos*, p. 125. Roth, *Medieval Jewish Civilization*, p. 226.

27 Kamen, *Inquisición*, p. 449. Translation from Kamen, *Inquisition*, p. 354.

28 Carlos Carrete Parrondo (ed.), *Fontes Iudaeorum Regni Castellae*, vol. 2: *El tribunal de la Inquisition en el obispado de Soria (1486–1502)*, Salamanca, Universidad Pontificia, 1985, p. 23.

29 Raphael, loc. 600 (citing Capsali, *Seder Elihayu Zuta*, vol. 1).

30 Roth, *Medieval Jewish Civilization*, p. 241.

31 Raphael, loc. 2248 (citing Joseph Hacohen, *Vale of Tears*).

32 Ibid., loc. 2762 (citing Samuel Usque, *Consolation for the Tribulations of Israel* (Consolagam As Tribulagoes de Israel), trans. Martin A-Cohen).

33 Nicolas Lopes Martínez, *Los judaizantes castellanos y la Inquisición en tiempo de Isabel la Católica*, Burgos, Imprenta de Aldecoa, 1954, p. 435.

34 Kamen, *Inquisition*, pp. 14, 35–6.

35 Haim Beinart, *Records of the Trials of the Spanish Inquisition in Ciudad Real*, 2 vols, Jerusalem, The Israel National Academy of Sciences and Humanities, 1974–7, vol. 2, pp. 10–12. Homza, *Spanish Inquisition*, pp. 27–9.

36 Beinart, *Records*, vol. 2, pp. 11, 14–15. Homza, *Spanish Inquisition*, p. 44.

37 Beinart, *Records*, vol. 2, pp. 9–40. Homza, *Spanish Inquisition*, 16n. Translation is the author's, with an excellent alternative translation of the whole trial at pp. 27–49.

38 Pulgar, *Crónicas*, Part 2, Chapter 120. Roth, *Medieval Jewish Civilization*, pp. 226, 230.

39 Azcona, *Isabel la Católica*, p. 511 (citing F. Cantera, 'Fernando de Pulgar y los conversos', *Sefarad*, vol. 4, pp. 295–348).

40 Azcona, *Isabel la Católica*, pp. 516–18.

41 Escudero, *Estudios sobre la Inquisición*, pp. 125. José Antonio Escudero, 'Los reyes católicos y el establicimiento de la Inquisicíon', Anvaro de Estudios Atlánticos, no. 50, 2004, p. 368. Gonzalo Martínez Díez, *Bulario de la Inquisición Española. Hasta la muerte de Fernando el Católico*, Madrid, Editorial Complutense, 1998, pp. 106–9. Azcona, *Isabel la Católica*, pp. 516–18. Kamen, *Inquisition*, p. 53.

42 Kamen, *Inquisition*, p. 58. Azcona, *Isabel la Católica*, pp. 517, 519.

43 Escudero, 'Los reyes católicos', p. 368.

44 Kamen, *Inquisición*, pp. 28, 44, 157.

45 Tarsicio de Azcona, 'Relaciones de Inocencio VIII con los Reyes Católicos según el Fondo Podocataro de Venecia', *Hispania Sacra*, no. 32, 1980, pp. 3–30.

46 Netanyahu, *Marranos*, pp. 206, 231 (citing the *Book of Complaints*).

47 Ibid., pp. 204–5, 282.

48 Ibid., p. 78. Roth, *Medieval Jewish Civilization*, p. 323.

49 Netanyahu, *Marranos*, p. 205.

50 Ibid., pp. 184, 286. Roth, *Medieval Jewish Civilization*, p. 323.

51 Alexander Marx, 'The Expulsion of the Jews from Spain: Two New Accounts', *Jewish Quarterly Review*, vol. 20, no. 2, January 1908, p. 256.

52 Netanyahu, *Marranos*, pp. 3, 189, 190, 236, 248, 284. Raphael, loc. 1946.

53 Netanyahu, *Origins*, pp. 995, 1003. Eloy Benito Ruano, *Los orígenes del problema converso*, Barcelona, El Albir, 1976, p. 110, for Bachiller Marcos García de la Mora's Memorial (Marquillos de Marambroz).

54 Claudio Guillén, 'Un padrón de conversos sevillanos (1510)', *Bulletin Hispanique*, vol. 58, no. 2, 1956, pp. 49–98. Roth, *Medieval Jewish Civilization*, p. 230, 232–3 (citing José de Sigüenza, *Historia de la Orden de San Jerónimo*, 1907). Kamen, *Inquisition*, pp. 183, 304–10.

55 Alonso de Fuentes, *Cuarenta cantos de diversas y peregrinas historias*, Seville, 1545, Canto noveno de la primera parte, fol. xliii. Escudero, *Estudios sobre la Inquisición*, pp. 338, 368, 371. Azcona, *Isabel la Católica*, p. 525.

56 Luis Suárez Fernández, *Judíos españoles en la Edad Media*, Madrid, Rialp, 1980, pp. 55–6. Netanyahu, *Origins*, p. 1088. Roth, *Medieval Jewish Civilization*, p. 283.

57 Raphael, locs 2508–18 (citing Isaac ibn Faradj). Marx, 'The Expulsion of the Jews from Spain', pp. 240–71.

CHAPTER 20: CRUSADE

1 Juan de Mata Carriazo, *Historia de la guerra de Granada*, in Menendez Pidal (ed.), *Historia de España*, XVII, vol. 1, Madrid, Espasa-Calpe, 1969, pp. 409–10 (citing *El Tumbo de los Reyes Católicos del Concejo de Sevilla*, docs 53, 54).

2 Ibid. Diego Clemencín, *Elogio a la reina Isabel la Católica e ilustraciones sobre varios asuntos de su reinado*, vol. 6, Madrid, Memorias de la Real Academia de la Historia', 1821, p. 577.

3 Carriazo, *Guerra*, p. 433 (citing *Tumbo Sevilla*, doc. 526).

4 Ibid., pp. 399, 409–10.

5 Ibid., p. 399.

6 Ibid., p. 403.

7 Ibid., p. 400.

8 Ibid., pp. 400–2, 406. L. P. Harvey, *Islam in Spain, 1250 to 1500*, Chicago, University of Chicago Press, 1990, p. 266.

9   Hernando de Baeza, *Relaciones de algunos sucesos*, ed. Emilio Lafuente y Alcántara, Madrid, Rivadeneyra, 1868, p. 7. Carriazo, *Guerra*, pp. 401, 406.

10   Baeza, *Relaciones*, p. 7. Andrés Bernáldez, *Historia de los Reyes Católicos don Fernando y doña Isabel*, in *Crónicas de los Reyes de Castilla*, ed. Cayetano Rosell, vol. 70, Madrid, Biblioteca de Autores Españoles, 1878, Chapter 56. Carriazo, *Guerra*, p. 473.

11   Carriazo, *Guerra*, p. 445–7.

12   Ibid., pp. 449, 453, 454 (citing *Tumbo Sevilla*, doc. 532).

13   Carriazo, *Guerra*, pp. 448–9.

14   Fernando del Pulgar, *Crónica de los Señores Reyes Católicos Don Fernando y Doña Isabel de Castilla y de Aragón*, in *Crónicas de los Reyes de Castilla*, vol. 3, ed. Cayetano Rosell, Madrid, Rivadeneyra, 1878, Part 3, Chapter 7. Carriazo, *Guerra*, p. 463.

15   Pulgar, *Crónica*, Part 3, Chapters 7–9. Tarsicio de Azcona, *Isabel la Católica. Estudio crítico de su vida y su reinado*, Madrid, Biblioteca de Autores Cristianos, 1993, p. 637. Carriazo, *Guerra*, pp. 463–5.

16   Carriazo, *Guerra*, pp. 465–7.

17   Pulgar, *Crónica*, Part 3, Chapter 9.

18   Carriazo, *Guerra*, pp. 469, 472.

19   Ibid., pp. 404–5, 469, 471–2.

20   Ibid., pp. 489–90, 494.

21   Bernáldez, *Historia de los Reyes Católicos*, Chapter 60, pp. 164–5. Carriazo, *Guerra*, pp. 489–94. Azcona, *Isabel la Católica*, pp. 639–42.

22   Baeza, *Relaciones*, p. 15.

23   Bernáldez, *Historia de los Reyes Católicos*, Chapter 60, p. 165. Carriazo, *Guerra*, p. 492.

24   Bernáldez, *Historia de los Reyes Católicos*, Chapter 60, pp. 168–9.

25   Fernando del Pulgar, *Letras*, ed. J. Domínguez Bordona, Madrid, Espasa-Calpe, 1958, p. 61. Carriazo, *Guerra*, p. 493.

26   Carriazo, *Guerra*, p. 494 (citing *Tumbo Sevilla*, doc. 618).

27   Ibid., pp. 499–500. Harvey, *Islam in Spain*, p. 278.

28   Carriazo, *Guerra*, p. 501.

29   Harvey, Islam in Spain, pp. 278–9. Carriazo, *Guerra*, pp. 501, 509.

30   Carriazo, *Guerra*, p. 508.

31   Ibid., pp. 512, 515, 521, 535. Azcona, *Isabel la Católica*, p. 643.

32   Bernáldez, *Historia de los Reyes Católicos*, Chapter 58.

33   Pulgar, *Crónica*, Part 3, Chapter 22. Carriazo, *Guerra*, pp. 525–6, 536–7, 674. Azcona, *Isabel la Católica*, p. 664–7.

34   Angus MacKay, *Spain in the Middle Ages: From Frontier to Empire, 1000–1500*, London, Macmillan, 1977, p. 215.

35 Peggy K. Liss, *Isabel the Queen: Life and Times*, Philadelphia, University of Pennsylvania Press, 2004, p. 77 (citing Rucquoi, 'Jeanne d'Arc', pp. 155–74). Azcona, *Isabel la Católica*, p. 644.

CHAPTER 21: THEY SMOTE US TOWN BY TOWN

1 Juan de Mata Carriazo, *Historia de la guerra de Granada*, in Menendez Pidal (ed.), *Historia de Espana*, XVII, vol. 1, Madrid, Espasa-Calpe, 1969, p. 554.

2 Ibid., pp. 554, 662.

3 Weston F. Cook Jr, 'The Cannon Conquest of Nasid Granada and the End of the *Reconquista*', in Donald J. Kagay and L. J. Andrew Villalon (eds), *Crusaders, Condottieri, and Cannon: Medieval Warfare in Societies around the Mediterranean*, Leiden and Boston, Brill, 2003, p. 261.

4 Carriazo, *Guerra*, p. 557.

5 Ibid., pp. 559–61.

6 Ibid., pp. 561–3.

7 Luis Suárez Fernández, *Judíos españoles en la Edad Media*, Madrid, Rialp, 1980, pp. 255–6. Roth, in Norman Roth (ed.), *Medieval Jewish Civilization: An Encyclopedia*, New York, Routledge, 2003, p. 283. Carriazo, *Guerra*, pp. 571–3.

8 Carriazo, *Guerra*, p. 573.

9 Cook, 'The Cannon Conquest of Nasid Granada', p. 274.

10 Ibid.

11 James T. Monroe, 'A Curious Morisco Appeal to the Ottoman Empire', *Al-Andalus*, vol. 31, 1966, pp. 281–303. P. S. van Koningsveld and G. A. Wiegers, 'The Islamic Statute of the Mudejars in the Light of a New Source', *Al-Qantara*, vol. 17, 1996, pp. 19–58. Carriazo, *Guerra*, p. 447.

12 Andrés Bernáldez, *Historia de los Reyes Católicos don Fernando y doña Isabel*, in *Crónicas de los Reyes de Castilla*, ed. Cayetano Rosell, vol. 70, Madrid, Biblioteca de Autores Españoles, 1878, Chapter 81. Cook, 'The Cannon Conquest of Nasid Granada', p. 253.

13 Joaquín Gil Sanjuan and Juan J. Toledo Navarro, 'Importancia de la artillería en la conquista de las poblaciones malagueñas (1485–1487)', *Baetica*, no. 30, 2008, pp. 315–18. Cook, 'The Cannon Conquest of Nasid Granada', p. 261.

14 Cook, 'The Cannon Conquest of Nasid Granada', p. 273.

15 Ibid., pp. 263, 275. Carriazo, *Guerra*, p. 649.

16 Carriazo, *Guerra*, pp. 623–37, 649, 655–9.

17 Bernáldez, *Historia de los Reyes Católicos*, Chapter 80. Carriazo, *Guerra*, pp. 643, 650, 655.

18 Bernáldez, *Historia de los Reyes Católicos*, Chapter 80. Carriazo, *Guerra*, pp. 664–5.

19 Cook, 'The Cannon Conquest of Nasid Granada', p. 276 (citing Pulgar).

20 Bernáldez, *Historia de los Reyes Católicos*, Chapter 81. Carriazo, *Guerra*, pp. 665–70.

CHAPTER 22: GOD SAVE KING BOABDIL!

1 Juan de Mata Carriazo, *Historia de la guerra de Granada*, in Menendez Pidal (ed.), *Historia de Espana*, XVII, vol. 1, Madrid, Espasa-Calpe, 1969, pp. 682–8.

2 Ibid., p. 693.

3 Ibid., pp. 696–8.

4 Hernando de Baeza, *Relaciones de algunos sucesos*, ed. Emilio Lafuente y Alcántara, Madrid, Rivadeneyra, 1868, p. 39.

5 Carriazo, *Guerra*, pp. 685–6, 699, 703, 705.

6 Ibid., p. 703.

7 Fernando del Pulgar, *Crónica de los Señores Reyes Católicos Don Fernando y Doña Isabel de Castilla y de Aragón*, in *Crónicas de los Reyes de Castilla*, vol. 3, ed. Cayetano Rosell, Madrid, Rivadeneyra, 1878, Part 3, Chapter 83. Carriazo, *Guerra*, pp. 703–7.

8 Carriazo, *Guerra*, p. 712.

9 Pulgar, *Crónica*, Part 3, Chapter 74. Carriazo, *Guerra*, pp. 707–12.

10 Pulgar, *Crónica*, Part 3, Chapter 75. Carriazo, *Guerra*, pp. 711, 715.

11 Pulgar, *Crónica*, Part 3, Chapters 82 and 85.

12 Ibid., Chapter 80–2 and 85. Carriazo, *Guerra*, pp. 716, 723.

13 Pulgar, *Crónica*, Part 3, Chapter 78. Andrés Bernáldez, *Historia de los Reyes Católicos don Fernando y doña Isabel*, in *Crónicas de los Reyes de Castilla*, ed. Cayetano Rosell, vol. 70, Madrid, Biblioteca de Autores Españoles, 1878, Chapter 84.

14 Bernáldez, *Historia de los Reyes Católicos*, Chapter 83.

15 Alonso de Palencia, *Guerra de Granada*, Alicante, Biblioteca Virtual Miguel de Cervantes, 1999, at http://www.cervantesvirtual.com/nd/ark:/59851/bmc833n9, Libro 7. Carriazo, *Guerra*, pp. 717, 721.

16 Pulgar, *Crónica*, Part 3, Chapters 88 and 92–3. Carriazo, *Guerra*, p. 717.

17 Bernáldez, *Historia de los Reyes Católicos*, Chapter 84.

18 Pulgar, *Crónica*, Part 3, Chapter 93. Carriazo, *Guerra*, pp. 718–21.

19 Pulgar, *Crónica*, Part 3, Chapter 93.

20 Ibid. Carriazo, *Guerra*, pp. 718–21, 722 (citing *Tumbo Sevilla*, doc. 1051).

21 Pulgar, *Crónica*, Part 3, Chapter 93. Carriazo, *Guerra*, p. 722.

22 Carriazo, *Guerra*, p. 723.

23 Ibid., p. 728.

24 Ibid., pp. 727–32.

25 Ibid., p. 775.

26   Ibid. (citing Garrido Atienza, *Las capitulaciones para la entrega de Granada*, pp. 173–4).

27   Ibid., p. 757.

28   Ibid., pp. 735, 756.

29   Ibid., p. 758.

30   Ibid., pp. 759–62.

31   Bernáldez, *Historia de los Reyes Católicos*, Chapter 112. Carriazo, *Guerra*, p. 764.

32   See Miguel Ángel Ladero Quesada, 'Las coplas de Hernando de Vera. Un caso de crítica al gobierno de Isabel la Católica', *Anuario de Estudios Atlánticos*, no. 14, 1968, pp. 365–81.

33   Pulgar, *Crónica*, Part 3, Chapter 120.

34   Álvaro Fernández de Córdova Miralles, *La Corte de Isabel I. Ritos y ceremonias de una reina (1474–1504)*, Madrid, Dykinson, 2002, p. 311.

35   Pulgar, *Crónica*, Part 3, Chapters 121–2.

36   *Colección de documentos inéditos*, vol. 8, pp. 402–10. Miguel Ángel Ladero Quesada, *Isabel I de Castilla. Siete ensayos sobre la reina, su entorno y sus empresas*, Madrid, Dykinson, 2012, pp. 168–9. Carriazo, *Guerra*, pp. 767, 771, 774.

37   Carriazo, *Guerra*, p. 786 (citing *Tumbo Sevilla*, doc. 1167).

CHAPTER 23: THE TUDORS

1   Álvaro Fernández de Córdova Miralles, *La Corte de Isabel I. Ritos y ceremonias de una reina (1474–1504)*, Madrid, Dykinson, 2002, p. 333.

2   Machado's Journal, in James Gairdner, *Memorials of King Henry the Seventh*, London, Longman, Brown, Green, Longmans & Roberts, 1858, p. 328.

3   Ibid., pp. 350–1.

4   Ibid., p. 341.

5   Ibid.

6   Ibid., pp. 166, 336.

7   Machado, pp. 328–32, 338.

8   Ibid., pp. 172, 343, 354. Córdova, *La Corte*, p. 337.

9   Bethany Aram, *Juana the Mad: Sovereignty and Dynasty in Renaissance Europe*, Baltimore, Johns Hopkins University Press, 2005, p. 23.

10   *Calendar of Letters, Despatches and State Papers relating to the negotiations between England and Spain preserved in the archives of Simancas and elsewhere* (hereafter *CSP Spain*) vol. 1, G. A. Bergenroth, Pascual de Gayangos and Garrett Mattingly, London, Longman, Green, Longmans & Roberts, 1862, p. 164.

11   Ibid., p. 11. Machado, pp. 343, 354.

12   Machado, p. 345.

13 Ibid., p. 347.

14 Córdova, *La Corte*, pp. 356–7.

15 Machado, p. 351.

16 *CSP Spain*, vol. 1, p. 34. See José Luis Orella Unzué, 'Las relaciones vascas con Inglaterra. Siglos XIV–XVI', *Lurralde*, no. 28, 2005, pp. 85–152.

CHAPTER 24: GRANADA FALLS

1 Fernando del Pulgar, *Crónica de los Señores Reyes Católicos Don Fernando y Doña Isabel de Castilla y de Aragón*, in *Crónicas de los Reyes de Castilla*, vol. 3, ed. Cayetano Rosell, Madrid, Rivadeneyra, 1878, Part 3, Chapter 130. Tarsicio de Azcona, 'El Príncipe don Juan, heredero de los Reyes Católicos, en el V centenario de su nacimiento (1478–1497)', *Cuadernos de Investigación Histórica*, no. 7, 1983, p. 223. Tarsicio de Azcona, *Isabel la Católica. Estudio crítico de su vida y su reinado*, Madrid, Biblioteca de Autores Cristianos, 1993, p. 659. Juan de Mata Carriazo, *Historia de la guerra de Granada*, in Menendez Pidal (ed.), *Historia de Espana*, XVII, vol. 1, Madrid, Espasa-Calpe, 1969, pp. 791–2.

2 Ana Isabel Carrasco Manchado, 'Discurso político propaganda en la corte de los Reyes Católicos (1474–1482)', doctoral thesis, Universidad Complutense de Madrid, 2000, at http://eprints.ucm.es/2525/, pp. 33–7, 134.

3 Peggy K. Liss, *Isabel the Queen: Life and Times*, Philadelphia, University of Pennsylvania Press, 2004, pp. 101–4. Anon, *Crónica Incompleta de los Reyes Católicos*, ed. Julio Puyol, Madrid, 1934, pp. 181, 304.

4 John Edwards, *Isabel la Católica. Poder y fama*, Madrid, Marcial Pons, 2004, p. 41.

5 Antonio de la Torre y del Cerro, *Cuentas de Gonzalo de Baeza, tesorero de Isabel la Católica*, Vol. 1, Madrid, Consejo Superior de Investigaciones Científicas, 1956, pp. 334, 347, 363. Azcona, *Isabel la Católica*, p. 658–60.

6 Carriazo, *Guerra*, pp. 792, 804.

7 Ibid., pp. 791–2, 804, 811–16, 823. Azcona, *Isabel la Católica*, p. 660. Miguel Ángel Ladero Quesada, *Isabel I de Castilla. Siete ensayos sobre la reina, su entorno y sus empresas*, Madrid, Dykinson, 2012, p. 167.

8 Andrés Bernáldez, *Historia de los Reyes Católicos don Fernando y doña Isabel*, in *Crónicas de los Reyes de Castilla*, ed. Cayetano Rosell, vol. 70, Madrid, Biblioteca de Autores Españoles, 1878, Chapter 101. Carriazo, *Guerra*, p. 820. Azcona, *Isabel la Católica*, p. 661.

9 Bernáldez, *Historia de los Reyes Católicos*, Chapter 101.

10 Carriazo, *Guerra*, p. 820.

11 Hernando de Baeza, *Relaciónes de algunos sucesos*, ed. Emilio Lafuente y Alcántara, Madrid, Rivadeneyra, 1868, p. 48. Carriazo, *Guerra*, pp. 824–5, 829.

12 Carriazo, *Guerra*, pp. 829–31.

13 Ibid.

14 Baeza, *Relaciónes*, p. 43.

15 Ibid., p. 44.

16 Carriazo, *Guerra*, p. 837.

17 Ibid., p. 844.

18 Ibid., pp. 838–40, 844.

19 James T. Monroe, 'A Curious Morisco Appeal to the Ottoman Empire', *Al-Andalus*, vol. 31, 1966, pp. 281–303. P. S. van Koningsveld and G. A. Wiegers, 'The Islamic Statute of the Mudejars in the Light of a New Source', *Al-Qantara*, vol. 17, 1996, pp. 19–58.

20 James Gairdner, *Three Fifteenth-Century Chronicles with Historical Memoranda by John Stowe*, Camden Society, London, 1880, at http://www.british-history.ac.uk/camden-record-soc/vol28, p. 87.

21 Carriazo, *Guerra*, pp. 827, 878.

CHAPTER 25: HANDOVER

1 Juan de Mata Carriazo, *Historia de la guerra de Granada*, in Menendez Pidal (ed.), *Historia de Espana*, XVII, vol. 1, Madrid, Espasa-Calpe, 1969, p. 884.

2 Francisco Medina de Mendoza, 'Vida del cardenal don Pedro González de Mendoza', in Real Academia de la Historia, *Memorial Histórico Española*, vol. 6, Madrid, 1853, pp. 289–90. Carriazo, *Guerra*, pp. 827, 878, 884, 888. Miguel Ángel Ladero Quesada, *Isabel I de Castilla. Siete ensayos sobre la reina, su entorno y sus empresas*, Madrid, Dykinson, 2012, pp. 175–6, 163.

3 Carriazo, *Guerra*, pp. 890–1.

4 Ibid., pp. 877, 887, 891–3.

5 Ibid., pp. 891–2.

6 Ibid., pp. 858–9, 866, 895.

7 Ibid., pp. 858, 873, 882, 896 n.2.

8 Ibid., p. 896.

9 María del Carmen Pescador del Hoyo (ed.), 'Cómo fue de verdad la toma de Granada, a la luz de un documento inédito', *Al-Andalus*, vol. 20, 1955, pp. 283–344.

10 Carriazo, *Guerra*, p. 876.

11 Ibid., pp. 875–7.

12 Ibid., p. 858.

13 Robert Irwin, *The Alhambra*, London, Profile Books, 2004, p. 57.

14   Ibid., pp. 46, 93.

15   Ibid., pp. 49, 44, 33, 52, 55.

16   Ibid., p. 41.

17   José Antonio García Luján, *El Generalife. Jardín del paraíso*, Granada, J. A. García, 2006, pp. 63–5.

18   Carriazo, *Guerra*, p. 878.

19   Ibid., pp. 903–11.

20   Ibid., p. 910.

21   Ladero Quesada, *Isabel*, pp. 167–8.

22   Isabelle Poutrin Reyes, 'Los derechos de los vencidos. Las capitulaciones de Granada', *Sharq al-Andalus*, vol. 19, 2008–10, pp. 11–34. Ladero Quesada, *Isabel*, pp. 167–9. Carriazo, *Guerra*, pp. 854, 858.

23   Carriazo, *Guerra*, pp. 850–4.

24   Poutrin, 'Los derechos de los vencidos', pp. 11–34.

25   Ibid. Carriazo, *Guerra*, p. 858.

26   Carriazo, *Guerra*, pp. 858, 861.

27   Ladero Quesada, *Isabel*, pp. 169–70.

28   Carriazo, *Guerra*, pp. 855–6, 877.

CHAPTER 26: EXPULSION OF THE JEWS

1   Tarsicio de Azcona, *Isabel la Católica. Estudio crítico de su vida y su reinado*, Madrid, Biblioteca de Autores Cristianos, 1993, p. 799, citing Abravanel's *Introduction to the former Prophets*. An alternative translation can be found at David Raphael (ed.), *The Expulsion 1492 Chronicles: Medieval Chronicles Relating to the Expulsion of the Jews from Spain and Portugal*, North Hollywood, CA, Carmi House (Kindle edn), 1992, loc 1296.

2   Raphael, loc. 662.

3   Azcona, *Isabel la Católica*, p. 799. Raphael, loc. 1328 (citing Isaac Abravanel, *Perush al Nebiim Rishonin*).

4   J. Contreras (ed.), *Inquisición Española. Nuevas aproximaciones*, Madrid, Centro de Estudios Inquisitoriales, 1987, pp. 3–8. Raphael, loc. 3586.

5   Jane Gerber, *The Jews of Spain: a history of the Sephardic experience*, The Free Press, New York, 1992, p. 136 (citing Solomon ibn Verga, *Shevet Yehuda*).

6   Joseph Pérez (ed.), *La inquisición española. Nuevas visiones, nuevos horizontes*, Madrid, Siglo XXI, 1980, pp. 11–22. Benzion Netanyahu, *The Origins of the Inquisition in Fifteenth Century Spain*, New York, New York Review Books, 2001, pp. 12, 62, 127, 1096. Miguel Ángel Ladero Quesada, *La España de los Reyes Catolicos*, Madrid, Alianza, 2014, p. 18. Fred Rosner, 'The Life of

Moses Maimonides, a Prominent Medieval Physician', *Einstein Quarterly*, 1995, pp. 125–8.

7   Netanyahu, *Origins*, p. 12. Pérez, *Inquisición*, p. 22.

8   Henry Kamen, *La Inquisición Española. Mito e historia crítica*, Barcelona, Crítica, 2013, p. 10.

9   Ariel Hessayon, review of François Soyer, *The Persecution of the Jews and Muslims of Portugal. King Manuel I and the End of Religious Tolerance (1496–7)*, at http://www.history.ac.uk/reviews/review/797.

10 Popplau in Javier Liske, *Viajes de extranjeros por España y Portugal en los siglos XV, XVI y XVII*, Madrid, Medina, 1878, pp. 55–6.

11 Pérez, *Inquisición española*, p. 27.

12 Ibid., pp. 24, 27, 30, 40, 65.

13 J. Valdeón Baruque, *Cristianos, judíos, musulmanes*, Barcelona, Crítica, 2006, p. 154.

14 Pérez, *Inquisición española*, p. 25.

15 Luis Suárez Fernández, *Documentos acerca de la expulsión de los judíos*, Aldecoa, Valladolid, 1964, p. 116.

16 Ibid., pp. 116, 124.

17 Pérez, *Inquisición española*, p. 56. J. M. Monsalvo Antón, *Teoría y evolución de un conflicto social. El antisemitismo en la corona de Castilla en la Baja Edad Media, Siglo XXI*, Madrid, 1985, pp. 256–7.

18 Pérez, *Inquisición española*, p. 61.

19 Raphael, loc. 105.

20 Henry Kamen, *The Spanish Inquisition: A Historical Revision*, New Haven, Yale University Press, 1998, p. 22.

21 Pérez, *Inquisición española*, pp. 31–2. Roth, in Norman Roth (ed.), *Medieval Jewish Civilization: An Encyclopedia*, New York, Routledge, 2003, pp. 318, 321. Kamen, *Inquisition*, pp. 17, 19, 22. Raphael, loc. 87.

22 Pérez, *Inquisición española*, p. 28.

23 María Fuencisla García Casar, 'Las comunidades judías de la Corona de Castilla al tiempo de la expulsión', in Ángel Alcalá (ed.), *Judíos, sefarditas, conversos. La expulsión de 1492 y sus consecuencias. Ponencias del Congreso Internacional celebrado en Nueva York en noviembre de 1992*, Valladolid, Ambito, 1995, p. 26.

24 Miguel Angel Motis Dolader, 'Las comunidades judías de la Corona de Aragón en el siglo XV', in Alcalá (ed.), *Judíos, sefarditas, conversos*, p. 45. Miguel Ángel Ladero Quesada, 'El número de judíos en la España de 1492', in Alcalá (ed.), *Judíos, sefarditas, conversos*, p. 171. Alexander Marx, 'The Expulsion of the Jews from Spain: Two New Accounts', *Jewish Quarterly Review*, vol. 20, no. 2, January 1908, pp. 246–7.

25 Suárez, *Documentos expulsión*, pp. 15, 119, 345, 781.

26 Ibid., pp. 15, 344–6 .

27 Ibid., pp. 13–14.

28 Roth, *Medieval Jewish Civilization*, p. 299.

29 Raphael, loc. 3166.

30 Suárez, *Documentos expulsión*, pp. 13–14 (citing De la Torre, *Un médico de los reyes católicos*, in Hispania XIV, 69).

31 Contreras, *Inquisición Española. Nuevas aproximaciones*, pp. 35–40. Azcona, *Isabel la Católica*, pp. 499, 785.

32 Contreras, *Inquisición Española. Nuevas aproximaciones*, pp. 36–8. Archivo General de Simancas, CCA, DIV, 1, 78, Memorial del Prior de Santa Cruz sobre las cosas que la Reina Católica debía remediar.

33 Pérez, *Inquisición española*, pp. 97–8. *Cortes de los antiguos reinos de León y Castilla, pub. por la Real Academia de la Historia*, vol. 4, Madrid, Rivadeneyra, 1882, p. 149.

34 Contreras, *Inquisición Española. Nuevas aproximaciones*, pp. 36–8.

35 Raphael, loc. 179. Suárez, *Documentos expulsión*, p. 24. Azcona, *Isabel la Católica*, pp. 786, 788.

36 María Antonia Bel Bravo, *Los Reyes Católicos y los judíos andaluces*, Granada, Biblioteca Chronica Nova de Estudios Históricos, 1989, pp. 160, 240. Ladero Quesada, 'El número de judíos en la España de 1492', p. 171.

37 Bel Bravo, *Los Reyes Católicos y los judíos andaluces*, pp. 241–2. Pérez, *Inquisición española*, p. 149.

38 Pérez, *Inquisición española*, p. 108. Raphael, locs 1990–3 (citing Solomon ibn Verga, *Shevet Yehuda*).

39 Pérez, *Inquisición española*, pp. 144–5.

40 Ibid., pp. 108, 151.

41 Ibid. pp. 146, 148.

42 Ibid., p. 149.

43 Ibid., pp. 150–1.

44 Ibid., p. 107.

45 Antoine de Lalaing, *Collection des voyages des souverains des Pays-Bas*, Gachard, Brussels, 1876, p. 453.

46 Pérez, *Inquisición española*, p. 107.

CHAPTER 27: THE VALE OF TEARS

1 Anon, *Cronicón de Valladolid*, Valladolid, Princiano, 1984, p. 195. Roth, in Norman Roth (ed.), *Medieval Jewish Civilization: An Encyclopedia*, New York, Routledge, 2003, p. 130.

2 Ariel Hessayon, review of François Soyer, *The Persecution of the Jews and Muslims of Portugal. King Manuel I and the End of Religious Tolerance (1496–7)*, at http://www.history.ac.uk/reviews/review/797. Joseph Pérez (ed.), *La inquisición española. Nuevas visiones, nuevos horizontes*, Madrid, Siglo XXI, 1980, p. 10.

3 David Raphael (ed.), *The Expulsion 1492 Chronicles: Medieval Chronicles Relating to the Expulsion of the Jews from Spain and Portugal*, North Hollywood, CA, Carmi House, 1992 (Kindle edn) loc. 683 (citing Elijah Capsali, *Seder Elihayu Zuta*, vol. 1).

4 Kevin Ingram (ed.), *The Conversos and Moriscos in Late Medieval Spain and Beyond*, vol. 2, Leiden, Brill, 2009, p. 26. Roth, *Medieval Jewish Civilization*, pp. 129–30. Miguel Ángel Ladero Quesada, *La Hermandad de Castilla. Cuentas y memoriales, 1480–1498*, Madrid, Real Academia de la Historia, 2005, p. 23.

5 Raphael, loc. 1913 (citing Joseph Hacker, 'New Chronicles on the Expulsion of the Jews from Spain: Its Causes and Consequences', pp. 201–28). Roth, *Medieval Jewish Civilization*, p. 8.

6 Raphael, loc. 1929 (citing *The De la Cavalleria Chronicle* in Hacker, 'New Chronicles', pp. 201–28).

7 Roth, *Medieval Jewish Civilization*, pp.300–3. Pérez, *Inquisición española*, p. 111.

8 Pérez, *Inquisición española*, p. 111.

9 Raphael, loc. 1340 (citing Isaac Abravanel, *Perush al Nebiim Rishonin*).

10 Ibid., loc. 659 (citing Capsali, *Seder Eliyahu Zuta*, vol. 1).

11 Ibid., loc. 1951 (citing Joseph Hacker, 'New Chronicles on the Expulsion of the Jews from Spain: Its Causes and Consequences', pp. 201–28).

12 Andrés Bernáldez, *Historia de los Reyes Católicos don Fernando y doña Isabel*, in *Crónicas de los Reyes de Castilla*, ed. Cayetano Rosell, Madrid, Biblioteca de Autores Españoles, 1878, Chapter 110.

13 Raphael, loc. 695 (citing Capsali, *Seder Eliyahu Zuta*, vol. 1).

14 Pérez, *Inquisición española*, p. 117. Raphael, locs. 332, 802, 825.

15 Bernáldez, *Historia de los Reyes Católicos*, Chapter 110.

16 Ibid.

17 Ibid.

18 François Soyer, *The Persecution of the Jews and Muslims of Portugal: King Manuel I and the End of Religious Tolerance (1496–7)*, Leiden, Brill, 2007, p. 111.

19 Bernáldez, *Historia de los Reyes Católicos*, Chapter 110. Soyer, *Persecution of the Jews and Muslims*, p. 105.

20 Bernáldez, *Historia de los Reyes Católicos*, Chapter 110. Pérez, *Inquisición española*, pp. 153–7. Raphael, loc. 2277.

21 Bernáldez, *Historia de los Reyes Católicos*, Chapter 110.

22 Raphael, loc. 683 (citing Capsali, *Seder Eliyahu Zuta*, vol. 1).

23 Isabel Montes Romero-Camacho, 'Judíos y mudéjares', *Medievalismo*, no. 14, 2004, pp. 253–4.

24 Raphael, loc. 2051 (citing Solomon ibn Verga, *Shevet Yehuda*).

25 Ibid., locs 2084–95 (citing Ibn Verga, *Shevet Yehuda*).

26 Ibid., loc. 1827.

27 Abraham Gross, *Iberian Jewry from Twilight to Dawn: The World of Rabbi Abraham Saba*, Leiden, Brill, 1995, pp. 11–14.

28 Bernáldez, *Historia de los Reyes Católicos*, Chapter 113.

29 Soyer, *Persecution of the Jews and Muslims*, p. 102.

30 Ibid., pp. 107–8, 111–12.

31 Ibid., p. 115.

32 Ibid., pp. 44, 117, 120–1. Gross, *Iberian Jewry*, pp. 5–7, 9–39.

33 Soyer, *Persecution of the Jews and Muslims*, pp. 126–30 (citing Damião de Góis, *Crónica do felicíssimo Rei D. Manuel*, vols 1–2, Coimbra, 1949, vol. 1, pp. 23–4).

34 Soyer, *Persecution of the Jews and Muslims*, pp. 122, 131. Gross, *Iberian Jewry*, p. 18.

35 Soyer, *Persecution of the Jews and Muslims*, p. 130.

36 Raphael, locs 2354–2407 (citing Nahum N. Glatzer, *A Jewish Reader: In Time and Eternity*, trans. Olga Marx). Soyer, *Persecution of the Jews and Muslims*, p. 113.

37 Bernáldez, *Historia de los Reyes Católicos*, Chapter 113.

38 Raphael, loc. 1689. Bernaldez, *Historia de los Reyes Católicos*, chapter 110.

39 Soyer, *Persecution of the Jews and Muslims*, p. 133. Luis Suárez Fernández, *Documentos acerca de la expulsión de los judíos*, Valladolid, Aldecoa, 1964, pp. 487–9 and 526–7.

40 Soyer, *Persecution of the Jews and Muslims*, p. 134 (citing Rui de Pina, *Crónica de D. João II*, p. 138).

41 Haim Beinart, 'Vuelta de judíos a España después de la expulsión', in Ángel Alcalá (ed.), *Judíos, sefarditas, conversos. La expulsión de 1492 y sus consecuencias. Ponencias del Congreso Internacional celebrado en Nueva York en noviembre de 1992*, Valladolid, Ambito, 1995, pp. 186, 191. Miguel Ángel Ladero Quesada, 'El número de judíos en la España de 1492', in Alcalá (ed.), *Judíos, sefarditas, conversos*, pp. 176–7.

42 Raphael, loc. 3415 (citing Abraham Ben Solomon (of Ardutiel), *Sefer Ha-Kabbalah*, in A. Neubauer (ed.), *Medieval Jewish Chronicles and Chronological Notes*, Oxford, 1887, vol. 1).

43 Ladero Quesada, 'El número de judíos en la España de 1492', pp. 176–7. Beinart, 'Vuelta de judíos a España después de la expulsión', pp. 177, 183–5. Tarsicio de Azcona, *Isabel la Católica. Estudio crítico de su vida y su reinado*, Madrid, Biblioteca de Autores Cristianos, 1993, p. 807n.

44 Suárez, *Documentos expulsión*, p. 116.

45 Raphael, locs 422–612.

46 Ibid., locs 600–8 (citing Capsali, *Seder Eliyahu Zuta*, vol. 1).

47 Ibid., loc. 2228 (citing Ibn Verga, *Shevet Yehuda*). Roth, *Medieval Jewish Civilization*, pp. 300–1. Soyer, *Persecution of the Jews and Muslims*, p. 107.

48 Raphael, loc. 1340 (citing Abravanel, *Perush al Nebiim Rishonin*). Pérez, *Inquisición española*, pp. 130–1, 136.

CHAPTER 28: THE RACE TO ASIA

1 Consuelo Varela, *Cristóbal Colón. Retrato de un hombre*, Barcelona, Alianza, 1992, pp. 37, 68, 149. Antonio Rumeu de Armas, *La Rábida y el descubrimiento de América*, Madrid, Ediciones Cultura Hispanica, 1968, p. 148.

2 Andrés Bernáldez, *Historia de los Reyes Católicos don Fernando y doña Isabel*, in *Crónicas de los Reyes de Castilla*, ed. Cayetano Rosell, vol. 70, Madrid, Biblioteca de Autores Españoles, 1878, Chapter 118.

3 Eufemio Lorenzo Sanz, *Salamanca en la vida de Colón*, Salamanca, Diputación Provincial, 1983, pp. 14–17.

4 Martín Fernández Navarrete, *Colección de los viages y descubrimientos que hicieron por mar los españoles desde fines del siglo XV*, vols 1–3, Madrid, Imprenta Real, 1825, vol. 1, p. 154. Francisco Javier Sánchez Cantón, *Libros, tapices y cuadros que coleccionó Isabel la Católica*, Madrid, Consejo Superior de Investigaciones Científicas, 1950, pp. 67, 82. Varela, *Retrato*, pp. 149–50.

5 Navarrete, *Viages*, vol. 1, p. 154.

6 Bartolomé de Las Casas, *Historia de las Indias*, vols 1–2, Madrid, Imprenta Ginesta, 1875, vol. 1, Chapter 12. Felipe Fernández-Armesto, *Columbus*, Oxford, Oxford University Press, 1991, pp. 30–1.

7 Samuel Eliot Morison, *The Great Explorers: The European Discovery of America*, Oxford, Oxford University Press, 1986, pp. 370.

8 Fernández-Armesto, *Columbus*, p. 54.

9 Las Casas, *Historia de las Indias*, vol. 1, Chapters 27 and 29. Antonio Rumeu de Armas, *Nueva luz sobre las capitulaciones de Santa Fe de 1492 concertadas entre los Reyes Católicos y Cristóbal Colón. Estudio Institucional y diplomático*, Madrid, Consejo Superior de Investigaciones Científicas, 1985, pp. 142–3. Varela, *Retrato*, pp. 59, 75.

10 Rumeu de Armas, *La Rábida*, pp. 13, 22, 27, 50–60. Fernández-Armesto, *Columbus*, p. 60. Varela, *Retrato*, p. 151.

11 Varela, *Retrato*, p. 151.

12 Ibid., pp. 149–51.

13 Consuelo Varela, *Textos y documentos completos*, Madrid, Alianza, 1992, p. 303. Andrés María Mateo, *Colón y Isabel la Católica*, Valladolid, Consejo Superior de Investigaciones Científicas, 1942, pp. 3–5.

14 Fernández-Armesto, *Columbus*, pp. 4, 17.

15 Bernáldez, *Historia de los Reyes Católicos*, Chapter 118.

16 Navarrete, *Viages*, vol. 1, p. 265.

17 Consuelo Varela, *La caída de Cristóbal Colón. El juicio de Bobadilla*, Barcelona, Marcial Pons, Ediciones de Historia, 2006, p. 70.

18 Varela, *Retrato*, pp. 99, 107.

19 Fernández-Armesto, *Columbus*, pp. 40, 64.

20 Thomas Suárez, *Shedding the Veil: Mapping the European Discovery of America and the World*, Singapore, World Scientific Publishing, 1992, p. 44.

21 Las Casas, *Historia de las Indias*, vol. 1, Chapter 31, p. 242. Felipe Fernández-Armesto, *Columbus on Himself*, Cambridge, MA, Hackett, 2010, p. 11. Varela, *Retrato*, p. 15.

22 Las Casas, *Historia de las Indias*, vol. 1, Chapter 31, p. 243.

23 Ibid., pp. 242–3.

24 Ibid., Chapter 32, p. 247.

25 Tarsicio de Azcona, *Isabel la Católica. Estudio crítico de su vida y su reinado*, Madrid, Biblioteca de Autores Cristianos, 1993, pp. 815–16.

26 María Montserrat León Guerrero, 'El segundo viaje colombino', doctoral thesis, University of Valladolid, 2002, p. 88.

27 Fernández-Armesto, *Columbus*, p. 62.

28 Ibid., pp. 62, 56.

29 León, 'Segundo viaje', pp. 89–90 (citing J. Varela, *El Tratado de Tordesillas*, p. 39). Fernández-Armesto, *Columbus*, p. 62.

30 Azcona, *Isabel la Católica*, pp. 831–2.

31 Las Casas, *Historia de las Indias*, Chapter 31, p. 243. http://www.mcu.es/archivos/docs/Novedades/capitulaciones_ACA.pdf. Juan Manzano Manzano, *La incorporación de las Indias a la Corona de Castilla*, Madrid, Ediciones Cultura Hispánica, 1948, p. 265. Azcona, *Isabel la Católica*, pp. 834–5.

32 Murga Sanz, pp. 298–9. István Szászdi León-Borja, 'El origen de la Armada de Vizcaya y el Tratado de las Alcáçovas', *Historia, instituciones, documentos*, no. 26, 1999, p. 563.

33 Antonio Rumeu de Armas, *La política indigenista de Isabel la Católica*, Valladolid, Instituto 'Isabel la Católica' de Historia Eclesiástica, 1969, pp. 203–7, 227–9.

34 Azcona, *Isabel la Católica*, pp. 819–20.

35 Manuel Lobo Cabrera, *La conquista de Gran Canaria (1478–1483)*, Las Palmas de Gran Canaria, Cabildo Insular de Gran Canaria, Departamento de Ediciones, 2012, p. 157. Miguel Ángel Ladero Quesada (ed.), *Edad Media*, vol. 2 of *Historia Militar de España*, Madrid, Ministerio de Defensa, 2013, pp. 352–3.

36 Lobo Cabrera, *Conquista de Gran Canaria*, pp. 153, 156.

37 Ibid., pp. 158–9.

38 Ibid., p. 178.

39 Ibid., pp. 152–3, 167, 169–75.

40 *Esclavos*, vol. 8 of *Documentos para la historia de Canarias*, Santa Cruz de Tenerife, Gobierno de Canarias, 2006, pp. 19, 23.

41 Hieronymus Münzer, *Viaje por España y Portugal (1494–1495)*, Madrid, Polifemo, 1991, p. 62.

42 Rumeu de Armas, *Política*, p. 38 and doc. 4.

43 Ibid., doc. 15.

44 Lobo Cabrera, *Conquista de Gran Canaria*, p. 182.

45 Fernández-Armesto, *Before Columbus*, pp. 212–14. Lobo Cabrera, *Conquista de Gran Canaria*, pp. 70–1, 186.

46 Rumeu de Armas, *La Rábida*, pp. 102–5.

47 Fernández-Armesto, *Columbus*, pp. 43–4.

48 León, 'Segundo viaje', p. 17.

49 Juan Gil and Consuelo Varela (eds), *Cartas de particulares a Colón y relaciones coetáneas*, Madrid, Alianza, 1984, p. 99. Fernández-Armesto, *Columbus*, pp. 53, 73.

CHAPTER 29: PARTYING WOMEN

1 Diego Clemencín, *Elogio a la reina Isabel la Católica e ilustraciones sobre varios asuntos de su reinado*, vol. 6, Madrid, Memorias de la Real Academia de la Historia, 1821, p. 371.

2 Ibid., pp. 351–71.

3 Ibid., p. 371.

4 Ibid.

5 Ibid., p. 375 and n. 11.

6 Álvaro Fernández de Córdova Miralles, *La Corte de Isabel I. Ritos y ceremonias de una reina (1474–1504)*, Madrid, Dykinson, 2002, pp. 356–7.

7 Fernando del Pulgar, *Crónica de los Señores Reyes Católicos Don Fernando y Doña Isabel de Castilla y de Aragón*, in *Crónicas de los Reyes de Castilla*, vol. 3, ed. Cayetano Rosell, Madrid, Rivadeneyra, 1878, Part 2, Chapter 24.

8 Ibid.

9 Córdova, *La Corte*, p. 153.

10 Bethany Aram, *Juana the Mad: Sovereignty and Dynasty in Renaissance Europe*, Baltimore, Johns Hopkins University Press, 2005, p. 18.

11 Machado Journal, in James Gairdner, *Chronicles of Henry VII*, p. 355.

12 Córdova, *La Corte*, p. 28 (citing Marineo Sículo).

13 Carmen Manso Porto, in Luis Suárez Fernández and Carmen Manso Porto (eds), *Isabel la Católica en la Real Academia de la Historia*, Madrid, Real

Academia de la Historia, 2004, pp. 194–5. Francisco Javier Sánchez Cantón, *Libros, tapices y cuadros que coleccionó Isabel la Católica*, Madrid, Consejo Superior de Investigaciones Científicas, 1950, p. 23. Gonzalo Fernández de Oviedo, *Batallas y quinquagenas*, ed. J. Pérez de Tudela y Bueso, vols 1, Madrid, pp. 481–6. Córdova, *La Corte*, pp. 74, 299. Gonzalo Fernández de Oviedo, *Libro de la Cámara Real del Príncipe don Juan e offiçios de su casa e seruiçio ordinario*, p. 107.

14 Córdova, *La Corte*, pp. 160, 166, 293, 299. Giles Tremlett, *Catherine of Aragon*, London, Faber & Faber, 2010, p. 93.

15 *CSP Spain*, vol. 1, p. 156.

16 Córdova, *La Corte*, p. 112.

17 Ibid., p. 127.

18 Aram, *Juana the Mad*, p. 23.

19 Juan Luis Vives, *The Education of a Christian Woman: A Sixteenth-Century Manual*, ed. and trans. Charles Fantazzi, Chicago, University of Chicago Press, 2000, p. 49.

20 See Oviedo, *Quinquagenas*.

21 Desiderius Erasmus, *The Epistles of Erasmus*, trans. Francis Morgan Nichols, vol. 3, London, Longmans, Green, 1901, p. 421.

22 Elisa Ruiz, 'El patrimonio gráfico de Isabel la Católica y sus fuentes documentales', *Signo: Revista de Historia de la Cultura Escrita*, no. 14, 2004, p. 133.

23 Alfonso Martínez de Toledo, Arcipreste de Talavera, *Corbacho, o Reprobación del amor mundano*, Biblioteca Virtual Miguel de Cervantes, at http://www.cervantesvirtual.com/servlet/SirveObras/01473958655714017554480/index.htm.1466, Chapter 13.

24 Francesc Eiximenis, *Carro de las donas*, ed. Carmen Clausell Nácher, Madrid, Fundación Universitaria Española, 2007, vol. 2, Chapter 19.

25 Córdova, *La Corte*, p. 299.

26 Ibid., pp. 74, 299 (citing Galindez de Carvajal). Sánchez, *Libros, tapices*, p. 23. Oviedo, *Quinquagenas*, pp. 233, 481–6. Oviedo, *Cámara*, pp. 29–31, 107.

27 Oviedo, *Cámara*, pp. 29–31, 107. Sánchez, *Libros, tapices*, p. 23.

28 Córdova, *La Corte*, p. 297.

29 Ibid., pp. 254, 275.

CHAPTER 30: A HELLISH NIGHT

1 Pietro Martire d'Anghiera, *Epistolario de Pedro Mártir de Anglería*, edited and translated by José López de Toro, Madrid, Imp. de Góngora, 1953–7, Letters 125 and 127.

2 Ibid., Letters 125–6.

3   Ibid., Letter 125.

4   Pere Miguel Carbonell, *Chròniques de Espanya, fins aci no divulades*, Barcelona,Carles Amoros, 1547. pp. 521–5.

5   Martire d'Anghiera, *Epistolario*, Letters 125–6.

6   Ibid., Letter 126.

7   Ibid., Letter 127.

8   Ibid., Letter 127.

9   Ibid., Letter 126.

10 Carbonell, *Chròniques de Espanya*, pp. 521–5. Peggy K. Liss, *Isabel the Queen: Life and Times*, Philadelphia, University of Pennsylvania Press, 2004, p. 348.

11 Gonzalo Fernández de Oviedo, *Libro de la Cámara Real del Príncipe don Juan e offiçios de su casa e seruiçio ordinario*, pp. 193–6.

CHAPTER 31: A NEW WORLD

1   Felipe Fernández-Armesto, *Columbus on Himself*, Cambridge, MA, Hackett, 2010, pp. 97–8 (citing Fernando Colón, *Historia del Almirante*, vol. 1, pp. 162–3).

2   María Montserrat León Guerrero, 'El segundo viaje colombino', doctoral thesis, University of Valladolid, 2002, p. 28.

3   Consuelo Varela, *Cristóbal Colón. Retrato de un hombre*, Barcelona, Alianza, 1992, pp. 167, 207–8. León, 'Segundo viaje', pp. 233–4. Martín Fernández Navarrete (ed.), *Colección de los viages y descubrimientos que hicieron por mar los españoles desde fines del siglo XV*, vols 1–3, Madrid, Imprenta Real, 1825, vol. 1, pp. 447–8.

4   See Antonio Rumeu de Armas, *Libro copiador de Cristóbal Colón. Estudio histórico-crítico y edición*, 2 vols, Madrid, Ministerio de Cultura, 1989.

5   Navarrete, *Viages*, vol. 1, p. 153.

6   Fernández-Armesto, *Columbus on Himself*, pp. 38–9.

7   Bartolomé de Las Casas, *Historia de las Indias*, vols 1–2, Madrid, Imprenta Ginesta, 1875, vol. 1, Chapter 36, p. 267.

8   Ibid., Chapter 39, p. 286. Christopher Columbus, *Diaro of 1492* at http://www.ems.kcl.ac.uk/content/etext/e019.html.

9   Las Casas, *Historia de las Indias*, vol. 1, Chapter 39, p. 287.

10 Ibid., p. 288.

11 Ibid., pp. 288–9.

12 Fernández-Armesto, *Columbus on Himself*, pp. 50–2.

13 Luis Suárez Fernández, *Expansión de la Fé*, Madrid, Rialp, 1990, p. 251.

14 Juan Gil and Consuelo Varela (eds), *Cartas de particulares a Colón y relaciones coetáneas*, Madrid, Alianza, 1984, p. 120.

15 Felipe Fernández-Armesto, *Columbus*, Oxford, Oxford University Press, 1991, p. 88.

16 Fernández-Armesto *Columbus on Himself*, p. 133.

17 Fernández-Armesto, *Columbus*, p. 87.

18 Navarrete, *Documentos*, vol. 2, pp. 24–5.

19 Las Casas, *Historia de las Indias*, vol. 1, Chapter 64, p. 415.

20 Felipe Fernández-Armesto, *Pathfinders: A Global History of Exploration*, Oxford, Oxford University Press, 2007, pp. 141–3, 157–8.

21 Ibid., pp. 127, 131–2, 145–6.

22 Ibid. Richard W. Kaeuper, *Chivalry and Violence in Medieval Europe*, p. 151. Jennifer G. Wollock, *Rethinking Chivalry and Courtly Love*, Santa Barbara, Praeger, 2011, p. 138.

CHAPTER 32: INDIANS, PARROTS AND HAMMOCKS

1 Juan Gil and Consuelo Varela (eds), *Cartas de particulares a Colón y relaciones coetáneas*, Madrid, Alianza, 1984, pp. 227, 235. María Montserrat León Guerrero, 'El segundo viaje colombino', doctoral thesis, University of Valladolid, 2002, pp. 28–33.

2 León, 'Segundo viaje', pp. 23–8.

3 Consuelo Varela, *Cristóbal Colón. Retrato de un hombre*, Barcelona, Alianza, 1992, p. 218.

4 Bartolomé de Las Casas, *Historia de las Indias*, vols 1–2, Madrid, Imprenta Ginesta, 1875, vol. 1, Chapter 78.

5 Ibid., p. 447.

6 Angus A. A. Mol, 'The Gift of the "Face of the Living": Shell Faces as Social Valuables in the Caribbean Late Ceramic Age', *Journal de la Société des Américanistes*, vol. 97, no. 2, 2011, pp. 6–7, at http://jsa.revues.org/11834.

7 León, 'Segundo viaje', pp. 33–4. Martín Fernández Navarrete (ed.), *Colección de los viages y descubrimientos que hicieron por mar los españoles desde fines del siglo XV*, vols 1–3, Madrid, Imprenta Real, 1825, vol. 2, p. 23.

8 Las Casas, *Historia de las Indias*, vol. 1, Chapter 78, p. 477. León, 'Segundo viaje', p. 36.

9 Álvaro Fernández de Córdova Miralles, *La Corte de Isabel I. Ritos y ceremonias de una reina (1474–1504)*, Madrid, Dykinson, 2002, p. 79 (citing F. Bermúdez de Pedraza, *Historia eclesiástica*).

10 León, 'Segundo viaje', p. 36 (citing Las Casas, *Historia de las Indias*, vol. 1, p. 478).

11 Felipe Fernández-Armesto, *Columbus*, Oxford, Oxford University Press, 1991, p. 89.

12 Luis Suárez Fernández, *Expansión de la Fé*, Madrid, Rialp, 1990, p. 251.

13 Mol, 'The Gift of the "Face of the Living" ', pp. 6–8.

14 León, 'Segundo viaje', pp. 53, 59.

15 Ibid., p. 42 (citing A. Allegretti, *Il diario delle cose di Siena dall'anno 1450 fino al 1496*).

16 Felipe Fernández-Armesto, *Columbus on Himself*, Cambridge, MA, Hackett, 2010, p. 101. Álvaro Fernández de Córdova Miralles, *Alejandro VI y los Reyes Católicos. Relaciones político-eclesiásticas (1492–1503)*, Rome, Edizioni Università della Santa Croce, 2005, p. 480.

17 Richard L. Kagan, *Clio and the Crown: The Politics of History in Medieval and Early Modern Spain*, Baltimore, Johns Hopkins University Press, 2009 (Kindle edn), pp. 51–2.

18 'John Cabot in Seville' from *The Smugglers' City*, Department of History, University of Bristol at http://www.bristol.ac.uk/Depts/History/Maritime/Sources/1494cabotseville.htm.

19 León, 'Segundo viaje', p. 68.

20 Ibid., p. 69 (citing AGI, 7 May 1493).

21 Ibid., pp. 72–3.

22 Ibid., pp. 70–4, 78, 84–8, 108–9, 111, 121, 179, 182.

23 Fernández-Armesto, *Columbus*, pp. 62, 56. León, 'Segundo viaje', pp. 89, 125n.

24 Consuelo Varela, *Los cuatro viajes. Testamento*, Barcelona, Alianza, 2007, p. 13.

25 León, 'Segundo viaje', pp. 95–104.

26 Ibid., pp. 116–19, 121–5, 191–4, 198. Férnandez-Armesto, *Columbus*, pp. 62, 56.

27 León, 'Segundo viaje', p. 110.

28 Ibid., pp. 200–1, 229–31, 242.

29 Consuelo Varela, *Textos y documentos*, Madrid, Alianza, 1992, p. 219.

30 León, 'Segundo viaje', pp. 232–3.

31 Ibid., pp. 229–37.

32 Ibid., pp. 173–9.

CHAPTER 33: DIVIDING UP THE WORLD

1 María Montserrat León Guerrero, 'El segundo viaje colombino', doctoral thesis, University of Valladolid, 2002, p. 402.

2 Felipe Fernández-Armesto, *Columbus*, Oxford, Oxford University Press, 1991, pp. 99–100. Martin Fernández Navarrete (ed.), *Colección de los viages y descubrimientos que hicieron por mar los españoles desde fines del siglo XV*, vols 1–3, Madrid, Imprenta Real, 1825, vol. 2, p. 155.

3   Ibid.

4   Miguel Ángel Ladero Quesada, *Isabel I de Castilla. Siete ensayos sobre la reina, su entorno y sus empresas*, Madrid, Dykinson, 2012, p. 208.

5   León, 'Segundo viaje', pp. 241–4.

6   Ibid., pp. 250–1.

7   Ibid., pp. 254–5, 258, 266–73. Consuelo Varela, *La caída de Cristóbal Colón. El juicio de Bobadilla*, Barcelona, Marcial Pons, Ediciones de Historia, 2006, p. 95.

8   León, 'Segundo viaje', pp. 256, 275–7.

9   Ibid., p. 451.

10 Christopher Columbus, *Memorial para los reyes católicos* at www.artic.ua.es/biblioteca/u53/documentos/1142.doc.

11 Ibid.

12 Ibid.

13 Ibid.

14 León, 'Segundo viaje', p. 287.

15 Ibid., p. 288. Christopher Columbus, *Memorial para los reyes católicos* at www.artic.ua.es/biblioteca/u53/documentos/1142.doc.

16 Antonio Rumeu de Armas, *La política indigenista de Isabel la Católica*, Valladolid, Instituto 'Isabel la Católica' de Historia Eclesiástica, 1969, pp. 314–15, 318, 341, 366–72, 396.

17 Gonzalo Fernández de Oviedo, *Libro de la Cámara Real del Príncipe don Juan e offiçios de su casa e seruiçio ordinario*, p. 122.

18 See Ildefonso Gutierrez Azopardo, 'Los papas en los inicios de la trata negrera', at http://www.africafundacion.org/spip.php?article1847.

19 Ibid.

20 León, 'Segundo viaje', pp. 290–2. www.artic.ua.es/biblioteca/u53/documentos/1142.doc.

21 León, 'Segundo viaje', p. 301.

22 Ibid., pp. 310–18, 325.

23 Ibid., pp. 328–41, 348, 358.

24 Ibid., pp. 382, 395, 399–402. 'Treaty between Spain and Portugal at Torsedillas', 7 June 1494, from Frances Gardiner Davenport, *European treaties bearing on the history of the United States to 1648*, Washington, Camegie Institution, 1917, at http://avalon.law.yale.edu/15th_century/mod001.asp.

25 Juan Gil and Consuelo Varela (eds), *Cartas de particulares a Colón y relaciones coetáneas*, Madrid, Alianza, 1984, p. 226.

26 Ibid., pp. 228–30.

27 León, 'Segundo viaje', pp. 451, 453.

28   Ibid., pp. 412–15, 422.

29   Bartolomé de Las Casas, *Historia de las Indias*, vols 1–2, Madrid, Imprenta Ginesta, 1875, vol. 2, Chapter 100, pp. 73–4.

30   León, 'Segundo viaje', pp. 424–9 (citing Colón, *Carta Relación del segundo viaje explorador al interior de la Española*), 435, 440–3.

31   Ibid., pp. 419–20. Navarrete, *Documentos*, vol. 1, p. 177.

32   León, 'Segundo viaje', pp. 420, 440, 467.

33   Ibid., pp. 450, 453, 457–60, 474–7. Fernández-Armesto, *Columbus*, p. 111. Gil and Varela, *Cartas*, pp. 264–5.

34   León, 'Segundo viaje', pp. 445, 468. Fernández-Armesto, *Columbus*, pp. 113–14.

35   León, 'Segundo viaje', pp. 462–5. Navarrete, *Colección de los viages y descubrimientos que hicieron por mar los españoles desde fines del siglo XV*, vols 1–3, Madrid, Imprenta Real, 1825, vol. 1, p. 186.

36   León, 'Segundo viaje', pp. 468–70.

37   Ibid., pp. 471–2, 479.

38   Antonio Rumeu de Armas, *Libro copiador de Cristóbal Colón. Estudio histórico-crítico y edición*, 2 vols, Madrid, Ministerio de Cultura, 1989, vol. 1, pp. 308–9.

39   Raúl Aguilar Rodas, *Cristóbal Colón. Realidad y ficción tras 500 años de su muerte 1506–2006*, Medellín, Panibérica, 2006, pp. 89–90.

40   Fernández-Armesto, *Columbus*, pp. 116–20. Felipe Fernández-Armesto, *Columbus on Himself*, Cambridge, MA, Hackett, 2010, p. 133.

41   Consuelo Varela, *Textos y documentos*, Madrid, Alianza, 1992, p. 197.

42   Navarrete, *Documentos*, vol. 1, p. 392.

43   Ibid., p. 393.

44   Ibid., p. 394.

CHAPTER 34: A NEW CONTINENT

1   Felipe Fernández-Armesto, *Columbus*, Oxford, Oxford University Press, 1991, pp. 117, 122. Laurence Bergreen, *Columbus: The Four Voyages*, New York, Viking Penguin, 2011, p. 323.

2   Martín Fernández Navarrete, *Colección de los viages y descubrimientos que hicieron por mar los españoles desde fines del siglo XV*, vols 1–3, Madrid, Imprenta Real, 1825, vol. 3, pp. 506–7.

3   Consuelo Varela, *Textos y documentos*, Madrid, Alianza, 1992, pp. 238–9. Fernández-Armesto, *Columbus*, pp. 123–9. Bergreen, *Columbus*, p. 248. Felipe Fernández-Armesto, *Colón*, Barcelona, Crítica, 1992, p. 187.

4   Fernández-Armesto, *Columbus*, p. 129.

5   Varela, *Textos y documentos*, p. 203.

6   Fernández-Armesto, *Columbus*, pp. 129–31. Fernández-Armesto, *Colón*, p. 194.

7   Bartolomé de Las Casas, *Historia de las Indias*, vols 1–2, Madrid, Imprenta Ginesta, 1875, vol. 2, Chapter 148. Bergreen, *Columbus*, pp. 249, 254.

8   Consuelo Varela, *La caída de Cristóbal Colón. El juicio de Bobadilla*, Barcelona, Marcial Pons, Ediciones de Historia, 2006, p. 43. Juan Gil and Consuelo Varela (eds), *Cartas de particulares a Colón y relaciones coetáneas*, Madrid, Alianza, 1984, pp. 271–6. Varela, *Textos y documentos*, pp. 255–6. Bergreen, *Columbus*, p. 260.

9   Las Casas, *Historia de las Indias*, vol. 2, Chapter 155.

10 Varela, *Textos y documentos*, p. 256.

11 Varela, *Bobadilla*, p. 39. George J. Armelagos et al., 'The Science Behind Pre-Columbian Evidence of Syphilis in Europe', *Evolutionary Anthropology*, vol. 21, no. 2, 2012, pp. 50–7. Nathan Nunn and Nancy Qian, 'The Columbian Exchange: A History of Disease, Food, and Ideas', *Journal of Economic Perspectives*, vol. 24, no. 2, 2010, pp. 163–88.

12 Felipe Fernández-Armesto, *Columbus on Himself*, Cambridge, MA, Hackett, 2010, p. 178.

13 Varela, *Textos y documentos*, p. 258.

14 Varela, *Bobadilla*, pp. 44–5. Fernández-Armesto, *Columbus*, p. 135 (citing Las Casas, *Historia de las Indias*, vol. 2, p. 257).

15 Varela, *Bobadilla*, p. 52.

16 Ibid., pp. 53–4.

17 Gil and Varela, *Cartas*, p. 329.

18 Varela, *Bobadilla*, pp. 72–3, 85.

19 Ibid., pp. 98–100, 104–5.

20 Ibid., pp. 111–14, 119.

21 Ibid., pp. 112–16.

22 Antonio Rumeu de Armas, *La política indigenista de Isabel la Católica*, Valladolid, Instituto 'Isabel la Católica' de Historia Eclesiástica, 1969, p. 396.

23 Navarrete, *Viages*, vol. 2, p. 331. Miguel Ángel Ladero Quesada, *Isabel I de Castilla. Siete ensayos sobre la reina, su entorno y sus empresas*, Madrid, Dykinson, 2012, p. 231.

24 Varela, *Bobadilla*, p. 116.

25 Ladero Quesada, *Isabel*, p. 231.

26 Ibid., pp. 226–7.

27 Varela, *Bobadilla*, p. 168. Las Casas, *Historia de las Indias*, vol. 2, pp. 511–12.

28 Varela, *Textos y documentos*, p. 264.

29 Ibid.

30 Navarrete, *Viages*, vol. 1, p. 421.

31 Varela, *Textos y documentos*, p. 271.

32 Varela, *Bobadilla*, pp. 169–71. María Montserrat León Guerrero, 'El segundo viaje colombino', doctoral thesis, University of Valladolid, 2002, pp. 85–6.

33 Varela, *Textos y documentos*, p. 303. Christopher Columbus, *Carta a los reyes* at http://www.ems.kcl.ac.uk/content/etext/e023.html.

34 Varela, *Bobadilla*, pp. 171–4.

35 Consuelo Varela, *Los cuatro viajes. Testamento*, Barcelona, Alianza, 2007, pp. 29–32. Fernández-Armesto, *Columbus on Himself*, p. 221. Varela, *Textos y documentos*, p. 317.

36 Varela, *Textos y documentos*, p. 317.

37 Las Casas, *Historia de las Indias*, vol. 2, Chapter 5. Varela, *Bobadilla*, p. 172. Fernández-Armesto, *Columbus on Himself*, pp. 220–1. Clarence H. Haring, 'American Gold and Silver Production in the First Half of the 16th Century', *Quarterly Journal of Economics*, vol. 29, no. 3, May 1915, p. 465.

38 Varela, *Los cuatro viajes*, pp. 31–2.

39 Gil and Varela, *Cartas*, p. 501.

40 Varela, *Textos y documentos*, pp. 328–9.

CHAPTER 35: BORGIA WEDDINGS

1 Luis Suárez Fernández, *El camino hacia Europa*, Madrid, Rialp, 1990, p. 15. Johann Burchard, *At the Court of the Borgia*, ed. Geoffrey Parker, London, Folio Society, 2002, pp. 64–7.

2 Christopher Hibbert, *The Borgias*, London, Constable, 2011 (Kindle edn), pp. 47–50.

3 Burchard, *Borgia*, pp. 64–7.

4 Mary Hollingsworth, *The Borgias: History's Most Notorious Dynasty*, London, Quercus, 2011 (Kindle edn), loc. 1660.

5 Ibid., loc. 1404.

6 Hibbert, *Borgias*, p. 50.

7 Ibid., pp. 51–2.

8 Suárez, *Europa*, pp. 13–15, 23–9. Álvaro Fernández de Córdova Miralles, *La Corte de Isabel I. Ritos y ceremonias de una reina (1474–1504)*, Madrid, Dykinson, 2002, p. 275.

9 Álvaro Fernandez de Córdova Miralles, *Alejandro VI y los Reyes Católicos. Relaciones político-eclesiásticas (1492–1503)*, Rome, Edizioni Università della Santa Croce, 2005, pp. 236, 476.

10 Suárez, *Europa*, p. 25 n. 42 (citing his own *Política internacional*, vol. 3, p. 105 n. 52). Córdova, *Alejandro VI*, p. 276.

11   Suárez, *Europa*, pp. 13–15, 18, 26, 34, 48, 56, 95, 198.

12   Burchard, *Borgia*, pp. 91–120. Hollingsworth, *Borgias*, locs 1792–1884.

13   Luis Suárez Fernández, 'La declaración de guerra a Francia por parte de los Reyes Católicos en 1494', *Archivum*, vol. 12, 1962, pp. 204, 207–9. Suárez, *Europa*, pp. 50–6. Hollingsworth, *Borgias*, locs 1923–1943. Antonio Rodríguez Villa, *Crónicas del Gran Capitan*, Bailly, Madrid, 1908, p. 30.

14   Suárez, *Europa*, p. 72.

15   Ibid., p. 64.

CHAPTER 36: ALL THE THRONES OF EUROPE

1   *CSP Spain*, vol. 1, pp. 43–51.

2   Ibid. Luis Suárez Fernández, *El camino hacia Europa*, Madrid, Rialp, 1990, p. 28.

3   *CSP Spain*, vol. 1, pp. 107–14.

4   Ibid.

5   Suárez, *Europa*, p. 103.

6   Ibid., pp. 26–7, 34, 48, 56. Luis Suárez Fernández, 'La declaración de guerra a Francia por parte de los Reyes Católicos en 1494', *Archivum*, vol. 12, 1962, p. 195. Bethany Aram, *Juana the Mad: Sovereignty and Dynasty in Renaissance Europe*, Baltimore, Johns Hopkins University Press, 2005, p. 186.

7   Suárez, *Europa*, pp. 67–8, 82, 86. Tarsicio de Azcona, *Isabel la Católica. Estudio crítico de su vida y su reinado*, Madrid, Biblioteca de Autores Cristianos, 1993, p. 891.

8   Carmen Manso Porto, in Luis Suárez Fernández and Carmen Manso Porto (eds), *Isabel la Católica en la Real Academia de la Historia*, Madrid, Real Academia de la Historia, 2004, pp. 194–5. Francisco Javier Sánchez Cantón, *Libros, tapices y cuadros que coleccionó Isabel la Católica*, Madrid, Consejo Superior de Investigaciones Científicas, 1950, p. 23. Gonzalo Fernández de Oviedo, *Batallas y quinquagenas*, ed. J. Pérez de Tudela y Bueso, vol 1, Madrid, 1983, pp. 481–6. Álvaro Fernández de Córdova Miralles, *La Corte de Isabel I. Ritos y ceremonias de una reina (1474–1504)*, Madrid, Dykinson, 2002, pp. 74, 299. Gonzalo Fernández de Oviedo, *Libro de la Cámara Real del Príncipe don Juan e offiçios de su casa e seruiçio ordinario*, p. 107.

9   Alfredo Alvar Ezquerra, *Isabel la Católica*, Madrid, Temas de Hoy, 2002, p. 132 (citing Pietro Martire d'Anghiera, *Epistolario de Pedro Mártir de Anglería*, edited and translated by José López de Toro, Madrid, Imp. de Góngora, 1953–7). Álvaro Fernández de Córdova Miralles, *Alejandro VI y los Reyes Católicos. Relaciones político-eclesiásticas (1492–1503)*, Rome, Edizioni Università della Santa Croce, 2005, p. 867.

10   Martire d'Anghiera, *Epistolario*, Letter 171.

11   Ibid.

12   Luis Suárez Fernández, *Política internacional de Isabel la Católica*, 6 vols, Valladolid, Instituto 'Isabel la Católica' de Historia Eclesiástica, 1965–72, vol. 4, p. 698. François Soyer, *The Persecution of the Jews and Muslims of Portugal: King Manuel I and the End of Religious Tolerance (1496–7)*, Leiden, Brill, 2007, p. 173.

13   Lalaing in Emilo García Rodríguez, 'Toledo y sus visitantes extranjeros hasta 1561', *Toletum: Boletín de la Real Academia de Bellas Artes y Ciencias Históricas de Toledo*, no. 1, 1955, p. 26.

14   Martire d'Anghiera, *Epistolario*, Letter 374.

15   Antonio de la Torre y del Cerro and Luis Suárez Fernández, *Documentos referentes a las relaciones con Portugal durante el reinado de los Reyes Católicos*, 3 vols, Valladolid, Consejo Superior de Investigaciones Científicas, 1960–3, vol. 3, pp. 13–18. Suárez, *Europa*, pp. 110–12. Soyer, *Persecution of the Jews*, p. 239. Javier Liske, *Viajes de extranjeros por España y Portugal en los siglos XV, XVI y XVII*, Madrid, Medina, 1878, p. 64.

16   De la Torre and Suárez, *Documentos Portugal*, vol. 3, p. 13.

17   Soyer, *Persecution of the Jews*, pp. 122, 188–90, 230–8.

18   Ibid., p. 192.

19   Ibid., pp. 14, 192, 194, 206, 209.

20   Abraham Gross, *Iberian Jewry from Twilight to Dawn: The World of Rabbi Abraham Saba*, Leiden, Brill, 1995, p. 9.

21   Soyer, *Persecution of the Jews*, pp. 16, 207.

22   Ibid., pp. 210, 217.

23   Ibid., p. 213.

24   Ibid., pp. 217–19.

25   Gross, *Iberian Jewry*, p. 10. Soyer, *Persecution of the Jews*, p. 229.

26   De la Torre and Suárez, *Documentos Portugal*, vol. 3, p. 10. Soyer, *Persecution of the Jews*, pp. 263–8.

CHAPTER 37: THOUGH WE ARE CLERICS ... WE ARE STILL FLESH AND BLOOD

1   See Juan Ruiz, Arcipreste de Hita, *Libro de buen amor*, Paris, Louis Michaud, undated, at http://www.cervantesvirtual.com/obra-visor/el-libro-de-buen-amor--o/html/ffoec418–82b1–11df-acc7–002185ce6064.html

2   María Sabina Álvarez Bezos, 'Violencia contra las mujeres en la castilla del final de la edad media. Documentos para el estudio de las mujeres como protagonistas de su historia', doctoral thesis, Universidad de Valladolid, 2013, pp. 293–7, at https://uvadoc.uva.es/bitstream/10324/4413/1/TESIS472–140224.pdf.

3   Álvaro Fernández de Córdova Miralles, *Alejandro VI y los Reyes Católicos. Relaciones político-eclesiásticas (1492–1503)*, Rome, Edizioni Università della Santa Croce, 2005, pp. 624–5.

4   José Sánchez Herrero, 'Amantes, barraganas, compañeras, concubinas clericales', *Clío y Crímen*, no. 5, 2008, p. 137.

5   Navagero in Jorge de Einghen et al., *Viajes por España de Jorge de Einghen, del Barón Leon de Rosmithal de Blatine, de Francisco Guicciardini y de Andrés Navajero; traducido, anotados y con un introducción por Antonio María Fabié*, Madrid, Librería de los Bibliófilos, 1889, p. 254. Hieronymus Münzer, *Viaje por España y Portugal (1494–1495)*, Madrid, Polifemo, 1991, p. 247. Córdova, *Alejandro VI*, p. 656.

6   Alonso de Palencia, *Crónica de Enrique IV*, ed. A. Paz y Meliá, 4 vols, Madrid, Revista de Archivos, 1904–8, Década 1, Libro 5, Chapter 8. Lucio Marineo Sículo, *Vida y hechos de los reyes Católicos*, Madrid, Atlas, 1943, pp. 73–4. Córdova, *Alejandro VI*, pp. 541–2.

7   Palencia, *Crónica de Enrique IV*, Década 1, Libro 7, Chapter 4. Córdova, *Alejandro VI*, p. 269 (citing Reinhard, 'Le népotisme. Fonctions et avatars d'une constante de l'histoire pontificale', in Reinhard, *Papauté, confessions, modernité*, pp. 69–98).

8   Córdova, *Alejandro VI*, pp. 276, 569–72, 608, 611. Marvin Lunenfeld, *The Council of Santa Hermandad: A Study of the Pacification Forces of Ferdinand and Isabela*, Coral Gables, FL, University of Miami Press, 1970, p. 212.

9   *Cortes de los antiguos reinos de León y Castilla, pub. por la Real Academia de la Historia*, vol. 4, Madrid, Rivadeneyra, 1882, p. 144. Córdova, *Alejandro VI*, pp. 625, 629. Álvarez Bezos, 'Violencia contra las mujeres', pp. 299–305.

10 John Edwards, *Isabel la Católica. Poder y fama*, Madrid, Marcial Pons, 2004, pp. 181–2, 192.

11 Popplau in Javier Liske, *Viajes de extranjeros por España y Portugal en los siglos XV, XVI y XVII*, Madrid, Medina, 1878, p. 8.

12 Indigo de Mendoza, *Coplas de vita Christi* at http://revistaliterariakatharsis.org/Coplas_de_Vita.pdf.

13 Córdova, *Alejandro VI*, p. 643.

14 Ibid., pp. 646–50.

15 Ibid., pp. 667–9.

16 Ibid., pp. 667–70.

17 Andrés Bernáldez, *Historia de los Reyes Católicos don Fernando y doña Isabel*, in *Crónicas de los Reyes de Castilla*, ed. Cayetano Rosell, vol. 70, Madrid, Biblioteca de Autores Españoles, 1878, Chapter 202.

18 Córdova, *Alejandro VI*, pp. 542–60, 673.

CHAPTER 38: JUANA'S FLEET

1   Alonso de Santa Cruz, *Crónica de los Reyes Católicos*, ed. Juan de Mata Carriazo, Seville, Publicaciones de la Escuela de Estudios Hispano-Americanos de Sevilla, 1951, Chapter 32. Miguel Ángel Ladero Quesada, *La Armada de Flandes. Un episodio en la política naval de los Reyes Católicos*, Madrid, Real Academia de la Historia, 2003, pp. 86, 104. Miguel Ángel Ladero Quesada, *Isabel I de Castilla. Siete ensayos sobre la reina, su entorno y sus empresas*, Madrid, Dykinson, 2012, pp. 115, 127.

2   Hieronymus Münzer, *Viaje por España y Portugal (1494–1495)*, Madrid, Polifemo, 1991, p. 44.

3   *Isabel la Católica. Magnificencia de un reinado*, p. 303. Ladero Quesada, *La Armada*, pp. 95–6, 148, 160–2. Ladero Quesada, *Isabel*, p. 128.

4   María Montserrat León Guerrero, 'La Armada de Flandes y el viaje de la Princesa Juana', *Revista de Estudios Colombinos*, no. 5, 2009, p. 57. Ladero Quesada, *Isabel*, p. 128.

5   León, 'La Armada de Flandes', p. 57.

6   Ladero Quesada, *La Armada*, pp. 63, 128.

7   Ladero Quesada, *Isabel*, pp. 128–30. Ladero Quesada, *La Armada*, p. 92.

8   Oviedo, *Cámara*, p. 165. Ladero Quesada, *Isabel*, p. 132.

9   Ladero Quesada, *Isabel*, p. 131.

10   Antonio Rumeu de Armas, *Itinerario de los Reyes Católicos, 1474–1516*, Madrid, Instituto Jerónimo Zurita, Biblioteca Reyes Católicos, 1974, pp. 227–8. Santa Cruz, *Crónica*, Chapter 32. Luis Suárez Fernández, *El camino hacia Europa*, Madrid, Rialp, 1990, pp. 82–3. John Edwards, *Isabel la Católica. Poder y fama*, Madrid, Marcial Pons, 2004, pp. 154–5.

11   Luis Suárez Fernández, *Política internacional de Isabel la Católica*, 6 vols, Valladolid, Instituto 'Isabel la Católica' de Historia Eclesiástica, 1965–72, vol. 4, doc. 177.

12   Santa Cruz, *Crónica*, Chapter 32. Ladero Quesada, *La Armada*, pp. 86, 104. Ladero Quesada, *Isabel*, p. 127. Suárez, *Política internacional*, vol. 4, doc. 178.

13   Santa Cruz, *Crónica*, Chapter 32. Ladero Quesada, *La Armada*, pp. 14, 104. Suárez, *Política internacional*, vol. 4, doc. 183.

14   *CSP Spain*, Supplement, pp. 54–62. Bethany Aram, *Juana the Mad: Sovereignty and Dynasty in Renaissance Europe*, Baltimore, Johns Hopkins University Press, 2005, pp. 35–6, 42, 54. Antonio Rodríguez Villa, *La Reina Doña Juana la Loca. Estudio histórico*, Madrid, Librería Murillo, 1892, pp. 185, 199.

15   Miguel Angel Zalama Rodríguez, 'Colon y Juana I. Los viajes por mar de la reina entre España y los Países Bajos', *Revista de Estudios Colombinos*,

no. 5, 2009, p. 42. Duque de Berwick y de Alba (ed.), *Correspondencia de Gutierre Gómez de Fuensalida. Embajador en Alemania, Flandes e Inglaterra (1496–1509)*, Madrid, Imprenta Alemana, 1907, p. ix.

16 Jean Molinet, *Chroniques*, 5, Paris, 1828, p. 64. Suárez, *Europa*, p. 108.

17 Molinet, *Chroniques*, p. 64. Suárez, *Europa*, p. 108.

18 Duque de Berwick y de Alba (ed.), *Correspondencia*, p. ix. Vicente Rodríguez Valencia, *Isabel la Católica en la opinión de españoles y extranjeros. Siglos XV al XX*, vol. 1: *Siglos XV al XVI*, Valladolid, Instituto 'Isabel la Católica' de Historia Eclesiástica, 1970, p. 20. Aram, *Juana the Mad*, pp. 34–5, 41, 47, 77. Suárez, *Política internacional*, vol. 4, doc. 188.

19 Molinet, *Chroniques*, p. 64. Suárez, *Política internacional*, vol. 5, docs 72 and 100. Aram, *Juana the Mad*, p. 42. Ladero Quesada, *La Armada*, pp. 114, 134.

20 Fuensalida, *Correspondencia*, pp. 139, 143.

CHAPTER 39: TWICE MARRIED, BUT A VIRGIN WHEN SHE DIED

1 Marino Sanuto, *I diarii di Marino Sanuto*, Venice, Fratelli Visentini Tipografi Editori, 1886, vol. 1, pp. 620–3.

2 Alonso de Santa Cruz, *Crónica de los Reyes Católicos*, ed. Juan de Mata Carriazo, 2 vols, Seville, Publicaciones de la Escuela de Estudios Hispano-Americanos de Sevilla, 1951, pp. 164–5. Álvaro Fernández de Córdova Miralles, *La Corte de Isabel I. Ritos y ceremonias de una reina (1474–1504)*, Madrid, Dykinson, 2002, pp. 289, 403. Garrett Mattingly, *Catherine of Aragon*, London, Jonathan Cape, 1942, p. 22. Emilo García Rodríguez, 'Toledo y sus visitantes extranjeros hasta 1561', *Toletum: Boletín de la Real Academia de Bellas Artes y Ciencias Históricas de Toledo*, no. 1, 1955, p. 17. Felipe Fernández-Armesto, *Ferdinand and Isabella*, New York, Dorset Press, 1991, p. 108.

3 Mattingly, *Catherine of Aragon*, p. 22.

4 Gonzalo Fernández de Oviedo, *Libro de la Cámara Real del Príncipe don Juan e offiçios de su casa e seruiçio ordinario*, p. 158.

5 Ibid., p. 111.

6 Córdova, *La Corte*, p. 150.

7 Oviedo, *Cámara*, pp. 197–8. Córdova, *La Corte*, p. 150. Juana María Arcelus, 'La Desconocida Librería de Isabel la Católica', in *Actes del X Congres Internacional de l'Associació Hispánica de Literatura Medieval*, ed. Rafael Alemany, Josep Lluís Martos and Josep Miquel Manzanaro, vol. 1, Alicante, 2005, pp. 296–7.

8 Tarsicio de Azcona, 'El Príncipe don Juan, heredero de los Reyes Católicos, en el V centenario de su nacimiento (1478–1497)', *Cuadernos de Investigación Histórica*, no. 7, 1983, p. 223.

9   Ibid., pp. 224–5. Antonio de la Torre y del Cerro, *Cuentas de Gonzalo de Baeza, tesorero de Isabel la Católica*, 2 vols, Madrid, Consejo Superior de Investigaciones Científicas, 1956, vol. 2, pp. 50–2. Oviedo, *Cámara*, p. 129.

10 Oviedo, *Cámara*, p. 111.

11 Arcelus, 'La Desconocida Librería', p. 299. Azcona, 'El Príncipe don Juan', pp. 226–7. See also Barbara F. Weissberger, *Isabel Rules: Constructing Queenship, Wielding Power*, Minneapolis, University of Minnesota Press, 2003.

12 Córdova, *La Corte*, p. 150 (citing *Blasón General*, fol. 18).

13 Azcona, 'El Príncipe don Juan', p. 243.

14 Pietro Martire d'Anghiera, *Epistolario de Pedro Mártir de Anglería*, edited and translated by José López de Toro, Madrid, Imp. de Góngora, 1953–7, Letters 176, 334 and 335. Ángel Rodríguez Sánchez, 'La muerte del Príncipe de Asturias, Señor de Salamanca', *Revista de Estudios Extremeños*, vol. 57, no. 1, 2001, p. 30.

15 Miguel Ángel Pérez Priego, 'Historia y literatura en torno al príncipe D. Juan, la "Representación sobre el poder del Amor" de Juan del Encina', in R. Beltrán, J. L. Canet and J. L. Sirera (eds), *Historias y ficciones. Coloquio sobre la literatura del siglo XV*, Valencia, Universitat-Departament de Filologia Espanyola, 1992, pp. 337–49.

16 Luis Suárez Fernández (ed.), *Isabel la Católica en la Real Academia de la Historia*, Madrid, Real Academia de la Historia, 2004, p. 85. Azcona, 'El Príncipe don Juan', p. 235.

17 Martire d'Anghiera, *Epistolario*, Letter 335.

18 Andrés Bernáldez, *Historia de los Reyes Católicos don Fernando y doña Isabel*, in *Crónicas de los Reyes de Castilla*, ed. Cayetano Rosell, vol. 70, Madrid, Biblioteca de Autores Españoles, 1878, Chapter 155. Rodríguez Sánchez, 'La muerte del Príncipe de Asturias', pp. 32, 44. Antonio Rumeu de Armas, *Itinerario de los Reyes Católicos, 1474–1516*, Madrid, Instituto Jerónimo Zurita, Biblioteca Reyes Católicos, 1974, p. 237. Santa Cruz, *Crónica*, p. 167.

19 Azcona, 'El Príncipe don Juan', pp. 234–6.

20 Bernáldez, *Historia de los Reyes Católicos*, Chapter 154.

21 Azcona, 'El Príncipe don Juan', p. 237. Arcadio de Larrea Palacios, *El Cancionero judío del norte de Marruecos*, Madrid, CSIC, 1952, pp. 68–9.

22 Tarsicio de Azcona, *Isabel la Católica. Estudio crítico de su vida y su reinado*, Biblioteca de Autores Cristianos, Madrid, 1993, p. 878 (citing *Libro de Cedulas* 2–2, fol. 325).

23 Bernáldez, *Historia de los Reyes Católicos*, Chapter 155.

24 Martire d'Anghiera, *Epistolario*, Letter 183.

25 Joseph Pérez, *Isabel y Fernando. Los Reyes Católicos*, San Sebastián, Nerea, 1997, p. 217.

26 Oviedo, *Cámara*, pp. 135, 136.

27 Rafael Ramírez de Arellano, *Historia de Córdoba desde su fundación hasta la muerte de Isabel la Católica, Ciudad Real, Tipografía del Hospicio Provincial*, vol. 4, 1919, p. 354. Pérez Priego, 'Historia y literatura', p. 341.

28 Azcona, *Isabel la Católica*, p. 879 n. 16 (citing Arellano, *Historia de Córdoba*, vol. 4, pp. 285–8). Arellano, *Historia de Córdoba*, vol. 4, pp. 354–7.

29 Duque de Berwick y de Alba (ed.), *Correspondencia de Gutierre Gómez de Fuensalida. Embajador en Alemania, Flandes e Inglaterra (1496–1509)*, Madrid, Imprenta Alemana, 1907, p. 7.

30 Bartolomé de Las Casas, *Historia de las Indias*, vols 1–2, Madrid, Imprenta Ginesta, 1875, vol. 1, Chapter 126.

31 Luis Suárez Fernández, '1500. Un giro radical en la política de los Reyes Católicos', *En la España Medieval*, no. 9, 1986, p. 1257.

32 Martire d'Anghiera, *Epistolario*, Letter 374.

33 Ibid., Letters 373–4.

34 Azcona, *Isabel la Católica*, p. 713.

CHAPTER 40: THE THIRD KNIFE-THRUST OF PAIN

1 Hieronymus Münzer, *Viaje por España y Portugal (1494–1495)*, Madrid, Polifemo, 1991, pp. 33–5. Antonio Rumeu de Armas, *Itinerario de los Reyes Católicos, 1474–1516*, Madrid, Instituto Jerónimo Zurita, Biblioteca Reyes Católicos, 1974, p. 254.

2 Münzer, *Viaje*, pp. 105, 113, 115, 127. José Antonio García Luján, *El Generalife. Jardín del paraíso*, Granada, J. A. García, 2006, p. 11.

3 Robert Irwin, *The Alhambra*, London, Profile Books, 2004, p. 55.

4 Isabelle Poutrin Reyes, 'Los derechos de los vencidos. Las capitulaciones de Granada', *Sharq al-Andalus*, vol. 19, 2008–10, pp. 13–18.

5 Pietro Martire d'Anghiera, *Epistolario de Pedro Mártir de Anglería*, edited and translated by José López de Toro, Madrid, Imp. de Góngora, 1953–7, Letter 199. Tarsicio de Azcona, *Isabel la Católica. Estudio crítico de su vida y su reinado*, Madrid, Biblioteca de Autores Cristianos, 1993, pp. 529, 880. Rumeu de Armas, *Itinerario*, p. 274.

6 Antonio de la Torre y del Cerro and Luis Suárez Fernández, *Documentos referentes a las relaciones con Portugal durante el reinado de los Reyes Católicos*, 3 vols, Valladolid, Consejo Superior de Investigaciones Científicas, 1960–3,

vol. 3, p. 30. François Soyer, *The Persecution of the Jews and Muslims of Portugal: King Manuel I and the End of Religious Tolerance (1496–7)*, Leiden, Brill, 2007, p. 278.

7　De la Torre and Suárez, *Documentos Portugal*, vol. 3, p. 30. Soyer, *Persecution of the Jews*, pp. 278–9. Damião de Góis, *Crónica do felicíssimo Rei D. Manuel*, vols 1–2, Coimbra, 1949, pp. 224–7.

8　Poutrin, 'Los derechos de los vencidos', p. 18.

9　Soyer, *Persecution of the Jews*, pp. 278–9.

10　Martire d'Anghiera, *Epistolario*, Letter 216.

11　Andrés Bernáldez, *Historia de los Reyes Católicos don Fernando y doña Isabel*, in *Crónicas de los Reyes de Castilla*, ed. Cayetano Rosell, vol. 70, Madrid, Biblioteca de Autores Españoles, 1878, Chapter 154. Martire d'Anghiera, *Epistolario*, Letter 216. Azcona, *Isabel la Católica*, pp. 526, 529.

CHAPTER 41: THE DIRTY TIBER

1　Johann Burchard, *At the Court of the Borgia*, ed. Geoffrey Parker, London, Folio Society, 2002, pp. 144–6.

2　Ibid.

3　Christopher Hibbert, *The Borgias*, London, Constable, 2011, p. 112.

4　Mary Hollingsworth, *The Borgias: History's Most Notorious Dynasty*, London, Quercus, 2011 (Kindle edn), locs 2128–39.

5　Ibid., locs 2268–87. Hibbert, *Borgias*, p. 119. Álvaro Fernández de Córdova Miralles, *Alejandro VI y los Reyes Católicos. Relaciones político-eclesiásticas (1492–1503)*, Rome, Edizioni Università della Santa Croce, 2005, p. 399.

6　Córdova, *Alejandro VI*, p. 397.

7　Hollingsworth, *Borgias*, loc. 2307.

8　Córdova, *Alejandro VI*, p. 400.

9　Luis Suárez Fernández, '1500. Un giro radical en la política de los Reyes Católicos', *En la España Medieval*, no. 9, 1986, p. 1265. Hollingsworth, *Borgias*, loc. 2503.

10　National Archives, PRO 31/11. *CSP Spain*, vol. 1, pp. 152, 156, 185–6, 198.

11　Mary Anne Everett Wood Green, *Letters of Royal and Illustrious Ladies of Great Britain*, 3 vols, London, Henry Colburn, 1846, vol. 1, p. 122. *CSP Spain*, vol. 1, p. 164.

12　National Archives, PRO 31/11. *CSP Spain*, vol. 1, pp. xci, 207.

13　Antonio de la Torre y del Cerro, *Cuentas de Gonzalo de Baeza, tesorero de Isabel la Católica*, vol. 1, Madrid, Consejo Superior de Investigaciones Científicas, 1956, pp. 266, 297, 428. Francisco Javier Sánchez Cantón,

Maestre Nicolás Francés, Madrid, CSIC, Instituto Diego Velázquez, 1964, pp. 41–65.

14   National Archives, PRO 31/11/3. *CSP Spain*, vol. 1, pp. 163, 179, 226, 258, 305. Garrett Mattingly, *Catherine of Aragon*, London, Jonathan Cape, 1942, p. 26. Alfredo Alvar Ezquerra, *Isabel la Catolica*, Madrid, Temas de Hoy, 2002, p. 322.

15   Thomas More, *Selected Letters*. Elizabeth Frances Rogers (ed.), New Haven, Yale University Press, 1961, p. 2.

16   Gordon Kipling (ed.), *The Receyt of The Ladie Kateryne*, Oxford, Oxford University Press for the Early English Text Society, 1990, p. 41.

17   Real Academia de Historia, MS 9–4674 (Veruela).

18   Edward Hall, *Hall's Chronicle – The union of the two noble and illustre famelies of Lancastre and Yorke (1548)*, London, J. Johnson, 1809, p. 494.

19   *CSP Spain*, vol. 1, p. 278. Álvaro Fernández de Córdova Miralles, *La Corte de Isabel I. Ritos y ceremonias de una reina (1474–1504)*, Madrid, Dykinson, 2002, p. 86.

20   *CSP Spain*, vol. 1, p. 360. National Archives, PRO 31/11/4.

21   A. H. Thomas and I. D. Thornley (eds), *The Great Chronicle of London*, Gloucester, Alan Sutton, 1983, p. 323.

22   Nicholas Pocock (ed.), *Records of the Reformation: The Divorce, 1527–33*, vol. 2, Oxford, Clarendon Press, 1870, pp. 426–8.

23   Giles Tremlett, *Catherine of Aragon*, London, Faber & Faber, 2010, pp. 63, 104.

24   *CSP Spain*, vol. 4, p. 572.

25   Stephan Ehses (ed.), *Römische Dokumente zur Geschichte der Ehescheidung Heinrichs VIII von England*, Paderborn, Ferdinand Schöningh, 1893, p. xliii. J. J. Scarisbrick, *Henry the Eighth*, London, Eyre Methuen, 1981, pp. 9–10.

CHAPTER 42: WE GERMANS CALL THEM RATS

1   Antoine de Lalaing, 'Relato del primer viaje de Felipe el Hermoso a España', in *Viajes de extranjeros por España y Portugal, desde los tiempos más remotos hasta fines del siglo XVI*, ed. J. García Mercadal, Madrid, 1952, pp. 247–8.

2   Ibid., p. 497.

3   Popplau in Javier Liske, *Viajes de extranjeros por España y Portugal en los siglos XV, XVI y XVII*, Madrid, Medina, 1878, p. 55.

4   Hieronymus Münzer, *Viaje por España y Portugal (1494–1495)*, Madrid, Polifemo, 1991, pp. 93–7, 103, 127.

5   Isabelle Poutrin Reyes, 'Los derechos de los vencidos. Las capitulaciones de Granada', *Sharq al-Andalus*, vol. 19, 2008–10, pp. 13–20.

6 Navagero in Jorge de Einghen et al., *Viajes por España de Jorge de Einghen, del Barón Leon de Rosmithal de Blatine, de Francisco Guicciardini y de Andrés Navajero; traducido, anotados y con un introducción por Antonio María Fabié*, Madrid, Librería de los Bibliófilos, 1889, p. 246. Noelia Silva Santa-Cruz, 'Maurofilia y mudejarismo en época de Isabel la Cátolica', in Fernando Checa Cremades (ed.), *Isabel la Católica. Magnificencia de un reinado. Quinto centenario de Isabel la Católica, 1504–2004*, Madrid, Sociedad Estatal de Conmemoraciones Culturales, 2004, pp. 143–5. Bernabé Cabañero Subiza, 'La Aljafería de Zaragoza', *Artigrama*, no. 22, 2007, p. 107.

7 Miguel Ángel Ladero Quesada, *Isabel I de Castilla. Siete ensayos sobre la reina, su entorno y sus empresas*, Madrid, Dykinson, 2012, pp. 159–61. Miguel Ángel Ladero Quesada, 'Los mudéjares de Castilla cuarenta años después', *En la España Medieval*, no. 33, 2010, p. 389.

8 Miguel Ángel Ladero Quesada, *Los mudéjares de Castilla en tiempos de Isabel I*, Madrid, Instituto 'Isabel la Católica' de Historia Eclesiástica, 1969, pp. 17–19. Jean-Pierre Molénat, 'Hornachos fin XVe–début XVIe siècles [Hornachos, Late 15th–Early 16th Century]', *En la España Medieval*, no. 31, 2008, pp. 161–76.

9 Isabel Montes Romero-Camacho, 'Las comunidades mudéjares en la Corona de Castilla durante el siglo XV', in *De mudéjares a moriscos. Una conversión forzada. Actas*, Instituto de Estudios Turolenses, Centro de Estudios Mudéjares, 2002, p. 461. Serafín de Tapia Sánchez, 'Los mudéjares de la Extremadura castellano-leonesa. Notas sobre una minoría dócil (1085–1502)', *Studia Historica*, no. 7, 1989, pp. 109–10. Serafín de Tapia Sánchez, 'Los judíos de Ávila en vísperas de la expulsión', *Sefarad*, no. 57/1, 1997, pp. 136, 145.

10 Angus MacKay, *Spain in the Middle Ages: From Frontier to Empire, 1000–1500*, London, Macmillan, 1977, pp. 215–18.

11 Ladero Quesada, *Isabel*, p. 176 (citing Anon, *Hechos del condestable Miguel Lucas de Iranzo*, Granada, Universidad de Granada, 2009).

12 Anon, *Hechos del condestable Miguel Lucas de Iranzo*, pp. 98–100, 111–12. José Julio Martín Romero, 'El Condestable Miguel Lucas en su crónica', *Revista de Filología Española*, vol. 91, 2011, pp. 129–58.

13 Silva Santa-Cruz, 'Maurofilia y mudejarismo', pp. 145, 143. Gonzalo Menéndez Pidal, *La España del siglo XIII. Leída en imágenes*, Madrid, Real Academia de la Historia, 1986, pp. 94–5.

14 Ladero Quesada, *Isabel*, pp. 176, 185–8. Álvaro Fernández de Córdova Miralles, *La Corte de Isabel I. Ritos y ceremonias de una reina (1474–1504)*, Madrid, Dykinson, 2002, p. 286.

15 Silva Santa-Cruz, 'Maurofilia y mudejarismo', pp. 145, 143–4. Barbara Fuchs, *Exotic Nation: Maurophilia and the Construction of Early Modern Spain*, Philadelphia, University of Pennsylvania Press, 2009, p. 70.

16 Ladero Quesada, *Isabel*, p. 159.

17 Münzer, *Viaje*, pp. xvi, 209.

18 Liske, *Viajes*, pp. 55–6.

19 Ladero Quesada, *Isabel*, pp. 159–61. Jose Bordes and Enrique Sanz, 'El protagonismo mudéjar en el comercio entre Valencia y el norte de Africa', in *De mudéjares a moriscos. Una conversión forzada. Actas*, Instituto de Estudios Turolenses, Centro de Estudios Mudéjares, 2002, pp. 275–81.

20 Ladero Quesada, *Isabel*, p. 162.

21 Ibid., pp. 161–2. P. S. van Koningsveld and G. A. Wiegers, 'The Islamic Statute of the Mudejars in the Light of a New Source', *Al-Qantara*, vol. 17, 1996, pp. 19–58. P. S. Koningsveld and G. A. Wiegers, 'Islam in Spain during the Early Sixteenth Century: The Views of Four Chief Judges in Cairo', *Orientations* 4, 1996, p. 140.

22 Ladero Quesada, *Isabel*, pp. 158–62. Koningsveld and Wiegers, 'Islam in Spain during the Early Sixteenth Century', p. 137.

23 François Soyer, *The Persecution of the Jews and Muslims of Portugal: King Manuel I and the End of Religious Tolerance (1496–7)*, Leiden, Brill, 2007, pp. 260–1 (citing Damião de Góis, *Crónica do felicíssimo Rei D. Manuel*, vols. 1–2, Coimbra, 1949, vol. 1, p. 43).

24 Ladero Quesada, *Isabel*, p. 160.

25 Ibid., pp. 159–62. Ladero Quesada, *Mudéjares*, p. 203.

26 Ladero Quesada, *Isabel*, pp. 170, 186–8, 200.

27 See François Martínez, 'Talavera/Cisneros. Dos posturas diferentes con un mismo fin ideológico', in *Actas del IX° Congreso Internacional de Sociocrítica*, Edmond Cros, Blanca Cardenas Fernandez and Juan Carlos Gonzalez Vidal (eds), Morelia, Universidad Michoacana, 2005. Luis del Mármol Carvajal, *Historia del rebelión y castigo de los moriscos del Reino de Granada*, Madrid, Imprenta de Sancha, 1797, p. 58.

28 Ladero Quesada, *Isabel*, p. 203.

29 Ibid., pp. 178–9.

30 Ibid., pp. 196–201, 254. Tarsicio de Azcona, *Isabel la Católica. Estudio crítico de su vida y su reinado*, Madrid, Biblioteca de Autores Cristianos, 1993, pp. 681, 685. Córdova, *La Corte*, pp. 671–2.

31 Azcona, *Isabel la Católica*, p. 686.

32 Ladero Quesada, *Isabel*, pp. 164, 170, 174. Azcona, *Isabel la Católica*, pp. 686–7, 689n. See also François Martínez, 'Talavera/Cisneros. Dos posturas diferentes con un mismo fin ideológico', in *Actas del IX°*

Congreso Internacional de Sociocrítica, Edmond Cros, Blanca Cardenas Fernandez and Juan Carlos Gonzalez Vidal (eds), Morelia, Universidad Michoacana, 2005.

33   Azcona, *Isabel la Católica*, pp. 687–9. Herrero del Collado, *Talavera y Cisneros: dos vivencias socio-religiosas en la conversión de los moros de Granada*, Madrid, Darek-Nyumba, 2001, p. 27. Ladero Quesada, *Isabel*, p. 171.

34   Azcona, *Isabel la Católica*, p. 689.

35   Herrero del Collado, *Talavera y Cisneros*, pp. 20, 64.

36   Ibid., pp. 20–1, 64. Alonso Fernández de Madrid, *Fray Hernando de Talavera*, Granada, Archivium, 1992, pp. lxiii–lxx, 47, 105. Ladero Quesada, *Isabel*, p. 171. Miguel Ángel Ladero Quesada, 'Los bautismos de los musulmanes granadinos en 1500', in *De mudéjares a moriscos. Una conversión forzada. Actas*, Instituto de Estudios Turolenses, Centro de Estudios Mudéjares, 2002, p. 489.

CHAPTER 43: THE END OF ISLAM?

1   L. P. Harvey, *Muslims in Spain, 1500 to 1614*, Chicago, University of Chicago Press, 2005, pp. 29–30. Pastore in Hernando de Talavera, *Católica impugnación del herético libelo maldito y descomulgado que fue divulgado en la ciudad de Sevilla* (with Francisco Marquez Villanueva and Stefania Pastore), Córdoba, Almuzara, 2012, p. xxxix. François Martínez, 'Talavera/Cisneros. Dos posturas diferentes con un mismo fin ideológico', *Actas del IXº Congreso Internacional de Sociocrítica*, Morelia, Mexico, 2003, p. 6.

2   Miguel Ángel Ladero Quesada, *Los mudéjares de Castilla en tiempos de Isabel I*, Madrid, Instituto 'Isabel la Católica' de Historia Eclesiástica, 1969, pp. 229–30. Tarsicio de Azcona, *Isabel la Católica. Estudio crítico de su vida y su reinado*, Madrid, Biblioteca de Autores Cristianos, 1993, pp. 691–2.

3   Ladero Quesada, *Mudéjares*, p. 228. Martínez, 'Talavera/Cisneros', p. 8. Alonso Fernández de Madrid, *Fray Hernando de Talavera*, Granada, Archivium, 1992, p. 56. Miguel Ángel Ladero Quesada, *Isabel I de Castilla. Siete ensayos sobre la reina, su entorno y sus empresas*, Madrid, Dykinson, 2012, p. 171. Harvey, *Muslims in Spain*, pp. 29–30. Azcona, *Isabel la Católica*, p. 692.

4   Miguel Ángel Ladero Quesada, 'Los bautismos de los musulmanes granadinos en 1500', in *De mudéjares a moriscos. Una conversión forzada. Actas*, Instituto de Estudios Turolenses, Centro de Estudios Mudéjares, 2002, pp. 494–5, 509–39, 542.

5   Maria Martínez, 'La creación de una moda propia en la España de los Reyes Católicos', *Aragón en la Edad Media*, no. 19, 2006, p. 380.

6   Azcona, *Isabel la Católica*, p. 692. Ladero Quesada, *Isabel*, p. 171.

7   Andrés Bernáldez, *Historia de los Reyes Católicos don Fernando y doña Isabel*, in *Crónicas de los Reyes de Castilla*, ed. Cayetano Rosell, vol. 70, Madrid, Biblioteca de Autores Españoles, 1878, Chapter 160.

8   Ladero Quesada, *Mudéjares*, p. 238.

9   Azcona, *Isabel la Católica*, p. 695.

10   Ladero Quesada, *Isabel*, p. 172. Ladero Quesada, 'Bautismos', p. 491.

11   Ladero Quesada, *Isabel*, p. 233.

12   Azcona, *Isabel la Católica*, p. 696.

13   Ladero Quesada, 'Bautismos', p. 492.

14   Ladero Quesada, *Isabel*, p. 172. Ladero Quesada, 'Bautismos', p. 492.

15   Tarsicio Herrero del Collado, *Talavera y Cisneros: dos vivencias socio-religiosas en la conversión de los moros de Granada*, Madrid, Darek-Nyumba, 2001. François Martínez, 'Talavera/Cisneros', p. 5.

16   Ladero Quesada, 'Bautismos', p. 493.

17   Ladero Quesada, *Isabel*, pp. 171–2. Ladero Quesada, *Mudéjares*, pp. 237, 305. Ladero Quesada, 'Bautismos', p. 486. Azcona, *Isabel la Católica*, p. 692.

18   Ladero Quesada, *Isabel*, pp. 172–3. Ladero Quesada, *Mudéjares*, pp. 241–2.

19   Ana Isabel Carrasco Manchado, 'Discurso político propaganda en la corte de los Reyes Católicos (1474–1482)', doctoral thesis, Universidad Complutense de Madrid, 2000, at http://eprints.ucm.es/2525/, pp. 226–7.

20   Azcona, *Isabel la Católica*, p. 697.

21   Emilio Meneses García, *Correspondencia del Conde de Tendilla. Biografía, estudio y transcripción*, vol. 1, Madrid, Real Academia de la Historia, 1973, pp. 299–300. Azcona, *Isabel la Católica*, p. 698. Ladero Quesada, *Mudéjares*, pp. 318–19.

22   Daniel Eisenberg, 'Cisneros y la quema de los manuscritos granadinos', *Journal of Hispanic Philology*, vol. 16, 1992, pp. 107–24 (citing contemporaries Juan de Vallejo and and Alvar Gómez de Castro).

23   Herrero del Collado, *Talavera y Cisneros*, p. 51.

24   Azcona, *Isabel la Católica*, p. 698.

25   Carrasco Manchado, 'Discurso', pp. 228–30, 234 and doc. 64.

26   Ibid., p. 234. Ladero Quesada, *Mudéjares*, p. 314.

27   François Soyer, *The Persecution of the Jews and Muslims of Portugal: King Manuel I and the End of Religious Tolerance (1496–7)*, Leiden, Brill, 2007, pp. 279–81.

28   Niccolò Machiavelli, *The Prince*, trans. George Bull, London, Penguin, 1999, p. 120. Miguel Ángel Ladero Quesada, 'Los mudéjares de Castilla

cuarenta años después', *En la España Medieval*, no. 33, 2010, pp. 389–40. Azcona, *Isabel la Católica*, pp. 699–701. Anon, *Tomo segundo de las Leyes de Recopilacion, que contiene los libros sexto, septimo, octavo i nono*, Madrid, Herederos de la Viuda de Juan Garcia Infanzón, 1772, p. 321.

29 Carrasco Manchado, 'Discurso', pp. 237–9.

30 Ibid., p. 238.

31 Luis del Mármol Carvajal, *Historia del rebelión y castigo de los moriscos del Reino de Granada*, Madrid, Imprenta de Sancha, 1797, pp. 123–365.

32 Pietro Martire d'Anghiera, *Epistolario de Pedro Mártir de Anglería*, edited and translated by José López de Toro, Madrid, Imp. de Góngora, 1953–7, Letter 215. Azcona, *Isabel la Católica*, p. 702 .

CHAPTER 44: THE SULTAN OF EGYPT

1 Luis García y García, *Una embajada de los Reyes Católicos a Egipto, según la 'Legatio Babylonica' y el 'Opus epistolarum' de Pedro Mártir de Anglería*, Valladolid, Instituto Jerónimo Zurita, 1947, pp. 32–50.

2 Ibid., pp. 32, 39–42, 48, 50, 52, 212. Pietro Martire d'Anghiera, *Epistolario de Pedro Mártir de Anglería*, edited and translated by José López de Toro, Madrid, Imp. de Góngora, 1953–7, Letter 223, cited in Manuel Moreno Alonso, 'El mundo por descubrir en la historiografía del Descubrimiento', in *Congreso de Historia del Descubrimiento (1492–1556). Actas*, vol. 4, 1992, p. 304. Luis Suárez Fernández, *Expansión de la Fé*, Madrid, Rialp, 1990, p. 221. Antonio de la Torre, *Documentos sobre relaciones internacionales de los Reyes Católicos*, vol. 6, Barcelona: Consejo Superior de Investigaciones Científicas, Patronato Marcelino Menéndez Pelayo, 1951, pp 266–70.

3 Hieronymus Münzer, *Viaje por España y Portugal (1494–1495)*, Madrid, Polifemo, 1991, pp. xvi, 209.

4 P. S. van Koningsveld and G. A. Wiegers, 'Islam in Spain during the Early Sixteenth Century: The Views of Four Chief Judges in Cairo', *Orientations* 4, 1996, p. 138. James T. Monroe, 'A Curious Morisco Appeal to the Ottoman Empire', *Al-Andalus*, vol. 31, 1966, pp. 281–303.

5 García y García, *Una embajada*, pp. 80, 82, 84, 98, 143.

6 Ibid., pp. 92, 98, 106, 122, 142–4, 150.

7 Ibid., p. 152.

8 Ibid., pp. 158–64.

9 Ibid., p. 168. Luis Suárez Fernández, 'Las relaciones de los reyes Católicos con Egipto', *En la España Medieval*, no. 1, 1980, p. 512.

10 Agustín Arce, 'Presencia de España en Jerusalem', *Boletín de la Real Academia de la Historia*, vol. 173, 1976, pp. 471–2. Suárez, 'Las relaciones de los reyes Católicos con Egipto', p. 514.

11 García y García, *Una embajada*, pp. 170–4, 212. Suárez, 'Las relaciones de los reyes Católicos con Egipto', pp. 514, 519.

12 Suárez, *Expansión de la Fé*, p. 222.

CHAPTER 45: LIKE A WILD LIONESS

1 Bethany Aram, *Juana the Mad: Sovereignty and Dynasty in Renaissance Europe*, Baltimore, Johns Hopkins University Press, 2005, p. 53.

2 Miguel Ángel Ladero Quesada, *Isabel I de Castilla. Siete ensayos sobre la reina, su entorno y sus empresas*, Madrid, Dykinson, 2012, p. 134.

3 Aram, *Juana the Mad*, p. 53.

4 Ibid., pp. 55–6. Ladero Quesada, *Isabel*, pp. 134–5. *CSP Spain*, Supplement, pp. 54–62.

5 Luis Suárez Fernández, *El camino hacia Europa*, Madrid, Rialp, 1990, p. 204. Ladero Quesada, *Isabel*, p. 147. Aram, *Juana the Mad*, p. 56.

6 Aram, *Juana the Mad*, pp. 59, 68.

7 Ladero Quesada, *Isabel*, p. 147.

8 Aram, *Juana the Mad*, p. 56.

9 Ibid., pp. 59–60.

10 Navagero in Jorge de Einghen et al., *Viajes por España de Jorge de Einghen, del Barón Leon de Rosmithal de Blatine, de Francisco Guicciardini y de Andrés Navajero; traducido, anotados y con un introducción por Antonio María Fabié*, Madrid, Librería de los Bibliófilos, 1889, p. 364.

11 Antoine de Lalaing, 'Relato del primer viaje de Felipe el Hermoso a España', in *Viajes de extranjeros por España y Portugal, desde los tiempos más remotos hasta fines del siglo XVI*, ed. J. García Mercadal, Madrid, 1952, pp. 452, 481. Lalaing, *Collection des voyages des souverains des Pays-Bas*, Gachard, Brussels, 1876, p. 150. Suárez, *Europa*, pp. 227, 245.

12 Lalaing, 'Relato', pp. 481–6. Fernando Checa Cremades (ed.), *Isabel la Católica. Magnificencia de un reinado. Quinto centenario de Isabel la Católica, 1504–2004*, Madrid, Sociedad Estatal de Conmemoraciones Culturales, 2004, p. 294. Aram, *Juana the Mad*, pp. 60–1.

13 Ladero Quesada, *Isabel*, pp. 136, 147. Suárez, *Europa*, pp. 235–7.

14 Lalaing, 'Relato', p. 480. Aram, *Juana the Mad*, p. 62.

15 Marino Sanuto, *I diarii di Marino Sanuto*, vol 1, Venice, Fratelli Visentini Tipografi Editori, 1886, vol 4, p. 662. Aram, *Juana the Mad*, pp. 62–3. Suárez, *Europa*, pp. 248, 266. Lalaing, 'Relato', pp. 493–4. Tarsicio de Azcona, *Isabel la Católica. Estudio crítico de su vida y su reinado*, Madrid, Biblioteca de Autores Cristianos, 1993, p. 913.

16 Aram, *Juana the Mad*, pp. 64, 69–70. Lalaing, 'Relato', p. 495. Documentos inéditos para la Historia de España, Vol. 10, p. 35, Letter 250.

17 Aram, *Juana the Mad*, pp. 70–1.

18 Ibid., p. 72 (citing RAH Salazar A-11, fols 380v–381). Antonio Rodríguez Villa, *La Reina Doña Juana la Loca. Estudio histórico*, Madrid, Librería Murillo, 1892, p. 82.

19 Lorenzo de Padilla, *Crónica de Felipe I, Llamado el Hermoso, escrita por don Lorenzo de Padilla y dirigida al emperador Carlos V*, vol. 8 of *Colección de documentos inéditos para la historia de España*, Madrid, Imprenta de Calero, 1846, pp. 114–15. Antonio Rumeu de Armas, *Itinerario de los Reyes Católicos, 1474–1516*, Madrid, Instituto Jerónimo Zurita, Biblioteca Reyes Católicos, 1974, pp. 287, 296. Aram, *Juana the Mad*, pp. 69–71. Luis Suárez Fernández, *Política internacional de Isabel La Católica: estudio y documentos*, vol. 6, Valladolid, Universidad de Valladolid, 1965–2002, p. 131. Suárez, *Europa*, pp. 248, 262–5, 292. Ladero Quesada, *Isabel*, p. 136.

20 Felix de Llanos y Torriglia, 'Sobre la fuga frustrada de doña Juana la Loca', *Boletín de la Real Academia de la Historia*, vol. 102, 1933, p. 97.

21 Ibid. Rumeu de Armas, *Itinerario*, pp. 299–300.

22 Suárez, *Europa*, pp. 285, 295–9, 308, 310, 313–16, 319. Pietro Martire d'Anghiera, *Epistolario de Pedro Mártir de Anglería*, edited and translated by José López de Toro, Madrid, Imp. de Góngora, 1953–7, pp. 65–7. Padilla, *Crónica*, pp. 114–15.

23 Duque de Berwick y de Alba (ed.), *Correspondencia de Gutierre Gómez de Fuensalida. Embajador en Alemania, Flandes e Inglaterra (1496–1509)*, Madrid, Imprenta Alemana, 1907, p. 198. Suárez, *Europa*, pp. 329, 333–7. Aram, *Juana the Mad*, p. 74.

24 Fuensalida, *Correspondencia*, pp. 265, 267, 297–301.

25 Suárez, *Europa*, pp. 297–301, 339.

26 Fuensalida, *Correspondencia*, pp. 297–301.

CHAPTER 46: THE FINAL JUDGEMENT

1 Felix de Llanos y Torriglia, 'Sobre la fuga frustrada de doña Juana la Loca', *Boletín de la Real Academia de la Historia*, vol. 102, 1933, p. 259. Luis Suárez Fernández, *El camino hacia Europa*, Madrid, Rialp, 1990, p. 333. Peggy K. Liss, *Isabel the Queen: Life and Times*, Philadelphia, University of Pennsylvania Press, 2004, p. 213.

2 Gerardo Moraleja, *Historia de Medina del Campo*, Medina del Campo, Alaguero, 1971, pp. 45, 101, 103, 149. J. H. Elliott, *Imperial Spain 1469–1716*, London, Pelican, 1970, p. 124.

3 Antonio Sánchez del Barrio, *Comercio y ferias en tiempos de Isabel la Católica*, Alicante, Biblioteca Virtual Miguel de Cervantes, 2005, at http://www.

cervantesvirtual.com/obra-visor-din/comercio-y-ferias-en-tiempos-de-isabel-la-catlica-o/html/. Edwin S. Hunt and James M. Murray, *A History of Business in Medieval Europe, 1200–1550*, New York, Cambridge University Press, 1999, p. 194. Moraleja, *Historia*, pp. 141, 145, 149. Elliot, *Imperial Spain*, p. 120.

4   Duque de Berwick y de Alba (ed.), *Correspondencia de Gutierre Gómez de Fuensalida. Embajador en Alemania, Flandes e Inglaterra (1496–1509)*, Madrid, Imprenta Alemana, 1907, pp. 286–7.

5   Ibid.

6   Norman Davies, *Europe: A History*, Oxford, Oxford University Press, 1996, p. 383 (citing Johan Huizinga).

7   François Martínez, 'Talavera/Cisneros. Dos posturas diferentes con un mismo fin ideológico', *Actas del IX° Congreso Internacional de Sociocrítica*, Morelia, Mexico, 2003, pp. lxvii–lxxi. Miguel Ángel Ladero Quesada, 'Los bautismos de los musulmanes granadinos en 1500', in *De mudéjares a moriscos. Una conversión forzada. Actas*, Instituto de Estudios Turolenses, Centro de Estudios Mudéjares, 2002, p. 489. Tarsicio Herrero del Collado, *Talavera y Cisneros: dos vivencias socio-religiosas en la conversión de los moros de Granada*, Madrid, Darek-Nyumba, 2001, p. 64.

8   Liss, *Isabel*, p. 402.

9   Guicciardini in Jorge de Einghen et al., *Viajes por España de Jorge de Einghen, del Barón Leon de Rosmithal de Blatine, de Francisco Guicciardini y de Andrés Navajero; traducido, anotados y con un introducción por Antonio María Fabié*, Madrid, Librería de los Bibliófilos, 1889, pp. 211–12.

10 Liss, *Isabel*, p. 398.

11 Tarsicio de Azcona, *Isabel la Católica. Estudio crítico de su vida y su reinado*, Madrid, Biblioteca de Autores Cristianos, 1993, p. 937.

12 *CSP Spain*, vol. 1, p. 413. National Archives, PRO 31/11/4. Azcona, *Isabel la Católica*, p. 936.

13 James Gairdner, *Memorials of King Henry the Seventh*, London, Longman, Brown, Green, Longmans & Roberts, 1858, pp. 415–16. Moraleja, *Historia*, p. 102.

AFTERWORD: A BEAM OF GLORY

1   Simon Barton, *A History of Spain*, London, Palgrave Macmillan, 2009, p. 121, quoting Bernal Díaz del Castillo.

2   J. H. Elliott, *Imperial Spain 1469–1716*, London, Pelican, 1970, p. 153.

3   Bethany Aram, *Juana the Mad: Sovereignty and Dynasty in Renaissance Europe*, Baltimore, Johns Hopkins University Press, 2005, pp. 97–100.

J. H. Elliott, *Imperial Spain 1469–1716*, London, Pelican, 1970, p. 142. Hugh Thomas, *The Slave Trade, The History of the Atlantic Slave Trade, 1440–1870*, Weidenfeld & Nicolson, 2015 (Kindle edn), loc. 233.

4   Francis Bacon, *The Works of Francis Bacon* (ed. Basil Montagu), Philadelphia, Carey and Hart, 1841, vol 2, p. 438. Simon Barton, *A History of Spain*, London, Palgrave Macmillan, 2009 p. 112–3. J. H. Elliott, *Imperial Spain 1469–1716*, London, Pelican, 1970, pp. 153, 164.

5   Felipe Fernández-Armesto, *Pathfinders: A Global History of Exploration*, Oxford, Oxford University Press, 2007, p. 122.

6   A website devoted to her cause publishes twice-yearly electronic bulletins in which devotees claim she has heard their prayers and interceded on their behalf before God to cure ilnesses or allow them to pass exams. It can be found at http://www.reinacatolica.org/. The Spanish church continues to pressure Rome to proceed with the process, according to the same website.

BIBLIOGRAPHY

MANUSCRIPT COLLECTIONS
Biblioteca Nacional, Madrid
Real Academia de la Historia, Madrid
Archivo General de Simancas, Valladolid
The National Archives, London
British Library, London

CALENDARS AND DOCUMENT COLLECTIONS
Calendar of Letters, Despatches and State Papers relating to the negotiations
between England and Spain preserved in the archives of Simancas and
elsewhere, vols 1–5, Supplement and further Supplement to vols 1 and 2, ed.
G. A. Bergenroth, Pascual de Gayangos and Garrett Mattingly, London,
Longman, Green, Longman & Roberts, 1862.
Jewish History Sourcebook: The Expulsion from Spain, 1492 CE, at http://www.
fordham.edu/halsall/jewish/1492-jews-spain1.html.
Letters and Papers Illustrative of the Reigns of Richard III and Henry VII, 2 vols, ed.
James Gairdner, London, Longman, Green, Longman & Roberts, 1861.

SPANISH SOURCES
Agapito y Revilla, Juan, *Las calles de Valladolid. Nomenclátor histórico. Datos*
para la historia biográfica de Valladolid, Valladolid, Maxtor, 2004.
Aguilar Rodas, Raúl, *Cristóbal Colón. Realidad y ficción tras 500 años de su*
muerte 1506–2006, Medellín, Panibérica, 2006.
Alcalá, Ángel (ed.), *Judíos, sefarditas, conversos. La expulsión de 1492 y sus*
consecuencias. Ponencias del Congreso Internacional celebrado en Nueva York en
noviembre de 1992, Valladolid, Ambito, 1995.
Alvar Ezquerra, Alfredo, *Isabel la Católica*, Madrid, Temas de Hoy, 2002.
Álvarez Bezos, María Sabina, 'Violencia contra las mujeres en la castilla del
final de la edad media. Documentos para el estudio de las mujeres como

protagonistas de su historia', doctoral thesis, Universidad de Valladolid, 2013, at https://uvadoc.uva.es/bitstream/10324/4413/1/TESIS472–140224.pdf.

Álvarez Palenzuela, Vicente, *'Paz con Portugal'. La guerra civil castellana y el enfrentamiento con Portugal (1475–1479)*, Alicante, Biblioteca Virtual Miguel de Cervantes http://www.cervantesvirtual.com/obra-visor-din/la-guerra-civil-castellana-y-el-enfrentamiento-con-portugal-14751479–0/html/ (consulted 27 November 2014).

Anghiera, Pietro Martire d', *Epistolario de Pedro Mártir de Anglería*, edited and translated by José López de Toro, Madrid, Imp. de Góngora, 1953–7.

—, *Una embajada de los Reyes Católicos a Egipto, según la 'Legatio Babylonica' y el 'Opus Epistolarum' de Pedro Mártir de Anglería. Traducción*, ed. Luis García y García, Valladolid, Consejo Superior de Investigaciones Científicas, Instituto 'Jerónimo Zurita', Sección de Historia Moderna 'Simancas', 1947.

Anon, *Continuación de la Crónica de Pulgar por un autor anónimo*, ed. Cayetano Rosell, Madrid, Biblioteca de Autores Españoles, 1953.

Anon, *Crónica anónima de Enrique IV de Castilla, 1454–1474* (Crónica castellana), ed. M. P. Sánchez Parra, Madrid, Ediciones de la Torre, 1991.

Anon, *Crónica de don Álvaro de Luna*, Madrid, Espasa-Calpe, 1940.

Anon, *Crónica incompleta de los Reyes Católicos*, ed. Julio Puyol, Madrid, Tipografía de Archivos, 1934.

Anon, *Cronicón de Valladolid*, Valladolid, Princiano, 1984.

Anon, *Documentos relativos a la visita del Cardenal Adriano cuando pasó de España a Roma, elegido Papa. – Proceso de la reina da Catalina de Aragón, reina de Inglaterra. – Registrum abbatis monasterii verolen. 1480*, Veruela, Real Academia de la Historia, Manuscript 9–4674.

Anon, *Hechos del condestable Miguel Lucas de Iranzo*, Granada, Universidad de Granada, 2009.

Anon, *Las cortes de Castilla y León en la Edad Media*, ed. Cortes de Castilla y León, 1988.

Anon, *Tomo segundo de las Leyes de Recopilacion, que contiene los libros sexto, septimo, octavo i nono*, Madrid, Herederos de la Viuda de Juan Garcia Infanzón, 1772.

Antelo Iglesias, Antonio, 'Alfonso de Palencia. Historiografía y humanismo en la Castilla del siglo xv', *Espacio, Tiempo y Forma*, vol. 3, 1990, pp. 21–40.

Arce, Agustín, 'Presencia de España en Jerusalem', *Boletín de la Real Academia de la Historia*, vol. 173, 1976, pp. 469–79.

Arcelus, Juana María, 'La Desconocida Librería de Isabel la Católica', in *Actes del X Congres Internacional de l'Associació Hispánica de Literatura Medieval*, ed. Rafael Alemany, Josep Lluís Martos and Josep Miquel Manzanaro, vol. 1, Alicante, 2005, pp. 295–320.

Azcona, Tarsicio de, *Isabel la Católica. Estudio crítico de su vida y su reinado*, Madrid, Biblioteca de Autores Cristianos, 1964, 1993.

—, 'El Príncipe don Juan, heredero de los Reyes Católicos, en el V centenario de su nacimiento (1478–1497)', *Cuadernos de Investigación Histórica*, no. 7, 1983, pp. 219–44.

—, 'Relaciones de Inocencio VIII con los Reyes Católicos según el Fondo Podocataro de Venecia', *Hispania Sacra*, no. 32, 1980, pp. 3–30.

Baeza, Hernando de, *Relaciones de algunos sucesos*, ed. Emilio Lafuente y Alcántara, Madrid, Rivadeneyra, 1868.

Barrios Aguilera, Manuel, *Granada Morisca, la convivencia negada. Historia y textos*, Albolote, Comares, 2002.

Beinart, Haim, 'Vuelta de judíos a España después de la expulsión', in Ángel Alcalá (ed.), *Judíos, sefarditas, conversos. La expulsión de 1492 y sus consecuencias. Ponencias del Congreso Internacional celebrado en Nueva York en noviembre de 1992*, Valladolid, Ambito, 1995, pp. 181–94.

Bel Bravo, María Antonia, *Los Reyes Católicos y los judíos andaluces*, Granada, Biblioteca Chronica Nova de Estudios Históricos, 1989.

Benito Ruano, Eloy, *Los orígenes del problema converso*, Barcelona, El Albir, 1976.

—, *Toledo en el siglo XV. Vida política*, Madrid, Consejo Superior de Investigaciones Científicas, Escuela de Estudios Medievales, 1961.

Bernáldez, Andrés, *Historia de los Reyes Católicos don Fernando y doña Isabel*, in *Crónicas de los Reyes de Castilla*, ed. Cayetano Rosell, vol. 70, Madrid, Biblioteca de Autores Españoles, 1878.

—, *Memorias del reinado de los Reyes Católicos*, ed. Manuel Gómez Moreno and Juan de Mata Carriazo, Madrid, Real Academia de la Historia, 1962.

Bernis, Carmen, *Trajes y modas en la España de los Reyes Católicos*, Madrid, Consejo Superior de Investigaciones Científicas, 1978.

Berwick y de Alba, Duque de (ed.), *Correspondencia de Gutierre Gómez de Fuensalida. Embajador en Alemania, Flandes e Inglaterra (1496–1509)*, Madrid, Imprenta Alemana, 1907.

—, *Noticias históricas y genealógicas de los Estados de Montijo y Teba, según los documentos se sus archivos*, Madrid, Imprenta Alemana, 1915.

Bordes, José and Sanz, Enrique, 'El protagonismo mudéjar en el comercio entre Valencia y el norte de Africa', in *De mudéjares a moriscos. Una conversión forzada. Actas*, Instituto de Estudios Turolenses, Centro de Estudios Mudéjares, 2002, pp. 275–82.

Cabañero Subiza, Bernabé, 'La Aljafería de Zaragoza', *Artigrama*, no. 22, 2007, pp. 103–29.

Calvo Poyato, José, *Enrique IV el Impotente y el final de un época*, Barcelona, Planeta, 1993.

Cañas Gálvez, Francisco de Paula, *El itinerario de la corte de Juan II de Castilla (1418–1454)*, Madrid, Silex Ediciones, 2007.

——, 'Las Casas de Isabel y Juana de Portugal, reinas de Castilla. Organización, dinámica institucional y prosopografía (1447–1496)', in José Martínez Millán and María Paula Marçal Lourenço (eds), *Las relaciones discretas entre las Monarquías Hispana y Portuguesa. Las Casas de las Reinas (siglos XV–XIX)*, Madrid, Polifemo, 2008, vol. 1, pp. 9–10.

Carbonell, Pere Miguel, *Chròniques de Espanya, fins aci no divulades*, Barcelona, Carles Amoros, 1547.

Caro Baroja, Julio, *Los judíos en la España moderna y contemporánea*, vol. 1, Madrid, Ediciones Istmo, 1978.

Carrasco Manchado, Ana Isabel, 'Discurso político propaganda en la corte de los Reyes Católicos (1474–1482)', doctoral thesis, Universidad Complutense de Madrid, 2000, at http://eprints.ucm.es/2525/.

——, 'Propaganda política en los panegíricos poéticos de los Reyes Católicos. Una aproximación', *Anuario de Estudios Medievales*, vol. 25, no. 2 (1995), pp. 517–45.

Carrete Parrondo, Carlos (ed.), *Fontes Iudaeorum Regni Castellae*, vol. 2: *El tribunal de la Inquisition en el obispado de Soria (1486–1502)*, Salamanca, Universidad Pontificia, 1985.

Carrillo de Huete, Pedro, *Crónica del halconero de Juan II*, ed. Juan de Mata Carriazo y Arroquia, Madrid, Espasa-Calpe, 1946.

Chamorro Esteban, Alfredo, 'Ceremonial monárquico y rituales cívicos. Las visitas reales a Barcelona desde el siglo XV hasta el XVII', doctoral thesis, University of Barcelona, 2013.

Checa Cremades, Fernando et al., *Isabel la Católica. La magnificencia de un reinado. Quinto centenario de Isabel la Católica, 1504–2004*, Madrid, Sociedad Estatal de Conmemoraciones Culturales, 2004.

Clausell Nácher, Carmen, 'Carro de las donas (Valladolid, 1542). Estudio preliminary edición anotada', doctoral thesis, Departamento de Literatura Española, Universidad Autónoma de Barcelona, 2004, at http://www.tesisenxarxa.net/TDX-0608105–110729/.

Clemencín, Diego, *Elogio de la reina Católica Doña Isabel, al que siguen varias ilustraciones sobre su reinado*, Madrid, Sancha, 1821.

Collantes de Terán Sánchez, Antonio, *Sevilla en la Baja Edad Media*, Seville, Servicio de Publicaciones del Excmo. Ayuntamiento, 1977.

Colmenares, Diego de, *Historia de la insigne ciudad de Segovia y compendio de las historias de Castilla*, vol. 2, Segovia, Eduardo Baeza, 1984.

Contreras, J. (ed.), *Inquisición Española. Nuevas aproximaciones*, Madrid, Centro de Estudios Inquisitoriales, 1987.

Cortes de los antiguos reinos de León y Castilla, pub. por la Real Academia de la Historia, vol. 4, Madrid, Rivadeneyra, 1882.

Dormer, Diego, *Discursos varios*, Zaragoza, Herederos de Diego Dormer, 1683.

Doussinague, José Maria, *La política internacional de Fernando el Católico*, Madrid, Espasa-Calpe, 1944.

Doval, G., *Refranero temático español*, Madrid, Ediciones del Prado, 1998.

Edwards, John, *Isabel la Católica. Poder y fama*, Madrid, Marcial Pons, 2004.

Einghen, Jorge de et al., *Viajes por España de Jorge de Einghen, del Barón Leon de Rosmithal de Blatine, de Francisco Guicciardini y de Andrés Navajero; traducido, anotados y con un introducción por Antonio María Fabié*, Madrid, Librería de los Bibliófilos, 1889.

Eisenberg, Daniel, 'Cisneros y la quema de los manuscritos granadinos', *Journal of Hispanic Philology*, vol. 16, 1992, pp. 107–24.

Eiximenis, Francesc, *Carro de las donas. Valladolid, 1542 / adaptación del Llibre de les dones de Francesc Eiximenis O.F.M., realizada por el P. Carmona O.F.M.*, ed. Carmen Clausell Nácher, Madrid, Fundación Universitaria Española, 2007.

Enríquez del Castillo, Diego, *Crónica del rey don Enrique el Quarto de este nombre*, ed. A. Sánchez Martín, Valladolid, Universidad de Valladolid, 1994.

Esclavos, vol. 8 of *Documentos para la historia de Canarias*, Santa Cruz de Tenerife, Gobierno de Canarias, 2006.

Escudero, José Antonio, *Estudios sobre la Inquisición*, Madrid, Marcial Pons, 2005.

—, 'Los Reyes Católicos y el Establecimiento de la Inquisición', *Anuario de Estudios Atlánticos*, no. 50, 2004, pp. 357–93.

Fernández de Córdova Miralles, Álvaro, *Alejandro VI y los Reyes Católicos. Relaciones político-eclesiásticas (1492–1503)*, Rome, Edizioni Università della Santa Croce, 2005.

—, *La Corte de Isabel I. Ritos y ceremonias de una reina (1474–1504)*, Madrid, Dykinson, 2002.

—, 'Imagen de los Reyes Católicos en la Roma pontificia', *En la España Medieval*, no. 28, 2005, pp. 259–354.

Fernández de Madrid, Alonso, *Fray Hernando de Talavera*, Granada, Archivium, 1992.

Fernández de Oviedo, Gonzalo, *Libro de la Cámara Real del Príncipe don Juan e offiçios de su casa e seruiçio ordinario*, ed. Santiago Fabregat Barrios, Valencia, Universitat de Valencia, 2002.

—, *Batallas y quinquagenas*, ed. J. Pérez de Tudela y Bueso, 3 vols, Madrid, Real Academia de la Historia, 1983–2000.

Fernández Navarrete, Martín et al. (eds), *Colección de documentos inéditos para la historia de España*, 112 vols, various imprints, 1842–95.

—, *Colección de los viages y descubrimientos que hicieron por mar los españoles desde fines del siglo XV*, vols 1–3, Madrid, Imprenta Real, 1825.

Fernández Suárez, José Ramón, 'Luis Vives. Educador de los jóvenes ingleses', *ES: Revista de filología inglesa*, no. 17, 1993, pp. 141–50.

Fernández-Armesto, Felipe, *Colón*, Barcelona, Crítica, 1992.

—, *1492. El nacimiento de la modernidad*, Madrid, Debate, 2010.

Fita, Fidel, *Los Reys d'Aragó y la Seu de Girona des de l'any 1462 fins al 1482. Col.lecció d'actes capitulars*, Barcelona, Obradors & Sulé, 1873.

—, 'Historia hebrea. Documentos y monumentos', *Boletín de la Real Academia de la Historia*, tomo 16, Madrid, 1890, pp. 432–56.

Flor, Pedro, 'Un retrato desconocido de Isabel la Católica', *Archivo Español de Arte*, vol. 86, no. 341, January–March 2012, pp. 1–14.

Fuentes, Alonso de, *Cuarenta cantos de diversas y peregrinas historias*, Seville, 1545.

Galíndez de Carvajal, Lorenzo, *Crónica de Enrique IV*, ed. Juan Torres Fontes, Murcia, Consejo Superior de Investigaciones Científicas, 1946.

García Casar, María Fuencisla, 'Las comunidades judías de la Corona de Castilla al tiempo de la expulsión', in Ángel Alcalá (ed.), *Judíos, sefarditas, conversos. La expulsión de 1492 y sus consecuencias. Ponencias del Congreso Internacional celebrado en Nueva York en noviembre de 1992*, Valladolid, Ambito, 1995, pp. 21–31.

García Luján, José Antonio, *El Generalife. Jardín del paraíso*, Granada, J. A. García, 2006.

García Rodríguez, Emilio, 'Toledo y sus visitantes extranjeros hasta 1561', *Toletum: Boletín de la Real Academia de Bellas Artes y Ciencias Históricas de Toledo*, no. 1, 1955, pp. 5–37.

García y García, Luis, *Una embajada de los Reyes Católicos a Egipto, según la 'Legatio Babylonica' y el 'Opus epistolarum' de Pedro Mártir de Anglería*, Valladolid, Instituto Jerónimo Zurita, 1947.

Gil, Juan and Varela, Consuelo (eds), *Cartas de particulares a Colón y relaciones coetáneas*, Madrid, Alianza, 1984.

Gil Sanjuan, Joaquín and Toledo Navarro, Juan J., 'Importancia de la artillería en la conquista de las poblaciones malagueñas (1485–1487)', *Baetica*, no. 30, 2008, pp. 311–31.

Góis, Damião de, *Crónica do felicíssimo Rei D. Manuel*, 4 vols, Coimbra, Universidade de Coimbra, 1949.

Goméz-Moreno, Manuel, 'Joyas arabes de la Reina Catolica', *Al-Andalus*, vol. 8, 1943, pp. 473–5.

González García, Casimiro, *Datos para la historia biográfica de Valladolid*, 2 vols, Valladolid, Maxtor, 2003.

Gonzálvez Ruíz, Ramón, 'Las bulas de la catedral de Toledo y la imprenta incunable castellana', *Toletum: Boletín de la Real Academia de Bellas Artes y Ciencias Históricas de Toledo*, no. 18, 1985, pp. 9–180.

Gracia Dei, Pedro, *Blasón General y Nobleza del Universo*, Madrid, Murillo, 1882.

—, *La crianza y virtuosa doctrina*, ed. A. Paz y Meliá, *Opúsculos literarios de los siglos XIV y XV*, Madrid, Sociedad de Bibliofilos Españoles, 1892.

Grau, M., 'Así fue coronada Isabel la Católica', *Estudios Segovianos*, no. 1, 1949, pp. 20–39. (See reprint *Polvo de Archivos. Páginas para la historia de Segovia*, Segovia, Caja de Ahorros, 1973, pp. 17–26.)

Guichot, Joaquín, *Historia de la Ciudad de Sevilla*, vol. 1, Seville, Imp. Gironés y Orduña, 1875.

Guillén, Claudio, 'Un padrón de conversos sevillanos (1510)', *Bulletin Hispanique*, vol. 65, no. 1, 1963.

Gutierrez Azopardo, Ildefonso, 'Los papas en los inicios de la trata negrera', at http://www.africafundacion.org/spip.php?article1847.

Herrero del Collado, Tarsicio, *Talavera y Cisneros: dos vivencias socio-religiosas en la conversión de los moros de Granada*, Madrid, Darek-Nyumba, 2001.

Jones, R. O., 'Isabel la Católica y el amor cortés', *Revista de Literatura*, vol. 21, no. 41–2, 1962, pp. 55–64.

Kamen, Henry, *La Inquisición Española. Mito e historia crítica*, Barcelona, Crítica, 2013.

Ladero Quesada, Manuel Fernando, 'Recibir princesas y enterrar reinas (Zamora 1501 y 1504)', *Espacio, tiempo y forma. Serie III. Historia medieval*, no. 13, 2000, pp. 119–38.

Ladero Quesada, Miguel Ángel (ed.), *Edad Media*, vol. 2 of *Historia militar de España*, Madrid, Ministerio de Defensa, 2013.

—, 'El número de judíos en la España de 1492', in Ángel Alcalá (ed.), *Judíos, sefarditas, conversos. La expulsión de 1492 y sus consecuencias. Ponencias del Congreso Internacional celebrado en Nueva York en noviembre de 1992*, Valladolid, Ambito, 1995, pp. 170–80.

—, *Isabel I de Castilla. Siete ensayos sobre la reina, su entorno y sus empresas*, Madrid, Dykinson, 2012.

—, 'Isabel la Católica vista por sus contemporáneos', *En la España Medieval*, no. 29, 2006, pp. 225–86.

—, *La Armada de Flandes. Un episodio en la política naval de los Reyes Católicos*, Madrid, Real Academia de la Historia, 2003.

—, *La España de los Reyes Católicos*, Madrid, Alianza, 2014.

—, *La Hermandad de Castilla. Cuentas y memoriales, 1480–1498*, Madrid, Real Academia de la Historia, 2005.

—, 'Las coplas de Hernando de Vera. Un caso de crítica al gobierno de Isabel la Católica', *Anuario de Estudios Atlánticos*, no. 14, 1968, pp. 365–81.

—, 'Los bautismos de los musulmanes granadinos en 1500', in *De mudéjares a moriscos. Una conversión forzada. Actas*, Instituto de Estudios Turolenses, Centro de Estudios Mudéjares, 2002, pp. 481–542.

—, 'Los mudéjares de Castilla cuarenta años después', *En la España Medieval*, no. 33, 2010, pp. 383–424.

—, Los mudéjares de Castilla en la Edada Media Baja, in *Historia. Instituciones. Documents*. No 5, Seville, 1978, pp. 284–8.

—, *Los mudéjares de Castilla en tiempos de Isabel*, Madrid, Instituto 'Isabel la Católica' de Historia Eclesiástica, 1969.

Lafuente, Modesto, *Historia general de España*, vol. 6, Barcelona, Montaner y Simón, 1888.

Lalaing, Antoine de, 'Relato del primer viaje de Felipe el Hermoso a España', in *Viajes de extranjeros por España y Portugal, desde los tiempos más remotos hasta fines del siglo XVI*, ed. J. García Mercadal, Madrid, Aguilar, 1952.

Larrea Palacios, Arcadio de, *El Cancionero judío del norte de Marruecos*, Madrid, CSIC, 1952.

Las Casas, Bartolomé de, *Historia de las Indias*, vols 1–2, Madrid, Imprenta Ginesta, 1875.

León Guerrero, María Montserrat, 'El segundo viaje colombino', doctoral thesis, University of Valladolid, 2002. Available at http://media.cervantesvirtual. com/s3/BVMC_OBRAS/ff7/e02/4c8/2b1/11d/fac/c70/021/85c/e60/ 64/mimes/ff7e024c-82b1-11df-acc7-002185ce6064.pdf

—, 'La Armada de Flandes y el viaje de la Princesa Juana', *Revista de Estudios Colombinos*, no. 5, 2009, pp. 53–62.

Liske, Javier, *Viajes de extranjeros por España y Portugal en los siglos XV, XVI y XVII*, Madrid, Medina, 1878.

Llanos y Torriglia, Félix de, *Así llegó a reinar Isabel la Católica*, Madrid, Editorial Voluntad, 1927.

—, *Catalina de Aragón, Reina de Inglaterra*, Madrid, Imprentas Helénicas, 1914.

—, *En el hogar de los Reyes Católicos y cosas de sus tiempos*, Madrid, Ediciones Fax, 1946.

—, 'Sobre la fuga frustrada de doña Juana la Loca', *Boletín de la Real Academia de la Historia*, vol. 102, 1933, pp. 97–114.

Llorca, Bernardino, *Bulario pontificio de la Inquisición española en su período constitucional (1478–1525), según los fondos del Archivo Histórico nacional de Madrid*, Rome, Pontificia Università Gregoriana, 1949.

Lobo Cabrera, Manuel, *La conquista de Gran Canaria (1478–1483)*, Las Palmas de Gran Canaria, Cabildo Insular de Gran Canaria, Departamento de Ediciones, 2012.

López Martínez, Nicolás, *Los judaiʒantes castellanos y la Inquisición en tiempo de Isabel la Católica*, Burgos, Imprenta de Aldecoa, 1954.

Lorenzo Sanz, Eufemio, *Salamanca en la vida de Colón*, Salamanca, Diputación Provincial, 1983.

Maganto Pavón, Emilio, 'Enrique IV de Castilla (1454–1474). Un singular enfermo urológico. Retrato morfológico y de la personalidad de Enrique IV "El Impotente" en las crónicas y escritos contemporáneos', *Archivos Españoles de Urología*, vol. 56, no. 3, 2003, pp. 211–54.

Manrique, Jorge, *Cancionero*, Madrid, Pérez Dubrull, 1885.

Manzano Manzano, Juan, *La incorporación de las Indias a la Corona de Castilla*, Madrid, Ediciones Cultura Hispánica, 1948.

Marañón, Gregorio, *Ensayo biológico sobre Enrique IV de Castilla y su tiempo*, Madrid, Boletín de la Real Academia 22, 1930.

Maravall, J. A., *Estado moderno y mentalidad social (siglos XV a XVII)*, Madrid, Revista de Occident, 1972.

Marineo Sículo, Lucio, *Vida y hechos de los reyes Católicos*, Madrid, Atlas, 1943.

Mármol Carvajal, Luis del, *Historia del rebelión y castigo de los moriscos del Reino de Granada*, Madrid, Imprenta de Sancha, 1797.

Márquez de la Plata y Ferrándiz, Vicenta María, *Mujeres renacentistas de la corte de Isabel la Católica*, Madrid, Editoral Castalia, 2005.

Martín, José-Luis, *Enrique IV de Castilla. Rey de Navarra, Príncipe de Cataluña*, San Sebastián, Nerea, 2003.

—, *Isabel la Católica. Sus hijas y las damas de su corte, modelos de doncellas, casadas y viudas, en el Carro de las donas (1542)*, Avila, J.-L. Martín, 2001.

Martín Romero, José Julio, 'El Condestable Miguel Lucas en su crónica', *Revista de Filología Española*, vol. 91, 2011, pp. 129–58.

Martínez de Toledo, Alfonso, *Arcipreste de Talavera, Corbacho, o Reprobación del amor mundano*, Biblioteca Virtual Miguel de Cervantes, at http://www.cervantesvirtual.com/obra-visor/arcipreste-de-talavera-o-corbacho – o/html/fedfb970–82b1–11df-acc7–002185ce6064_2.html

Martínez, Francisco Javier, Introduction to Alonso Fernandez de Madrid, *Fray Hernando de Talavera*, Granada, Archivium, 1992.

Martínez, François, 'Talavera/Cisneros. Dos posturas diferentes con un mismo fin ideológico', in *Actas del IX° Congreso Internacional de Sociocrítica*, Edmond Cros, Blanca Cardenas Fernandez, Juan Carlos Gonzalez Vidal (eds), Morelia, Universidad Michoacana, 2005.

Martínez, María, 'La creación de una moda propia en la España de los Reyes Católicos', *Aragón en la Edad Media*, no. 19, 2006, pp. 343–80.

Martínez Díez, Gonzalo, *Bulario de la Inquisición Española. Hasta la muerte de Fernando el Católico*, Madrid, Editorial Complutense, 1998.

Martínez Millán, José and Marçal Lourenço, María Paula, *Las relaciones discretas entre las Monarquías Hispana y Portuguesa. Las Casas de las Reinas (siglos XV–XIX)*, Madrid, Polifemo, 2008.

Mártir de Anglería, Pedro. *See* Anghiera, Pietro Martire d'.

Mata Carriazo, Juan de, *Historia de la guerra de Granada*, in Menendez Pidal (ed.), *Historia de Espana*, XVII, vol. 1, Madrid, Espasa-Calpe, 1969.

Mateo, Andrés María, *Colón e Isabel la Católica*, Valladolid, Consejo Superior de Investigaciones Científicas, 1942.

Medina y Mendoza, Francisco, 'Vida del cardenal don Pedro González de Mendoza', in Real Academia de la Historia, *Memorial Histórico Española*, vol. 6, Madrid, 1853, pp. 147–310.

Memorias de don Enrique IV de Castilla. Contiene la colección diplomática del mismo rey compuesta y ordenada por la Real Academia de la Historia, ed. Duque de Berwick y de Alba, Madrid, Fortanet, 1913.

Menéndez Pidal, Gonzalo, *La España del siglo XIII. Leída en imágenes*, Madrid, Real Academia de la Historia, 1986.

Meneses García, Emilio, *Correspondencia del Conde de Tendilla. Biografía, estudio y transcripción*, vol. 1, Madrid, Real Academia de la Historia, 1973.

Molénat, Jean-Pierre, 'Hornachos fin XVe–début XVIe siècles [Hornachos, Late 15th–Early 16th Century]', *En la España Medieval*, no. 31, 2008, pp. 161–76.

Molinet, Jean, *Chroniques*, Vol. 5, Paris, 1828.

Monsalvo Antón, J. M., *Teoría y evolución de un conflicto social. El antisemitismo en la corona de Castilla en la Baja Edad Media*, Siglo XXI, Madrid, 1985.

Montalvo, Juan José, *De la Historia de Arévalo y sus sexmos*, 2 volumes, Valladolid, Imprenta Castellana, 1928.

Montes Romero-Camacho, Isabel, 'Judíos y mudéjares', *Medievalismo* no. 14, 2004, pp. 241–74.

—, 'Las comunidades mudéjares en la Corona de Castilla durante el siglo XV', in *De mudéjares a moriscos. Una conversión forzada. Actas*, Instituto de Estudios Turolenses, Centro de Estudios Mudéjares, 2002, pp. 367–480.

Moraleja, Gerardo, *Historia de Medina del Campo*, Medina del Campo, Alaguero, 1971.

Morales, Carmen Alicia, *Isabel de Barcelos. Su importancia en la niñez de Isabel de Castilla*, Arévalo, Cuadernos de Cultura y Patrimonio, no. 14, Arévalo, La Alhóndiga – Asociación de Cultura y Patrimonio, 2012.

—, *Isabel de Castilla. Una psicobiografía*, San Juan, Puerto Rico, Adoquín, 2013 (Kindle edn).

Motis Dolader, Miguel Ángel, 'Las comunidades judías de la Corona de Aragón en el siglo XV', in Ángel Alcalá (ed.), *Judíos, sefarditas, conversos. La expulsión de 1492 y sus consecuencias. Ponencias del Congreso Internacional celebrado en Nueva York en noviembre de 1992*, Valladolid, Ambito, 1995, pp. 32–54.

Münzer, Hieronymus, *Viaje por España y Portugal (1494–1495)*, Madrid, Polifemo, 1991.

Nieto Soria, José Manuel, 'El "poderío real absoluto" de Olmedo (1445) a Ocaña (1469). La monarquía como conflicto', *En la España Medieval*, no. 21, 1998, pp. 159–228.

——, 'La renovación de la historia política en la investigación medieval. Las relaciones de poder', *Relaciones de poder en Castilla: el ejemplo de Cuenca*, Cuenca, 1997, pp. 37–64.

Olivera Santos, César, *Las Cortes de Castilla y León y la crisis del Reino*, Valladolid, Cortes de Castilla y León, 1986.

Olivetto, Georgina, 'Un testimonio de la crónica de Enrique IV atribuida por Nicolás Antonio a Fernando del Pulgar', *Cuadernos de Historia de España*, vol. 82, 2008, pp. 55–98.

Orella Unzué, José Luis, 'Las relaciones vascas con Inglaterra. Siglos XIV–XVI', *Lurralde*, no. 28, 2005, pp. 85–152.

Ortiz de Zúñiga, Diego, *Anales eclesiásticos y seculares de la muy noble y muy leal ciudad de Sevilla*, vol. 3, Madrid, Imprenta Real, 1796.

Padilla, Lorenzo de, *Crónica de Felipe I, Llamado el Hermoso, escrita por don Lorenzo de Padilla y dirigida al emperador Carlos V*, in vol. 8 of Navarrete et al. (eds), *Colección de documentos inéditos para la historia de España*, Madrid, Imprenta de Calero, 1846.

Palencia, Alonso de, *Crónica de Enrique IV*, 5 vols, ed. A. Paz y Meliá, Biblioteca de Autores Españoles, Madrid, Atlas, 1904.

——, *Cuarta década de Alonso de Palencia*, ed. J. López de Toro, 2 vols, Madrid, Real Academia de la Historia, 1970–4.

——, *Gesta hispaniensia ex annalibus suorum dierum collecta*, ed. B. Tate and J. Lawrance, 2 vols, Madrid, Real Academia de la Historia, 1999.

——, *Guerra de Granada*, Alicante, Biblioteca Virtual Miguel de Cervantes, 1999, at http://www.cervantesvirtual.com/nd/ark:/59851/bmc833n9.

Palma, Bachiller, *Divina retribución sobre la caída de España en tiempo del noble rey Don Juan el Primero*, Madrid, Bibliófilos Españoles, 1879.

Parrilla, Carmen, 'Un cronista olvidado. Juan de Flores, autor de la Crónica incompleta de los Reyes Católicos', in Alan Deyermond and Ian Macpherson (eds), *The Age of the Catholic Monarchs, 1475–1516*, Special

Issue of *Bulletin of Hispanic Studies*, Liverpool, Liverpool University Press, 1989, pp. 123–33.

Pastor, Ludwig, *Historia de los Papas desde fines de la Edad Media*, Barcelona, Gustavo Gili, 1910.

Pastor Bodmer, Isabel, *Grandeza y tragedia de un valido. La muerte de Don Álvaro de Luna. Estudios y documentos*, 2 vols, Madrid, Caja Madrid, 1992.

Paz y Meliá, Antonio, *El cronista Alonso de Palencia. Su vida y sus obras. Sus décadas y las crónicas contemporáneas*, Madrid, Hispanic Society of America, 1914.

Pérez, Joseph, *Isabel y Fernando. Los Reyes Católicos*, San Sebastián, Nerea, 1997.

—, *La España de los Reyes Católicos*, Madrid, Arlanza, 2004.

—, *La inquisición española. Nuevas visiones, nuevos horizontes*, Madrid, Siglo XXI, 1980.

Pérez de Guzmán, Fernán, *Crónica de Juan II*, in *Crónicas de los Reyes de Castilla*, vol. 2, ed. Cayetano Rosell, Madrid, Rivadeneyra, 1887.

Pérez de Guzmán y Gallo, Juan, 'Noticias históricas y genealógicas de los Estados de Montijo y Teba, según los documentos de sus archivos', *Boletín de la Real Academia de la Historia*, vol. 67, December 1915, pp. 562–78 and Alicante, Biblioteca Virtual Miguel de Cervantes, 2008, at http://www.cervantesvirtual.com/obra/noticias-historicas-y-genealogicas-de-los-estados-de-montijo-y-teba-segun-los-documentos-de-sus-archivos-las-publica-el-duque-de-berwick-y-de-alba-escudo-ducal-madrid-imprenta-alemana-fuencarral-137–1915–0/)

Pérez Priego, Miguel Ángel, 'Historia y literatura en torno al príncipe D. Juan, la "Representación sobre el poder del Amor" de Juan del Encina', in R. Beltrán, J. L. Canet and J. L. Sirera (eds), *Historias y ficciones. Coloquio sobre la literatura del siglo XV*, Valencia, Universitat-Departament de Filologia Espanyola, 1992, pp. 337–49.

Pescador del Hoyo, María del Carmen (ed.), 'Cómo fue de verdad la toma de Granada, a la luz de un documento inédito', *Al-Andalus*, vol. 20, 1955, pp. 283–344.

Poutrin Reyes, Isabelle, 'Los derechos de los vencidos. Las capitulaciones de Granada', *Sharq al-Andalus*, vol. 19, 2008–10, pp. 11–34.

Pulgar, Fernando del, *Claros varones de Castilla y Letras*, Madrid, Jerónimo Ortega, 1789.

—, *Crónica de los Señores Reyes Católicos Don Fernando y Doña Isabel de Castilla y de Aragón*, in *Crónicas de los Reyes de Castilla*, vol. 3, ed. Cayetano Rosell, Madrid, Rivadeneyra, 1878.

—, *Letras*, ed. J. Domínguez Bordona, Madrid, Espasa-Calpe, 1958.

Ramírez de Arellano, Rafael, *Historia de Córdoba desde su fundación hasta la muerte de Isabel la Católica*, Ciudad Real, Tipografía del Hospicio Provincial, vol. 4, 1919.

Rodríguez Molina, José, 'Poder político de los arzobispos de Toledo en el siglo XV', in Antonio Luis Cortés Peña, José Luis Betrán Moya and Eliseo Serrano (eds), *Religión y poder en la Edad Moderna*, Granada, Universidad de Granada, 2005, pp. 11–36.

Rodríguez Sánchez, Ángel, 'La muerte del Príncipe de Asturias, Señor de Salamanca', *Revista de Estudios Extremeños*, vol. 57, no. 1, 2001, pp. 23–48.

Rodríguez Valencia, Vicente, *Isabel la Católica en la opinión de españoles y extranjeros. Siglos XV al XX*, vol. 1: *Siglos XV al XVI*, Valladolid, Instituto 'Isabel la Católica' de Historia Eclesiástica, 1970.

—, *Perfil moral de Isabel la Católica*, Valladolid, Instituto 'Isabel la Católica' de Historia Eclesiástica, 1974.

—, and Suárez Férnandez, Luis, *Matrimonio y derecho sucesorio de Isabel la Católica*, Valladolid, Facultad de Teología de Oña, 1960.

Rodríguez Villa, Antonio, *La Reina Doña Juana la Loca. Estudio histórico*, Madrid, Librería Murillo, 1892.

—, *Crónicas del Gran Capitan*, Bailly, Madrid, 1908.

Rucquoi, Adeline, *Valladolid en la Edad Media*, 2 vols, Valladolid, Junta de Castilla y León, Consejería de Educación y Cultura, 1997.

Ruiz, Elisa, 'El patrimonio gráfico de Isabel la Católica y sus fuentes documentales', *Signo: Revista de Historia de la Cultura Escrita*, no. 14, 2004, pp. 89–138.

Ruiz, Juan, Arcipreste de Hita, *Libro de buen amor*, Paris, Louis Michaud, undated, at http://www.cervantesvirtual.com/obra-visor/el-libro-de-buen-amor-0/html/ffoec418–82b1–11df-acc7–002185ce6064.html

Ruiz Benavent, Remedios, *Palacio de don Gutierre de Cárdenas en Ocaña*, Madrid, Editorial Visión Libros, 2006.

Rumeu de Armas, Antonio, *Itinerario de los Reyes Católicos, 1474–1516*, Madrid, Instituto Jerónimo Zurita, Biblioteca Reyes Católicos, 1974.

—, *La política indigenista de Isabel la Católica*, Valladolid, Instituto 'Isabel la Católica' de Historia Eclesiástica, 1969.

—, *La Rábida y el descubrimiento de América*, Madrid, Ediciones Cultura Hispanica, 1968.

—, *Libro copiador de Cristóbal Colón. Estudio histórico-crítico y edición*, 2 vols, Madrid, Ministerio de Cultura, 1989.

—, *Nueva luz sobre las capitulaciones de Santa Fe de 1492 concertadas entre los Reyes Católicos y Cristóbal Colón. Estudio Institucional y diplomático*, Madrid, Consejo Superior de Investigaciones Científicas, 1985.

Salazar y Castro, Luis de, *Historia genealógica de la Casa de Lara, justifcada con instrumentos y escritores de inviolable fe*, Madrid, Imprenta Real, for Mateo de Llanos y Guzmán, 1698.

Salvador Miguel, Nicasio, 'Isabel, Infanta de Castilla, en la corte de Enrique IV (1461–1467). Formación y entorno literario', in *Actes del XX Congres Internacional de l'Associació Hispánica de Literatura Medieval*, Alacant, Institui Interuniversitari de Filologia Valenciana 'Symposia Philologica', vol. 1, 2005, pp. 185–212.

Sánchez Cantón, Francisco Javier, *Libros, tapices y cuadros que coleccionó Isabel la Católica*, Madrid, Consejo Superior de Investigaciones Científicas, 1950.

—, *Maestre Nicolás Francés*, Madrid, CSIC, Instituto Diego Velázquez, 1964.

Sánchez del Barrio, Antonio, *Comercio y ferias en tiempos de Isabel la Católica*, Alicante, Biblioteca Virtual Miguel de Cervantes, 2005 at http://www.cervantesvirtual.com/obra-visor-din/comercio-y-ferias-en-tiempos-de-isabel-la-catlica-o/html/

Sánchez Dueñas, Blas, 'Una particular visión de la mujer en el siglo XV. Jardín de Nobles Doncellas de Fray Martín de Córdoba', *Boletín de la Real Academia de Córdoba*, no. 141, 2001, pp. 291–9.

Sánchez Herrero, José, 'Amantes, barraganas, compañeras, concubinas clericales', *Clío y Crímen*, no. 5, 2008, pp. 106–37.

Santa Cruz, Alonso de, *Crónica de los Reyes Católicos*, ed. Juan de Mata Carriazo, 2 vols, Seville, Publicaciones de la Escuela de Estudios Hispano-Americanos de Sevilla, 1951.

Sarasola, Modesto, *Viscaya y los Reyes Católicos*, Madrid, Consejo Superior de Investigaciones Científicas, Patronato Marcelino Menéndez Pelayo, 1950.

Segura Graiño, Cristina, 'Derechos sucesorios al trono de la mujeres en la Corona de Aragón', *Mayurqa*, no. 22(2), 1989, pp. 591–600.

Silva Santa-Cruz, Noelia, 'Maurofilia y mudejarismo en época de Isabel la Cátolica', in Fernando Checa Cremades (ed.), *Isabel la Católica. Magnificencia de un reinado. Quinto centenario de Isabel la Católica, 1504–2004*, Madrid, Sociedad Estatal de Conmemoraciones Culturales, 2004, pp. 141–54.

Sobrino, Miguel, *Catedrales. Las biografías desconocidas de los Grandes Templos de España*, Madrid, La Esfera de los Libros, 2009.

Suárez Fernández, Luis, '1500. Un giro radical en la política de los Reyes Católicos', *En la España Medieval*, no. 9, 1986, pp. 1249–66.

—, *Documentos acerca de la expulsión de los judíos*, Valladolid, Aldecoa, 1964.

—, *El camino hacia Europa*, Madrid, Rialp, 1990.

—, *Enrique IV de Castilla. La difamación como arma política*, Barcelona, Ariel, 2001.

——, *Expansión de la Fé*, Madrid, Rialp, 1990.

——, *Fernando el Católico*, Barcelona, Ariel, 2013.

——, *Isabel I*, Barcelona, Ariel, 2000.

——, *Judíos españoles en la Edad Media*, Madrid, Rialp, 1980.

——, *La conquista del trono*, Madrid, Rialp, 1989.

——, 'La declaración de guerra a Francia por parte de los Reyes Católicos en 1494', *Archivum*, vol. 12, 1962, pp. 193–209.

——, 'Las relaciones de los reyes Católicos con Egipto', *En la España Medieval*, no. 1, 1980, pp. 507–19.

——, *Los Reyes Católicos*, Barcelona, Ariel, 2004.

——, *Política internacional de Isabel la Católica: estudio y documentos*, 6 vols, Valladolid, Instituto 'Isabel la Católica' de Historia Eclesiástica, 1965–72.

——, Carmen Manso Porto and Abraham Rubio Celada (eds), *Isabel la Católica en la Real Academia de la Historia*, Madrid, Real Academia de la Historia, 2004.

Szászdi León-Borja, István, 'El origen de la Armada de Vizcaya y el Tratado de las Alcáçovas', *Historia, instituciones, documentos*, no. 26, 1999, pp. 547–74.

Takimoto, Kayoko, 'De secretario a cronista real. Fernando de Pulgar, oficial real de la corona de Castilla del siglo XV', *Hiyoshi Review of the Humanities*, no. 23, 2008, pp. 351–77, at http://koara.lib.keio.ac.jp/xoonips/modules/xoonips/detail.php?koara_id=AN10065043-20080531-0351.

Talavera, Hernando de, *Católica impugnación del herético libelo maldito y descomulgado que fue divulgado en la ciudad de Sevilla* (with Francisco Marquez Villanueva and Stefania Pastore), Córdoba, Almuzara, 2012.

Tapia Sánchez, Serafín de, 'Los judíos de Ávila en vísperas de la expulsión', *Sefarad*, no. 57/1, 1997, pp. 135–78.

——, 'Los mudéjares de la Extremadura castellano-leonesa. Notas sobre una minoría dócil (1085–1502)', *Studia Historica*, no. 7, 1989, pp. 96–125.

Torre y del Cerro, Antonio de la, *Documentos sobre relaciones internacionales de los reyes Católicos*, 6 volumes, Barcelona, Patronato Marcelino Menéndez Pelayo, 1949–66.

——, *La Casa de Isabel la Católica*, Madrid, Consejo Superior de Investigaciones Científicas, 1954.

——, 'Maestros de los hijos de los Reyes Católicos', *Hispania*, no. 63, 1956, pp. 256–66.

——, 'Un médico de los Reyes Católicos', *Hispania*, no. 14, 1944, pp. 66–72.

—— and Eugenia Alsina (eds), *Cuentas de Gonzalo de Baeza, tesorero de Isabel la Católica*, 2 vols, Madrid, Consejo Superior de Investigaciones Científicas, 1955–6.

—— and Luis Suárez Fernández (eds), *Documentos referentes a las relaciones con Portugal durante el reinado de los Reyes Católicos*, 3 vols, Valladolid, Consejo Superior de Investigaciones Científicas, 1960–3.

Torres Fontes, Juan, *Don Pedro Fajardo, adelantado mayor del reino de Murcia*, Madrid, Consejo Superior de Investigaciones Científicas, 1953.

——, 'Dos fechas de España en Murcia', *Anales de la Universidad de Murcia*, vol. 6, 1946, pp. 641–8.

—— (ed.), *Estudio de la 'Crónica de Enrique IV' del Dr. Galíndez de Carvajal*, Murcia, Sucesores de Nogués, 1946.

Val Valdivieso, María Isabel del, *Isabel I de Castilla (1451–1504)*, Madrid, Ediciones del Orto, 2005.

——, 'Isabel, *Infanta* and Princess of Castile', in David A. Boruchoff (ed.), *Isabel la Católica, Queen of Castile: Critical Essays*, New York and Basingstoke, Palgrave Macmillan, 2003, pp. 41–56.

——, *Isabel la Católica. Princesa (1468–1474)*, Valladolid, Instituto 'Isabel la Católica' de Historia Eclesiástica, 1974.

——, 'La educación de las mujeres en la corte de Isabel la Católica', *Nara Historical Journal (Nara Shien)*, no. 52, February 2007.

Valdeón Baruque, J., *Cristianos, judíos, musulmanes*, Barcelona, Crítica, 2006.

——, 'Judíos y conversos en la Castilla Medieval', in Fernando Checa Cremades (ed.), *Isabel la Católica. Magnificencia de un reinado. Quinto centenario de Isabel la Católica, 1504–2004*, Madrid, Sociedad Estatal de Conmemoraciones Culturales, 2004, pp. 63–74.

——, *Los conflictos sociales en el reino de Castilla en los siglos XIV y XV*, Madrid, Siglo XXI, 1975.

Valera, Diego de, *Crónica de los Reyes Católicos*, ed. Juan de Mata Carriazo, Madrid, José Molina, 1927.

——, *Epístolas*, Madrid, Sociedad de Bibliófilos, 1878.

——, *Memorial de diversas hazañas, crónica de Enrique IV*, in *Crónicas de los Reyes de Castilla* (ed. Cayetano Rosell), vol. 3, Madrid, Rivadeneyra, 1878.

Varela, Consuelo, *Cristóbal Colón. Retrato de un hombre*, Barcelona, Alianza, 1992.

——, *La caída de Cristóbal Colón. El juicio de Bobadilla*, Barcelona, Marcial Pons, Ediciones de Historia, 2006.

——, *Los cuatro viajes. Testamento*, Barcelona, Alianza, 2007.

—— (ed.), *Textos y documentos completos*, Madrid, Alianza, 1992.

—— (ed.), *Textos y documentos completos. Relaciones de viajes, cartas y memoriales*, Madrid, Alianza, 1984.

Vicens Vives, Jaime, *Historia crítica de la vida y reinado de Fernando II de Aragón*, Zaragoza, Institución Fernando el Católico, 2007.

—, *Juan II de Aragón. Monarquía y revolución*, Barcelona, Editorial Teide, 1953.

Villacampa, Carlos G., *Grandezas de Guadalupe. Estudios sobre la historia y las bellas artes del gran monasterio extremeño*, Madrid, C. Vallinas, 1924.

Villaseñor Sebastián, 'Fernando, La corte literaria de Juan de Zúñiga y Pimentel (Plasencia, 1459–1504 Guadalupe)', *Anales de Historia del Arte*, 2013, vol. 23, Núm. Especial (II).

Zalama Rodríguez, Miguel Ángel, 'Oro, perlas, brocados … La ostentación en el vestir en la corte de los Reyes Católicos', *Revista de Estudios Colombinos*, no. 8, 2012, pp. 13–22.

—, 'Colon y Juana I. Los viajes por mar de la reina entre España y los Países Bajos', *Revista de Estudios Colombinos*, no. 5, 2009, p. 42.

Zurita, Jerónimo, *Anales de Aragón*, ed. Ángel Canellas López et al., Zaragoza, Institución Fernando el Católico, at http://ifc.dpz.es/publicaciones/ver/id/2448.

—, *Historia del rey Don Fernando el Católico. De las empresas, y ligas de Italia*, ed. José Javier Iso et al., Zaragoza, Oficina de Domingo de Portonariis, y Ursino impresor de la Sacra, Real, y Católica Majestad, y del reino de Aragón, Zaragoza, 1580 at http://ifc.dpz.es/publicaciones/ver/id/2423.

SOURCES IN ENGLISH AND LANGUAGES OTHER THAN SPANISH

Anderson, Perry, *Lineages of the Absolutist State*, New York and London, Verso, 2013.

Anon, 'Original Documents Relating to Queen Katharine of Aragon', *Gentleman's Magazine*, 42, New series, December 1854, p. 572.

Aram, Bethany, *Juana the Mad: Sovereignty and Dynasty in Renaissance Europe*, Baltimore, Johns Hopkins University Press, 2005.

Armelagos, George J. et al. 'The Science Behind Pre-Columbian Evidence of Syphilis in Europe', *Evolutionary Anthropology*, vol. 21, no. 2, 2012, pp. 50–7.

Bacon, Francis, *The Works of Francis Bacon* (ed. Basil Montagu), Philadelphia, Carey and Hart, 1841, 3 volumes.

Barnett, Richard (ed.), *The Sephardi Heritage: Essays on the History and Cultural Contribution of the Jews of Spain and Portugal*, vol. 1: *The Jews in Spain and Portugal Before and After the Expulsion of 1492*, London, Vallentine Mitchell, 1971.

Barton, Simon, *A History of Spain*, London, Palgrave Macmillan, 2009.

—, *Conquerors, Brides, and Concubines: Interfaith Relations and Social Power in Medieval Iberia*, Philadelphia, University of Pennsylvania Press, 2015.

Beinart, Haim, 'The Conversos Community of Fifteenth-Century Spain', in Richard Barnett (ed.), *The Sephardi Heritage: Essays on the History and*

Cultural Contribution of the Jews of Spain and Portugal, vol. 1: *The Jews in Spain and Portugal Before and After the Expulsion of 1492*, London, Vallentine Mitchell, 1971, pp. 425–56.

—, *Records of the Trials of the Spanish Inquisition in Ciudad Real*, 2 vols, Jerusalem, The Israel National Academy of Sciences and Humanities, 1974–7.

Blackmore, Josiah and Hutcheson, Gregory S., *Queer Iberia: Sexualities, Cultures, and Crossings from the Middle Ages to the Renaissance*, Durham, NC, and London, Duke University Press, 1999.

Boruchoff, David A., 'Historiography with License: Isabel, the Catholic Monarch and the Kingdom of God', in David A. Boruchoff (ed.), *Isabel la Católica, Queen of Castile: Critical Essays*, New York and Basingstoke, Palgrave Macmillan, 2003, pp. 225–94.

— (ed.), *Isabel la Católica, Queen of Castile: Critical Essays*, New York and Basingstoke, Palgrave Macmillan, 2003.

Britnell, Richard and Dodds, Ben, *Agriculture and Rural Society after the Black Death: Common Themes*, Hatfield, University of Hertfordshire Press, 2008.

Brundage, James, *Law, Sex, and Christian Society in Medieval Europe*, Chicago, University of Chicago Press, 1987.

Burchard, Johann, *At the Court of the Borgia*, ed. Geoffrey Parker, London, Folio Society, 2002.

Columbus, Christopher, *Select Letters of Christopher Columbus: With Other Original Documents, Relating to His Four Voyages to the New World*, ed. Richard Henry Major, 2 vols, London, Printed for the Hakluyt Society, 1847.

Cook Jr, Weston F., 'The Cannon Conquest of Nasid Granada and the End of the *Reconquista*', in Donald J. Kagay and L. J. Andrew Villalon (eds), *Crusaders, Condottieri, and Cannon: Medieval Warfare in Societies around the Mediterranean*, Leiden and Boston, Brill, 2003, pp. 253–84.

Cunningham, Sean, *Henry VII*, London, Routledge, 2007.

Davies, Norman, *Europe: A History*, Oxford, Oxford University Press, 1996.

Earenfight, Theresa (ed.), *Queenship and Political Power in Medieval and Early Modern Spain*, Burlington, VT, Ashgate, 2005.

—, 'Two Bodies, One Spirit: Isabel and Fernando's Construction of Monarchical Partnership', in Barbara F. Weissberger (ed.), *Queen Isabel I of Castile: Power, Patronage, Persona*, Woodbridge, Suffolk, Tamesis, 2008, pp. 3–18.

Edwards, John, *Ferdinand and Isabella*, Profiles in Power series, Harlow, Pearson Longman, 2005.

—, *Torquemada and the Inquisitors*, Stroud, Tempus, 2005.

Ehses, Stephan (ed.), *Römische Dokumente zur Geschichte der Ehescheidung Heinrichs VIII von England*, Paderborn, Ferdinand Schöningh, 1893.

Elliott, J. H., *Imperial Spain 1469–1716*, London, Pelican, 1970.

Ellis, Henry (ed.), *Original Letters Illustrative of English History*, 1st ser., 3 vols, 2nd ser., 4 vols, 3rd ser., 4 vols, London, Harding, Triphook & Lepard, 1824.

Erasmus, Desiderius, *The Epistles of Erasmus*, trans. Francis Morgan Nichols, vol. 3, London, Longmans, Green, 1901.

Fernández-Armesto, Felipe, *Before Columbus: Exploration and Colonisation from the Mediterranean to the Atlantic, 1229–1492*, Philadelphia, University of Pennsylvania Press, 1987.

—, *Columbus*, Oxford, Oxford University Press, 1991.

—, *Columbus on Himself*, Cambridge, MA, Hackett, 2010.

—, *Ferdinand and Isabella*, New York, Dorset Press, 1991.

—, *Pathfinders: A Global History of Exploration*, Oxford, Oxford University Press, 2007.

Fuchs, Barbara, *Exotic Nation: Maurophilia and the Construction of Early Modern Spain*, Philadelphia, University of Pennsylvania Press, 2009.

Gairdner, James, *Henry VII*, London, Macmillan, 1889.

—, *Memorials of King Henry the Seventh*, London, Longman, Brown, Green, Longmans & Roberts, 1858.

— (ed.), *Three Fifteenth-Century Chronicles with Historical Memoranda by John Stowe*, Camden Society, London, 1880, at http://www.british-history.ac.uk/camden-record-soc/vol28.

Gerber, Jane, *The Jews of Spain: A History of the Sephardic Experience*, The Free Press, New York, 1992, p. 136 (citing Solomon ibn Verga, *Shevet Yehuda*).

Gross, Abraham, *Iberian Jewry from Twilight to Dawn: The World of Rabbi Abraham Saba*, Leiden, Brill, 1995.

Hall, Edward, *Hall's Chronicle – The union of the two noble and illustre famelies of Lancastre and Yorke (1548)*, London, J. Johnson, 1809.

Haring, Clarence H., 'American Gold and Silver Production in the First Half of the 16th Century', *Quarterly Journal of Economics*, vol. 29, no. 3, May 1915, pp. 433–79.

Harvey, L. P., *Islam in Spain, 1250 to 1500*, Chicago, University of Chicago Press, 1990.

—, *Muslims in Spain, 1500 to 1614*, Chicago, University of Chicago Press, 2005.

Hessayon, Ariel, review of François Soyer, *The Persecution of the Jews and Muslims of Portugal. King Manuel I and the End of Religious Tolerance (1496–7)*, at http://www.history.ac.uk/reviews/review/797.

Hibbert, Christopher, *The Borgias*, London, Constable, 2011 (Kindle edn).

Hollingsworth, Mary, *The Borgias: History's Most Notorious Dynasty*, London, Quercus, 2011 (Kindle edn).

Homza, Lu Ann, *The Spanish Inquisition 1478–1614*, Indianapolis, Hackett, 2006.

Hunt, Edward S. and Murray, James M., *A History of Business in Medieval Europe, 1200–1550*, New York, Cambridge University Press, 1999.

Ingram, Kevin (ed.), *The Conversos and Moriscos in Late Medieval Spain and Beyond*, vol. 2, Leiden, Brill, 2009.

Irwin, Robert, *The Alhambra*, London, Profile Books, 2004.

Kagan, Richard L., *Clio and the Crown: The Politics of History in Medieval and Early Modern Spain*, Baltimore, Johns Hopkins University Press, 2009 (Kindle edn).

Kamen, Henry, *The Spanish Inquisition: A Historical Revision*, New Haven, Yale University Press, 1998.

Kipling, Gordon (ed.), *The Receyt of The Ladie Kateryne*, Oxford, Oxford University Press for the Early English Text Society, 1990.

Koningsveld, P. S. van and Wiegers, G. A., 'Islam in Spain during the Early Sixteenth century. The Views of the Four Chief Judges in Cairo (Introduction, translation and Arabic Text)', in O. Zwartjes, G.J. van Gelder and E. de Moor (eds), *Poetry, Politics and Polemics. Cultural Transfer between the Iberian Peninsula and North Africa*, Amsterdam, Atlanta, 1997, pp. 133–52 and in *Orientations* 4, 1996.

—, 'The Islamic Statute of the Mudejars in the Light of a New Source', *Al-Qantara*, vol. 17, 1996, pp. 19–58.

Lalaing, Antoine de, *Collection des voyages des souverains des Pays-Bas*, Gachard, Brussels, 1876.

Lea, Henry Charles, *History of the Inquisition of Spain*, 4 volumes, New York and London, Macmillan, 1906–7.

Liss, Peggy K., *Isabel the Queen: Life and Times*, Philadelphia, University of Pennsylvania Press, 2004.

Lunenfeld, Marvin, *The Council of Santa Hermandad: A Study of the Pacification Forces of Ferdinand and Isabela*, Coral Gables, FL, University of Miami Press, 1970.

Machiavelli, Niccolò, *The Prince*, trans. George Bull, London, Penguin, 1999.

MacKay, Angus, *Spain in the Middle Ages: From Frontier to Empire, 1000–1500*, London, Macmillan, 1977.

Marx, Alexander, 'The Expulsion of the Jews from Spain: Two New Accounts', *Jewish Quarterly Review*, vol. 20, no. 2, 1908, pp. 240–71.

Mattingly, Garrett, *Catherine of Aragon*, London, Jonathan Cape, 1942.

Mol, Angus A. A., 'The Gift of the "Face of the Living": Shell Faces as Social Valuables in the Caribbean Late Ceramic Age', *Journal de la Société des Américanistes*, vol. 97, no. 2, 2011, pp. 7–43, at http://jsa.revues.org/11834.

Monroe, James T., 'A Curious Morisco Appeal to the Ottoman Empire', *Al-Andalus*, vol. 31, 1966, pp. 281–303.

More, Thomas, *Selected Letters*, Elizabeth Frances Rogers (ed.), New Haven, Yale University Press, 1961.

Morison, Samuel Eliot, *The Great Explorers: The European Discovery of America*, Oxford, Oxford University Press, 1986.

Netanyahu, Benzion, *The Marranos of Spain: From the Late 14th to the Early 16th Century*, Ithaca, NY, Cornell University Press, 1999.

—, *The Origins of the Inquisition in Fifteenth Century Spain*, New York, New York Review Books, 2001.

Nicolas, Nicholas Harris, *Privy Purse Expenses of Elizabeth of York: Wardrobe Accounts of Edward the Fourth*, London, William Pickering, 1830.

Nunn, Nathan and Qian, Nancy, 'The Columbian Exchange: A History of Disease, Food, and Ideas', *Journal of Economic Perspectives*, vol. 24, no. 2, 2010, pp. 163–88.

Ombelet, Willem and Van Robays, Johan, 'History of Human Artificial Insemination', *Facts, Views & Vision*, Monograph, 2010, pp. 1–5 at http://www.fvvo.be/assets/97/13-Ombelet_Et_al.pdf

Pérez de Guzmán, Fernán, *Pen Portraits of Illustrious Castilians*, trans. Marie Gillette and Loretta Zehngut, Washington, DC, Catholic University Press, 2003.

Pocock, Nicholas (ed.), *Records of the Reformation: The Divorce, 1527–33*, 2 vols, Oxford, Clarendon Press, 1870.

Raphael, David (ed.), *The Expulsion 1492 Chronicles: Medieval Chronicles Relating to the Expulsion of the Jews from Spain and Portugal*, North Hollywood, CA, Carmi House (Kindle edn), 1992.

Rosner, Fred, 'The Life of Moses Maimonides, a Prominent Medieval Physician', *Einstein Quarterly*, vol. 19, 2002, pp.125–8.

Roth, Norman (ed.), *Medieval Jewish Civilization: An Encyclopedia*, New York, Routledge, 2003.

—, *Conversos, Inquisition, and the Expulsion of the Jews from Spain*, Madison, University of Wisconsin Press, 2002

Rubin, Nancy, *Isabella of Castile: The First Renaissance Queen*, Lincoln, NB, ASJA Press, 2004.

Rucquoi, Adeline, *De Jeanne d'Arc à Isabelle la Catholique. L'image de la France en Castille au XVe siècle*, *Journal des Savants*, vol. 1, no. 1, January–June 1990, pp. 155–74.

Sanuto, Marino, *I diarii di Marino Sanuto*, vols 1, 14, 15, 16, 17, 39, 54, Venice, Fratelli Visentini Tipografi Editori, 1879–86.

Scarisbrick, J. J., *Henry the Eighth*, London, Eyre Methuen, 1981.

Shadis, Miriam, *Berenguela of Castile (1180–1246) and Political Women in the High Middle Ages*, New York, Palgrave Macmillan, 2009.

Silleras-Fernández, Nuria, *Power, Piety, and Patronage in Late Medieval Queenship: Maria de Luna*, New York, Palgrave Macmillan, 2009.

Soyer, François, *The Persecution of the Jews and Muslims of Portugal: King Manuel I and the End of Religious Tolerance (1496–7)*, Leiden, Brill, 2007.

Strickland, Agnes, *Lives of the Queens of England*, Philadelphia, Blanchard & Lea, 1852.

Suárez, Thomas, *Shedding the Veil: Mapping the European Discovery of America and the World*, Singapore, World Scientific Publishing, 1992.

Thacker, Eugene, *The Global Genome: Biotechnology, Politics and Culture*, Cambridge, MA, and London, MIT Press, 2006.

Thomas, Hugh, *Rivers of Gold: The Rise of the Spanish Empire, from Columbus to Magellan*, London, Penguin, 2010.

—, *The Golden Age: The Spanish Empire of Charles V*, London, Penguin, 2011.

—, *The Slave Trade, The History of the Atlantic Slave Trade, 1440–1870* (Kindle edn), Weidenfeld & Nicolson, 2015.

Thomas, A. H. and Thornley, I. D. (eds), *The Great Chronicle of London*, Gloucester, Alan Sutton, 1983.

Tremlett, Giles, *Catherine of Aragon*, London, Faber & Faber, 2010.

Vives, Juan Luis, *The Education of a Christian Woman: A Sixteenth-Century Manual*, ed. and trans. Charles Fantazzi, Chicago, University of Chicago Press, 2000.

—, *Vives: On Education. A translation of the tradendis disciplinis of Juan Luis Vives together with an Introduction by Foster Watson*, Cambridge, Cambridge University Press, 1913.

Watson, Foster (ed.), *Vives and the Renascence Education of Women*, London, Arnold, 1912.

Weissberger, Barbara F., ' "¡A tierra, puto!": Alfonso de Palencia's Discourse of Effeminacy', in Josiah Blackmore and Gregory S. Hutcheson (eds), *Queer Iberia: Sexualities, Cultures, and Crossings from the Middle Ages to the Renaissance*, Durham, NC, and London, Duke University Press, 1999, pp. 291–324.

—, *Isabel Rules: Constructing Queenship, Wielding Power*, Minneapolis, University of Minnesota Press, 2003.

— (ed.), *Queen Isabel I of Castile: Power, Patronage, Persona*, Woodbridge, Suffolk, Tamesis, 2008.

Wollock, Jennifer G., *Rethinking Chivalry and Courtly Love*, Santa Barbara, Praeger, 2011.

Wood, Mary Anne Everett, *Letters of Royal and Illustrious Ladies of Great Britain*, 3 vols, London, Henry Colburn, 1846.

Wroe, Ann, *Perkin: A Story of Deception*, London, Jonathan Cape, 2003.

ACKNOWLEDGEMENTS

My deepest gratitude goes to those academic historians who have been so generous with their time and thoughts. Professors Felipe Fernández-Armesto at Notre Dame and Simon Barton at Exeter University were both kind enough to read through parts of the manuscript of this book, commenting and critiquing. I am especially thankful to Professor Fernández-Armesto for his thoughtful commentary, and for putting me right on several matters. The final version of this book is, of course, mine – including any errors and, especially, my conclusion on Isabella's place in history, her usurpation of the crown, the emergence of race and what today we call 'racism' as issues during her reign, and the concentration of power in her court as an authoritarian precursor to absolutism.

I am grateful to Professor David Raphael and Esther Carmi for permission to use extracts from translations of the Hebrew chronicles published in his *The Expulsion 1492 Chronicle: An Anthology of Chronicles Relating to the Expulsion of the Jews from Spain and Portugal*. This remains the most valuable first-hand source in English on the Sephardic Jewish experience of expulsion. Professor Lu Ann Homza at William and Mary and Hackett Publishing generously also offered permission to cite from her *Spanish Inquisition, 1478–1614: An Anthology of Sources* though – after finding the original material – I eventually opted to follow the principle of translating myself wherever possible. I continue to recommend Professor Homza's book to those wanting a deeper immersion in first-hand sources on the Inquisition. Likewise, Professor Fernández-Armesto's *Columbus on*

Himself provides fine alternative, and full, translations to Columbus's writing. Pedro Flor at the Universidad Nova in Lisbon, Portugal, has discovered what I consider to be an important addition to the small number of surviving Isabella portraits and kindly answered my queries on the subject. I am grateful for his help and hope the National Gallery in London will revise its catalogue accordingly. Librarians and archivists at the Biblioteca Nacional in Madrid, the Real Academia de la Historia, the British Library and the National Archives have all provided valuable support.

Much of this book depends on the published work of the academic masters of fifteenth- and sixteenth-century Spanish history – including Tarsicio de Azcona, Miguel Angel Ladero Quesada, Luis Suárez Fernández, Consuelo Varela, Álvaro Fernández de Córdova Miralles, J.H. Elliott and Felipe Fernández-Armesto, to name just a few. I would also like to thank those who have made their PhD theses, or versions of them, available – including Córdova Miralles on Pope Alexander VI (Rodrigo Borgia) and the Catholic monarchs, Maria Montserrat León Guerrero on Columbus's second voyage, Ana Isabel Carrasco Manchado on propaganda and Carmen Alicia Morales's fascinating *Psiquobiografía*. I am just one of many people who await Teresa Tinsley's thesis on Hernando de Baeza with great interest, and thank her for sharing thoughts.

The team at Bloomsbury has been patient, painstaking and creative, so many thanks to Michael Fishwick, Bill Swainson, Anna Simpson, Marigold Atkey, Kate Quarry, David Atkinson and Angelique Tran Van Sang. Peter James has lived up to his fame as one of Britain's best copy editors and thanks also go to Catherine Best for her careful proofreading. My agent Georgina Capel has, as ever, been both a guide and a rock. Walter Donohue also generously and disinterestedly applied his publisher's mind to an early version of the text. Special thanks go to that most perspicacious of readers, Katharine Scott, and to those who have participated in many dinner-table conversations about Isabella of Castile – Lucas and Samuel Tremlett.

INDEX